Sociology and Religion

Sociology and Religion

A Collection of Readings

ANDREW M. GREELEY
University of Chicago

HarperCollinsCollegePublishers

Acquisitions Editor: Alan McClare
Project Coordination: Ruttle, Shaw & Wetherill, Inc.
Text and Cover Designer: Nancy Sabato
Electronic Production Manager: Valerie A. Sawyer
Desktop Administrator: Hilda Koparanian
Manufacturing Manager: Helene G. Landers
Electronic Page Makeup: American–Stratford Graphic Services, Inc.
Printer and Binder: R. R. Donnelley & Sons Company
Cover Printer: The Lehigh Press, Inc.

Sociology and Religion: A Collection of Readings

Library of Congress Cataloging-in-Publication Data

Sociology and religion: a collection of readings / Andrew Greeley.
      p.   cm.
   Includes bibliographical references.
   ISBN 0-06-501881-8
   1. Religion and sociology. I. Greeley, Andrew M.

BL60.S62 1995	94-7907
306.6—dc20	CIP

95 96 97 98   9 8 7 6 5 4 3 2 1

Contents

Section 8 American Religion 337

Preface

....

This volume is intended to be a resource kit, a kind of toolbox for faculty and students in upper-division (graduate/undergraduate) courses on the sociology of religion. It is intended to make available to students some of the most interesting writings of great sociologists, particulary because the law of the land forbids the copying of these works for classroom use. Because of this purpose, I have made the following decisions:

1. I have included more than enough selections to keep the class busy for a term. Faculty will be able to choose which selections are pertinent for the design of the course.
2. I have cast my net wide to include selections from many disciplines besides sociology—anthropology, psychology, and history of religions, for example.
3. Because I believe it is impossible to edit a collection of readings, save from a perspective of one's own, I have chosen to be explicit in my perspective, thus giving faculty and students a chance to disagree and even fight with me. There is nothing more conducive to an interesting course than a lot of disagreement.
4. In particular, I feel that sociologists of religion have ignored for too long the experiential aspect of religion. Therefore, I include many selections on religious experience.
5. I also believe that there has been too much word-spinning, in the sociology of religion (by which I mean so-called theory that is neither testable nor tested). Therefore I include many empirical selections though not with complex mathematical methodology.
6. I am extremely skeptical about the so-called "secularization theory," which is a horrific example of word-spinning, undisciplined by the slightest contact with data.

My own perspective on the sociology of religion is that religion begins in "hope-renewal" experiences, that these experiences are coded in narrative symbols that purport to explain the meaning of life and provide templates for living, that these experiences and narratives are shared with and shaped by communities, which provide the individual with repertories of symbols that predispose to experiences and provide interpretations for them, and that these communities act out their shared stories in religious ritual. Thus, before religion becomes doctrine and devotion and code, it is experience, image, story, community and ritual—the latter four of which help to shape further experiences. The process is not linear, but circular, a circle in which the analyst can enter at any point.

Moreover, the narrative symbols that encode religious experiences in the shapes and forms provided by the religious heritage, also shape behavior patterns in the world beyond the formal boundaries of religion—politics, economics, and social action.

My perspective is shaped by the work of Clifford Geertz, William James, Rudolph Otto, and David Tracy, none of whom are formally sociologists—though Geertz is a conduit back to Max Weber and Emile Durkheim, the father founders of not only sociology of religion, but of sociology. I make no apologies for the catholicity of the sources of my perspective—one takes insight where one can find it.

Nor, do I apologize for including my own empirical work in many of the selections. Data are data no matter where one finds them.

Finally I want to express my gratitude to my administrative assistant, Mary Kotecki, my research assistants, Julie Durkin Montague and Elizabeth Durkin, and to my editors at HarperCollins, Alan McClare and Michael Kimball. I am also grateful to the anonymous reviewers who encourged the work and made many helpful suggestions, including cutting the volume down to proper size. In addition to recommending cuts, very wisely I think, the reviewers suggested additions—which if made would have increased the book back to its original size.

I finally had to follow my own instincts, flawed as they may be, about what articles to use. It is quite impossible to provide a comprehensive reader in the sociology of religion, one that will contain all the articles necessary to satisfy everyone. So this is a reader that contains the material that I find interesting and helpful—and for which I do not make the impossible claim that it is comprehensive.

Andrew M. Greeley

Sociology and Religion

1

WHAT IS RELIGION?
The Search of the Classic Tradition

Serious, critical, and nontheological reflection on religion has presumably gone on for as long as there has been religion. But as a formal activity, which preoccupied many thinkers and writers, it was a nineteenth-century phenomenon. The men who engaged in such reflection, all of them brilliant and some of them geniuses, provided the raw materials out of which came contemporary social science.

One could divide them into two categories: those who sought to explain religion, and those who thought to explain it away. Marx and Freud, and perhaps Durkheim, can be included in the latter category, while Weber, Simmel, Otto, and especially William James belong in the former.

Many of these thinkers were concerned about the persistence of religion, its ability to survive despite the onslaught of science. Some, most notably Freud, thought religion would slowly disappear. Others, Durkheim for example, thought it would survive, but with a very limited area of competence. Still others, Weber and Simmel, found it hard to imagine a world without religion.

Most of these men were at most agnostics, Freud and Marx atheists. Only William James asked a question that sociology (and his psychology), as such, cannot answer: is religion true? James' answer was, in effect, "I think so, but if you don't think so, I can't force you to agree with me."

The search for the meaning of religion in these classic thinkers (as interpreted and clarified by their contemporary disciples) continues to define the terms of sociology's attempt to understand religion. They are to be read, not because they were right, not because what they say is the final word, but because it is within the context of the questions that they ask—perennial questions, perhaps—that our search continues.

....

THE OPIATE OF THE PEOPLE—KARL MARX

Karl Marx (1818–1883) was a dialectical materialist; he combined the Hegelian idea that reality emerges from an endless series of contradictions with Ludwig Feurbach's materialism, the belief that matter was the only and ultimate reality. Hegel was wrong, Marx argued, not about dialectics, but about making the dialectic spiritual. The ultimate reality is not spirit (or *Spirit*) but matter. Political and social reality is shaped by struggles between social classes over control of the material modes of production.

Because there is no such thing as spirit, religion must be an illusion, part of the "superstructure" of reality generated by underlying reality of the material substructure. It is one of the techniques that the ruling class (whoever controls the modes of production) uses to keep the subject class under control. It is an opiate, a drug that immobilizes the subject class with the hope of a spiritual reward as a substitute for material possessions.

Marx was more than just a philosopher, however. He was also a messianic prophet who preached to the workers of the world the need to throw off the chains of oppression with which the bourgeoisie (the ruling class) had bound them. It was therefore not enough to reveal that religion was an illusion. Religion must be denounced as the enemy of the working class. To throw off its chains, the working class must dispose of religion. Hence the prophetic fervor of his attack on religion. Curiously enough, his own Marxist philosophy would eventually become a quasi-religion in its own right and Marx himself the Moses of the new faith. In a nice historical irony that that faith was used in Eastern Europe to control the people and to provide its own promise of an eventual materialist paradise. Marxism itself had become an opiate for the people, one that worked only when enforced at gunpoint.

Obviously, Marx had a point. Religion has often been a tool in the hands of rulers and a means for cowing people into submission.

Marx owed his popularity to the incisiveness of his historical analysis, the toughness of his materialism, and the enthusiasm of his vision. Precisely because he admitted only material reality, his doctrine was considered to be scientific; and precisely because of the seeming inevitability of the dialectic that he described, those who followed his faith believed that they would triumph, they would "bury" capitalism as once boasted by Nikita Khrushchev, Soviet party boss in the late 1950s and early 1960s.

After the collapse of the Iron Curtain in 1990, the weaknesses of Marxism were revealed to everyone. But Marx's notion that religion was a means of social domination and control can stand alone and does not need the rest of his philosophical system to sustain it. Religion still seems to promise "pie in the sky when you die" as a substitute for social justice while you are still alive. Much of the skepticism of many intellectuals about religion is based on an implicit Marxist premise—men and women would like to believe in God and therefore they do. In fact, however, these observers would say, religion is nothing more than wish-fulfillment, and indeed is wish-fulfillment that blinds men and women to injustice.

This argument has appeal to some clergy, particularly those Catholic clergy for whom liberation theology and "identification with the poor" is an effort to prove that there is more to religion than just spiritual promises and pious devotions. It may be that the last Marxist in the world will be a Catholic priest, perhaps even a Jesuit, and one with a tenured faculty appointment at a Catholic university.

One is struck as one reads the attack on religion by Karl Marx by how "unscientific" it is by the standards of contemporary social science. He asserts, but does not prove. He attacks, but does not provide evidence. He argues fiercely, but his arguments are aprioristic and deductive. If science requires the possibility of falsification for verification to become possible—and that is how scientists today would define their work—then Marx's comments on religion are hardly scientific. But the passion of his moral outrage can still stir the emotions.

Questions for Reflection and Discussion

1. In what ways does religion become a drug?
2. Why have so many men and women been persuaded by Marx's attack on religion?
3. Why have some clergy become Marxists? How does his critique appeal to them?
4. How would one go about testing Marx's argument empirically?

Part 1

CONTRIBUTION TO THE CRITIQUE OF HEGEL'S PHILOSOPHY OF RIGHT
Karl Marx

For Germany the *criticism of religion* is in the main complete, and criticism of religion is the premise of all criticism.

Source: The Marx-Engels Reader. Edited by Robert C. Tucker. New York: Norton, 1972.

The *profane* existence of error is discredited after its *heavenly oratio pro aris et focis** has been rejected. Man, who looked for a superman in the fantastic reality of heaven and found nothing there but the *reflexion* of himself, will no longer be disposed to find but the *semblance* of himself, the non-human [*Unmensch*] where he seeks and must seek his true reality.

The basis of irreligious criticism is: *Man makes religion,* religion does not make man. In other words, religion is the self-consciousness and self-feeling of man who has either not yet found himself or has already lost himself again. But *man* is no abstract being squatting outside the world. Man is *the world of man,* the state, society. This state, this society, produce religion, *a reversed world-consciousness,* because they are *a reversed world.* Religion is the general theory of that world, its encyclopaedic compendium, its logic in a popular form, its spiritualistic *point d'honneur,* its enthusiasm, its moral sanction, its solemn completion, its universal ground for consolation and justification. It is *the fantastic realization* of the human essence because the *human essence* has no true reality. The struggle against religion is therefore mediately the fight against *the other world,* of which religion is the spiritual *aroma.*

Religious distress is at the same time the *expression* of real distress and the *protest* against real distress. Religion is the sigh of the oppressed creature, the heart of a heartless world, just as it is the spirit of a spiritless situation. It is the *opium* of the people.

The abolition of religion as the *illusory* happiness of the people is required for their *real* happiness. The demand to give up the illusions about its condition is the *demand to give up a condition which needs illusions.* The criticism of religion is therefore *in embryo the criticism of the vale of woe,* the *halo* of which is religion.

Criticism has plucked the imaginary flowers from the chain not so that man will wear the chain without any fantasy or consolation but so that he will shake off the chain and cull the living flower. The criticism of religion disillusions man to make him think and act and shape his reality like a man who has been disillusioned and has come to reason, so that he will revolve round himself and therefore round his true sun. Religion is only the illusory sun which revolves round man as long as he does not revolve round himself.

The task of history, therefore, once the *world beyond the truth* has disappeared, is to establish the *truth of this world.* The immediate *task of philosophy,* which is at the service of history, once the *saintly form* of human self-alienation has been unmasked, is to unmask self-alienation in its *unholy forms.* Thus the criticism of heaven turns into the criticism of the earth, the *criticism of religion* into the *criticism of right* and the *criticism of theology* into the *criticism of politics.*

The following exposition—a contribution to that work—bears immediately not on the original, but on a copy, the German *philosophy* of state and of right, for the single reason that it is written in *Germany.*

---

*Speech for the altars and hearths.—Ed.

If one wanted to proceed from the *status quo* itself in Germany, even in the only appropriate way, i.e., negatively, the result would still be an *anachronism*. Even the negation of our political present is already covered with dust in the historical lumber-room of modern nations. If I negate the powdered pigtail, I still have an unpowdered pigtail. If I negate the German state of affairs in 1843, then, according to the French computation of time, I am hardly in the year 1789, and still less in the focus of the present.

Yes, German history flatters itself with a movement which no people in the heaven of history went through before it or will go through after it. For we shared the restorations of the modern nations although we had not shared their revolutions. We were restored, first because other nations dared to carry out a revolution and second because other nations suffered a counter-revolution, the first time because our rulers were afraid, and the second because our rulers were not afraid. Led by our shepherds, we never found ourselves in the company of freedom except once—on the *day of its burial*.

A school which legalizes the baseness of today by the baseness of yesterday, a school that declares rebellious every cry of the serf against the knout once that knout is a time-honoured, ancestral, historical one, a school to which history only shows its *a posteriori* as the God of Israel did to his servant Moses—the *historical school of right*—would hence have discovered German history had it not been a discovery of German history itself. Shylock, but Shylock the servant, it swears on its bond, its historical bond, its Christian-Germanic bond, to have every pound of flesh cut from the heart of the people.

Part 2

THESES ON FEUERBACH
Karl Marx

I

The chief defect of all hitherto existing materialism—that of Feuerbach included—is that the thing [*Gegenstand*], reality, sensuousness, is conceived only in the form of the *object* [*Objekt*] or of *contemplation* [*Anschauung*], but not as *human sensuous activity, practice*, not subjectively. Hence it happened that the

Source: The Marx-Engels Reader. Edited by Robert C. Tucker. New York: Norton, 1972.

active side, in contradistinction to materialism, was developed by idealism—but only abstractly, since, of course, idealism does not know real, sensuous activity as such. Feuerbach wants sensuous objects, really differentiated from the thought-objects, but he does not conceive human activity itself as *objective* [*gegenständliche*] activity. Hence, in the *Essence of Christianity,* he regards the theoretical attitude as the only genuinely human attitude, while practice is conceived and fixed only in its dirty-judaical form of appearance. Hence he does not grasp the significance of "revolutionary," of "practical–critical," activity.

II

The question whether objective [*gegenständliche*] truth can be attributed to human thinking is not a question of theory but a *practical* question. In practice man must prove the truth, that is, the reality and power, the this-sidedness [*Diesseitigkeit*] of his thinking. The dispute over the reality or non-reality of thinking which is isolated from practice is a purely *scholastic* question.

III

The materialist doctrine that men are products of circumstances and upbringing, and that, therefore, changed men are products of other circumstances and changed upbringing, forgets that it is men that change circumstances and that the educator himself needs educating. Hence, this doctrine necessarily arrives at dividing society into two parts, of which one is superior to society (in Robert Owen, for example).

　　The coincidence of the changing of circumstances and of human activity can be conceived and rationally understood only as *revolutionizing practice.*

IV

Feuerbach starts out from the fact of religious self-alienation, the duplication of the world into a religious, imaginary world and a real one. His work consists in the dissolution of the religious world into its secular basis. He overlooks the fact that after this work is completed the chief thing still remains to be done. For the fact that the secular foundation detaches itself from itself and establishes itself in the clouds as an independent realm is really only to be explained by the self-cleavage and self-contradictoriness of this secular basis. The latter must itself, therefore, first be understood in its contradiction, and then revolutionized in practice by the removal of the contradiction. Thus, for instance, once the earthly family is discovered to be the secret of the holy family, the former must then itself be criticized in theory and revolutionized in practice.

V

Feuerbach, not satisfied with *abstract thinking,* appeals to *sensuous contemplation;* but he does not conceive sensuousness as *practical,* human-sensuous activity.

VI

Feuerbach resolves the religious essence into the *human* essence. But the human essence is no abstraction inherent in each single individual. In its reality it is the ensemble of the social relations.

Feuerbach, who does not enter upon a criticism of this real essence, is consequently compelled:

1. To abstract from the historical process and to fix the religious sentiment [*Gemüt*] as something by itself and to presuppose an abstract—*isolated*—human individual.
2. The human essence, therefore, can with him be comprehended only as "genus," as an internal, dumb generality which merely *naturally* unites the many individuals.

VII

Feuerbach, consequently, does not see that the "religious sentiment" is itself a *social product,* and that the abstract individual whom he analyzes belongs in reality to a particular form of society.

VIII

Social life is essentially *practical.* All mysteries which mislead theory to mysticism find their rational solution in human practice and in the comprehension of this practice.

IX

The highest point attained by *contemplative* materialism, that is, materialism which does not understand sensuousness as practical activity, is the contemplation of single individuals in "civil society."

X

The standpoint of the old materialism is "civil" society; the standpoint of the new is *human* society, or socialized humanity.

XI

The philosophers have only *interpreted* the world, in various ways; the point however, is to *change* it.

Reading 2

....

RELIGION AS NEUROSIS—SIGMUND FREUD

In a certain sense, Freud and Marx are at the opposite ends of the argument about human suffering. Marx saw suffering as the result of the oppression of one social class by another. Freud (1856–1939) saw it as the result of unresolved childhood conflicts. Marx called for revolution, Freud for psychoanalysis. Marx wanted the workers to throw off the chains of bourgeoisie oppression. Freud wanted the patient to throw off the domination of the neurotic super-ego. Marx exhorted his followers to social action, Freud prescribed long and painful self-examination.

But both were atheists, both were materialists, both rejected the spiritual, both believed that materialism was necessary for science and that their respective analyses were "scientific," indeed, the only possible science. Both began movements that often have looked like substitute religions, even substitute churches. Both often looked and acted like the Moses of their new faiths. Both have had enormous influence on how men and women, including many who are anything but Marxists or Freudians, think about religion.

For Freud, religion is essentially neurotic, a regression to childhood behavior patterns of guilt and dependency, based either on humankind's collective guilt about the murder of a father by the primal horde (in *Totem and Taboo*) or on the human need to transfer control of life to a father figure (as in *Moses and Monotheism*). Religion, therefore, reinforces the control of the superego—the childish self with its feelings of guilt—over the reality principle, the mature self. In the process of discharging guilt and breaking free of dependency, psychoanalysis should free a person from the religious illusion.

Freud no more proves the truth of this analysis of religion than Marx proved the truth of his analysis. The brilliance of his insight is taken to be sufficient proof, a posture that no responsible modern scientist could possibly accept. Yet it is certainly clear to both clinicians, who must work every day with the emotionally troubled, and to ordinary people that religion is often the focus if not the cause of much neurosis, especially if religion is linked to conflicts with one's parents. God becomes the father, the church becomes the mother, and guilt over one's failures to be what parents want one to be becomes the source of neurotic feelings of "sinfulness."

Some religious leaders often seem to be only too willing to become substitutes for parents and thus targets for neurotic guilt and anger. Just as Marx was entirely correct that religion often was (and is) a drug to narcotize the oppressed, so Freud was entirely correct that religious faith and fervor are often the result of guilt and dependency.

The question remains, however, of whether that is all that religion does. Is religion ever radical instead of reactionary? Are religious men and women ever relatively free of neurosis? Freud never really bothered to try to respond to the latter question, just as Marx never bothered to respond to the former question. For both men, in fact, the questions never arose because on *apriori* grounds there was no point in asking them.

Questions for Reflection and Discussion

1. How do parent figures and religious figures become confused?
2. Why is religion such an easy target for neurosis?
3. What do you think of Freud's argument about Moses?
4. How would you design a study to test Freud's theory about religion?

MOSES AND MONOTHEISTIC RELIGION
Sigmund Freud

THE PROGRESS IN SPIRITUALITY

To achieve lasting psychical effects in a people it is obviously not sufficient to assure them that they were specially chosen by God. This assurance must be proved if they are to attach belief to it and draw their conclusions from that belief. In the religion of Moses the Exodus served as such a proof; God, or Moses in his name, did not tire of citing this proof of favour. The feast of the Passover was established to keep this event in mind, or, rather, an old feast was endowed with this memory. Yet it was only a memory. The Exodus itself belonged to a dim past. At the time the signs of God's favour were meagre enough; the fate of the people of Israel would rather indicate his disfavour. Primitive peoples used to depose or even punish their gods if they did not fulfil their duty of granting them victory, fortune, and comfort. Kings have often been treated similarly to gods in every age; the ancient identity of king and god—that is, their common origin—thus becomes manifest. Modern peoples also are in the habit of thus getting rid of their kings if the splendour of their reign is dulled by defeats accompanied by the loss of land and money. Why the people of Israel, however, adhered to their God all the more devotedly the worse they were treated by him—that is a question which we must leave open for the moment.

It may stimulate us to inquire whether the religion of Moses had given the people nothing but an increase in self-confidence through the consciousness of

Source: Sigmund Freud, *Moses and Monotheism,* Translated from the German by Katherine Jones. New York: Vintage Books, 1958. Copyright 1939.

being "chosen." The next element is indeed easily found. Their religion also gave to the Jews a much more grandiose idea of their God or, to express it more soberly, the idea of a more august God. Whoever believed in this God took part in his greatness, so to speak, might feel uplifted himself. This may not be quite obvious to unbelievers, but it may be illustrated by the simile of the high confidence a Briton would feel in a foreign land made unsafe by revolt, a confidence in which a subject of some small Continental state would be entirely lacking. The Briton counts on his government to send a warship if a hair of his head is touched, and also on the rebels' knowing very well that this is so, while the small state does not even own a warship. The pride in the greatness of the British Empire has therefore one of its roots in the consciousness of the greater security and protection that a British subject enjoys. The same may be true of the idea of the great God, and—since one would hardly presume to assist God in his conduct of the world—pride in the greatness of God goes together with that of being "chosen."

Among the precepts of Mosaic religion is one that has more significance than is at first obvious. It is the prohibition against making an image of God, which means the compulsion to worship an invisible God. I surmise that in this point Moses surpassed the Aton religion in strictness. Perhaps he meant to be consistent; his God was to have neither a name nor a countenance. The prohibition was perhaps a fresh precaution against magic malpractices. If this prohibition was accepted, however, it was bound to exercise a profound influence. For it signified subordinating sense perception to an abstract idea; it was a triumph of spirituality over the senses; more precisely, an instinctual renunciation accompanied by its psychologically necessary consequences.

To make more credible what at first glance does not appear convincing we must call to mind other processes of similar character in the development of human culture. The earliest among them, and perhaps the most important, we can discern only in dim outline in the obscurity of primeval times. Its surprising effects make it necessary to conclude that it happened. In our children, in adult neurotics, as well as in primitive people, we find the mental phenomenon which I have called the belief in the "omnipotence of thoughts." We judge it to be an over-estimation of the influence which our mental faculties—the intellectual ones in this case—can exert on the outer world by changing it. All magic, the predecessor of science, is basically founded on these premises. All magic of words belongs here, as does the conviction of the power connected with the knowledge and the pronouncing of a name. We surmise that "omnipotence of thoughts" was the expression of the pride mankind took in the development of language, which had brought in its train such an extraordinary increase in the intellectual faculties. There opened then the new realm of spirituality where conceptions, memories, and deductions became of decisive importance, in contrast to the lower psychical activity which concerned itself with the immediate perceptions of the sense organs. It was certainly one of the most important stages on the way to becoming human.

Another process of later time confronts us in a much more tangible form. Under the influence of external conditions—which we need not follow up here and which in part are also not sufficiently known—it happened that the matri-archal structure of society was replaced by a patriarchal one. This naturally brought with it a revolution in the existing state of the law. An echo of this revolution can still be heard, I think, in the *Oresteia* of Æschylus. This turning from the mother to the father, however, signifies above all a victory of spirituality over the senses—that is to say, a step forward in culture, since maternity is proved by the senses whereas paternity is a surmise based on a deduction and a premise. This declaration in favour of the thought-process, thereby raising it above sense perception, was proved to be a step charged with serious consequences.

Some time between the two cases I have mentioned, another event took place which shows a closer relationship to the ones we have investigated in the history of religion. Man found that he was faced with the acceptance of "spiritual" forces—that is to say, such forces as cannot be apprehended by the senses, particularly not by sight, and yet having undoubted, even extremely strong effects. If we may trust to language, it was the movement of the air that provided the image of spirituality, since the spirit borrows its name from the breath of wind (*animus, spiritus,* Hebrew *ruach* = smoke). The idea of the soul was thus born as the spiritual principle in the individual. Observation found the breath of air again in the human breath, which ceases with death; even today we talk of a dying man breathing his last. Now the realm of spirits had opened for man, and he was ready to endow everything in nature with the soul he had discovered in himself. The whole world became animated, and science, coming so much later, had enough to do in disestablishing the former state of affairs and has not yet finished this task.

Through the Mosaic prohibition, God was raised to a higher level of spirituality; the door was opened to further changes in the idea of God, of which I shall speak later. At present another of its effects will occupy us. All such progress in spirituality results in increasing self-confidence, in making people proud so that they feel superior to those who have remained in the bondage of the senses. We know that Moses had given the Jews the proud feeling of being God's chosen people; by dematerializing God a new, valuable contribution was made to the secret treasure of the people. The Jews preserved their inclination towards spiritual interests. The political misfortune of the nation taught them to appreciate the only possession they had retained, their written records, at its true value. Immediately after the destruction of the Temple in Jerusalem by Titus, Rabbi Jochanan ben Sakkai asked for permission to open at Jabneh the first school for the study of the Torah. From now on, it was the Holy Book, and the study of it, that kept the scattered people together.

So much is generally known and accepted. I only wished to add that this whole development, so characteristic of the Jews, had been initiated by Moses' prohibition against worshipping God in a visible form.

The preference which through two thousand years the Jews have given to spiritual endeavour has, of course, had its effect; it has helped to build a dike against brutality and the inclination to violence which are usually found where athletic development becomes the ideal of the people. The harmonious development of spiritual and bodily activity, as achieved by the Greeks, was denied to the Jews. In this conflict their decision was at least made in favour of what is culturally the more important. . . .

RENUNCIATION VERSUS GRATIFICATION

It is not at all obvious why progress in spirituality and subordination of the senses should raise the self-confidence of a person as well as of a nation. This seems to presuppose a definite standard of value and another person or institution who uses it. For an explanation we turn to an analogous case in the psychology of the individual, which we have learned to understand.

When the Id makes an instinctual demand of an erotic or aggressive nature on a human being, the most simple and natural response for the Ego, which governs the apparatus for thinking and muscle innervation, is to satisfy this by an action. This satisfaction of the instinct is felt as pleasure by the Ego, just as not satisfying this instinct would undoubtedly become a source of discomfort. Now, it may happen that the Ego eschews satisfaction of the instinct because of external obstacles—namely, when it realizes that the action in question would bring in its course serious danger to the Ego. Such a refraining from satisfaction, an "instinctual renunciation" because of external obstacles—as we say, in obedience to the reality-principle—is never pleasurable. The instinctual renunciation would bring about a lasting painful tension if we did not succeed in diminishing the strength of the instinctual urge itself through a displacement of energy. This instinctual renunciation may also be forced on us, however, by other motives, which we rightly call inner ones. In the course of individual development a part of the inhibiting forces in the outer world becomes internalized; a standard is created in the Ego which opposes the other faculties by observation, criticism, and prohibition. We call this new standard the *Super-ego*. From now on, the Ego, before undertaking to satisfy the instincts, has to consider not only the dangers of the outer world, but also the objections of the Super-ego, and has therefore more occasion for refraining from satisfying the instinct. While, however, instinctual renunciation for external reasons is only painful, renunciation for internal reasons, in obedience to the demands of the Super-ego, has another economic effect. It brings besides the inevitable pain a gain in pleasure to the Ego— as it were, a substitutive satisfaction. The Ego feels uplifted; it is proud of the renunciation as of a valuable achievement. We think we can follow the mechanism of this gain in pleasure. The Super-ego is the successor and representative of the parents (and educators) who superintended the actions of the individual in his first years of life; it perpetuates their functions almost without a change. It keeps the Ego in lasting dependence and exercises a steady pressure. The Ego is concerned, just as it was in childhood, to retain the love of its master, and it feels his appreciation as a relief and satisfaction, his reproaches as pricks of conscience. When the Ego has made the sacrifice to the Super-ego of renouncing an instinctual satisfaction, it expects to be rewarded by being loved all the more. The consciousness of deserving this love is felt as pride. At a time when the authority was not yet internalized as Super-ego the relation between the threatened loss of love and the instinctual demand would have been the same. A feeling of security and satisfaction results if out of love to one's parents one achieves an instinctual renunciation. This good feeling could acquire the peculiar narcissistic character of pride only after the authority itself had become a part of the Ego.

How does this explanation of gaining satisfaction through instinctual renunciation help us in understanding the process we wish to study—namely, the increase of self-confidence that accompanies progress in spirituality? Apparently they help very little, for the circumstances here are very different. There is no instinctual enunciation, and there is no second person or higher standard for whose benefit the sacrifice is made. The second statement will soon appear doubtful. One might say that the great man is the authority for whose sake the effort is made, and since the great man achieves this because he is a father substitute we need not be surprised if he is allotted the role of Super-ego in mass psychology. This would, therefore, hold good for the man Moses in his relationship to the Jewish people. In other points, however, there would seem to be no proper analogy. The progress in spirituality consists in deciding against the direct sense perception in favour of the so-called higher intellectual processes— that is to say, in favour of memories, reflection, and deduction. An example of this would be the decision that paternity is more important than maternity, although the former cannot be proved by the senses as the latter can. This is why the child has to have the father's name and inherit after him. Another example would be: our God is the greatest and mightiest, although he is invisible like the storm and the soul. Rejecting a sexual or aggressive instinctual demand seems to be something very different from this. In many examples of progress in spirituality—for instance, in the triumph of father-right—we cannot point to the authority that provides the measure for what is to be valued the more highly. In this case it cannot be the father himself, since it is only this progress that raises him to the rank of an authority. We are therefore confronted with the phenomenon that during the development of mankind the world of the senses becomes gradually mastered by spirituality, and that man feels proud and uplifted by each such step in progress. One does not know, however, why this should be so. Still later it happens that spirituality itself is overpowered by the altogether mysterious emotional phenomenon of belief. This is the famous *credo quia absurdum,* and whoever has compassed this regards it as the highest achievement. Perhaps what is common to all these psychological situations is something else. Perhaps man declares simply that the higher achievement is what is more difficult to attain, and his pride in it is only narcissism heightened by his consciousness of having overcome difficulty.

These considerations are certainly not very fruitful, and one might think that they have nothing to do with our investigation into what determined the character of the Jewish people. This would be only to our advantage, but that this train of thought has all the same to do with our problem is shown by a fact that will occupy us later more extensively. The religion that began with the prohibition against making an image of its God has developed in the course of centuries more and more into a religion of instinctual renunciation. Not that it demands sexual abstinence; it is content with a considerable restriction of sexual freedom. God, however, becomes completely withdrawn from sexuality and raised to an ideal of ethical perfection. Ethics, however, means restriction of instinctual gratification. The Prophets did not tire of maintaining that God demands nothing else from his people but a just and virtuous life—that is to say, abstention from the gratification of all impulses that, according to our present-day moral standards, are to be condemned as vicious. And even the exhortation to believe in God seems to recede in comparison with the seriousness of these ethical demands. Instinctual renunciation thus appears to play a prominent part in religion, although it had not been present in it from the beginning.

Here is the place to make a statement which should obviate a misunderstanding. Though it may seem that instinctual renunciation, and the ethics based on it, do not belong to the essence of religion, still they are genetically closely related to religion. Totemism, the first form of religion of which we know, contains as an indispensable part of its system a number of laws and prohibitions which plainly mean nothing else but instinctual renunciation. There is the worship of the totem, which contains the prohibition against killing or harming it; exogamy (that is to say, the renunciation of the passionately desired mothers and sisters of the horde); the granting of equal rights to all members of the brother horde (that is, the restriction of the impulse to settle their rivalry by brute force). In these rules we have to discern the first beginnings of a moral and social order. It does not escape our notice that here two different motivations come into play. The first two prohibitions work in the direction of what the murdered father would have wished; they, so to speak, perpetuate his will. The third law, the one giving equal rights to the brothers, ignores the father's wishes. Its sense lies in the need of preserving permanently the new order which was established after the death of the father. Otherwise reversion to the former state would have been inevitable. Here social laws became separated from others which, we might say, originated directly from a religious context.

In the abbreviated development of the human individual the most important events of that process are repeated. Here also it is the parents' authority—essentially that of the all-powerful father, who wields the power of punishment—that demands instinctual renunciation on the part of the child and determines what is allowed and what is forbidden. What the child calls "good" or "naughty" becomes later, when society and Super-ego take the place of the parents, "good," in the sense of moral, or "evil," virtuous or vicious. But it is still the same thing: instinctual renunciation through the presence of the authority which replaced and continued that of the father.

Our insight into these problems becomes further deepened when we investigate the strange conception of sanctity. What is it really that appears "sacred" compared with other things which we respect highly and admit to be important and significant? On the one hand the connection between the sacred and the religious is unmistakable; it is so stressed as to be obvious. Everything connected with religion is sacred; it is the very core of sanctity. On the other hand our judgment is disturbed by the numerous attempts to lay claim to the character of holiness by so many other things—persons, institutions, and procedures that have little to do with religion. These endeavours are often plainly tendentious. Let us proceed from the feature of prohibition which adheres so closely to religion. The sacred is obviously something that must not be touched. A sacred prohibition has a very strong affective note, but actually it has no rational motivation. For why should it be such a specially hideous crime to commit incest with a daughter or sister, so much more so than any other sexual relations? When we ask for an explanation we shall surely be told that all our feelings cry out against such a crime. Yet all this means is that the prohibition is taken to be self-evident, that we do not know how to explain it.

That such an explanation is illusory can easily be proved. What is reputed to offend our feelings used to be a general custom—one might say, a sacred tradition—in the ruling families of the ancient Egyptians and other peoples. It went without saying that each Pharaoh found his first and foremost wife in his sister, and the successors of the Pharaohs, the Greek Ptolemies, did not hesitate to follow this example. So far we seem to discern that incest—in this case between brother and sister—was a prerogative forbidden to ordinary mortals and reserved for kings who represented the gods on earth. The world of the Greek and Germanic myths also took no exception to these incestuous relationships. We may surmise that the anxious concern for "family" in our higher nobility is a remnant of that old privilege, and we observe that, as a consequence of inbreeding continued through many generations in the highest social circles, the crowned heads of Europe today consist in effect of one family.

To point to the incest of gods, kings, and heroes helps to dispose of another attempt at explanation—namely, the one that would explain the horror of incest biologically and reduce it to an instinctive knowledge of the harmfulness of inbreeding. It is not even certain, however, that there lies any danger in inbreeding, let alone that primitive races recognized it and guarded against it. The uncertainty in determining permitted and prohibited relationships is another argument against presupposing a "natural feeling" as an original motive for the horror of incest.

Our reconstruction of prehistory forces another explanation on us. The law of exogamy, the negative expression of which is the fear of incest, was the will of the father and continued it after his murder. Hence the strength of its affectivity and the impossibility of a rational motivation—in short, its sacredness. I should confidently anticipate that an investigation of all other cases of sacred prohibitions would lead to the same result as that of the horror of incest—namely, that what is sacred was originally nothing but the perpetuated will of the primeval father. This would also elucidate the ambivalence of the word, hitherto inexplicable, which expresses the conception of sacredness. It is the ambivalence which governs the relationship to the father. "Sacer" does not only mean "sacred," "blessed," but also something that we can only translate by "accursed," "worthy of disgust" (*"auri sacra fames"*). The will of the father, however, was not only something which one must not touch, which one had to hold in high honour, but also something which made one shudder because it necessitated a painful instinctual renunciation. When we hear that Moses "sanctified" his people by introducing the custom of circumcision, we now understand the deep-lying meaning of this pretension. Circumcision is the symbolical substitute of castration, a punishment which the primeval father dealt his sons long ago out of the fullness of his power; and whosoever accepted this symbol showed by so doing that he was ready to submit to the father's will, although it was at the cost of a painful sacrifice.

To return to ethics: we may say in conclusion that a part of its precepts is explained rationally by the necessity of marking off the rights of the community to the individual, those of the individual to the community, and those of individuals to one another. What, however, appears mysterious, grandiose, and mystically self-evident owes its character to its connection with religion, its origin in the will of the father.

THE TRUTH IN RELIGION

How we who have little belief envy those who are convinced of the existence of a Supreme Power, for whom the world holds no problems because he himself has created all its institutions! How comprehensive, exhaustive, and final are the doctrines of the believers compared with the laboured, poor, and patchy attempts at explanation which are the best we can produce! The Divine Spirit, which in itself is the ideal of ethical perfection, has planted within the soul of men the knowledge of this ideal and at the same time the urge to strive towards it. They feel immediately what is high and noble and what low and mean. Their emotional life is measured by the distance from their ideal. It affords them high gratification when they—in perihelion, so to speak—come nearer to it; and they are punished by severe distress when—in aphelion—they have moved farther away from it. All this is so simply and unshakably established. We can only regret it if certain experiences of life and observations of nature have made it impossible to accept the hypothesis of such a Supreme Being. As if the world had not enough problems, we are confronted with the task of finding out how those who have faith in a Divine Being could have acquired it, and whence this belief derives the enormous power that enables it to overwhelm Reason and Science.[1]

Let us return to the more modest problem that has occupied us so far. We set out to explain whence comes the peculiar character of the Jewish people which in all probability is what has enabled that people to survive until today. We found that the man Moses created their character by giving to them a religion which heightened their self-confidence to such a degree that they believed

---

[1] An allusion to the passage in *Faust*: *"Verachte nur Vernunft und Wissenschaft."*—*Translator.*

themselves to be superior to all other peoples. They survived by keeping aloof from the others. Admixture of blood made little difference, since what kept them together was something ideal—the possession they had in common of certain intellectual and emotional values. The Mosaic religion had this effect (1) because it allowed the people to share in the grandeur of its new conception of God, (2) because it maintained that the people had been "chosen" by this great God and was destined to enjoy the proofs of his special favour, and (3) because it forced upon the people a progress in spirituality which, significant enough in itself, further opened the way to respect for intellectual work and to further instinctual renunciations.

This, then, is the conclusion we have attained, but although I do not wish to retract anything I have said before, I cannot help feeling that it is somehow not altogether satisfactory. The cause does not, so to speak, accord with the result. The fact we are trying to explain seems to be incommensurate with everything we adduce by way of explanation. Is it possible that all our investigations have so far discovered not the whole motivation, but only a superficial layer, and that behind this lies hidden another very significant component? Considering how extraordinarily complicated all causation in life and history is, we should have been prepared for something of that kind.

The path to this deeper motivation starts at a certain passage in the previous discussion. The religion of Moses did not achieve its effects immediately, but in a strangely indirect manner. This does not mean that it did not itself produce the effect. It took a long time, many centuries, to do so; that goes without saying where the development of a people's character is concerned. Our modification, however, refers to a fact which we have taken from the history of Jewish religion or, if one prefers, introduced into it. I said that the Jewish people shook off the religion of Moses after a certain time; whether they did so completely or whether they retained some of its precepts we cannot tell. In accepting the supposition that during the long period of the fight for Canaan, and the struggles with the peoples settled there, the Jahve religion did not substantially differ from the worship of the other Baalim, we stand on historical ground, in spite of all the later tendentious attempts to obscure this shaming state of affairs. The religion of Moses, however, had not perished. A sort of memory of it had survived, obscured and distorted, but perhaps supported by individual members of the priest caste through the ancient scripts. It was this tradition of a great past that continued to exert its effect from the background; it slowly attained more and more power over the minds of the people, and at last succeeded in changing the God Jahve into the God of Moses and in bringing again to life the abandoned religion Moses had instituted centuries before.

Earlier in this book I have discussed the hypothesis that would seem to be inevitable if we are to find comprehensible such an achievement on the part of tradition.

THE RETURN OF THE REPRESSED

There are a number of similar processes among those which the analytic investigation of mental life has made known to us. Some of them are termed pathological; others are counted among the varieties of the normal. This matters little, however, for the limits between the two are not strictly defined, and the mechanisms are to a certain extent the same. It is much more important whether the changes in question take place in the Ego itself or whether they confront it as alien; in the latter case they are called symptoms.

Religion as Society's Self-Worship— Emile Durkheim

Marxism and Freudianism, in attenuated format, pervade the atmosphere of modern thought. They shape, however implicitly, the response of many men and women to religion: it is an illusion, created either by the infrastructure of society (the modes of production) or the superstructure of the self (the rigid, controlling super-ego). Emile Durkheim (1858–1917) is not so well known and certainly not so influential. But among sociologists who study religion, Durkheim is far more influential than either Marx or Freud. The latter discuss religion in passing as part of their larger theories of the human condition and dismiss it as an illusion. Durkheim, however, made religion the central concern of his sociology and can be considered in many respects the founder of not only sociology of religion, but also of empirical sociology. In his book *Suicide* (1897), he begins with an empirical question: Why are suicide rates lower for Catholics than for Protestants? His answer is that Catholicism as a community exerts stronger social control than does Protestantism. Catholic suicide rates are, by the way, still lower than Protestant rates, almost a century after Durkheim's analysis.

In his *Elementary Forms of the Religious Life* (1912), Durkheim considers the religion of the Australian aborigines and asks what role it plays in their lives. His startling, original, and creative explanation of religion is that it is society worshipping itself as it experiences itself in the "effervescence" of religious rituals. The experience of the ritual creates religion instead of vice versa.

Durkheim calls these rituals "collective representations" because in them the community becomes conscious of itself as a reality that transcends the personality of the individual members—as for a secular example in a football pep rally. The energies released in such situations become or seem to become a reality distinct from that of the participants. When the rituals are religious—a Catholic Mass, a Jewish High Holiday ceremony, a Protestant revival service— the celebrants encounter what seems to be a religious reality and assume that it is a "supernatural" figure. In fact, they merely encounter society as a collective agent, generating enthusiasm and fervor. Worship of God is in fact nothing more than society worshipping itself. Durkheim has had a tremendous impact on both sociologists and anthropologists. Rituals do not merely reflect religious fervor, they create it. Religions with strong ritual systems have more control on the behavior of their members than do other religions. Thus, Eider, in a study of elderly people showed that those who practiced Catholicism or Judaism (as opposed to Protestantism) had better health and that Jews and Catholics even "postponed" their deaths until after important religious festivals (Christmas, Easter, High Holidays, and Passover). Durkheim established beyond any possibility of doubt that ritual and imagery were of enormous religious importance and that, to a very considerable extent, they shaped religion and religious response.

Like Marx before him and Freud after him, Durkheim was ultimately a reductionist. In explaining, religion, he explained it away. Unlike Marx and Freud, Durkheim, however, was not hostile to religion. Quite the contrary, he was perfectly prepared to see religion as useful and necessary. It could and should continue, though it should abandon the field of explanations about the world to science. He seemed unwilling to face the fact that those who, like himself, saw what religion really was—society's self-worship—would have an insidious effect on the faith of less sophisticated people. It is fair to say that religion as something more than ritual has survived despite Durkheim's analysis. While no serious social-science student of religion today can ignore Durkheim's conclusions, there are relatively few who accept his analysis without considerable qualification.

Questions for Reflection and Discussion

1. Can you explain why Durkheim's analysis of religion is so appealing?
2. What does he leave out of his analysis?
3. Would you be able to respond to a follower of Durkheim who insisted that religion is "nothing but" society worshipping itself?
4. Describe some "collective representations" that you have experienced. Did even the secular ones seem partially religious?

THE ELEMENTARY FORMS OF THE RELIGIOUS LIFE
Emile Durkheim

I

The theorists who have undertaken to explain religion in rational terms have generally seen in it before all else a system of ideas, corresponding to some determined object. This object has been conceived in a multitude of ways: nature, the

Source: Emile Durkheim, *The Elementary Forms of the Religious Life: A Study in Religious Sociology.* Translated from the French by Joseph Ward Swain. London: G. Allen and Unwin, Ltd; New York: The Macmillan Company, 1915.

infinite, the unknowable, the ideal, etc.; but these differences matter but little. In any case, it was the conceptions and beliefs which were considered as the essential elements of religion. As for the rites, from this point of view they appear to be only an external translation, contingent and material, of these internal states which alone pass as having any intrinsic value. This conception is so commonly held that generally the disputes of which religion is the theme turn about the question whether it can conciliate itself with science or not, that is to say, whether or not there is a place beside our scientific knowledge for another form of thought which would be specifically religious.

But the believers, the men who lead the religious life and have a direct sensation of what it really is, object to this way of regarding it, saying that it does not correspond to their daily experience. In fact, they feel that the real function of religion is not to make us think, to enrich our knowledge, nor to add to the conceptions which we owe to science others of another origin and another character, but rather, it is to make us act, to aid us to live. The believer who has communicated with his god is not merely a man who sees new truths of which the unbeliever is ignorant; he is a man who is *stronger*. He feels within him more force, either to endure the trials of existence, or to conquer them. It is as though he were raised above the miseries of the world, because he is raised above his condition as a mere man; he believes that he is saved from evil, under whatever form he may conceive this evil. The first article in every creed is the belief in salvation by faith. But it is hard to see how a mere idea could have this efficacy. An idea is in reality only a part of ourselves; then how could it confer upon us powers superior to those which we have of our own nature? Howsoever rich it might be in affective virtues, it could add nothing to our natural vitality; for it could only release the motive powers which are within us, neither creating them nor increasing them. From the mere fact that we consider an object worthy of being loved and sought after, it does not follow that we feel ourselves stronger afterwards; it is also necessary that this object set free energies superior to these which we ordinarily have at our command and also that we have some means of making these enter into us and unite themselves to our interior lives. Now for that, it is not enough that we think of them; it is also indispensable that we place ourselves within their sphere of action, and that we set ourselves where we may best feel their influence; in a word, it is necessary that we act, and that we repeat the acts thus necessary every time we feel the need of renewing their effects. From this point of view, it is readily seen how that group of regularly repeated acts which form the cult get their importance. In fact, whoever has really practised a religion knows very well that it is the cult which gives rise to these impressions of joy, of interior peace, of serenity, of enthusiasm which are, for the believer, an experimental proof of his beliefs. The cult is not simply a system of signs by which the faith is outwardly translated; it is a collection of the means by which this is created and recreated periodically. Whether it consists in material acts or mental operations, it is always this which is efficacious.

Our entire study rests upon this postulate that the unanimous sentiment of the believers of all times cannot be purely illusory. Together with a recent apologist of the faith[1] we admit that these religious beliefs rest upon a specific experience whose demonstrative value is, in one sense, not one bit inferior to that of scientific experiments, though different from them. We, too, think that "a tree is known by its fruits," and that fertility is the best proof of what the roots are worth. But from the fact that a "religious experience," if we choose to call it this, does exist and that it has a certain foundation—and, by the way, is there any experience which has none?—it does not follow that the reality which is its foundation conforms objectively to the idea which believers have of it. The very fact that the fashion in which it has been conceived has varied infinitely in different times is enough to prove that none of these conceptions express it adequately. If a scientist states it as an axiom that the sensations of heat and light which we feel correspond to some objective cause, he does not conclude that this is what it appears to the senses to be. Likewise, even if the impressions which the faithful feel are not imaginary, still they are in no way privileged intuitions; there is no reason for believing that they inform us better upon the nature of their object than do ordinary sensations upon the nature of bodies and their properties. In order to discover what this object consists of, we must submit them to an examination and elaboration analogous to that which has substituted for the sensuous idea of the world another which is scientific and conceptual.

This is precisely what we have tried to do, and we have seen that this reality, which mythologies have represented under so many different forms, but which is the universal and eternal objective cause of these sensations *sui generis* out of which religious experience is made, is society. We have shown what moral forces it develops and how it awakens this sentiment of a refuge, of a shield and of a guardian support which attaches the believer to his cult. It is that which raises him outside himself; it is even that which made him. For that which makes a man is the totality of the intellectual property which constitutes civilization, and civilization is the work of society. Thus is explained the preponderating role of the cult in all religions, whichever they may be. This is because society cannot make its influence felt unless it is in action, and it is not in action unless the individuals who compose it are assembled together and act in common. It is by common action that it takes consciousness of itself and realizes its position; it is before all else an active cooperation. The collective ideas and sentiments are even possible only owing to these exterior movements which symbolize them, as we have established. Then it is action which dominates the religious life, because of the mere fact that it is society which is its source. . . .

Religious forces are therefore human forces, moral forces. It is true that since collective sentiments can become conscious of themselves only by fixing themselves upon external objects, they have not been able to take form without adopting some of their characteristics from other things: they have thus acquired a sort of physical nature; in this way they have come to mix themselves with the

---

[1]William James, *The Varieties of Religious Experience.*

life of the material world, and then have considered themselves capable of explaining what passes there. But when they are considered only from this point of view and in this role, only their most superficial aspect is seen. In reality, the essential elements of which these collective sentiments are made have been borrowed by the understanding. It ordinarily seems that they should have a human character only when they are conceived under human forms;[2] but even the most impersonal and the most anonymous are nothing else than objectified sentiments. . . .

Some reply that men have a natural faculty for idealizing, that is to say, of substituting for the real world another different one, to which they transport themselves by thought. But that is merely changing the terms of the problem; it is not resolving it or even advancing it. This systematic idealization is an essential characteristic of religions. Explaining them by an innate power of idealization is simply replacing one word by another which is the equivalent of the first; it is as if they said that men have made religions because they have a religious nature. Animals know only one world, the one which they perceive by experience, internal as well as external. Men alone have the faculty of conceiving the ideal, of adding something to the real. Now where does this singular privilege come from? Before making it an initial fact or a mysterious virtue which escapes science, we must be sure that it does not depend upon empirically determinable conditions.

The explanation of religion which we have proposed has precisely this advantage, that it gives an answer to this question. For our definition of the sacred is that it is something added to and above the real: now the ideal answers to this same definition; we cannot explain one without explaining the other. In fact, we have seen that if collective life awakens religious thought on reaching a certain degree of intensity, it is because it brings about a state of effervescence which changes the conditions of psychic activity. Vital energies are overexcited, passions more active, sensations stronger; there are even some which are produced only at this moment. A man does not recognize himself; he feels himself transformed and consequently he transforms the environment which surrounds him. In order to account for the very particular impressions which he receives, he attributes to the things with which he is in most direct contact properties which they have not, exceptional powers and virtues which the objects of everyday experience do not possess. In a word, above the real world where his profane life passes he has placed another which, in one sense, does not exist except in thought, but to which he attributes a higher sort of dignity than to the first. Thus, from a double point of view it is an ideal world.

The formation of the ideal world is therefore not an irreducible fact which escapes science; it depends upon conditions which observation can touch; it is a natural product of social life. For a society to become conscious of itself and maintain at the necessary degree of intensity the sentiments which it thus attains, it must assemble and concentrate itself. Now this concentration brings about an

---

[2]It is for this reason that Frazer and even Preuss set impersonal religious forces outside of, or at least on the threshold of religion, to attach them to magic.

exaltation of the mental life which takes form in a group of ideal conceptions where is portrayed the new life thus awakened; they correspond to this new set of psychical forces which is added to those which we have at our disposition for the daily tasks of existence. A society can neither create itself nor recreate itself without at the same time creating an ideal. This creation is not a sort of work of supererogation for it, by which it would complete itself, being already formed; it is the act by which it is periodically made and remade. Therefore when some oppose the ideal society to the real society, like two antagonists which would lead us in opposite directions, they materialize and oppose abstractions. The ideal society is not outside of the real society; it is a part of it. Far from being divided between them as between two poles which mutually repel each other, we cannot hold to one without holding to the other. For a society is not made up merely of the mass of individuals who compose it, the ground which they occupy, the things which they use and the movements which they perform, but above all is the idea which it forms of itself. It is undoubtedly true that it hesitates over the manner in which it ought to conceive itself; it feels itself drawn in divergent directions. But these conflicts which break forth are not between the ideal and reality, but between two different ideals, that of yesterday and that of to-day, that which has the authority of tradition and that which has the hope of the future. There is surely a place for investigating whence these ideals evolve; but whatever solution may be given to this problem, it still remains that all passes in the world of the ideal.

Thus the collective ideal which religion expresses is far from being due to a vague innate power of the individual, but it is rather at the school of collective life that the individual has learned to idealize. It is in assimilating the ideals elaborated by society that he has become capable of conceiving the ideal. It is society which, by leading him within its sphere of action, has made him acquire the need of raising himself above the world of experience and has at the same time furnished him with the means of conceiving another. For society has constructed this new world in constructing itself, since it is society which this expresses. Thus both with the individual and in the group, the faculty of idealizing has nothing mysterious about it. It is not a sort of luxury which a man could get along without, but a condition of his very existence. He could not be a social being, that is to say, he could not be a man, if he had not acquired it. It is true that in incarnating themselves in individuals, collective ideals tend to individualize themselves. Each understands them after his own fashion and marks them with his own stamp; he suppresses certain elements and adds others. Thus the personal ideal disengages itself from the social ideal in proportion as the individual personality develops itself and becomes an autonomous source of action. But if we wish to understand this aptitude, so singular in appearance, of living outside of reality, it is enough to connect it with the social conditions upon which it depends.

Therefore it is necessary to avoid seeing in this theory of religion a simple restatement of historical materialism: that would be misunderstanding our thought to an extreme degree. In showing that religion is something essentially social, we do not mean to say that it confines itself to translating into another language the material forms of society and its immediate vital necessities. It is true that we take it as evident that social life depends upon its material foundation and bears its mark, just as the mental life of an individual depends upon his nervous system and in fact his whole organism. But collective consciousness is something more than a mere epiphenomenon of its morphological basis, just as individual consciousness is something more than a simple efflorescence of the nervous system. In order that the former may appear, a synthesis *sui generis* of particular consciousnesses is required. Now this synthesis has the effect of disengaging a whole world of sentiments, ideas and images which, once born, obey laws all their own. They attract each other, repel each other, unite, divide themselves, and multiply, though these combinations are not commanded and necessitated by the condition of the underlying reality. The life thus brought into being even enjoys so great an independence that it sometimes indulges in manifestations with no purpose or utility of any sort, for the mere pleasure of affirming itself. We have shown that this is often precisely the case with ritual activity and mythological thought.[3] . . .

That is what the conflict between science and religion really amounts to. It is said that science denies religion in principle. But religion exists; it is a system of given facts; in a word, it is a reality. How could science deny this reality? Also, in so far as religion is action, and in so far as it is a means of making men live, science could not take its place, for even if this expresses life, it does not create it; it may well seek to explain the faith, but by that very act it presupposes it. Thus there is no conflict except upon one limited point. Of the two functions which religion originally fulfilled, there is one, and only one, which tends to escape it more and more: that is its speculative function. That which science refuses to grant to religion is not its right to exist, but its right to dogmatize upon the nature of things and the special competence which it claims for itself for knowing man and the world. As a matter of fact, it does not know itself. It does not even know what it is made of, nor to what need it answers. It is itself a subject for science, so far is it from being able to make the law for science! And from another point of view, since there is no proper subject for religious speculation outside that reality to which scientific reflection is applied, it is evident that this former cannot play the same rôle in the future that it has played in the past.

However, it seems destined to transform itself rather than to disappear. . . .

---

[3]On this same question, see our article, "Représentations individuelles et représentations collectives," in the *Revue de Métaphysique,* May, 1898.

Reading 4

THE FUNCTION OF FUNERALS—
BRONISLAW MALINOWSKI

Malinowski (1884–1942) was a Polish anthropologist who worked in the Trobriand Islands in South Pacific during WWI. His approach to religion is "functionalist." He was not so much concerned with explaining religion as a global phenomenon as he was with describing the function of specific religious activities in society. His description of the funeral ritual here excerpted is a classic in social research and could as easily be applied to a funeral service in a contemporary American church or synagogue as to a primitive people in Melanesia. The ritual reintegrates the social network after the trauma of loss and enables life to continue. Malinowski built on the work of Durkheim, who also described funeral rites, though not so precisely or powerfully, but he did not fall into reductionism. The dangers of functionalism are that the analyst plays God, explaining what people are doing from the point of view of one who understands their "real" if unperceived motivations. In unskilled hands, functionalism can become supercilious and arrogant. Malinowksi, however, was far too sophisticated to succumb to such a temptation. His "primitives" are more or less deliberately creating emotions that reintegrated society. Their ritual is not so much producing a "supernatural" that they can adore, but an attempt to heal wounds in the social fabric.

It seems to the editor of this volume that the Irish wake—now infrequent in Ireland but persisting in somewhat attenuated form in the United States—is a spectacular example of "mortuary ritual." The drinking and singing and dancing in the cottage where the dead body rests (described in the Dublin ballad, "Tim Finnegan's Wake"), to say nothing of the love-making in the fields around the cottage were deliberate acts of defiance aimed at death. The social network was reintegrated by shouting at the top of one's lungs, "Screw you, Death!" It is one way to do it.

Questions for Reflection and Discussion

1. Are not the funeral rites described by Malinowski inherently deceptive, a way of escaping the somber fact of death?
2. Would it not be easier on mourners if there were no such rituals?
3. Analyze with Malinowski's model a funeral rite in which you participated.
4. Do you think that such rituals today are hollow and empty for many who participate in them?

DEATH AND THE REINTEGRATION OF THE GROUP
Bronislaw Malinowski

Of all sources of religion, the supreme and final crisis of life—death—is of the greatest importance. Death is the gateway to the other world in more than the literal sense. According to most theories of early religion, a great deal, if not all, of religious inspiration has been derived from it—and in this orthodox views are on the whole correct. Man has to live his life in the shadow of death, and he who clings to life and enjoys its fullness must dread the menace of its end. And he who is faced by death turns to the promise of life. Death and its denial—Immortality—have always formed, as they form today, the most poignant theme of man's forebodings. The extreme complexity of man's emotional reactions to life finds necessarily its counterpart in his attitude to death. Only what in life has been spread over a long space and manifested in a succession of experiences and events is here at its end condensed into one crisis which provokes a violent and complex outburst of religious manifestations.

Even among the most primitive peoples, the attitude towards death is infinitely more complex and, I may add, more akin to our own, than is usually assumed. It is often stated by anthropologists that the dominant feeling of the survivors is that of horror at the corpse and of fear of the ghost. This twin attitude is even made by no less an authority than Wilhelm Wundt the very nucleus of all religious belief and practice. Yet this assertion is only a half-truth, which means no truth at all. The emotions are extremely complex and even contradictory; the dominant elements, love of the dead and loathing of the corpse, passionate attachment to the personality still lingering about the body and a shattering fear of the gruesome thing that has been left over, these two elements seem to mingle and play into each other. This is reflected in the spontaneous behavior and in the ritual proceedings at death. In the tending of the corpse, in the modes of its disposal, in the post-funerary and commemorative ceremonies, the nearest relatives, the mother mourning for her son, the widow for her husband, the child for the parent, always show some horror and fear mingled with pious love, but never do the negative elements appear alone or even dominant.

The mortuary proceedings show a striking similarity throughout the world. As death approaches, the nearest relatives in any case, sometimes the whole community, forgather by the dying man, and dying, the most private act which a man can perform, is transformed into a public, tribal event. As a rule, a certain differentiation takes place at once, some of the relatives watching near the corpse, others making preparations for the pending end and its consequences, others again performing perhaps some religious acts at a sacred spot. Thus in certain parts of Melanesia the real kinsmen must keep at a distance and only rel-

Source: Bronislaw Malinowski. *Magic, Science and Religion,* Garden City, New York: Doubleday, pp. 47–53. Copyright 1948 by The Free Press.

atives by marriage perform the mortuary services, while in some tribes of Australia the reverse order is observed.

As soon as death has occurred, the body is washed, anointed and adorned, sometimes the bodily apertures are filled, the arms and legs tied together. Then it is exposed to the view of all, and the most important phase, the immediate mourning begins. Those who have witnessed death and its sequel among savages and who can compare these events with their counterpart among other uncivilized peoples must be struck by the fundamental similarity of the proceedings. There is always a more or less conventionalized and dramatized outburst of grief and wailing in sorrow, which often passes among savages into bodily lacerations and the tearing of hair. This is always done in a public display and is associated with visible signs of mourning, such as black or white daubs on the body, shaven or disheveled hair, strange or torn garments.

The immediate mourning goes on round the corpse. This, far from being shunned or dreaded, is usually the center of pious attention. Often there are ritual forms of fondling or attestations of reverence. The body is sometimes kept on the knees of seated persons, stroked and embraced. At the same time these acts are usually considered both dangerous and repugnant, duties to be fulfilled at some cost to the performer. After a time the corpse has to be disposed of. Inhumation with an open or closed grave; exposure in caves or on platforms, in hollow trees or on the ground in some wild desert place; burning or setting adrift in canoes—these are the usual forms of disposal.

This brings us to perhaps the most important point, the two-fold contradictory tendency, on the one hand to preserve the body, to keep its form intact, or to retain parts of it: on the other hand the desire to be done with it, to put it out of the way, to annihilate it completely. Mummification and burning are the two extreme expressions of this two-fold tendency. It is impossible to regard mummification or burning or any intermediate form as determined by mere accident of belief, as a historical feature of some culture or other which has gained its universality by the mechanism of spread and contact only. For in these customs is clearly expressed the fundamental attitude of mind of the surviving relative, friend or lover, the longing for all that remains of the dead person and the disgust and fear of the dreadful transformation wrought by death.

One extreme and interesting variety in which this double-edged attitude is expressed in a gruesome manner is sarco-cannibalism, a custom of partaking in piety of the flesh of the dead person. It is done with extreme repugnance and dread and usually followed by a violent vomiting fit. At the same time it is felt to be a supreme act of reverence, love, and devotion. In fact it is considered such a sacred duty that among the Melanesians of New Guinea, where I have studied and witnessed it, it is still performed in secret, although severely penalized by the white Government. The smearing of the body with the fat of the dead, prevalent in Australia and Papuasia is, perhaps, but a variety of this custom.

In all such rites, there is a desire to maintain the tie and the parallel tendency to break the bond. Thus the funerary rites are considered as unclean and soiling, the contact with the corpse as defiling and dangerous, and the performers have to wash, cleanse their body, remove all traces of contact, and perform ritual lustrations. Yet the mortuary ritual compels man to overcome the repugnance, to conquer his fears, to make piety and attachment triumphant, and with it the belief in a future life, in the survival of the spirit.

And here we touch on one of the most important functions of religious cult. In the foregoing analysis I have laid stress on the direct emotional forces created by contact with death and with the corpse, for they primarily and most powerfully determine the behavior of the survivors. But connected with these emotions and born out of them, there is the idea of the spirit, the belief in the new life into which the departed has entered. And here we return to the problem of animism with which we began our survey of primitive religious facts. What is the substance of a spirit, and what is the psychological origin of this belief?

The savage is intensely afraid of death, probably as the result of some deep-seated instincts common to man and animals. He does not want to realize it was an end, he cannot face the idea of complete cessation, of annihilation. The idea of spirit and of spiritual existence is near at hand, furnished by such experiences as are discovered and described by Tylor. Grasping at it, man reaches the comforting belief in spiritual continuity and in the life after death. Yet this belief does not remain unchallenged in the complex, double-edged play of hope and fear which sets in always in the face of death. To the comforting voice of hope, to the intense desire of immortality, to the difficulty, in one's own case, almost the impossibility, of facing annihilation there are opposed powerful and terrible forebodings. The testimony of the senses, the gruesome decomposition of the corpse, the visible disappearance of the personality—certain apparently instinctive suggestions of fear and horror seem to threaten man at all stages of culture with some idea of annihilation, with some hidden fears and forebodings. And here into this play of emotional forces, into this supreme dilemma of life and final death, religion steps in, selecting the positive creed, the comforting view, the culturally valuable belief in immortality, in the spirit independent of the body, and in the continuance of life after death. In the various ceremonies at death, in commemoration and communion with the departed, and worship of ancestral ghosts, religion gives body and form to the saving beliefs.

Thus the belief in immortality is the result of a deep emotional revelation, standardized by religion, rather than a primitive philosophic doctrine. Man's conviction of continued life is one of the supreme gifts of religion, which judges and selects the better of the two alternatives suggested by self-preservation—the hope of continued life and the fear of annihilation. The belief in spirits is the result of the belief in immortality. The substance of which the spirits are made is the full-blooded passion and desire for life, rather than the shadowy stuff which haunts his dreams and illusions. Religion saves man from a surrender to death and destruction, and in doing this it merely makes use of the observations of dreams, shadows, and visions. The real nucleus of animism lies in the deepest emotional fact of human nature, the desire for life.

Thus the rites of mourning, the ritual behavior immediately after death, can be taken as pattern of the religious act, while the belief in immortality, in the continuity of life and in the nether world, can be taken as the prototype of an act of faith. Here, as in the religious ceremonies previously described, we find self-contained acts, the aim of which is achieved in their very performance. The ritual despair, the obsequies, the acts of mourning, express the emotion of the bereaved and the loss of the whole group. They endorse and they duplicate the natural feelings of the survivors, they create a social event out of a natural fact. Yet, though in the acts of mourning, in the mimic despair of wailing, in the treatment of the corpse and in its disposal, nothing ulterior is achieved, these acts fulfill an important function and possess a considerable value for primitive culture.

What is this function? The imitation ceremonies we have found fulfill theirs in sacralizing tradition; the food cults, sacrament and sacrifice bring man into communion with providence, with the beneficent forces of plenty; totemism standardizes man's practical, useful attitude of selective interest towards his surroundings. If the view here taken of the biological function of religion is true, some such similar role must also be played by the whole mortuary ritual.

The death of a man or woman in a primitive group, consisting of a limited number of individuals, is an event of no mean importance. The nearest relatives and friends are disturbed to the depth of their emotional life. A small community bereft of a member, especially if he be important, is severely mutilated. The whole event breaks the normal course of life and shakes the moral foundations of society. The strong tendency on which we have insisted in the above description: to give way to fear and horror, to abandon the corpse, to run away from the village, to destroy all the belongings of the dead one—all these impulses exist, and if given way to would be extremely dangerous, disintegrating the group, destroying the material foundations of primitive culture. Death in a primitive society is, therefore, much more than the removal of a member. By setting in motion one part of the deep forces of the instinct of self-preservation, it threatens the very cohesion and solidarity of the group, and upon this depends the organization of that society, its tradition, and finally the whole culture. For if primitive man yielded always to the disintegrating impulses of his reaction to death, the continuity of tradition and the existence of material civilization would be made impossible.

We have seen already how religion, by sacralizing and thus standardizing the other set of impulses, bestows on man the gift of mental integrity. Exactly the same function it fulfills also with regard to the whole group. The ceremonial of death which ties the survivors to the body and rivets them to the place of death, the beliefs in the existence of the spirit, in its beneficent influences or malevolent intentions, in the duties of a series of commemorative or sacrificial ceremonies—in all this religion counteracts the centrifugal forces of fear, dismay, demoralization, and provides the most powerful means of reintegration of the group's shaken solidarity and of the re-establishment of its morale.

In short, religion here assures the victory of tradition and culture over the mere negative response of thwarted instinct.

Reading 5

A REPLY TO MARX—MAX WEBER

Max Weber (1864–1920), according to most sociologists is the giant who did more to shape contemporary sociology than any other of the founding geniuses. Much of his life's work was an implicit dialogue with Karl Marx in which Weber argued against materialistic determinism. His best known work, *The Protestant Ethic and the Spirit of Capitalism* (1922), (here excerpted) argues that while religion may be shaped by social institutions (such as the modes of production), it also shapes them. The work ethic ("inner worldly asceticism") is perhaps the result of capitalism, but it also shaped it. Capitalism, is in part the product of a religious ethic.

There is much debate about what exactly Weber meant. Indeed the production of books purporting to explain Weber has become a cottage industry among sociologists. Several conclusions about what Weber did *not* mean seem, however, to be generally accepted:

1. Weber did not believe that Protestantism caused capitalism. Something very much like the capitalist system of plowing profits back into the enterprise already existed in the medieval Italian city states.
2. He did not believe that all forms of Protestantism encouraged the "vocation" of the work ethic. Indeed the Reformers were diligent in their condemnation of greed.
3. He did not believe that religious affiliation still necessarily correlated with the work ethic—though his evidence did show that there was more stress on education in the Protestant regions of Germany than in the Catholic.
4. He did not believe that without the Reformation, capitalism would not have emerged.

What did he mean?

Weber believed that there was an affinity between the kind of work habits that capitalism requires and the ethical emphasis of certain kinds of Protestantism, particularly Calvinism. This affinity created a situation in which those who possesses such an ethic would become leaders in the capitalist enterprise and to some extent shape its development. Eventually the ethic (which Weber did not like) would become so powerful and pervasive in capitalist society that it would no longer correlate with religion.

His analysis then is cautious, complex, and low key. Marx said the economic organization of society shaped religion, that the latter was little more than an epiphenomon. Weber did *not* reply that the truth was the other way around. Rather, he replied that matters were more complicated and that both religion and economic organization were capable to some extent of shaping one another.

Such an analysis does not provide the sort of rallying cry around which revolutions are organized. But it does correspond to the gray, problematic nature of ordinary reality with what a common-sense answer would be to the question of whether religion shapes economic structure or economic structure shapes religion.

Weber's reply in language much simpler than the heavy Teutonic academic rhetoric, which he would have preferred, is that both are capable of influencing each other. It is an insight that seems so self-evident as to be trivial, except that since Marx, millions of people rejected it. Moreover it completely recasts the issue of religion in modern society. In Weber's view of things, religion was not merely the result of collective experiences of higher powers (though it surely could be that too). Religion was also a road map, which explained the meaning of life and provided directions for how men and women ought to live It is fair to say that this understanding of religion has shaped sociology and the sociology of religion ever since. There are still reductionists, men and women who insisted that religion is "nothing but. . . ." However, after Max Weber that position is a difficult one to take.

Questions for Reflection and Discussion

1. In your experience, do Protestants and Catholics in fact have different approaches to life and work?
2. What do you think of "inner worldly asceticism?" Is it a good way to live? What are its advantages and disadvantages?
3. Is Weber "blaming" capitalism on Protestants?
4. If the Reformation had not happened, would there still be capitalism? What might it be like?

THE PROTESTANT ETHIC AND THE SPIRIT OF CAPITALISM
Max Weber

In order to understand the connection between the fundamental religious ideas of ascetic Protestantism and its maxims for everyday economic conduct, it is

Source: Max Weber, "Asceticism and the Spirit of Capitalism," from Max Weber, *The Protestant Ethic and the Spirit of Capitalism,* New York: Scribner's, 1958, pp. 155–183.

necessary to examine with especial care such writings as have evidently been derived from ministerial practice. For in a time in which the beyond meant everything, when the social position of the Christian depended upon his admission to the communion, the clergyman, through his ministry, Church discipline, and preaching, exercised an influence (as a glance at collections of *consilia, casus conscientiæ,* etc., shows) which we modern men are entirely unable to picture. In such a time the religious forces which express themselves through such channels are the decisive influences in the formation of national character.

For the purposes of this chapter, though by no means for all purposes, we can treat ascetic Protestantism as a single whole. But since that side of English Puritanism which was derived from Calvinism gives the most consistent religious basis for the idea of the calling, we shall, following our previous method, place one of its representatives at the centre of the discussion. Richard Baxter stands out above many other writers on Puritan ethics, both because of his eminently practical and realistic attitude, and, at the same time, because of the universal recognition accorded to his works, which have gone through many new editions and translations. He was a Presbyterian and an apologist of the Westminister Synod, but at the same time, like so many of the best spirits of his time, gradually grew away from the dogmas of pure Calvinism. At heart he opposed Cromwell's usurpation as he would any revolution. He was unfavourable to the sects and the fanatical enthusiasm of the saints, but was very broad-minded about external peculiarities and objective towards his opponents. He sought his field of labour most especially in the practical promotion of the moral life through the Church. In the pursuit of this end, as one of the most successful ministers known to history, he placed his services at the disposal of the Parliamentary Government, of Cromwell, and of the Restoration, until he retired from office under the last, before St. Bartholomew's day. His *Christian Directory* is the most complete compendium of Puritan ethics, and is continually adjusted to the practical experiences of his own ministerial activity. In comparison we shall make use of Spener's *Theologische Bedenken,* as representative of German Pietism, Barclay's *Apology* for the Quakers, and some other representatives of ascetic ethics, which, however, in the interest of space, will be limited as far as possible.

Now, in glancing at Baxter's *Saints' Everlasting Rest,* or his *Christian Directory,* or similar works of others, one is struck at first glance by the emphasis placed, in the discussion of wealth and its acquisition, on the ebionitic elements of the New Testament. Wealth as such is a great danger; its temptations never end, and its pursuit is not only senseless as compared with the dominating importance of the Kingdom of God, but it is morally suspect. Here asceticism seems to have turned much more sharply against the acquisition of earthly goods than it did in Calvin, who saw no hindrance to the effectiveness of the clergy in their wealth, but rather a thoroughly desirable enhancement of their prestige. Hence he permitted them to employ their means profitably. Examples of the condemnation of the pursuit of money and goods may be gathered without end from Puritan writings, and may be contrasted with the late mediæval ethical literature, which was much more open-minded on this point.

Moreover, these doubts were meant with perfect seriousness; only it is necessary to examine them somewhat more closely in order to understand their true ethical significance and implications. The real moral objection is to relaxation in the security of possession, the enjoyment of wealth with the consequence of idleness and the temptations of the flesh, above all of distraction from the pursuit of a righteous life. In fact, it is only because possession involves this danger of relaxation that it is objectionable at all. For the saints' everlasting rest is in the next world; on earth man must, to be certain of his state of grace, "do the works of him who sent him, as long as it is yet day." Not leisure and enjoyment, but only activity serves to increase the glory of God, according to the definite manifestations of His will.

Waste of time is thus the first and in principle the deadliest of sins. The span of human life is infinitely short and precious to make sure of one's own election. Loss of time through sociability, idle talk, luxury, even more sleep than is necessary for health, six to at most eight hours, is worthy of absolute moral condemnation. It does not yet hold, with Franklin, that time is money, but the proposition is true in a certain spiritual sense. It is infinitely valuable because every hour lost is lost to labour for the glory of God. Thus inactive contemplation is also valueless, or even directly reprehensible if it is at the expense of one's daily work. For it is less pleasing to God than the active performance of His will in a calling. Besides, Sunday is provided for that, and, according to Baxter, it is always those who are not diligent in their callings who have no time for God when the occasion demands it.

Accordingly, Baxter's principal work is dominated by the continually repeated, often almost passionate preaching of hard, continuous bodily or mental labour. It is due to a combination of two different motives. Labour is, on the one hand, an approved ascetic technique, as it always has been in the Western Church, in sharp contrast not only to the Orient but to almost all monastic rules the world over. It is in particular the specific defence against all those temptations which Puritanism united under the name of the unclean life, whose role for it was by no means small. The sexual asceticism of Puritanism differs only in degree, not in fundamental principle, from that of monasticism; and on account of the Puritan conception of marriage, its practical influence is more far-reaching than that of the latter. For sexual intercourse is permitted, even within marriage, only as the means willed by God for the increase of His glory according to the commandment, "Be fruitful and multiply." Along with a moderate vegetable diet and cold baths, the same prescription is given for all sexual temptations as is used against religious doubts and a sense of moral unworthiness: "Work hard in your calling." But the most important thing was that even beyond that labour came to be considered in itself the end of life, ordained as such by God. St. Paul's "He who will not work shall not eat" holds unconditionally for everyone. Unwillingness to work is symptomatic of the lack of grace. . . .

This worldly Protestant asceticism, as we may recapitulate up to this point, acted powerfully against the spontaneous enjoyment of possessions; it restricted consumption, especially of luxuries. On the other hand, it had the psychological effect of freeing the acquisition of goods from the inhibitions of traditionalistic ethics. It broke the bonds of the impulse of acquisition in that it not only legalized it, but (in the sense discussed) looked upon it as directly willed by God. The campaign against the temptations of the flesh, and the dependence on external things, was, as besides the Puritans the great Quaker apologist Barclay expressly says, not a struggle against the rational acquisition, but against the irrational use of wealth.

But this irrational use was exemplified in the outward forms of luxury which their code condemned as idolatry of the flesh, however natural they had appeared to the feudal mind. On the other hand, they approved the rational and utilitarian uses of wealth which were willed by God for the needs of the individual and the community. They did not wish to impose mortification on the man of wealth, but the use of his means for necessary and practical things. The idea of comfort characteristically limits the extent of ethically permissible expenditures. It is naturally no accident that the development of a manner of living consistent with that idea may be observed earliest and most clearly among the most consistent representatives of this whole attitude toward life. Over against the glitter and ostentation of feudal magnificence which, resting on an unsound economic basis, prefers a sordid elegance to a sober simplicity, they set the clean and solid comfort of the middle-class home as an ideal.

On the side of the production of private wealth, asceticism condemned both dishonesty and impulsive avarice. What was condemned as covetousness, Mammonism, etc., was the pursuit of riches for their own sake. For wealth in itself was a temptation. But here asceticism was the power "which ever seeks the good but ever creates evil"; what was evil in its sense was possession and its temptations. For, in conformity with the Old Testament and in analogy to the ethical valuation of good works, asceticism looked upon the pursuit of wealth as an end in itself as highly reprehensible; but the attainment of it as a fruit of labour in a calling was a sign of God's blessing. And even more important: the religious valuation of restless, continuous, systematic work in a worldly calling, as the highest means to asceticism, and at the same time the surest and most evident proof of rebirth and genuine faith, must have been the most powerful conceivable lever for the expansion of that attitude toward life which we have here called the spirit of capitalism.

When the limitation of consumption is combined with this release of acquisitive activity, the inevitable practical result is obvious: accumulation of capital through ascetic compulsion to save. The restraints which were imposed upon the consumption of wealth naturally served to increase it by making possible the productive investment of capital. How strong this influence was is not, unfortunately, susceptible of exact statistical demonstration. In New England the connection is so evident that it did not escape the eye of so discerning a historian as Doyle. But also in Holland, which was really only dominated by strict Calvinism for seven years, the greater simplicity of life in the more seriously religious circles, in combination with great wealth, led to an excessive propensity to accumulation.

That, furthermore, the tendency which has existed everywhere and at all times, being quite strong in Germany today, for middle-class fortunes to be absorbed into the nobility, was necessarily checked by the Puritan antipathy to the feudal way of life, is evident. English Mercantilist writers of the seventeenth century attributed the superiority of Dutch capital to English to the circumstance that newly acquired wealth there did not regularly seek investment in land. Also, since it is not simply a question of the purchase of land, it did not there seek to transfer itself to feudal habits of life, and thereby to remove itself from the possibility of capitalistic investment. The high esteem for agriculture as a peculiarly important branch of activity, also especially consistent with piety, which the Puritans shared, applied (for instance in Baxter) not to the landlord, but to the yeoman and farmer, in the eighteenth century not to the squire, but the rational cultivator. Through the whole of English society in the time since the seventeenth century goes the conflict between the squirearchy, the representatives of "merrie old England," and the Puritan circles of widely varying social influence. Both elements, that of an unspoiled naïve joy of life, and of a strictly regulated, reserved self-control, and conventional ethical conduct are even today combined to form the English national character. Similarly, the early history of the North American Colonies is dominated by the sharp contrast of the adventurers, who wanted to set up plantations with the labour of indentured servants, and live as feudal lords, and the specifically middle-class outlook of the Puritans.

As far as the influence of the Puritan outlook extended, under all circumstances—and this is, of course, much more important than the mere encouragement of capital accumulation—it favoured the development of a rational bourgeois economic life; it was the most important, and above all the only consistent influence in the development of that life. It stood at the cradle of the modern economic man.

To be sure, these Puritanical ideals tended to give way under excessive pressure from the temptations of wealth, as the Puritans themselves knew very well. With great regularity we find the most genuine adherents of Puritanism among the classes which were rising from a lowly status, the small bourgeois and farmers, while the *beati possidentes,* even among Quakers, are often found tending to repudiate the old ideals. It was the same fate which again and again befell the predecessor of this worldly asceticism, the monastic asceticism of the Middle Ages. In the latter case, when rational economic activity had worked out its full effects by strict regulation of conduct and limitation of consumption, the wealth accumulated either succumbed directly to the nobility, as in the time before the Reformation, or monastic discipline threatened to break down, and one of the numerous reformations became necessary.

In fact the whole history of monasticism is in a certain sense the history of a continual struggle with the problem of the secularizing influence of wealth. The same is true on a grand scale of the worldly asceticism of Puritanism. The great revival of Methodism, which preceded the expansion of English industry toward the end of the eighteenth century, may well be compared with such a monastic reform. We may hence quote here a passage from John Wesley himself which might well serve as a motto for everything which has been said above. For it shows that the leaders of these ascetic movements understood the seemingly paradoxical relationships which we have here analysed perfectly well, and in the same sense that we have given them. He wrote: "I fear, wherever riches have increased, the essence of religion has decreased in the same proportion. Therefore I do not see how it is possible, in the nature of things, for any revival of true religion to continue long. For religion must necessarily produce both industry and frugality, and these cannot but produce riches. But as riches increase, so will pride, anger, and love of the world in all its branches. How then is it possible that Methodism, that is, a religion of the heart, though it flourishes now as a green bay tree, should continue in this state? For the Methodists in every place grow diligent and frugal; consequently they increase in goods. Hence they proportionately increase in pride, in anger, in the desire of the flesh, the desire of the eyes, and the pride of life. So, although the form of religion remains, the spirit is swiftly vanishing away. Is there no way to prevent this—this continual decay of pure religion? We ought not to prevent people from being diligent and frugal; *we must exhort all Christians to gain all they can, and to save all they can; that is, in effect, to grow rich.*" . . .

A specifically bourgeois economic ethic had grown up. With the consciousness of standing in the fullness of God's grace and being visibly blessed by Him, the bourgeois business man, as long as he remained within the bounds of formal correctness, as long as his moral conduct was spotless and the use to which he put his wealth was not objectionable, could follow his pecuniary interests as he would and feel that he was fulfilling a duty in doing so. The power of religious asceticism provided him in addition with sober, conscientious, and unusually industrious workmen, who clung to their work as to a life purpose willed by God. . . .

One of the fundamental elements of the spirit of modern capitalism, and not only of that but of all modern culture: rational conduct on the basis of the idea of the calling, was born—that is what this discussion has sought to demonstrate—from the spirit of Christian asceticism. One has only to re-read the passage from Franklin, quoted at the beginning of this essay, in order to see that the essential elements of the attitude which was there called the spirit of capitalism are the same as what we have just shown to be the content of the Puritan worldly asceticism, only without the religious basis, which by Franklin's time had died away. The idea that modern labour has an ascetic character is of course not new. Limitation to specialized work, with a renunciation of the Faustian universality of man which it involves, is a condition of any valuable work in the modern world; hence deeds and renunciation inevitably condition each other today. This fundamentally ascetic trait of middle-class life, if it attempts to be a way of life at all, and not simply the absence of any, was what Goethe wanted to teach, at the height of his wisdom, in the *Wanderjahren,* and in the end which he gave to the life of his *Faust.* For him the realization meant a renunciation, a departure from an age of full and beautiful humanity, which can no more be repeated in the course of our cultural development than can the flower of the Athenian culture of antiquity.

The Puritan wanted to work in a calling; we are forced to do so. For when asceticism was carried out of monastic cells into everyday life, and began to dominate worldly morality, it did its part in building the tremendous cosmos of the modern economic order. This order is now bound to the technical and economic conditions of machine production which today determine the lives of all the individuals who are born into this mechanism, not only those directly concerned with economic acquisition, with irresistible force. Perhaps it will so determine them until the last ton of fossilized coal is burnt. In Baxter's view the care for external goods should only lie on the shoulders of the "saint like a light cloak, which can be thrown aside at any moment." But fate decreed that the cloak should become an iron cage.

Since asceticism undertook to remodel the world and to work out its ideals in the world, material goods have gained an increasing and finally an inexorable power over the lives of men as at no previous period in history. Today the spirit of religious asceticism—whether finally, who knows?—has escaped from the cage. But victorious capitalism, since it rests on mechanical foundations, needs its support no longer. The rosy blush of its laughing heir, the Enlightenment, seems also to be irretrievably fading, and the idea of duty in one's calling prowls about in our lives like the ghost of dead religious beliefs. Where the fulfilment of the calling cannot directly be related to the highest spiritual and cultural values, or when, on the other hand, it need not be felt simply as economic compulsion, the individual generally abandons the attempt to justify it at all. In the field of its highest development, in the United States, the pursuit of wealth, stripped of its religious and ethical meaning, tends to become associated with purely mundane passions, which often actually give it the character of sport.

No one knows who will live in this cage in the future, or whether at the end of this tremendous development entirely new prophets will arise, or there will be a great rebirth of old ideas and ideals, or, if neither, mechanized petrification, embellished with a sort of convulsive self-importance. For of the last stage of this cultural development, it might well be truly said: "Specialists without spirit, sensualists without heart; this nullity imagines that it has attained a level of civilization never before achieved.". . .

....

Religion as a Search for Meaning— Talcott Parsons

Talcott Parsons (1902–1979), who taught at Harvard University for several decades, was the most influential American sociologist of his generation, both because of his books and because of his classroom work with many who would teach sociology in major American universities. He did his graduate work in Germany and there studied Max Weber. When he returned to the United States, he translated some of Weber's writing into English. Using Weber as a source and inspiration, he developed an elaborate theory of human social behavior as "purposive social action"—an approach directly antagonistic to materialism and determinism, especially of the Marxist variety.

His literary style was, alas, opaque and sometimes virtually unintelligible. His Marxist critics, especially during the 1960s, took glee in ridiculing and satirizing Parsons, whom they accused of underwriting the social order and of providing no room in his system for social change, to say nothing of revolution.

The excerpted essay, written in 1944, does not suffer from heaviness of style (which students insisted did not affect his classroom lectures). Moreover, it foreshadows his later theory that human behavior is shaped to some considerable (though not total) extent by the meaning that humans attach to their lives. Humans, to anticipate Parsons' student Clifford Geertz, are interpreting animals. Their behavior depends on their interpretations.

The essay also neatly and deftly combines the work of the earlier classic theorists with that of Weber to develop a theory of religion as providing an answer to the "problem of meaning." The "function" of religion is to give meaning to life—a notion with which most humans would have little trouble agreeing, but which seems to have escaped the classic theorists.

If life needs explanation, if humans require meaning to shape their lives, then there will always be religion, if not for everyone, then for most humans.

Parsons' brief synthesis has itself provided meaning for the working of sociologists of religion ever since. While often they have been content to look at devotion figures to see whether the influence of religion is waxing or waning, they cannot pretend finally that those are the important issues about religion. To study religion as a sociologist finally means to ask how religious meaning systems influence human behavior.

Questions for Reflection and Discussion

1. Do you think that Parsons's synthesis is artificial? Why or why not?
2. If you were trying to write a synthesis based on the readings so far, is there anything you want to add to Parsons?
3. Could there be a "secular religion," a system of beliefs that explained life satisfactorily and did not need to postulate any "supernatural?" What might that religion look like?
4. Despite Parsons, don't most people live and work automatically without any need for meaning?

RELIGION AND THE PROBLEM OF MEANING
Talcott Parsons

Malinowski shows quite clearly that neither ritual practices, magical or religious, nor the beliefs about supernatural forces and entities integrated with them can be treated simply as a primitive and inadequate form of rational techniques or scientific knowledge; they are qualitatively distinct and have quite different functional significance in the system of action (see Malinowski, 1926). Durkheim (1915; see also Parsons, 1937, ch. 11), however, went farther than Malinowski in working out the specific character of this difference, as well as in bringing out certain further aspects of the functional problem. Whereas Malinowski tended to focus attention on functions in relation to action in a situation, Durkheim became particularly interested in the problem of the specific attitudes exhibited towards supernatural entities and ritual objects and actions. The results of this study he summed up in the fundamental distinction between the sacred and the profane. Directly contrasting the attitudes appropriate in a ritual context with those towards objects of utilitarian significance and their use in fields of rational technique, he found one fundamental feature of the sacred to be its radical dissociation from any utilitarian context. The sacred is to be treated with a certain specific attitude of respect, which Durkheim identified with the appropriate attitude towards moral obligations and authority. If the effect of the prominence which Durkheim gives to the conception of the sacred is strongly to reinforce the significance of Malinowski's observation that the two systems are not confused but are in fact treated as essentially separate, it also brings out even more sharply than did Malinowski the inadequacy of the older

Source: T. Parsons, *Essays in Sociological Theory,* Free Press of Glencoe, 1954, pp. 204–10. (First published 1944.)

approach to this range of problems which treated them entirely as the outcome of intellectual processes in ways indistinguishable from the solution of empirical problems. Such treatment could not but obscure the fundamental distinction upon which Durkheim insisted.

The central significance of the sacred in religion, however, served to raise in a peculiarly acute form the question of the source of the attitude of respect. Spencer, for instance, had derived it from the belief that the souls of the dead reappear to the living, and from ideas about the probable dangers of association with them. Max Müller and the naturalist school, on the other hand, had attempted to derive all sacred things in the last analysis from personification of certain phenomena of nature which were respected and feared because of their intrinsically imposing or terrifying character. Durkheim opened up an entirely new line of thought by suggesting that it was hopeless to look for a solution of the problem on this level at all. There was in fact no common intrinsic quality of things treated as sacred which could account for the attitude of respect. In fact, almost everything from the sublime to the ridiculous has in some society been treated as sacred. Hence the source of sacredness is not intrinsic; the problem is of a different character. Sacred objects and entities are symbols. The problem then becomes one of identifying the referents of such symbols. It is that which is symbolized and not the intrinsic quality of the symbol which becomes crucial.

At this point Durkheim became aware of the fundamental significance of his previous insight that the attitude of respect for sacred things was essentially identical with the attitude of respect for moral authority. If sacred things are symbols, the essential quality of that which they symbolize is that it is an entity which would command moral respect. It was by this path that Durkheim arrived at the famous proposition that society is always the real object of religious veneration. In this form the proposition is certainly unacceptable, but there is no doubt of the fundamental importance of Durkheim's insight into the exceedingly close integration of the system of religious symbols of a society and the patterns sanctioned by the common moral sentiments of the members of the community. In his earlier work (see also Parsons, 1937, chs. 8 and 10) Durkheim had progressed far in understanding the functional significance of an integrated system of morally sanctioned norms. Against this background the integration he demonstrated suggested a most important aspect of the functional significance of religion. For the problem arises, if moral norms and the sentiments supporting them are of such primary importance, what are the mechanisms by which they are maintained other than external processes of enforcement? It was Durkheim's view that religious ritual was of primary significance as a mechanism for expressing and reinforcing the sentiments most essential to the institutional integration of the society. It can readily be seen that this is closely linked to Malinowski's view of the significance of funeral ceremonies as a mechanism for reasserting the solidarity of the group on the occasion of severe emotional strain. Thus Durkheim worked out certain aspects of the specific relations between religion and social structure more sharply than did Malinowski, and in addition put the problem in a different functional perspective in that he applied it to the society as a whole in abstraction from particular situations of tension and strain for the individual.

One of the most notable features of the development under consideration lay in the fact that the cognitive patterns associated with religion were no longer, as in the older positivism, treated as essentially given points of reference, but were rather brought into functional relationship with a variety of other elements of social system of action. Pareto in rather general terms showed their interdependence with the sentiments. Malinowski contributed the exceedingly important relation to particular types of human situation, such as those of uncertainty and death. He in no way contradicted the emphasis placed by Pareto on emotional factors or sentiments. These, however, acquire their significance for specifically structured patterns of action only through their relation to specific situations. Malinowski was well aware in turn of the relation of both these factors to the solidarity of the social group, but this aspect formed the center of Durkheim's analytical attention. Clearly, religious ideas could only be treated sociologically in terms of their interdependence with all four types of factors.

There were, however, still certain serious problems left unsolved. In particular, neither Malinowski nor Durkheim raised the problem of the relation of these factors to the variability of social structure from one society to another. Both were primarily concerned with analysis of the functioning of a given social system without either comparative or dynamic reference. Furthermore, Durkheim's important insight into the role of symbolism in religious ideas might, without further analysis suggest that the specific patterns, hence their variations, were of only secondary importance. Indeed, there is clearly discernible in Durkheim's thinking in this field a tendency to circular reasoning in that he tends to treat religious patterns as a symbolic manifestation of "society," but at the same time to define the most fundamental aspect of society as a set of patterns of moral and religious sentiment.

Max Weber (1930) approached the whole field in very different terms. In his study of the relation between Protestantism and capitalism, his primary concern was with those features of the institutional system of modern Western society which were most distinctive in differentiating it from the other great civilizations. Having established what he felt to be an adequate relation of congruence between the cognitive patterns of Calvinism and some of the principal institutionalized attitudes towards secular roles of our own society, he set about systematically to place the material in the broadest possible comparative perspective through studying especially the religion and social structure of China, India and ancient Judea (Weber, 1921; see also Parsons, 1937, chs. 15 and 17). As a generalized result of these studies, he found it was not possible to reduce the striking variations of patterns in the level of religious ideas in these cases to any features of an independently existent social structure or economic situation, though he continually insisted on the very great importance of situational factors in a number of different connexions.[1] These factors, however, served only

---

[1]See especially his treatment of the role of the balance of social power in the establishment of the ascendancy of the Brahmans in India, and of the international position of the people of Israel in the definition of religious problems for the prophetic movement.

to pose the problems with which great movements of religious thought have been concerned. But the distinctive cognitive patterns were only understandable as the result of a cumulative tradition of intellectual effort in grappling with the problems thus presented and formulated.

For present purposes, even more important than Weber's views about the independent causal significance of religious ideas is his clarification of their functional relation to the system of action. Following up the same general line of analysis which provides one of the major themes of Pareto's and Malinowski's work, Weber made clear above all that there is a fundamental distinction between the significance for human action of problems of empirical causation and what, on the other hand, he called the "problem of meaning." In such cases as premature death through accident, the problem of *how* it happened in the sense of an adequate explanation of empirical causes can readily be solved to the satisfaction of most minds and yet leave a sense not merely of emotional but of cognitive frustration with respect to the problem of *why* such things must happen. Correlative with the functional need for emotional adjustment to such experiences as death is a cognitive need for understanding, for trying to have it "make sense." Weber attempted to show that problems of this nature, concerning the discrepancy between normal human interest and expectations in any situation or society and what actually happens are inherent in the nature of human existence. They always pose problems of the order which on the most generalized line have come to be known as the problem of evil, of the meaning of suffering, and the like. In terms of his comparative material, however, Weber shows there are different directions of definition of human situations in which rationally integrated solutions of these problems may be sought. It is differentiation with respect to the treatment of precisely such problems which constitute the primary modes of variation between the great systems of religious thought.

Such differences as, for instance, that between the Hindu philosophy of Karma and transmigration and the Christian doctrine of Grace with their philosophical backgrounds are not of merely speculative significance. Weber is able to show, in ways which correlate directly with the work of Malinowski and Durkheim, how intimately such differences in doctrine are bound up with practical attitudes towards the most various aspects of everyday life. For if we can speak of a need to understand ultimate frustrations in order for them to "make sense," it is equally urgent that the values and goals of everyday life should also "make sense." A tendency to integration of these two levels seems to be inherent in human action. Perhaps the most striking feature of Weber's analysis is the demonstration of the extent to which precisely the variations in socially sanctioned values and goals in secular life correspond to the variations in the dominant religious philosophy of the great civilizations.

It can be shown with little difficulty that those results of Weber's comparative and dynamic study integrate directly with the conceptual scheme developed as a result of the work of the other writers. Thus Weber's theory of the positive significance of religious ideas is in no way to be confused with the earlier naively rationalistic positivism. The influence of religious doctrine is not exerted through the actor's coming to a conviction and then acting upon it in a rational sense. It is rather, on the individual level, a matter of introducing a determinate structure at certain points in the system of action where, in relation to the situation men have to face, other elements, such as their emotional needs, do not suffice to determine specific orientations of behavior. In the theories of Malinowski and Durkheim, certain kinds of sentiments and emotional reactions were shown to be essential to a functioning social system. These cannot stand alone, however, but are necessarily integrated with cognitive patterns; for without them there could be no coordination of action in a coherently structured social system. This is because functional analysis of the structure of action shows that situations must be subjectively defined, and the goals and values to which action is oriented must be congruent with these definitions, must that is, have "meaning."

References

Durkheim, E. (1915), *The Elementary Forms of the Religious Life* (trans. J. Swain), Allen and Unwin, and Macmillan.

Durkheim, E. (1933), *The Division of Labor in Society* (trans. G. Simpson), Macmillan.

Malinowski, B. (1926), '*Magic, science, and religion*', in J. Needham. ed. *Science, Religion and Reality*, Macmillan, pp. 19–84.

Parsons, T. (1937), *The Structure of Social Action*, Free Press of Glencoe.

Weber, M. (1921), *Gesammelte Aufsätze zur Religionssoziologie*, Mohr.

Weber, M. (1930), *The Protestant Ethic and the Spirit of Capitalism*, Allen and Unwin.

RELIGION AS A CULTURAL SYSTEM— CLIFFORD GEERTZ

The editor of this book first encountered Clifford Geertz's (born 1926) essay on "Religion as a Cultural System" in a classroom lecture at the University of Chicago in 1961 and was dazzled by it. He continues to be dazzled. With intellectual balance, elegant language, and profound insight, Geertz has pulled together the diverse elements of the classic tradition and developed the Paronian synthesis into a full statement that still stands as one of the most important contributions to the social-scientific study of religion in the second half of the twentieth Century.

For Geertz, religion is a set of symbols (narrative symbols, I would add), which claim to possess a unique factuality and thus reveal the general order of existence—to explain what life is all about—and to account especially for the suffering, injustice, and death that are part of the human condition. "Myth," by the way is another name for a narrative symbol. To say that a story is a myth is not to say that it is necessarily fictional. It means rather that the story purports to explain what life means. So even if it isn't true in the literal sense, it attempts to be True in the revelatory sense—to illumine existence and indirectly explain it.

A religion then is a meaning system, it purports to explain what life is all about. Geertz's definition of religion (which comes, like all good definitions, after much investigation instead of before any investigation) is more Weberian than Durkheimian, though he extends Weber's concept of meaning beyond anything that Weber imagined. Indeed the symbols and their unique reality are collectively engendered and collectively reinforced—so Durkheim is honored and respected—but religion is not reduced to a collective effervescence or to society's discovering of itself as an other which deserves to be respected and honored. Rather, it is one of the templates that shape humankind's perception of reality and its pilgrimage through the confusion of life.

Other cultural systems that Geertz has studied in his career include ideology, ethics ("ethos is the flip side of the coin of mythos"), art, common sense, and law. Each cultural system is an attempt to impose order on the chaos of life and suggests appropriate paths through that chaos. Religion is, if not the most important of these cultural systems, the most ultimate because it attempts to answer the most basic and fundamental questions about what life means.

Geertz's perspective represents what has become the approach of many American sociologists who study religion. These scholars make no attempt to explain religion and perhaps to explain it away. Nor do they try to explain why religion persists despite scientific progress. They do not make predictions about the eventual decline of religion. Rather now it is understood that religion exists to give the ultimate meanings of life and the task of the social scientist is to understand what those meanings are, how they are passed on from generation to generation, and what effect they have on human values and behaviors.

Questions for Reflection and Discussion

1. What are the advantages and disadvantages of Geertz's approach to religion?
2. Can you think of any lacunae in this approach?
3. Ought organized religion be concerned about scholarship within Geertz's paradigm?
4. What symbols of which you are aware purport to explain the mysteries of injustice, suffering, and death?

RELIGION AS A CULTURAL SYSTEM
Clifford Geertz

> *Any attempt to speak without speaking any particular language is not more hopeless than the attempt to have a religion that shall be no religion in particular. . . . Thus every living and healthy religion has a marked idiosyncrasy. Its power consists in its special and surprising message and in the bias which that revelation gives to life. The vistas it opens and the mysteries it propounds are another world to live in; and another world to live in—whether we expect ever to pass wholly over into it or no—is what we mean by having a religion.*
>
> SANTAYANA, *Reason in Religion*

II

As we are to deal with meaning, let us begin with a paradigm: viz., that sacred symbols function to synthesize a people's ethos—the tone, character, and quality of their life, its moral and aesthetic style and mood—and their world view— the picture they have of the way things in sheer actuality are, their most comprehensive ideas of order. In religious belief and practice a group's ethos is rendered intellectually reasonable by being shown to represent a way of life ideally

Source: Clifford Geertz, *The Interpretation of Cultures*, New York: Basic Books. 1973.

adapted to the actual state of affairs the world view describes, while the world view is rendered emotionally convincing by being presented as an image of an actual state of affairs peculiarly well-arranged to accommodate such a way of life. This confrontation and mutual confirmation has two fundamental effects. On the one hand, it objectivizes moral and aesthetic preferences by depicting them as the imposed conditions of life implicit in a world with a particular structure, as mere common sense given the unalterable shape of reality. On the other, it supports these received beliefs about the world's body by invoking deeply felt moral and aesthetic sentiments as experiential evidence for their truth. Religious symbols formulate a basic congruence between a particular style of life and a specific (if, most often, implicit) metaphysic, and in so doing sustain each with the borrowed authority of the other.

Phrasing aside, this much may perhaps be granted. The notion that religion tunes human actions to an envisaged cosmic order and projects images of cosmic order onto the plane of human experience is hardly novel. But it is hardly investigated either, so that we have very little idea of how, in empirical terms, this particular miracle is accomplished. We just know that it is done, annually, weekly, daily, for some people almost hourly; and we have an enormous ethnographic literature to demonstrate it. But the theoretical framework which would enable us to provide an analytic account of it, an account of the sort we can provide for lineage segmentation, political succession, labor exchange, or the socialization of the child, does not exist.

Let us, therefore, reduce our paradigm to a definition, for, although it is notorious that definitions establish nothing, in themselves they do, if they are carefully enough constructed, provide a useful orientation, or reorientation, of thought, such that an extended unpacking of them can be an effective way of developing and controlling a novel line of inquiry. They have the useful virtue of explicitness: they commit themselves in a way discursive prose, which, in this field especially, is always liable to substitute rhetoric for argument, does not. Without further ado, then, a *religion* is:

1. *a system of symbols which acts to*
2. *establish powerful, pervasive, and long-lasting moods and motivations in men by*
3. *formulating conceptions of a general order of existence and*
4. *clothing these conceptions with such an aura of factuality that*
5. *the moods and motivations seem uniquely realistic.*

A SYSTEM OF SYMBOLS WHICH ACTS TO . . .

Such a tremendous weight is being put on the term "symbol" here that our first move must be to decide with some precision what we are going to mean by it. This is no easy task, for, rather like "culture," "symbol" has been used to refer to a great variety of things, often a number of them at the same time.

In some hands it is used for anything which signifies something else to someone: dark clouds are the symbolic precursors of an on-coming rain. In others it is used only for explicitly conventional signs of one sort or another: a red flag is a symbol of danger, a white of surrender. In others it is confined to something which expresses in an oblique and figurative manner that which cannot be stated in a direct and literal one, so that there are symbols in poetry but not in science, and symbolic logic is misnamed. In yet others, however, it is used for any object, act, event, quality, or relation which serves as a vehicle for a conception—the conception is the symbol's "meaning"—and that is the approach I shall follow here.[1] The number 6, written, imagined, laid out as a row of stones, or even punched into the program tapes of a computer, is a symbol. But so also is the Cross, talked about, visualized, shaped worriedly in air or fondly fingered at the neck, the expanse of painted canvas called "Guernica" or the bit of painted stone called a churinga, the word "reality," or even the morpheme "-ing." They are all symbols, or at least symbolic elements, because they are tangible formulations of notions, abstractions from experience fixed in perceptible forms, concrete embodiments of ideas, attitudes, judgments, longings, or beliefs. To undertake the study of cultural activity—activity in which symbolism forms the positive content—is thus not to abandon social analysis for a Platonic cave of shadows, to enter into a mentalistic world of introspective psychology or, worse, speculative philosophy, and wander there forever in a haze of "Cognitions," "Affections," "Conations," and other elusive entities. Cultural acts, the construction, apprehension, and utilization of symbolic forms, are social events like any other; they are as public as marriage and as observable as agriculture.

They are not, however, exactly the same thing; or, more precisely, the symbolic dimension of social events is, like the psychological, itself theoretically abstractable from those events as empirical totalities. There is still, to paraphrase a remark of Kenneth Burke's, a difference between building a house and drawing up a plan for building a house, and reading a poem about having children by marriage is not quite the same thing as having children by marriage.[2] Even though the building of the house may proceed under the guidance of the plan or—a less likely occurrence—the having of children may be motivated by a reading of the poem, there is something to be said for not confusing our traffic with symbols with our traffic with objects or human beings, for these latter are not in themselves symbols, however often they may function as such.[3] No matter how deeply interfused the cultural, the social, and the psychological may be in the everyday life of houses, farms, poems, and marriages, it is useful to distinguish them in analysis, and, so doing, to isolate the generic traits of each against the normalized background of the other two.

---

[1]S. Langer, *Philosophy in a New Key,* 4th ed. (Cambridge, Mass., 1960).

[2]K. Burke, *The Philosophy of Literary Form* (Baton Rouge, La.: Louisiana State University Press, 1941), p. 9.

[3]The reverse mistake, especially common among neo-Kantians such as Cassirer, of taking symbols to be identical with, or "constitutive of," their referents is equally pernicious. [Cf. E. Cassirer, *The Philosophy of Symbolic Forms* (New Haven: 1953–1957), 3 vols.] "One can point to the moon with one's finger," some, probably well-invented, Zen Master is supposed to have said, "but to take one's finger for the moon is to be a fool."

So far as culture patterns, that is, systems or complexes of symbols, are concerned, the generic trait which is of first importance for us here is that they are extrinsic sources of information. By "extrinsic," I mean only that—unlike genes, for example—they lie outside the boundaries of the individual organism as such in that intersubjective world of common understandings into which all human individuals are born, in which they pursue their separate careers, and which they leave persisting behind them after they die. By "sources of information," I mean only that—like genes—they provide a blueprint or template in terms of which processes external to themselves can be given a definite form. As the order of bases in a strand of DNA forms a coded program, a set of instructions, or a recipe, for the synthesis of the structurally complex proteins which shape organic functioning, so culture patterns provide such programs for the institution of the social and psychological processes which shape public behavior. Though the sort of information and the mode of its transmission are vastly different in the two cases, this comparison of gene and symbol is more than a strained analogy of the familiar "social heredity" sort. It is actually a substantial relationship, for it is precisely because of the fact that genetically programmed processes are so highly generalized in men, as compared with lower animals, that culturally programmed ones are so important; only because human behavior is so loosely determined by intrinsic sources of information that extrinsic sources are so vital. To build a dam a beaver needs only an appropriate site and the proper materials—his mode of procedure is shaped by his physiology. But man, whose genes are silent on the building trades, needs also a conception of what it is to build a dam, a conception he can get only from some symbolic source—a blueprint, a textbook, or a string of speech by someone who already knows how dams are built—or, of course, from manipulating graphic or linguistic elements in such a way as to attain for himself a conception of what dams are and how they are built.

This point is sometimes put in the form of an argument that cultural patterns are "models," that they are sets of symbols whose relations to one another "model" relations among entities, processes or what-have-you in physical, organic, social, or psychological systems by "paralleling," "imitating," or "simulating" them.[4] The term "model" has, however, two senses—an "of" sense and a "for" sense—and though these are but aspects of the same basic concept they are very much worth distinguishing for analytic purposes. In the first, what is stressed is the manipulation of symbol structures so as to bring them, more or less closely, into parallel with the pre-established nonsymbolic system, as when we grasp how dams work by developing a theory of hydraulics or constructing a flow chart. The theory or chart models physical relationships in such a way— that is, by expressing their structure in synoptic form—as to render them apprehensible; it is a model of "reality." In the second, what is stressed is the manipulation of the nonsymbolic systems in terms of the relationships expressed in the symbolic, as when we construct a dam according to the specifications implied in

---

[4]K. Craik, *The Nature of Explanation* (Cambridge, 1952).

an hydraulic theory or the conclusions drawn from a flow chart. Here, the theory is a model under whose guidance physical relationships are organized: it is a model *for* "reality." For psychological and social systems, and for cultural models that we would not ordinarily refer to as "theories," but rather as "doctrines," "melodies," or "rites," the case is in no way different. Unlike genes, and other nonsymbolic information sources, which are only models *for*, not models *of*, culture patterns have an intrinsic double aspect: they give meaning, that is, objective conceptual form, to social and psychological reality both by shaping themselves to it and by shaping it to themselves.

It is, in fact, this double aspect which sets true symbols off from other sorts of significative forms. Models *for* are found, as the gene example suggests, through the whole order of nature; for wherever there is a communication of pattern, such programs are, in simple logic, required. Among animals, imprint learning is perhaps the most striking example, because what such learning involves is the automatic presentation of an appropriate sequence of behavior by a model animal in the presence of a learning animal which serves, equally automatically, to call out and stabilize a certain set of responses genetically built into the learning animal.[5] The communicative dance of two bees, one of which has found nectar and the other of which seeks it, is another, somewhat different, more complexly coded, example.[6] Craik has even suggested that the thin trickle of water which first finds its way down from a mountain spring to the sea and smooths a little channel for the greater volume of water that follows after it plays a sort of model *for* function.[7] But models *of*—linguistic, graphic, mechanical, natural, etc., processes which function not to provide sources of information in terms of which other processes can be patterned, but to represent those patterned processes as such, to express their structure in an alternative medium—are much rarer and may perhaps be confined, among living animals, to man. The perception of the structural congruence between one set of processes, activities, relations, entities, and so on, and another set for which it acts as a program, so that the program can be taken as a representation, or conception—a symbol—of the programmed, is the essence of human thought. The intertransposability of models *for* and models *of* which symbolic formulation makes possible is the distinctive characteristic of our mentality.

... To Establish Powerful, Pervasive, and Long-lasting Moods and Motivations In Men By ...

So far as religious symbols and symbol systems are concerned this intertransposability is clear. The endurance, courage, independence, perseverance, and passionate willfulness in which the vision quest practices the Plains Indian are

---

[5] K. Lorenz, *King Solomon's Ring* (London, 1952).

[6] K. von Frisch, "Dialects in the Language of the Bees," *Scientific American*, August 1962.

[7] Craik, *Nature of Explanation*.

the same flamboyant virtues by which he attempts to live: while achieving a sense of revelation he stabilizes a sense of direction.[8] The consciousness of defaulted obligation, secreted guilt, and, when a confession is obtained, public shame in which Manus' seance rehearses him are the same sentiments that underlie the sort of duty ethic by which his property-conscious society is maintained: the gaining of an absolution involves the forging of a conscience.[9] And the same self-discipline which rewards a Javanese mystic staring fixedly into the flame of a lamp with what he takes to be an intimation of divinity drills him in that rigorous control of emotional expression which is necessary to a man who would follow a quietistic style of life.[10] Whether one sees the conception of a personal guardian spirit, a family tutelary, or an immanent God as synoptic formulations of the character of reality or as templates for producing reality with such a character seems largely arbitrary, a matter of which aspect, the model *of* or model *for,* one wants for the moment to bring into focus. The concrete symbols involved—one or another mythological figure materializing in the wilderness, the skull of the deceased household head hanging censoriously in the rafters, or a disembodied "voice in the stillness" soundlessly chanting enigmatic classical poetry—point in either direction. They both express the world's climate and shape it.

They shape it by inducing in the worshipper a certain distinctive set of dispositions (tendencies, capacities, propensities, skills, habits, liabilities, pronenesses) which lend a chronic character to the flow of his activity and the quality of his experience. A disposition describes not an activity or an occurrence but a probability of an activity being performed or an occurrence occurring in certain circumstances: "When a cow is said to be a ruminant, or a man is said to be a cigarette-smoker, it is not being said that the cow is ruminating now or that the man is smoking a cigarette now. To be a ruminant is to tend to ruminate from time to time, and to be a cigarette-smoker is to be in the habit of smoking cigarettes."[11] Similarly, to be pious is not to be performing something we would call an act of piety, but to be liable to perform such acts. So, too, with the Plains Indian's bravura, the Manus' compunctiousness, or the Javanese's quietism, which, in their contexts, form the substance of piety. The virtue of this sort of view of what are usually called "mental traits" or, if the Cartesianism is unavowed, "psychological forces" (both unobjectionable enough terms in themselves) is that it gets them out of any dim and inaccessible realm of private sensation into that same well-lit world of observables in which reside the brittleness of glass, the inflammability of paper, and, to return to the metaphor, the dampness of England.

So far as religious activities are concerned (and learning a myth by heart is as much a religious activity as detaching one's finger at the knuckle), two some-

---

[8]R. H. Lowie, *Primitive Religion* (New York, 1924).

[9]R. F. Fortune, *Manus Religion* (Philadelphia, 1935).

[10]C. Geertz, *The Religion of Java* (Glencoe, Ill., 1960).

[11]G. Ryle, *The Concept of Mind* (London and New York, 1949).

what different sorts of disposition are induced by them: moods and motivations. . . .

The major difference between moods and motivations is that where the latter are, so to speak, vectorial qualities, the former are merely scalar. Motives have a directional cast, they describe a certain overall course, gravitate toward certain, usually temporary, consummations. But moods vary only as to intensity: they go nowhere. They spring from certain circumstances but they are responsive to no ends. Like fogs, they just settle and lift; like scents, suffuse and evaporate. When present they are totalistic: if one is sad everything and everybody seems dreary; if one is gay, everything and everybody seems splendid. Thus, though a man can be vain, brave, willful, and independent at the same time, he can't very well be playful and listless, or exultant and melancholy, at the same time. Further, where motives persist for more or less extended periods of time, moods merely recur with greater or lesser frequency, coming and going for what are often quite unfathomable reasons. But perhaps the most important difference, so far as we are concerned, between moods and motivations is that motivations are "made meaningful" with reference to the ends toward which they are conceived to conduce, whereas moods are "made meaningful" with reference to the conditions from which they are conceived to spring. We interpret motives in terms of their consummations, but we interpret moods in terms of their sources. We say that a person is industrious because he wishes to succeed; we say that a person is worried because he is conscious of the hanging threat of nuclear holocaust. And this is no less the case when the interpretations are ultimate. Charity becomes Christian charity when it is enclosed in a conception of God's purposes; optimism is Christian optimism when it is grounded in a particular conception of God's nature. The assiduity of the Navaho finds its rationale in a belief that, since "reality" operates mechanically, it is coercible; their chronic fearfulness finds its rationale in a conviction that, however "reality" operates, it is both enormously powerful and terribly dangerous.[12]

... BY FORMULATING CONCEPTIONS OF A GENERAL ORDER OF EXISTENCE AND ...

That the symbols or symbol systems which induce and define dispositions we set off as religious and those which place those dispositions in a cosmic framework are the same symbols ought to occasion no surprise. For what else do we mean by saying that a particular mood of awe is religious and not secular, except that it springs from entertaining a conception of all-pervading vitality like mana and not from a visit to the Grand Canyon? Or that a particular case of asceticism is an example of a religious motivation, except that it is directed toward the achievement of an unconditioned end like nirvana and not a conditioned one like weight-reduction? If sacred symbols did not at one and the same time induce

---

[12]C. Kluckhohn, "The Philosophy of the Navaho Indians," in *Ideological Differences and World Order,* ed. F. S. C. Northrop (New Haven, 1949), pp. 356–384.

dispositions in human beings and formulate, however obliquely, inarticulately, or unsystematically, general ideas of order, then the empirical differentia of religious activity or religious experience would not exist. A man can indeed be said to be "religious" about golf, but not merely if he pursues it with passion and plays it on Sundays: he must also see it as symbolic of some transcendent truths. And the pubescent boy gazing soulfully into the eyes of the pubescent girl in a William Steig cartoon and murmuring, "There is something about you, Ethel, which gives me a sort of religious feeling," is, like most adolescents, confused. What any particular religion affirms about the fundamental nature of reality may be obscure, shallow, or, all too often, perverse; but it must, if it is not to consist of the mere collection of received practices and conventional sentiments we usually refer to as moralism, affirm something. If one were to essay a minimal definition of religion today, it would perhaps not be Tylor's famous "belief in spiritual beings," to which Goody, wearied of theoretical subtleties, has lately urged us to return, but rather what Salvador de Madariaga has called "the relatively modest dogma that God is not mad."[13]

Usually, of course, religions affirm very much more than this: we believe, as James remarked, all that we can and would believe everything if we only could.[14] The thing we seem least able to tolerate is a threat to our powers of conception, a suggestion that our ability to create, grasp, and use symbols may fail us, for were this to happen, we would be more helpless, as I have already pointed out, than the beavers. The extreme generality, diffuseness, and variability of man's innate (that is, genetically programmed) response capacities means that without the assistance of cultural patterns he would be functionally incomplete, not merely a talented ape who had, like some underprivileged child, unfortunately been prevented from realizing his full potentialities, but a kind of formless monster with neither sense of direction nor power of self-control, a chaos of spasmodic impulses and vague emotions. Man depends upon symbols and symbol systems with a dependence so great as to be decisive for his creatural viability and, as a result, his sensitivity to even the remotest indication that they may prove unable to cope with one or another aspect of experience raises within him the gravest sort of anxiety:

> [Man] can adapt himself somehow to anything his imagination can cope with; but he cannot deal with Chaos. Because his characteristic function and highest asset is conception, his greatest fright is to meet what he cannot construe—the "uncanny," as it is popularly called. It need not be a new object; we do meet new things, and "understand" them promptly, if tentatively, by the nearest analogy, when our minds are functioning freely; but under mental stress even perfectly familiar things may become suddenly disorganized and give us the horrors. Therefore our most important assets are always the symbols of our general *orientation* in nature, on the earth, in society, and in what we are doing: the symbols of our *Weltanschauung* and *Lebensanschauung*. Consequently, in a

---

[13]J. Goody, "Religion and Ritual: The Definition Problem," *British Journal of Psychology* 12 (1961):143–164.

[14]W. James, *The Principles of Psychology,* 2 vols. (New York, 1904).

primitive society, a daily ritual is incorporated in common activities, in eating, washing, fire-making, etc., as well as in pure ceremonial; because the need of reasserting the tribal morale and recognizing its cosmic conditions is constantly felt. In Christian Europe the Church brought men daily (in some orders even hourly) to their knees, to enact if not to contemplate their assent to the ultimate concepts.[15]

There are at least three points where chaos—a tumult of events which lack not just interpretations but *interpretability*—threatens to break in upon man: at the limits of his analytic capacities, at the limits of his powers of endurance, and at the limits of his moral insight. Bafflement, suffering, and a sense of intractable ethical paradox are all, if they become intense enough or are sustained long enough, radical challenges to the proposition that life is comprehensible and that we can, by taking thought, orient ourselves effectively within it—challenges with which any religion, however "primitive," which hopes to persist must attempt somehow to cope.

Of the three issues, it is the first which has been least investigated by modern social anthropologists (though Evans-Pritchard's classic discussion of why granaries fall on some Azande and not on others, is a notable exception).[16] Even to consider people's religious beliefs as attempts to bring anomalous events or experiences—death, dreams, mental fugues, volcanic eruptions, or marital infidelity—within the circle of the at least potentially explicable seems to smack of Tyloreanism or worse. But it does appear to be a fact that at least some men— in all probability, most men—are unable to leave unclarified problems of analysis merely unclarified, just to look at the stranger features of the world's landscape in dumb astonishment or bland apathy without trying to develop, however fantastic, inconsistent, or simple-minded, some notions as to how such features might be reconciled with the more ordinary deliverances of experience. Any chronic failure of one's explanatory apparatus, the complex of received culture patterns (common sense, science, philosophical speculation, myth) one has for mapping the empirical world, to explain things which cry out for explanation tends to lead to a deep disquiet—a tendency rather more widespread and a disquiet rather deeper than we have sometimes supposed since the pseudoscience view of religious belief was, quite rightfully, deposed. After all, even that high priest of heroic atheism, Lord Russell, once remarked that although the problem of the existence of God had never bothered him, the ambiguity of certain mathematical axioms had threatened to unhinge his mind. And Einstein's profound dissatisfaction with quantum mechanics was based on a—surely religious— inability to believe that, as he put it, God plays dice with the universe.

But this quest for lucidity and the rush of metaphysical anxiety that occurs when empirical phenomena threaten to remain intransigently opaque is found on much humbler intellectual levels. Certainly, I was struck in my own work, much more than I had at all expected to be, by the degree to which my more

---

[15]Langer, *Philosophy in a New Key,* p. 287. Italics in original.

[16]E. Evans-Pritchard, *Witchcraft, Oracles and Magic Among the Azande* (Oxford, 1937).

animistically inclined informants behaved like true Tyloreans. They seemed to be constantly using their beliefs to "explain" phenomena: or, more accurately, to convince themselves that the phenomena were explainable within the accepted scheme of things, for they commonly had only a minimal attachment to the particular soul possession, emotional disequilibrium, taboo infringement, or bewitchment hypothesis they advanced and were all too ready to abandon it for some other, in the same genre, which struck them as more plausible given the facts of the case. What they were *not* ready to do was abandon it for no other hypothesis at all; to leave events to themselves.

And what is more, they adopted this nervous cognitive stance with respect to phenomena which had no immediate practical bearing on their own lives, or for that matter on anyone's. When a peculiarly shaped, rather large toadstool grew up in a carpenter's house in the short space of a few days (or, some said, a few hours), people came from miles around to see it, and everyone had some sort of explanation—some animist, some animatist, some not quite either—for it. Yet it would be hard to argue that the toadstool had any social value in Radcliffe-Brown's sense, or was connected in any way with anything which did and for which it could have been standing proxy, like the Andaman cicada.[17] Toadstools play about the same role in Javanese life as they do in ours, and in the ordinary course of things Javanese have about as much interest in them as we do. It was just that this one was "odd," "strange," "uncanny"—*aneh*. And the odd, strange, and uncanny simply must be accounted for—or, again, the conviction that it *could be accounted for* sustained. One does not shrug off a toadstool which grows five times as fast as a toadstool has any right to grow. In the broadest sense the "strange" toadstool did have implications, and critical ones, for those who heard about it. It threatened their most general ability to understand the world, raised the uncomfortable question of whether the beliefs which they held about nature were workable, the standards of truth they used valid.

Nor is this to argue that it is only, or even mainly, sudden eruptions of extraordinary events which engender in man the disquieting sense that his cognitive resources may prove unavailing or that this intuition appears only in its acute form. More commonly it is a persistent, constantly re-experienced difficulty in grasping certain aspects of nature, self, and society, in bringing certain elusive phenomena within the sphere of culturallly formulatable fact, which renders man chronically uneasy and toward which a more equable flow of diagnostic symbols is consequently directed. It is what lies beyond a relatively fixed frontier of accredited knowledge that, looming as a constant background to the daily round of practical life, sets ordinary human experience in a permanent context of metaphysical concern and raises the dim, back-of-mind suspicions that one may be adrift in an absurd world:

> Another subject which is matter for this characteristic intellectual enquiry [among the Iatmul] is the nature of ripples and waves on the surface of water. It is said secretly that men, pigs, trees, grass—all the objects in the world—are

---

[17]A. R. Radcliffe-Brown, *Structure and Function in Primitive Society* (Glencoe, Ill., 1952).

only patterns of waves. Indeed there seems to be some agreement about this, although it perhaps conflicts with the theory of reincarnation, according to which the ghost of the dead is blown as a mist by the East Wind up the river and into the womb of the deceased's son's wife. Be that as it may—there is still the question of how ripples and waves are caused. The clan which claims the East Wind as a totem is clear enough about this: the Wind with her mosquito fan causes the waves. But other clans have personified the waves and say that they are a person (Kontummali) independent of the wind. Other clans, again, have other theories. On one occasion I took some Iatmul natives down to the coast and found one of them sitting by himself gazing with rapt attention at the sea. It was a windless day, but a slow swell was breaking on the beach. Among the totemic ancestors of his clan he counted a personified slit gong who had floated down the river to the sea and who was believed to cause the waves. He was gazing at the waves which were heaving and breaking when no wind was blowing, demonstrating the truth of his clan myth.[18]

The second experiential challenge in whose face the meaningfulness of a particular pattern of life threatens to dissolve into a chaos of thingless names and nameless things—the problem of suffering—has been rather more investigated, or at least described, mainly because of the great amount of attention given in works on tribal religion to what are perhaps its two main loci: illness and mourning. Yet for all the fascinated interest in the emotional aura that surrounds these extreme situations, there has been, with a few exceptions such as Lienhardt's recent discussion of Dinka divining, little conceptual advance over the sort of crude confidence-type theory set forth by Malinowski: viz., that religion helps one to endure "situations of emotional stress" by "open[ing] up escapes from such situations and such impasses as offer no empirical way out except by ritual and belief into the domain of the supernatural."[19] The inadequacy of this "theology of optimism," as Nadel rather dryly called it, is, of course, radical.[20] Over its career religion has probably disturbed men as much as it has cheered them; forced them into a head-on, unblinking confrontation of the fact that they are born to trouble as often as it has enabled them to avoid such a confrontation by projecting them into sort of infantile fairy-tale worlds where—Malinowski again—"hope cannot fail nor desire deceive."[21] With the

---

[18]G. Bateson, *Naven*, 2nd ed. (Stanford, 1958). That the chronic and acute forms of this sort of cognitive concern are closely interrelated, and that responses to the more unusual occasions of it are patterned on responses established in coping with the more usual is also clear fron Bateson's description, however, as he goes on to say: "On another occasion I invited one of my informants to witness the developnent of photographic plates. I first desensitized the plates and then developed them in an open dish in moderate light, so that my informant was able to see the gradual appearance of the images. He was much interested, and some days later made me promise never to show this process to members of other clans. Kontum-mali was one of his ancestors, and he saw in the process of photographic development the actual embodiment of ripples into images, and regarded this as a demonstration of the clan's secret."

[19]G. Lienhardt, *Divinity and Experience* (Oxford, 1961), p. 151ff; B. Malinowski, *Magic, Science and Religion* (Boston, 1948), p. 67.

[20]S. F. Nadel, "Malinowski on Magic and Religion," in *Man and Culture*, ed. R. Firth (London, 1957), pp. 189–208.

[21]Malinowski, *Magic, Science and Religion* (Boston, 1948), p. 67.

possible exception of Christian Science, there are few if any religious traditions, "great" or "little," in which the proposition that life hurts is not strenuously affirmed, and in some it is virtually glorified:

> She was an old [Ba-Ila] woman of a family with a long genealogy. Leza, "the Besetting One," stretched out his hand against the family. He slew her mother and father while she was yet a child, and in the course of years all connected with her perished. She said to herself, "Surely I shall keep those who sit on my thighs." But no, even they, the children of her children, were taken from her. . . . Then came into her heart a desperate resolution to find God and ask the meaning of it all. . . . So she began to travel, going through country after country, always with the thought in her mind: "I shall come to where the earth ends and there I shall find a road to God and I shall ask him: 'What have I done to thee that thou afflictest me in this manner?'" She never found where the earth ends, but though disappointed she did not give up her search, and as she passed through the different countries they asked her, "What have you come for, old woman?" And the answer would be, "I am seeking Leza." "Seeking Leza! For what?" "My brothers, you ask me! Here in the nations is there one who suffers as I have suffered?" And they would ask again, "How have you suffered?" "In this way. I am alone. As you see me, a solitary old woman; that is how I am!" And they answered. "Yes, we see. That is how you are! Bereaved of friends and husband? In what do you differ from others? The Besetting-One sits on the back of every one of us and we cannot shake him off." She never obtained her desire; she died of a broken heart.[22]

As a religious problem, the problem of suffering is, paradoxically, not how to avoid suffering but how to suffer, how to make of physical pain, personal loss, wordly defeat, or the helpless contemplation of others' agony something bearable, supportable—something, as we say, sufferable. It was in this effort that the Ba-Ila woman—perhaps necessarily, perhaps not—failed and, literally not knowing how to feel about what had happened to her, how to suffer, perished in confusion and despair. Where the more intellective aspects of what Weber called the Problem of Meaning are a matter affirming the ultimate explicability of experience, the more affective aspects are a matter of affirming its ultimate sufferableness. As religion on one side anchors the power of our symbolic resources for formulating analytic ideas in an authoritative conception of the overall shape of reality, so on another side it anchors the power of our, also symbolic, resources for expressing emotions—moods, sentiments, passions, affections, feelings—in a similar conception of its pervasive tenor, its inherent tone and temper. For those able to embrace them, and for so long as they are able to embrace them, religious symbols provide a cosmic guarantee not only for their ability to comprehend the world, but also, comprehending it, to give a precision to their feeling, a definition to their emotions which enables them, morosely or joyfully, grimly or cavalierly, to endure it. . . .

The problem of suffering passes easily into the problem of evil, for if suffering is severe enough it usually, though not always, seems morally undeserved

---

[22]C. W. Smith and A. M. Dale, *The Ila-Speaking Peoples of Northern Rhodesia* (London, 1920), p. 197ff.; quoted in P. Radin, *Primitive Man as a Philosopher* (New York, 1957), pp. 100–101.

as well, at least to the sufferer. But they are not, however, exactly the same thing—a fact I think Weber, too influenced by the biases of a monotheistic tradition in which, as the various aspects of human experience must be conceived to proceed from a single, voluntaristic source, man's pain reflects directly on God's goodness, did not fully recognize in his generalization of the dilemmas of Christian theodicy Eastward. For where the problem of suffering is concerned with threats to our ability to put our "undisciplined squads of emotion" into some sort of soldierly order, the problem of evil is concerned with threats to our ability to make sound moral judgments. What is involved in the problem of evil is not the adequacy of our symbolic resources to govern our affective life, but the adequacy of those resources to provide a workable set of ethical criteria, normative guides to govern our action. The vexation here is the gap between things as they are and as they ought to be if our conceptions of right and wrong make sense, the gap between what we deem various individuals deserve and what we see that they get—a phenomenon summed up in that profound quatrain:

> The rain falls on the just
> And on the unjust fella;
> But mainly upon the just,
> Because the unjust has the just's umbrella. . . .

Thus the problem of evil, or perhaps one should say the problem *about* evil, is in essence the same sort of problem of or about bafflement and the problem of or about suffering. The strange opacity of certain empirical events, the dumb senselessness of intense or inexorable pain, and the enigmatic unaccountability of gross iniquity all raise the uncomfortable suspicion that perhaps the world, and hence man's life in the world, has no genuine order at all—no empirical regularity, no emotional form, no moral coherence. And the religious response to this suspicion is in each case the same: the formulation, by means of symbols, of an image of such a genuine order of the world which will account for, and even celebrate, the perceived ambiguities, puzzles, and paradoxes in human experience. The effort is not to deny the undeniable—that there are unexplained events, that life hurts, or that rain falls upon the just—but to deny that there are inexplicable events, that life is unendurable, and that justice is a mirage. The principles which constitute the moral order may indeed often elude men, as Lienhardt puts it, in the same way as fully satisfactory explanations of anomalous events or effective forms for the expression of feeling often elude them. What is important, to a religious man at least, is that this elusiveness be accounted for, that it be not the result of the fact that there are no such principles, explanations, or forms, that life is absurd and the attempt to make moral, intellectual, or emotional sense out of experience is bootless. The Dinka can admit, in fact insist upon, the moral ambiguities and contradictions of life as they live it because these ambiguities and contradictions are seen not as ultimate, but as the "rational," "natural," "logical" (one may choose one's own adjective here, for none of them is truly adequate) outcome of the moral structure of reality which the myth of the withdrawn "Divinity" depicts, or as Lienhardt says, "images."

The Problem of Meaning in each of its intergrading aspects (how these aspects in fact intergrade in each particular case, what sort of interplay there is between the sense of analytic, emotional, and moral impotence, seems to me one of the outstanding, and except for Weber untouched, problems for comparative research in this whole field) is a matter of affirming, or at least recognizing, the inescapability of ignorance, pain, and injustice on the human plane while simultaneously denying that these irrationalities are characteristic of the world as a whole. And it is in terms of religious symbolism, a symbolism relating man's sphere of existence to a wider sphere within which it is conceived to rest, that both the affirmation and the denial are made.[23]

... AND CLOTHING THOSE CONCEPTIONS WITH SUCH AN AURA OF FACTUALITY THAT ...

There arises here, however, a more profound question: how is it that this denial comes to be believed? How is it that the religious man moves from a troubled perception of experienced disorder to a more or less settled conviction of fundamental order? Just what does "belief" mean in a religious context? Of all the problems surrounding attempts to conduct anthropological analysis of religion this is the one that has perhaps been most troublesome and therefore the most often avoided, usually by relegating it to psychology, that raffish outcast discipline to which social anthropologists are forever consigning phenomena they are unable to deal with within the framework of a denatured Durkheimianism. But the problem will not go away, it is not "merely" psychological (nothing social is), and no anthropological theory of religion which fails to attack it is worthy of the name. We have been trying to stage Hamlet without the Prince quite long enough.

It seems to me that it is best to begin any approach to this issue with frank recognition that religious belief involves not a Baconian induction from everyday experience—for then we should all be agnostics—but rather a prior acceptance of authority which transforms that experience. The existence of bafflement, pain, and moral paradox—of The Problem of Meaning—is one of the things that drives men toward belief in gods, devils, spirits, totemic principles, or the spiritual efficacy of cannibalism (an enfolding sense of beauty or a dazzling perception of power are others), but it is not the basis upon which those beliefs rest, but rather their most important field of application. . . .

But to speak of "the religious perspective" is, by implication, to speak of one perspective among others. A perspective is a mode of seeing, in that extend-

---

[23]This is *not,* however, to say that everyone in every society does this; for as the immortal Don Marquis once remarked, you don't have to have a soul unless you really want one. The oft-heard generalization that religion is a human universal embodies a confusion between the probably true (though on present evidence unprovable) proposition that there is no human society in which cultural patterns that we can, under the present definition or one like it, call religious are totally lacking, and the surely untrue proposition that all men in all societies are, in any meaningful sense of the term, religious. But if the anthropological study of religious commitment is underdeveloped, the anthropological study of religious noncommitment is nonexistent. The anthropology of religion will have come of age when some more subtle Malinowski writes a book called "Belief and Unbelief (or even "Faith and Hypocrisy") in a Savage Society."

ed sense of "see" in which it means "discern," "apprehend," "understand," or "grasp." It is a particular way of looking at life, a particular manner of construing the world, as when we speak of an historical perspective, a scientific perspective, an aesthetic perspective, a common-sense perspective, or even the bizarre perspective embodied in dreams and in hallucinations.[24] The question then comes down to, first, what is "the religious perspective" generically considered, as differentiated from other perspectives; and second, how do men come to adopt it.

If we place the religious perspective against the background of three of the other major perspectives in terms of which men construe the world—the common-sensical, the scientific, and the aesthetic—its special character emerges more sharply. What distinguishes common sense as a mode of "seeing" is, as Schutz has pointed out, a simple acceptance of the world, its objects, and its processes as being just what they seem to be—what is sometimes called naive realism—and the pragmatic motive, the wish to act upon that world so as to bend it to one's practical purposes, to master it, or so far as that proves impossible, to adjust to it.[25] The world of everyday life, itself, of course, a cultural product, for it is framed in terms of the symbolic conceptions of "stubborn fact" handed down from generation to generation, is the established scene and given object of our actions. Like Mt. Everest it is just there, and the thing to do with it, if one feels the need to do anything with it at all, is to climb it. In the scientific perspective it is precisely this givenness which disappears. Deliberate doubt and systematic inquiry, the suspension of the pragmatic motive in favor of disinterested observation, the attempt to analyze the world in terms of formal concepts whose relationship to the informal conceptions of common sense become increasingly problematic—there are the hallmarks of the attempt to grasp the world scientifically. And as for the aesthetic perspective, which under the rubric of "the aesthetic attitude" has been perhaps most exquisitely examined, it involves a different sort of suspension of naive realism and practical interest, in that instead of questioning the credentials of everyday experience, one merely ignores that experience in favor of an eager dwelling upon appearances, an engrossment in surfaces, an absorption in things, as we say, "in themselves": "The function of artistic illusion is not 'make-believe' . . . but the very opposite,

---

[24]The term "attitude" as in "aesthetic attitude" or "natural attitude" is another, perhaps more common term for what I have here called "perspective." [For the first, see C. Bell, *Art*, London, 1914; for the second, though the phrase is originally Husserl's, see A. Schutz, *The Problem of Social Reality*, vol. 1 of *Collected Papers* (The Hague, 1962).] But I have avoided it because of its strong subjectivist connotations, its tendency to place the stress upon a supposed inner state of an actor rather than on a certain sort of relation—a symbolically mediated one—between an actor and a situation. This is not to say, of course, that a phenomenological analysis of religious experience, if cast in intersubjective, nontranscendental, genuinely scientific terms [e.g., W. Percy, "Symbol, Consciousness and Intersubjectivity," *Journal of Philosophy* 15 (1958):631–641] is not essential to a full understanding of religious belief, but merely that that is not the focus of my concern here. "Outlook," "frame of reference," "frame of mind," "orientation," "stance," "mental set," and so on, are other terms sometimes employed, depending upon whether the analyst wishes to stress the social, psychological, or cultural aspects of the matter.

[25]Schutz, *The Problem of Social Reality.*

disengagement from belief—the contemplation of sensory qualities without their usual meanings of 'here's that chair', 'that's my telephone' . . . etc. The knowledge that what is before us has no practical significance in the world is what enables us to give attention to its appearance as such."[26] And like the common sensical and the scientific (or the historical, the philosophical, and the artistic), this perspective, this "way of seeing" is not the product of some mysterious Cartesian chemistry, but is induced, mediated, and in fact created by means of curious quasi objects—poems, dramas, sculptures, symphonies— which, dissociating themselves from the solid world of common sense, take on the special sort of eloquence only sheer appearances can achieve.

The religious perspective differs from the common-sensical in that, as already pointed out, it moves beyond the realities of everyday life to wider ones which correct and complete them, and its defining concern is not action upon those wider realities but acceptance of them, faith in them. It differs from the scientific perspective in that it questions the realities of everyday life not out of an institutionalized scepticism which dissolves the world's givenness into a swirl of probabilistic hypotheses, but in terms of what it takes to be wider, nonhypothetical truths. Rather than detachment, its watchword is commitment; rather than analysis, encounter. And it differs from art in that instead of effecting a disengagement from the whole question of factuality, deliberately manufacturing an air of semblance and illusion, it deepens the concern with fact and seeks to create an aura of utter actuality. It is this sense of the "really real" upon which the religious perspective rests and which the symbolic activities of religion as a cultural system are devoted to producing, intensifying, and so far as possible, rendering inviolable by the discordant revelations of secular experience. It is, again, the imbuing of a certain specific complex of symbols—of the metaphysic they formulate and the style of life they recommend—with a persuasive authority which, from an analytic point of view, is the essence of religious action.

Which brings us, at length, to ritual. For it is in ritual—that is, consecrated behavior—that this conviction that religious conceptions are veridical and that religious directives are sound is somehow generated. It is in some sort of ceremonial form—even if that form be hardly more than the recitation of a myth, the consultation of an oracle, or the decoration of a grave—that the moods and motivations which sacred symbols induce in men and the general conceptions of the order of existence which they formulate for men meet and reinforce one another. In a ritual, the world as lived and the world as imagined, fused under the agency of a single set of symbolic forms, turn out to be the same world, producing thus that idiosyncratic transformation in one's sense of reality to which Santayana refers in my epigraph. Whatever role divine intervention may or may not play in the creation of faith—and it is not the business of the scientist to pronounce upon such matters one way or the other—it is, primarily at least, out of the context of concrete acts of religious observance that religious conviction emerges on the human plane. . . .

---

[26]S. Langer, *Feeling and Form* (New York, 1953), p. 49.

... THAT THE MOODS AND MOTIVATIONS SEEM UNIQUELY REALISTIC

But no one, not even a saint, lives in the world religious symbols formulate all of the time, and the majority of men live in it only at moments. The everyday world of common-sense objects and practical acts is, as Schutz says, the paramount reality in human experience—paramount in the sense that it is the world in which we are most solidly rooted, whose inherent actuality we can hardly question (however much we may question certain portions of it), and from whose pressures and requirements we can least escape.[27] A man, even large groups of men, may be aesthetically insensitive, religiously unconcerned, and unequipped to pursue formal scientific analysis, but he cannot be completely lacking in common sense and survive. The dispositions which religious rituals induce thus have their most important impact—from a human point of view—outside the boundaries of the ritual itself as they reflect back to color the individual's conception of the established world of bare fact. The peculiar tone that marks the Plains vision quest, the Manus confession, or the Javanese mystical exercise pervades areas of the life of these peoples far beyond the immediately religious, impressing upon them a distinctive style in the sense both of a dominant mood and a characteristic movement. The interweaving of the malignant and the comic, which the Rangda–Barong combat depicts, animates a very wide range of everyday Balinese behavior, much of which, like the ritual itself, has an air of candid fear narrowly contained by obsessive playfulness. Religion is sociologically interesting not because, as vulgar positivism would have it, it describes the social order (which, in so far as it does, it does not only very obliquely but very incompletely), but because, like environment, political power, wealth, jural obligation, personal affection, and a sense of beauty, it shapes it.

The movement back and forth between the religious perspective and the common-sense perspective is actually one of the more obvious empirical occurences on the social scene, though, again, one of the most neglected by social anthropologists, virtually all of whom have seen it happen countless times. Religious belief has usually been presented as a homogeneous characteristic of an individual, like his place of residence, his occupational role, his kinship position, and so on. But religious belief in the midst of ritual, where it engulfs the total person, transporting him, so far as he is concerned, into another mode of existence, and religious belief as the pale, remembered reflection of that experience in the midst of everyday life are not precisely the same thing, and the failure to realize this has led to some confusion, most especially in connection with the so-called primitive-mentality problem. . . .

The recognition and exploration of the qualitative difference—an empirical, not a transcendental difference—between religion pure and religion applied, between an encounter with the supposedly "really real" and a viewing of ordinary experience in light of what that encounter seems to reveal, will, therefore,

---

[27]Schutz, *The Problem of Social Reality*, p. 226ff.

take us further toward an understanding of what a Bororo means when he says "I am a parakeet," or a Christian when he says "I am a sinner," than either a theory of primitive mysticism in which the commonplace world disappears into a cloud of curious ideas or of a primitive pragmatism in which religion disintegrates into a collection of useful fictions. The parakeet example, which I take from Percy, is a good one.[28] For, as he points out, it is unsatisfactory to say either that the Bororo thinks he is literally a parakeet (for he does not try to mate with other parakeets), that his statement is false or nonsense (for, clearly, he is not offering—or at least not only offering—the sort of class-membership argument which can be confirmed or refuted as, say, "I am a Bororo" can be confirmed or refuted), or yet again that it is false scientifically but true mythically (because that leads immediately to the pragmatic fiction notion which, as it denies the accolade of truth to "myth" in the very act of bestowing it, is internally self-contradictory). More coherently it would seem to be necessary to see the sentence as having a different sense in the context of the "finite province of meaning" which makes up the religious perspective and of that which makes up the common-sensical. In the religious, our Bororo is "really" a "parakeet," and given the proper ritual context might well "mate" with other "parakeets"—with metaphysical ones like himself, not commonplace ones such as those which fly bodily about in ordinary trees. In the common-sensical perspective he is a parakeet in the sense—I assume—that he belongs to a clan whose members regard the parakeet as their totem, a membership from which, given the fundamental nature of reality as the religious perspective reveals it, certain moral and practical consequences flow. A man who says he is a parakeet is, if he says it in normal conversation, saying that, as myth and ritual demonstrate, he is shot through with parakeetness and that this religious fact has some crucial social implications—we parakeets must stick together, not marry one another, not eat mundane parakeets, and so on, for to do otherwise is to act against the grain of the whole universe. It is this placing of proximate acts in ultimate contexts that makes religion, frequently at least, socially so powerful. It alters, often radically, the whole landscape presented to common sense, alters it in such a way that the moods and motivations induced by religious practice seem themselves supremely practical, the only sensible ones to adopt given the way things "really" are.

Having ritually "lept" (the image is perhaps a bit too athletic for the actual facts—"slipped" might be more accurate) into the framework of meaning which religious conceptions define, and the ritual ended, returned again to the common-sense world, a man is—unless, as sometimes happens, the experience fails to register—changed. And as he is changed, so also is the common-sense world, for it is now seen as but the partial form of a wider reality which corrects and completes it.

But this correction and completion is not, as some students of "comparative religion" would have it, everywhere the same in content. The nature of the bias

---

[28]W. Percy, "The Symbolic Structure of Interpersonal Process," *Psychiatry* 24 (1961):39–52.

religion gives to ordinary life varies with the religion involved, with the particular dispositions induced in the believer by the specific conceptions of cosmic order he has come to accept. On the level of the "great" religions, organic distinctiveness is usually recognized, at times insisted upon to the point of zealotry. But even at its simplest folk and tribal levels—where the individuality of religious traditions has so often been dissolved into such desiccated types as "animism," "animatism," "totemism," "shamanism," "ancestor worship," and all the other insipid categories by means of which ethnographers of religion devitalize their data—the idiosyncratic character of how various groups of men behave because of what they believe they have experienced is clear. A tranquil Javanese would be no more at home in guilt-ridden Manus than an activist Crow would be in passionless Java. And for all the witches and ritual clowns in the world, Rangda and Barong are not generalized but thoroughly singular figurations of fear and gaiety. What men believe is as various as what they are—a proposition that holds with equal force when it is inverted.

It is this particularity of the impact of religious systems upon social systems (and upon personality systems) which renders general assessments of the value of religion in either moral or functional terms impossible. The sorts of moods and motivations which characterize a man who has just come from an Aztec human sacrifice are rather different from those of one who has just put off his Kachina mask. Even within the same society, what one "learns" about the essential pattern of life from a sorcery rite and from a commensal meal will have rather diverse effects on social and psychological functioning. One of the main methodological problems in writing about religion scientifically is to put aside at once the tone of the village atheist and that of the village preacher, as well as their more sophisticated equivalents, so that the social and psychological implications of particular religious beliefs can emerge in a clear and neutral light. And when that is done, overall questions about whether religion is "good" or "bad," "functional" or "dysfunctional," "ego strengthening" or "anxiety producing," disappear like the chimeras they are, and one is left with particular evaluations, assessments, and diagnoses in particular cases. There remains, of course, the hardly unimportant questions of whether this or that religious assertion is true, this or that religious experience genuine, or whether true religious assertions and genuine religious experiences are possible at all. But such questions cannot even be asked, much less answered, within the self-imposed limitations of the scientific perspective.

III

For an anthropologist, the importance of religion lies in its capacity to serve, for an individual or for a group, as a source of general, yet distinctive, conceptions of the world, the self, and the relations between them, on the one hand—its model *of* aspect—and of rooted, no less distinctive "mental" dispositions—its model *for* aspect—on the other. From these cultural functions flow, in turn, its social and psychological ones.

Religious concepts spread beyond their specifically metaphysical contexts to provide a framework of general ideas in terms of which a wide range of experience—intellectual, emotional, moral—can be given meaningful form. The Christian sees the Nazi movement against the background of The Fall which, though it does not, in a causal sense, explain it, places it in a moral, a cognitive, even an affective sense. An Azande sees the collapse of a granary upon a friend or relative against the background of a concrete and rather special notion of witchcraft and thus avoids the philosophical dilemmas as well as the psychological stress of indeterminism. A Javanese finds in the borrowed and reworked concept of *rasa* ("sense–taste–feeling–meaning") a means by which to "see" choreographic, gustatory, emotional, and political phenomena in a new light. A synopsis of cosmic order, a set of religious beliefs, is also a gloss upon the mundane world of social relationships and psychological events. It renders them graspable.

But more than gloss, such beliefs are also a template. They do not merely interpret social and psychological processes in cosmic terms—in which case they would be philosophical, not religious—but they shape them. In the doctrine of original sin is embedded also a recommended attitude toward life, a recurring mood, and a persisting set of motivations. The Azande learns from witchcraft conceptions not just to understand apparent "accidents" as not accidents at all, but to react to these spurious accidents with hatred for the agent who caused them and to proceed against him with appropriate resolution. *Rasa,* in addition to being a concept of truth, beauty, and goodness, is also a preferred mode of experiencing, a kind of affectless detachment, a variety of bland aloofness, an unshakable calm. The moods and motivations a religious orientation produces cast a derivative, lunar light over the solid features of a people's secular life.

The tracing of the social and psychological role of religion is thus not so much a matter of finding correlations between specific ritual acts and specific secular social ties—though these correlations do, of course, exist and are very worth continued investigation, especially if we can contrive something novel to say about them. More, it is a matter of understanding how it is that men's notions, however implicit, of the "really real" and the dispositions these notions induce in them, color their sense of the reasonable, the practical, the humane, and the moral. How far they do so (for in many societies religion's effects seem quite circumscribed, in others completely pervasive), how deeply they do so (for some men, and groups of men, seem to wear their religion lightly so far as the secular world goes, while others seem to apply their faith to each occasion, no matter how trivial), and how effectively they do so (for the width of the gap between what religion recommends and what people actually do is most variable cross-culturally)—all these are crucial issues in the comparative sociology and psychology of religion. Even the degree to which religious systems themselves are developed seems to vary extremely widely, and not merely on a simple evolutionary basis. In one society, the level of elaboration of symbolic formulations of ultimate actuality may reach extraordinary degrees of complexity and systematic articulation; in another, no less developed socially, such formulations may remain primitive in the true sense, hardly more than congeries of fragmentary by-beliefs and isolated images, of sacred reflexes and spiritual pictographs. One need only think of the Australians and the Bushmen, the Toradja and the Alorese, the Hopi and the Apache, the Hindus and the Romans, or even the Italians and the Poles, to see that degree of religious articulateness is not a constant even as between societies of similar complexity.

The anthropological study of religion is therefore a two-stage operation: first, an analysis of the system of meanings embodied in the symbols which make up the religion proper, and, second, the relating of these systems to social-structural and psychological processes. My dissatisfaction with so much of contemporary social anthropological work in religion is not that it concerns itself with the second stage, but that it neglects the first, and in so doing takes for granted what most needs to be elucidated. To discuss the role of ancestor worship in regulating political succession, of sacrificial feasts in defining kinship obligations, of spirit worship in scheduling agricultural practices, of divination in reinforcing social control, or of initiation rites in propelling personality maturation, are in no sense unimportant endeavors, and I am not recommending they be abandoned for the kind of jejune cabalism into which symbolic analysis of exotic faiths can so easily fall. But to attempt them with but the most general, common-sense view of what ancestor worship, animal sacrifice, spirit worship, divination, or initiation rites are as religious patterns seems to me not particularly promising. Only when we have a theoretical analysis of symbolic action comparable in sophistication to that we now have for social and psychological action, will we be able to cope effectively with those aspects of social and psychological life in which religion (or art, or science, or ideology) plays a determinant role.

Reading 8

....

THE "HOLY"—RUDOLPH OTTO

The classic writers, for all their emphasis on experience in religious rituals, paid very little attention to religious experience as such. Even Geertz, whose theory of religion as a culture system is one of the most important works on the sociology of religion in the final half of this century, and whose other work brilliantly analyzes religious experience (in Bali for example), does not integrate into his theory a view on how experience shapes the symbols that explain the "real" or how these symbols in their turn shape further religious experiences. For the German theologian Rudolph Otto (1869–1937) the essence of religion was the experience of *"The Idea of the Holy"* (*Das Heilige* 1917), the "totally other," the "numinous," which was both fascinating and terrifying. Human beings are religious because they encounter, sometimes intensely, sometimes very gently the numinous, which both frightens them and fascinates them. Such experiences may occur in collective rituals, in relationships with others, or in personal and solitary encounters. Once one has encountered the "totally other" all questions about the value and validity of religion are swept aside. Nothing that is merely an illusion can be so intimidating and yet so attractive.

Otto neatly describes human ambivalence toward the sacred (which will be the subject of the next section of readings), which is both intimidating and appealing, but from which humans cannot escape once they have encountered it.

For some people (about a third according to my research on such experiences in contemporary America), the experience is spectacular, time stands still, the whole cosmos rushes into the person and she or he perceives the unity of the cosmos and the person's place within it, he or she is filled with light and love and laughter and knows that everything will be "all right."

For others the experience is less spectacular, but still powerful enough to confirm religious faith. Yet others' (including the present editor) experiences of the numinous are so mild that they are hardly noticed.

Does everyone have at least mild experiences of the numinous? Perhaps not, but it seems safe to say that most people do. The question then arises as to whether this terrifying and intriguing totally other is real or merely a creation of the imagination and the needs of the person having the experience. The classic writers in varying degrees would be skeptical of such experiences. They would admit the power of the encounter with the numinous, but suggest that there is no need to postulate an actual numen or Numen to account for the experience. Biological, psychological, and sociological dynamisms provide adequate explanations.

One would have a hard time winning an argument on that point with one who had been, let us say, knocked off a horse by the numinous. Nonetheless, while sociology cannot accept on its own terms the existence of the totally other, neither can it prove that experiences of the numinous are either wish-fulfillment or self-deception. An understanding of the dynamics of such experiences do not necessarily establish that there is not a Numen at work, which chooses to reveal itself through such dynamics. To Otto, the sociologist must reply, perhaps and then again perhaps not. If wise and sensitive, however, the sociologist will not ridicule those who claim such experiences, but like Otto (and William James, whom we will meet in the next reading) listen carefully to what they say and try to learn what kinds of people have such experiences and what impact they have on human life.

Voltaire said that man creates God in his own image and likeness. Perhaps it would be more accurate to say that humans create God in the image and likeness of the numen that they have experienced.

Questions for Reflection and Discussion

1. Have you ever encountered the numinous? What was the experience like?
2. If you have had such an experience, how would you persuade a skeptic that it was real?
3. If you have not had such an experience, how would you challenge someone who claimed to have one?
4. Can you think of any criteria for testing such experiences?

THE IDEA OF THE HOLY
Rudolph Otto

'NUMEN' AND THE 'NUMINOUS'

'Holiness'—'the holy'—is a category of interpretation and valuation peculiar to the sphere of religion. It is, indeed, applied by transference to another sphere—that of ethics—but it is not itself derived from this. While it is complex, it contains a quite specific element or 'moment', which sets it apart from 'the rational' in the meaning we gave to that word above, and which remains inexpressible—an ἄρρητον or *ineffabile*—in the sense that it completely eludes apprehension in terms of concepts. The same thing is true (to take a quite different region of experience) of the category of the beautiful.

Source: Rudolf Otto, *The Idea of the Holy: An Inquiry into the Non-rational Factor in the Idea of the Divine and its Relation to the Rational,* 2nd. edition, London: Oxford University Press, 1952.

Now these statements would be untrue from the outset if 'the holy' were merely what is meant by the word, not only in common parlance, but in philosophical, and generally even in theological usage. The fact is we have come to use the words 'holy', 'sacred' (*heilig*) in an entirely derivative sense, quite different from that which they originally bore. We generally take 'holy' as meaning 'completely good'; it is the absolute moral attribute, denoting the consummation of moral goodness. In this sense Kant calls the will which remains unwaveringly obedient to the moral law from the motive of duty a 'holy' will; here clearly we have simply the *perfectly moral* will. In the same way we may speak of the holiness or sanctity of duty or law, meaning merely that they are imperative upon conduct and universally obligatory.

But this common usage of the term is inaccurate. It is true that all this moral significance is contained in the word 'holy', but it includes in addition—as even we cannot but feel—a clear overplus of meaning, and this it is now our task to isolate. Nor is this merely a later or acquired meaning; rather, 'holy', or at least the equivalent words in Latin and Greek, in Semitic and other ancient languages, denoted first and foremost *only* this overplus: if the ethical element was present at all, at any rate it was not original and never constituted the whole meaning of the word. Any one who uses it to-day does undoubtedly always feel 'the morally good' to be implied in 'holy'; and accordingly in our inquiry into that element which is separate and peculiar to the idea of the holy it will be useful, at least for the temporary purpose of the investigation, to invent a special term to stand for 'the holy' *minus* its moral factor or 'moment', and, as we can now add, minus its 'rational' aspect altogether. . . .

Accordingly, it is worth while, as we have said, to find a word to stand for this element in isolation, this 'extra' in the meaning of 'holy' above and beyond the meaning of goodness. By means of a special term we shall the better be able, first, to keep the meaning clearly apart and distinct, and second, to apprehend and classify connectedly whatever subordinate forms or stages of development it may show. For this purpose I adopt a word coined from the Latin *numen*. *Omen* has given us 'ominous', and there is no reason why from *numen* we should not similarly form a word 'numinous'. I shall speak, then, of a unique 'numinous' category of value and of a definitely 'numinous' state of mind, which is always found wherever the category is applied. This mental state is perfectly *sui generis* and irreducible to any other; and therefore, like every absolutely primary and elementary datum, while it admits of being discussed, it cannot be strictly defined. There is only one way to help another to an understanding of it. He must be guided and led on by consideration and discussion of the matter through the ways of his own mind, until he reach the point at which 'the numinous' in him perforce begins to stir, to start into life and into consciousness. We can co-operate in this process by bringing before his notice all that can be found in other regions of the mind, already known and familiar, to resemble, or again to afford some special contrast to, the particular experience we wish to elucidate. Then we must add: 'This X of ours is not precisely *this* experience, but akin to this one and the opposite of that other. Cannot you now realize for yourself what it is?' In other words our X cannot, strictly speaking, be taught, it can only be evoked, awakened in the mind; as everything that comes 'of the spirit' must be awakened. . . .

'MYSTERIUM TREMENDUM'

The Analysis of 'Tremendum'

We said above that the nature of the numinous can only be suggested by means of the special way in which it is reflected in the mind in terms of feeling. 'Its nature is such that it grips or stirs the human mind with this and that determinate affective state.' We have now to attempt to give a further indication of these determinate states. We must once again endeavour, by adducing feelings akin to them for the purpose of analogy or contrast, and by the use of metaphor and symbolic expressions, to make the states of mind we are investigating ring out, as it were, of themselves.

Let us consider the deepest and most fundamental element in all strong and sincerely felt religious emotion. Faith unto salvation, trust, love—all these are there. But over and above these is an element which may also on occasion, quite apart from them, profoundly affect us and occupy the mind with a wellnigh bewildering strength. Let us follow it up with every effort of sympathy and imaginative intuition wherever it is to be found, in the lives of those around us, in sudden, strong ebullitions of personal piety and the frames of mind such ebullitions evince, in the fixed and ordered solemnities of rites and liturgies, and again in the atmosphere that clings to old religious monuments and buildings, to temples and to churches. If we do so we shall find we are dealing with something for which there is only one appropriate expression, 'mysterium tremendum.' The feeling of it may at times come sweeping like a gentle tide, pervading the mind with a tranquil mood of deepest worship. It may pass over into a more set and lasting attitude of the soul, continuing, as it were, thrillingly vibrant and resonant, until at last it dies away and the soul resumes its 'profane', non-religious mood of everyday experience. It may burst in sudden eruption up from the depths of the soul with spasms and convulsions, or lead to the strangest excitements, to intoxicated frenzy, to transport, and to ecstasy. It has its wild and demonic forms and can sink to an almost grisly horror and shuddering. It has its crude, barbaric antecedents and early manifestations, and again it may be developed into something beautiful and pure and glorious. It may become the hushed, trembling, and speechless humility of the creature in the presence of—whom or what? In the presence of that which is a *mystery* inexpressible and above all creatures.

It is again evident at once that here too our attempted formulation by means of a concept is once more a merely negative one. Conceptually *mysterium* denotes merely that which is hidden and esoteric, that which is beyond conception or understanding, extraordinary and unfamiliar. The term does not define the object more positively in its qualitative character. But though what is enunciated in the word is negative, what is meant is something absolutely and intensely positive. This pure positive we can experience in feelings, feelings which our discussion can help to make clear to us, in so far as it arouses them actually in our hearts.

1. The Element of Awefulness

To get light upon the positive *'quale'* of the object of these feelings, we must analyse more closely our phrase *mysterium tremendum,* and we will begin first with the adjective.

Tremor is in itself merely the perfectly familiar and 'natural' emotion of *fear.* But here the term is taken, aptly enough but still only by analogy, to denote a quite specific kind of emotional response, wholly distinct from that of being afraid, though it so far resembles it that the analogy of fear may be used to throw light upon its nature. There are in some languages special expressions which denote, either exclusively or in the first instance, this 'fear' that is more than fear proper. The Hebrew *hiqdīsh* (hallow) is an example. To 'keep a thing holy in the heart' means to mark it off by a feeling of peculiar dread, not to be mistaken for any ordinary dread, that is, to appraise it by the category of the numinous. But the Old Testament throughout is rich in parallel expressions for this feeling. Specially noticeable is the '*ēmāh*' of Yahweh ('fear of God'), which Yahweh can pour forth, dispatching almost like a daemon, and which seizes upon a man with paralysing effect. It is closely related to the δεῖμα πανικόν of the Greeks. Compare Exod. xxiii. 27: 'I will send my fear before thee, and will destroy all the people to whom thou shalt come . . . '; also Job ix. 34; xiii. 21 ('let not his fear terrify me'; 'let not thy dread make me afraid'). Here we have a terror fraught with an inward shuddering such as not even the most menacing and overpowering created thing can instil. It has something spectral in it. . . .

2. The element of 'Overpoweringness' ('majestas')

We have been attempting to unfold the implications of that aspect of the *mysterium tremendum* indicated by the adjective, and the result so far may be summarized in two words, constituting, as before, what may be called an 'ideogram', rather than a concept proper, viz. 'absolute unapproachability'.

It will be felt at once that there is yet a further element which must be added, that, namely, of 'might', 'power', 'absolute overpoweringness'. We will take to represent this the term *majestas,* majesty—the more readily because anyone with a feeling for language must detect a last faint trace of the numinous still clinging to the word. The *tremendum* may then be rendered more adequately *tremenda majestas,* or *'awful majesty'.* This second element of majesty may continue to be vividly preserved, where the first, that of unapproachability, recedes and dies away, as may be seen, for example, in mysticism. It is especially in relation to this element of majesty or absolute overpoweringness that the creature-consciousness, of which we have already spoken, comes upon the scene, as a sort of shadow or subjective reflection of it. Thus, in contrast to 'the overpowering' of which we are conscious as an object over against the self, there is the feeling of one's own submergence, of being but 'dust and ashes' and nothingness. And this forms the numinous raw material for the feeling of religious humility. . . .[1]

3. The Element of 'Energy' or Urgency

There is, finally, a third element comprised in those of *tremendum* and *majestas*, awefulness and majesty, and this I venture to call the 'urgency' or 'energy' of the numinous object. It is particularly vividly perceptible in the ὀργή or 'wrath'; and it everywhere clothes itself in symbolical expressions—vitality, passion, emotional temper, will, force, movement,[2] excitement, activity, impetus. These features are typical and recur again and again from the daemonic level up to the idea of the 'living' God. We have here the factor that has everywhere more than any other prompted the fiercest opposition to the 'philosophic' God of mere rational speculation, who can be put into a definition. And for their part the philosophers have condemned these expressions of the energy of the numen, whenever they are brought on to the scene, as sheer anthropomorphism. In so far as their opponents have for the most part themselves failed to recognize that the terms they have borrowed from the sphere of human conative and affective life have merely value as analogies, the philosophers are right to condemn them. But they are wrong, in so far as, this error notwithstanding, these terms stood for a genuine aspect of the divine nature—its non-rational aspect—a due consciousness of which served to protect religion itself from being 'rationalized' away. . . .

The element of 'energy' reappears in Fichte's speculations on the Absolute as the gigantic, never-resting, active world-stress, and in Schopenhauer's daemonic 'Will'. At the same time both these writers are guilty of the same error that is already found in myth; they transfer 'natural' attributes, which ought only to be used as 'ideograms' for what is itself properly beyond utterance, to the non-rational as real qualifications of it, and they mistake symbolic expressions of feelings for adequate concepts upon which a 'scientific' structure of knowledge may be based. . . .

THE ANALYSIS OF 'MYSTERIUM'

We gave to the object to which the numinous consciousness is directed the name *mysterium tremendum,* and we then set ourselves first to determine the meaning of the adjective *tremendum*—which we found to be itself only justified by analogy—because it is more easily analysed than the substantive idea *mysterium*. We have now to turn to this, and try, as best we may, by hint and suggestion, to get to a clearer apprehension of what it implies.

---

[1]Cf. R. R. Marett, 'The Birth of Humility', in *The Threshold of Religion,* 2nd ed., 1914. [Tr.]

[2]The 'mobilitas Dei' of Lactantius.

4. The 'Wholly Other'

It might be thought that the adjective itself gives an explanation of the substantive; but this is not so. It is not merely analytical; it is a synthetic attribute to it; i.e. *tremendum* adds something not necessarily inherent in *mysterium*. It is true that the reactions in consciousness that correspond to the one readily and spontaneously overflow into those that correspond to the other; in fact, anyone sensitive to the use of words would commonly feel that the idea of 'mystery' (*mysterium*) is so closely bound up with its synthetic qualifying attribute 'aweful' (*tremendum*) that one can hardly say the former without catching an echo of the latter, 'mystery' almost of itself becoming 'aweful mystery' to us. But the passage from the one idea to the other need not by any means be always easy. The elements of meaning implied in 'awefulness' and 'mysteriousness' are in themselves definitely different. The latter may so far preponderate in the religious consciousness, may stand out so vividly, that in comparison with it the former almost sinks out of sight; a case which again could be clearly exemplified from some forms of mysticism. Occasionally, on the other hand, the reverse happens, and the *tremendum* may in turn occupy the mind without the *mysterium*.

This latter, then, needs special consideration on its own account. We need an expression for the mental reaction peculiar to it; and here, too, only one word seems appropriate, though, as it is strictly applicable only to a 'natural' state of mind, it has here meaning only by analogy: it is the word 'stupor'. *Stupor* is plainly a different thing from *tremor*; it signifies blank wonder, an astonishment that strikes us dumb, amazement absolute.[3] Taken, indeed, in its purely natural sense, *mysterium* would first mean merely a secret or a mystery in the sense of that which is alien to us, uncomprehended and unexplained; and so far *mysterium* is itself merely an ideogram, an analogical notion taken from the natural sphere, illustrating, but incapable of exhaustively rendering, our real meaning. Taken in the religious sense, that which is 'mysterious' is—to give it perhaps the most striking expression—the 'wholly other' (θάτερον, *anyad, alienum*), that which is quite beyond the sphere of the usual, the intelligible, and the familiar, which therefore falls quite outside the limits of the 'canny', and is contrasted with it, filling the mind with blank wonder and astonishment. . . .

In accordance with laws of which we shall have to speak again later, this feeling or consciousness of the 'wholly other' will attach itself to, or sometimes be indirectly aroused by means of, objects which are already puzzling upon the 'natural' plane, or are of a surprising or astounding character; such as extraordinary phenomena or astonishing occurrences or things in inanimate nature, in

---

[3]Compare also *obstupefacere*. Still more exact equivalents are the Greek θάμβος and θάμβεῖν. The sound θ α μ β (*thamb*) excellently depicts this state of mind of blank, staring wonder. And the difference between the moments of *stupor* and *tremor* is very finely suggested by the passage, Mark x. 32 (cf. *infra*, p. 158). On the other hand, what was said above of the facility and rapidity with which the two moments merge and blend is also markedly true of θάαμβος, which then becomes a classical term for the (ennobled) awe of the numinous in general. So Mark xvi. 5 is rightly translated by Luther 'und sie entsetzten sich', and by the English Authorized Version 'and they were affrighted'.

the animal world, or among men. But here once more we are dealing with a case of association between things specifically different—the 'numinous' and the 'natural' moments of consciousness—and not merely with the gradual enhancement of one of them—the 'natural'—till it becomes the other. As in the case of 'natural fear' and 'daemonic dread' already considered, so here the transition from natural to daemonic amazement is not a mere matter of degree. But it is only with the latter that the complementary expression *mysterium* perfectly harmonizes, as will be felt perhaps more clearly in the case of the adjectival form 'mysterious'. No one says, strictly and in earnest, of a piece of clockwork that is beyond his grasp, or of a science that he cannot understand: 'That is "mysterious" to me.'

It might be objected that the mysterious is something which is and remains absolutely and invariably beyond our understanding, whereas that which merely eludes our understanding for a time but is perfectly intelligible in principle should be called, not a 'mystery', but merely a 'problem'. But this is by no means an adequate account of the matter. The truly 'mysterious' object is beyond our apprehension and comprehension, not only because our knowledge has certain irremovable limits, but because in it we come upon something inherently 'wholly other', whose kind and character are incommensurable with our own, and before which we therefore recoil in a wonder that strikes us chill and numb.[4]

This may be made still clearer by a consideration of that degraded offshoot and travesty of the genuine 'numinous' dread or awe, the fear of ghosts. Let us try to analyse this experience. We have already specified the peculiar feeling-element of 'dread' aroused by the ghost as that of 'grue', grisly horror.[5] Now this 'grue' obviously contributes something to the attraction which ghost-stories exercise, in so far, namely, as the relaxation of tension ensuing upon our release from it relieves the mind in a pleasant and agreeable way. So far, however, it is not really the ghost itself that gives us pleasure, but the fact that we are rid of it. But obviously this is quite insufficient to explain the ensnaring attraction of the ghost-story. The ghost's real attraction rather consists in this, that of itself and in an uncommon degree it entices the imagination, awakening strong interest and curiosity; it is the weird thing itself that allures the fancy. But it does this, not because it is 'something long and white' (as someone once defined a ghost), nor yet through any of the positive and conceptual attributes which fancies about ghosts have invented, but because it is a thing that 'doesn't really exist at all', the 'wholly other', something which has no place in our scheme of reality but belongs to an absolutely different one, and which at the same time arouses an irrepressible interest in the mind.

---

[4]In *Confessions*, ii. 9. I, Augustine very strikingly suggests this stiffening, benumbing element of the 'wholly other' and its contrast to the rational aspect of the numen; the *dissimile* and the *simile*:

'Quid est illud, quod interlucet mihi et percutit cor meum sine laesione? Et inhorresco et inardesco. *Inhorresco*, in quantum *dissimilis* ei sum. Inardesco, in quantum similis ei sum.'

('What is that which gleams through me and smites my heart without wounding it? I am both a-shudder and a-glow. A-shudder, in so far as I am unlike it, a-glow in so far as I am like it.')

[5]*gruseln, gräsen.*

But that which is perceptibly true in the fear of ghosts, which is, after all, only a caricature of the genuine thing, is in a far stronger sense true of the 'daemonic' experience itself, of which the fear of ghosts is a mere off-shoot. And while, following this main line of development, this element in the numinous consciousness, the feeling of the 'wholly other', is heightened and clarified, its higher modes of manifestation come into being, which set the numinous object in contrast not only to everything wonted and familiar (i.e. in the end, to nature in general), thereby turning it into the 'supernatural', but finally to the world itself, and thereby exalt it to the 'supramundane', that which is above the whole world-order.

In mysticism we have in the 'beyond' (ἐπέκεινα) again the strongest stressing and over-stressing of those non-rational elements which are already inherent in all religion. Mysticism continues to its extreme point this contrasting of the numinous object (the numen), as the 'wholly other', with ordinary experience. Not content with contrasting it with all that is of nature or this world, mysticism concludes by contrasting it with Being itself and all that 'is', and finally actually calls it 'that which is nothing'. By this 'nothing' is meant not only that of which nothing can be predicated, but that which is absolutely and intrinsically other than and opposite of everything that is and can be thought. But while exaggerating to the point of paradox this *negation* and contrast—the only means open to conceptual thought to apprehend the *mysterium*—mysticism at the same time retains the *positive quality* of the 'wholly other' as a very living factor in its over-brimming religious emotion.

But what is true of the strange 'nothingness' of our mystics holds good equally of the *sūnyam* and the *sūnyatā*, the 'void' and 'emptiness' of the Buddhist mystics. This aspiration for the 'void' and for becoming void, no less than the aspiration of our western mystics for 'nothing' and for becoming nothing, must seem a kind of lunacy to anyone who has no inner sympathy for the esoteric language and ideograms of mysticism, and lacks the matrix from which these come necessarily to birth. To such an one Buddhism itself will be simply a morbid sort of pessimism. But in fact the 'void' of the eastern, like the 'nothing' of the western, mystic is a numinous ideogram of the 'wholly other'.

These terms 'supernatural' and 'transcendent'[6] give the appearance of positive attributes, and, as applied to the mysterious, they appear to divest the *mysterium* of its originally negative meaning and to turn it into an affirmation. On the side of conceptual thought this is nothing more than appearance, for it is obvious that the two terms in question are merely negative and exclusive attributes with reference to 'nature' and the world or cosmos respectively. But on the side of the feeling-content it is otherwise; that *is* in very truth positive in the highest degree, though here too, as before, it cannot be rendered explicit in conceptual terms. It is through this positive feeling-content that the concepts of the 'transcendent' and 'supernatural' become forthwith designations for a unique

---

[6]Literally, supramundane: *überweltlich*.

'wholly other' reality and quality, something of whose special character we can *feel*, without being able to give it clear conceptual expression.

THE ELEMENT OF FASCINATION

The qualitative *content* of the numinous experience, to which 'the mysterious' stands as *form*, is in one of its aspects the element of daunting 'awefulness' and 'majesty', which has already been dealt with in detail; but it is clear that it has at the same time another aspect, in which it shows itself as something uniquely attractive and *fascinating*.

These two qualities, the daunting and the fascinating, now combine in a strange harmony of contrasts, and the resultant dual character of the numinous consciousness, to which the entire religious development bears witness, at any rate from the level of the 'daemonic dread' onwards, is at once the strangest and most noteworthy phenomenon in the whole history of religion. The daemonic-divine object may appear to the mind an object of horror and dread, but at the same time it is no less something that allures with a potent charm, and the crea-ture, who trembles before it, utterly cowed and cast down, has always at the same time the impulse to turn to it, nay even to make it somehow his own. The 'mystery' is for him not merely something to be wondered at but something that entrances him; and beside that in it which bewilders and confounds, he feels a something that captivates and transports him with a strange ravishment, rising often enough to the pitch of dizzy intoxication; it is the Dionysiac-element in the numen.

The ideas and concepts which are the parallels or 'schemata' on the ra-tional side of this non-rational element of 'fascination' are love, mercy, pity, comfort; these are all 'natural' elements of the common psychical life, only they are here thought as absolute and in completeness. But important as these are for the experience of religious bliss or felicity, they do not by any means exhaust it. It is just the same as with the opposite experience of religious infelicity—the experience of the ὀργή or 'wrath' of God:—both alike contain fundamentally non-rational elements. Bliss or beatitude is more, far more, than the mere nat-ural feeling of being comforted, of reliance, of the joy of love, however these may be heightened and enhanced. Just as 'wrath', taken in a purely rational or a purely ethical sense, does not exhaust that profound element of *awefulness* which is locked in the mystery of deity, so neither does 'graciousness' exhaust the profound element of *wonderfulness* and rapture which lies in the mysterious beatific experience of deity. The term 'grace' may indeed be taken as its aptest designation, but then only in the sense in which it is really applied in the lan-guage of the mystics, and in which not only the 'gracious intent' but 'something more' is meant by the word. This 'something more' has its antecedent phases very far back in the history of religions. . . .

'Eye hath not seen, nor ear heard, neither have entered into the heart of man, the things which God hath prepared for them that love him.' Who does

not feel the exalted sound of these words and the 'Dionysiac' element of transport and fervour in them? It is instructive that in such phrases as these, in which
consciousness would fain put its highest consummation into words, 'all images
fall away' and the mind turns from them to grasp expressions that are purely
negative. And it is still more instructive that in reading and hearing such words
their merely negative character simply is not noticed; that we can let whole
chains of such negations enrapture, even intoxicate us, and that entire hymns—
and deeply impressive hymns—have been composed, in which there is really
nothing positive at all! All this teaches us the independence of the positive content of this experience from the implications of its overt conceptual expression,
and how it can be firmly grasped, thoroughly understood, and profoundly
appreciated, purely in, with, and from the feeling itself.

Mere love, mere trust, for all the glory and happiness they bring, do not
explain to us that moment of rapture that breathes in our tenderest and most
heart-felt hymns of salvation, as also in such eschatological hymns of longing as
that Rhyme of St. Bernard in which the very verses seem to dance.

Urbs Sion unica, mansio mystica, condita coelo,
Nunc tibi gaudeo, nunc tibi lugeo, tristor, anhelo,
Te, quia corpore non queo, pectore saepe penetro;
Sed caro terrea, terraque carnea, mox cado retro.
Nemo retexere, nemoque promere sustinet ore,
Quo tua moenia, quo capitolia plena nitore.
Id queo dicere, quo modo tangere pollice coelum,
Ut mare currere, sicut in aere figere telum.
Opprimit omne cor ille tuus decor, O Sion, O Pax.
Urbs sine tempore, nulla potest fore laus tibi mendax.
O nova mansio, te pia concio, gens pia munit,
Provehit, excitat, auget, identitat, efficit, unit.[7]

This is where the living 'something more' of the *fascinans,* the element of
fascination, is to be found. It lives no less in those tense extollings of the blessing of salvation, which recur in all religions of salvation, and stand in such
remarkable contrast to the relatively meagre and frequently childish import of
that which is revealed in them by concept or by image. Everywhere salvation is
something whose meaning is often very little apparent, is even wholly obscure,
to the 'natural' man; on the contrary, *so far as he understands it,* he tends to find
it highly tedious and uninteresting, sometimes downright distasteful and repugnant to his nature, as he would, for instance, find the beatific vision of God in

---

[7]'O Sion, thou city sole and single, mystic mansion hidden away in the heavens, now I rejoice in
thee, now I moan for thee and mourn and yearn for thee; thee often I pass through in the heart,
as I cannot in the body, but being but earthly flesh and fleshly earth soon I fall back. None can
disclose or utter in speech what plenary radiance fills thy walls and thy citadels. I can as little tell
of it as I can touch the skies with my finger, or run upon the sea or make a dart stand still in the
air. This thy splendour overwhelms every heart, O Sion, O Peace! O timeless City, no praise can
belie thee. O new dwelling-place, thee the concourse and people of the faithful erects and exalts,
inspires and increases, joins to itself, and makes complete and one.'

our own doctrine of salvation, or the *henōsis* of 'God all in all' among the mystics. 'So far as he understands', be it noted; but then he does not understand it in the least. Because he lacks the inward teaching of the Spirit, he must needs confound what is offered him as an expression for the experience of salvation—a mere ideogram of what is felt, whose import it hints at by analogy—with 'natural' concepts, as though it were itself just such an one. And so he 'wanders ever farther from the goal'.

It is not only in the religious feeling of longing that the moment of fascination is a living factor. It is already alive and present in the moment of 'solemnity', both in the gathered concentration and humble submergence of private devotion, when the mind is exalted to the holy, and in the common worship of the congregation, where this is practised with earnestness and deep sincerity, as, it is to be feared, is with us a thing rather desired than realized. It is this and nothing else that in the solemn moment can fill the soul so full and keep it so inexpressibly tranquil. Schleiermacher's assertion[8] is perhaps true of it, as of the numinous consciousness in general, viz. that it cannot really occur alone on its own account, or except combined and penetrated with rational elements. But, if this be admitted, it is upon other grounds than those adduced by Schleiermacher; while, on the other hand, it may occupy a more or less predominant place and lead to states of calm ($\dot{\eta}\sigma\upsilon\chi\acute{\iota}\alpha$) as well as of transport, in which it *almost* of itself wholly fills the soul. But in all the manifold forms in which it is aroused in us, whether in eschatological promise of the coming kingdom of God and the transcendent bliss of Paradise, or in the guise of an entry into that beatific reality that is 'above the world'; whether it come first in expectancy or pre-intimation or in a present experience ('When I but *have* Thee, I ask no question of heaven and earth'); in all these forms, outwardly diverse but inwardly akin, it appears as a strange and mighty propulsion towards an ideal good known only to religion and in its nature fundamentally non-rational, which the mind knows of in yearning and presentiment, recognizing it for what it is behind the obscure and inadequate symbols which are its only expression. And this shows that above and beyond our rational being lies hidden the ultimate and highest part of our nature, which can find no satisfaction in the mere allaying of the needs of our sensuous, physical, or intellectual impulses and cravings. The mystics called it the basis or ground of the soul. . . .

---

[8]*Glaubenslehre*, § 5.

Section 2 THE LURE OF THE SACRED

Most humans, it would appear, have been aware of another dimension, which lurks at the fringes of life. Some are more aware of it than others. Some seem overwhelmed, even obsessed by it, others barely perceive it or perhaps perceive it not at all. This "other dimension" is mysterious, wonderful, appealing, and frightening. It is pregnant with both meaning and threat. One name for it is "the sacred."

Rudolph Bultman, a German Protestant theologian once very fashionable and now very much out of fashion, said that when you controlled electricity with a flick of a lightswitch, it was difficult to feel any awe for lightning. Modern humans, understanding the nature of electrical discharge and knowing about negative ions are, in such a view, simply unimpressed by a spectacular thunderstorm. Hence, that which was once sacred has been deprived of its awsomeness and has become profane.

Perhaps Bultman did not find a thunderstorm exciting. Perhaps some of his students had become sufficiently prosaic that they no longer paid any attention to storms. But the question remains as to whether or not they were simply dullards and whether or not thunderstorms can be exciting when you understand their scientific explanation. As long as human experiences produce awe and wonder and surprise and admiration and fear, the phenomenona still hint at the sacred, the "other," no matter how advanced scientific knowledge may become.

The borders of the "other" may change, but the "other" still lurks nearby. Whether there was any more awe in the primitive societies that Mircea Eliade describes in these selections than there is in our society remains to be seen.

In any event the "totally other," as Rudolph Otto named it, still has the capacity to stir both terror and fascination for many modern humans and with that fact sociology must deal.

Reading 9

SACRED TIME—MIRCEA ELIADE

Mircea Eliade, Romanian by birth, was by young adulthood, a novelist, mystic, linguist, diplomat, and perhaps the most brilliant student of the "history of religions" in the twentieth century. Unlike some of his predecessors (in a field that was for many years called "comparative religion"), he was not interested either in debunking Christianity or in arguing that all religions were essentially the same. Unlike Joseph Campbell, he did not see a single hero with a thousand faces, but many heroes who had similar faces but very different stories. Jesus and Buddha were both saviors in a certain sense, but their stories were very different. Mary, Venus, Brigid, Aurora were all spring goddesses, whose youthful faces and bodies represent the promise of new life. But their stories are very different. (Brigid was assimilated to Mary by the early Irish Christians who called her "Mary of the Gaels" and thought she was the mother of Jesus reincarnate).

So, too, there are many water ceremonies, and they are all about life, but they tell different stories about the origins and meaning of life.

Among the many phenomena that impinge on human consciousness, there are some that because of their enormous importance and power usually have been interpreted by humans as revealing in a special way the work of the deities: water, fire, sun, moon, food and drink, sex, birth, and death. These realities become "sacraments," hints of the gods at work and around them humans have built the rituals through which they join in the original creative activity of the gods.

Thus, humans may plant their fields as part of a ritual dance, and husband and wife may even make love in the fields to link their crops with the ultimate powers of fertility that "in that time" created the earth and its fertility.

Note that there is a certain "fiction," an act of "make-believe," a kind of "fantasy" at work in such sacrament making. The love-making in the fields, for example, is an act of physical union between a man and a woman, indistinguishable in the act itself from other acts of love between them; that it represents in this particular case a link to the gods' life-giving actions depends on their "pretense" that it is a very special kind of sexual congress. Such a pretense may well make it special. The sacred tree is a tree. An outsider would think it is a tree like any other tree. But the members of the tribe "pretend" that it is the *axis mundi,* the link between heaven and earth, and thus make it special.

Such "pretense" is not an attempt to deceive. It is rather the investment of certain objects, events, and persons with a special interpretation. Myth making and sacrament making is interpretative behavior.

For Eliade, this world was but a pale reflection of what happened "in that time" and human religion is in substantial part an attempt to maintain contact with the Really Real, which exists "in that time." In the present worldly time, we exist as if trapped in a labyrinth, cut off from the source of life. The editor of this collection felt for many years that Eliade's radical platonism was more a metaphor than a statement of his literal belief. However, Eliade autographed a copy of his autobiographical novel, *The Forbidden Forest,* to the editor with the words, "who is also trapped in the labyrinth."

The editor was reminded of G.K. Chesteron's reaction after he finished reading Eliot's "The Waste Land." He threw the book across the room and announced to the world, "I'll be damned if I ever felt that way!"

The cycle of the seasons guarantees that time is sacred in contemporary society. The various religious festivals of the Jewish and Christian traditions, linked as they are to the passage of the seasons, demonstrate that some times are more important than other times. So, too, do the secular feasts—such as Thanksgiving and New Years Day and the Fourth of July—which take some of their content and symbolism from their place in the seasonal calendar. Some will argue that the festivals are not as sacred as they used to be. But this argument presumes that our predecessors were somehow different from us and that their festivals were more purely religious than ours. Human nature however has not changed. It would be a mistake to think that the singing and dancing and love-making that characterized festivals in earlier cultures were not enjoyable for those who participated in them—just as the sacred and the secular are interwoven in our festivals today (such as Christmas). Then and now, that some times are sacred does not mean that they are not secular, too.

Rituals carried out in sacred time are often dramatic representations of the narrative symbols that Geertz says are what religion is. The sacred rituals represent the symbols to the people who participate in the rituals, renewing their power and importance. It is not necessary that these be seen as a reflection of some past "in that time" (though obviously even our secular feasts in America recall the foundational moments of the republic), but they do recall the critical moments in the religious tradition, such as the birth of Jesus, or the Sinai experience of the Jews. And the celebrations do recall those events and make them present again for the celebrants.

This essay shows how much we have in common with our ancestors.

Questions for Reflection and Discussion

1. How is sacred time different from ordinary time?
2. Why do humans seem to need sacred time?
3. How do our sacred times differ from those peoples about whom Eliade writes?

SACRED TIME AND MYTHS
Mircea Eliade

PROFANE DURATION AND SACRED TIME

For religious man time too, like space, is neither homogeneous nor continuous. On the one hand there are the intervals of a sacred time, the time of festivals (by far the greater part of which are periodical); on the other there is profane time, ordinary temporal duration, in which acts without religious meaning have their setting. Between these two kinds of time there is, of course, solution of continuity; but by means of rites religious man can pass without danger from ordinary temporal duration to sacred time.

One essential difference between these two qualities of time strikes us immediately: *by its very nature sacred time is reversible* in the sense that, properly speaking, it is *a primordial mythical time made present.* Every religious festival, any liturgical time, represents the reactualization of a sacred event that took place in a mythical past, "in the beginning." Religious participation in a festival implies emerging from ordinary temporal duration and reintegration of the mythical time reactualized by the festival itself. Hence sacred time is indefinitely recoverable, indefinitely repeatable. From one point of view it could be said that it does not "pass," that it does not constitute an irreversible duration. It is an ontological, Parmenidean time; it always remains equal to itself, it neither changes nor is exhausted. With each periodical festival, the participants find the same sacred time—the same that had been manifested in the festival of the previous year or in the festival of a century earlier; it is the time that was created and sanctified by the gods at the period of their *gesta,* of which the festival is precisely a reactualization. In other words the participants in the festival meet in it *the first appearance of sacred time,* as it appeared *ab origine, in illo tempore.* For the sacred time in which the festival runs its course did not exist before the divine *gesta* that the festival commemorates. By creating the various realities that today constitute the world, the gods *also founded sacred time,* for the time contemporary with a creation was necessarily sanctified by the presence and activity of the gods.

Hence religious man lives in two kinds of time, of which the more important, sacred time, appears under the paradoxical aspect of a circular time, reversible and recoverable, a sort of eternal mythical present that is periodically reintegrated by means of rites. This attitude in regard to time suffices to distinguish religious from nonreligious man; the former refuses to live solely in what, in modern terms, is called the historical present; he attempts to regain a sacred time that, from one point of view, can be homologized to eternity.

Source: Mircea Eliade, *The Sacred and The Profane: The Nature of Religion.* Translated from the French by Willard R. Trask. New York: Harper & Row, 1961, Copyright 1959.

What time is for the nonreligious man of modern societies would be more difficult to put into a few words. We do not intend to discuss the modern philosophies of time nor the concepts that modern science uses in its own investigations. Our aim is to compare not systems or philosophies but existential attitudes and behaviors. Now, what it is possible to observe in respect to a nonreligious man is that he too experiences a certain discontinuity and heterogeneity of time. For him too there is the comparatively monotonous time of his work, and the time of celebrations and spectacles—in short, "festal time." He too lives in varying temporal rhythms and is aware of times of different intensities; when he is listening to the kind of music that he likes or, being in love, waits for or meets his sweetheart, he obviously experiences a different temporal rhythm from that which he experiences when he is working or bored.

But, in comparison with religious man, there is an essential difference. The latter experiences intervals of time that are "sacred," that have no part in the temporal duration that precedes and follows them, that have a wholly different structure and origin, for they are of a primordial time, sanctified by the gods and capable of being made present by the festival. This transhuman quality of liturgical time is inaccessible to a nonreligious man. This is as much as to say that, for him, time can present neither break nor mystery; for him, time constitutes man's deepest existential dimension; it is linked to his own life, hence it has a beginning and an end, which is death, the annihilation of his life. However many the temporal rhythms that he experiences, however great their differences in intensity, nonreligious man knows that they always represent a human experience, in which there is no room for any divine presence.

For religious man, on the contrary, profane temporal duration can be periodically arrested; for certain rituals have the power to interrupt it by periods of a sacred time that is nonhistorical (in the sense that it does not belong to the historical present). Just as a church constitutes a break in plane in the profane space of a modern city, the service celebrated inside it marks a break in profane temporal duration. It is no longer today's historical time that is present—the time that is experienced, for example, in the adjacent streets—but the time in which the historical existence of Jesus Christ occurred, the time sanctified by his preaching, by his passion, death, and resurrection. But we must add that this example does not reveal all the difference between sacred and profane time; Christianity radically changed the experience and the concept of liturgical time, and this is due to the fact that Christianity affirms the historicity of the person of Christ. The Christian liturgy unfolds in a *historical time sanctified by the incarnation of the Son of God.* The sacred time periodically reactualized in pre-Christian religions (especially in the archaic religions) is a *mythical time,* that is, a primordial time, not to be found in the historical past, an *original time,* in the sense that it came into existence all at once, that it was not preceded by another time, because no time could exist *before the appearance of the reality narrated in the myth.*

It is this archaic conception of mythical time that is of chief concern to us. We shall later see how it differs from the conceptions held by Judaism and Christianity.

TEMPLUM-TEMPUS

We shall begin our investigation by presenting certain facts that have the advantage of immediately revealing religious man's behavior in respect to time. First of all, an observation that is not without importance: in a number of North American Indian languages the term world (= Cosmos) is also used in the sense of year. The Yokuts say "the world has passed," meaning "a year has gone by." For the Yuki, the year is expressed by the words for earth or world. Like the Yokuts, they say "the world has passed" when a year has passed. This vocabulary reveals the intimate religious connection between the world and cosmic time. The cosmos is conceived as a living unity that is born, develops, and dies on the last day of the year, to be reborn on New Year's Day. We shall see that this *rebirth* is a *birth,* that the cosmos is reborn each year because, at every New Year, time begins *ab initio*.

The intimate connection between the cosmos and time is religious in nature: the cosmos is homologizable to cosmic time (= the Year) because they are both sacred realities, divine creations. Among some North American peoples this cosmic-temporal connection is revealed even in the structure of sacred buildings. Since the temple represents the image of the world, it can also comprise a temporal symbolism. We find this, for example, among the Algonquins and the Sioux. As we saw, their sacred lodge represents the universe; but at the same time it symbolizes the year. For the year is conceived as a journey through the four cardinal directions, signified by the four doors and four windows of the lodge. The Dakotas say: "The Year is a circle around the world"—that is, around their sacred lodge, which is an *imago mundi*.[1]

A still clearer example is found in India. We saw that the erection of an altar is equivalent to a repetition of the cosmogony. The texts add that "the fire altar is the year" and explain its temporal system as follows: the 360 bricks of the enclosure correspond to the 360 nights of the year, and the 360 *yajusmati* bricks to the 360 days (*Shatapatha Brāhmana*, X, 5, 4, 10; etc.). This is as much as to say that, with the building of each fire altar, not only is the world remade but the year is built too; in other words, *time is regenerated by being created anew*. But then, too, the year is assimilated to Prajāpati, the cosmic god; consequently, with each new altar Prajāpati is reanimated—that is, the sanctity of the world is strengthened. It is not a matter of profane time, of mere temporal duration, but of the sanctification of cosmic time. What is sought by the erection of the fire altar is to sanctify the world, hence to place it in a sacred time.

We find a similar temporal symbolism as part of the cosmological symbolism of the Temple at Jerusalem. According to Flavius Josephus (*Ant. Jud.,* III, 7, 7), the twelve loaves of bread on the table signified the twelve months of the year and the candelabrum with seventy branches represented the decans (the zodiacal division of the seven planets into tens). The Temple was an *imago mundi;* being at the Center of the World, at Jerusalem, it sanctified not only the entire cosmos but also cosmic life—that is, time.

---

[1] Werner Müller, *Die blaue Hütte,* Wiesbaden, 1954, p. 133.

Hermann Usener has the distinction of having been the first to explain the etymological kinship between *templum* and *tempus* by interpreting the two terms through the concept of "intersection," (*Schneidung, Kreuzung*).[2] Later studies have refined the discovery: "*templum* designates the spatial, *tempus* the temporal aspect of the motion of the horizon in space and time."[3]

The underlying meaning of all these facts seems to be the following: for religious man of the archaic cultures, *the world is renewed annually:* in other words, *with each new year it recovers* its original sanctity, the sanctity that it possessed when it came from the Creator's hands. This symbolism is clearly indicated in the architectonic structure of sanctuaries. Since the temple is at once the holy place par excellence and the image of the world, it sanctifies the entire cosmos and also sanctifies cosmic life. This cosmic life was imagined in the form of a circular course; it was identified with the year. The year was a closed circle; it had a beginning and an end, but it also had the peculiarity that it could be reborn in the form of a *new* year. With each New Year, a time that was "new," "pure," "holy"—because not yet worn—came into existence.

But time was reborn, began again, because with each New Year the world was created anew. In the preceding chapter we noted the considerable importance of the cosmogonic myth as paradigmatic model for every kind of creation and construction. We will now add that the cosmogony equally implies the creation of time. Nor is this all. For just as the cosmogony is the archetype of all creation, cosmic time, which the cosmogony brings forth, is the paradigmatic model for all other times—that is, for the times specifically belonging to the various categories of existing things. To explain this further: for religious man of the archaic cultures, every creation, every existence begins in time; *before a thing exists, its particular time could not exist.* Before the cosmos came into existence, there was no cosmic time. Before a particular vegetable species was created, the time that now causes it to grow, bear fruit, and die did not exist. It is for this reason that every creation is imagined as having taken place *at the beginning of time, in principio.* Time gushes forth with the first appearance of a new category of existents. This is why myth plays such an important role; as we shall show later, the way in which a reality came into existence is revealed by its myth.

ANNUAL REPETITION OF THE CREATION

It is the cosmogonic myth that tells how the cosmos came into existence. At Babylon during the course of the *akītu* ceremony, which was performed during the last days of the year that was ending and the first days of the New Year, the *Poem of Creation*, the *Enuma elish*, was solemnly recited. This ritual recitation reactualized the combat between Marduk and the marine monster Tiamat, a combat that took place *ab origine* and put an end to chaos by the final victory of the god. Marduk created the cosmos from Tiamat's dismembered body and

---

[2] H. Usener, Götternamen, 2nd ed., Bonn 1920, pp 191ff.
[3] Werner Müller, Kreis and Kreuz, Berlin, 1938, p. 39; cf. also pp. 33ff.

created man from the blood of the demon Kingu, Tiamat's chief ally. That this commemoration of the Creation was in fact a *reactualization* of the cosmogonic act is shown both by the rituals and in the formulas recited during the ceremony.

The combat between Tiamat and Marduk, that is, was mimed by a battle between two groups of actors, a ceremonial that we find again among the Hittites (again in the frame of the dramatic scenario of the New Year), among the Egyptians, and at Ras Shamra. The battle between two groups of actors *repeated the passage from chaos to cosmos,* actualized the cosmogony. The mythical event became *present* once again. "May he continue to conquer Tiamat and shorten his days!" the priest cried. The combat, the victory, and the Creation took place *at that instant, hic et nunc.*

Since the New Year is a reactualization of the cosmogony, it implies *starting time over again at its beginning,* that is, restoration of the primordial time, the "pure" time, that existed at the moment of Creation. This is why the New Year is the occasion for "purifications," for the expulsion of sins, of demons, or merely of a scapegoat. For it is not a matter merely of a certain temporal interval coming to its end and the beginning of another (as a modern man, for example, thinks); it is also a matter of abolishing the past year and past time. Indeed, this is the meaning of ritual purifications; there is more than a mere "purification"; the sins and faults of the individual and of the community as a whole are annulled, *consumed as by fire.*

The Nawrōz—the Persian New Year—commemorates the day that witnessed the creation of the world and man. It was on the day of Nawrōz that the "renewal of the Creation" was accomplished, as the Arabic historian al-Bīrūnī expressed it. The king proclaimed: "Here is a new day of a new month of a new year; what time has worn must be renewed." Time had worn the human being, society, the cosmos—and this destructive time was profane time, duration strictly speaking; it had to be abolished in order to reintegrate the mythical moment in which the world had come into existence, bathed in a "pure," "strong," and sacred time. The abolition of profane past time was accomplished by rituals that signified a sort of "end of the world." The extinction of fires, the return of the souls of the dead, social confusion of the type exemplified by the Saturnalia, erotic license, orgies, and so on, symbolized the retrogression of the cosmos into chaos. On the last day of the year the universe was dissolved in the primordial waters. The marine monster Tiamat—symbol of darkness, of the formless, the nonmanifested—revived and once again threatened. The world that had existed for a whole year *really* disappeared. Since Tiamat was again present, the cosmos was annulled; and Marduk was obliged to create it once again, after having once again conquered Tiamat.[4]

The meaning of this periodical retrogression of the world into a chaotic modality was this: all the "sins" of the year, everything that time had soiled and worn, was annihilated in the physical sense of the word. By symbolically par-

---

[4] For New Year rituals, cf. *Myth,* pp. 55 ff.

ticipating in the annihilation and re-creation of the world, man too was created anew; he was reborn, for he began a new life. With each New Year, man felt freer and purer, for he was delivered from the burden of his sins and failings. He had reintegrated the fabulous time of Creation, hence a sacred and strong time—sacred because transfigured by the presence of the gods, strong because it was the time that belonged, and belonged only, to the most gigantic creation ever accomplished, that of the universe. Symbolically, man became contemporary with the cosmogony, he was present at the creation of the world. In the ancient Near East, he even participated actively in its creation (cf. the two opposed groups, representing the god and the marine monster).

It is easy to understand why the memory of that marvelous time haunted religious man, why he periodically sought to return to it. *In illo tempore* the gods had displayed their greatest powers. *The cosmogony is the supreme divine manifestation,* the paradigmatic act of strength, superabundance, and creativity. Religious man thirsts for the real. By every means at his disposal, he seeks to reside at the very source of primordial reality, when the world was *in statu nascendi.* . . .

SACRED HISTORY, HISTORY, HISTORICISM

Let us recapitulate:

Religious man experiences two kinds of time—profane and sacred. The one is an evanescent duration, the other a "succession of eternities," periodically recoverable during the festivals that made up the sacred calendar. The liturgical time of the calendar flows in a closed circle; it is the cosmic time of the year, sanctified by the works of the gods. And since the most stupendous divine work was the creation of the world, commemoration of the cosmogony plays an important part in many religions. The New Year coincides with the first day of Creation. The year is the temporal dimension of the cosmos. "The world has passed" expresses that a year has run its course.

At each New Year the cosmogony is reiterated, the world re-created, and to do this is also to create time—that is, to regenerate it by beginning it anew. This is why the cosmogonic myth serves as paradigmatic model for every creation or construction; it is even used as a ritual means of healing. By symbolically becoming contemporary with the Creation, one reintegrates the primordial plenitude. The sick man becomes well because he begins his life again with its sum of energy intact.

The religious festival is the reactualization of a primordial event, of a sacred history in which the actors are the gods or semidivine beings. But sacred history is recounted in the myths. Hence the participants in the festival become contemporaries of the gods and the semidivine beings. They live in the primordial time that is sanctified by the presence and activity of the gods. The sacred calendar periodically regenerates time, because it makes it coincide with the *time of origin,* the strong, pure time. The religious experience of the festival—that is, participation in the sacred—enables man periodically to live in the presence of the gods. This is the reason for the fundamental importance of myths in all pre-Mosaic religions, for the myths narrate the *gesta* of the gods and these *gesta* constitute paradigmatic models for all human activities. In so far as he imitates his gods, religious man lives in the *time of origin,* the time of the myths. In other words, he emerges from profane duration to recover an unmoving time, eternity.

Since, for religious man of the primitive societies, myths constitute his sacred history, he must not forget them; by reactualizing the myths, he approaches his gods and participates in sanctity. But there are also tragic divine histories, and man assumes a great responsibility toward himself and toward nature by periodically reactualizing them. Ritual cannibalism, for example, is the consequence of a tragic religious conception.

In short, through the reactualization of his myths, religious man attempts to approach the gods and to participate in *being:* the imitation of paradigmatic divine models expresses at once his desire for sanctity and his ontological nostalgia.

In the primitive and archaic religions the eternal repetition of the divine exploits is justified as an *imitatio dei.* The sacred calendar annually repeats the same festivals, that is, the commemoration of the same mythical events. Strictly speaking, the sacred calendar proves to be the "eternal return" of a limited number of divine *gesta*—and this is true not only for primitive religions but for all others. The festal calendar everywhere constitutes a periodical return of the same primordial situations and hence a reactualization of the same sacred time. For religious man, reactualization of the same mythical events constitutes his great hopes for with each reactualization he again has the opportunity to transfigure his existence, to make it like its divine model. In short, for religious man of the primitive and archaic societies, the eternal repetition of paradigmatic gestures and the eternal recovery of the same mythical time of origin, sanctified by the gods, in no sense implies a pessimistic vision of life. On the contrary, for him it is by virtue of this eternal return to the sources of the sacred and the real that human existence appears to be saved from nothingness and death.

The perspective changes completely when the sense of *the religiousness of the cosmos becomes lost.* This is what occurs when, in certain more highly evolved societies, the intellectual élites progressively detach themselves from the patterns of the traditional religion. The periodical sanctification of cosmic time then proves useless and without meaning. The gods are no longer accessible through the cosmic rhythms. The religious meaning of the repetition of paradigmatic gestures is forgotten. But *repetition emptied of its religious content necessarily leads to a pessimistic vision of existence.* When it is no longer a vehicle for reintegrating a primordial situation, and hence for recovering the mysterious presence of the gods, that is, *when it is desacralized,* cyclic time becomes terrifying: it is seen as a circle forever turning on itself, repeating itself to infinity.

This is what happened in India, where the doctrine of cosmic cycles (*yugas*) was elaborately developed. A complete cycle, a *mahāyuga,* comprises 12,000 years. It ends with a dissolution, a *pralaya,* which is repeated more drastically (*mahāpralaya,* the Great Dissolution) at the end of the thousandth cycle. For the paradigmatic schema "creation–destruction–creation–etc." is reproduced *ad infinitum*. The 12,000 years of a *mahāyuga* were regarded as divine years, each with a duration of 360 years, which gives a total of 4,320,000 years for a single cosmic cycle. A thousand such *mahāyugas* make up a *kalpa* (form); 14 *kalpas* make up a *manvantāra* (so named because each *manvantāra* is supposed to be ruled by Manu, the mythical Ancestor-King.) A *kalpa* is equivalent to a day in the life of Brahma: a second *kalpa* to a night. One hundred of these "years" of Brahma, in other words 311,000 milliards of human years, constitute the life of Brahma. But even this duration of the god's life does not exhaust time, for the gods are not eternal and the cosmic creations and destructions succeed one another forever.[5]

This is the true eternal return, the eternal repetition of the fundamental rhythm of the cosmos—its periodical destruction and re-creation. In short, *it is the primitive conception of the Year-Cosmos, but emptied of its religious content*. Obviously, the doctrine of *yugas* was elaborated by intellectual élites, and if it became a pan-Indian doctrine, we must not suppose that it revealed its terrifying aspect to all the peoples of India. It was chiefly the religious and philosophical élites who felt despair in the presence of cyclic time repeating itself *ad infinitum*. For to Indian thought, this eternal return implied eternal return to existence by force of *karma,* the law of universal causality. Then, too, time was homologized to the cosmic illusion (*māyā*), and the eternal return to existence signified indefinite prolongation of suffering and slavery. In the view of these religious and philosophical élites, the only hope was nonreturn-to-existence, the abolition of karma; in other words, final deliverance (*moksha*), implying a transcendence of the cosmos.[6]

Greece too knew the myth of the eternal return, and the Greek philosophers of the late period carried the conception of circular time to its furthest limits. To quote the perceptive words of H. C. Puech: "According to the celebrated Platonic definition, time, which is determined and measured by the revolution of the celestial spheres, is the moving image of unmoving eternity, which it imitates by revolving in a circle. Consequently all cosmic becoming, and, in the same manner, the duration of this world of generation and corruption in which we live, will progress in a circle or in accordance with an indefinite succession of cycles in the course of which the same reality is made, unmade, and remade in conformity with an immutable law and immutable alternatives. Not only is the same sum of existence preserved in it, with nothing being lost and nothing created, but in addition certain thinkers of declining antiquity—Pythagoreans, Stoics, Platonists—reached the point of admitting that within each of these cycles of duration, of these *aiones*, these *aeva*, the same situations are reproduced that have already been produced in previous cycles and will be reproduced in subsequent cycles—*ad infinitum*. No event is unique, occurs once and for all (for example, the condemnation and death of Socrates), but it has

---

[5]Cf. Eliade, *Myth*, pp. 113 ff.; see also *id., Images et symboles*. Paris, 1952, pp. 80 ff.

[6]This transcendence is achieved through the "fortunate instant" (kahaza), which implies a sort of sacred time that permits emergence from time: see *Images et symboles,* pp. 10 ff.

occurred, occurs, and will occur, perpetually; the same individuals have appeared, appear, and will reappear at every return of the cycle upon itself. Cosmic duration is repetition and *anakuklosis,* eternal return."[7]

Compared with the archaic and palaeo-oriental religions, as well as with the mythic-philosophical conceptions of the eternal return, as they were elaborated in India and Greece, Judaism presents an innovation of the first importance. For Judaism, time has a beginning and will have an end. The idea of cyclic time is left behind. Yahweh no longer manifests himself in *cosmic time* (like the gods of other religions) but in a *historical time,* which is irreversible. Each new manifestation of Yahweh in history is no longer reducible to an earlier manifestation. The fall of Jerusalem expresses Yahweh's wrath against his people, but it is no longer the same wrath that Yahweh expressed by the fall of Samaria. His gestures are *personal* interventions in history and reveal their deep meaning *only for his people,* the people that Yahweh had *chosen.* Hence the historical event acquires a new dimension; it becomes a *theophany.*[8]

Christianity goes even further in valorizing *historical time.* Since God was *incarnated,* that is, since he took on a *historically conditioned human existence,* history acquires the possibility of being sanctified. The *illud tempus* evoked by the Gospels is a clearly defined historical time—the time in which Pontius Pilate was Governor of Judaea—but it was *sanctified by the presence of Christ.* When a Christian of our day participates in liturgical time, he recovers the *illud tempus* in which Christ lived, suffered, and rose again—but it is no longer a mythical time, it is the time when Pontius Pilate governed Judaea. For the Christian, too, the sacred calendar indefinitely rehearses the same events of the existence of Christ—but these events took place in history; they are no longer facts that happened at the *origin of time,* "in the beginning." (But we should add that, for the Christian, time begins anew with the birth of Christ, for the Incarnation establishes a new situation of man in the cosmos). This is as much as to say that history reveals itself to be a new dimension of the presence of God in the world. History becomes *sacred history* once more—as it was conceived, but in a mythical perspective, in primitive and archaic religions.[9]

Christianity arrives, not at a *philosophy* but at a *theology* of history. For God's interventions in history, and above all his Incarnation in the historical person of Jesus Christ, have a transhistorical purpose—the *salvation* of man.

Hegel takes over the Judaeo-Christian ideology and applies it to universal history in its totality: the universal spirit *continually* manifests itself in historical events and manifests itself *only* in historical events. Thus *the whole* of history becomes a theophany; everything that has happened in history *had to happen as it did,* because the universal spirit so willed it. The road is thus opened to the various forms of twentieth-century historicistic philosophies. Here our present investigation ends, for all these new valorizations of time and history belong to

---

[7]Henri Charles Peuch, "La gnose et le temps," *Eranos-Jahrbuch,* XX. 1952, pp. 60–61.
[8]Cf. Eliade, *Myth,* pp. 102 ff., on the valorization of history in Judaism, especially by the prophets.
[9]Cf. Eliade, *Images et symboles,* pp. 222 ff.

the history of philosophy. Yet we must add that historicism arises as a decomposition product of Christianity; it accords decisive importance to the historical event (which is an idea whose origin is Christian) but to the *historical event as such,* that is, by denying it any possibility of revealing a transhistorical, soteriological intent.[10]

As for the conceptions of time on which certain historicistic and existentialist philosophies have insisted, the following observation is not without interest: although no longer conceived as a circle, time in these modern philosophies once again wears the terrifying aspect that it wore in the Indian and Greek philosophies of the eternal return. Definitively descralized, time presents itself as a precarious and evanescent duration, leading irremediably to death.

---

[10]On the difficulties of historicism, see *Myth,* pp. 147 ff.

SACRED PLACE—MIRCEA ELIADE

Just as sacred time is that time when the barriers between humankind and the gods becomes permeable, so sacred space is the locale where the boundaries between humans and their deities become thin. God is everywhere but She or He is especially available in a church—which in European Christianity usually was built in the central plaza of the town. Just as humans have a need or at least a propensity to see the passage of time divided into more important and less important segments, so they are inclined to divide space into the ordinary and extraordinary, even in the secular world. The Lincoln Memorial is not the same as the neighborhood shopping mall. The Christmas tree, fraught with mythological meanings, remains an important center for family festivities at Christmas. The space around the tree takes on a special aura; indeed the lights and the ornaments are designed precisely to create that aura. Even most secularists decorate Christmas trees.

Do we invest as much reverence or awe in our sacred places as in our sacred times? Perhaps we over-estimate how reverent earlier cultures were. In any event, Christians and Jews and Muslims, for example, still treat their houses of worship as very special places. Attempts at desecration produce reactions or horror and rage. We may have more sophisticated explanations of why a place is holy than did our ancestors who built New Grange or Stonehenge, but it would be unwise to argue that they were more primitive or we more sophisticated in our regard for such places.

Eliade's descriptions of sacred time and sacred place seem almost to exist in a different category of analysis than most sociological discussions of the sacred, as we shall see in subsequent essays. While times and places of awe are common enough in the human condition and in the experiences of most humans, they seem to be foreign to sociological analysis—which is why sociologists should listen more carefully to scholars such as Eliade. The sacred is alive and well not merely in "New Age" phenomena but in the ordinary life, even the secular life, of most Americans. Sociologists who ignore it do so at their own risk, the risk of misunderstanding religion.

Questions for Reflection and Discussion

1. Describe some of your experiences (if any) of sacred place?
2. Granted that some of the customs described in the excerpt are more than a little strange, can you find something in common with their experiences of sacred space and your own?

3. Can you integrate Eliade's analysis of the Sacred with Rudolph Otto's description?
4. What are the similarities and differences between Eliade and Durkheim?

SACRED SPACE AND MAKING THE WORLD SACRED
Mircea Eliade

HOMOGENEITY OF SPACE AND HIEROPHANY

For religious man, space is not homogeneous; he experiences interruptions, breaks in it; some parts of space are qualitatively different from others. "Draw not nigh hither," says the Lord to Moses; "put off thy shoes from off thy feet, for the place whereon thou standest is holy ground" (Exodus, 3, 5). There is, then, a sacred space, and hence a strong, significant space; there are other spaces that are not sacred and so are without structure or consistency, amorphous. Nor is this all. For religious man, this spatial nonhomogeneity finds expression in the experience of an opposition between space that is sacred—the only *real* and *really* existing space—and all other space, the formless expanse surrounding it.

It must be said at once that the religious experience of the nonhomogeneity of space is a primordial experience, homologizable to a founding of the world. It is not a matter of theoretical speculation, but of a primary religious experience that precedes all reflection on the world. For it is the break effected in space that allows the world to be constituted, because it reveals the fixed point, the central axis for all future orientation. When the sacred manifests itself in any hierophany, there is not only a break in the homogeneity of space: there is also revelation of an absolute reality, opposed to the nonreality of the vast surrounding expanse. The manifestation of the sacred ontologically founds the world. In the homogeneous and infinite expanse, in which no point of reference is possible and hence no *orientation* can be established, the hierophany reveals an absolute fixed point, a center.

So it is clear to what a degree the discovery—that is, the revelation—of a sacred space possesses existential value for religious man; for nothing can begin, nothing can be *done*, without a previous orientation—and any orientation implies acquiring a fixed point. It is for this reason that religious man has always sought to fix his abode at the "center of the world." *If the world is to be lived in,* it must be *founded*—and no world can come to birth in the chaos of the

Source: Mircea Eliade, *The Sacred and the Profane: The Nature of Religion.* Translated from the French by Willard R. Trask. New York: Harper & Row, 1961. Copyright 1959.

homogeneity and relativity of profane space. The discovery or projection of a fixed point—the center—is equivalent to the creation of the world; and we shall soon give some examples that will unmistakably show the cosmogonic value of the ritual orientation and construction of sacred space.

For profane experience, on the contrary, space is homogeneous and neutral; no break qualitatively differentiates the various parts of its mass. Geometrical space can be cut and delimited in any direction; but no qualitative differentiation and, hence, no orientation are given by virtue of its inherent structure. We need only remember how a classical geometrician defines space. Naturally, we must not confuse the *concept* of homogeneous and neutral geometrical space with the *experience* of profane space, which is in direct contrast to the experience of sacred space and which alone concerns our investigation. The *concept* of homogeneous space and the history of the concept (for it has been part of the common stock of philosophical and scientific thought since antiquity) are a wholly different problem, upon which we shall not enter here. What matters for our purpose is the *experience* of space known to nonreligious man—that is, to a man who rejects the sacrality of the world, who accepts only a profane existence, divested of all religious presuppositions.

It must be added at once that such a profane existence is never found in the pure state. To whatever degree he may have desacralized the world, the man who has made his choice in favor of a profane life never succeeds in completely doing away with religious behavior. This will become clearer as we proceed; it will appear that even the most desacralized existence still preserves traces of a religious valorization of the world.

But for the moment we will set aside this aspect of the problem and confine ourselves to comparing the two experiences in question—that of sacred space and that of profane space. The implications of the former experience have already been pointed out. Revelation of a sacred space makes it possible to obtain a fixed point and hence to acquire orientation in the chaos of homogeneity, to "found the world" and to live in a real sense. The profane experience, on the contrary, maintains the homogeneity and hence the relativity of space. No *true* orientation is now possible, for the fixed point no longer enjoys a unique ontological status; it appears and disappears in accordance with the needs of the day. Properly speaking, there is no longer any world, there are only fragments of a shattered universe, an amorphous mass consisting of an infinite number of more or less neutral places in which man moves, governed and driven by the obligations of an existence incorporated into an industrial society.

Yet this experience of profane space still includes values that to some extent recall the nonhomogeneity peculiar to the religious experience of space. There are, for example, privileged places, qualitatively different from all others—a man's birthplace, or the scenes of his first love, or certain places in the first foreign city he visited in youth. Even for the most frankly nonreligious man, all these places still retain an exceptional, a unique quality; they are the "holy places" of his private universe, as if it were in such spots that he had received the revelation of a reality *other* than that in which he participates through his ordinary daily life.

This example of crypto-religious behavior on profane man's part is worth noting. In the course of this book we shall encounter other examples of this sort of degradation and desacralization of religious values and forms of behavior. Their deeper significance will become apparent later.

THEOPHANIES AND SIGNS

To exemplify the nonhomogeneity of space as experienced by nonreligious man, we may turn to any religion. We will choose an example that is accessible to everyone—a church in a modern city. For a believer, the church shares in a different space from the street in which it stands. The door that opens on the interior of the church actually signifies a solution of continuity. The threshold that separates the two spaces also indicates the distance between two modes of being, the profane and the religious. The threshold is the limit, the boundary, the frontier that distinguishes and opposes two worlds—and at the same time the paradoxical place where those worlds communicate, where passage from the profane to the sacred world becomes possible.

A similar ritual function falls to the threshold of the human habitation, and it is for this reason that the threshold is an object of great importance. Numerous rites accompany passing the domestic threshold—a bow, a prostration, a pious touch of the hand, and so on. The threshold has its guardians—gods and spirits who forbid entrance both to human enemies and to demons and the powers of pestilence. It is on the threshold that sacrifices to the guardian divinities are offered. Here too certain palaeo-oriental cultures (Babylon, Egypt, Israel) situated the judgment place. The threshold, the door *show* the solution of continuity in space immediately and concretely; hence their great religious importance, for they are symbols and at the same time vehicles of *passage* from the one space to the other.

What has been said will make it clear why the church shares in an entirely different space from the buildings that surround it. Within the sacred precincts the profane world is transcended. On the most archaic levels of culture this possibility of transcendence is expressed by various *images of an opening;* here, in the sacred enclosure, communication with the gods is made possible; hence there must be a door to the world above, by which the gods can descend to earth and man can symbolically ascend to heaven. We shall soon see that this was the case in many religions; properly speaking, the temple constitutes an opening in the upward direction and ensures communication with the world of the gods.

Every sacred space implies a hierophany, an irruption of the sacred that results in detaching a territory from the surrounding cosmic milieu and making it qualitatively different. When Jacob in his dream at Haran saw a ladder reaching to heaven, with angels ascending and descending on it, and heard the Lord speaking from above it, saying: "I am the Lord God of Abraham," he awoke and was afraid and cried out: "How dreadful is this place: this is none other but the house of God, and this is the gate of heaven." And he took the stone that had been his pillow, and set it up as a monument, and poured oil on the top of it. He called the place Beth-el, that is, house of God (Genesis, 28, 12–19). The symbolism implicit in the expression "gate of heaven" is rich and complex: the theophany that occurs in a place consecrates it by the very fact that it makes it open above—that is, in communication with heaven, the paradoxical point of passage from one mode of being to another. We shall soon see even clearer examples—sanctuaries that are "doors of the gods" and hence places of passage between heaven and earth.

Often there is no need for a theophany or hierophany properly speaking; some *sign* suffices to indicate the sacredness of a place. "According to the legend, the *marabout* who founded El-Hamel at the end of the sixteenth century stopped to spend the night near a spring and planted his stick in the ground. The next morning, when he went for it to resume his journey, he found that it had taken root and that buds had sprouted on it. He considered this a sign of God's will and settled in that place."[1] In such cases the *sign,* fraught with religious meaning, introduces an absolute element and puts an end to relativity and confusion. *Something* that does not belong to this world has manifested itself apodictically and in so doing has indicated an orientation or determined a course of conduct.

When no sign manifests itself, it is *provoked.* For example, a sort of *evocation* is performed with the help of animals: it is they who *show* what place is fit to receive the sanctuary or the village. This amounts to an evocation of sacred forms or figures for the immediate purpose of establishing an *orientation* in the homogeneity of space. A *sign* is asked, to put an end to the tension and anxiety caused by relativity and disorientation—in short, to reveal an absolute point of support. For example, a wild animal is hunted, and the sanctuary is built at the place where it is killed. Or a domestic animal—such as a bull—is turned loose; some days later it is searched for and sacrificed at the place where it is found. Later the altar will be raised there and the village will be built around the altar. In all these cases, the sacrality of a place is revealed by animals. This is as much as to say that men are not free to *choose* the sacred site, that they only seek for it and find it by the help of mysterious signs.

These few examples have shown the different means by which religious man receives the revelation of a sacred place. In each case the hierophany has annulled the homogeneity of space and revealed a fixed point. But since religious man cannot live except in an atmosphere impregnated with the sacred, we must expect to find a large number of techniques for consecrating space. As we saw, the sacred is pre-eminently the *real,* at once power, efficacity, the source of life and fecundity. Religious man's desire to live *in the sacred* is in fact equivalent to his desire to take up his abode in objective reality, not to let himself be paralyzed by the never-ceasing relativity of purely subjective experiences, to live in a real and effective world, and not in an illusion. This behavior is documented on every plane of religious man's existence, but it is particularly evident in his desire to move about only in a sanctified world, that is, in a sacred space. This is the

---

[1]René Basset in *Revue des Traditions Populaires,* XXII, 1907, p. 287.

reason for the elaboration of techniques of *orientation* which, properly speaking, are techniques for the *construction* of sacred space. But we must not suppose that *human* work is in question here, that it is through his own efforts that man can consecrate a space. In reality the ritual by which he constructs a sacred space is efficacious in the measure in which *it reproduces the work of the gods*. But the better to understand the need for ritual construction of a sacred space, we must dwell a little on the traditional concept of the "world": it will then be apparent that for religious man every world is a sacred world.

CHAOS AND COSMOS

One of the outstanding characteristics of traditional societies is the opposition that they assume between their inhabited territory and the unknown and indeterminate space that surrounds it. The former is the world (more precisely, our world), the cosmos; everything outside it is no longer a cosmos but a sort of "other world," a foreign, chaotic space, peopled by ghosts, demons, "foreigners" (who are assimilated to demons and the souls of the dead). At first sight this cleavage in space appears to be due to the opposition between an inhabited and organized—hence cosmicized—territory and the unknown space that extends beyond the frontiers, on one side there is a cosmos, on the other a chaos. But we shall see that if every inhabited territory is a cosmos, this is precisely because it was first consecrated, because, in one way or another, it is the work of the gods or is in communication with the world of the gods. The world (that is, our world) is a universe within which the sacred has already manifested itself, in which, consequently, the break-through from plane to plane has become possible and repeatable. It is not difficult to see why the religious moment implies the cosmogonic moment. The sacred reveals absolute reality and at the same time makes orientation possible; hence it *founds the world* in the sense that it fixes the limits and establishes the order of the world.

All this appears very clearly from the Vedic ritual for taking possession of a territory; possession becomes legally valid through the erection of a fire altar consecrated to Agni. "One says that one is installed when one has built a fire altar *[gārhapatya]* and all those who build the fire altar are legally established" (*Shatapatha Brāhmana.* VII, 1, 1, 1–4). By the erection of a fire altar Agni is made present, and communication with the world of the gods is ensured: the space of the altar becomes a sacred space. But the meaning of the ritual is far more complex, and if we consider all of its ramifications we shall understand why consecrating a territory is equivalent to making it a cosmos, to *cosmicizing* it. For, in fact, the erection of an altar to Agni is nothing but the reproduction—on the microcosmic scale—of the Creation. The water in which the clay is mixed is assimilated to the primordial water; the clay that forms the base of the altar symbolizes the earth; the lateral walls represent the atmosphere, and so on. And the building of the altar is accompanied by songs that proclaim which cosmic region has just been created (*Shatapatha Brāhmana* I, 9, 2, 29, etc.). Hence the erection of a fire altar—which alone validates taking possession of a new territory—is equivalent to a cosmogony.

An unknown, foreign, and unoccupied territory (which often means, "unoccupied by our people") still shares in the fluid and larval modality of chaos. By occupying it and, above all, by settling in it, man symbolically transforms it into a cosmos through a ritual repetition of the cosmogony. What is to become "our world" must first be "created," and every creation has a paradigmatic model—the creation of the universe by the gods. When the Scandinavian colonists took possession of Iceland *(land-náma)* and cleared it, they regarded the enterprise neither as an original undertaking nor as human and profane work. For them, their labor was only repetition of a primordial act, the transformation of chaos into cosmos by the divine act of creation. When they tilled the desert soil, they were in fact repeating the act of the gods who had organized chaos by giving it a structure, forms, and norms.[2]

Whether it is a case of clearing uncultivated ground or of conquering and occupying a territory already inhabited by "other" human beings, ritual taking possession must always repeat the cosmogony. For in the view of archaic societies everything that is not "our world" is not yet a world. A territory can be made ours only by creating it anew, that is, by consecrating it. This religious behavior in respect to unknown lands continued, even in the West, down to the dawn of modern times. The Spanish and Portuguese conquistadores, discovering and conquering territories, took possession of them in the name of Jesus Christ. The raising of the Cross was equivalent to consecrating the country, hence in some sort to a "new birth." For through Christ "old things are passed away; behold, all things are become new" (II Corinthians, 5, 17). The newly discovered country was "renewed," "recreated" by the Cross.

CONSECRATION OF A PLACE—REPETITION OF THE COSMOGONY

It must be understood that the cosmicization of unknown territories is always a consecration; to organize a space is to repeat the paradigmatic work of the gods. The close connection between cosmicization and consecration is already documented on the elementary levels of culture—for example, among the nomadic Australians whose economy is still at the stage of gathering and small-game hunting. According to the traditions of an Arunta tribe, the Achilpa, in mythical times the divine being Numbakula cosmicized their future territory, created their Ancestor, and established their institutions. From the trunk of a gum tree Numbakula fashioned the sacred pole *(kauwa-auwa)* and, after anointing it with blood, climbed it and disappeared into the sky. This pole represents a cosmic axis, for it is around the sacred pole that territory becomes habitable, hence is transformed into a world. The sacred pole consequently plays an important role

---

[2]Cf. Mircea Eliade. *The Myth of the Eternal Return,* New York, Pantheon Books, Bollingen Series XLVI, 1954, pp. 11 ff. Cited hereafter as *Myth.*

ritually. During their wanderings the Achilpa always carry it with them and choose the direction they are to take by the direction toward which it bends. This allows them, while being continually on the move, to be always in "their world" and, at the same time, in communication with the sky into which Numbakula vanished.

For the pole to be broken denotes catastrophe; it is like "the end of the world," reversion to chaos. Spencer and Gillen report that once, when the pole was broken, the entire clan were in consternation; they wandered about aimlessly for a time, and finally lay down on the ground together and waited for death to overtake them.[3]

This example admirably illustrates both the cosmological function of the sacred pole and its soteriological role. For on the one hand the *kauwa-auwa* reproduces the pole that Numbakula used to cosmicize the world, and on the other the Achilpa believe it to be the means by which they can communicate with the sky realm. Now, human existence is possible only by virtue of this permanent communication with the sky. The world of the Achilpa really becomes *their* world only in proportion as it reproduces the cosmos organized and sanctified by Numbakula. Life is not possible without an opening toward the transcendent; in other words, human beings cannot live in chaos. Once contact with the transcendent is lost, existence in the world ceases to be possible—and the Achilpa let themselves die.

To settle in a territory is, in the last analysis, equivalent to consecrating it. When settlement is not temporary, as among the nomads, but permanent, as among sedentary peoples, it implies a vital decision that involves the existence of the entire community. Establishment in a particular place, organizing it, inhabiting it, are acts that presuppose an existential choice—the choice of the universe that one is prepared to assume by "creating" it. Now, this universe is always the replica of the paradigmatic universe created and inhabited by the gods; hence it shares in the sanctity of the gods' work. . . .

TEMPLE, BASILICA, CATHEDRAL

In the great oriental civilizations—from Mesopotamia and Egypt to China and India—the temple received a new and important valorization. It is not only an *imago mundi;* it is also interpreted as the earthly reproduction of a transcendent model. Judaism inherited this ancient oriental conception of the temple as the copy of a celestial work of architecture. In this idea we probably have one of the last interpretations that religious man has given to the primary experience of sacred space in contrast to profane space. Hence we must dwell a little on the perspectives opened by this new religious conception.

To summarize the essential data of the problem: If the temple constitutes an *imago mundi,* this is because the world, as the work of the gods, is sacred. But

---

[3]B. Spencer and F. J. Gillen, *The Arunta,* London, 1926, J, p. 388.

the cosmological structure of the temple gives room for a new religious valorization; as house of the gods, hence holy place above all others, the temple continually resanctifies the world, because it at once represents and contains it. In the last analysis, *it is by virtue of the temple that the world is resanctified in every part.* However impure it may have become, the world is continually purified by the sanctity of sanctuaries.

Another idea derives from this increasingly accepted ontological difference between the *cosmos* and *its sanctified image,* the temple. This is the idea that the sanctity of the temple is proof against all earthly corruption, by virtue of the fact that the architectural plan of the temple is the work of the gods and hence exists in heaven, near to the gods. The transcendent models of temples enjoy a spiritual, incorruptible celestial existence. Through the grace of the gods, man attains to the dazzling vision of these models, which he then attempts to reproduce on earth. The Babylonian king Gudea saw in a dream the goddess Nidaba showing him a tablet on which were written the names of the beneficent stars, and a god revealed the plan of the temple to him.[4] Sennacherib built Ninevah according to "the plan established from most distant times in the configuration of the Heavens." This means not only that celestial geometry made the first constructions possible, but above all that since the architectonic models were in heaven, they shared in the sacrality of the sky.

For the people of Israel, the models of the tabernacle, of all the sacred utensils, and of the temple itself had been created by Yahweh, who revealed them to his chosen, to be reproduced on earth. Thus Yahweh says to Moses: "And let them make me a sanctuary; that I may dwell among them. According to all that I shew thee, after the pattern of the tabernacle, and the pattern of all the instruments thereof, even so shall ye make it" (Exodus, 25, 8–9). "And look that thou make them after their pattern, which was shewed thee in the mount" (*ibid.,* 25, 40). When David gives his son Solomon the plans for the Temple buildings, the tabernacle, and all the utensils, he assures him that "all this . . . the Lord made me understand in writing by his hand upon me" (II Chronicles, 28, 19). He must, then, have seen the celestial model created by Yahweh from the beginning of time. This is what Solomon affirms: "Thou hast commanded me to build a temple upon thy holy mount, and an altar in the city wherein thou dwellest, a resemblance of the holy tabernacle which thou hast prepared from the beginning" (Wisdom of Solomon, 9, 8).

The Heavenly Jerusalem was created by God at the same time as Paradise, hence *in aeternum.* The city of Jerusalem was only an approximate reproduction of the transcendent model; it could be polluted by man, but the model was incorruptible, for it was not involved in time. "This building now built in your midst is not that which is revealed with Me, that which was prepared beforehand here from the time when I took counsel to make Paradise, and showed it to Adam before he sinned" (II Baruch, 4, 3–7; trans. R. H. Charles[5]).

---

[4]Cf. Eliade, *Myth,* pp. 7–8.

[5]R. H. Charles, ed., *The Apocrypha and Pseudepigrapha of the Old Testament in English,* Oxford 1943, Vol. II, p. 482.

The Christian basilica and, later, the cathedral take over and continue all these symbolisms. On the one hand, the church is conceived as imitating the Heavenly Jerusalem, even from patristic times: on the other, it also reproduces Paradise or the celestial world. But the cosmological structure of the sacred edifice still persists in the thought of Christendom; for example, it is obvious in the Byzantine church. "The four parts of the interior of the church symbolize the four cardinal directions. The interior of the church is the universe. The altar is paradise, which lay in the East. The imperial door to the altar was also called the Door of Paradise. During Easter week, the great door to the altar remains open during the entire service: the meaning of this custom is clearly expressed in the Easter Canon: 'Christ rose from the grave and opened the doors of Paradise unto us.' The West on the contrary, is the realm of darkness, of grief, of death, the realm of the eternal mansions of the dead, who await the resurrection of the flesh and the Last Judgment. The middle of the building is the earth. According to the views of Kosmas Indikopleustes, the earth is rectangular and is bounded by four walls, which are surmounted by a dome. The four parts of the interior of the church symbolize the four cardinal directions."[6] As "copy of the cosmos," the Byzantine church incarnates and at the same time sanctifies the world.

SOME CONCLUSIONS

From the thousands of examples available to the historian of religions, we have cited only a small number but enough to show the varieties of the religious experience of space. We have taken our examples from different cultures and periods, in order to present at least the most important mythological constructions and ritual scenarios that are based on the experience of sacred space. For in the course of history, religious man has given differing valorizations to the same fundamental experience. We need only compare the conception of the sacred space (and hence of the cosmos) discernible among the Australian Achilpa with the corresponding conceptions of the Kwakiutl, the Altaic peoples, or the Mesopotamians, to realize the differences among them. There is no need to dwell on the truism that, since the religious life of humanity is realized in history, its expressions are inevitably conditioned by the variety of historical moments and cultural styles. But for our purpose it is not the infinite variety of the religious experiences of space that concerns us but, on the contrary, their elements of unity. Pointing out the contrast between the behavior of nonreligious man with respect to the space in which he lives and the behavior of religious man in respect to sacred space is enough to make the difference in structure between the two attitudes clearly apparent.

If we should attempt to summarize the result of the descriptions that have been presented in this chapter, we could say that the experience of sacred space makes possible the "founding of the world": where the sacred manifests itself in

---

[6]Hans Sellmayr. *Die Entstehung der Kathedrale,* Zurich, 1950, p. 119.

space, *the real unveils itself,* the world comes into existence. But the irruption of the sacred does not only project a fixed point into the formless fluidity of profane space, a center into chaos; it also effects a break in plane, that is, it opens communication between the cosmic planes (between earth and heaven) and makes possible ontological passage from one mode of being to another. It is such a break in the heterogeneity of profane space that creates the center through which communication with the transmundane is established, that, consequently, founds the world, for the center renders *orientation* possible. Hence the manifestation of the sacred in space has a cosmological valence; every spatial hierophany or consecration of a space is equivalent to a cosmogony. The first conclusion we might draw would be: *the world becomes apprehensible as world, as cosmos, in the measure in which it reveals itself as a sacred world.*

Every world is the work of the gods, for it was either created directly by the gods or was consecrated, hence cosmicized, by men ritually reactualizing the paradigmatic act of Creation. This is as much as to say that religious man can live only in a sacred world, because it is only in such a world that he participates in being, that he has a *real existence.* This religious need expresses an unquenchable ontological thirst. Religious man thirsts for *being.* His terror of the chaos that surrounds his inhabited world corresponds to his terror of nothingness. The unknown space that extends beyond his world—an uncosmicized because unconsecrated space, a mere amorphous extent into which no orientation has yet been projected, and hence in which no structure has yet arisen—for religious man, this profane space represents absolute nonbeing. If, by some evil chance, he strays into it, he feels emptied of his ontic substance, as if he were dissolving in Chaos, and he finally dies.

This ontological thirst is manifested in many ways. In the realm of sacred space which we are now considering, its most striking manifestation is religious man's will to take his stand at the very heart of the real, at the Center of the World—that is, exactly where the cosmos came into existence and began to spread out toward the four horizons, and where, too, there is the possibility of communication with the gods; in short, precisely where he is *closest to the gods.* We have seen that the symbolism of the center is the formative principle not only of countries, cities, temples, and palaces but also of the humblest human dwelling, be it the tent of a nomad hunter, the shepherd's yurt, or the house of the sedentary cultivator. This is as much as to say that every religious man places himself at the Center of the World and by the same token at the very source of absolute reality, as close as possible to the opening that ensures him communication with the gods.

But since to settle somewhere, to inhabit a space, is equivalent to repeating the cosmogony and hence to imitating the work of the gods, it follows that, for religious man, every existential decision to situate himself in space in fact constitutes a religious decision. By assuming the responsibility of creating the world that he has chosen to inhabit, he not only cosmicizes chaos but also sanctifies his little cosmos by making it like the world of the gods. Religious man's profound nostalgia is to inhabit a "divine world," is his desire that his house shall be like the house of the gods, as it was later represented in temples and sanctuaries. In short, this religious nostalgia expresses *the desire to live in a pure and holy cosmos, as it was in the beginning, when it came fresh from the Creator's hands.*

The experience of sacred time will make it possible for religious man periodically to experience the cosmos as it was *in principio,* that is, at the mythical moment of Creation.

3 RELIGIOUS EXPERIENCES

Some people experience the "other" or "extra" dimension. Or at least they think they do, and their conviction is itself is a proper object for social-science research, whether the social scientist believes in the possibility of such experience or not. There are probably many different kinds of experiences of an encounter with the "totally other." In this section, only two varieties are discussed because so little is known about the subject—the spectacular religious experience which is usually called mystical or ecstatic, and the ordinary religious experience of hope renewal, which some writers call a "limit" or "horizon" experience. Whether these two types of experience differ in kind or only in degree probably does not matter for the present purpose.

About a third of Americans appear to have had the former experience and nine out of ten appear to have had the latter.

While there is no disposition to deny the occurrence of mystical or ecstatic experiences—even Freud, Marx, and Weber acknowledge that they occur—there is considerable difference of opinion about what causes them and whether they are signs of emotional disturbance or of mental health. The empirical research described in this section suggests that they at least correlate with mental health.

There is also a debate about whether or not religious experiences, of whatever variety, tell us anything about the nature of the cosmos and the meaning of life. Are they nothing more than a deceptive (or self-deceptive) propensity to hope, which the evolutionary process has programmed in the only organism of which we know that is aware of its own mortality? Or are they hints of an explanation?

Regardless of how this question is answered, there can be little question that religious experiences—mystical or "limit"—are an important, indeed probably essential, aspect of human religion.

Reading 11

THE NATURE OF MYSTICISM—PHILIP H. ENNIS AND F. C. HAPPOLD

Philip Ennis, who was at the time on the staff of the National Opinion Research Center, and F.C. Happold, an editor of an anthology of mystical experiences, both describe the phenomenon, the former in social-science terms, the latter in religious terms. Ennis establishes that Freud, Marx, Mannheim, and Weber—all giants of the classic era—recognized the occurrence and importance of such experiences. Ennis then cites Marghanita Laski's study of mystics, which confirms the enormous impact that such experiences can have on human life and argues that ecstasy can be and often has been a revolutionary and even dangerous event which threatens the social order. Therefore, society struggles to control the ecstatic. While some people need ecstatic variation from the ordinary, nonetheless there is a struggle between the ecstatic and the ordinary that parallels and may even overlap with the struggle between the social classes.

Instead of Max Weber, Happold makes the medieval mystic John Ruysbroeck his starting point. Happold is much more interested in the experience itself than on its societal impact, and on how it transforms the life of the person than he is on the struggle for social control of ecstasy.

But clearly from very different perspectives and very different concerns, both men are describing the same phenomenon. They both agree that it is religious and that it is extremely important for those who experience it. Neither writes of the ecstatic as a crazy person.

Yet, despite the recognition of ecstasy by the classic writers and despite the obvious religious and sociological importance of the phenomenon, main-line sociology pays little attention to it and discussion of ecstasy is not to be found in most books on the sociology of religion.

Some people might think that sociologists are afraid to deal with mysticism.

Questions for Reflection and Discussion

1. What do you think Ennis's basic attitude is toward ecstasy?
2. What do you think Happold's basic attitude is?
3. What agreement do you see between them?
4. What disagreement?

Part 1

ECSTASY AND EVERYDAY LIFE
Philip H. Ennis

The concept of ecstasy seems to be scattered widely in the writings that constitute the core of modern social theory. Though not expressed directly by some theorists, it is for example an important idea in Freud's *Civilization and its Discontents;* it is discussed in Weber's writings, but it is almost entirely absent in the writings of Marx. This absence will be examined subsequently.

The theme of ecstasy is also found in Mannheim. It is so delightfully upsetting and unexpected in the midst of Mannheim's impenetrable sociological jargon that his formulation merits quotation.

> It is that achieving from time to time a certain distance from his own situation and from the world is one of the fundamental traits of man as truly a human being. A man for whom nothing exists beyond his immediate situation is not fully human ... We have inherited from our past (the need) of severing from time to time all connection with life and with the contingencies of our existence. We shall designate this ideal by the term 'ecstacy.'[1]

There is a recognition of the same need in Weber's analysis of religion. His awesome virtuosity and perceptivity finds in the religions of the world what he terms a *mystical* element, which always turns out to contain an emotional experience in the here and now, and which always has behind it, "a stand toward something in the actual world which is experienced as specifically 'senseless.'"[2] There is in this mystical state, he says, something beyond our empirical world of sense experience, a state which he contrasts to the action-in-this-world of *aestheticism.* "Mysticism," Weber continues, "intends a state of possession not action, and the individual is *not* a tool but a *vessel* of the divine."[3] The specifically religious context of Weber's mystical state is readily assimilated into Mannheim's concept of ecstasy.

Freud began his *Civilization and its Discontents* with the story of a friend (Romain Rolland) to whom he had sent a manuscript of *The Future of an Illusion,* his analysis of religion in terms of the family drama. Rolland replied that he agreed with Freud's thesis, but was sorry that Freud had not appreciated the roots, the ultimate source of religious experience which consisted of:

Source: Journal for the Scientific Study of Religion Vol. VI, 1, 1967
[1]Karl Mannheim, *Essays on the Sociology of Culture* (New York: Oxford, 1956), p. 210.
[2]H. H. Gerth and C. Wright Mills, *Max Weber: Essays in Sociology* (New York: Oxford, 1946), p. 281.
[3]*Ibid.,* p. 325.

A peculiar feeling, which never leaves him personally, a feeling which he would like to call a sensation of 'eternity,' a feeling as of something limitless, unbounded something 'oceanic.' It is purely subjective experience not an article of belief. . . . [4]

It seems quite clear that the "oceanic feeling" is of the same family of experiences Mannheim and Weber discuss. Yet Freud says, "I cannot discover this oceanic feeling myself." Why was this? A clue comes from Freud himself. After a brief exchange of letters in which Freud asks Rolland if he would mind his using the remark in the introduction to this book, Freud then amplifies his published statement that he never experienced ecstasy by privately describing his reluctance and inability to approach mysticism as a result of "an uncertain blending of Hellenic love of proportion, Jewish sobriety, and philistine timidity."[5] These reasons, perhaps *deliberately* literary and ironic as a joke shared with Rolland, become somewhat tangential when the familiar but irresistible comparisons to Karl Marx are rehearsed.

Both Freud and Marx were middle class assimilated Jews in a Germanic culture.[6] Both had achieved learned professional status but both were rejected by strategic sectors of their society, professionally and socially. In turn, both men rejected a great deal of that society and in particular their religious heritage. Both totally introjected into their personalities an ideology of their own manufacture, an ideology founded on the premises and directives of 19th Century science. Both headed social movements seeking to translate that ideology into new social relationships. The leadership of these movements brought them directly into the world of contentious action but at times took them out of that world into a world of contemplation, and personal reflection. The relationship between leadership of such social movements and their solitary creativity suggests that in some fashion a mode of behavior that both sublimates and expresses the needs for transcendence can be achieved. It is as if there cannot be *ecstatic* transcendence for men who have made their own worlds.

These few examples point to the concept of ecstasy as an individual experience of great importance, probably of limited duration and counterposed to everyday life. This relationship to everyday life is the point of departure for the sociological analysis of the idea, but I will initially try to indicate the ecstasy-everyday life relationship by invoking two literary observations. The first is I. A. Richard's major premise, expressed by his early book, *The Principles of Literary Criticism,* that aesthetic appreciation, particularly poetry, and common sense, everyday experience were not qualitatively different but drew upon a common

---

[4]Sigmund Freud, *Civilization and its Discontents* (London: Hogarth Press, 1953), pp. 7, 8.

[5]*Letters of Sigmund Freud,* selected and edited by Ernest L. Freud (New York: Basic Books, 1960), p. 302. It is interesting that Freud invokes his Jewish heritage here against the appeals of mysticism, when according to David Bakan, Freud himself was a product, albeit a distilled one, of the Chasidic Cabbalist tradition of East European Jewry. *Sigmund Freud and the Jewish Mystical Tradition* (Princeton: Van Nostrand, 1958).

[6]From some points of view, including a religious or an ethnic one, neither of the two, especially Marx, can be considered as Jewish. But this is a complex issue that need not be pursued here.

shared humanity, that poetry was only a refined and a more densely packed version of that humanity.[7] The second is the remark attributed to Paul Valery to the effect that he would not write a novel because he could not bring himself to say, "the Marquise descended from her carriage."[8]

We have here more than the usual clash between poet and critic; we have an abbreviated contrast between ecstasy and everyday life; flat and mundane prose vs. the poetic heights—both drawn, however, from a common core of meaning. Bound together they influence one another, but require separation and distinction for each to have its own fulfillment.

INSTITUTIONALIZATION OF ECSTASY

The sociological problem arises when we ask how society institutionalizes this motivational state the entire thrust of which is to break through all institutional enclosures.

In principle it is quite easy to make an ecstasy machine. You build, in an empty lot, a high circular fence with a small door. Inside the fence, there is either a deep well that goes down to nowhere or a high ladder that goes up to nowhere. The direction is a matter of taste. Then you let people in a few at a time—you can't let everyone in because someone has to watch the store. Before you let them down into the well or up into the ladder, you tie a rope around their waist to make sure you can get them back. Since the capacity for ecstasy varies among individuals, as does their height and weight, people can climb down or up as far as they like to find their level of ecstatic satisfaction.

This, in essence, is the architectural model of the cathedral, the theatre, the lover's couch and the bottle. For separately and in various combinations, the institutions of religion, the arts, of love, and finally alcohol and other drugs have all been charged at one point or another in history with the mission of being the vehicle of legitimate ecstatic transcendence.

These are not the only forms containing ecstatic behavior, of course. Three others might be mentioned briefly; first is the political community itself, with the symbols and actuality of state power as the core ecstatic object. Second is the world of rational mastery, the institutions of science and industry, in short, *work*. Even though work in the everyday world appears the very antithesis of the state of ecstasy, there are interesting modulations between the two that conceivably could be effective for some people. Finally, there is insanity and psy-

---

[7] I. A. Richards, *The Principles of Literary Criticism* (London; Routledge & Paul, 1959), ch. 2.

[8] This is, of course, a recurrent argument. A peculiarly coincidental repetition occurs in Leo Spitzer's essay, "Three Poems on Ecstasy" in his Essays on *English and American Literature* (Princeton Press, 1962), in which he practices the art of "explication du texte" on three poems concerned with ecstatic states as a direct and avowed rebuttal to Karl Shapiro's pronounciamento that a poem could not and should not be subject to meaning and meaningful interpretation.

chosis. This path to transcendence has enjoyed a recent vogue, but it seems too disorderly for the fastidious and too irreversible for many to emulate.[9]

WHY INSTITUTIONALIZATION IS UNSTABLE

It is also quite clear in principle why the institutionalization of ecstatic experience is inherently unstable. First, there is the problem of the *rope*. Societies in general, and institutions sanctioning ecstatic experience in particular, are reluctant to lose control over their members and are especially ferocious toward anyone reaching directly for ecstasy by short-cutting the proper channels, that is, trying to do without the rope. There are, generally, firm rules defining the occasions and conditions under which transcendence is legitimate and possible. Release from the world becomes thereby immediately enmeshed in the workings of the world. Even on this simple level the rules governing the expression of ecstasy begin to generate tensions within the ecstasy-giving institutions for as the rope chafes, people begin to look around for some new place where there will be no rope. This includes the tendencies to *leave* the ecstasy park, but of more importance is the "inward migration" toward the direct unmediated source of ecstasy. Cabbalist, Protestant fundamentalist, and Catholic miracle producers, all share this tendency to some extent.

Second, there is the question of the *permit* to build your ecstasy park in the empty lot. If you have the mayor's permission, and especially if he grants you a monopoly on the ecstasy business, you become part of the Establishment, and the condition under which you allow people down into the well includes an implicit loyalty oath to the mayor, or at least a disclaimer that participants belong to any subversive organization. But since the individual's urge for transcendent experience is shaped to some extent both in its content and in its intensity by his fate in the world, those *disaffected* from legitimate authority are not likely to come for their release to your official lot.

Monopolization of the modes of ecstatic expression by one institution is a particularly unstable situation. The domination of Western Europe up to the Reformation by the joint power of feudal aristocracy and the Church, illustrates this quite well, for during those long centuries, countermovements ceaselessly rose and fell, ranging from the courts of love to the witch cults.[10] Each sought alternative and subversive outlets for the ecstatic urges of their followers. In addition there were spontaneous mass cataclysms of hysterical fervor, for example, the dancing manias and the response to itinerant preachers who stood apart from the official church hierarchy and raised waves of emotional release with their evangelism.

---

[9]The spread of LSD and related drugs attests to the attraction of this mode of transcendence and to the wonders of nature and science and to the resistance of "society" to uncontrolled release from its constraints.

[10]See Denis de Rougemont, *Love in the Western World* (New York: Harcourt, Brace, 1940), and Margaret Alice Murray, *The Witch-Cult in Western Europe* (Oxford: Clarendon Press, 1921).

If on the other hand, your ecstasy park fails to get a permit or never tried to get one in the first place, it is in for obvious trouble. You are a threat to the status quo because you are likely to attract a clientele with such an admixture of "genuine" ecstasy needs and disaffection from the secular order, that the enterprise will be ambivalently strained toward either secular involvement of a revolutionary order or towards a rejection of wordly affairs altogether. If the first direction prevails, the power structures will force you either to declare all-out war, to sell out in some form of compromise, or to dry up. If the other worldly direction prevails there will be attrition among those who really have some secular motivation, and you will be consequently attacked by the legitimated ecstatic institutions.

Finally, there is this problem; suppose your ecstacy park is legitimate, but in *competition* with others. This is the situation of the modern pluralistic society with separation of church and state, a diversity of religions, and variety of secular attractions. The key to institutional stability here turns on economic considerations. How are you going to pay the rent, except through charging a fee for the privilege of using the ladder or the well? Therefore you've got to keep your clientele from going down the street. The competition is keen; you scout out your rival and discover he has installed a Coke machine next to his ecstasy well. Not to be outdone, you redesign your well with an ascending and descending escalator and advertise that you provide ecstasy easier and faster. The competition responds with a juke box and dance floor; you counter with a reading room and social club.

What has happened is that in order to survive, the institutions of ecstasy incorporate the techniques and the content of the secular world and above all the tactics of the market place.[11] One of the most important of these tactics is to attach the clientele to your institution by as many *different* needs as possible so that they are held by a *variety* of obligations and dependencies. In doing so, the distinction between everyday life and the social setting of transcendent experience blurs and one of two things will happen: people will simply go elsewhere, or if they stay, they will lower their level of aspiration for a truly transcendent experience and be content with a diminished version of it, one that is available anywhere down the street, thus deepening the vicious cycle of instability.

The difficulties of institutionalizing ecstatic experience are not exhausted by these problems. Since the motivational sources of ecstatic states are probably so varied and the occasions for expressing them so diverse that few, if any, ecstasy parks have either the capacity or desire to distinguish among them, or even between the genuine ecstatic response and the variety of other escapist states resulting from the abrasions of everyday life.

Eager for converts and driven to maintain their clientele, most ecstasy parks are thus willing to accept anyone on almost any grounds. This undoubtedly engenders a distortion toward the acceptance of more "escapist" behavior depending on the size of the population that simply seeks relief from the everyday world.

---

[11]This is tangentially related of course to the familiar processes of transforming sect into church.

At the same time *since* ecstatic motivations demand the institution's services for only a limited time, they are likely to, and do, serve a variety of other needs. For example, the functions of love and religion beyond that of providing a legitimate enclosure for ecstatic expression are too numerous and obvious to name. These other functions, however, threaten to infuse the provision of ecstasy with their more mundane considerations. In sum: the social fate of ecstasy is a precarious one.

MORE DURABLE HOUSING FOR ECSTASY

What are the general conditions which provide stability for the housing of ecstatic experience? Some clues come from anthropological and recent psychological thinking. An important example is Jane Belo's study, *Trance in Bali,* which begins in these words:

> The Balinese are a people whose everyday behavior is measured, controlled, graceful, tranquil. Emotion is not easily expressed. Dignity and adherence to the rules of decorum are customary. At the same time, they show a susceptibility and a facility for going into states of trance, states in which *there* is an altered consciousness and behavior springing from a deeper level of the personality is manifested . . . Ruth Benedict who made the classical distinction between Apollonian and Dionysian configurations of culture went over our material with great care and came to the conclusion that the distinction could not be applied to Balinese culture. Their customary pose and moderation resembles the Apollonian, while the outbreak into trance, approved and recognized in the culture, is nearer to the Dionysian.[12]

After an extended description of the variety of trance behaviors and ceremonies, of the history and recruitment of the trance practitioner and their many functions, she concludes with the view that the public performance of ritualized trance behavior was seen by the Balinese as "an attestation of the power of the gods,"[13] and that this power of the gods to invade a person—or rather for the person to absorb the gods—established communication between the upper world and that of the living, and thereby served to relieve the anxiety of the people.

Three points are particularly important here. First, ecstatic behavior—and these trance states are clearly related to what we have been talking about—*has consequences,* not entirely, if at all, envisaged by either their practitioners. In this case, it is, individually, anxiety or tension reduction, and, collectively, a communal reassertion of the basic values of the society, the reality and presence of the gods, and their purifying beneficence.

Second, the social setting of ecstasy need not be a solitary individual event, but can be assimilated into a *public performance* in which both audience and

---

[12]Jane Belo, *Trance in Bali* (New York: Columbia University, 1960).
[13]*Ibid.*

performer are involved. Indeed, Benjamin Hunningher's *Origin of the Theater* asks the question as to the relation between the primitive ecstatic cults and the latter more formalized worship of Dionysis. His answer, in part is that the "very ecstacy aroused by the rites, leads into portrayal, the core and primary characteristic of dramatic art. Through ecstasy, as the word itself indicates, the cultist can step outside of himself and start on the road to the presentation of other characters."[14]

Third, and more implicit, is the *alternation of states*. Both religious and theatrical modes of ecstatic participation discussed above involve an important patterning, a shift from everyday life to elevated states. Octavio Paz in his poetically and intellectually compelling book, *The Labyrinth of Solitude,* makes this more explicit. He analyzes Mexican thought and character by a match of three meditations on the essence of Mexican life—everyday and ecstatic—with the three great periods of Mexican history. He says:

> While the Mexican tries to create closed worlds in his politics and in the arts, he wants modesty, prudence, and a ceremonious reserve to rule over his everyday life.[15]

He contrasts this with *fiesta* in a way immediately reminiscent of Bali. He says:

> It is significant that a country as sorrowful as ours should have so many and such joyous fiestas. Their frequency, their brilliance and excitement, the enthusiasm with which we take part, all suggest that without them we would explode. They free us, *if only momentarily* (my emphasis, P. H. E.) from the thwarted impulses, the inflammable desires that we carry within us. But the Mexican fiesta is not merely a return to an original state of formless and normless liberty; the Mexican is not seeking to return, but to escape from himself, to exceed himself.[16]

Most of these hints about the subjective nature of ecstasy, its origins, nature and consequences can be traced in an infuriating, but important book called *"Ecstasy," A Study of Some Secular and Religious Experiences.*[17] It was written by Marghanita Laski, an English novelist who, without training or very much expertise, devised a questionnaire which she administered to sixty-three of her friends and acquaintances, and collected passages from forty-nine writers describing their ecstatic experiences. Anyone who wants to know in more detail than they need, what ecstasies are like and how they happen, should consult Miss Laski's relentlessly pursued analysis. The important points I think are these: Among these relatively well educated Englishmen and women, art, nature, sexual love and religion, in that order, account for the onset of about two-thirds of the ecstatic experiences. The duration of the experience is quite brief—a few

---

[14]Benjamin Hunningher, *Origin of the Theatre* (The Hague, Holland: M. Nyhoff, 1955).

[15]Octavio Paz, *The Labyrinth of Solitude* (New York: Grove Press, Inc., 1961), p. 34–35.

[16]*Ibid.,* p. 52–53.

[17]Marghanita Laski, *Ecstasy, A Study of Some Religious and Secular Experiences* (Bloomington, Indiana: Indiana University Press, 1961), p. 9.

moments typically. About 40 per cent of the respondents had experienced ecstasy less than ten times, 40 per cent had had an experience from ten to one hundred times and the remaining 10 per cent had it over a hundred times. There were not important differences in the ecstasies of men vs. women, or Christians vs. non-believers, but the more intellectual and creative people seemed to have more intense ecstatic experiences. The content of the experience involves quasi-physical feelings, e.g., upward movement, expansion, lightness, etc. The main content of the experiences ranges from what she calls adamic states of renewal, and purification, a sense of a new world, through experiences of knowledge and/or contact with a deeper reality (or God) to union ecstasies, i.e., the extension and loss of the self, joining with something or somebody.

But by far the major idea of Miss Laski's work is her concept of "over-belief," an unwarranted and powerful acceptance, beyond ordinary rationality, of some idea, experience or value which occurs as the result of the extraordinary quality of the ecstatic state. Miss Laski suggests that this over-belief can be the seed of utopian thought, of high moral purpose, of spiritually informed conduct; in short:

> Some ecstasies have as their result the discovery of a continuing and often expanding focus of value in the trigger to the experience.[18]

I would extend her view by identifying ecstatic experience—in conjunction with its unsatisfactory institutional home—as a major engine of social and cultural change.

There are two links missing from the Laski analysis that make this argument stronger. The first is the empirical connection between the quality of everyday life and ecstatic behavior. As yet there is no study that I know of that does connect these two modes of being. The study that conjoins the two should be on someone's research agenda.

The second missing link is the accumulation of recent psychological evidence on the necessity for humans to have a varied stimulus environment.

Donald Fiske and Salvatore Maddi's book, *Functions of Varied Experience*, indicates that on the basic level of perception, and on higher levels of personal stability and learning, alternation of stimulus environments is an important factor.[19] One implication of this presumably universal human characteristic appears to be that alternation of *intensity* of experience is also likely to be a necessity for people. Thus, if a society basically did one thing most of the time—say hunt or fish or criticize—then at some other time during the day or week or whatever time cycle was resonant with their psyche and their culture, they would have to do something different—different in the same way that the people of Bali experienced the trance performances and the people of Mexico participate in fiestas as breaks in an orderly and controlled everyday mode of life.

---

[18] *Ibid.*, p. 370.

[19] Donald Fiske and Salvatore Maddi, *Functions of Varied Experience* (Homewood, Illinois: Dorsey Press, 1961).

One plausible guess is that the more homogeneous the everyday life of a people is, the more visibly different and socially coordinated will be their ecstatic release from that routine.[20] When we have come to the high state of role differentiation and consequent variety of role behavior in which people participate in an advanced urbanized, industrialized culture, then there is a great deal of alternation of styles of behavior from work and play, office to family room, committee room to pool room. Such alternation might absorb the deeper quest for enlarged experience.

However, the variety of experiences in everyday life, its joys and suffering, activity and quiet, giving and taking, do not exhaust the range of variation that people appear to need and which at one pole includes the ecstatic transcendence beyond everyday life. This is the same position that Marghanita Laski reaches and the position from which Mannheim began. Everyday life does not exhaust the human state; ecstatic transcendence is part of our nature, and must, thereby be part of our civilization. This is also the position of Joseph Piper in his rereading of Plato's Phaedrus which deals with the varieties of divine manias, enthusiasms, or in our terms, ecstasies.

> If then, you acknowledge that all this—receptivity to God's speech, liberating and purifying conversion, ... the stirring of the soul by the rationally incomprehensible and ungovernable power of art (I interrupt the quote here to add what is later included in the forms of mania, that of Erotic transcendence)—if you acknowledge that all these things constitute the true wealth of man, you agree that mania, madness, enthusiasm are not at variance with the dignity of man, but are instead essential to a truly human life.[21]

A SOCIOLOGICAL PROPOSITION

Thus I conclude with this sociological proposition: along with the conflict of social groups for power, most familiarly stated in Marxian terms as the struggle of social classes for control of the means of production, there is another, equally pervasive, but perhaps less visible struggle. It is the ceaseless battle of organized powers of society for control and monopoly over the means of ecstatic expression.

These two dynamics of social change have been historically only slightly related; perhaps the correlation between the two battles is closer than we imagine. One possible confrontation of the two is foreshadowed in Mexico, where in the introduction to his shattering *Children of Sanchez*, Oscar Lewis says:

> ... the political stability of Mexico is grim testimony to the great capacity for misery and suffering of the ordinary Mexican. But even the Mexican capacity

---

[20]Given the general unpredictability of social life, the opposite is likely to be true in some places and in some times.

[21]Joseph Piper, *Enthusiasm and Divine Madness* (New York: Harcourt, Brace & World, Inc., 1964), p. 70.

for suffering has its limits and unless ways are found to achieve a more equitable distribution of the growing national wealth . . . we may expect social upheavals sooner or later.[22]

There is very little expression of ecstatic release in the autobiographies of Sanchez' children; one feels mainly the grimness. Yet almost as a reply, Octavio Paz connects the social and ecstatic revolution. He says:

History has the cruel reality of a nightmare, and the grandeur of man consists in his making beautiful and lasting works out of the real substance of that nightmare. Or to put it another way, it consists in transforming the nightmare into vision; in freeing ourselves from the shapeless horror of reality—if only for an instant—by means of creation.[23]

Part 2

THE NATURE OF MYSTICAL EXPERIENCE
F. C. Happold

In *The Sparkling Stone* Ruysbroeck describes four ascending religious types, under the names of the hirelings, the faithful servants, the secret friends, and the hidden sons of God.

The *hirelings,* he says, are 'those who love themselves so inordinately that they will not serve God save for their own profit and because of their own reward'. These 'dwell in bondage and in their own selfhood; for they seek, and aim, at their own in all they do'.

The *faithful servants* are those who serve God in the outward and active life. They love and serve God in their own way and have, in some degree, subdued the dictates of self, but they have not yet learned to turn wholly inward. Consequently they are divided in heart, unstable in mind, and easily swayed by joy and grief in temporal things.

Though he [the faithful servant] may live according to the commandments of God, inwardly he abides in darkness. He lives more in the world of the senses than of the spirit.

The *secret friends* are those who have conquered self and entered on the inward life, which is for them 'an upward stirring exercise of love'. They have

---

Source: F.C. Happold, *Mysticism: A Study and an Anthology,* Baltimore, Maryland: Penguin Books, 1970.

[22]Oscar Lewis, *The Children of Sanchez* (New York: Vintage Book, 1961). p. xxx–xxxi.

[23]Paz, *op. cit.,* p. 104.

not as yet, however, become fully inward men. They possess their inwardness, in Ruysbroeck's term, as an *attribute,*

> ... for they have, as images and intermediaries, between themselves and God, their own being and their own activity. And though in their loving adherence they feel united with God, yet, in their union, they always feel a difference and otherness between God and themselves. For the simple passing into the Bare and Wayless they do not know and love; and therefore their highest inward life ever remains in Reason and Ways.
>
> How great [continues Ruysbroeck] is the difference between the secret friend and the *hidden son.* For the friend makes only loving, living, and measured ascents towards God. But the son presses on to lose his own life upon the summits in that simplicity which knoweth not itself. [Only when] we and all our selfhood die in God do we become his hidden sons.

The highest state of the mystic life can only be reached when there has been a complete death of the selfhood, when all images and intermediaries have been abandoned, and when a man has entered that Dark Silence, that Nothingness, that Wayless Way, where the hidden sons of God lose and, at the same time, find themselves.

One may be a 'faithful servant' of God without being in any sense a mystic or having known any sort of mystical illumination; nor does an awakening of the transcendental sense necessarily result in mystical insight, still less in the birth of a contemplative. The state of dark contemplation, known by the 'hidden sons of God', is one which few are capable of attaining. True mysticism, however, begins in an awakening of the transcendental sense, that sense of something beyond material phenomena which lies at the root of all religious feeling. But it is only the beginning; there must be something more.

No one chooses to be a mystic of his own volition. He must undergo some sort of experience which is of sufficient intensity to lead to an expansion of normal consciousness and perception, so that there comes to him a new vision of reality which dominates his life and thought. He must experience some sort of 'conversion'.

The illumination may be gradual, almost imperceptible, or sudden and violent. If there is a sudden conversion, a swift, overwhelming experience, it is usually preceded by and is the result of a long period of restlessness, uncertainty, and mental stress. The classic example of sudden conversion and illumination, resulting in a complete change of outlook and life, is that of St Paul on the road to Damascus. Yet here, though the actual change was abrupt, there seems to have been a period of mental stress leading up to it. If not, what is the meaning of the words, 'Saul, Saul, why persecutest thou me? It is hard for thee to kick against the goad'?

There was a long, hard struggle in the mind of St Francis of Assisi between the life of the world and the call of the spirit, which lasted for several years, before the illumination in the little, ruinous church of San Damiano, when (in the words of Thomas of Celano):

... being led by the Spirit he went in to pray; and he fell down before the Crucifix in devout supplication, and having been smitten by unwonted visitations, found himself another man than he who had gone in.

St Paul and St Francis were true mystics, adepts in the spiritual life. In this Study we are, however, concerned with the whole range of mystical consciousness. I have, therefore, as a prologue to the Anthology, which forms the second section of the book, included descriptions of a number of experiences, clearly mystical in character, of men and women who are in no sense contemplatives. Each contains one or more of the characteristics marks of mystical states which have been described in earlier pages. Let us consider some of them.

Consider first the vivid, illuminating experience which came to Warner Allen between two notes of a symphony and which he describes in his book, *The Timeless Moment*. In it one finds not only that sense of the oneness of everything which has been noted as typical of a mystical state, but also the feeling of absorption without loss of identity, the feeling of ceasing to be oneself and yet at the same time discovering what one is convinced is one's true self. There is also the feeling of amazement, of intense joy and peace, and, at the same time, intense unworthiness, which is also typical.

Consider next the experience of the adolescent boy on the cricket field.

What had been merely an outside became an inside. The objective was somehow transformed into a completely subjective fact, which was experienced as 'mine', but on a level where the world had no meaning; for 'I' was no longer the familiar ego.*

Here is the typical reconciliation of the polar opposites of 'outside' and 'inside', of 'objective' and 'subjective', and the sense of the familiar phenomenal self being not the real self. Though at the time his background of experience prevented him from understanding the meaning of what he had seen, its effect on him can be gauged by the fact that he was able to describe it so exactly and vividly many years later.

The experience of Winifred Holtby,* knowing, from what the doctors had told her, that the work she loved was at an end and that she had not long to live, is typical of one particular type of mystical experience, the vision of a Love which is inherent, though not obvious, in the texture of the universe, which once glimpsed brings peace, acceptance, joy, and faith, and enables a man or woman to say with confidence that 'there is nothing anywhere in the world or without that can make us afraid'.

The small girl in the orchard* can only use phrases such as 'I saw the heavens open' and 'so it's like this; now I know what Heaven is like, now I know what they mean in church'.

John Buchan, later Lord Tweedsmuir and Governor-General of Canada, in his autobiography, *Memory Hold-the-Door* tells of his own experience in these words:

---

*All these passages are printed in Section 1 of the Anthology.

Then and there came on me the hour of revelation. . . . Scents, sights, and sounds blended into a harmony so perfect that it transcended human expression, even human thought. It was like a glimpse of the peace of eternity.*

The hour of revelation! Mystical states are more than states of feeling, they are states of knowledge.

The experience which befell Dr R. M. Bucke at the age of thirty-five and which dominated all his later thinking is described as follows:

Directly afterwards there came upon me a sense of exultation, of immense joyousness, accompanied or immediately followed by an intellectual illumination quite impossible to describe.

It was this experience which enabled him in his book, *Cosmic Consciousness* (Innes, Philadelphia, 1905), to write one of the clearest and most precise descriptions of that intellectual illumination, that new access of knowledge, which comes through mystical intuition, a knowledge which reveals aspects of the universe not accessible to the intellect:

Like a flash there is presented to his consciousness a conception (a vision) of the meaning and drift of the universe. He does not come to believe merely; but he sees and knows that the cosmos, which to the self-conscious mind seems made up of dead matter, is in fact far otherwise—is in truth a living presence. He sees that the life which is in man is eternal . . . that the foundation principle of the world is what we call love. . . . Especially does he obtain such a conception of *the whole*—as makes the old attempts mentally to grasp the universe and its meaning petty and ridiculous.

None of these experiences are experiences of mystics in the restricted sense of the word, i.e. those who have ascended the Mount of Contemplation. Yet can one doubt that they are of the same character and spring from the same source as that described by St Augustine, one of the greatest of Western contemplatives, in the famous passage in his *Confessions*:

Thus with the flash of one trembling glance it [the soul] arrived at THAT WHICH IS. And then I saw Thy invisible things understood by the things that are made. But I could not fix my gaze thereon; and my infirmity being struck back, I was thrown again on my wonted habits, carrying along with me only a loving memory thereof, and a longing for what I had, as it were, perceived the odour of, but was not yet able to feed on.†

The difference between the mystic, in the wide sense, as the term is here used, and the contemplative is thus one of degree. The primary experience and the primary effect are the same. Those called to that high state of spirituality named Contemplation, by a greater concentration and a more thorough purgation, attain to a state of consciousness, in which that which for those not called to the following of this way is only occasional and spasmodic can become so frequent, so much a way of life, that, in the words of St John of the Cross already quoted, 'the soul has it in its power to abandon itself, *whenever it wills,* to this sweet sleep of love'.

---

†Anthology, Section 13.

Reading 12

A Way of Knowing—William James

No one has improved on William James' *Varieties* as a description of the mystical experience. It is for him above all an experience of *knowing*, "noetic," in his term. Passive, transient, beyond description, it conveys powerful and exciting insights into what existence means. Such experiences do not by any means guarantee personal stability or mental health. They do not make a person easy to live with or a devout and regular church member. But they are nonetheless profoundly religious interludes in the basic sense of the word: religion explains what life means.

Unlike Ennis and like Happold, James seems to incline to think that something positive must be said about the mystic's knowledge. Neither mystics or non-mystics can claim a monopoly on truth. Both must listen to one another. The scientist must realize that it is possible that the mystic knows something about reality that is important in the search for truth even though the methods of science cannot attain it.

James is very "catholic" in this excerpt and indeed in the whole of the *Varieties*. He seems to revel in the fact that there are many different forms of knowledge, each of them with its own validity, each with the responsibility to acknowledge the domain of the other.

Curiously enough, Ennis in his essay does not mention William James. Nor for that matter does Happold. In the second half of the twentieth century it almost seems that the *Varieties* no longer exists, especially in sociology and most especially in the sociology of religion. The journals abound in articles about small religious cults, about "secularization," and about the alleged rise or decline of religious devotion. Yet sociologists have paid very little attention to either William James (although the offices of Harvard University sociologists are housed in a hall named after him) or the ecstatic component of religion.

Questions for Reflection and Discussion

1. Compare James with Ennis. Why do you think Ennis does not cite him?
2. Do you think that a theory of religion which omits mystical experiences is deficient? In what respect?
3. How important do you think experience—not necessarily ecstatic—is in religious life?

MYSTICISM
William James

Over and over again in these lectures I have raised points and left them open and unfinished until we should have come to the subject of Mysticism. Some of you, I fear, may have smiled as you noted my reiterated postponements. But now the hour has come when mysticism must be faced in good earnest, and those broken threads wound up together. One may say truly, I think, that personal religious experience has its root and centre in mystical states of consciousness; so for us, who in these lectures are treating personal experience as the exclusive subject of our study, such states of consciousness ought to form the vital chapter from which the other chapters get their light. Whether my treatment of mystical states will shed more light or darkness, I do not know, for my own constitution shuts me out from their enjoyment almost entirely, and I can speak of them only at second hand. But though forced to look upon the subject so externally, I will be as objective and receptive as I can; and I think I shall at least succeed in convincing you of the reality of the states in question, and of the paramount importance of their function.

First of all, then, I ask, What does the expression 'mystical states of consciousness' mean? How do we part off mystical states from other states?

The words 'mysticism' and 'mystical' are often used as terms of mere reproach, to throw at any opinion which we regard as vague and vast and sentimental, and without a base in either facts or logic. For some writers a 'mystic' is any person who believes in thought-transference, or spirit-return. Employed in this way the word has little value: there are too many less ambiguous synonyms. So, to keep it useful by restricting it, I will do what I did in the case of the word 'religion,' and simply propose to you four marks which, when an experience has them, may justify us in calling it mystical for the purpose of the present lectures. In this way we shall save verbal disputation, and the recriminations that generally go therewith.

1. *Ineffability.*—The handiest of the marks by which I classify a state of mind as mystical is negative. The subject of it immediately says that it defies expression, that no adequate report of its contents can be given in words. It follows from this that its quality must be directly experienced; it cannot be imparted or transferred to others. In this peculiarity mystical states are more like states of feeling than like states of intellect. No one can make clear to another who has never had a certain feeling, in what the quality or worth of it consists. One must have musical ears to know the value of a symphony; one must have been in love one's self to understand a lover's state of mind. Lacking the heart or ear, we cannot interpret the musician or the lover justly, and are even likely to consider him

Source: William James, *The Varieties of Religious Experience: A Study in Human Nature,* New York: Longmans, Green and Co., 1902.

weak-minded or absurd. The mystic finds that most of us accord to his experiences an equally incompetent treatment.

2. *Noetic quality.*—Although so similar to states of feeling, mystical states seem to those who experience them to be also states of knowledge. They are states of insight into depths of truth unplumbed by the discursive intellect. They are illuminations, revelations, full of significance and importance, all inarticulate though they remain; and as a rule they carry with them a curious sense of authority for after-time.

These two characters will entitle any state to be called mystical, in the sense in which I use the word. Two other qualities are less sharply marked, but are usually found. These are:—

3. *Transiency.*—Mystical states cannot be sustained for long. Except in rare instances, half an hour, or at most an hour or two, seems to be the limit beyond which they fade into the light of common day. Often, when faded, their quality can but imperfectly be reproduced in memory; but when they recur it is recognized; and from one recurrence to another it is susceptible of continuous development in what is felt as inner richness and importance.

4. *Passivity.*—Although the oncoming of mystical states may be facilitated by preliminary voluntary operations, as by fixing the attention, or going through certain bodily performances, or in other ways which manuals of mysticism prescribe; yet when the characteristic sort of consciousness once has set in, the mystic feels as if his own will were in abeyance, and indeed sometimes as if he were grasped and held by a superior power. This latter peculiarity connects mystical states with certain definite phenomena of secondary or alternative personality, such as prophetic speech, automatic writing, or the mediumistic trance. When these latter conditions are well pronounced, however, they may be no recollection whatever of the phenomenon, and it may have no significance for the subject's usual inner life, to which, as it were, it makes a mere interruption. Mystical states, strictly so called, are never merely interruptive. Some memory of their content always remains, and a profound sense of their importance. They modify the inner life of the subject between the times of their recurrence. Sharp divisions in this region are, however, difficult to make, and we find all sorts of gradations and mixtures.

These four characteristics are sufficient to mark out a group of states of consciousness peculiar enough to deserve a special name and to call for careful study. Let it then be called the mystical group.

Our next step should be to gain acquaintance with some typical examples. Professional mystics at the height of their development have often elaborately organized experiences and a philosophy based thereupon. But you remember what I said in my first lecture: phenomena are best understood when placed within their series, studied in their germ and in their over-ripe decay, and compared with their exaggerated and degenerated kindred. The range of mystical experience is very wide, much too wide for us to cover in the time at our disposal. Yet the method of serial study is so essential for interpretation that if we really wish to reach conclusions we must use it. I will begin, therefore, with phenomena which claim no special religious significance, and end with those of which the religious pretensions are extreme.

The simplest rudiment of mystical experience would seem to be that deepened sense of the significance of a maxim or formula which occasionally sweeps over one. "I've heard that said all my life," we exclaim, "but I never realized its full meaning until now." "When a fellow-monk," said Luther, "one day repeated the words of the Creed: 'I believe in the forgiveness of sins,' I saw the Scripture in an entirely new light; and straightaway I felt as if I were born anew. It was as if I had found the door of paradise thrown wide open."[1] This sense of deeper significance is not confined to rational propositions. Single words,[2] and conjunctions of words, effects of light on land and sea, odors and musical sounds, all bring it when the mind is tuned aright. Most of us can remember the strangely moving power of passages in certain poems read when we were young, irrational doorways as they were through which the mystery of fact, the wildness and the pang of life, stole into our hearts and thrilled them. The words have now perhaps become mere polished surfaces for us; but lyric poetry and music are alive and significant only in proportion as they fetch these vague vistas of a life continuous with our own, beckoning and inviting, yet ever eluding our pursuit. We are alive or dead to the eternal inner message of the arts according as we have kept or lost this mystical susceptibility.

A more pronounced step forward on the mystical ladder is found in an extremely frequent phenomenon, that sudden feeling, namely, which sometimes sweeps over us, of having 'been here before,' as if at some indefinite past time, in just this place, with just these people, we were already saying just these things. As Tennyson writes:

> "Moreover, something is or seems,
> That touches me with mystic gleams,
> Like glimpses of forgotten dreams—
>
> "Of something felt, like something here;
> Of something done, I know not where;
> Such as no language may declare."[3]

Sir James Crichton-Browne has given the technical name of 'dreamy states' to these sudden invasions of vaguely reminiscent consciousness. They bring a sense of mystery and of the metaphysical duality of things, and the feeling of an enlargement of perception which seems imminent but which never completes

---

[1] Newman's *Securus judicat orbis terrarum* is another instance.

[2] 'Mesopotamia' is the stock comic instance.—An excellent old German lady, who had done some traveling in her day, used to describe to me her *Sebrsucht* that she might yet visit 'Philadelphia,' whose wondrous name had always haunted her imagination. Of John Foster it is said that "single words (as *chalcedony*), or the names of ancient heroes, had a mighty fascination over him. 'At any time the word *hermit* was enough to transport him.' The words *woods* and *forests* would produce the most powerful emotion." Foster's Life, by Ryland, New York, 1846, p. 3.

[3] The Two Voices.

itself. In Dr. Crichton-Browne's opinion they connect themselves with the perplexed and scared disturbances of self-consciousness which occasionally precede epileptic attacks. I think that this learned alienist takes a rather absurdly alarmist view of an intrinsically insignificant phenomenon. He follows it along the downward ladder, to insanity; our path pursues the upward ladder chiefly. The divergence shows how important it is to neglect no part of a phenomenon's connections, for we make it appear admirable or dreadful according to the context by which we set it off.

Somewhat deeper plunges into mystical consciousness are met with in yet other dreamy states. Such feelings as these which Charles Kingsley describes are surely far from being uncommon, especially in youth:—

> "When I walk the fields, I am oppressed now and then with an innate feeling that everything I see has a meaning, if I could but understand it. And this feeling of being surrounded with truths which I cannot grasp amounts to indescribable awe sometimes. . . . Have you not felt that your real soul was imperceptible to your mental vision, except in a few hallowed moments?"[4]

A much more extreme state of mystical consciousness is described by J. A. Symonds; and probably more persons than we suspect could give parallels to it from their own experience.

> "Suddenly," writes Symonds, "at church, or in company, or when I was reading, and always, I think, when my muscles were at rest, I felt the approach of the mood. Irresistibly it took possession of my mind and will, lasted what seemed an eternity, and disappeared in a series of rapid sensations which resembled the awakening from anaesthetic influence. One reason why I disliked this kind of trance was that I could not describe it to myself. I cannot even now find words to render it intelligible. It consisted in a gradual but swiftly progressive obliteration of space, time, sensation, and the multitudinous factors of experience which seem to qualify what we are pleased to call our Self. In proportion as these conditions of ordinary consciousness were subtracted, the sense of an underlying or essential consciousness acquired intensity. At last nothing remained but a pure, absolute, abstract Self. The universe became without form and void of content. But Self persisted, formidable in its vivid keenness, feeling the most poignant doubt about reality, ready, as it seemed, to find existence break as breaks a bubble round about it. And what then? The apprehension of a coming dissolution; the grim conviction that this state was the last state of the conscious Self, the sense that I had followed the last thread of being to the verge of the abyss, and had arrived at demonstration of eternal Maya or illusion, stirred or seemed to stir me up again. The return to ordinary conditions of sentient existence began by my first recovering the power of touch, and then by the gradual though rapid influx of familiar impressions and diurnal interests. At last I felt myself once more a human being; and though the riddle of what is meant by life remained unsolved, I was thankful for this return from the abyss—this deliverance from so awful an initiation into the mysteries of skepticism.

---

[4]Charles Kingsley's Life, i. 55, quoted by Inge: Christian Mysticism, London, 1899, p. 341.

"This trance recurred with diminishing frequency until I reached the age of twenty-eight. It served to impress upon my growing nature the phantasmal unreality of all the circumstances which contribute to a merely phenomenal consciousness. Often have I asked myself with anguish, on waking from that formless state of denuded, keenly sentient being, Which is the unreality?—the trance of fiery, vacant, apprehensive, skeptical Self from which I issue, or these surrounding phenomena and habits which veil that inner Self and build a self of flesh-and-blood conventionality? Again, are men the factors of some dream, the dream-like unsubstantiality of which they comprehend at such eventful moments? What would happen if the final stage of the trance were reached?"... [5]

... Certain aspects of nature seem to have a peculiar power of awakening such mystical moods.[6] Most of the striking cases which I have collected have occurred out of doors. Literature has commemorated this fact in many passages of great beauty—this extract, for example, from Amiel's Journal Intime:—

"Shall I ever again have any of those prodigious reveries which sometimes came to me in former days? One day, in youth, at sunrise, sitting in the ruins of the castle of Faucigny; and again in the mountains, under the noonday sun, above Lavey, lying at the foot of a tree and visited by three butterflies; once more at night upon the shingly shore of the Northern Ocean, my back upon the sand and my vision ranging through the milky way;—such grand and spacious, immortal, cosmogonic reveries, when one reaches to the stars, when one owns the infinite! Moments divine, ecstatic hours; in which our thought flies from world to world, pierces the great enigma, breathes with a respiration broad, tranquil, and deep as the respiration of the ocean, serene and limitless as the blue firmament; ... instants of irresistible intuition in which one feels one's self great as

---

[5]H. F. Brown: J. A. Symonds, a Biography, London, 1895, pp. 29–31, abridged.

[6]The larger God may then swallow up the smaller one. I take this from Starbuck's manuscript collection:—
"I never lost the consciousness of the presence of God until I stood at the foot of the Horseshoe Falls, Niagara. Then I lost him in the immensity of what I saw. I also lost myself, feeling that I was an atom too small for the notice of Almighty God."

I subjoin another similar case from Starbuck's collection:—
"In that time the consciousness of God's nearness came to me sometimes. I say God, to describe what is indescribable. A presence, I might say, yet that is too suggestive of personality, and the moments of which I speak did not hold the consciousness of a personality, but something in myself made me feel myself a part of something bigger than I, that was controlling. I felt myself one with the grass, the trees, birds, insects, everything in Nature. I exulted in the mere fact of existence, of being a part of it all—the drizzling rain, the shadows of the clouds, the tree-trunks, and so on. In the years following, such moments continued to come, but I wanted them constantly. I knew so well the satisfaction of losing self in a perception of supreme power and love, that I was unhappy because that perception was not constant."

The cases quoted in my third lecture, pp. 66, 67, 70, are still better ones of this type. In her essay, The Loss of Personality, in The Atlantic Monthly (vol. lxxxv. p. 195), Miss Ethel D. Puffer explains that the vanishing of the sense of self, and the feeling of immediate unity with the object, is due to the disappearance, in these rapturous experiences, of the motor adjustments which habitually intermediate between the constant background of consciousness (which is the Self) and the object in the foreground, whatever it may be. I must refer the reader to the highly instructive article, which seems to me to throw light upon the psychological conditions, though it fails to account for the rapture or the revelation-value of the experience in the Subject's eyes.

the universe, and calm as a god. . . . What hours, what memories! The vestiges they leave behind are enough to fill us with belief and enthusiasm, as if they were visits of the Holy Ghost."[7]

Here is a similar record from the memoirs of that interesting German idealist, Malwida von Meysenbug:—

"I was alone upon the seashore as all these thoughts flowed over me, liberating and reconciling; and now again, as once before in distant days in the Alps of Dauphiné, I was impelled to kneel down, this time before the illimitable ocean, symbol of the Infinite. I felt that I prayed as I had never prayed before, and knew now what prayer really is: to return from the solitude of individuation into the consciousness of unity with all that is, to kneel down as one that passes away, and to rise up as one imperishable. Earth, heaven, and sea resounded as in one vast world-encircling harmony. It was as if the chorus of all the great who had ever lived were about me. I felt myself one with them, and it appeared as if I heard their greeting: 'Thou too belongest to the company of those who overcome.'"[8]

The well-known passage from Walt Whitman is a classical expression of this sporadic type of mystical experience.

"I believe in you, my Soul . . .
Loaf with me on the grass, loose the stop from your throat; . . .
Only the lull I like, the hum of your valved voice.
I mind how once we lay, such a transparent summer morning.
Swiftly arose and spread around me the peace and knowledge that pass all
* the argument of the earth,*
And I know that the hand of God is the promise of my own,
And I know that the spirit of God is the brother of my own,
And that all the men ever born are also my brothers and the women my
* sisters and lovers,*
And that a kelson of the creation is love."[9]

I could easily give more instances, but one will suffice. I take it from the Autobiography of J. Trevor.[10]

---

[7]Op. cit., i. 43–44.

[8]Memoiren einer Idealistin, 5te Auflage, 1900, iii. 166. For years she had been unable to pray, owing to materialistic belief.

[9]Whitman in another place expresses in a quieter way what was probably with him a chronic mystical perception: "There is," he writes, "apart from mere intellect, in the make-up of every superior human identity, a wondrous something that realizes without argument, frequently without what is called education (though I think it the goal and apex of all education deserving the name), an intuition of the absolute balance, in time and space, of the whole of this multifariousness, this revel of fools, and incredible make-believe and general unsettledness, we call *the world*; a soul-sight of that divine clue and unseen thread which holds the whole congeries of things, all history and time, and all events, however trivial, however momentous, like a leashed dog in the hand of the hunter. [Of] such soul-sight and root-centre for the mind mere optimism explains only the surface." Whitman charges it against Carlyle that he lacked this perception. Specimen Days and Collect, Philadelphia, 1882, p. 174.

[10]My Quest for God, London, 1897, pp. 268, 269, abridged.

"One brilliant Sunday morning, my wife and boys went to the Unitarian Chapel in Macclesfield. I felt it impossible to accompany them—as though to leave the sunshine on the hills, and go down there to the chapel, would be for the time an act of spiritual suicide. And I felt such need for new inspiration and expansion in my life. So, very reluctantly and sadly, I left my wife and boys to go down into the town, while I went further up into the hills with my stick and my dog. In the loveliness of the morning, and the beauty of the hills and valleys, I soon lost my sense of sadness and regret. For nearly an hour I walked along the road to the 'Cat and Fiddle,' and then returned. On the way back, suddenly, without warning, I felt that I was in Heaven—an inward state of peace and joy and assurance indescribably intense, accompanied with a sense of being bathed in a warm glow of light, as though the external condition had brought about the internal effect—a feeling of having passed beyond the body, though the scene around me stood out more clearly and as if nearer to me than before, by reason of the illumination in the midst of which I seemed to be placed. This deep emotion lasted, though with decreasing strength, until I reached home, and for some time after, only gradually passing away."

The writer adds that having had further experiences of a similar sort, he now knows them well.

"The spiritual life," he writes, "justifies itself to those who live it; but what can we say to those who do not understand? This, at least, we can say, that it is a life whose experiences are proved real to their possessor, because they remain with him when brought closest into contact with the objective realities of life. Dreams cannot stand this test. We wake from them to find that they are but dreams. Wanderings of an overwrought brain do not stand this test. These highest experiences that I have had of God's presence have been rare and brief—flashes of consciousness which have compelled me to exclaim with surprise—God is *here!*—or conditions of exaltation and insight, less intense, and only gradually passing away. I have severely questioned the worth of these moments. To no soul have I named them, lest I should be building my life and work on mere phantasies of the brain. But I find that, after every questioning and test, they stand out to-day as the most real experiences of my life, and experiences which have explained and justified and unified all past experiences and all past growth. Indeed, their reality and their far-reaching significance are ever becoming more clear and evident. When they came, I was living the fullest, strongest, sanest, deepest life. I was not seeking them. What I was seeking, with resolute determination, was to live more intensely my own life, as against what I knew would be the adverse judgment of the world. It was in the most real seasons that the Real Presence came, and I was aware that I was immersed in the infinite ocean of God."[11]

Even the least mystical of you must by this time be convinced of the existence of mystical moments as states of consciousness of an entirely specific quality, and of the deep impression which they make on those who have them. A Canadian psychiatrist, Dr. R. M. Bucke, gives to the more distinctly characterized of these phenomena the name of cosmic consciousness. "Cosmic consciousness in its more striking instances is not," Dr. Bucke says, "simply an

---

[11]Op. cit., pp. 256, 257, abridged.

expansion or extension of the self-conscious mind with which we are all familiar, but the superaddition of a function as distinct from any possessed by the
average man as *self*-consciousness is distinct from any function possessed by one
of the higher animals."

"The prime characteristic of cosmic consciousness is a consciousness of the cosmos, that is, of the life and order of the universe. Along with the consciousness
of the cosmos there occurs an intellectual enlightenment which alone would
place the individual on a new plane of existence—would make him almost a
member of a new species. To this is added a state of moral exaltation, an indescribable feeling of elevation, elation, and joyousness, and a quickening of the
moral sense, which is fully as striking, and more important than is the enhanced intellectual power. With these come what may be called a sense of immortality, a consciousness of eternal life, not a conviction that he shall have
this, but the consciousness that he has it already." [12]

It was Dr. Bucke's own experience of a typical onset of cosmic consciousness in his own person which led him to investigate it in others. He has printed
his conclusions in a highly interesting volume, from which I take the following
account of what occurred to him:—

"I had spent the evening in a great city, with two friends, reading and discussing
poetry and philosophy. We parted at midnight. I had a long drive in a hansom
to my lodging. My mind, deeply under the influence of the ideas, images, and
emotions called up by the reading and talk, was calm and peaceful. I was in a
state of quiet, almost passive enjoyment, not actually thinking, but letting ideas,
images, and emotions flow of themselves, as it were, through my mind. All at
once, without warning of any kind, I found myself wrapped in a flame-colored
cloud. For an instant I thought of fire, an immense conflagration somewhere
close by in that great city; the next, I knew that the fire was within myself.
Directly afterward there came upon me a sense of exultation, of immense joyousness accompanied or immediately followed by an intellectual illumination
impossible to describe. Among other things, I did not merely come to believe,
but I saw that the universe is not composed of dead matter, but is, on the contrary, a living Presence; I became conscious in myself of eternal life. It was not a
conviction that I would have eternal life, but a consciousness that I possessed
eternal life then; I saw that all men are immortal; that the cosmic order is such
that without any peradventure all things work together for the good of each
and all; that the foundation principle of the world, of all the worlds, is what we
call love, and that the happiness of each and all is in the long run absolutely
certain. The vision lasted a few seconds and was gone; but the memory of it
and the sense of the reality of what it taught has remained during the quarter of
a century which has since elapsed. I knew that what the vision showed was
true. I had attained to a point of view from which I saw that it must be true.
That view, that conviction, I may say that consciousness, has never, even during
periods of the deepest depression, been lost." [13]

---

[12]Cosmic Consciousness: a study in the evolution of the human mind. Philadelphia, 1901, p. 2.
[13]Loc. cit., pp. 7, 8. My quotation follows the privately printed pamphlet which preceded Dr.
Bucke's larger work, and differs verbally a little from the text of the latter.

. . . This incommunicableness of the transport is the keynote of all mysticism. Mystical truth exists for the individual who has the transport, but for no one else. In this, as I have said, it resembles the knowledge given to us in sensations more than that given by conceptual thought. Thought, with its remoteness and abstractness, has often enough in the history of philosophy been contrasted unfavorably with sensation. It is a commonplace of metaphysics that God's knowledge cannot be discursive but must be intuitive, that is, must be constructed more after the pattern of what in ourselves is called immediate feeling, than after that of proposition and judgment. But *our* immediate feelings have no content but what the five senses supply; and we have seen and shall see again that mystics may emphatically deny that the senses play any part in the very highest type of knowledge which their transports yield.

In the Christian church there have always been mystics. Although many of them have been viewed with suspicion, some have gained favor in the eyes of the authorities. The experiences of these have been treated as precedents, and a codified system of mystical theology has been based upon them, in which everything legitimate finds its place.[14] The basis of the system is 'orison' or meditation, the methodical elevation of the soul towards God. Through the practice of orison the higher levels of mystical experience may be attained. It is odd that Protestantism, especially evangelical Protestantism, should seemingly have abandoned everything methodical in this line. Apart from what prayer may lead to, Protestant mystical experience appears to have been almost exclusively sporadic. It has been left to our mind-curers to reintroduce methodical meditation into our religious life.

The first thing to be aimed at in orison is the mind's detachment from outer sensations, for these interfere with its concentration upon ideal things. Such manuals as Saint Ignatius's Spiritual Exercises recommend the disciple to expel sensation by a graduated series of efforts to imagine holy scenes. The acme of this kind of discipline would be a semi-hallucinatory mono-ideism—an imaginary figure of Christ, for example, coming fully to occupy the mind. Sensorial images of this sort, whether literal or symbolic, play an enormous part in mysticism.[15] But in certain cases imagery may fall away entirely, and in the very highest raptures it tends to do so. The state of consciousness becomes then insusceptible of any verbal description. Mystical teachers are unanimous as to this. Saint John of the Cross, for instance, one of the best of them, thus describes the condition called the 'union of love,' which, he says, is reached by 'dark contemplation.' In this the Deity compenetrates the soul, but in such a hidden way that the soul—

---

[14]Görres's Christliche Mystik gives a full account of the facts. So does Ribet's Mystique Divine, 2 vols., Paris, 1890. A still more methodical modern work is the Mystica Theologia of Vallgornera, 2 vols., Turin, 1890.

[15]M. Récéjac, in a recent volume, makes them essential. Mysticism he defines as "the tendency to draw near to the Absolute morally, *and by the aid of Symbols*." See his Fondements de la Connaissance mystique, Paris, 1897, p. 66. But there are unquestionably mystical conditions in which sensible symbols play no part.

"finds no terms, no means, no comparison whereby to render the sublimity of the wisdom and the delicacy of the spiritual feeling with which she is filled. . . . We receive this mystical knowledge of God clothed in none of the kinds of images, in none of the sensible representations, which our mind makes use of in other circumstances. Accordingly in this knowledge, since the senses and the imagination are not employed, we get neither form nor impression, nor can we give any account or furnish any likeness, although the mysterious and sweet-tasting wisdom comes home so clearly to the inmost parts of our soul. Fancy a man seeing a certain kind of thing for the first time in his life. He can understand it, use and enjoy it, but he cannot apply a name to it, nor communicate any idea of it, even though all the while it be a mere thing of sense. How much greater will be his powerlessness when it goes beyond the senses! This is the peculiarity of the divine language. The more infused, intimate, spiritual, and supersensible it is, the more does it exceed the senses, both inner and outer, and impose silence upon them. . . . The soul then feels as if placed in a vast and profound solitude, to which no created thing has access, in an immense and boundless desert, desert the more delicious the more solitary it is. There, in this abyss of wisdom, the soul grows by what it drinks in from the well-springs of the comprehension of love, . . . and recognizes, however sublime and learned may be the terms we employ, how utterly vile, insignificant, and improper they are, when we seek to discourse of divine things by their means."[16]

I cannot pretend to detail to you the sundry stages of the Christian mystical life.[17] Our time would not suffice, for one thing; and moreover, I confess that the subdivisions and names which we find in the Catholic books seem to me to represent nothing objectively distinct. So many men, so many minds: I imagine that these experiences can be as infinitely varied as are the idiosyncrasies of individuals.

The cognitive aspects of them, their value in the way of revelation, is what we are directly concerned with, and it is easy to show by citation how strong an impression they leave of being revelations of new depths of truth. Saint Teresa is the expert of experts in describing such conditions, so I will turn immediately to what she says of one of the highest of them, the 'orison of union.'

"In the orison of union," says Saint Teresa, "the soul is fully awake as regards God, but wholly asleep as regards things of this world and in respect of herself. During the short time the union lasts, she is as it were deprived of every feeling, and even if she would, she could not think of any single thing. Thus she needs to employ no artifice in order to arrest the use of her understanding: it remains

---

[16]Saint John of the Cross: The Dark Night of the Soul, book ii. ch. xvii., in Vie et Œuvres, 3me édition, Paris, 1893, iii. 428–432. Chapter xi. of book ii. of Saint John's Ascent of Carmel is devoted to showing the harmfulness for the mystical life of the use of sensible imagery.

[17]In particular I omit mention of visual and auditory hallucinations, verbal and graphic automatisms, and such marvels as 'levitation,' stigmatization, and the healing of disease. These phenomena, which mystics have often presented (or are believed to have presented), have no essential mystical significance, for they occur with no consciousness of illumination whatever, when they occur, as they often do, in persons of non-mystical mind. Consciousness of illumination is for us the essential mark of 'mystical' states.

so stricken with inactivity that she neither knows what she loves, nor in what manner she loves, nor what she wills. In short, she is utterly dead to the things of the world and lives solely in God. . . . I do not even know whether in this state she has enough life left to breathe. It seems to me she has not; or at least that if she does breathe, she is unaware of it. Her intellect would fain understand something of what is going on within her, but it has so little force now that it can act in no way whatsoever. So a person who falls into a deep faint appears as if dead. . . .

"Thus does God, when he raises a soul to union with himself, suspend the natural action of all her faculties. She neither sees, hears, nor understands, so long as she is united with God. But this time is always short, and it seems even shorter than it is. God establishes himself in the interior of this soul in such a way, that when she returns to herself, it is wholly impossible for her to doubt that she has been in God, and God in her. This truth remains so strongly impressed on her that, even though many years should pass without the condition returning, she can neither forget the favor she received, nor doubt of its reality. If you, nevertheless, ask how it is possible that the soul can see and understand that she has been in God, since during the union she has neither sight nor understanding, I reply that she does not see it then, but that she sees it clearly later, after she has returned to herself, not by any vision, but by a certitude which abides with her and which God alone can give her. I knew a person who was ignorant of the truth that God's mode of being in everything must be either by presence, by power, or by essence, but who, after having received the grace of which I am speaking, believed this truth in the most unshakable manner. So much so that, having consulted a half-learned man who was as ignorant on this point as she had been before she was enlightened, when he replied that God is in us only by 'grace,' she disbelieved his reply, so sure she was of the true answer; and when she came to ask wiser doctors, they confirmed her in her belief, which much consoled her. . . .

"But how, you will repeat, *can* one have such certainty in respect to what one does not see? This question, I am powerless to answer. These are secrets of God's omnipotence which it does not appertain to me to penetrate. All that I know is that I tell the truth; and I shall never believe that any soul who does not possess this certainty has ever been really united to God."[18]

The kinds of truth communicable in mystical ways, whether these be sensible or supersensible, are various. Some of them relate to this world,—visions of the future, the reading of hearts, the sudden understanding of texts, the knowledge of distant events, for example; but the most important revelations are theological or metaphysical.

"Saint Ignatius confessed one day to Father Laynez that a single hour of meditation at Manresa had taught him more truths about heavenly things than all the teachings of all the doctors put together could have taught him. . . . One day in orison, on the steps of the choir of the Dominican church, he saw in a distinct manner the plan of divine wisdom in the creation of the world. On another occasion, during a procession, his spirit was ravished in God, and it was

---

[18]The Interior Castle, Fifth Abode, ch. i., in Œuvres, translated by Bouix, iii. 421–424.

given him to contemplate, in a form and images fitted to the weak understanding of a dweller on the earth, the deep mystery of the holy Trinity. This last vision flooded his heart with such sweetness, that the mere memory of it in after times made him shed abundant tears."[19]

Similarly with Saint Teresa. "One day, being in orison," she writes, "it was granted me to perceive in one instant how all things are seen and contained in God. I did not perceive them in their proper form, and nevertheless the view I had of them was of a sovereign clearness, and has remained vividly impressed upon my soul. It is one of the most signal of all the graces which the Lord has granted me. . . . The view was so subtle and delicate that the understanding cannot grasp it."[20]

She goes on to tell how it was as if the Deity were an enormous and sovereignly limpid diamond, in which all our actions were contained in such a way that their full sinfulness appeared evident as never before. On another day, she relates, while she was reciting the Athanasian Creed,—

"Our Lord made me comprehend in what way it is that one God can be in three Persons. He made me see it so clearly that I remained as extremely surprised as I was comforted, . . . and now, when I think of the holy Trinity, or hear It spoken of, I understand how the three adorable Persons form only one God and I experience an unspeakable happiness."

On still another occasion, it was given to Saint Teresa to see and understand in what wise the Mother of God had been assumed into her place in Heaven.[21]

---

[19]Bartoli-Michel: Vie de Saint Ignace de Loyola, i. 34–36. Others have had illuminations about the created world, Jacob Boehme, for instance. At the age of twenty-five he was "surrounded by the divine light, and replenished with the heavenly knowledge; insomuch as going abroad into the fields to a green, at Görlitz, he there sat down, and viewing the herbs and grass of the field, in his inward light he saw into their essences, use, and properties, which was discovered to him by their lineaments, figures, and signatures." Of a later period of experience he writes: "In one quarter of an hour I saw and knew more than if I had been many years together at an university. For I saw and knew the being of all things, the Byss and the Abyss, and the eternal generation of the holy Trinity, the descent and original of the world and of all creatures through the divine wisdom. I knew and saw in myself all the three worlds, the external and visible world being of a procreation or extern birth from both the internal and spiritual worlds; and I saw and knew the whole working essence, in the evil and in the good, and the mutual original and existence; and likewise how the fruitful bearing womb of eternity brought forth. So that I did not only greatly wonder at it, but did also exceedingly rejoice, albeit I could very hardly apprehend the same in my external man and set it down with the pen. For I had a thorough view of the universe as in a chaos, wherein all things are couched and wrapt up, but it was impossible for me to explicate the same." Jacob Behmen's Theosophic Philosophy, etc., by Edward Taylor, London, 1691, pp. 425, 427, abridged. So George Fox: "I was come up to the state of Adam in which he was before he fell. The creation was opened to me; and it was showed me, how all things had their names given to them, according to their nature and virtue. I was at a stand in my mind, whether I should practice physic for the good of mankind, seeing the nature and virtues of the creatures were so opened to me by the Lord." Journal, Philadelphia, no date, p. 69. Contemporary 'Clairvoyance' abounds in similar revelations. Andrew Jackson Davis's cosmogonies, for example, or certain experiences related in the delectable 'Reminiscences and Memories of Henry Thomas Butterworth,' Lebanon, Ohio, 1886.

[20]Vie, pp. 581, 582.

[21]Loc. cit., p. 574.

The deliciousness of some of these states seems to be beyond anything known in ordinary consciousness. It evidently involves organic sensibilities, for it is spoken of as something too extreme to be borne, and as verging on bodily pain.[22] But it is too subtle and piercing a delight for ordinary words to denote. God's touches, the wounds of his spear, references to ebriety and to nuptial union have to figure in the phraseology by which it is shadowed forth. Intellect and senses both swoon away in these highest states of ecstasy. "If our under-standing comprehends," says Saint Teresa, "it is in a mode which remains unknown to it, and it can understand nothing of what it comprehends. For my own part, I do not believe that it does comprehend, because, as I said, it does not understand itself to do so. I confess that it is all a mystery in which I am lost."[23] In the condition called *raptus* or ravishment by theologians, breathing and circulation are so depressed that it is a question among the doctors whether the soul be or be not temporarily dissevered from the body. One must read Saint Teresa's descriptions and the very exact distinctions which she makes, to per-suade one's self that one is dealing, not with imaginary experiences, but with phenomena which, however rare, follow perfectly definite psychological types.

To the medical mind these ecstasies signify nothing but suggested and imitated hypnoid states, on an intellectual basis of superstition, and a corporeal one of degeneration and hysteria. Undoubtedly these pathological conditions have existed in many and possibly in all the cases, but that fact tells us nothing about the value for knowledge of the consciousness which they induce. To pass a spiritual judgment upon these states, we must not content ourselves with superficial medical talk, but inquire into their fruits for life.

Their fruits appear to have been various. Stupefaction, for one thing, seems not to have been altogether absent as a result. You may remember the helpless-ness in the kitchen and schoolroom of poor Margaret Mary Alacoque. Many other ecstatics would have perished but for the care taken of them by admiring followers. The 'other-worldliness' encouraged by the mystical consciousness makes this over-abstraction from practical life peculiarly liable to befall mystics in whom the character is naturally passive and the intellect feeble; but in native-ly strong minds and characters we find quite opposite results. The great Spanish mystics, who carried the habit of ecstasy as far as it has often been carried, appear for the most part to have shown indomitable spirit and energy, and all the more so for the trances in which they indulged.

Saint Ignatius was a mystic, but his mysticism made him assuredly one of the most powerfully practical human engines that ever lived. Saint John of the Cross, writing of the intuitions and 'touches' by which God reaches the sub-stance of the soul, tells us that—

---

[22]Saint Teresa discriminates between pain in which the body has a part and pure spiritual pain (Interior Castle, 6th Abode, ch. xi.). As for the bodily part in these celestial joys, she speaks of it as "penetrating to the marrow of the bones, whilst earthly pleasures affect only the surface of the senses. I think," she adds, "that this is a just description, and I cannot make it better." Ibid., 5th Abode, ch. i.

[23]Vie, p. 198.

"They enrich it marvelously. A single one of them may be sufficient to abolish at a stroke certain imperfections of which the soul during its whole life had vainly tried to rid itself, and to leave it adorned with virtues and loaded with supernatural gifts. A single one of these intoxicating consolations may reward it for all the labors undergone in its life—even were they numberless. Invested with an invincible courage, filled with an impassioned desire to suffer for its God, the soul then is seized with a strange torment—that of not being allowed to suffer enough."[24]

Saint Teresa is as emphatic, and much more detailed. You may perhaps remember a passage I quoted from her in my first lecture.[25] There are many similar pages in her autobiography. Where in literature is a more evidently veracious account of the formation of a new centre of spiritual energy, than is given in her description of the effects of certain ecstasies which in departing leave the soul upon a higher level of emotional excitement?

"Often, infirm and wrought upon with dreadful pains before the ecstasy, the soul emerges from it full of health and admirably disposed for action . . . as if God had willed that the body itself, already obedient to the soul's desires, should share in the soul's happiness. . . . The soul after such a favor is animated with a degree of courage so great that if at that moment its body should be torn to pieces for the cause of God, it would feel nothing but the liveliest comfort. Then it is that promises and heroic resolutions spring up in profusion in us, soaring desires, horror of the world, and the clear perception of our proper nothingness. . . . What empire is comparable to that of a soul who, from this sublime summit to which God has raised her, sees all the things of earth beneath her feet, and is captivated by no one of them? How ashamed she is of her former attachments! How amazed at her blindness! What lively pity she feels for those whom she recognizes still shrouded in the darkness! . . . She groans at having ever been sensitive to points of honor, at the illusion that made her ever see as honor what the world calls by that name. Now she sees in this name nothing more than an immense lie of which the world remains a victim. She discovers, in the new light from above, that in genuine honor there is nothing spurious, that to be faithful to this honor is to give our respect to what deserves to be respected really, and to consider as nothing, or as less than nothing, whatsoever perishes and is not agreeable to God. . . . She laughs when she sees grave persons, persons of orison, caring for points of honor for which she now feels profoundest contempt. It is suitable to the dignity of their rank to act thus, they pretend, and it makes them more useful to others. But she knows that in despising the dignity of their rank for the pure love of God they would do more good in a single day than they would effect in ten years by preserving it. . . . She laughs at herself that there should ever have been a time in her life when she made any case of money, when she ever desired it. . . . Oh! if human beings might only agree together to regard it as so much useless mud, what harmony would then reign in the world! With what friendship we would all treat each

[24]Œuvres, ii. 320.
[25]Above, p. 21.

other if our interest in honor and in money could but disappear from earth! For my own part, I feel as if it would be a remedy for all our ills."[26]

Mystical conditions may, therefore, render the soul more energetic in the lines which their inspiration favors. But this could be reckoned an advantage only in case the inspiration were a true one. If the inspiration were erroneous, the energy would be all the more mistaken and misbegotten. So we stand once more before that problem of truth which confronted us at the end of the lectures on saintliness. You will remember that we turned to mysticism precisely to get some light on truth. Do mystical states establish the truth of those theological affections in which the saintly life has its root? . . .

I have now sketched with extreme brevity and insufficiency, but as fairly as I am able in the time allowed, the general traits of the mystic range of consciousness. *It is on the whole pantheistic and optimistic, or at least the opposite of pessimistic. It is anti-naturalistic, and harmonizes best with twice-bornness and so-called other-worldly states of mind.*

My next task is to inquire whether we can invoke it as authoritative. Does it furnish any *warrant for the truth* of the twice-bornness and supernaturality and pantheism which it favors? I must give my answer to this question as concisely as I can.

In brief my answer is this,—and I will divide it into three parts:—

1. Mystical states, when well developed, usually are, and have the right to be, absolutely authoritative over the individuals to whom they come.
2. No authority emanates from them which should make it a duty for those who stand outside of them to accept their revelations uncritically.
3. They break down the authority of the non-mystical or rationalistic consciousness, based upon the understanding and the senses alone. They show it to be only one kind of consciousness. They open out the possibility of other orders of truth, in which, so far as anything in us vitally responds to them, we may freely continue to have faith.

I will take up these points one by one.

1.

As a matter of psychological fact, mystical states of a well-pronounced and emphatic sort *are* usually authoritative over those who have them. They have been 'there,' and know. It is vain for rationalism to grumble about this. If the mystical truth that comes to a man proves to be a force that he can live by, what mandate have we of the majority to order him to live in another way? We can throw him into a prison or a madhouse, but we cannot change his mind—we commonly attach it only the more stubbornly to its beliefs. It mocks our utmost

---

[26]Vie, pp. 229, 200, 231–233, 243.

efforts, as a matter of fact, and in point of logic it absolutely escapes our jurisdiction. Our own more 'rational' beliefs are based on evidence exactly similar in
nature to that which mystics quote for theirs. Our senses, namely, have assured
us of certain states of fact; but mystical experiences are as direct perceptions of
fact for those who have them as any sensations ever were for us. The records
show that even though the five senses be in abeyance in them, they are absolutely sensational in their epistemological quality, if I may be pardoned the bar-
barous expression,—that is, they are face to face presentations of what seems
immediately to exist.

The mystic is, in short, *invulnerable,* and must be left, whether we relish it
or not, in undisturbed enjoyment of his creed. Faith, says Tolstoy, is that by
which men live. And faith-state and mystic state are practically convertible
terms.

2.

But I now proceed to add that mystics have no right to claim that we ought to
accept the deliverance of their peculiar experiences, if we are ourselves outsiders
and feel no private call thereto. The utmost they can ever ask of us in this life is
to admit that they establish a presumption. They form a consensus and have an
unequivocal outcome; and it would be odd, mystics might say, if such a unanimous type of experience should prove to be altogether wrong. At bottom, however, this would only be an appeal to numbers, like the appeal of rationalism the
other way; and the appeal to numbers has no logical force. If we acknowledge
it, it is for 'suggestive,' not for logical reasons: we follow the majority because
to do so suits our life. . . .

Once more, then, I repeat that non-mystics are under no obligation to
acknowledge in mystical states a superior authority conferred on them by their
intrinsic nature.[27]

3.

Yet, I repeat once more, the existence of mystical states absolutely overthrows
the pretension of non-mystical states to be the sole and ultimate dictators of
what we may believe. As a rule, mystical states merely add a supersensuous

---

[27]In chapter i. of book ii. of his work Degeneration, 'Max Nordau' seeks to undermine all mysticism by exposing the weakness of the lower kinds. Mysticism for him means any sudden perception of hidden significance in things. He explains such perception by the abundant uncompleted
associations which experiences may arouse in a degenerate brain. These give to him who has the
experience a vague and vast sense of its leading further, yet they awaken no definite or useful consequent in his thought. The explanation is a plausible one for certain sorts of feeling of significance; and other alienists (Wernicke, for example, in his Grundriss der Psychiatrie, Theil ii.,
Leipzig, 1896) have explained 'paranoiac' conditions by a laming of the association-organ. But
the higher mystical flights, with their positiveness and abruptness, are surely products of no such
merely negative condition. It seems far more reasonable to ascribe them to inroads from the subconscious life, of the cerebral activity correlative to which we as yet know nothing.

meaning to the ordinary outward data of consciousness. They are excitements like the emotions of love or ambition, gifts to our spirit by means of which facts already objectively before us fall into a new expressiveness and make a new connection with our active life. They do not contradict these facts as such, or deny anything that our senses have immediately seized.[28] It is the rationalistic critic rather who plays the part of denier in the controversy, and his denials have no strength, for there never can be a state of facts to which new meaning may not truthfully be added, provided the mind ascend to a more enveloping point of view. It must always remain an open question whether mystical states may not possibly be such superior points of view, windows through which the mind looks out upon a more extensive and inclusive world. The difference of the views seen from the different mystical windows need not prevent us from entertaining this supposition. The wider world would in that case prove to have a mixed constitution like that of this world, that is all. It would have its celestial and its infernal regions, its tempting and its saving moments, its valid experiences and its counterfeit ones, just as our world has them; but it would be a wider world all the same. We should have to use its experiences by selecting and subordinating and substituting just as is our custom in this ordinary naturalistic world; we should be liable to error just as we are now; yet the counting in of that wider world of meanings, and the serious dealing with it, might, in spite of all the perplexity, be indispensable stages in our approach to the final fullness of the truth.

In this shape, I think, we have to leave the subject. Mystical states indeed wield no authority due simply to their being mystical states. But the higher ones among them point in directions to which the religious sentiments even of non-mystical men incline. They tell of the supremacy of the ideal, of vastness, of union, of safety, and of rest. They offer us *hypotheses,* hypotheses which we may voluntarily ignore, but which as thinkers we cannot possibly upset. The supernaturalism and optimism to which they would persuade us may, interpreted in one way or another, be after all the truest of insights into the meaning of this life.

"Oh, the little more, and how much it is; and the little less, and what worlds away!" It may be that possibility and permission of this sort are all that the religious consciousness requires to live on. In my last lecture I shall have to try to persuade you that this is the case. Meanwhile, however, I am sure that for many of my readers this diet is too slender. If supernaturalism and inner union with the divine are true, you think, then not so much permission, as compulsion to believe, ought to be found. Philosophy has always professed to prove religious truth by coercive argument; and the construction of philosophies of this kind has always been one favorite function of the religious life, if we use this term in the large historic sense. But religious philosophy is an enormous subject, and in my next lecture I can only give that brief glance at it which my limits will allow.

---

[28]They sometimes add subjective *audita et visa* to the facts, but as these are usually interpreted as transmundane, they oblige no alteration in the facts of sense.

Reading 13

ONLY THE FACTS: SURVEY RESEARCH ON ECSTASY—ANDREW M. GREELEY

In 1972, with a grant from the Henry Luce Foundation, my colleague William C. McCready and I (and I switch to the first person in reporting my own work) began a study of the American religious situation. One of our concerns was the phenomenon of mysticism, which (like sexual behavior) had never been the subject of a national probability sample survey in which the respondents reflected the whole American population with a high degree of probability and within a margin of error of a couple of percentage points.

Our goal was to take mysticism out of the descriptive books like the *Varieties* and Margarina Laski's account of the experiences of a self-selected sample and determine whether any traces of mysticism could be found among typical Americans. Is ecstasy a phenomenon that may have existed in the faintly Edwardian era of William James, but which has no place in busy, secularized, contemporary America?

We found that almost a third of the American population had experienced one interlude of ecstasy and that one out of six had such experiences several times. Moreover we also discovered that ecstasy correlates positively with psychological well being and mental health. For a substantial component of Americans ecstasy is "normal" and good for you.

Despite an article in the *New York Times* magazine, the response of the sociological fraternity was underwhelming. As far as I am aware, not a single book on the sociology of religion made any use of our findings—although subsequent work by Sir Alastair Hardy and David Hay of the University of Nottingham replicated our findings in Great Britain and an international study in the early 1980s found a range of proportions reporting mysticism in the different countries, but no country where it did not occur.

In the late 1980s, the question was asked again for several years in National Opinion Research Center's (NORC's) General Social Survey. The rate of mysticism (or at least the rate of those affirming mystical experiences) had actually increased.

At the risk of sounding bitter, it must be said that sociology of religion in the United States couldn't care less. It has clearly decided that intense religious experiences are not proper subject matter for sociological research, an imposition of boundaries on the field, that I find inexplicable.

In any event, the experience described by Ennis and Happold and James (and all the writers whom James quotes) is commonplace in contemporary America.

Questions for Reflection and Discussion

1. Do the statistics on mystical experience surprise you? Why or why not?
2. What weaknesses do you see in the research reported?
3. What further research would you like to see done?
4. Why do you think sociologists of religion ignore this research?

THE SOCIOLOGY OF THE PARANORMAL: A RECONNAISANCE
Andrew M. Greeley

MYSTICISM

While orthodox social science has paid relatively little attention to the parapsychological, there is almost an embarrassment of riches on the subject of the mystical. Indeed the capital building of all American social science is named after William James, whose *Varieties of Religious Experience* is the classic study of mysticism in the United States. Psychologists and anthropologists have always been interested in the subject, though as we shall note, sociologists seem unaware of it. Furthermore, much of the interest on the part of psychologists has consisted in efforts to explain away such experiences.

First, what are the experiences like? Some descriptions may be helpful as a way to begin our analysis. They portray far more graphically than statistical data the sort of experience we are trying to understand.

Those who have been through a mystical experience tell us that there is nothing in the world quite like it. In his classic work, William James recounts an experience of James Russell Lowell:

> I had a revelation last Friday evening, I was at Mary's, and happening to say something of the presence of spirits (of whom, I said, I was often dimly aware), Mr. Putnam entered into an argument with me on spiritual matters. As I was speaking, the whole system rose up before me like a vague destiny looming from the Abyss. I never before so clearly felt the Spirit of God in me and around me. The whole room seemed to me full of God. The air seemed to waver to and fro with the presence of Something I knew not what. I spoke with the calmness and clearness of a prophet. I cannot tell you what this revelation was. I have

Source: Andrew M. Greeley, *The Sociology of the Paranormal: A Reconnaissance,* Beverly Hills, California: Sage Publications, 1975.

not yet studied it enough. But I shall perfect it one day, and then you shall hear it and acknowledge its grandeur [James, 1958: 67].

He then turns to two even more detailed descriptions of similar events. The first concerns the experience of a clergyman:

I remember the night, and almost the very spot on the hilltop, where my soul opened out, as it were, into the Infinite, and there was a rushing together of the two worlds, the inner and the outer. It was deep calling unto deep,—the deep that my own struggle had opened up within being answered by the unfathomable deep without, reaching beyond the start. I stood alone with Him who had made me, and all the beauty of the world, and love, and sorrow, and even temptation. I did not see Him, but felt the perfect unison of my spirit with His. The ordinary sense of things around me faded. For the moment nothing but an ineffable joy and exaltation remained. It is impossible fully to describe the experience. It was like the effect of some great orchestra when all the separate notes have melted into one swelling harmony that leaves the listener conscious of nothing save that his soul is being wafted upwards, and almost bursting with its own emotion. The perfect stillness of the night was thrilled by a more solemn silence. The darkness held a presence that was all the more felt because it was not seen. I could not any more have doubted that *He* was there than that I was. Indeed, I felt myself to be, if possible, the less real of the two.

My highest faith in God and truest idea of him were then born in me. I have stood upon the Mount of Vision since, and felt the Eternal round about me. But never since has there come quite the same stirring of the heart. Then, if ever, I believe, I stood face to face with God, and was born anew of his spirit. There was, as I recall it, no sudden change of thought or belief, except that my early crude conception had, as it were, burst into flower. There was no destruction of the old, but a rapid, wonderful unfolding. Since that time no discussion that I have heard of the proofs of God's existence has been able to shake my faith. Having once felt the presence of God's spirit, I have never lost it again for long. My most assuring evidence of his existence is deeply rooted in that hour of vision, in the memory of that supreme experience, and in the conviction, gained from reading and reflection, that something the same has come to all who have found God. I am aware that it may justly be called mystical. I am not enough acquainted with philosophy to defend it from that or any other charge. I feel that in writing of it I have overlaid it with words rather than put it clearly to your thought. But, such as it is, I have described it as carefully as I now am able to do [James, 1958: 67–68].

James translated this account from the original French written by a Swiss:

I was in perfect health: we were on our sixth day of tramping, and in good training. We had come the day before from Sixt to Trient by Buet. I felt neither fatigue, hunger, nor thirst, and my state of mind was equally healthy. I had had at Forlaz good news from home; I was subject to no anxiety, either near or remote, for we had a good guide, and there was not a shadow of uncertainty about the road we should follow. I can best describe the condition in which I was by calling it a state of equilibrium. When all at once I experienced a feeling of being raised above myself, I felt the presence of God—I tell of the thing just as I was conscious of it—as if his goodness and his power were penetrating me altogether. The throb of emotion was so violent that I could barely tell the boys to pass on and not wait for me. I then sat down on a stone, unable to stand any longer, and my eyes overflowed with tears. I thanked God that in the course of my life he had taught me to know him, that he sustained my life and took pity both on the insignificant creature and on the sinner that I was. I begged him ardently that my life might be consecrated to the doing of his will. I felt his reply, which was that I should do his will from day to day, in humility and poverty, leaving him, the Almighty God, to be judge of whether I should some time be called to bear witness, more conspicuously. Then, slowly, the ecstasy left my heart; that is, I felt that God had withdrawn the communion which he had granted, and I was able to walk on, but very slowly, so strongly was I still possessed by the interior emotion. Besides, I had wept uninterruptedly for several minutes, my eyes were swollen, and I did not wish my companions to see me. The state of ecstasy may have lasted four or five minutes, although it seemed at the time to last much longer. My comrades waited for me ten minutes at the cross of Barine, but I took about twenty-five or thirty minutes to join them, for as well as I can remember, they said that I had kept them back for about half an hour. The impression had been so profound that in climbing slowly the slope I asked myself if it were possible that Moses on Sinai could have had a more intimate communication with God. I think it well to add that in this ecstasy of mine, God had neither form, color, odor, nor taste; moreover, that the feeling of his presence was accompanied with no determinate localization. It was rather as if my personality had been transformed by the presence of a *spiritual spirit*. But the more I seek words to express this intimate intercourse, the more I feel the impossibility of describing the thing by any of our usual images. At bottom the expression most apt to render what I felt is this: God was present, though invisible; he fell under no one of my senses, yet my consciousness perceived him [James, 1958: 68–69].

These are obviously spectacular events. Most of us would be inclined to believe that these kinds of intense experience happened only in the past or only in primitive regions today.

F. C. Happold (1964) has compiled one of the best anthologies of mysticism presently available. He describes such an experience in his own life:

It happened in my room in Peterhouse on the evening of 1 February 1913, when I was an undergraduate at Cambridge. If I say that Christ came to me I should be using conventional words which would carry no precise meaning; for Christ comes to men and women in different ways. When I tried to record the experience at the time I used the imagery of the vision of the Holy Grail; it seemed to me to be like that. There was, however, no sensible vision. There was just the room, with its shabby furniture and the fire burning in the grate and the red-shaded lamp on the table. But the room was filled by a Presence, which in a strange way was both about me and within me, like light or warmth. I was overwhelmingly possessed by Someone who was not myself, and yet I felt I was more myself than I had ever been before. I was filled with an intense happiness, and almost unbearable joy, such as I had never known before and have never known since. And over all was a deep sense of peace and security and certainty [Happold, 1964: 133–134].

Happold, mind you, was a very commonsensical British headmaster, a hero awarded a DSO for service during the First World War, and a quintessential Anglo-Saxon—not the sort who would be given to flimflam. Nor was John Buchan, Scottish novelist and diplomat, exactly what we would consider a mystical type. Yet:

> I had been ploughing all day in the black dust of the Lichtenburg roads, and had come very late to a place called the eye of Malmani—Malmani Oog—the spring of a river which presently loses itself in the Kalahari. We watered our horses and went supperless to bed. Next morning I bathed in one of the Malmani pools—and icy cold it was—and then basked in the early sunshine while breakfast was cooking. The water made a pleasant music, and near by was a covert of willows filled with singing birds. Then and there came on me the hour of revelation, when, though savagely hungry, I forgot about breakfast. Scents, sights, and sounds blended into a harmony so perfect that it transcended human expression, even human thought. It was like a glimpse of the peace of eternity [Happold, 1964: 131].

The moments of ecstasy can come in strange places—particularly for Englishmen it seems—drab rooms, African landscapes, and even on a cricket field:

> The thing happened one summer afternoon, on the school cricket field, while I was sitting on the grass, waiting my turn to bat. I was thinking about nothing in particular, merely enjoying the pleasures of midsummer idleness. Suddenly, and without warning, something invisible seemed to be drawn across the sky, transforming the world about me into a kind of tent of concentrated and enhanced significance. What had been merely an outside became an inside. The objective was somehow transformed into a completely subjective fact, which was experienced as "mine," but on a level where the word had no meaning; for "I" was no longer the familiar ego. Nothing more can be said about the experience, it brought no accession of knowledge about anything except, very obscurely, the knower and his way of knowing. After a few minutes there was a "return to normalcy." The event made a deep impression on me at the time; but, because it did not fit into any of the thought patterns—religious, philosophical, scientific—with which, as a boy of fifteen, I was familiar, it came to seem more and more anomalous, more and more irrelevant to "real life," and was finally forgotten [Happold, 1964: 130].

Finally, one contemporary American poet proves that even in the city of Chicago, County of Cook, State of Illinois, the mystical light still shines:

PRAYER OF SOMEONE WHO HAS BEEN THERE BEFORE

After the last time
    when I finally turned from flight
    and from somewhere came the strength
       to go back
I rummaged the ruins
    a refugee picking through bombed belongings
       for what surely was destroyed
and began again.

When a child tests the ice for skating,
he checks for thickness not for smoothness.
He will endure the bumps
as long as he does not drown.
        Out of fear of falling in
        I grew my new life
            thick and rough
             with an alarm system on the heart
             and an escape hatch in the head.
It was as spontaneous
as a military campaign.
      I love in small amounts
        like a sick man sipping whiskey.
Hope was sensibly bracketed. Is there any other way?
      Each day was lived within its limits.
        Each job swallowed quickly.
        Perhaps it was not all-out embracement
                of life—
        the position of crucifixion—
      but neither was it the hunched
        and jabbing stance of the boxer.
   There was courtesy   and consideration
      and manners.
It was not that bad.
      What's more—it was necessary.
      What's important—it was mine.
Now this.
This thing   this feeling
     This unpardonable intrusion
        which had no part to play
        but played it anyway
   All those things scrupulously screened out
            want in.
And I can sense it coming,
      a second coming,
        a second shattering.
   Someone   Something   is at me once more,
        mocking my defenses,
     wrenching my soul.
        God damn it!
Is it you again, Lord?

      —JOHN SHEA (a previously unpublished poem,
         used with the permission of the poet)

What is one to make of such extraordinary, vivid, and apparently overwhelming phenomena? William James notes four common characteristics in such experiences:

1. *Ineffability*. Mystical union is something that defies expression. It is a state of feeling that must be directly experienced and cannot be transferred or imparted to others. In James' words,

> One must have musical ears to know the value of a symphony; one must have been in love one's self to understand a lover's state of mind. Lacking the heart or ear, we cannot interpret the musician or the lover justly, and are even likely to consider him weak-minded or absurd. The mystic finds that most of us accord to his experiences an equally incompetent treatment [James, 1958: 293].

2. *Noetic quality*. The mystic has an overwhelming experience of understanding. He sees things with a fantastic clarity. (This is a point that is reported very often in experiences of drug-induced ecstasy.) Maslow tells us that in the "peak-experiences" he studied, the person involved sees the unity of the universe and his own integration with it. One need only read Teilhard de Chardin's *Letters from a Traveller* to realize that he was a mystic whose entire world view, so brilliantly expressed in many books, was simply an attempt to explicate a profound mystical insight. In James' words: "They are states of insights into depths of truth unplumbed by the discursive intellect. They are illuminations, revelations, full of significance and importance, all inarticulate though they remain; and as a rule they carry with them a curious sense of authority for aftertime" (James, 1958: 293).

3. *Transiency*. The mystical experience is transient. In her empirical research Marghanita Laski reports that the ecstatic interlude was very brief indeed—a few moments, a few minutes at the most—though there was an added time of "coming back down to earth" after the episode. James comments: "Mystical states cannot be sustained for long. Except in rare instances, half an hour, or at most an hour or two, seems to be the limit beyond which they fade into the light of common day" (James, 1958: 293). I suspect that he includes in his definition not only the moments of ecstasy themselves but that which Laski calls "the afterglow." When one's experience has "faded into the light of common day," then even the aftereffects have pretty well vanished, and it may be difficult to even remember what the experience was like. As James says, "Often, when faded, their quality can but imperfectly be reproduced in memory; but when they recur it is recognized; and from one recurrence to another it is susceptible of continuous development in what is felt as inner richness and importance" (James, 1958: 193). There is, then, some kind of continuity between such experiences, though when one is not immediately involved in the experience, the thread of continuity seems lost; in fact, it is there, though unrecognized.

4. Finally, mystical experiences are marked by *passivity*. There may be all sorts of things one may do to induce a mystical experience—prayer, meditation, hypnosis, listening to music, taking drugs, imposing intense discipline on the

senses—but these are all by way of preparation; they merely put one in a state where something else seems to happen, where another power seems to take over. As James observes:

> Although the oncoming of mystical states may be facilitated by preliminary voluntary operations, as by fixing the attention, or going through certain bodily performances, or in other ways which manuals of mysticism prescribe; yet when the characteristic sort of consciousness once has set in, the mystic feels as if his own will were in abeyance, and indeed sometimes as if he were grasped and held by a superior power [James, 1958: 193].

Something besides the conscious, self-controlling reality principle is operating. According to the great mystics of the Christian tradition, God himself intervenes. But while I believe that in a certain sense such an assertion might be the truth, one need not postulate some special divine intervention. In fact, what is happening is that deep powers in the human personality, normally latent, take over and produce in us experiences of knowledge and insight that are simply not available in daily life. But more of that in a later section.

In another mysticism classic, Richard M. Bucke, writing in 1901 and himself, unlike James, a mystic, describes a "cosmic consciousness" that is similar to the paradigm of James:

1. "The person, suddenly, without warning, has a sense of being immersed in a flame, or rose-colored cloud, or perhaps rather a sense that the mind is itself filled with such a cloud of haze" (Bucke, 1972: 86). (This experience of light, though not reported by all mystics, seem to be widespread. Indeed, as Mircea Eliade notes, it is to be found in almost all other cultures. So, too, is the sense of being "caught in flame." See, for example, Richard Rolle, *The Fire of Love*, Penguin edition, 1972.)

2. The ecstatic is possessed by joy, for he perceives that all things are well. As Bucke puts it.

> He is, as it were, bathed in an emotion of joy, assurance, triumph, "salvation." The last word is not strictly correct if taken in its ordinary sense, for the feeling, when fully developed, is not that a particular act of salvation is affected, but that no special "salvation" is needed, the scheme upon which the world is built, being itself sufficient [Bucke, 1972:87].

3. Bucke also records, as does James, an experience of intellectual illumination: "Like a flash there is presented . . . a clear conception (a vision) in outline of the meaning and drift of the universe. He does not come to believe merely; but he sees and knows that the cosmos, which to the Self-Conscious mind seems to be made up of dead matter, is in fact far otherwise—is in very truth a living presence (Bucke, 1972: 87). Bucke adds later,

> He sees that the life which is in man is eternal, as all life is eternal; that the soul of man is as immortal as God is; that the universe is so built and ordered that without and peradventure all things work together for the good of each and all; that the foundation principle of the world is what we call love, and that the happiness of every individual is in the long run absolutely certain [Bucke, 1972: 87].

Bucke wrote from within the Christian religious tradition. Mystics almost universally report an "illumination" as part of their experience, but it is usually an illumination within the context of the world view to which they are committed (or which they have absorbed through their culture). As Marghanita Laski's research makes clear, not all mystics are religious men and women, and for many of them the illumination is not necessarily a confirmation of the benignity or graciousness of the universe. And some mystical experiences, especially those that are drug-induced, lead to a very pessimistic or even despairing world view.

4. Bucke also contends that in the moment of Cosmic Consciousness there comes "a sense of immortality," an "elimination of the fear of death" and "the sense of sin," and, finally, even that it adds "change to the personality" and a change in the appearance that may "amount to a veritable 'transfiguration'" (Bucke, 1972: 88–89). All of this, he argues, occurs because the mystic knows without learning and from the mere fact of his illumination "(1) that the universe is not a dead machine but a living presence; (2) that in its essence and tendency it is infinitely good; (3) that individual existence is continuous beyond what is called death" (Bucke, 1972:90).

An Oriental mystic might choose to use different belief systems to explicate what happens in a mystical interlude. Thus, instead of describing life beyond death, he might choose to stress the integration of the self into some higher, more immutable reality. But there can be little doubt that both Bucke and the Oriental would be discussing what would be fundamentally the same kind of experience.

The British philosopher-mathematician-political expert and self-confessed universal genius Bertrand Russell was not sympathetic to mystics, but he did discuss them, seeing four characteristics of such experiences:

1. There is a better way of gaining information than through the senses.
2. There is a unity of all things.
3. There is no reality to time.
4. All evil is mere appearance [Russell, 1925: 9].

Of all the contemporary psychologists who have addressed themselves to mystical phenomena. Abraham Maslow (1972) is the most sympathetic and the most perceptive, His book *Religions, Values, and Peak-Experiences* (Ohio State University Press, 1964) ought to be read by those interested in mystical phenomena. The most characteristic quality of the peak-experience, according to Maslow, is that the universe is "perceived as an integrated and unified whole." This experience is not merely verbal or intellectual but pervades the being and is "so profound and shaking . . . that it can change the person's character . . . forever after" (Maslow, 1972: 357). When one perceives that the universe is a unified whole and that one has a place in it, one can overcome extreme mental stress, and Maslow reports that one of his patients was permanently cured of chronic anxiety neurosis and another of obsessional thoughts of suicide.

During the peak-experience, a kind of knowledge occurs that Maslow calls "B-cognition":

In the peak-experiences, we become more detached, more objective, and are more able to perceive the world as if it were independent not only of the perceiver but even of human beings in general. The perceiver can more readily look upon nature as if it were there in itself and for itself, not simply as if it were a human playground put there for human purposes. He can more easily refrain from projecting human purposes upon it. In a word, he can see it in its own Being (as an end in itself) rather than as something to be used or something to be afraid of or something to wish for or to be reacted to in some other personal, human, self-centered way [Maslow, 1972: 359].

The person who has a peak-experience can be, at least temporarily, "self-forgetful, egoless, unselfish." He experiences a moment in which he is validated and self-justified. Despite the disorientation of time and space, he sees the world as beautiful, good, desirable, worthwhile, and is even able to accept and understand evil itself as having a proper place in the world. Maslow argues that the peak-experience is always a beautiful one, though he admits that his methods of research might reveal only raptures, failing to uncover experiences of pessimism and despair, which surely are part of drug-induced ecstasies and may also occur in "intellectual" ecstasies.

Maslow's peak-experiences are eminently positive:

In the peak-experience, such emotions as wonder, awe, reverence, humility, surrender, and even worship before the greatness of the experience are often reported. This may go so far as to involve thoughts of death in a peculiar way. Peak-experiences can be so wonderful that they can parallel the experience of dying, that is of an eager and happy dying. It is a kind of reconciliation and acceptance of death. Scientists have never considered as a scientific problem the question of the "good death"; but here in these experiences, we discover a parallel to what has been considered to be the religious attitude toward death, i.e., humility or dignity before it, willingness to accept it, possibly even a happiness with it [Maslow, 1972: 362].

Maslow goes on to say that in "peak-experiences, the dichotomies, polarities, and conflicts of life are transcended or resolved" (Maslow, 1972: 362). There is a loss, though transient, of fear, anxiety, inhibition, of defense and control, of perplexity, confusion, conflict, of delay and restraint. The profound fear of disintegration, of insanity, of death, all tend to disappear for the moment. For Maslow, the peak-experience is "a visit to a personally defined heaven from which the person then returns to earth." Upon his return, the person "feels himself more than at other times to be the responsible, active, the creative center of his own activities and of his own perceptions, more self-determined, more of a free agent, with more 'free will' than at other times" (Maslow, 1972: 362–363).

Until recently psychologists have been much less tolerant of mystical experience than Maslow; mostly they seem to have devoted considerable energy to "explaining" it, which usually means explaining it away. Although the alleged mystical revival has persuaded some psychologists on the fringes of the counterculture to be more sympathetic to the mystic, hostility toward him still persists. Thus, for example, in an article in *Psychedelic Drugs*, Mortimer Ostow concludes by seeing mysticism as a result of the same psychic mechanism as psychosis:

> Antinomianism, mysticism and psychosis share the same psychic mechanism, namely, disparagement and abandonment of the world in which the individual lives, followed by a commitment to a "new world." They differ in the degree to which this process is pursued in concert with others; in the degree to which the change in attitude is reflected in overt action; and in the degree to which the process is initiated by personal idiosyncratic difficulty as contrasted with response to excessive social pressure. All three modes may be facilitated by the use of hallucinogenic drugs because these drugs facilitate the kind of mental dissociation which is involved in the two-phase process which is common to all. The drugs produce this mental dissociation by impairing the function of the temporal lobe mechanism which converts perception in the service of instinctual need to cognitive apperception in the service of intellectual function and true object relation [Ostow, 1969: 185].

And in a more recent article yet to be published, Ostow delivers a devastating critique of mysticism as "primary narcissism":

> Confronted with an inacceptable [sic] reality, intrapsychic, personal or social, the individual turns his back on that reality, excluding it from his consciousness and psychically destroying it. He replaces it with a new inner reality which he has so designed that it gratifies rather than frustrates him. This process represents a rebirth, a return to a state of mind characteristic of his infancy, when he was able to deal with frustration and disappointment by retreating to a world of fantasy and when he was blessed with a firm and intimate union with his parents [Ostow, 1974: 8].

Ostow says later:

> He reinterprets what he sees of the external world as a representation of the inner world and thereby he makes it possible for himself to tolerate the external world. In a sense, the latter is made more palatable by being "flavored" by the inner world and its affects [Ostow, 1974: 10].

Mysticism in Ostow's view is not entirely schizophrenic:

> While the mystic may seem to be following in the footsteps of the schizophrenic in that he retreats from outer reality to inner reality, he does not go all the way in his retreat: he differs from the schizophrenic in three important ways. First, his retreat is facultative rather than obligatory. Second, it is partial rather than complete. Third, he finds it possible, frequently desirable, to associate with the others who share his view of the world, that is, he participates in mystical fraternities. Schizophrenics, on the other hand, are rarely able to form or maintain affectionate ties with others [Ostow, 1974: 12].

Ostow's paper, like so much psychoanalytic literature, is innocent of evidence. Presumably one is given his wisdom distilled from clinical experience. Still, it would be nice to have data. Or as Kurt Reinhardt observes,

> there is this important difference [between mystical and pathological states of mind]: while the exaltation, the mental and emotional strain and the patterns of

thinking and doing that are observed in connection with several forms of mental disease are in all instances followed by distraction, exhaustion, and a general impoverishment of the mind, the genuine mystical experience brings in its wake effects of a totally different kind: a simplicity of mind that derives from a rich and deeply recollected mental activity, and a heightened intensity of purpose and resolve [Reinhardt, 1957: VII].

One must search extensively through the sociological literature to find even the slightest hint that there are such things as mystic experience. Bourque (1969) and Bourque and Back (1970, 1971) have studied "transcendental experiences." Marghanita Laski (1968) did an amateur though intelligent study of a nonrepresentative sample of friends and acquaintances. Philip Ennis (1967) has written a theoretical article on ecstatic experiences. Beyond these few, however, sociologists seem to be uninterested in the subject. Ennis notes that most of the idols to whom sociologists burn incense (Marx, Freud, Weber, Durkheim, Mannheim) were all aware of the phenomenon of "oceanic" experiences. Our own probing and poking amongst our colleagues would suggest that not all of them are as insensitive to the paranormal or the mystical as the two who directed the research described in this monograph. Still it seems fair to say that the generally implicit assumption among orthodox social scientists, particularly among sociologists, is that ecstasy may be interesting if you are concerned with drugs or the counterculture, but that it is not sufficiently widespread in American society to justify the collection of systematic data on the subject. If one is studying Bali, then, yes, of course one would be interested in ecstasy, but in the United States of America? Most people are watching television.

Let us make clear the assumptions of our own research:

1. We were prepared to take the ecstatic at his own word that his experience is cognitive. He assures us that he *sees,* that indeed he sees things the way they *really are.* It is up to the psychologists of perception to determine just what perceptual phenomena are involved (and they should tell us that on the basis of research, not a priori reasoning). It is up to the philosophers and theologians to tell us whether what the ecstatic thinks he sees is really the way things really are. We are interested in the correlates, the antecedents, and the consequences of such experiences. And we assume that the experience will have antecedents and consequences whether the mystical experience is a breaking through to the ultimate reality or merely a psychotic episode.

2. We also would define the ecstatic experience as "religious." It is not ecclesiastical or doctrinal in the formal sense, but religious as it has been defined by Thomas Luckmann (1967) and Clifford Geertz (1966,1969): religion is a set of symbols that purport to provide a unique interpretive scheme to explain the ultimate reality. The mystic is religious whether he goes to church or not, whether he professes any doctrine or not, because he claims to have seen and to know the way things really are. His cognition in the ecstatic interlude is religious cognition in the sense that it is a cognition of the ultimate order of things.

3. Like all experiences the ecstatic interlude has its antecedents in the respondent's past. Since we have defined it as a religious experience in the Geertzian and Luckmannian sense, we also assume that the ecstatic experience,

like all religious phenomena, will be strongly influenced by the relationships among the triad of mother, father, and child in the infancy, childhood, and adolescent years. It will be affected by the quantity and quality of the religious life of the parents.

4. We also assume that there will be consequences in attitudes and behaviors from such experiences, at least for those who have them frequently. "Ethos," as Geertz remarked, "is the flip-side of the coin of mythos." Our notions of how one ought to behave are direct consequences of our convictions about the nature of the cosmos in which we find ourselves constrained to behave. If the ecstatic experience is as powerful as those who have experienced it claim, there seems every reason to assume that at least those who have such experiences frequently will be different in some fashion in their values and behaviors from those who do not.

5. Finally, we assume that—and here we have the evidence of the Bourque and Back research—ecstatic experience is not all that infrequent in American society. That social science does not examine a phenomenon does not compel us to conclude that the phenomenon does not exist.

One can approach this enterprise with alternative sets of hypotheses culled from the disorganized and impressionistic literature on the subject.

1. The ecstatic is an oppressed, unhappy, rigid person who is looking for reassurance and release, which his interlude of self-induced withdrawal provides.

2. The ecstatic is one who has had a "peak-experience" that unleashes, however temporarily, the most creative and generous human resources.

First of all, Table 1 shows that mystical experience (insofar as it is measured by our question) is relatively widespread in the population. Thirty-five percent of the American people report that they have had such an experience at least once or twice. Twelve percent report it "several times," and five percent "often." Some seventy million Americans, then, have experienced some kind of ecstatic interlude (in the literal sense of the word that they were "lifted out of themselves"). Ten million people have these experiences frequently. It is problematic, of course, that all seventy million who have had such experiences, or even the ten million who have them frequently, have undergone the intense ecstatic interludes described in the beginning of this section. In a subsequent section we shall try to sort out those whose experiences have apparently been intense and who might well fit into the category of ecstatic described by James, Russell, Bucke, and Maslow.

There is (Table 2) some correlation between mystical experience and age. Unlike those who experience psi, the mystics are somewhat more likely to be older, with the most frequent report of such experiences coming from those who are in their fifties (43 percent). It is worth noting, however, that the differences are not great, and that those in their seventies are only three percentage points more likely to report a mystical experience than those in their teens. However, even the moderate correlation with age suggests that the mystical revival among the young may be simply a figment of the journalistic imagination.

TABLE 1
Mystical Experiences in a National Sample of Americans

Questionnaire Item	Response				
	Never in My Life	Once or Twice	Several Times	Often	I Cannot Answer This Question
Have you ever felt as though you were very close to a powerful, spiritual force that seemed to lift you out of yourself ...	61	18	12	5	3

TABLE 2
Mystical Experiences of Americans by Age

(PERCENT EVER)	
Age	Mystical Experience
Teens (54)	32
Twenties (388)	33
Thirties (253)	33
Forties (246)	38
Fifties (288)	43
Sixties (184)	36
Seventies (113)	35
Average	36

Protestants (Table 3) and "others" are the most likely to report a mystical experience (in excess of two-fifths of both groups). Jews are less likely than Protestants to have had such interludes, but both Jews and those with no religion are still more likely than Catholics to have them. As Professor McCready remarked to me, "If you have Canon Law and an infallible pope, maybe you don't need mystical experience." Surely one would not know from the education most contemporary Catholics receive that Catholicism presides over an

TABLE 3

Mystical Experiences of Americans by Religious Affiliation, Protestant Denomination, and Religio-Ethnicity

(PERCENT EVER)

Affiliation	Percent	Protestant Denomination	Percent	Religio-Ethnicity	Percent
Protestant (889)	43	Baptist (282)	43	Protestant British (167)	45
Catholic (361)	24	Methodist (181)	40	German (131)	37
Jew (29)	29	Lutheran (101)	37	Scandinavian (47)	34
Other (98)	45	Presbyterian (74)	46	Irish (72)	51
None (46)	29	Episcopalian (35)	50	American (87)	40
		Other (173)	47	Catholic Irish (47)	38
		No denomination (40)	52	German (48)	19
				Italian (52)	25
				Polish (43)	18
				Spanish-speaking (33)	15
				Jew (28)	27

ancient mystical heritage. Indeed, some of the greatest of the medieval mystics were English Catholics.

One might expect that the Baptists and the fundamentalists would be most likely to have mystical experiences. In fact, though, it is the nondenominational Protestants and the Episcopalians who are the most likely to report ecstatic interludes. Indeed more than half of both groups have had such experiences. Both the Presbyterians and the "other" Protestants are more likely to experience ecstasy than are Baptists. The notion of mysticism as a fundamentalist experience is badly shaken in this table.

If mystics came from socially oppressed groups, one would expect them to be disproportionately young, female, black, lower income. In fact, however, mystics are more likely to be over forty, male, college-educated, and making over $10,000 a year (Table 4). They are, however, substantially more likely to be black (.52) and to be Protestant (.53).

TABLE 4

Measures of Association Between Mystical Experiences "Often" and Demographic Variables, Family Relationships, and Life Satisfaction and Religious Ladders

(YULE'S Q)

Demographic Variables	Yule's Q	Family Relationship	Yule's Q	Life Phase	Life Satisfaction[a]	Religious Satisfaction[b]
Age (over 40)	.35***	Closeness between mother and father	.04	Child	.15	.16
Sex (female)	-.19*	Closeness between respondent and mother	.29**	Teenager	.32***	.47***
Race (black)	.52***	Closeness between respondent and father	.19*	Now	.31***	.68***
Religion (Protestant)	.53***	Mother's church attendance almost every week or more	.00	Five years from now	.33***	.73***
Education (college)	.33***	Father's church attendance almost every week or more	.44***			
Income (over $10,000)	.18*	Joyousness of father's religion	.36***			
		Joyousness of mother's religion	.43***			
n = (75) (1392)						

[a] A ten-point scale between "the best your life could be" and "the worst your life could be."
[b] A ten-point scale between "the most religious you could be" and "the least religious you could be."
*** = .001
** = .01
* = .05

Those who think of mystics as being unhappy, maladjusted people seeking release would predict that mystics come from rigid, harsh, and inflexible families. Our own assumptions, based on the theoretical perspective we derived from the work of Luckmann and Geertz and from McCready's (1973) research led us to expect, rather, a background of warm family relationship and a joyous approach to religion. Table 4 seems to support our approach. While there is no association between ecstasy and closeness between parents (much to our surprise), there are strong associations with closeness between the respondent and parents, with mother's church attendance, and with the joyousness of both parents' religious approach (at least as the respondent remembered that approach).

McCready's research has indicated that for the transmission of religious behavior the father is considerably more important than the mother. However, Table 4 suggests that as far as ectasy in adult life goes, the mother may well be more important than the father. In any case, growing up in a supportive and religiously joyous family atmosphere turns out to be conducive to frequent mystical experience.

It is also conducive to a general satisfaction with one's life (Table 4). As a child the mystic was notably above the average in his life satisfactions, but in the teen years and at "the present time," as well as in his expectations for five years from now, he is substantially above the average. Furthermore, while he does not remember his childhood to be more religious than the rest of our respondents, his adolescence, his present, and his future religious situation are described as substantially more religious than the rest of the population. The fact that both his satisfaction and his religious behavior seem to move notably above the average in his adolescent years suggests the possibility that mystical experiences may have begun then, or perhaps may have been more self-consciously perceived at that time. (One mystic we interviewed cannot recall a time in his life when he did not have such experiences.) Much of the autobiographical literature of mystics does indeed begin with a description of an adolescent experience.

Our data scarcely suggest repressed, unhappy, rigid, guilt-ridden, puzzled people. It could well be, of course, that the conflicts are deeply repressed in their personalities. It is also difficult to say whether the mystical experience induced life satisfaction or whether a higher life satisfaction created a personality open to mystical experience. But our data at least raise the possibility that mysticism may well be good for you. Surely the findings presented in Table 5 would confirm such a hunch.

There is a correlation of .34 between mystical experience and positive affect on the Bradburn psychological well-being scale (Bradburn and Caplovitz, 1965) and a correlation of $-.31$ on a negative affect scale (which means that mystics are low on negative affect). The result of this combination is a very high .4 association between mystical experience and balance affect or "happiness." While their marriages are no better and no worse than the rest of the population, the frequent mystic reports a state of psychological well-being substantially higher than the national average. We would suggest that this is a finding of considerable importance.

TABLE 5

Measures of Association Between Mystical Experience "Often" and Psychological Well-Being, Certain Social Values, and Basic Belief Systems

	(YULE'S Q)
Psychological Well-Being[a]	
Positive affect	.34***
Negative affect	−.31***
Balance affect	.40***
Positive marriage	.09
Negative marriage	.04
Marriage balance	.05
Certain Social Values	
Racism	−.27**
Conservative authoritarianism	−.09
Liberal authoritarianism	−.13
Basic Belief Systems	
Agnosticism	−.31***
Survival	.72***
Religious optimism	.49***
Hopefulness	.44***
Secular optimism	.19*
Gratitude	.04

[a]Bradburn "happiness" Scales (Brandburn, 1969)
*** = .001
* = .05

Furthermore, white mystics are also substantially less likely to be racist than the national population (Table 5). Whether mystical interludes "cause" their racial enlightenment or whether tolerance and openness to mystical experience are both related to antecedent cultural and psychological factors is difficult to say on the basis of our survey. Whatever the flow of causality, the negative correlation between ecstasy and racism seems to be another refutation of the theory that ecstatics are rigid, haunted, unhappy people.

We would also expect that if the basic belief system measures do indeed get at fundamental orientations toward the cosmos, there would be relationships between these belief systems and mystical experience. More specifically we would expect those who are high on the religious optimism and survival scales to be more likely to have such experiences; those high on the agnosticism scales would be less likely to have them. It also seemed reasonable to assume that those with high survival measures would be the most likely of all to have such experiences because their approach to religion suggests more depth than the easily optimistic approaches. The data in Table 5 generally support these assumptions.

TABLE 6

Triggers of Mystical Experience for Those who have had One or More

Trigger	Percent
Listening to music	49
Prayer	48
Beauties of nature such as sunset	45
Moments of quiet reflection	42
Attending church service	41
Listening to sermon	40
Watching little children	34
Reading the Bible	31
Being alone in church	30
Reading a poem or a novel	21
Childbirth	20
Sexual lovemaking	18
Your own creative work	17
Looking at a painting	15
Something else	13
Physical exercise	1
Drugs	0

It is those who score high on survival and on religious optimism who are the most likely to be frequent mystics. In addition, there is a very high correlation (.72) between the survival scale and a mystical experience. One would be hard put to say with certainty which way the relationship runs. Are hopeful people more likely to be open to ecstatic experience, or are those who have had ecstatic experiences more hopeful as a result? We suspect that the childhood religious environment produces a hopeful religious orientation which in turn creates an openness to mystical experience which then deepens and strengthens hope for survival.

We might add in passing that the relationship reported in Table 5 provides some validation for the basic belief system measures themselves. One would expect that if the basic belief scales had any use at all they would differentiate on mystics who are in one respect "religiously sensitive" individuals. Our expectations seem to be borne out.

There is probably no way of wording a question about a mystical experience that will be perfectly satisfactory—surely not one that could be administered in a national survey. There are, we suppose, some people who can get profoundly shook up emotionally when a 46-year-old George Blanda puts the ball between the uprights for the ten thousandth time, or when Henry Aaron knocks the baseball over the center field wall for the seven hundred and fifteenth time or so. We therefore tried to determine what triggered the experience and how people would describe it (or them). Table 6 presents the rank order of triggers (for all of those who had at least one mystical experience). The beauties of nature, moments of

TABLE 7

"Descriptors" of Mystical Experience for Those who have had One or More

"Descriptor"	Percent
A feeling of deep and profound peace	55
A certainty that all things would work out for the good	48
Sense of my own need to contribute to others	43
A conviction that love is at the center of everything	43
Sense of joy and laughter	43
An experience of great emotional intensity	38
A great increase in my understanding and knowledge	32
A sense of the unity of everything and my own part in it	29
A sense of a new life or living in a new world	27
A confidence in my own personal survival	27
A feeling that I couldn't possibly describe what was happening to me	26
The sense that all the universe is alive	25
The sensation that my personality has been taken over by something much more powerful than I am	24
A sense of tremendous personal expansion, either psychological or physical	22
A sensation of warmth or fire	22
A sense of being alone	19
A loss of concern about worldly problems	19
A sense that I was being bathed in light	14
A feeling of desolation	8
Something else	4

quiet reflection, church services and sermons were all mentioned by two-fifths of those who had such experiences. Interestingly enough, none of our sample reported that the experience was drug-induced, suggesting at least the possibility that mysticism need not rely on hallucinogenic drugs at all.

Among the descriptions of mystical experience (Table 7), feelings of peace, a certainty that all things work out, a sense of need to contribute to others, a conviction that love is the center of everything, and a sense of joy and laughter were mentioned by more than two-fifths of those who had had such experiences—a finding in keeping with Abraham Maslow's descriptions of core religious experiences, as well as many of the autobiographical accounts of the mystics themselves. It is interesting to note that one-fifth of the respondents reported a sense of being alone, and eight percent a feeling of desolation. We will investigate this "dark night of the soul" aspect of mysticism later.

Most of the literature on mysticism suggests that the experience itself is brief, although there may be a halo effect before it and a relatively lengthy pleasant period of "coming back down to earth" after it. Table 8 makes clear that most of those who have had ecstatic experiences recalled them as being relatively brief. More than 60 percent report that they were of less than an hour's duration, and 37 percent said the experience lasted for only a few minutes.

TABLE 8

Duration of Mystical
Experience (Percent)

A few minutes or less	37
Ten or fifteen minutes	13
Half an hour	6
An hour	5
Several hours	9
A day or more	21
No answer	8

In summary, the data we have presented in this section indicate that ecstatic interludes are widespread in the population and that they are described by those who have experienced them in terms not unlike those used to describe the "classic" mystical episodes with which we began the section. No evidence was found in our data to confirm the image of the mystic as someone who is escaping from reality or as a quasi-schizophrenic. Mystics (unlike psychics) are more likely to be male; they are also more likely to be better educated than nonmystics, more successful economically, less racist, and substantially higher on scores of psychological well-being. It may be argued by those who think the mystics are running away from reality that their flight has been so successful that they look like people who have made a healthy, psychologically satisfying adjustment to reality. If this is the case, no doubt the respondents themselves are also deceived about their flight from reality, and no survey could uncover their psychological maladjustment; one would need either personality tests or in-depth interviews.

Of course, if the high levels of psychological well-being reported by our mystic respondents represent a successful, escape from the torments of life on the planet earth, we should all be lucky to find such an effective method of coping!

Section

4

FOLK RELIGION

The lofty theological precepts and the elegant ceremonials that characterize the great world religions often seem insufficient to their followers. They need something more to cope with the problems and uncertainties of life. The "totally other" may be admirable, but often She or He does not seem inclined to help His or Her followers deal with daily challenges and anxieties. So people return to older religious forms, superstitious and magical, which have persisted from the nature religions and coexist with the doctrines and practices of the world religions. When a seemingly abstract God does not reply, people ask why not and turn to a more concrete God who seems perfectly willing to make a deal with you.

The Pygmy people of the rain forest leave a basket of food for their god so that he will continue to like them. They thus diminish the uncertainty of life—how much more problematic it would be if they didn't leave the food! So with the folk religionists. They reduce the anxieties of life by participating in rituals and practices that guarantee that a god will take care of them no matter what the danger. The selections in this section that describe the Marian folk cults all emphasize that the cult is a response to danger—the plague, the Moors, Godless Liberalism, Communism, or the hostility of Americans to the immigrants. The folk religions seek the reassurance of magic especially in troubled times, perhaps as a form of bet-hedging against the possibility that the God of the universal religious has forgotten about them or perhaps is busy elsewhere.

The folk religionist seeks an advantage in the game of life, special knowledge and special power which, as it were, will give her or him a head start.

Reading 14

....

THE PERSISTENCE OF FOLK RELIGION—
GUSTAV MENSCHING

Folk religion is a term that normally means the survival of residues of past religion into the present world, where they mix either with universal religions or secularism to provide an alternative religion for those who are dissatisfied with the options. The various blends of West African religion, Christianity, and secularism in contemporary Brazil, such as the Machumbe cult or the Voodoo cult in Haiti, are examples that are more pagan than Christian. The cult of the Lady of Guadeloupe (a pagan goddess converted to Christianity in Spain before she migrated to Mexico) seems to come down on the Christian side of the line.

The two essays by Gustav Mensching add another meaning to the word. Folk religion in its more primary sense is the religion of a folk, of a community, of a clan or a tribe. The deity belongs to the tribe, indeed is virtually a member of the tribe and hence no deep reflection is necessary on the nature of the god or of the possibility that he might be shared with others. In Mensching's view, this simple, concrete, local religion may evolve into something more elaborate, reflective, and even universal as the tribe acquires the time and the experience to reflect on the nature of the deity. The tough old Semitic warrior god of the pre-Sinai Hebrews must come a long way to be the God of the Hebrew prophets, who belongs to no people and to all peoples, who demands ethical justice instead of sacrifices, and who suffers because of, in, and for His people.

But the development of a universal religion does not mean the end of folk religion. It persists as a residue, espically attractive and appealing, because of its simplicity and its promises, to the modern masses who are cut off from the high religion of their churches.

One may doubt that there is a need to postulate an alienated "mass" to account for folk religion in the modern world. The nice thing about the god of the folk is that you can deal with him. He is responsive to and can be coerced by your magic. You say the right prayers, offer the right gifts, invoke the right lesser deities, and He will oblige by giving you what you want as His end of the bargain.

Yahweh in his later forms would not play the game that way. Nor would the other universalistic deities who emerged in the millennium before the common era, in what Karl Jaspers the German philosopher calls the "axial era"—the era of the world religions.

There are many times in the course of a human life for which and many humans for whom a God who is free of matter and who asserts passionate love, but leaves you in a state of ambiguity, is not acceptable. At those times and for those people, the folk god is an attractive alternative, and magic instead of ethical justice seems by far the better way to go. As subsequent readings in this section will show, folk religion is alive and well.

Questions for Reflection and Discussion

1. Do folk religions necessarily become universal religions? Under what circumstances do they become universal?
2. Why do surviving folk religions have so much appeal?
3. The examples in this section are mostly of Catholic folk religions. Are there any Protestant or Jewish or Islamic folk cults?
4. Why is Catholicism apparently prone to the invasion of folk superstitions?

Part 1

FOLK AND UNIVERSAL RELIGION
Gustav Mensching

1. FOLK RELIGION

We distinguish basic structures of religion and religious types within them. We come upon the phenomenon of basic structures when we investigate the historical circumstance that there are some religions which are confined to a single folk and others which have spread among many peoples. There are *folk religions* and *world religions*. The difference thus suggested among historical religions by no means has to do with territorial diffusion alone. Rather it rests upon a deeper structural differentiation of religion itself.

First it must be noted that, in folk religion of every kind, the *folk*, or in nature-religion the tribe, but in any case a vital community, is the carrier of the religion. The individual has not yet discovered himself but has a life quite bound up with that of the collectivity. On this foundation the historically earliest religious communities are of the vital type: family—and house—community, sib

Source: Gustav Mensching, "Folk and Universal Religion" (from *Die Religion,* Curt E. Schwab, Stuttgart, 1959, 65–77).

and tribe, folk and state. In early religion there are no specific religious communities aside from the vital, given communities of birth. But these vital communities for their part have a sacred stamp and are at the same time religious communities.

The second structural factor in folk religion is that in that religion the "salvation" afforded consists in the condition of positive relationships of the folk community to the divinities that appertain to it. This condition of salvation of the folk community, into which the individual is born, and whose maintenance is the duty of the members of the folk society, is a mystic "life" which binds all together and to separate one's self from which means actual death. "The human being who precedes history or exists outside it leads . . . a double life. One is the unheeded life whose beginning is actual birth . . . the other is the true life, which begins with a rite . . . These two lives are not separate." (C. H. Ratschow, *Magie und Religion,* 1946, p. 43.)

The gods of folk religion are exclusively related to a particular folk and limited to that folk as their province of domination, so to put it. This holds not only for the folk as a whole but also for the vital communities that constitute it: family and sib, tribe and clan also have their proper gods. These gods accordingly lack universality. The idea of one's own gods is thus wholly reconcilable with the view that other peoples have gods proper to them. In the Israelite religion, for example, the claim of the Moabites against that of the Israelite God Jahweh is delimited and recognized. But there prevails between the folk and its divinities a strictly and exclusively binding relationship. Defection to foreign divinities is, thus, repeatedly designated in Israel as seriously sinful. Folk religion is in consequence of this by no means tolerant. But we are confronted by a typically folk-religious intolerance which I designate as inner-religious intolerance; for toward the outside one is tolerant insofar as one does not dispute the existence or right to existence of foreign gods.

The peculiarity of the particular folk involved and the relationship to the folk is substantially more clearly marked out in folk religion than in the universal religions. While the universal religions are in principle supra-national and owe their diffusion and ability to diffuse to this supra-national character, there is naturally and quite directly reflected in the folk religions the special spirit of the folk. This is especially clear (other factors, such as peculiarity of cultus, outlook on the gods, and the like, aside) in what is considered good and bad, in a word in *folk-religious* ethics. In the Teutonic religion, for example, ethical values are related to the weal and woe of the sib, so that the sib is the value standard of good and bad. The same relationship is present in the pre-Mohammedan folk religion of the Arabic tribes. And in Japanese Shinto serious "celestial sins" consist in offense against the interests of the folk community. The "ten commandments" of the Old Testament, also, are explicit folk-law, in which in the fourth commandment the continued existence of the folk is made contingent upon proper conduct toward father and mother and thus upon maintenance of the family. But aside from this relationship of ethic to folk, it may be shown in detail through comparison of the value-tables of different folk religions that, through "preference" of one value over other recognized ethical values, the special spirit of the individual folk religion is determined. As another characteristic of the folk-religious ethic and thereby of the structure of the folk religion itself may be added the circumstance that the recognized ethical values (like the idea of God itself) still neither have nor claim universal validity. The above stressed folk connection of ethics thus means not only that values are related to the welfare and security of the folk but also that they have validity only within the domain of the particular folk. The stranger to folk and sib has no claim to friendly conduct: he is "hostis" (stranger and enemy), and the laws of behavior valid within the folk context are of no effect in relation to him. There is also lacking within the folk religious context the perception of the universality of ethical values and of their *unconditioned* validity—a validity unrestricted by the object of the ethical act or disposition. Good and evil are not yet absolute good and evil, but still the relatively good and evil, that which is valuable or harmful for the welfare and survival of the folk.

As the external circumstance of restriction to a folk points to fundamental structures which determine the character and limits of folk religion, so on the other hand the observation of the external *fate* of the folk religion within the folk world leads to a far more important recognition of essential changes in human existence itself. A glance at the history of religion shows that nearly all the folk religions experienced the fate of being replaced by universal religions. In detail, this happened in different ways. We can distinguish three different ways of replacement of aboriginal folk religion through a universal religion.

One set of folk religions evolved in the course of their history, in their later period, universal tendencies that came out of themselves, although with a maintenance of their folk-determined limited form and their own folk-religious tradition. This is the case, for example, in India. Universal tendencies indeed emerge early in the Vedas. We already encounter the intuition of the One in the earlier Rigveda. The many folk gods disappear behind the One (whether personally or neutrally conceived) and become simply names for the One. "The singers designate what is merely one by many names—Agni, Mitra, Matarishvan." In the Upanishads the basic structure is already that of universal religion, but the folk-religious *form* has remained. And also in Hinduism, which essentially builds on the Vedic tradition, we deal with pure universal religion (aside from the primitive folk religion of the broad masses, which is also maintained in every universal religion as "folk belief"), but again in the form of folk religion. The folk-religious tradition is not overcome; but it no longer determines essence, although it continues to determine external form. Similarly the *Israelite* religion offers in its evolution the picture of a self-universalizing religion. The real folk religion was founded through Moses on the demonistic foundation that remains clearly visible in the Old Testament in the worship of animals, the dead, ancestors, trees, springs, and stars. Through Moses the individual tribes became a single folk with a conscious and religiously experienced fate under a common God, Jahweh. Jahweh is unequivocally the folk god of Israel.

Through the agency of the great prophets of the eighth century before Christ there begins the universalization of the Israelite religion. But this religion preserves its folk-religious form into the present. The folk religion of *Iran* also won through the prophet Zarathustra a universal character but kept its folk-religious form. In Greece, where every polis had its gods, it was the great tragedians who proclaimed a universal idea of God. Here indeed we have an example of the second form of universalization.

In a second set of folk religions universalization occurs as the folk religion is replaced or complemented by a foreign universal religion. This occurred, for example, in Greece by the agency of the mystery religions coming from abroad, which also came to Rome and appeared beside the Roman folk religion (the latter, for its part, never developed its own universal tendencies). The same process also occurred in Japan: the folk religion of Shintoism was complemented, from 552 A.D. on, by the foreign universal religion of Buddhism.

In a third set of folk religions, there occurred the establishment of a supranational *world religion*. On the ground of Indian folk religion Buddha founded Buddhism. On the ground of the Israelite folk religion and on that of the Arabic folk religion, Christianity and Islam were founded by Jesus and Mohammed respectively. Each of these three world religions came into a peculiar relationship to the field of its own folk-religious origin. The tension between Indian folk-religion and Buddhism led to the overcoming of Buddhism in the Indian field of origin. In the Israelite religious world also the tension, already present in the lifetime of Christianity's founder, between Israelite folk religion and Christianity, was preserved. In contrast to Buddhism in India, Christianity in Palestine never won a victory but remained a foreign religion which neither displaced nor complemented the original religion. But Buddhism, too, was influential in India only perhaps for a millennium. Then it wandered as a foreign religion into the Far East. Only on the ground of the Arabic folk religion did Islam come to replace the aboriginal religion.

In all cases, then, actual folk religion in religious history was replaced by universal religion. That occurred in a later time. The folk religions are early religions. But it is not enough simply to record this historical circumstance. It rests upon a structural change in the mode of existence of men themselves and thus upon *anthropological* presuppositions. There are precise correspondences between the mode of existence of early men and religious structure. Early man, as we may say briefly in connection with important work by G. van der Leeuw (*Der Primitive Mensch und die Religion,* 1937), lives in the unity of an undivided and unexamined life. He does not stand over against the world, but lives in it, and the fullness of powers that animate the world fills him also. In this stage, there is little that separates subject and object, or indeed object and object. Man is essentially participant in everything. The contours of things in the external world are fluid. In the depths of all phenomena and of man himself there is an ultimate essential identity. In brief, early man is not yet isolated from the elementary unity of life, has not yet fathomed himself as an ego and a self released from community and life-unity. Folk religion corresponds to this stage of human existence, for it is the religion of *unexamined elementary unity*. The various interpretations of the folk-religious stage of belief may be corrected from this perspective. One may characterize the stage of folk religion, with Paul, as a "time of ignorance," which was then overcome through the universal-religious knowledge of one's own religion. In terms of the science of religion it must be said that this theological interpretation does not do justice to historical circumstance. Anthropologically speaking, a universal religion would not have been possible in early times. We shall analyze the structure of universal religion in the next section. It will then be plain that as folk religion corresponded precisely to early human existence, so universal religion, which is a religion of later time, again corresponds to the *transformed* existence of recent man. The emergence of universal religion thus occurred in an historical moment in which it was a human necessity, since, to be sure, folk religion no longer answered man's condition.

But it is not only the flat theological interpretation of folk religion which now becomes corrected. The rationalistic interpretation of the course of religious history is corrected by the above perspective. Historical religions cannot be looked upon as variations, of essentially the same order, of a "natural religion," for there are profound structural differences among religions—differences that are left out of account in the abstraction of a meager "natural religion" as the common religion of man. The historical necessity of the transition from folk to universal religion may be perceived directly from the cognition of anthropological presuppositions.

2. UNIVERSAL RELIGION

In the analysis of universal religion, we may also begin with external phenomena which point to profound inner laws and factors. The universality of the religions of which we affirm that they also have an inner structural community is in the first place external: these religions go beyond the boundaries of their religio-historical field of origin or their folk or country and diffuse among many different peoples without regard to race, culture, speech, or other distinctiveness. There is still another observation that points from the external to concealed laws. It is not only in regard to space (diffusion to many lands and peoples) but also in regard to time that the phenomenon of universal religion presents itself to us as a problem. The universal religions emerge in the history of religion at nearly the same time. Rudolf Otto, in another connection and from different viewpoints, first referred to "the law of parallels in the history of religion." Otto speaks of the transition from myth to logos, from mythology to theology, and thinks that this significant step occurred nearly everywhere at the same time among civilized men—between 800 and 500 B.C. In my judgment, the phenomenon Otto had in view can be better described as a transition from the structure of folk religion to that of universal religion. In Greece, this transition took place in the period between Hesiod and Plato. Pythagoras founded his order in 530 B.C. Confucius died in China about 470 B.C. Lao-tse lived some centuries later, according to recent opinion. This development begins in India in the era of the Upanishads, about 800 B.C., and Buddha was alive in 500 B.C. In Israel also the same period is involved, for the prophets paved the way for the universalization of folk religion in the eighth century B.C. Even in Persia the reform of folk religion by Zarathustra probably falls in these same centuries. These parallels in time are strange. In the same centuries there stirs everywhere among men the longing for a new form of religion. What happened? Clearly, a *fundamental change in human existence* itself set in. But let us first be clear on what the structure of universal religion, which takes account of this altered situation in the human mode of existence, consists of.

The decisively new feature in the structure of universal religion is that in this religion it is no longer the collectivity, as in folk religion, but the *individual* who is the subject of religion. Whereas the individual in folk religion was a member of the over-arching community, through which he lived and in whose "sanctity" he participated, in all universal religion we encounter the individual who has become conscious of himself and presents distinctive religious problems.

For this is now the second fundamental factor: no longer is sanctity a given thing, sanctity that one could lose in folk religion in exceptional cases if one got detached from the salvation-community of folk and sib, but *the condition of non-salvation* is the given thing, and indeed a *personal* condition of non-salvation in which the individual finds himself. Salvation is desired, as is contact with divinity or the unity that is no longer given with membership in the great vital communities of sib and folk into which everyone is born. The vital community, indeed, lost its sacred character in later time and became profane. The individual himself perceives himself as detached from the numinous primitive ground of existence. Man did indeed become in growing measure master of the world and its powers as he became subject and the external world increasingly became object. But in his surrender to the world and its goods he lost elemental contact with the numinous world above. Therefore the individual must win anew a soteriological contact which had only to be cultivated and maintained in folk religion. Also on the ground of the individualized universal religion, in a later stage of organization, the effort is made to produce a situation analogous to that of folk religion, insofar as man wins salvation through membership in an objective soteriological organization (the church).

In universal religion *man* is the object of the message of salvation. Thereby a de-nationalization of religious concern takes place. We deal with the need for depth in human existence, flatly, and thus with every man's need. Universal religion is therefore not only externally universal, but has primarily an inner universality, in that it concerns everyone. And therefore in universal religion everywhere a universal offer of salvation is proclaimed over against the existing state of non-salvation. Salvation and man's existence depend on the taking up of this offer.

The universal message encounters a folk-differentiated humanity. The supranational proclamation of universal religion therefore had everywhere to be melted down. Re-minting and minting anew were necessary for all universal religions and were carried out everywhere in East and West. The universal message of salvation is consequently international in content, but in its form it appears in the history of religion in a variety of stampings, according to the spirit of the peoples it conquered. The folk-differentiation of mankind is thus no boundary for the diffusion of a universal religion; for, as the history of religion shows, it is certainly possible for other peoples to appropriate a universal religion which is foreign to them as regards its field of origin. Two thirds of mankind profess a foreign religion. The absolute limit of appropriation lies rather in men themselves, in their religious capacity for understanding or the lack thereof. The great founders of religions have meditated on the fact of their wide-reaching failure or of the downright unbelief which they encountered among men, and adduced an explanation correspondent with the basic character of their message. Buddha construed unbelief in such fashion as to understand it as a sign of immaturity in man's long journey of rebirth. Even the unbeliever will in time attain knowledge when he has attained the necessary stage of maturity. Jesus spoke of the calling to belief by the Father in Heaven, and similarly Mohammed conceived unbelief as the effect of a quite incalculable act of will on the part of the arbitrary Allah. But in any case there are assumed here firm barriers, immovable by men.

A further characteristic of universal religion lies in *the totality of its claim.* The religion of salvation claims the entire personality and existence of man. It is not a matter of modification on the periphery of human life, but of a profound level of existence, from out of which all sectors of human existence receive their new influence.

Folk religion also bound its members totally, for the existence of the secondary individual depended on the community of the folk, whose life was his life. In early religion also, man lives a full and redeemed life only when he lives a "united existence." This redemptive union, however, is given in antecedent folk-solidarity.

In the universal religion of later times there goes forth to the given isolation of the individual the message of salvation. This also aspires to achieve a "united existence," on a new basis, to be sure. But it can do so only if it penetrates to the depth where the disturbance of unity has taken place. Mysticism and prophecy, the two fundamental forms of universal religions, both claim, each in characteristic fashion, the whole man to the very roots of his existence: mysticism as it strives for the elimination of individual being, the merging of the individual in the One; prophecy as it seeks to re-establish the unity-in-belief (of the individual isolated and living remote from God) with the personally conceived savior–deity.

Universal religion, which has in actuality spread among numerous peoples, carries within itself the *tendency to diffusion.* In the pure folk religion, whose divinities are nationally and territorially delimited, there naturally does not exist the object of converting other peoples to one's own religion. On the contrary, the knowledge of one's own gods appears here as a value that puts one at an advantage over other people and that one would therefore rather keep secret than impart. Thus the Romans, for example, called out unknown gods from a besieged city in an act of "evocation" in order to take away divine aid from the besieged. In the folk religion with a universal content the tendency to diffusion is already manifest, as in Judaism, which in the time of Christ had conquered seven per cent of the inhabitants of the Roman Empire. This mission of Judaism broke down in view of the pure religious universalism of Christianity, since the

Jewish religion held firm to the specifically folk-religious demand of entrance into the national community of the Jews. On these grounds the substantially universal religion of the Jews could not become a world religion. The same is true of Confucianism, for this too represented specifically Chinese outlooks and claims, side by side with a substantial universality (especially in the realm of ethics). It is thus evident that everywhere that universal contents emerge in a folk religion a tendency to diffusion becomes apparent. But this tendency nevertheless fails: not by reason of historical accident but out of innermost necessity, for on the one hand the universal content has not yet attained the depth in which the universally unredeemed condition of the existential isolation of latter-day man is shown, and on the other this same content, insofar as it is already universal, has not yet transcended its national boundaries and so failed to find understanding among alien peoples.

In the case of genuine world religions, on the other hand, these conditions are fulfilled. They touch upon the unredeemed condition of *man* and transcend the nation. The tendency to diffusion is omnipresent in them and has been everywhere successfully realized, to be sure in differing degrees. The difference in intensity of the desire to missionize is contingent on the essential structure of the universal religion. Mystic religions, which rather incline toward concealment (compare the arcana-discipline in the mystery religions), are less disposed to mission than the prophetic religions. Buddhism as a mystic world religion has nowhere represented a hard Either–Or, as have Islam and Christianity, the prophetic world religions. Buddhism, rather, has considered foreign notions of deity as pre-stages of the Buddhist knowledge of salvation and built them into its own system. But the prophetic religions are strictly exclusive and therefore sought the radical destruction of all alien religions in order to make the prophetic ones all-dominant. Hence Buddhism appears everywhere *beside* other religions. In Japan it came as a universal religion beside genuine Shintoism; in China beside Confucianism and Taoism; and in India, its land of origin, it remained existent, to be sure as a dwindling minority religion, beside Hinduism and Islam.

Part 2

THE MASSES, FOLK BELIEF AND UNIVERSAL RELIGION
Gustav Mensching

The masses have a peculiar connection with universal religion, for on the one hand, to be sure, they do not understand the ideas of high religion, and on the other hand (partly out of their distortion of ideas, partly out of a primeval folk-religious heritage), they create a religion of their own which we call folk belief. We understand the term "masses" here in the sense of Gustave LeBon. The basic tendencies of the masses adduced by LeBon are indeed to the point, but they do not exhaust the character of the masses in general, and the purely religious primitive tendencies of the masses are not discussed by LeBon. Nevertheless, we may, in broad connection with LeBon's analysis, cite a number of general mass tendencies which, religiously speaking, work out in such fashion that they lead directly to folk belief and make the latter comprehensible.

1. Our problem is the comportment of the masses within a high religion. It must be added at once that this must be *organized* high religion, in order for the problem to arise, for as long as high religion is and remains a matter of individuals who are deeply moved personally, masses in our sense have nothing to do with it. In that case, high religion is what it is supposed to be in its purity, a matter of conscious personal decision. And the communal religious structures of pure high religion are communities of committed individuals, but certainly not mass structures. This, LeBon has quite left out of consideration. For him, every union of divers persons is a mass, which without further specification is subject to the laws of the mass spirit. The view which we here defend is that the high-religious communal structures *may* become "massified." But they need not necessarily do so. *Organized* high religion, for example in the form of a church, on the other hand, has to do with masses, since it stands unqualifiedly open to all and actually has the tendency to take up within itself as many people as possible—and therefore the masses. But what are the tendencies of the masses which operate religiously?

(a) The masses are not moved by rational considerations but by dim, subconscious motives and feelings. The consequence is that the individual in the mass largely loses his individuality and independence. Thus the level of the masses is lowered to a primitive stage and becomes disposed toward the taking on of primitive forms of belief.

Source: A translation in abridged form from Gustav Mensching, *Soziologie der Religion,* Bonn: Ludwig Röhrscheid, 1947, pp. 137–148.

(b) The masses are credulous. The unusual and fantastic arouse their imaginative propensity and find credence with them. Hence the masses very easily construct legends and demand miracles of all sorts. They are most readily influenced by concrete representations and graphic events or reports of events. They ask for large guarantees, for the certainty of the visible and the empirically experienceable. Here there emerges incapacity for symbolic thought.

(c) The masses are one-sided. They cannot, in independent judgment, form a differentiated opinion, but can only accept or reject wholesale what they find in various doctrines. Only *unqualified* truths are accepted by them. Doubt and probing effort to attain truth and certainty are alien to them.

(d) The masses may be ethically good or bad. They show no necessary tendency to the ethically good. They are only externally subject to influence in either direction. They need external moral leadership. And they allow themselves to be guided by what "people" do, again with abandonment of one's own judgment and of rational and moral testing of convention. The moral level of the masses is actually very low. Organized high religion is wont to aim for a lowered ethics of the masses, for a lesser perfection beside the greater perfection of the virtuosos of piety.

(e) Tradition has great power over the masses. They abide by the usual and the accustomed with great tenacity. They guard against change and innovation and connect these with the sentiment of sacrilege. They clothe customary forms in a sacred invulnerability, on which the practical effect of transactions in the holy is made to depend. And here we already have the basic tendency of the masses which is decisive for folk belief: the primitive magical attitude.

(f) The masses are a sociological residue from the stage of the sacred folk community. The magical world-view corresponds to the latter; and in early time this world-view is mixed with religion, just as it is found in the masses in high religion. Primitive magical religion, again, is the most important factor in folk belief.

(g) Finally, the desire to be led and for leaders characterizes the masses, religious as well as other masses. The religious masses demand authoritative leadership by the representatives of a religious organization to whom nearly divine power and virtue are imputed. Priests are the leaders of the religious. They and the organizations they serve are expert in the handling of the masses.

2. The belief of the masses, "folk belief" in its most general and basic features, can be derived and understood from these most general tendencies.

(a) First we may note the amazing *sameness* of folk belief. In terms of content, folk beliefs everywhere in the world of religion resemble one another most astonishingly. As examples, Chinese and Indian folk belief are very similar. Frazer has referred to the universal sameness of folk belief and noted that in India the religion of the common people was really a belief in an immense number of spirits, many, if not most of them, malicious and harmful. He has remarked that as in Europe (under a veneer of Christianity) so in the Orient, belief in magic and witchcraft, in spirits and kobolds has constantly maintained itself popularly.

(b) The foundation of folk belief is magic. The masses believe in powers and forces that can be influenced by magical practice. The idea of mana is alive everywhere in the folk belief of religions. With the dynamic conception of mana there is often bound up a personalistic notion. "Power" appears in personal form, in large numbers of spirits, toward whom the appropriate behavior is on the lines of magical conjuring. It is obvious that many elements within the masses are especially disposed toward this elementary magic: women, standing closer to the primitive forces of life and more influenced by feeling than men; among occupational classes, peasants, whose life work brings them more closely into contact with and arouses presentiments about the dark and mysterious powers of the earth; hunters and sailors, whose occupations make them feel their dependence upon powers they cannot control by reason and vocational skills; soldiers, men hourly threatened by death who have always been ready to ensure themselves against the deadly shot by means of magical folk belief.

(c) All folk belief has a pronouncedly eudemonistic character. Happiness and prosperity, personal success of every kind—these are the aims served by the folk belief of all times and peoples. (Thus it comes about that folk belief degrades religious credo and cultus to the status of instrumentalities of earthly welfare, within high religion oriented to quite different things such as the salvation of the soul. The primitive reward—and—punishment theme, reckoning with the compensation of earthly merits, plays an important role in all folk belief.) The kind of installation a Japanese may have in the way of a Buddha-altar in a wall niche is designed for the happiness and prosperity of his family. A niche for a deity reminds us of the corner for God in Catholic and especially in Bavarian houses. But in both East and West this sort of installation arises from the primitive need for the proximity and solid presence of the holy.

(d) Here we come upon a further essential element of all folk belief: the nearness and differentiation and vividness of the divine reflect a primitive religious tendency of all masses. The inaccessible remoteness of the high-religious *single* divinity everywhere arouses in the masses the same feeling of aloneness and evokes the desire for mediation, for differentiation, for specialization of the divinely all-powerful in the form of an abundance of celestial beings which shall be close to man. This tendency of the masses is shown in Islam. As against the remote God in all his majesty and arbitrariness, the simple man of the masses feels the need for nearness through mediating powers. High Islamic religion does not satisfy the need of the masses. From the same tendency arises the cult of saints of the Catholic Church. The saints are near and trustworthy helpers in distress in life's daily concerns, who have their precisely delimited functional spheres.

(e) The desire for leadership noted above as a general tendency of the masses meets, in organized high religion, with the propensity to leadership and rule everywhere peculiar to the clergy. The organized priesthood therefore takes over, in all places, the handling of the masses as it demands and achieves their full subordination—for the demand corresponds to the masses' own disposition. But then the belief of these subordinated, subject masses—folk belief—becomes incorporated into the system of high religion.

In universal religion that has become firmly organized there necessarily arises a folk belief of the masses which maintains itself unchanged through the millennia since the masses also remain identical with themselves. If we look about us in the world of high religion we encounter everywhere the same mass belief that has been characterized in principle above.

1. Primitive folk belief again made its way into the old Mazdaism of Zoroaster. Mazdaism is indeed as much an example of the arousal of magic as it is of the reversion of the high-religious monotheism of Zoroaster to an outright polytheism.

2. Buddhism likewise everywhere shows the emergence of magical-primitive folk belief. Particularly within the church organization of Lamaism in Tibet, the entire world of folk religion is present in baffling profusion. Holy objects are built into or allowed entry into the figures of gods and saints in order to make them ritually effective. Thereby magical mana-power is conferred. All cult objects need this power and receive it by a consecration carried out according to set prescriptions. The characteristic instruments for typically folk-religious mechanization of piety are prayer-wheels, which, with the motion given by wind or water, effect increase of the virtues earned by their builders.

But folk belief again and again breaks through in other areas of Buddhism, for example in the Shingon and Tendai sects of Japan. (Tendai was founded by Dengyo Daishi, 767–822; Shingon by Kobo Daishi, 744–835.) Both built a tremendous system of ritual magic and prayer for all man's conceivable hurts and wishes: against illnesses, labor in birth, danger of fire, drought, robbery, apparitions, spirits of the forest, evil dreams, and so on. All sorts of apparatus are used to carry out the rituals involved.

Even the reform sect founded by Nichiren (born 1222 A.D.), which sought to keep itself free from magical folk belief, was not spared a re-awakening thereof. Amulets, all sorts of talismans, magical formulas, and magical transactions were widely diffused, and all this expression of folk belief was supported even by the priestly group which attended to mass dispositions.

The situation was similar in the Shin sect of Japanese Buddhism. Before the reformers, Honen Shonin (born 1133 A.D.) and Shinran Shonin (born 1173 A.D.) founded the Shin sect, religion was overgrown with all the forms of folk belief. Conjuring, recitation of sutras for the dead, oracles, interpretations of dreams, drawing of lots, magical choice of propitious days, astrology, divination, and so on, were widespread. The folk themselves were busy with calling upon the name of Buddha, with the reading and copying of holy texts, with pilgrimages, with offerings of flowers and incense, with the making of bells and temple paraphernalia and entire temples. They were preoccupied with vows and ascetic exercises. At the beginning of the twelfth century, the Tantric practices of the "left hand" spread for the first time in the above mentioned Shingon sect. This Tantrism regarded sexual union as means for the attainment of Buddhahood. Such was the orientation of the Tachikawa sect, which made rapid gains in those days. And in the recent past, also, shortly before 1868, the end of the Tokugawa period and the beginning of Japan's new political and religious order, there existed among the broad masses a folk belief ingeniously exploited by the Buddhist and Shintoist priesthood—although this belief has so little to do with higher religious ideas that it cannot in a strict sense be imputed to either Buddhism or Shintoism.

3. The same situation confronts us in Islam. Mohammed himself, believing in jinn and magical powers, made considerable concessions to folk belief, which accordingly developed the more profusely. Exorcism was a common substitute for medical science. Amulets with verses from the Koran or with symbolic, magically effective verses were worn. White magic is the special domain of dervishes. In the Islamic saint-cult, old cults repressed by Islam live on and fulfil the need of the masses to bridge over the distance to the one remote God through mediating powers. Belonging to a religious order is valued by the masses as a potent means for the attainment of blessings in this world and the next. Members of the orders, in Islamic folk belief, dispose of a power of giving benediction, lending incomparable efficacy to amulets, pleas, and prescriptions. Some of the orders owe their particular success among the masses to the belief that their members eat snakes and scorpions without being harmed, can swallow fire and fragments of glass, and are invulnerable to weapons.

4. The Christian church organization, which actively opened itself to the masses, was of course also not spared folk belief. There are the holy objects employed by the folk for magical—eudemonistic uses, like holy water, willow catkin, amulets, rosaries, candles, bells, and so on. Primitive folk belief is evident in the multiplication of prayers recommended by the church; for here prayer itself becomes a meritorious sacrificial performance and can be employed for various purposes. But this signifies that the meaning of the Our Father, for example, which is expressed in supplications is no longer attended to and the prayer is employed in its wholeness for concrete purposes, as becomes evident from the phrase "to say an Our Father for someone." Also in processions with the various ends that are to be gained by them, we confront ancient magical folk belief. As in Islam, so also in Catholicism the abstract monotheism of primitive Christianity is replaced by large numbers of holy powers and persons, by saints, angels, and archangels, and at the top of the celestial hosts there is the queen of heaven, Mary, the "Mother of God," to whom the most ardent forms of the Catholic cult are addressed.

The masses are a constant folk-religious residue. They remain the oppressive majority in universal religion also, and, on the basis of folk-religious primitive experience and driven by the primitive tendencies of religious masses, they believe in folk-religious manner and with folk-religious intention. However different religions are, folk-belief is similar in all the high religions. The primitive and ancient experiences of mankind are everywhere the same, and later men for the most part never transcend them. Differentiation first sets in over this elementary human stratum.

Reading 15

MADONNAS THAT MAIM—MICHAEL CARROLL

The religion of Southern Italy—the *Mezzogiorno*—Michael Carroll argues, is different from that of the rest of the country because the Counter Reformation reforms were never fully implemented there. For many of those who live in this region, the folk religion was close to the Mary worship condemned by the Reformers—and may still be. There are scores of different Madonnas, each one with her own shrine, her own devotions, and her own powers, to each one of which the local people were (and perhaps still are) deeply loyal. But no Madonna cult is stranger or more bizarre than that that is marked by beating, maiming, and tongue dragging. Somewhat like the flagellant cults of medieval Europe and the contemporary American Southwest, these rites seem to go far beyond the boundaries of Catholism—while still maintaining some link to it. The official Church opposes these cults and stamps them out where it can (as it did in northern New Mexico in recent years). Yet the tradition lingers on, a residue of older folk traditions in the Roman Catholic heritage, and it exercises special appeal in those areas where life is bleak and hard and where the formal control of the institutional church has never been strong.

Why drag your tongue in the dust? For the same reason you offer little gifts to the goddess of the sea in Rio de Janeiro on New Years Day: it is the thing to do. It is what secret knowledge prescribes as the appropriate action to obtain what one wants from the deity. There is a lot more going on in these cults than simply the impulse to magic. They require special circumstances, special hardships, special kinds of personality, and perhaps even special geography.

They are paradoxically cults in which those who already suffer greatly impose yet more suffering on themselves to win respite from suffering.

Questions for Reflection and Discussion

1. How does masochism become connected to religion?
2. What in the social and economic situation in southern Italy creates an environment for such devotions?
3. Does this essay provide an insight about what the "Ages of Faith" were like in Europe?"
4. Do you remember the flagellant scene from Bergman's film, "The Seventh Seal?" How does it fit with Carroll's description?

MEZZOGIORNO MASOCHISM
Michael Carroll

The first edition of Sir James Frazer's *The Golden Bough* was published in 1890 and became an instant success with the educated public in the English-speaking world. Frazer suggested in that book that ritual slaying had once been central to primitive religion. Originally, Frazer argued, ritual slaying involved a divine king who was slain and replaced, and the purpose of the rite was to renew the forces of nature with which the divine king was linked. Over time, the ritual slaying of the divine king gave rise to myths about gods who died and were reborn and to annual rituals in which the representative of a god was slain and replaced. Given the immense popularity of Frazer's theory in the 1890s, it was no wonder that, when Sir Edward Clodd gave his presidential address to the Folk-Lore Society of England in 1895, he would give examples of ritual slaying that had "survived" into the modern era. In fact, he came up with three such examples.

Two of these were isolated incidents that were manifestly a response to an extreme situation. In the first case, some peasants in Russia had drugged a beggar and then torn out his heart and lungs for use in rites designed to end a famine. The second case occurred in Rumania, also during a time of famine, and involved two teenaged boys who had drowned an infant. But it is Clodd's third case that is the most interesting and that provoked controversy. This case involved an event that was repeated annually and was not, therefore, done *in extremis*. Further, it was tied to a recognized European religion, namely, Catholicism. In fact, it occurred in Italy during Holy Week. In Clodd's words:

> Mr. Grant Allen told me that when he was last in Italy, he was informed by the Rev. W. Pulling, well known as the author of *Dame Europa's School,* and editor of Murray's *Handbook to Italy,* that "in a village in the Abruzzi the young men draw lots once a year to decide which should die for Christ. Whoever drew the fatal lot was secretly killed by another, equally drawn for the purpose, before the next Good Friday. It was accounted a great honour to die for Christ. Although these facts are known to the Government, it is unable to catch the perpetrator, because none will betray him." Mr. Allen had forgotten the name of the village, but no doubt Mr. Pulling would supply it (Clodd 1895: 57).

Clodd expressed no doubts whatever about the veracity of the report, despite the fact that he had received it thirdhand and despite the suspicious absence of the name of the village in question. Nor was the appeal of this Frazerian fancy limited to Clodd. The next year, in the postscript to an article on executed criminals and folk medicine, Mabel Peacock (1896: 282), who was at that time a regular contributor to *Folk-Lore*, repeated the "ritual slaying in the Abruzzi" story without any qualification.

Source: Michael P. Carroll, *Madonnas That Maim: Popular Catholicism in Italy since the Fifteenth Century,* Baltimore, MD: The Johns Hopkins University Press, 1992.

English Catholic commentators saw Clodd's remarks as just one more example of the antipathy toward religion generally and Catholicism in particular that was characteristic of so many modern scientists (e.g., Britten 1898). But most of the outrage generated by Clodd's remarks were felt in Italy. An Italian anthropologist, Antonio De Nino, sent off a letter to *Folk-Lore* in which he related that he had himself inquired of Canon Pullen what the name of the mysterious village was and learned that it was Gioia del Colle (De Nino 1897). This was not a village at all, De Nino noted, but rather a large market town of 20,000 people, and it was located in Puglia, not Abruzzo. More important, De Nino's inquiries had turned up no accounts at all similar to those reported by Pullen. In a longer article written for an Italian anthropological journal, De Nino (1898) printed extracts from communications received from politicians and scholars who had lived in or near Gioia del Colle for most of their lives. All denied ever hearing about anything that even smacked of ritual slaying, and all were outraged that this libel would be leveled against a civilized society like Italy. To counter the charge that there was a conspiracy of silence that the local police could not penetrate, De Nino inspected (or had inspected) the police logs for all Holy Thursdays between 1850 and 1865 and found no murder victims reported on those days.

The last word in the fiasco, so far as I can tell, came from Grant Allen (1899), who complained of having been brought into the dispute. Allen said that he had simply passed along as fact a story that he had been told as fact by Canon Pullen, an English clergyman and noted editor of English guidebooks to Italy. Allen inadvertently linked the story to Frazer by mentioning that Pullen had related the story during the course of a conversation about *The Golden Bough*. But Allen's disclaimers notwithstanding, he could not resist this closing sentence: "Until Canon Pullen gives his informant's name, and enables us to examine that informant, I shall continue to believe that the story *may* have some foundation of truth, because it is hardly likely that anyone could invent a tale so wholly in accord with the rest of our knowledge unless he were a skilled student of customs." The remark "so wholly in accord with the rest of our knowledge" meant that it was consistent with Frazer's well-known theory, and this is obviously what predisposed Allen—and Clodd—to accept it at face value. The fact that no further correspondence or articles on the subject were printed in *Folk-Lore* suggests that most investigators, unlike Allen, decided that the report was untrue.

Despite their differences, both Allen and De Nino agreed on one thing: either the report of ritual slaying was true or it was a fabrication. The obvious third possibility, which nobody seems to have explored at the time, is that the report was Canon Pullen's misinterpretation of something that actually occurred, a misinterpretation heavily influenced by Pullen's commitment to the "truth" of Frazer's general theory. If so, what was that "something"?

BLOODY RITUALS

Cleto Corrain and Pierluigi Zampini (1970: 187) suggest that Pullen's account was a garbled description of one of the many bloody rituals that took place in the South at the turn of the century and in which people did mutilate themselves. For example, in some communities in Calabria during Holy Week, two groups of men were to be found in the streets. The first, clothed only in loincloths, ran through the streets cutting themselves with bits of glass or with bloodletting instruments borrowed from barbers. They drew so much blood, they were "as red as shrimp" (Venturi 1901: 359). The second group, called Inchiovati, walked through the streets in silent procession with arms extended and bound to a length of wood. Their hands seemed nailed (*inchiodati*, in standard Italian) to these crosspieces, just as Christ was nailed to his cross.

But it was not just during Holy Week that such bloody rituals occurred. At Guardia Sanframondi near Benevento (in Campania), such rituals took place during the procession held on 21 August in honor of the Assunta, Mary's Assumption into heaven (see De Blasio 1903). Here the first of the two groups who walked in procession were the *disciplinanti*. These wore white chemises and carried a scourge in their right hands and either a crucifix or a human skull (often with bits of dried skin still attached) in their left. The second group were called the *battenti a sangue*. They also wore white chemises, but these were opened at the front. The *battenti a sangue* carried a piece of cork in which were embedded small metal pins, and they used this device to beat their chests until blood appeared. Bloody rituals such as these also occurred in Puglia, the location of Canon Pullen's reported ritual slaying (Corrain and Zampini 1970: 187).

Perhaps surprisingly, these rituals are still being practiced. An acquaintance in Italy, Andrew Mutter, has sent me two photographs. The first is a color photo that appeared in *Il Venerdi di Repubblica*, a Rome magazine, on 13 October 1989. It had been taken at Guardia Sanframondi during the festa of the Assunta the preceding August. The photo shows a man wearing a white hood and a white chemise and holding a cork studded with pins. The chemise is unbuttoned at the front. The man's chest clearly appears lacerated, while the lower half of the chemise seems drenched in blood. Other men, also holding studded pieces of cork and with lacerations on their chests, are standing in the background. These images match perfectly the descriptions that appear in A. De Blasio's (1903) account of the same festa at the turn of this century. The second picture was taken by an acquaintance of Mutter's during a visit to Nocera Terinese, a village in Calabria, during Holy Week in 1989. It shows a man wearing a crown of thorns, a sweater, and a loincloth. The backs of his legs are covered with blood, as are the steps on which he is standing. He seems to be lacerating himself with two hand-held devices that look like the studded pieces of cork used at Guardia Sanframondi.

In light of all this, it seems likely that Canon Pullen had stumbled across a report of one of these bloody southern Italian rituals and had "made sense of it" using Frazer's then-very-popular theory. While this reconstruction allows us to lay aside any suggestion of a true ritual slaying, we are still left with some pretty extreme and regular examples of self-punishment and self-mutilation in public rituals. This masochistic element needs to be explained.

A REGIONAL DIFFERENCE?

The first task is to decide if such rituals are distinctively southern. If we focus on flagellation alone, the answer is clearly no. After all, the medieval Flagellant Movement broke out in Perugia and from there spread to the rest of northern Italy. Furthermore, most of the *disciplinati* confraternities established in the wake of the Flagellant Movement were established in northern, not southern, Italy. Although public flagellation became less and less part of these northern *disciplinati* ceremonies, here again (as in the case of magic) this may only reflect the vulnerability of northern communities to the dictates of the Church hierarchy, whose Tridentine commitment to order and control usually predisposed them against such public displays. Similarly, the fact that flagellation continued to be practiced in the South until quite recently possibly only reflects that the *chiese ricettizie* insulated southern communities from Tridentine reformers.

But we come to a somewhat different conclusion if we consider flagellation as just one of a range of similar behaviors. Italian investigators regularly note that virtually all forms of popular Catholicism in the South are permeated by a strong penitential emphasis (e.g. Mazzacane and Lombardi Satriani 1974: 43–44). But *penitential* is far too mild a word to describe what has gone on in southern Italy over the centuries. Saying five Our Fathers and five Hail Marys is penitential; what we find in southern Italy is a extraordinary strong masochistic emphasis, across a wide range of devotional activities. Masochism appears in the North but mainly in connection with individual mystics who mutilate themselves in private. When public rituals involving masochism do appear in the North, as in the case of the public flagellations of the early *disciplinati* confraternities, they stand out precisely because they are so dissimilar from most of the other religious rituals.

What is distinctive about popular Catholicism in southern Italy is the diversity of masochistic rituals, their widespread appeal, and the fact that they have continued until recently. While some of these masochistic practices, like flagellation, have been borrowed from other areas of Italy, other masochistic practices seem to have developed more autochthonously.

TONGUE DRAGGING

Tongue dragging is a form of religious behavior that has appeared all over southern Italy. In Sicilia, it is called "la lingua a strascinuni" (Pitrè 1978: 2: 249; Candura 1971: 401), and in Basilicata, "lingere lingua terram" (Cilento 1975:

247). Undoubtedly, other terms are used in other regions. Whatever the terminology, the central features of the practice are everywhere the same: a person goes down on all fours, usually at the threshold of the church, and moves forward while dragging his or her tongue along the pavement of the church. This last action is to be done with sufficient force that the tongue is lacerated and made to bleed. If a sufficiently large number of people engage in tongue dragging during a particular festa, the floor of the church will be covered with bloody stripes. A manuscript written in 1608 and preserved in the archives of the sanctuary dedicated to the Madonna dell'Arco near Naples gives a good account of the practice:

> In order to fulfil a vow or to ask for favors, several of those who come to this Holy House go down on their knees at the entrance to the church. They then move forward, on their knees and with their tongues to the ground, until they reach the chapel and altar of the Madonna. At times, this tongue dragging is done with such fervor that their tongues are lacerated, and they leave the floor of the church looking like the scene of a bloody massacre. (D'Antonio 1979: 43).

Tongue dragging continued to be practiced at this particular sanctuary until the 1930s, at which time a determined effort was made to stamp it out. Nino D'Antonio (1979: 49) suggests that high Church authorities were behind the drive to eliminate the practice, but Giuseppe De Lutiis (1973: 100) is likely correct in saying that the practice was suppressed by the government because it was at odds with the image of a "virile" Italy favored by the Fascist regime. Even so, Annabella Rossi (1969: 92–93) reports that tongue dragging was practiced at a variety of Mezzogiorno sanctuaries, including that dedicated to the Madonna dell'Arco, until the 1950s, and that individual instances of the practice could still be observed at several Mezzogiorno sanctuaries in the 1960s.

The practice of tongue dragging was by no means uniform from region to region. In some Sicilian communities, those dragging their tongues proceeded forward along the floor of the church in pairs; a friend or relative stood between them and guided them with a kerchief passed under the tongue dragger's armpits. In other Sicilian communities, there was one such guide per tongue dragger (Pitrè 1896; 1978: 2: 249; Candura 1971). At the sanctuary dedicated to the Madonna Incoronata at Foggia (in Puglia), pilgrims began dragging their tongues from some point on the ground beyond the church, rather than just at the threshold (Cipriani, Rinaldi, and Sobrero 1979: 76). Giuseppe Pitrè (1896: 19) reports the case of a woman in Sicilia who dragged her tongue from the boundaries of the community up to the main altar of the local church, a distance of about one kilometer. In his study of Italian immigrants in New York City, Robert Orsi (1985: xii–xiv) reports that a tongue dragger, usually a woman, would be dragged forward in the church by the members of her family. Since most of these immigrants were originally from the Naples area, it seems likely that they were repeating a pattern common there. In the Abruzzo, devotees obtained favors from San Pantaleo by dragging their tongues along the floor of the church, making sure that the tongue became lacerated in the process (Pitrè 1883). When they reached the statue of the saint, they would kiss it, thereby marking it with the blood that flowed from their lacerated tongues. In what is likely a concession to modern notions of hygiene, tongue draggers at the sanctuary of the Madonna del Pollino in the Basilicata during the 1960s were sometimes preceded by someone who wiped the pavement with a cloth (Rossi 1969: 20).

Virtually every commentator trying to convey the essence of popular Catholicism in southern Italy mentions tongue dragging. When recalling his adolescence in the Basilicata during the 1920s, Nicola Cilento (1975: 247) writes of being unable to erase certain religious images from his mind. One of these is tongue dragging. To convey the nature of the "superstitions" associated with the practice of Catholicism in the South, L. Villari (1902: 121) names three things: the San Gennaro miracle at Naples, miraculous statues ("countless curt-sying Madonnas and nodding saints"), and tongue dragging. In his account of Mezzogiorno piety during the eighteenth and nineteenth centuries, Pietro Borzomati (1973: 627) singles out the tongue dragging practiced at the sanctu-ary dedicated to San Michele on the Gargano peninsula (in Puglia) as a particu-larly clear example of the fanaticism associated with this piety. Tongue dragging is also mentioned in literary works seeking to convey a sense of southern Italian Catholicism. It is prominent among the many devotional horrors that Gabriele D'Annunzio (1956: 246) caused his protagonists to observe at a southern sanc-tuary, and the practice is described as well in Ignazio Silone's *Bread and Wine* (1937: 233–34).

Scholarly and literary judgments of this particular practice are invariably neg-ative. Terms like *dehumanizing, bestial, brutal, disgusting,* and *savage* are rou-tinely and liberally used in all commentaries. Unlike, say, the festas devoted to patron saints, tongue dragging is not romanticized by commentators. Yet surpris-ingly, no one has yet asked the obvious question: if tongue dragging is indeed such a bestial and brutish practice, then why has it flourished in the South, despite the near-constant opposition of high Church authorities? The obvious answer is that there is something about tongue dragging particularly appealing to southerners, something missed by the elites who sniff "bestial" and "brutish" and then look away from the event itself. Indeed, in the next chapter I argue that tongue drag-ging does epitomize southern Italian Catholicism, since it gratifies a psychological desire that in many ways is the motive force behind this type of Catholicism.

For the moment, I simply note that the widespread popularity of tongue dragging *is* a distinctively southern Italian phenomena. Outside the Mezzogiorno, I have found references to the practice only in a few sanctuaries in Lazio in cen-tral Italy, an area on the border of the Mezzogiorno (Rossi 1969: 254–80). There are occasional references to "kissing the ground" in the North, but the strong emphasis upon lacerating and mutilating the tongue is always absent.

A PANORAMA OF MASOCHISTIC PRACTICES

Although tongue dragging epitomizes southern Italian Catholicism for many commentators, what most of all distinguishes southern Italian festas from their northern counterparts is the simultaneous presence of several different masochistic behaviors. Such simultaneity is captured in an anonymous account recorded in the eighteenth century and reproduced in the *Archivio per le tradizioni popolari* in the late nineteenth century:

> The spirit of religion [which characterizes the people of Sardegna] also gives rise to the austerity of the public penances practiced in many communities on the occasion of important festas. Some people come [to the festa] from a long way away, barefoot, and with their heads uncovered. Others appear in the habit of a confraternity, with the cowls covering their face. These slash their shoulders violently, using a razor-sharp instrument, and so mark with their blood all the spaces over which they pass. Some of the women, not wearing any veil on their head and with their hair dishevelled, go on their knees from the door of the church up to the altar. Other women do this while dragging their tongue on the ground as well. In several communities, there exist confraternities in which the prior punishes some failing on the part of a member by making him hang a large stone around his neck for the entire period of the [religious] services, and each member accepts this with humility. (Lumbroso 1886: 18)

Although the author is writing about Sardegna, the same report could equally apply to the entire Mezzogiorno. Annabella Rossi (1969) studied fifty-four "liturgical" cults that flourished in the Mezzogiorno during the 1960s. She calls them "liturgical," because each cult was organized around a madonna or saint legitimated by the Church, and each was localized in a sanctuary administered by Catholic clergy. Three of the rituals that appear with some regularity have a clear masochistic component (ibid., 254–58). These three rituals, and the number of sanctuaries at which each ritual was practiced, are:

1. moving on one's knees from the threshold of the sanctuary up to the relevant altar, all the while striking oneself on the chest and asking pardon for one's sins (forty-three sanctuaries),
2. walking barefoot some portion of the journey to the sanctuary (forty-four sanctuaries), and
3. tongue dragging on the pavement in the church (eight sanctuaries).

Interviews conducted by Rossi also make it clear that tongue dragging was common at these sanctuaries within living memory.

Rossi also studied ten extraliturgical cults. Half of these were organized around living seers and half around people who were dead. To say that they were extraliturgical is not to say that they were completely outside the Church. On the contrary, most of these ten cults had received legitimation from Church authorities. One of these cults, for example, was organized about Marietta D'Agostino, and we have already seen how this seer came to be legitimized. Another was organized around the body of Beato Giulio, a monk who had died in 1601 and whose body was conserved in an urn kept in the sanctuary at Montevergine (Campania). A third was organized around Giacomo Izzo, a seer who was in constant contact with the Madonna and who received his followers in the sanctuary of Maria Santissima della Ruota del Monti, a sanctuary that Izzo managed by authority of the local bishop. Another cult was organized about the mummified body of a man who had been discovered beneath the pavement of a church in Bonito (Campani) and subsequently kept in an urn located in that same church. And so on. The only thing that clearly distinguishes Rossi's extraliturgical cults from her liturgical cults is that the extraliturgical cults were not organized around a madonna or saint recognized by the official Church. With this in mind, it is worth noting that the masochistic practices Rossi observed in connection with liturgical cults were not associated with any of the extraliturgical cults.

Rossi's data suggest, therefore, that the masochistic practices of southern Italian festas in honor of a madonna or saint are not simply folk elements that would find their way into any religious ceremony. On the contrary, there seems to be an affinity between these practices and the concepts of *saint* and *madonna*. There is, in other words, something in the veneration of the saints and madonnas of southern Italy that elicits masochistic behavior in a way that the veneration of seers and other beings who are not saints or madonnas does not— and this needs to be explained.

Reading 16

THE MADONNA OF ITALIAN HARLEM— ROBERT ORSI

With the compassionate objectivity of an insider who has an outsider's training, Robert Orsi describes the street festival of Easter Harlem (portrayed with colorful detail in the "Godfather" series) in honor of Our Lady of Mount Carmel and then explains the street theology behind it. In doing so, he also helps us to understand how the Madonna cults of the past (though hardly all of them) were compatible with the Catholic tradition. All the components of folk religion are there—threat (from the American society), special knowledge (the mother love of God was on the side of the Italian immigrants), and special devotions (celebration of that mother love in a gorgeous street festival).

Even the notion of suffering, toned down from the cult of the Madonnas that maim, and less masochistic than in the cult of the Marian apparitions, often is present; but here it is the suffering of a community that supports one another along with the support of the Mother who loves them.

In Orsi's description the role of the Madonna in Catholicism seems more benign and humane than in other selections, perhaps because he is able to describe the cult from the inside and perhaps because the East Harlem ceremony is a celebration, an event suffused with a spirit of joy and hope. The Madonna here is truly a madonna, a gentle mother who loves her Child and her children with a love that is, indeed, fierce, but also gentle and tender.

As a rehabilitation of a cult that the official Church of New York (mostly Irish) never liked and never understood, Orsi's work is a brilliant success. It also helps to comprehend the positive side of the enormous appeal of the Mother of Jesus within the Catholic tradition.

Questions for Reflection and Discussion

1. Explain the street theology of the festival. Why did it hold so much appeal for those who practiced it?
2. Have you ever been to one of these Italian street festivals? What was it like?
3. How does Orsi win our sympathy for the festival?
4. Why is the celebratory component so important in the festival and perhaps in our sympathy for it?

Part 1

THE DAYS AND NIGHTS OF THE FESTA
Robert Orsi

Shortly after midnight on July 16, the great bell high in the campanile of the church of Our Lady of Mount Carmel on 115th Street announced to East Harlem that the day of the festa had begun. It was a solemn moment; the voice of the bell seemed more vibrant and sonorous on this night. The sound touched every home in Italian Harlem. It greeted the devout already arriving from the other boroughs and from Italian communities in Connecticut, New Jersey, Pennsylvania, and even California. The sound filled Jefferson Park, where pilgrims who were not fortunate enough to have *compari* or family in East Harlem were camping out. In the church, the round of masses had begun and would continue until the following midnight, each mass expressing either gratitude for a grace bestowed or a plea for comfort and assistance. Italian Harlem was ready and excited: "In alto i cuori, oggi è la grande, memorabile, solenne giornata del XVI Luglio."

The Italians of East Harlem had been preparing for the festa for weeks. They had a special responsibility to host friends and relatives who came from out of town. The homes of Italian Harlem had been scrubbed clean, the windows had been washed and the floor polished. Residents had bought and cooked special foods in anticipation of the arrival of their guests. One participant described the scene in the homes like this:

> I remember my father, every year, people came from Paterson, New Jersey, there was a group of these people from our *paese* who lived there, they would come every time, they would sleep in our house, and eat and drink for four days, five days, going on. And everybody in the neighborhood had to clean their house that week, the week before, new curtains, and everything; it was the feast of Mount Carmel.

The time of the festa was long and undefined. Some people say it lasted two or three days, others say a week, even two weeks. It was a celebration that knew no time. As one participant expressed this, "It started July 16th and went on for about a week. . . . These things went on and on, for hours and hours."

Italian Harlem slept little during the days of the festa. Children played with their cousins from New Haven and Boston and then fell asleep in the laps of the adults, who stayed up all night talking and eating. People went out into the crowded streets at two or three in the morning to go to confession or to attend a special mass at the church that had been offered to *la Madonna* for the health

Source: Robert Anthony Orsi. *The Madonna of 115th Street: Faith and Community in Italian Harlem, 1880–1950,* New York: Yale University Press, 1985.

of their mother or in the hope of finding a job. When they returned, there was more eating and talking and visiting.

Then sometime in the early afternoon of July 16, people would begin walking over to the church. They were dressed in their finest clothes, particularly the children, whose new outfits their families had bought at considerable sacrifice but also with the fierce determination that the family should make *bella figura* in the community and show proper *rispetto* for the Virgin on her feast day. According to Garibaldi Lapolla, "the whole colony had emptied into the thoroughfares, jostling, guff-awing, shouting, shuffling back and forth." Italians living in relative isolation in West Harlem made their way eastward. The crowds walked beneath fire escapes decorated with crepe, American flags, and the Italian tricolor, and under arches of colored lights. Colorful blankets were hung out of the windows. The streets of Italian Harlem had been especially cleaned for the occasion, and local restauranteurs had set up tables outside where the people could stop for some refreshment at, in the words of advertisements in the parish bulletin, special festa prices, though we are not told whether this meant they paid more or less for their food.

Italian popular faith in both Italy and America sought the streets to express itself, and the street life of the festa was dense. Men stood in groups in front of storefront regional social clubs, getting ready to march in the procession, proud of their regional identification and secure in the company of their fellows. Boys from the different neighborhoods within East Harlem went to the church in groups—the Pleasant Avenue crowd, the guys from 109th Street. Girls went with their families. The day held the promise of flirting and meeting, furtive in the earlier history of the celebration, much more open in the 1930s and 1940s. Men and women gambled during the festa, privately and publicly playing games of chance. During the 1920s an old Jewish man wandered through the crowd with a Yiddish-speaking white parrot on his arm; the parrot had been taught to say in Italian, "Come, Italians," and predicted fortunes by drawing cards from a deck.

Vendors of religious articles set up booths along the sidewalks, competing for business with the thriving local trade in religious goods. The booths were filled with wax replicas of internal human organs and with models of human limbs and heads. Someone who had been healed—or hoped to be healed—by the Madonna of headaches or arthritis would carry wax models of the afflicted limbs or head, painted to make them look realistic, in the big procession. The devout could also buy little wax statues of infants. Charms to ward off the evil eye, such as little horns to wear around the neck and little red hunchbacks, were sold alongside the holy cards, statues of Jesus, Mary, and the saints, and the wax body parts.

The most sought-after items were the big and enormously heavy candles that the faithful bought, carried all through the blistering July procession, and then donated to the church. There was a wax factory at 431 East 115th Street, and candles were available at several stores on the block near the church. According to one of my informants: "They sold candles. They did a *tremendous* business in candles for years." In the June 1929 issue of the parish bulletin, in time for that year's celebration, Nicola Sabatini, who owned a religious articles shop at the prime location of 410 East 115th Street, advertised: "The faithful who need candles of any size, votive articles of wax and silver, and other religious articles can get them here directly at reasonable prices and made to their specifications." The weights of the candles chosen by the people corresponded to the seriousness of the grace they were asking, and this was carefully specified in the vows made to the Madonna. A bad problem or a great hope required an especially heavy candle and weights could reach fifty or sixty pounds or more. Sometimes the candles weighed as much as the person for whom prayers and sacrifices were being offered. In 1923, for example, Giuseppe Caparo, sixty-nine years old, who had recently fallen from the fifth floor of a building without hurting himself, offered the Madonna a candle weighing as much as he did, 185 pounds. If, as often happened, the candles were too long or too heavy to be carried by one person, other family members and friends would share the burden.

The most characteristic sensuous facts of the Mount Carmel festa were the smell and taste of food. In the homes, in the streets, and in the restaurants, the festa of Our Lady of Mount Carmel had a taste. Big meals, *pranzi,* were cooked in the homes, and after the festa, family, friends, and neighbors would gather for long and boisterous meals. During the day, snacks of hard-boiled eggs, sausage, and pastry were ready at home. But it was in the street that the real eating took place. From the street vendors the devout could buy beans boiled in oil and red pepper, hot waffles, fried and sugared dough, boiled corn, ice cream, watermelon, sausage, "tempting pies filled with tomato, red pepper and garlic," bowls of pasta, dried nuts, nougat candy, raisins, tinted cakes, and "pastry rings glistening in the light." Beer and wine were drunk, to the horror of those who came from New York's better neighborhoods to watch the lower classes at play.

The crowds slowly made their way to the Church of Our Lady of Mount Carmel on 115th Street between First and Pleasant avenues. The front of the church was decorated with colored lights that traced the outline of the facade and spelled out "Nostra Signora del Monte Carmelo." It was on the steps of the church that the intensity and diversity of the day were at their extreme. Penitents crawled up the steps on their hands and knees, some of them dragging their tongues along the stone. Thousands of people were jammed onto 115th Street in front of the church in the crushing July heat and humidity. Nuns and volunteers from the parish moved through the crowd to help those who succumbed. Many of the pilgrims stood barefoot on the scalding pavement; many had walked barefoot to the shrine through the night from the Bronx and Brooklyn— a barefoot and wearying trek through the long hours of the morning. They took off their shoes as an act of penance, as a demonstration of rispetto for the Virgin, and because they considered the place holy. The crowd had been gathering since midnight, and as the time of the procession neared—la Madonna would soon leave the church and come out among her people—the excitement sizzled like the heat.

There were outsiders in the crowd in front of the church. Irish and German Catholics, who dominated the neighborhood in the early days of the festa and still maintained a presence in East Harlem during the years of Italian ascendency, came to watch. It is likely that in the late nineteenth and early twentieth centuries many of these Irish and German onlookers were the men and woman who supervised and bossed the Italians on the job. The wealthy strolled over from West Harlem to enjoy the exotic spectacle. Jews came both from the East Harlem working-class community and the wealthier Jewish community on the West Side. In the earliest period, in the late nineteenth and early twentieth centuries, blacks came from West Harlem, some of them to pray at the shrine. Irish police kept the peace.

In the afternoon, after the solemn high mass, parish and neighborhood societies began to take their places in front of the church in preparation for the procession. The members of the Congregation of Mount Carmel were there, together with the women of the Altar Sodality and the girls of the Children of Mary; also represented, until they gradually faded away after the Second World War, were the regional societies from the neighborhood that held their annual, smaller feste at Mount Carmel. Bands lined up at intervals in the procession, and throughout the march they played Italian and American music. Behind the societies, a large statue of the Madonna—not the one from the high altar, which left the church only on very special occasions, but a second statue—was mounted on a float which had been decorated with flowers and white ribbons. An honor guard of little girls and young unmarried women clothed in white surrounded the Madonna. Dressed in their best suits or, later in the history of the devotion, in rented tuxedos, the young men from the Holy Name society who would be pulling the float through the streets of East Harlem—a task that was viewed as a great honor and privilege—lined up in front of the Madonna. When everyone was in place, the banner of the Congregazione del Monte Carmelo was carried out by male members of the congregation. Then, at a signal from the priests and with an explosion of music and fireworks, the procession began.

The great Mount Carmel parade, with thousands of marchers, several bands, trailing incense and the haunting sounds of southern Italian religious chanting, made its way up and down every block in the "Italian quarter" of Harlem. Until the late 1940s, the banner was carried down to 102d Street and up to 124th Street, passing under windows filled with the devout. Two processions were necessary to reach all the streets of Italian Harlem: the first went south from the church; the second, on the evening of the 16th, went north. As the neighborhood shrank, so did the procession, gradually withdrawing to the blocks around the church itself. It weaved in and out of the blocks between Third Avenue on the west and Pleasant Avenue on the east. Immediately behind the banner walked women chanting; men and women walked in segregated groups in the procession until at least the 1940s. People of all ages marched. Children helped support the old, who marched on, grimly fulfilling vows made perhaps decades before. Daughters walked arm-in-arm and barefoot with their mothers, sharing the responsibility of the vow.

At the head of the procession marched *i prominenti,* members of the East Harlem and New York elite. This group included judges, lawyers, doctors, local politicians, and prominent funeral directors. Before this elite emerged in the 1920s, the festa was presided over by local merchants and businessmen—men of material success who had "made America," in the popular expression—who valued the prestige and rispetto that came from being known as a sponsor of the procession. These merchants paid for the fireworks that were set off on street corners near their stores when la Madonna passed. As soon as economic capacity matched social aspiration, which allowed Italians to send their children to school, the entire grammar school of Our Lady of Mount Carmel marched in the procession by grade.

As la Madonna slowly made her way through the streets of East Harlem, the devout standing on the sidewalks in front of their tenements kicked off their shoes and joined the procession. Fireworks that had been strung along the trolley tracks were lit as la Madonna approached, making a carpet of noise and smoke for her. In the days before the community was powerful enough to make arrangements, the procession was forced to stop while the trolley cars rumbled past. Above the procession, as it moved down Third Avenue, the thunder of the elevated train drowned out the music. Pushcart vendors saluted as the Madonna was carried past the great outdoor Italian market on First Avenue. Women and girls shouted entreaties over the heads of the crowd to their patroness; others cried aloud, arms outstretched, fingers spread. Noise, smoke, people shoving to get closer, the city's public transportation bearing down on them, children lighting firecrackers—all this, and men and women were still able to kneel on the gritty sidewalk as the statue or banner passed and, pulling a shawl of silence and respect around themselves, bow to la Madonna.

From time to time la Madonna was forced to stop in the street by her faithful. Lapolla tells of one woman who threw herself at the base of the "wandering shrine" to beg help for her family. Before the community, she identified her need, described the details of the situation that had brought her to the feet of la Madonna, and made her request. Others pushed their way through the crowd, or pushed their children through the crowd, to pin money onto the banner. In front of the image was a small box into which people threw money and jewelry. The contributions of the faithful on the day of the festa, even in the days of poverty, were considerable; it was this money that permitted the frequent beautification of the church.

At the very rear of the procession walked the penitents. All of them walked barefoot; some crawled along on their hands and knees; many had been walking all night. For the most part, it was the women who walked barefoot on the searing pavement, though one of my informants told me that men would do this if their wives insisted. In his words, "You do that, or you don't get any food." Women bore huge and very heavy altars of candles arranged in tiered circles ("like a wedding cake," one of my East Harlem sources told me) and balanced on their heads with the poise that had enabled them and their mothers to carry jugs of water and loaves of bread on their heads in southern Italy. Sometimes white ribbons extended out from the tiered candles and were held by little girls in white communion outfits. Some of the people in the rear had disheveled hair and bloodied faces, and women of all ages walked with their hair undone. Some people wore special robes—white robes with a blue sash like Mary's or Franciscan-style brown robes knotted at the waist with a cord; they had promised to wear these robes during the procession, though some had promised to wear their *abitini* for several months, or even a year. Although the rear of the procession was the area designated for these practices, a penitential motif characterized the entire procession and, indeed, the entire day.

This behavior was governed by the vows people made to la Madonna. The seriousness with which these promises were made and kept simply cannot be overemphasized. All my East Harlem sources told me, matter-of-factly, that people did all this, that they came to East Harlem—and kept coming even when Italians grew frightened of Spanish Harlem and knew that the neighborhood was no longer theirs—because they had made a vow. One of my sources described the promise like this:

> You see, these elderly women would make a vow, you know, they would pray for something, say, if I ever get what I'm praying for . . . you know, a son was sick or someone had died [at this point, another former East Harlem resident interjected, "Like some kind of a penance"], and they would make a vow . . . they'd say, maybe for five Mount Carmels we would march with the procession without shoes. In other words, do some sort of a penance to repay for the good that they'd gotten.

In later years, as the older generation passed away or became too sick to come to the festa, their children came and kept their promises for them.

When the tour of Italian Harlem was over, the procession returned to the doors of the church, where la Madonna was greeted with a round of fireworks and, in the earlier days, gunshot. Then the people lined up to wait for hours for their turn to enter the sanctuary and present their petitions or express their gratitude to their protectress, who waited for them on her throne on the altar of the downstairs church until 1923 and then in splendor on the main altar of the newly built sanctuary. Around her, hundreds of candles blazed and, until the late 1930s, the altar was piled high with wax body parts melting in the heat.

The people had come to be healed. The mood in the sanctuary was tense and charged, the crowd dense but quiet, the heat overpowering. Frequently the pilgrims broke spontaneously into hymns and prayers in the Virgin's honor. One man who witnessed this moment of the festa in 1939 wrote that the people were weeping when they came to the altar and that they spoke "with incomprehensible words and deep sighs." Others laughed at the altar in joyful and uncontrollable gratitude for a grace received. The lame were carried in and the old were helped to the front. Men and women lit vigil lights for the intentions of their family and friends, in the United States and in Italy.

When, after the long wait outside and then the difficult passage to the altar, the pilgrims, predominantly women, were able to push through to la Madonna's throne, they lay at her feet the burdens they had been carrying during the procession. They gave the heavy candles and the body parts to the priests and nuns waiting at the altar; they also gave gifts of money and gold. The 1939 souvenir journal saw these gifts in the context of the people's lives: "Every offer represents a sorrowful tale of great sufferings, of unexpected joys and of eternal gratitude. Each heart is enclosed in that offer. Tight in their trembling hands it represents the fruit of their labour [sic,] and for many it probably represents their daily sacrifice."

Occasionally the following scene would be enacted. A woman (this penance was never undertaken by men, according to my sources) would begin crawling on her hands and knees from the back of the church toward the main altar, dragging her tongue along the pavement as she went. If she got tired or was unable to bend over far enough to lick the floor, members of her family would come and carry her along. The clergy discouraged this practice, and it seems to have disappeared for the most part by the 1920s.

Men and women from the neighborhood volunteered to help the pilgrims, an involvement which they viewed as their annual responsibility and privilege. One woman, who has participated in many feste at Mount Carmel, told me: "Naturally, when you're in a family you want to be as helpful as you possibly can, so where the help was needed, we went. It isn't that, nothing is forced, it was all voluntary, and if you're going to do something voluntary, you have to do it with all your heart, otherwise don't do it." She and her friends in the Children of Mary used to greet the pilgrims as they came into the sanctuary, they took their names and addresses for the parish records, ran the church's religious article shop, and handed out scapulars. Others moved through the crowd outside making sure that all went well.

These volunteers also accepted the small bundles of clothing thrust over the altar rail by women. In the earliest years of the devotion, it was customary for a woman who had had a child healed by the Madonna to bring that child to the festa dressed in the best clothes she could afford, often straining family resources to buy a new outfit especially for the occasion. Sometime during the day, the woman would find a private place in the church and change the child into more ordinary clothes, which she had carried along with her. Then she would make her way to the altar and offer the new clothes as a gesture of gratitude to the Madonna and an offering to be distributed to the poor of the parish.

The pilgrims had only a moment at the altar because others were pushing up behind them. From the priests on the altar they received a scapular, which they valued as protection from all harm. They paused for a brief moment to say a prayer to la Madonna, and then they made their way back outside. The line waiting in the July night stretched down 115th Street to First Avenue, where it went along for blocks.

The day of the festa did not end with the visit to the sanctuary. At night there were concerts, at first in Sulzer Park on 126th Street and Second Avenue and then, after 1902, in Jefferson Park, and people danced in the streets of Italian Harlem until early morning. Meat, donated by local butchers, was raffled off in the evening in the park. The residents of the neighborhood prepared feasts for their visitors, and all night family and neighbors dropped by to eat and celebrate. Men and women who grew up in East Harlem but left it in the 1940s and 1950s still remember the feast day of Our Lady of Mount Carmel as a very special time, a time of gaiety and parties that lasted for a week, but also a time of serious religious dedication.

At the heart of this joy and longing was the figure of la Madonna del Carmine. The statue that still stands high above the main altar is a lifelike representation of a young Mediterranean woman holding a small child. The Madonna's first gown, which she wore until her coronation in 1904, was decorated with rings, watches, earrings, and chains, all given to her by men and women who believed she had helped them in a moment of terrible difficulty or pain; and her statue, until it was moved into the upper church, was surrounded by canes, crutches, braces, and wax body parts left there as signs of their gratitude by people she had healed. Both mother and child have real hair, long, thick, and very beautiful; la Madonna's hair flows down over her shoulders. The woman's figure is full. She has broad hips and an ample bosom. Her face is round, though not heavy, and her neck is delicate. She wears pendant earrings. The child she holds is the Infant Jesus. His hair resembles his mother's, thick and very long, as Italian women would often keep their sons' hair until they were four or five years old. Both mother and son are holding scapulars. The statue resembles those in Salerno, Naples, Avellino, and in small towns throughout southern Italy.

The questions we must now ask are: What did this devotion mean to the immigrants and their children in the new land? What role did it play in the history of East Harlem? How could this devotion not only survive the sea change but take on a new and powerful life in New York City? What does the devotion reveal about the immigrants' values and hopes? What does it teach us about the nature of their religious faith?

And how was it that a beautiful peasant woman not only presided over a community along the East River but every year summoned thousands of Italians to Harlem?

Part 2

THE THEOLOGY OF THE STREETS
Robert Orsi

Southern Italian popular religion gave voice to the despair of men and women long oppressed—oppressed with peculiar, sadistic ingenuity—and reinforced attitudes of resignation and fear, as well as a sense of the perversity of reality. All

Source: Robert Anthony Orsi, *The Madonna of 115th Street: Faith and Community in Italian Harlem, 1880–1950,* New York: Yale University Press, 1985.

of this was certainly present in the devotion to the Madonna of 115th Street—
but this is not the whole story. The immigrants were people strong enough to
leave southern Italy and to struggle with the many hardships of migration to
secure "Christian" lives for themselves and their families; their religious vision
expressed both fear and courage, exile and security, submission and defiance.
Every July 16, the soul of a people was revealed in East Harlem. In the devotion
to Mount Carmel, as it spilled out of the homes and onto the streets of Italian
Harlem, we are offered a unique opportunity to read the theology of a people.

There are problems with such an effort, of course. The theology of the men
and women of Italian Harlem would be implicit only, evident for the most part
in gestures and attitudes, and so difficult to systemize. But it would simply not
be true to say that these people were silent about such things or that their theology was merely a corruption of a poor assimilation of Catholic doctrine. They
thought and talked about God and the saints constantly, they wondered about
the meaning of their lives, they pondered their place in the scheme of things.
Having set the festa in its proper place at the center of Italian Harlem, it becomes
possible to understand popular theology critically, in the context of the total life
of the community. Theology has a full context now; what is known of the whole
life of the culture will inform and restrain what can be said about its theology.

This popular religious thinking was strongly shaped by a Catholic sensibility, although not necessarily by the Catholic church, Italian or American. The
immigrants and their offspring were resolutely Catholic, a Catholicism woven
deep into the fabric of their family lives. One not wholly sympathetic Protestant
pastor noted in 1917 that the immigrants could not bear being accused of dis-
loyalty to the Catholic church. Other observers concurred: whether or not the
immigrants went to church regularly or sent their children to parochial schools,
they were clear in tenaciously understanding themselves as, and calling themselves, Catholics.

This Catholicism, however, had little to do with the church, which in the
mezzogiorno was known as part of the system of oppression and in the United
States seemed eager, though unable, to reproduce the caste system the people
had known in Italy. The anger of the immigrants toward the American Catholic
church is clear in the history of Italian Harlem. The people greatly resented
being compelled to worship their Madonna in the lower church. An old Italian
resident of East Harlem told Marie Concistre in the early 1930s:

> In 1886 the Italians in East Harlem lived within a radius of about a quarter of a
> mile. There was only one church to go to and that was what we used to call the
> "American Church" at East 115th Street (now the renowned Madonna of
> Mount Carmel Church). In those days we Italians were allowed to worship
> only in the basement part of the church, a fact which was not altogether to our
> liking. But the neighborhood became more and more Italian—Now Our Lady
> of Mt. Carmel Church is our very own.

In another souvenir journal, published in 1927, it was noted that Italians who
came to East Harlem from all over the United States found "everything good,
everything beautiful," with one great exception "that venerated image for which

you have labored so much should not be in the lower church, but on high, in the upper church." The author of this little sketch concurred, "The observation was just, the lament reasonable." Elsewhere the lower church is described in angry terms as "without light and air, small and with an inconvenient entrance without a bell tower, the glass case [enshrining the Madonna] set upon weak little walls under a cover of zinc, corroded by time."

The people knew, of course, that the leaders of the American church downtown frowned upon their devotion, upon this public display of a Catholicism that was viewed as pagan and primitive. There is a spirit of defiance in popular spirituality. Dalia was revered in the neighborhood for showing the Madonna and her people the rispetto they had come to America to secure and for putting an end to the humiliation of *la chiesa inferiore*. This spiritual defiance is essential if religious experience is to serve, as we saw it did in Italian Harlem, as a mode of popular self-expression: it allows the people to claim their religious experience as their own and to affirm the validity of their values.

The troubled history of the mezzogiorno and the complex problems of the Italian American domus left their marks on popular religiosity in Italian Harlem. The vows made to the Madonna could at times (though not as often as people think) be little more than a crude bartering with the divine, an attempt at bribing destiny. There are instances where the people mechanically checked off a list of payments to the various divine figures, always careful to give the Madonna a little more. In such cases, the relationship with the divine became a mere patron–client relationship, and the Madonna a kind of divine enforcer to be treated respectfully out of fear alone. Furthermore, the manipulation of suffering to gain the attention of the divine and secure special favors often seemed, and may have been, pathological in its origins and consequences. At times the people seemed to want to bind themselves to the divine with a covenant of pain.

The gambling that invariably took place at Italian American feste vividly expresses this side of the devotion. The people of Italian Harlem played games of chance in the presence of the Madonna. They also made deals with her, wagering their pain and discomfort to win some prize they had long been hoping for. At these moments the Madonna became the symbol of fate, of the powerful forces which southern Italians saw pressing down on them and their families, and the festa became a sacred bazaar at which the people anxiously watched the wheel of fortune spinning, literally and spiritually, in the streets.

The street theologians had much more to say than this, however. Most clearly they proclaimed that suffering and sacrifice were the essential links between themselves and the divine. Their own suffering was used to create a deep bond of sympathy with the redemptive suffering at the heart of Christianity. Each July, in a distant recapitulation of Calvary, the immigrants marched through East Harlem bearing heavy burdens of wax. Churches throughout Italy, and the Church of the Madonna on 115th Street, display in small corner niches the *ecce homo*, a bust of the suffering Christ, so that people can see the suffering of the man and sense the commonality of their pain with his. In the summons "Behold this human being," Italians recognized the truth of their own lives, and this recognition became the ground of their religious experience. Identification with the suffering of Christ and the Madonna became the people's way of participating in the central mystery of the Christian faith.

In the Church of Saint Ann, which was (and still is) one of the major stops on the pilgrimage route of the procession through East Harlem, there is a striking statue of the Madonna. Dressed in a real and heavy black dress identical to those worn in mourning by the older Italian women of Harlem, Mary stands at the railing of the side altar. She is easily mistaken for a woman at prayer. She is at the foot of the cross, and her face wears an expression of great and violent grief. Dark circles are painted around her eyes and her mouth is open in sorrow. This statue was a favorite shrine for men and women, but especially for women, during the festa. The Madonna is close enough to be touched, so that people bringing their sorrows to this image of the suffering divine could reach out and clutch her dress in their fists. In this way, the people of Italian Harlem and the Madonna appeared to be clinging to each other in their troubles.

This kind of devotion enjoys a considerable heritage. For centuries Catholic Europe had known the tradition of the intimately portrayed and experienced suffering divine, expressed most forcefully in Spanish gothic crucifixes, Italy's sorrowing *pietà*, and the stigmata of Francis and most recently of Padre Pio. In the devotion to the Madonna of 115th Street, which takes its place in this tradition, the people used the facts and trials of their lives as their way of faith. It was a faith of the quotidian sanctified: the people's own lives became the way of faith; their suffering, the nexus with divine suffering and, through that, the way to the hope of redemption.

The people's awareness of and participation in the great Christian dialectic of suffering and redemption was strikingly revealed in a ritual popular at Mount Carmel in the period under consideration. On Good Friday, the figure of Jesus was taken down from the huge and special cross used for the occasion and carried around the church on the shoulders of young women, recalling Anna Ruddy's comment that these were the burden-bearers of Italian Harlem. Once again the divine, in this case the suffering divine, was in motion among the people. On Easter Sunday, this same Christ, hands outstretched and nail pocked, not a special Resurrection figure, was displayed in glory on the altar. The people were expressing here an intimate sense of the movement from suffering to triumph.

As we have seen, the movement from suffering to sacrifice during the festa was a movement toward freedom: by embracing suffering on the day of the festa and on behalf of their families and the Madonna, the men and women of Italian Harlem were declaring their human freedom and dignity. The Italians in Harlem and elsewhere respected suffering and acknowledged its inescapable place in their lives. In the words of one of my sources, the people believed "they had to suffer. They'd be surprised if they didn't have to suffer." The people's ritual sacrifice was usually a literal reenactment of their real suffering. In a broader sense, the very atmosphere of discomfort and suffering on the day of the celebration paralleled the conditions of la miseria. The official historian of the devotion equated the early conditions of the immigrants' lives in New York with la miseria and located the origins of the devotion and its emphasis on sacrifice in this continuity of experience. But significantly, in this new-world document sacrifice means triumph—it was what was required of the immigrants if they would prevail in their struggle against adversity in their new home, a struggle which, it is emphasized, they undertook themselves. In the devotion, the people recapitulated and sanctified this central dynamic of immigration, and as they did so they entered into the essential Christian mystery of the movement from suffering to redemption. Their own suffering thus undertaken became the pathway to the encounter with the divine. And through transformed suffering, the people articulated their acceptance and transcendence of suffering. Religious sacrifice, as observed earlier, is the human claim of self-respect in the face of suffering. . . .

As they insisted on a personal God who could know the hidden sorrows of their lives, the Italians of East Harlem revealed a sense of the insufficiency of a male God. Women seemed to doubt that a male God could understand their needs and hopes and so they turned to another, complementary divine figure whose life was one of suffering for her child, a story that resonated deeply with the economy of Italian American family life. There was a popular Mariology in Italian Harlem that was quite different from official versions but consistent with a long European popular tradition: the women in the community believed that Mary had suffered the pains of childbirth, that she had menstruated, and that she worried constantly about her child. They felt that she could understand and help them because she had shared their most private experiences and because she was as powerful—and as powerless—as they were. Furthermore, the community knew the power and authority of women, and they expected to see this reflected in the ordering of the divine. The arrangements of Italian Harlem's heaven were similar to the arrangements of its life on earth.

The divine had many faces for the people of Italian Harlem. The Madonna's gaze was sometimes warm and maternal, welcoming her children into their mamma's domus to find peace and rest; but the Madonna was also an unpredictable and fierce woman who had to be propitiated with pain. Jesus, who seems a much less complex divine figure than his mother in the popular theology of Italian Harlem, was a suffering and dutiful son. Saint Anthony and other saints, like Ann, Cosmos and Damian, and Joseph, were familiar figures who behaved much the way one's earthly relations and comari and compari did—sometimes they seemed to have power and be dependable, at other times they showed no respect and so deserved none in return. . . .

The festa, moreover, articulated, celebrated, and confirmed the people's belief that destiny, however terrible it might be, was a shared destiny. It confirmed the communion of people and saints, living and dead, present and absent, that Italians viewed as so essential to the good life. As one of my sources proudly told me when explaining why elderly Italians insisted on remaining in East Harlem even after it had become "dangerous" in the eyes of their upwardly aspirant children, "Italians need people." If there was one thing the festa of July 16 gave Italian Harlem it was people.

So the street theologians proclaimed that divine and human are in a relationship of mutual responsibility and reciprocity; that the divine needs the human as the human needs the divine; that Christ's redeeming blood established an intimacy between heaven and the domus; that the power of the divine is awesome, not always comprehensible from the perspective of the human and to be approached with love and fear; that the divine is bound to behave with rispetto toward the human; that living and dead, holy and human exist together in the communion of saints; that what God proposes men and women must respect, though they are also free to entreat the divine for help and support; that reality is communal, not individual, and destiny shared; that suffering can become triumph. The Italians brought an ancient religious heritage to the community along the East River; and the American Catholics of the downtown church, dazzled by the prospects of success at last in the United States and embarrassed by this Mediterranean spirituality spilling onto the streets and into the awareness of Americans, might have learned from listening to the voices of the streets.

The fusion of sacred and profane, of the serious and the apparently trivial, troubled observers of the festa, who were offended by the noise and food and emotion in the presence of the sacred. Yet as we back off from the festa and see it in all its lived intensity, in the conflict and tension as well as the hope and reverence of the people's new lives, hear the prayers and cries and laughter, and smell the steam of sausage and peppers cooking under colored lights, we sense that this sustaining of opposites is probably the epiphany of the entire meaning of the festa. These people took all the pain and hope of their lives and brought them to a divine mother, who lived not only in the faith of their present but in the faith of their past as well, as she merged in their memories with their own mothers. They carried all this into her house, which they had built. On the streets they claimed and in the homes they sanctified, they prayed to be healed of the hurts they knew would come on those streets and in those homes. They begged to be nurtured through another year. And they knew that the path to the divine was the same dense and trying and joyous and painful path that they trod every day.

SECULARIZATION:
THE DECLINE OF RELIGION

The notion that men and women are less religious than they used to be and that the churches are not as important as they used to be is so widespread that it has become the conventional wisdom in American society. Those who oppose religion celebrate its decline. Religious leaders lament that people are not as virtuous as they used to be. The fact is that there is little evidence to back up this thesis. Indeed as Roger Finke and Rodney Stark contend in a selection in a subsequent section, there is considerable evidence that Americans are more religious than they used to be.

The editor of this volume makes no secret of his contempt of the theory, which routinely provides no data for either a *terminus a quo* or a *terminus ad quem*. Most versions of it exist only on the "theoretical" level—which is to say that they are an exercise in word spinning, which does not generate hypotheses that can be either verified or falsified. In the absence of the possibility of falsification, then verification is also impossible. The testing of hypotheses need not be done with survey data. Any evidence will do. But the secularization theorists seem to have a positive horror for evidence—either of the great religious faith that existed at a specified time in the past or of the great decline of faith from that time to the present.

Secularized relative to what?

The Rome of the Caesars, the Ottos, or the Borgias? The Paris of the Louises? The London of the Restoration, or the Regency?

There is less religion now present in America, and it is less influential on society than in those times and places?

Gimme a break!

Religion Isn't What It Used to Be—Bryan Wilson and Thomas Luckmann

The "secularization" theory in all its many forms argues, in effect, that religion is not a important as it used to be. Either levels of human devotion and faith have declined or the Churches don't have as much influence on the social order as they once had. Usually such theories are both imprecise about when religion and the Churches had more influence than now and what evidence there is to support the notion that there was a time—any time—when men and women were more devout. That there was a time when faith was stronger is assumed as a self-evident point of departure. In other areas of sociology, such an argument would be considered a form of the "good old days" or "golden age" fallacy. Yet in the sociology of religion, the assumption escapes unchallenged.

Writers such as Bryan Wilson, who analyze at great length and in agonizing detail (and in Wilson's case with evident hostility to both religion and the Churches) the decline of religion are never challenged to prove their assertions and especially never questioned about their assumption that there was once an age of faith. Religion it would seem is everywhere in decline and religious institutions have their backs to the walls and these truths are so self-evident that it is unnecessary to offer proof.

Thomas Luckmann's approach is more sensitive and more sophisticated. Religion has become "invisible"; that is, it exercises influence in the interstistes of the modern corporate society. None of the major sectors of society—government, industry, finance, the media, the military—are any longer influenced by Church or religion, but faith may still be important in personal lives—though in Western European countries even that seems no longer to be true. In the ages of faith, religion or at least organized religion made its presence felt in all areas of human behavior. Now it has impact only on family life—that is to say, it has become invisible.

The problem with this paradigm is that it both assumes that, at some unspecified time in the past, religion did exercise considerable influence in other sectors of society and because it is no longer formally represented in those sectors it no longer exercises such influence.

Whether bishops ruled kings or kings ruled bishops at various times in the past is a question that must be answered empirically of specific times and places. In Czarist Russia, the Church was always subservient to the state. In the West, some popes did dispose emperors and some emperors did dispose popes. How often the conflicts between the Church and State were really about religion and how often about power is also a question that is open to empirical analysis. Moreover, if the Church is able to influence family relationships, it may be able to inculcate its principles and convictions in such a way that it still has a powerful if indirect influence on other sectors of life.

In other words, the secularization "theory" compares two "ideal" situations—one in which the Church dominated the rest of society to a second in which it has no impact at all—without ever carefully investigating either of the two times in question to determine the actual relationship between religion and life. However, we know enough today about, let us say, medieval history to know that it was hardly an era of either great religious devotion or great moral virtue.

Despite these grave weaknesses, the secularization theory still dominates the sociology of religion and has become the accepted conventional wisdom about religion for the American media. The fact that religion still survives and is still important to many if not most people does not seem to matter.

Questions for Reflection and Discussion

1. Compare Wilson and Luckmann. What do they have in common and how do they differ?
2. Does the influence of religion equate with the influence of the Churches?
3. What proof is there that religion had all that much influence on human behavior in the past?
4. What proof is there that it has all that little influence today?

Part 1

RELIGION IN SECULAR SOCIETY
Bryan Wilson

The concept of the Church, as it has been understood in the social sense, is one which acquired its full meaning and realization in European feudal society. It claimed within a given territory, the monopoly of spiritual power, just as the state claimed the monopoly of political and military power. In European history one Church presided over several nascent states and this but reflected its claim to transcendence and universality. For, although in the age of more emphatic nationalism the Church tended to become closely identified with the state, and this was especially true in Protestant Christendom—indeed to the point of accepting the dominant authority of the state—the earlier conception was of a Church unconfined by national or ethnic boundaries. But the Church relied, for

Source: B. R. Wilson, 'Conclusion', Religion in Secular Society, Watts, 1966, pp. 221–33.

the effective recognition of its claim to a monopoly of spiritual power, on the coercive power of the political authority.

As the institutions of society grew apart, and as religious institutions and functionaries lost, first their control of, and later much of their access to, various social activities—diplomacy, education, the regulation of trade, etc., so the civil authority gained in power, and, having less need for the good offices of the Church, was less disposed to protect its ancient privileges. The emergence of new classes with new skills and resources, who were unaccommodated in the Church, but whose social importance sometimes won for them the protection of princes, created a pluralism which became the first properly instituted invasion (there had been many unlegitimated invasions before) of the Church's claim to spiritual monopoly as far as the temporal sovereign's writ could run.

The ecclesiological theory of the Church remained. But once tolerance was extended to organized dissenters the Church, sociologically viewed, was reduced to the status of a denomination, albeit for a very long time a dominant and privileged denomination. In America, despite the 'establishment' of particular confessions in various states, denominationalism was, from the very creation of the federation, the norm. Religious pluralism has its official foundation stone in the American constitution, although its modern beginnings go back to sixteenth- and early seventeenth-century Europe. The growth of religious diversity in the United States made evident the untenability of the social concept of 'the Church' in that society, although those religious organizations which inherited the ecclesiology and the associated liturgical practices, continued to behave as if they were in fact Churches. In political and social affairs, of course, they could not do so.

In Europe, where Established Churches did persist in most countries, loss of effective authority affected the Churches even in societies where there was near unanimity of religious belief. In Germany, Scandinavia, Holland, Switzerland and Britain, Protestantism created the conditions for an earlier manifestation of religious tolerance than occurred in Catholic countries, but as religion lost political influence, dissent, even in Catholic countries, became increasingly tolerated. More important, anti-clericalism became a significant manifestation of political radicalism.

What was begun by the tolerance necessary in increasingly diversified societies, was continued by the process of secularization itself. When large numbers effectively ceased to be religious, all religious movements were reduced to the status of denominations and sects. The process was, inevitably, the more painful in those societies in which the fiction of the concept of the Church had persisted. In America secularization drained the religious content, without too radically affecting the form, of religious institutions. So persistent indeed were the forms, that in that pluralistic society, sects could expect, especially in the nineteenth century when expansion and optimism were so manifest, to graduate into denominations and even to acquire for themselves the liturgical, architectural and (sometimes) the ecclesiastical styles which had previously been exclusively associated with those more ancient religious institutions which had in the past been—and which still laid claim to being—Churches. Thus some commentators have, mistaking the form for the social reality, been prepared, rather inappropriately, to discuss the process not as one of denominationalism, but as one 'from sect to Church'. Church was, however, merely the high status towards which some sects were aspiring, without, however, any realistic prospect of attaining it.

In the secular society there are, strictly speaking, no Churches. There are denominations, some of which have special historic privileges, and some of which suffer some historic liabilities (for example, the preclusion of Roman Catholics from certain offices of state in England). But whereas denominational claims are, given the high level of manifest public support, sustainable in America, even these become difficult to sustain in Europe where the secularization process has not merely (or not so markedly) drained away the content of religious beliefs but has also caused public support to ebb. In some European countries those religious institutions which once boasted the name and the reality of Churches are, with secularization, faced with being reduced to the status of sects; that is to say, of being reduced to relatively small, heterodox groups who believe and practise things which are alien to the majority. They differ from sects, however, in lacking the intensity of commitment.

It is in response to this circumstance of secularization that the Churches of the past have sought to shore up their claims to status. Their dominant stratagem has been ecumenicalism. Since what secularization has eroded has been the intensity of specific belief, the sense of superiority and apartness, this solution has been all the easier to accept. Clearly, in this process, those Churches which have remained largest and which have managed to maintain their more traditional practices have some advantage. The ritual dance of ecumenism emphasizes steps known as 'drawing together' and 'growing together'. A close observer of the dance might notice that the gyrations and revolutions of some of the dancers are far more numerous in a short space of time than those of others. The attempt to discover a more firmly legitimated basis of faith and order—beginning with the Tractarian movement of the nineteenth century in England—has led to an attempt to restore the security of the past, however much of it may be done in the name of action appropriate to the present. The sentiments of returning to the first century of Christianity come readily to the lips of modern churchmen, even when they are emphasizing the need for change to keep up with the twentieth century, and restoring liturgical practices from the twelfth or thirteenth centuries (see Paul, 1964, and Wilson, 1965).

Yet if it is the Roman Church which, liturgically, ecclesiastically, and theologically stands to gain, it can do so in these departments only by surrendering control in others. What affects liturgy and ecclesiology and theology as an academic discipline, affects only the Church. It has little consequence for society at large. Where ethics are concerned, however, matters are rather different. The secular society, with its acceptance of more technical and scientific procedures, will not brook interference of the traditional kind, in, for example, matters relating to marriage and birth. It may eventually also reassert the control it was steadily acquiring until the past decade perhaps, over education, as the financial demands of modern education steadily outstrip the resources of private agencies—even of religious organizations. Other religious movements have in the main abandoned the attempt to influence society in these matters except by pious injunction. Eventually the Roman Church must do the same.

Ecumenicalism, then, is a response which might save the Churches from becoming sects, since 'from Church to sect' would appear to be the order of the day for religious organizations in secular society. Sects have always been anathema to churchmen, indeed to most Christians, even including those who, in the eyes of other Christians and of the secular world, are themselves sectarians. And this, even though there can be no doubt that the intensity of religious commitment, the most individually influential and pervasive religious view of the world undoubtedly exists in sectarian movements. Enthusiasm has never had much appeal to churchmen, and lay intensity has often been a matter for concern and reproach among those who have become professionals of religious organizations. The ecumenical alternative to sectarianism—although Christianity was certainly sectarian in the now so-popular first century—is associated with the liturgical revival and the reassertion of the episcopacy even in denominations which began by disavowing both.

Both have a special appeal to the professionals of the Churches. They improve the claim to social status on the part of the ministry; they emphasize the antiquity of the religious role and hence reassure its performers of the legitimacy, permanence and usefulness of their chosen calling. Liturgicalism reasserts the monopoly of the professional, by providing him with the equivalent of skills and techniques which he alone is licensed to practise. Episcopacy ensures the promotion prospects of the cleric, and perpetuates the claim to high dignity, association with ruling *élites* and the maintenance of the religious institution in some nominal position of high social importance.

Given an organization with all the capacity for persistence displayed by the Churches—their claims on latent sentiment, their operation at crucial times of personal and familial crisis, their association with the kinship structure, and especially with the childhood of many people—one sees the clerical profession as a self-perpetuating incumbency. The forces of ecumenism are clerical forces, and the forces of the new ritualist movement are clerical forces. We witness the struggles of a professional for survival in the Protestant countries of Europe. The choice is principally between the loss of organizations, positions and social influence, as in the case of sects, or the maintenance of organizations, the multiplication of positions, the reassertion of professional expertise, and the close identification with the cultural goals and styles of secular society, as in the case of religious institutions in America. There is a third position and it appeals to a minority of the clergy in Europe. As the ministry becomes an entrenched but increasingly functionless intelligentsia, so this minority interprets its role increasingly as involvement with social and political affairs. From the secure base of religious livings, they sally forth on what are largely political crusades. This is the tradition of dissent, of course (even though it is often Anglican and Lutheran clergy who are involved), but it is not religious dissent. It is the use of a religious base for political action. In general, the choice of the clergy has been ecumenicalism, liturgicalism and the attempt to identify with the goals of secular society and to show where religious organization (even if not religious ideas and values) fits in.

The social basis which facilitates the development of ecumenicalism is the diminishing diversity of society. The disappearance of ethnic, regional and pronounced stratificational differences reduces the significance of the religious divisions which reflected them. That significance has, of course, been affected, too, by the process of secularization itself. Were secularization not involved it might be possible to predict a return to the Durkheimian case of a unitary religion expressing the social solidarity, cohesion and shared values of an undiversified society. Those functions of religion were manifested in a simple society, but we can seriously doubt whether, even with a less diversified society of the future, and with ecumenism, we shall in any sense return to the position in which religion would operate as the integrative agency of modern society.

The whole significance of the secularization process is that society does not, in the modern world, derive its values from certain religious preconceptions which are then the basis for social organization and social action. It is rather that ecumenical religion will, as Herberg suggests it does in America, merely reflect the values which stem from social organization itself. Even with its votaries in contemporary society, religion does not begin to compare in its influence with the total religious world view which prevailed in simple society, and the subsumption of all activities and all institutions in the religious orientation of the world. The diversification of society destroyed the dominance of religion, and redistributed its functions. The diminution of diversity (and it is a diminution in only certain areas, in fact) does not restore religion to its former pre-eminence, nor return to it the functions which it once performed.

Social cohesion, and some measure of social consensus—at least concerning innumerable patterns of action in everyday life—must prevail in all continuing societies which are not experiencing anarchy. But even if this cohesion were attributed to the primacy of shared patterns of values, norms, conventions and orientations to the world laid deep in the socialization process, still one need not suppose these values to be specifically religious or to be today actively supported by religious commitment and religious organization. It is clear, of course, that they owe, in origin and development, much to religious conceptions of society of the past.

We may rather turn to the complex dovetailing of our institutional arrangements; to the mixture of inducement and coercion which prevails within the work order of our society; to the largely autonomous body of duly instituted law; to the elaborate interaction of supply, demand, knowledge of the market, and knowledge of consumers, which structure much of the provision of a modern economy, to see what it is that maintains the cohesion of contemporary society. That certain values, norms, and conventions enter into this highly intricate picture is self-evident. That they have a primacy or a determinacy seems very much more disputable. That they are ultimately religious ideas, and rest on religious practice and institutions for their validity and legitimacy, seems highly questionable.

Social cohesion is but one of the functions which have been generally ascribed to religion. In this essay no attempt has been made to examine the fulfilment of these functions in modern society, but what has perhaps become broadly apparent is that the secular society does not appear to depend in any direct way on the maintenance of religious thinking, practices or institutions. In a society with diminished diversity in public affairs, and the relegation of various moral matters to the private domain, religion, too, may have become a largely private concern. Indeed religionists have increasingly tended to describe religion as an individual matter, and a personal matter. Such has been the drift especially of the more evangelical branches of Christianity. Does religion, then, become merely a matter for private predilection? Or a matter of individual demand for emotional support in circumstances of extremity? Do we then see a return, for the mass of men, to the occasional conformity of the past? Those occasions being primarily the occasions of trauma in the life cycle of the individual or of the nuclear family.

There is, however, one function which appears to have been vitally performed particularly by the Protestant manifestations of Christianity, and which assumed great importance in the development of modern society. The voluntary act of religious association implicit in Protestantism—in its various denominations and in many of its sects—entailed a distinctive commitment of goodwill to a group which was neither specifically kinsfolk nor neighbours. Without the primary affectivity of kinship relations, this goodwill had none the less to be manifested. Clearly, the implications for such a response are deeply laid in earlier Christianity: they are found in the parable of the Samaritan, and in the oft repeated dictum, 'We love him because he first loved us' which has applications for relations within the fraternity as well as for the relations of man to his God.

In Protestantism, however, was reacquired the voluntary character of earliest Christianity, and this has been of importance for the development of modern society. But Protestantism added something more to the detached goodwill which was implied in the formation of voluntary religious societies, and this it did by transcendental reinterpretation of the social roles of the new trading strata which were becoming important in late fifteenth- and early sixteenth-century Europe. The work ethic which was emphasized in Calvinism, in Puritanism generally and subsequently in Methodism and the various Holiness sects, was an ethic which rested on an essentially extraneous motivation to be committed to work. The disinterested devotion to the calling, relied on the detachment of work and material reward, and the assertion that work was a spiritual activity and a moral obligation. The strong informal assumption was that, whatever material ends were gained, the real end of fulfilling one's calling in this world was a heavenly reward. It was the uncertainty of that reward in Calvinism, and the strong informal assumption that, although God's will could not be known, achievement in this world was an intimation of the real blessings which God would bestow in the next, which induced the disposition to work (see Weber, 1930; Yinger, 1946; Parsons, 1949).

Thus, with work regarded as a religious and moral duty, material reward is, at least ideologically, displaced. A disinterested commitment is established. But, as Max Weber stressed, once these work dispositions had been established, and society had been resocialized for a new work order, the religious agent of this change was no longer necessary for its continuance.[1] Role performance, in the post-Protestant society, comes to rely on a secularized value structure in which work is no longer a sacred calling. Today a man works without the higher sense of purpose which the Protestant ethic communicated. Protestantism replaced the immediate material inducement to work by a more remote spiritual one, and this was perhaps a necessary ideological justification for that age; but in so doing it created a more involved nexus between what a man did and his reward for it. His remote prospective spiritual interest became effectively a type of disinterested commitment in the everyday activity of his life. The disappearance of a religious interpretation of economic activity may mean that role performance is now evinced without specific commitment and without devotion. The nakedness of the interest relation is borne home. Work, which ceased to be part of a life itself with the passing of agrarian society (that is for farmers), became a *calling* and was recognized as a distinctive activity of life, sanctified in religious terms, and was gradually transformed into being a *job,* supported strictly by the institutional order and an unmediated interest relationship.

It might be maintained that this development, which is clearly part of the secularization process, is itself part of the process of man's increasing rationality, his recognition of 'real' facts. One might, however, also ask whether work is made more bearable for the worker and its performance more valuable for society if disinterested devotion is lacking. Unreligious societies have attempted to find other ways of motivating men, of winning their disinterested goodwill: it is not clear that any appeals have been more effective than was that of the Protestant ethic.[2]

Disinterested devotion, or disinterested goodwill, has, however, significance for other things besides work relations. Although Victorian industrialism would not have been possible without a widely diffused work ethic, there may be a time when, in an age of automation, society's work order will function without these ingrained habits of work of the past. Even then, however, disinterested devotion might still be necessary to society's functioning, at least as the radical alternative to institutional coercion. Anyone who has compared the pattern of civic and political life in underdeveloped countries with those of advanced society must be impressed by the differing degrees of disinterested commitment and detached goodwill which prevails in advanced society, and the extent to which advanced societies rely on their dispositions for their normal functioning. The maintenance of public order and social control depend, in large measure, on the diffusion of disinterested goodwill, and on a certain level of public and individual honesty (as distinct from the purely communal honesty which prevails in simple,

---

[1]See Weber (1930), p. 70. At the end of Weber (1961, p. 270). he remarks, 'The religious root of modern economic humanity is dead, today the concept of the calling is a *caput mortuum* in the world.'

[2]In this connexion, see Bendix (1956); and for an examination of some of these issues in a very different culture context, see Bellah (1957).

often even in peasant, societies). The extension of kin group and neighbourhood affectivity in generalized and impersonal goodwill, has been an achievement which has kept the corruption, crime, nepotism of modern society within bounds. It has facilitated a pattern of very general socialization—all class, regional and ecological differences notwithstanding—in which a strongly internalized sense of impersonal individual honesty has been very widely created. And in all of this the teachings of Christianity, and originally the implications of the teachings of Protestantism in particular and the voluntarism of denominational allegiance, have played perhaps the more important parts. Less advanced people rely very much more on the social control of the group, on public surveillance of individual behaviour; when those societies are urbanized and industrialized, bribery and corruption become widespread patterns of public behaviour. [...]

Secular society has little direct regard for religion. It would be too early to say that it functioned without it, or that it could ever do so. The secular society of the present, in which religious thinking, practices and institutions have but a small part, is none the less the inheritor of values, dispositions and orientations from the religious past. The completely secularized society has not yet existed. Whether indeed our own type of society will effectively maintain public order, without institutional coercion once the still persisting influence of past religion wanes even further, remains to be seen. It may be, that in response to the growing institutionalism, impersonality and bureaucracy of modern society, religion will find new functions to perform—but that, perhaps, would be not the religion which accepts the values of the new institutionalism, the religion of ecumenism, but the religion of the sects.

References

Bellah, R. N. (1957), *Tokugawa Religion*, Free Press.
Bendix, R. (1956), *Work and Authority in Industry*, Wiley.
Parsons, T. (1949), *The Structure of Social Action*, Free Press, 2nd edn.
Paul, L. (1964), *Deployment and Payment of the Clergy*, Church Information Office.
Weber, M. (1930), *The Protestant Ethic and the Spirit of Capitalism*, Allen and Unwin.
Weber, M. (1961), *General Economic History*, Collier.
Wilson, B. (1965), 'The Paul Report examined', *Theology*, vol. 68, no. 536, pp. 89–103.
Yinger, J. M. (1946), *Religion in the Struggle for Power*, Duke University Press.

Part 2

THE DECLINE OF CHURCH-ORIENTED RELIGION
Thomas Luckmann

During the past decades, and especially in the last ten years, many studies of churches, sects and denominations accumulated. Most studies originated in the United States, Germany, France, Belgium, England and the Netherlands, with a few coming from other countries such as Italy and Austria. In the European countries research concentrated, with a few exceptions, on Catholicism and the established or quasi-established Protestant churches. In the United States the sects received the major share of attention, although Judaism, Catholicism and the major Protestant denominations were not completely neglected.[1]

Despite the large number of studies it is not without difficulty that one may proceed to generalizations about the location of church-oriented religion in modern industrial society. With some exaggeration one may venture the remark that the wealth of data—in the absence of a common theoretical framework—proves to be more of an embarrassment than an advantage. Since most studies have concentrated on sociographic details it is easier to discern the local, regional, national and doctrinal peculiarities of the churches than the common social characteristics of church-oriented religion. To add to the difficulties, some authors have ecclesiastic if not theological commitments. It is, therefore, sometimes necessary to disentangle the data from a certain bias in interpretation. The fact that we cannot present all findings in detail here compounds the difficulties. If we are to gain an overall picture of church-oriented religion in modern society as a first step toward an understanding of religion in the contemporary world, we must face the risk of some oversimplification. In order to minimize this risk, we shall present only such generalizations as are based on convergent rather than on isolated findings. Even after taking this precaution it is to be admitted that the generalizations cannot be taken as proven beyond all doubt. They are, however, conclusions favored by the weight of available evidence.[2]

In Europe it is common knowledge that the country is more 'religious' than the city. This is generally borne out by the findings of research in the sociology of religion. From church attendance figures to religious burial reports, various

---

Source: T. Luckmann, *The Invisible Religion,* Macmillan, 1967, pp. 28–37.

[1]Notable are Fichter's studies of Catholic parishes. Fichter was influential in initiating the trend from purely sociographic studies to parish sociology and his studies served as a model for most recent Catholic as well as Protestant parish investigations. Cf. Fichter (1951 and 1954).

[2]Considering the limitations of this study an attempt to document the following by a complete bibliography would be impossible. A large bibliography can be found in Goldschmidt and Matthes (1962). For reviews of the field, see Glock (1959), Honigsheim (1957), Hunt (1958), Le Bras (1960), Goldschmidt, Griener and Schelsky (1959) and Lambert (1960).

statistics which can be taken as indicative of church-oriented religion show consistently higher averages for rural than for urban areas. On the basis of such statistics only a small proportion of the urban population can be described as church-oriented. It is of some interest to note, however, that there is a long-range trend toward a decrease of church-oriented religion in rural regions, too. Consequently, the difference in church-oriented religion, while not completely leveled, is smaller now than several decades ago. It hardly needs to be added that this is merely part of a more general process. The transformations in the distribution of church-oriented religion are linked to increasing economic interpenetration of city and country, the growing rationalization of farming, the diffusion of urban culture to the country through mass media and so forth. It should be noted, however, that these transformations do not proceed at an even rate. In addition to local and regional circumstances of economic and political character the specifically 'religious' historical tradition of a region or congregation may speed up or retard the process.

According to another item of common knowledge women are more 'religious' than men and the young and old more 'religious' than other age groups. Research findings indicate that such opinions need to be revised at least in part. Indeed, women generally do better than men on various indices of church-oriented religion, and the middle generation is, in fact, characterized by lower participation and attendance rates than the young and the old. It is significant, however, that working women as a category tend to resemble men more closely in church orientation than, for example, housewives do. This hardly supports the view that women, children and old people have something like a natural inclination for church-oriented religion. The findings represent an important aspect of the social distribution of church-oriented religion rather than being indicative of the psychology of sex and age. In general terms, we may say, that the degree of involvement in the work processes of modern industrial society correlates negatively with the degree of involvement in church-oriented religion. It is obvious, of course, that the degree of involvement in such processes is in turn linked with age- and sex-roles.

The involvement of the working population in church-oriented religion—while lower than that of the rest of the population—is, however, itself significantly differentiated. Among the various occupational groups can be found important differences in participation. The indices are generally higher for agricultural, white-collar and some professional groups. These differences coincide roughly with the distribution of church-oriented religion among social classes. Farmers, peasants and those elements of the middle classes which are basically survivals of the traditional bourgeoisie and petite bourgeoisie are marked by a degree of involvement in church-oriented religion which is disproportionately higher than that of the working class.

In addition to church attendance, opinions on doctrinal matters and so forth, some recent studies in the sociology of religion also investigated participation in various nonritual activities of the churches, ranging from youth clubs to charitable enterprises. These studies indicate that in Europe only a small fraction of the members of congregations join activities that lie outside of the ritual functions of the churches. While those participating in these functions—whom we may collectively call the ritual core of the congregation—represent only a relatively small part of the nominal membership of the parish, they are yet more numerous than those otherwise active in the church. The size of that latter group, the hard core of active members, varies from region to region and from one denomination to the other. It can be said that the major factors determining these differences are the ecology of the community and the distribution of social classes and occupational groups within the parish. The role which these factors play in the selection of the 'hard core' from the congregational membership as a whole, however, is not as important as the role these same factors play in the initial recruitment of the congregation from the reservoir of merely nominal members.

While some aspects of the relation between society and church-oriented religion are common knowledge, there can be little doubt that for the industrial countries of Western Europe the findings of the recent sociology of religion describe this relation with more precision. They establish a clear connexion between the distribution of church-oriented religion and a number of demographic and other sociologically relevant variables. In the foregoing we described the most important of these. We must, however, draw attention to the fact that the figures vary from country to country and from denomination to denomination. By most criteria Catholicism exhibits higher rates of participation than Protestantism. Some part of this variation can be attributed to differences in the degree of industrialization characterizing Catholic and Protestant countries, respectively, to the presence or absence of a tradition of militant socialism, to different forms of church–state relations and other factors. At the same time, there are considerable national and regional differences which cannot be attributed directly to demographic, economic or political factors. The level of participation in church-oriented religion seems to be exceptionally low in the case of Anglicanism. Or, to refer to another example, there are differences in the level of participation among French Catholic dioceses which can be attributed in part to sociologically rather intangible historical traditions. Note should be taken also of another factor, neglected in our present summary, that seems to be involved in the distribution of church-oriented religion: the proportion of the members of a denomination in the total population. With certain exceptions, so-called diaspora congregations are characterized by relatively high attendance and participation figures.

These remarks should not obscure the over-riding influence of economic, political and class variables in determining the distribution of church-oriented religion in present-day Western Europe. Before we proceed to draw conclusions about religion in modern society, the European data must be compared with the findings of research on religion in the United States.

For several reasons such comparison is difficult. First, the great variety of institutional expressions of religion in America has not yet been thoroughly and systematically investigated, although at least the major and most typical expressions and some of the sects, fascinating to the sociologist for one reason or another, did receive attention. Second, among the studies that were carried out some were guided by a pronounced positivistic bias. The third and most important reason is the unique social and religious history of America. For this, more than for any other reason, caution is indicated in summary characterizations of church religion in America, especially if they are to be used for comparison with the European findings. A sizeable number of processes and circumstances find no close parallel in European social history; for example, the absence of a feudal past and of a peasantry, the peculiar complex of conditions known as the frontier experience, the successive ethnically and denominationally distinct waves and strata of immigration, the rapid and nearly convulsive processes of urbanization and industrialization, the Negro problem and the early establishment of a dominant middle-class outlook and way of life. The religious history of the country includes equally distinct circumstances: the Puritan period, the early separation of church and state, followed by a persistent and peculiarly intimate relation between politics and religion, the era of revival movements, the prodigious development of sects and the transformation of sects into denominations.

If one views the findings of research on church religion in America against this historical background, it is surprising that they exhibit so much similarity to the European data. It is true that, at first, this similarity is not obvious. Fewer people seem to be involved in church religion than in Europe—if one bases the comparison on the European conception of nominal membership. Conversely, and no matter what criteria one uses, the figures for participation and involvement are much higher for the United States. The difference is especially striking in the case of Protestantism, since Catholic participation rates are relatively high in Europe, too.

Yet, on closer inspection, it appears that the same general factors determine the over-all social location of church religions although the levels of participation may differ. The participation rates are again higher for Catholicism than Protestantism, especially if, in the latter case, one considers the major denominations rather than some of the smaller sects. And, again, differences between rural and urban areas can be found. The contrast between city and country exhibits a more complex pattern than in Europe and is not as striking, mainly because of Catholic concentrations in many metropolitan areas. The differences between men and women also follow the same lines, with the exception of the Jews. These differences, too, are less sharply drawn than in Europe. The differences in the involvement of the generations in church religion follow the European example only in part. Here, a number of factors, especially the pull of Sunday-school children on the parents—most pronounced in suburbia—complicates the basic pattern.

From the findings on church involvement of different occupational groups no consistent picture emerges. In any case, the data are too scarce to permit any generalizations. One may, perhaps, suspect that in this instance some deviations from the European pattern may be present. The differences between classes with respect to religion are less pronounced than in Europe. This may be attributable in part to the fact that class differences are less pronounced—and certainly less conspicuous—in general, despite an underlying structural similarity in the social stratification of the Western European countries and the United States. Although the major churches and denominations are, at the very least, middle-class oriented, the relatively sharp cleavage between a church-oriented middle class and an unchurched working class does not exist. This is, of course, not surprising, since the working class today merges almost imperceptibly into the outlook, way of life and religious pattern of the middle classes to a much greater extent than in Europe, although there are some indications of a process of *embourgeoisement* in the European working class. Such differences as still exist in the recruitment of church members and in participation are overlaid by the peculiarly American differentiation of prestige among the denominations. These differences find expression in the composition of membership of the denominations. Significantly enough, however, the status differences in the membership of the denominations are popularly much exaggerated. In this connexion the Negro–White cleavage in Protestant churches and congregations deserves to be mentioned. These observations are not valid for one social stratum: the rural and urban proletariat, the term not being understood in its Marxist sense. It consists in large part of Negroes, Puerto Ricans, Mexicans and others. This stratum is socially almost completely invisible and nearly unchurched. Even Catholicism, whose influence on the working class generally appears to be stronger than that of Protestantism, appears to have lost or is loosing its hold on this stratum. But this stratum is not part of the middle-class oriented working population and those parts that are not unchurched tend to be attracted to sects that are marginal to Protestantism both theologically and in its orientation to society.

Ethnic churches played a significant role in American religious history. Today, ethnic churches for persons of European background have either disappeared or are of subordinate importance. Only churches linked to racial minorities persist on the religious scene. Their function depends, of course, on the position of the minorities in American society.

One of the most important developments in American church religion is the process of doctrinal leveling. It can be safely said that within Protestantism doctrinal differences are virtually irrelevant for the members of the major denominations. Even for the ministry traditional theological differences seem to have an ever-decreasing importance. More significant is the steady leveling of the differences between Catholicism, Protestantism and Judaism. This process should not be taken as a result of a serious theological *rapprochement*. Furthermore, several areas of fairly sharp friction remain between Catholicism and the other religious bodies, especially in matters of public policy. There can be little doubt, however, that Catholicism, Protestantism and Judaism are jointly characterized by similar structural transformations—a bureaucratization along rational businesslike lines—and accommodation to the 'secular' way of life. In consequence of the historical link between this way of life and the Protestant ethos, the accommodation of Protestantism, as represented by its major denomination, has perhaps gone farther than that of the other religious bodies. It seems, however, that the difference is superficial (cf. Herberg, 1955). It is to be noted that, despite the trend toward a leveling of ideological differences and the increasing irrelevance of doctrine for the membership, the *social* differences in the traditions of

Protestantism, Catholicism and Judaism continue to play a role. According to some findings they may be destined for perpetuation by endogamy. The way of life and the social basis for some central dimensions of subjective identification remain linked to subcultures designated by religious labels (cf. Lenski, 1961).

These observations may be summarized as follows. There are some aspects of church religion in America which are either unique or at least conspicuously different from the European situation. With one exception—the relatively high involvement of Americans in church religion—the differences seem less significant than the similarities. The correlations of various indices of involvement in church religion with demographic and ecological variables as well as with social role and status configurations follow a similar pattern in the European and American findings. This pattern represents the social location of church religion in the industrial countries of the West. If we may take these countries as paradigmatic, the pattern invites the conclusion that church-oriented religion has become a marginal phenomenon in modern society.

This conclusion meets one serious difficulty in the previously mentioned deviation from the pattern. The most 'modern' of the countries under discussion, the United States, shows the highest degree of involvement in church religion. To compound the difficulties, the high American figures of overt participation represent, in all likelihood, a fairly recent upward movement rather than a decrease from a yet higher previous level. In the face of these circumstances it is obvious that no simple unilinear and one-dimensional theory of 'secularization' in modern society can be maintained.

The difficulty is only apparent. In order to resolve it, it is only necessary to take into account the differences in the character of church religion in Europe and America. In Europe church religion did not undergo radical inner transformations and became restricted to a minor part of the population. As it continued to represent and mediate the traditional universe of religious ideas, its social base shrunk characteristically to that part of the population which is peripheral to the structure of modern society: the peasantry, the remnants of the traditional bourgeoisie and petite bourgeoisie within the middle classes, which are not— or no longer or not yet—involved in the typical work processes of industrial and urban society.[3]

In the United States, on the other hand, church religion has a broad middle-class distribution. The middle classes are, *in toto,* anything but peripheral to the modern industrial world. The distribution of church religion in America, nevertheless, does not represent a reversal of the trend toward 'secularization'—that is, a resurgence of traditional church religion. It is rather the result of a radical inner change in American church religion. This change consists in the adoption of the *secular* version of the Protestant ethos by the churches which, of course, did not result from concerted policy but is rather a product of a unique constellation of factors in American social and religious history.[4]

---

[3]For an interpretation, see Tenbruck (1959); cf. also Koester (1959), esp. p. 108.

[4]A study which traces the symptoms of these changes has been done by Schneider and Dornbusch (1958).

Whereas religious ideas originally played an important part in the shaping of the American Dream, today the secular ideas of the American Dream pervade church religion. The cultural, social and psychological functions which the churches perform for American society as a whole as well as for its social groups, classes, and individuals would be considered 'secular' rather than 'religious' in the view the churches traditionally held of themselves.[5] Comparing the European and American findings on the social location of church religion and allowing for the differences in the character of church religion in European and American society we are led to the conclusion that traditional church religion was pushed to the periphery of 'modern' life in Europe while it became more 'modern' in America by undergoing a process of internal secularization. This conclusion requires further interpretation.

The configuration of meaning which constitutes the symbolic reality of traditional church religion appears to be unrelated to the culture of modern industrial society. It is certain, at least, that internalization of the symbolic reality of traditional religion is neither enforced nor, in the typical case, favored by the social structure of contemporary society. This fact alone suffices to explain why traditional church religion moved to the margin of contemporary life. The findings contradict the notion that the challenge of overt antichurch ideologies plays an important role. If the churches maintain their institutional claim to represent and mediate the traditional religious universe of meaning, they survive primarily by association with social groups and social strata which continue to be oriented toward the values of a past social order. If, on the other hand, the churches accommodate themselves to the dominant culture of modern industrial society they necessarily take on the function of legitimating the latter. In the performance of this function, however, the universe of meaning traditionally represented by the churches becomes increasingly irrelevant. In short, the so-called process of secularization has decisively altered either the social location of church religion or its inner universe of meaning. As we have formulated it, it may appear that these two alternatives are mutually exclusive. This is the case only for their hypothetical, extreme forms. In fact, less radical transformations of both the social location and the meaning universe of church religion may occur jointly.

References

Berger, P. (1961), *The Noise of Solemn Assemblies*, Doubleday.
Fichter, J. H. (1951), *Southern Parish*, vol. 1, University of Chicago Press.
Fichter, J. H. (1954), *Social Relations in the Urban Parish*, University of Chicago Press.
Glock, C. Y. (1959), 'The sociology of religion', in R. K. Merton, L. Broom and L. S. Cottrell, eds., *Sociology Today*, Basic Books, pp. 153–77.
Goldschmidt, D., Greiner, F. and Schelsky, H. (1959), *Soziologie der Kirchengemeinde*, Enke, Stuttgart.
Goldschmidt, D., and Matthes, J. (1962), Probleme der Religionssoziologie, *Kölner Zeitschrift für Soziologie und Sozialpsychologie*, special issue no. 6.

---

[5]For a description and interpretation of these functions, see Berger (1961).

Herberg, W. (1955), *Protestant, Catholic, Jew,* Doubleday.

Honigsheim, P. (1957), 'Sociology of religion—complementary analyses of religious institutions', in H. Becker and A. Boskoff, eds., *Modern Sociological Theory in continuity and change,* Dryden, pp. 450–81.

Hunt, C. L. (1958), 'The sociology of religion', in J. S. Roucek, ed., *Contemporary Sociology,* Philosophical Library, New York.

Koester, R. (1959), *Die Kirchentreuen,* Enke, Stuttgart.

Lambert, R. D. (1960), 'Current trends in religion', *Ann. Amer. Soc. polit. soc. Scien.,* vol. 332, pp. 146–55.

Le Bras, G. (1960), 'Problémes de la Sociologie des Religions', in G. Gurvitch, ed., *Traité de la Sociologie,* vol. 2, Presses Universitaires de France, pp. 79–102.

Lenski, G. (1961). *The Religious Factor,* Doubleday.

Schneider, L., and Dornbusch, S. M. (1958), *Popular Religion—Inspirational Books in America,* University of Chicago Press.

Tenbruck, F. (1959), 'Die Kirchengemeinde in der enkirchlichten Gesellschaft', in D. Goldschmidt, F. Greiner and H. Schelsky, eds., *Soziologie der Kirchengemeinde,* Enke, Stuttgart.

Reading 18

THE SOCIAL FORMS OF RELIGION—
THOMAS LUCKMANN

In this essay, Luckmann moves back in history from an era vaguely medieval to a much more primitive time when religion and society were largely undifferentiated. In such simple societies there was no conscious distinction between religion and the rest of the social order, in part because not even the concepts necessary to make that decision were available. Presumably virtually everyone in the tribe showed up for the annual fertility festival, though human nature being what it was and is, they participated in the festival with varying amounts of enthusiasm and faith.

Luckmann's analysis is interesting and useful, though one wonders how long such simple societies survived. Surely the emergence of religious specialists of one sort or another—medicine men, witch doctors, and shamans—must have come very early. It also must be understood that when participation in and public acceptance of the religious symbols was to a very great extent not a free choice, but something one did almost automatically, religious devotion as we would understand it today is not necessarily more authentic. As Clifford Geertz once remarked to the editor of this volume, there is no reason to think that the blend of faith and hypocrisy was all that much different than it is today.

One could argue that, quite the contrary, conscious choice of religious behavior produces more authentic religion (as we would understand it) than does the opposite.

Questions for Reflection and Discussion

1. Do you think those for whom religious behavior is almost automatic are more religious than those who accept it as a matter of free choice?
2. Were the "primitives" more religious than we are?
3. Does the differentiation of religion that Luckmann describes in fact mean a weakening of religion?
4. In the relatively undifferentiated societies that Luckmann describes, does religion control society or society control religion?

THE SOCIAL FORMS OF RELIGION
Thomas Luckmann

In the sociological theory of religion it is customary to define certain ideas—for example, those dealing with the "supernatural"—as religious and, then, to attach that label to the groups and institutions that seem primarily concerned with the codification, maintenance and propagation of such ideas. This appeared to us as a theoretically impermissible short cut. In order to avoid it we felt obliged to begin with a specification of the universal anthropological condition of religion before turning to the question of how religion becomes a distinct part of social reality; that is, how it is objectivated socially. With this aim in mind we gave a brief account of the origin of meaning-systems in general, and symbolic universes, in particular, in social processes. We found that the construction of meaning-systems rested on detachment and integration and that these phenomena presupposed the reciprocity of face-to-face situations and the continuity of social relations, respectively. The formal description of the structure of social processes in which meaning-systems originated also specified the conditions for the individuation of consciousness and conscience. The formal argument led us to the similarly formal conclusion that an organism becomes a Self by constructing, with others, an "objective and moral universe of meaning." We said that the organism transcends its biological nature by developing a Self and felt justified in calling that process fundamentally religious.

Presently we must reconsider the validity of this conclusion. Because we first had to account for the conditions under which meaning-systems could emerge, we had to restrict our analysis to the constitutive elements of the social processes in which consciousness and conscience are individuated and meaning-systems constructed. We had to leave out of our consideration the historical priority of meaning-systems to any particular human organism.

The conclusion to which our formal analysis led us is, therefore, valid only on the level of general anthropological discourse. We had to restrict our analysis to this level, temporarily, for an obvious reason. The historical existence of meaning-systems is the result of universe-constructing activities of successive generations. Had we started out with the proposition that universes of meaning are historically given, we could not have avoided an infinite regression in our analysis. We did avoid it by giving, first, a formal description of the general conditions under which universes of meaning are constructed. Now we have reached the point, however, at which we may abandon our initial and self-imposed restriction and give due attention to an empirical fact that we so far disregarded.

Empirically, human organisms do not construct "objective" and moral universes of meaning from scratch—they are born into them. This means that

Source: Thomas Luckmann, *The Invisible Religion: The Transformation of Symbols in Industrial Society,* New York: The Macmillan Co., 1967.

human organisms normally transcend their biological nature by internalizing a historically given universe of meaning, rather than by constructing universes of meaning. This implies, further, that a human organism does not confront other human organisms; it confronts Selves. While we so far described the formal structure only of the social processes in which a Self emerges, we must now add that these processes are always filled with "content." To put it differently, the human organism becomes a Self in concrete processes of socialization. These processes exhibit the formal structure previously described *and* mediate, empirically, a historical social order. We suggested before that the transcendence of biological nature by human organisms is a fundamentally religious process. We may now continue by saying that socialization, as the concrete process in which such transcendence is achieved, is fundamentally religious. It rests on the universal anthropological condition of religion, individuation of consciousness and conscience in social processes, and is actualized in the internalization of the configuration of meaning underlying a historical social order. We shall call this configuration of meaning a world view.

The world view transcends the individual in several ways. It is a historical reality which precedes the individuation of any organism's consciousness and conscience. Once it is internalized it becomes a subjective reality for the individual and circumscribes for him the range of meaningful and potentially meaningful experience. Thus it determines his orientation in the world and exerts an influence upon his conduct that is as profound as it is taken for granted and, therefore, unnoticed. In addition, the world view exerts an indirect and "external" influence upon the conduct of the individual by means of institutionalized and noninstitutionalized social controls which reflect the social order and its underlying configuration of meaning. The world view is, consequently, an objective and historical (transcendent), as well as a subjective (immanent), reality for the individual.

Under certain circumstances the world view may reach a further level of transcendence. Since the social order is apprehended as valid and obligatory regardless of person, place and situation, it can be understood as a manifestation of a transcendent and universal order, as a *cosmion* reflecting a cosmos. It may be added that the procedure by which a world view is assigned the status of universality and the transcendence of the social order is explicitly articulated typically serves as a mechanism of great significance in the legitimation of an established social order.

The very fact that the world view is a socially objectivated historical reality explains its crucial function for the individual. Instead of constructing a rudimentary system of meaning the individual draws upon a reservoir of significance. The world view, as the result of universe-constructing activities of successive generations, is immeasurably richer and more differentiated than the interpretive schemes that could be developed from scratch by individuals. Its stability, as a socially objectivated reality, is immeasurably greater than that of individual streams of consciousness. The world view, as a transcendent moral universe, has an obligatory character that could not be approximated in the immediate context of social relations.

Individual existence derives its meaning from a transcendent world view. The stability of the latter makes it possible for the individual to grasp a sequence of originally disjointed situations as a significant biographical whole. The world view as a historical matrix of meaning spans the life of the individual and the life of generations. We may say, in sum, that the historical priority of a world view provides the empirical basis for the "successful" transcendence of biological nature by human organisms, detaching the latter from their immediate life context and integrating them, as persons, into the context of a tradition of meaning. We may conclude, therefore, that the world view, as an "objective" and historical social reality, performs an essentially religious function and define it as an *elementary social form of religion*. This social form is universal in human society.

The world view is an encompassing system of meaning in which socially relevant categories of time, space, causality and purpose are superordinated to more specific interpretive schemes in which reality is segmented and the segments related to one another. In other words, it contains a "natural" logic as well as a "natural" taxonomy. It is important to note that both the logic and the taxonomy have a pragmatic as well as a moral dimension. We say that the logic and the taxonomy contained in a world view are "natural" because they are taken for granted in their totality without question. Only particular items, especially in the content of taxonomic areas, can become doubtful within the lifetime of an individual. As long as the social structure and the social order remain in existence, the logic, at least, survives the passing of many generations. In stable societies, however, not only the logic but also the taxonomy gives the appearance of permanence and rigidity.

In connection with these observations it should be stressed that socialization consists in the internalization of the world view as an encompassing configuration of meaning. The learning of particular items of content is, of course, part of the process and the part which can be apprehended as a conscious performance. In contrast, the internalization of the encompassing configuration of meaning, while containing the acquisition of particular items of content, is not conscious in the same sense. It can be observed only as the formation of an individual "style" of thinking and acting that is relatively independent of the particular characteristics of a given situation and that can be attributed only to the "character" of a person.

The world view is objectivated in society in various forms. Some socially approved and significant ways of orientation in nature and society manifest themselves in stylized forms of movement, gesture and expression that are transmitted from generation to generation. Some socially significant moral ideas and values are represented by symbols of various kinds; for example, flags, icons, totems. The most important form in which a world view is socially objectivated, however, is language. Before showing why this is the case a remark on the relation of world view and language is in order.

At first, one might be tempted to consider the social structure in its totality as an objectivation of the world view. The social structure as a system of performances is, indeed, oriented by the world view. But performances are acts of individuals and one should not disregard the fact that they are directly based upon a substratum of "meaningless" physiological processes, biological needs, and so forth. On the other hand, performances are determined directly or indirectly by institutional controls. Despite the fact that institutional controls reflect in some fashion the configuration of meaning underlying the world view, the fact cannot be ignored that norms can be and are enforced regardless of what is subjectively meaningful to an individual. It would be, therefore, imprecise as well as confusing to consider the social structure as a "straightforward" objectivation of the world view. The world view stands in a dialectic relationship with the social structure. It originates in human activities that are at least partly institutionalized. It is transmitted over the generations in processes that are, again, at least partly dependent on institutions. Conversely, performances and institutions depend on the continuous internalization of a world view.

We said that the most important objectivation of the world view is to be found in language. A language contains the most comprehensive and, at the same time, most highly differentiated system of interpretation. This system can be internalized, in principle, by any member of society, and all experiences of all members can be potentially located in that system. The logic and the taxonomy contained in the world view are stabilized in the syntax and the semantic structure of the language. It is obvious, therefore, that in the analysis of the objectivating function of language its semantic and syntactic levels are of more immediate consequence than its phonology. It is just as obvious, however, that it is the embodiment of sense in sound which fixes and stabilizes interpretive schemes and makes the latter continuously and routinely available.

We said earlier that socialization consists, concretely, in the learning of particular items of content but that these are only elements in the internalizations of an encompassing configuration of meaning. Analogously, the learning of particular linguistic elements, while essential and the only directly observable and conscious process, is subordinate to the internalization of what we may call, adopting Wilhelm von Humboldt's concept, the inner form of language.

The explicit rules and codifications, corresponding roughly to what in linguistics are called "phenotypes," are, of course, objectivations in the strict sense. At least as important, however, are the contextual elements in the linguistic analysis of reality, the "cryptotypes." The explicit and the contextual elements together constitute the inner form of language—the latter may be said to represent a comprehensive model of the universe.

As the individual acquires his mother tongue and internalizes its inner form, he takes over the "natural" logic and taxonomy of a historical world view. The world view, as a reservoir of ready-made solutions and as a matrix of procedures for solving problems, routinizes and stabilizes the individual's memory, thinking, conduct and perception in a manner that is inconceivable without the mediation of language. Through language the world view serves the individual as a source of meaning that is continuously available—both internally and socially.

We defined the world view as an elementary social form of religion. This definition rests on two assumptions which we tried to establish in the foregoing analysis: that the world view performs an essentially religious function and that it is part of socially objectivated reality. One difficulty, however, that may be read into this definition still needs to be clarified.

The world view, as an encompassing system of meaning, contains typifications, interpretive schemes and recipes for conduct on different levels of generality. Those on the lower levels refer to routine affairs and matters of everyday life (such as, the west wind brings rain; don't eat raw pork). Taken by themselves they appear too trivial to deserve to be designated as "religious." But our analysis—at least up to the present point—does not imply that any single element of the world view, trivial or otherwise, is "religious." No single interpretive scheme performs a religious function. It is, rather, the world view as a whole, as a unitary matrix of meaning, that provides the historical context within which human organisms form identities, thereby transcending biological nature.

It will be, therefore, advisable to add an explicit reminder of this fact to the definition of the world view as a social form of religion and say that it is both elementary and *nonspecific*. Perhaps it is superfluous to point out that the nonspecific quality of the world view—as a social form of religion—is connected with another previously mentioned circumstance. The world view is universal in human society and has no special or distinct institutional basis. It stands, rather, in a dialectic relationship to the social structure as a whole. Important as it was to establish the religious function and the social "objectivity" of the world view, the sociological theory of religion, interested in specific forms of religion in society, cannot rest content at that point. We must, therefore, now turn to the question of what additional and distinctly articulated forms religion may assume in society and how such forms are to be derived from the elementary and nonspecific objectivation of religion in the world view.

Although we just said that the world view as a whole performs a religious function and that no single element of the world view is to be designated as religious, we must presently qualify this statement. Within the world view a domain of meaning can become articulated that deserves to be called religious. This domain consists of symbols which represent an essential "structural" trait of the world view as a whole—to wit, its inner hierarchy of significance. It is the fact that this domain stands for the religious function of the world view as a whole that justifies calling it religious.

The typifications, interpretive schemes and models of conduct contained in a world view are not discrete and isolated units of meaning. They are arranged in a hierarchy of significance. Formally speaking, this hierarchical arrangement of meaning is an essential "structural" trait of the world view. The concrete arrangement of the elements in a historical world view, however, is a characteristic that distinguishes it empirically from other historical world views. The extraordinary richness of the permutations of meaning and the historical variety of the hierarchies of significance preclude a detailed analysis. We shall have to restrict ourselves to a formal outline of the argument, illustrating, rather than systematically documenting the argument, by occasional examples.

On the lowest level of the world view are typifications of concrete objects and events in the world of everyday life (trees, rocks, dogs, walking, running, eating, green, round, etc., etc.). These typifications are applied routinely and in an attitude of familiarity in the course of unproblematic experiences. While they aid in the articulation of such experiences, they instil little significance into them. The interpretive schemes and recipes for conduct on the next higher level are based on the typifications of the first level, but contain, in addition, significant elements of pragmatic *and* "moral" evaluation (such as, maize does not grow where aloe grows; pork is inferior meat; there should be no marriage between first-degree cousins; if invited for dinner take flowers to the lady of the house). Such schemes and recipes are also applied in taken-for-granted processes of orientation in everyday life, but are charged with some significance that points "beyond" the individual experience and are capable of functioning as "motives." To this level are superordinated more general interpretive schemes and models of conduct which chart a morally significant course of thought and conduct against a background of problematic alternatives (such as, early to bed and early to rise keeps a man healthy, wealthy and wise; a true warrior does not shrink from pain; and a lady does not smoke in public). The application of these models and interpretive schemes in concrete instances depends on an element of reflection—as slight as that may be—and is, typically, accompanied by a subjective realization of the "moral" significance involved. These models and schemes are closely linked to evaluations and prescriptions formulated in terms of encompassing biographical categories (such as, he lived and died a man). These are related, in turn, to a superordinated level of interpretation referring to social and historical wholes (such as, a just social order; the beaver clan) that claim jurisdiction over individual conduct.

Thus, as one moves from the lower to the higher levels of meaning in a world view, one finds a decrease of familiar and variable concreteness that is met with unthinking routine and an increase of generally obligatory models whose concrete application involves some "choice." This complex hierarchy of significance is a "structural" trait of the world view. As we indicated earlier, it is capable of articulation. Such articulation is necessarily indirect: The hierarchy of significance underlying the world view as a whole finds expression in *specific* representations. These representations implicitly stand for the global sense of the world view but refer, explicitly, to a distinct level of reality—a level in which ultimate significance is located. Thus a "structural" trait of the world view becomes a part of its "contents."

The routines of everyday life "make sense" in graduated biographical, social and historical strata of meaning. Daily life is apprehended as being subordinated to levels of significance that transcend everyday life. Everyday routines are part and parcel of a familiar world. This is a world which can be managed by ordinary action. Its "reality" can be grasped by the ordinary senses of ordinary men. The "reality" of the world of everyday life is concrete, unproblematic and, as we may say, "profane." The strata of significance to which everyday life is ultimately referred, however, are neither concrete nor unproblematic. Their "reality" manifests itself in various ways which are only partially accessible to the insight of ordinary men. That "reality" cannot be dealt with habitually;

indeed, it is beyond the control of ordinary men. The domain transcending the world of everyday life is experienced as "different" and mysterious. If the characteristic quality of everyday life is its "profaneness," the quality that defines the transcendent domain is its "sacredness."

The relation between the world of everyday life and the sacred domain is indirect. Many graduated strata of meaning mediate between the trivial and "profane" routines and the "ultimate" significance of a biography, a social tradition, and so forth. There is another type of experience which results from a breakdown of the routine of everyday life. It ranges from helplessness in the face of natural events to death and is typically accompanied by anxiety or ecstasy or a mixture of both. Experiences of that type are apprehended, as a rule, as direct manifestations of the reality of the sacred domain. Thus both the ultimate significance of everyday life and the meaning of extraordinary experiences are located in this "different" and "sacred" domain of reality.

While the two domains tend to become polarized, they are necessarily apprehended as being related in some manner. This relationship ranges from a relatively high degree of segregation between a profane world and a sacred cosmos to a high degree of interpenetration. Animism, totemism and eschatology are some of the more typical systematic elaborations of this relationship.

Since the sacred cosmos is taken to manifest itself in the profane world in some form, there is no insurmountable obstacle to an articulation of the transcendent domain in the world of everyday life. The articulation depends, however, on the "limited" objective possibilities of expression that characterize the profane world. Consequently there is a tendency to consider such expression as "ultimately" inadequate. Again one finds a variety of more or less systematic positions on this question, ranging from the view that the sacred cosmos manifests itself in concrete and visible enclaves in the profane world to highly sophisticated theories of the roles which language, icons, and so forth perform in expressing the "inexpressible."

We must now qualify the statement that the articulation of the sacred cosmos depends on the possibilities of ordinary expression. It is valid in a purely formal sense: The sacred cosmos is, of course, socially objectivated in the same media in which the world view as a whole is objectivated—that is, in performances, images and language. Formally speaking, rituals are performances, sacred icons are images, divine names are words. Yet there is a difference. Performances such as a manner of eating and a procedure of planting do indeed embody an aspect of the world view. The meaning of such performances is, however, first and foremost, pragmatic. They have a purpose in the context of everyday life proper, but only indirectly are they integrated into "higher" levels of significance. Ritual acts, on the other hand, which embody an element of the sacred cosmos, are—strictly speaking—meaningless within the immediate context of everyday life. Their purpose refers *directly* to the sacred cosmos. Sacrifices, rites of passage, burial rites, and such like represent ultimate significance without what we may term intermediate levels of translation into the profane context of everyday routine. *Mutatis mutandis,* this also holds for language, the most important medium of objectivation of the world view in general as well as of the sacred cosmos. The formulation of interpretive schemes and models of conduct in everyday life depends, primarily, upon the straightforward referential function of language. The linguistic articulation of a sacred cosmos, however, rests upon what we may term the symbolic potential of language which appears in the personification of events, the formation of divine names, the construction of "different" realities by metaphorical transposition, and so forth. In contrast to ordinary use the symbolic use of language is typically accompanied by an element of ecstasy and frequently leads to a theory of inspiration.

In sum, language combines with ritual acts and icons in the articulation of a sacred cosmos. The most prominent objectivated features of this cosmos are a sacred calendar, a sacred topography and ritual enactments of the sacred tradition of social groups, as well as ritual acts instilling sacred significance into individual biographies. Further elaborations of the sacred cosmos may take the form of thematically rather specific condensation of critical problems of social and individual life in dance, epos, drama.

The embodiments of the sacred cosmos—which we shall call religious representations—authoritatively bestow sense to individual life. The authority of religious representations cannot be derived from the content of a given sacred theme taken in isolation. It rests upon the hierarchy of significance of the world view as a whole and, ultimately, upon the transcendent quality of the latter. The integrating function of the world view as a whole is performed in concrete processes of socialization by specific religious representations. The effectiveness of specific religious themes in shaping individual consciousness and in bestowing significance upon individual biographies, however, does not originate in the explicit, historically variable content of the themes but in the hierarchy of significance which these themes indirectly represent. The explicitly articulated transcendence of a sacred cosmos in relation to the world of everyday life stands for the transcendence of a socially articulated world view in relation to the subjective stream of consciousness. Correspondingly, the specifically articulated religious themes in the process of socialization stand for socialization as a total process of religious individuation.

We may say, in summary, that the hierarchy of significance which characterizes the world view as a whole and which is the basis of the religious function of the world view is articulated in a distinct superordinated layer of meaning within the world view. By means of symbolic representations that layer refers explicitly to a domain of reality that is set apart from the world of everyday life. This domain may be appropriately designated as a sacred cosmos. The symbols which represent the reality of the sacred cosmos may be termed religious representations because they perform, in a specific and concentrated way, the broad religious function of the world view as a whole. The world view in its totality was defined earlier as a universal and nonspecific social form of religion. Consequently, the configuration of religious representations that form *a sacred universe* is to be defined as a *specific historical social form of religion*.

The sacred cosmos is part of the world view. It is socially objectivated in the same manner as the world view as a whole, the special symbolic quality of religious representations notwithstanding. This means that the sacred cosmos forms part of the objective social reality without requiring a distinct and specialized institutional basis. As part of the world view the sacred cosmos stands in a relationship with the social structure as a whole. The sacred cosmos permeates the various, more or less clearly differentiated, institutional areas such as kinship, the division of labor and the regulation of the exercise of power. The sacred cosmos determines directly the entire socialization of the individual and is relevant for the total individual biography. To put it differently, religious representations serve to legitimate conduct in the full range of social situations.

Without analyzing in detail the social-structural conditions for the elaboration and maintenance of a sacred cosmos, it can be observed generally that this social form of religion predominates in *relatively* "simple" societies. With this term we refer to societies with a low degree of institutional differentiation—more precisely, with a low degree of "autonomy" of separate institutional areas (roughly corresponding to what is referred to as "primitive fusion" by Redfield)—and a relatively homogeneous social distribution of the world view. In such societies the sacred cosmos is, in principle, equally accessible to all members of society and equally relevant to them. Since a genuinely homogeneous distribution of the world view is inconceivable, it is obvious that the equal accessibility and relevance of the sacred cosmos is in fact only approximated. No matter how "simple" a society is, it is characterized by some social differentiation, even if that differentiation is primarily institutionalized and articulated in terms of the kinship system. Whatever differentiation there is, it can, and typically does, serve as a basis for an unequal distribution not only of the other elements of the world view but also of the sacred cosmos.

We may say, nonetheless, that the sacred cosmos is a social form of religion which is characterized by segregation of specifically religious representations within the world view *without* specialization of an institutional basis for these representations. The sacred cosmos penetrates, perhaps in varying degrees, the relatively undifferentiated institutional spheres. The maintenance of the sacred cosmos as a social reality and its transmission from generation to generation depend upon general rather than institutionally specialized social processes.

The more "complex" a society, the more likely is it to develop distinct institutions supporting the objectivity and social validity of the sacred cosmos. Full specialization of an institutional basis for the sacred cosmos presupposes, however, a concurrence of circumstances that is historically unique. In relatively "simple" societies one may already find an incipient differentiation of social roles that are directly linked to the sacred cosmos. In the so-called higher civilizations the sacred cosmos generally rests on institutions that are at least partly differentiated from kinship institutions and the institutions regulating the exercise of power and the production and distribution of goods and services. Thus the classical civilizations of the Orient, Europe and the Americas are characterized by some form of institutionalized priesthood. Complete institutional specialization and "autonomy" of religion, with all their structural concomitants, however, emerged only in the Judaeo–Christian tradition of Western history. A somewhat remote parallel can be discerned in the Islamic world. Because we are understandably predisposed to identify institutionally specialized religion with religion *tout court,* it is important to stress the fact that the full development of this social form of religion presupposed an intricate pattern of structural and intellectual conditions.

A society can have a world view with a more or less clearly articulated sacred cosmos without having, at the same time, a special institutional basis that carries that cosmos. The establishment of specialized religious institutions, on the other hand, presupposes some degree of articulation of a sacred cosmos in the world view. Generally speaking one may say that the more pronounced the distinctness of the sacred cosmos, the likelier is the emergence of a specialized institutional basis for that cosmos.

The relation between the sacred cosmos as part of the world view and specialized religious institutions is not one-sided, however. An incipient differentiation of religious institutions as, for example, the emergence of a priesthood, favors and accelerates the segregation of specifically religious representations. Some events in the life of the group, such as the death of a chief, or in the life of the individual, the first hunt, are, of course, apprehended in all societies as having a distinctly higher significance than, for example, the routine planting of coconut trees or the ninety-seventh hunt. Nevertheless, the sharper such distinctions of significance (that is, the more clearly articulated the sacred cosmos), the greater is the likelihood that the events involved, and the knowledge appropriate to deal with such events, will be in charge of relatively specialized social roles. Conversely, the specialization of social roles that are directly linked to the sacred universe will enhance the division of reality into a sacred cosmos and a world of ordinary affairs and the segregation of religious representations from other fields of significance within the world view. Whereas the original articulation of the sacred cosmos does not, in principle, depend on institutional specialization, the formation of specifically religious social roles does presuppose the existence of an articulated sacred cosmos. General recognition of the special status of religious representations in the world view and specialization of religious roles in the social structure do, however, in fact support one another.

The articulation of a sacred cosmos in the world view is, therefore, a necessary but not a sufficient condition for institutional specialization of religion. In addition to this "cultural" prerequisite, several structural conditions must be met before a development toward institutional specialization of religion can set in. Differentiation of social roles whose specific and more or less exclusive task is the administration of knowledge and regulation of performances pertaining to the sacred universe can occur only in societies that fulfill the minimal *general* presuppositions for the evolution of a "complex" social structure. The technology of production and the division of labor must be sufficiently developed to permit the accumulation of surplus over the subsistence minimum. The surplus over the subsistence minimum, in turn, must be large enough to support further differentiation in the division of labor and to permit, more specifically, the growth of specialized bodies of experts. It should be noted, of course, that no matter how "simple" a society, different social roles carry a graduated charge of sacred significance. Thus, for example, fathers may be closer to things sacred than sons—but sons normally become fathers themselves. Or, to give another example, chiefs may possess a sacred quality that is not shared by the other members of the tribe—but chiefs perform many tasks that are only indirectly connected with the sacred cosmos. One may speak here of a preferential distribution of sacred qualities to social roles, but not of specialized religious roles. The sacred qualities remain integrated into the biographical cycle and are "fused" into the over-all role pattern. From such a state of affairs fully specialized religious roles are likely to develop only if the structural conditions presupposed in the removal of full-time "experts" from production are met.

A point that is closely related to the one just made concerns the circumstances surrounding the emergence of religious "theory." Increasing complexity of the division of labor, a large surplus over the subsistence minimum and a correspondingly more differentiated pattern of social stratification combine to produce an increasingly more heterogeneous social distribution of the world view. This means, among other things, that certain types of knowledge will be available only to socially designated experts. It means further that religious representations will be distributed in a pattern of growing inequality. Because of the place and function of the sacred cosmos in the world view, "everybody" will still participate, of course, in some manner in the configuration of religious representations long after other types of knowledge have become reserved for specialists. Thus, for example, the fisherman will know little of bow-making and the bow-maker little of fishing while both will share sacred knowledge although that knowledge may be inferior to that of the chief in degree. The systems of relevance attached to occupational roles, however, are likely to accentuate such differences in sacred knowledge. At a certain level of complexity of the social structure the social and occupational stratification leads to typical differences in socialization which also affect the acquisition of sacred knowledge. The resulting inequality in the distribution of religious representations will induce, at the very least, the consolidation of different versions of the sacred cosmos among occupational groups and social strata.

The more unequal the distribution of religious representations, the more is the integrating function of the sacred cosmos for the society as a whole threatened. This threat is countered by two mutually not exclusive procedures. The different versions of the sacred cosmos are standardized into an obligatory doctrine, and the existence of whatever differences in religious representations that may remain is explained by an account that is plausible in terms of the inner logic of the sacred cosmos. Now the problems that may lead to the codification of doctrine and the reinforcement of the plausibility of the sacred cosmos do not equally affect all members of a society. The problems arise most often in the transmission of the sacred cosmos from one generation to the next and in situations involving the incumbents of social roles that are charged with a relatively high degree of sacred significance. Such problems are much less likely to arise as long as religious representations are distributed in society in a fairly homogeneous fashion. The "logic" underlying the sacred cosmos is taken for granted because it is equally applicable to different social situations. The validity of that "logic" is reinforced by everybody. Thus the sacred cosmos and its underlying logic remain unproblematic. The chance of situations occurring in which the "logic" of the sacred universe is no longer self-explanatory increases, however, as the social distribution of religious representations grows more heterogeneous. Especially those involved in the transmission of the sacred universe to the next generation and the incumbents of social roles containing a relatively high degree of sacred significance are likely to find that the sacred cosmos and its "logic" require some elaboration in order to retain their plausibility. Thus the relation of religious representations to one another becomes the topic of more or less systematic reflection and interpretation. The meaningful coherence of the world view as a whole and of the sacred cosmos is worked out "theoretically" by a body of incipient experts. If these experts can be set aside from the production process, institutional specialization of religious "theory" proceeds apace. In sum, the structurally determined growth of codification and interpretation of the sacred cosmos significantly contributes to the differentiation of specialized religious roles.

It should be noted briefly that "extrinsic" factors may also encourage reflection about and systematic interpretation of a sacred cosmos. Thus, for example, the contact of different cultures typically produces situations in which the home-grown variety of a sacred universe confronts an imported religion. Such situations encourage "theoretical" efforts proving the superiority of the native religion or syncretizing the native and the imported religions in some way. More often than not this strengthens the trend toward institutional specialization of religion by provoking the establishment of defensive organizations of an incipiently ecclesiastic type.

With increasing specialization of religious roles laymen come to participate less and less directly in the sacred cosmos. Only the religious experts are in "full" possession of sacred knowledge. The application of that knowledge is the province of the experts and the laymen rely increasingly on the mediation of the experts in their relations with the sacred universe.

If religiously relevant conduct originally rests on fully internalized norms and general social controls, conformity in such matters is increasingly supervised by religious specialists in more "complex" societies. While religious representations originally served to legitimate conduct in all kinds of situations, increasing specialization of religion results in the transfer of social controls over "religious behavior" to specific institutions. The vested interests of religious experts in the recruitment and training of their successors, in the exclusion of laymen from the "higher" forms of sacred knowledge and in the defense of privileges against competing bodies of experts typically lead to the formation of some kind of "ecclesiastic" organization.

Institutional specialization as a social form of religion, we may say in summary, is characterized by standardization of the sacred cosmos in a well-defined doctrine, differentiation of full-time religious roles, transfer of sanctions enforcing doctrinal and ritual conformity to special agencies and the emergence of organizations of the "ecclesiastic" type.

Only if religion is localized in special social institutions does an antithesis between "religion" and "society" develop. Such localization is the necessary condition for the history of religious dogma and ecclesiastic organization as distinct from secular culture and "social," that is, nonreligious institutions. The history of the so-called higher civilizations shows a wide range of relationships between "religion" and "society" ranging from accommodation to conflict. Not only does the degree of institutional specialization of religion vary in these civilizations but also the position which religious institutions occupy in the social structure as a whole. Correspondingly, the antithesis between "religion" and "society" is etched sharply into the history of some of these societies while it remains in abeyance in others.

Religion originally serves in the integration of the social order and in the legitimation of the *status quo*. Institutionally specialized religion may become, however, a dynamic social force in some historical circumstances. Once the sacred universe and the "world" develop their own "logic" and once the latter is backed up by different institutions, tensions may develop between religious experience and the requirements of everyday affairs. Specifically religious communities may emerge, claiming loyalties that place their followers in conflict with "secular" institutions—or the members of other religious communities. The history of Christianity—also of Islam and Buddhism—documents a variety of attempts to find intellectual and structural solutions to such tensions and conflicts. These observations do not imply, of course, that institutionally specialized religion is an intrinsically "progressive" force. If anything, the opposite is true. But in contrast to other social forms of religion, institutional specialization of religion always contains the possibility of an antithesis between "religion" and "society." The latter may act as a catalyst of social change.

It should be noted again that institutional specialization of religion can be approximated in various degrees. The existence of a part-time priesthood, for example, may mark an incipient stage of institutional specialization. Theocracies may be considered an intermediate form of institutional specialization. The church in the Judaeo–Christian tradition of Western history, however, represents an extreme and historically unique case of institutional specialization of religion. It emerges from an extraordinarily sharp segregation of the sacred cosmos from the profane world in Hebrew theology, formulation of the inner logic of that cosmos in eschatological terms, heterogeneity of the world views, "culture conflicts" and syncretism in the areas in which Christianity arose, a fairly high degree of "autonomy" of political and economic institutions in the Roman Empire, etc., etc. The institutionalization of doctrine, the development of ecclesiastic organization and the differentiation of a religious community from society at large reached a degree that was not paralleled elsewhere. It should be also remembered, however, that in all societies characterized by this social form of religion, even if to a lesser degree, the segregation of the sacred cosmos in the world view is matched, to some extent, by specialization of religious roles in the social structure and by the existence of groups claiming a distinctly religious quality.

Reading 19

....

AN ARGUMENT ABOUT SECULARIZATION— THOMAS LUCKMANN AND ANDREW M. GREELEY

This (friendly) argument between Professor Luckmann and the editor (at a conference at the University of Chicago) illustrates not only the argument between those who think religion is not as important as it used to be and those who scream for proof that such is the case, it also illustrates the difference between "theory" as some theorists would define it and as empiricists would define it. The latter ("we" latter) insist that theories not only be testable—that they be subject to analysis that admits of falsification as well as verification— but that they in fact be tested.

The argument took place before the vicious wars that followed the break-up of Yugoslavia illustrated the continued power of religion acting directly upon the social order. It is not clear, however, whether such conflicts are, any more than were the Crusades, proof that men and women were in fact once more religious than they are now. Or that the relative peace among religious groups in the United States makes Americans any less religious than the Serbs or the Croats or the Bosnians.

Questions for Reflection and Discussion

1. Was Richard the Lion-Hearted a better Christian than Mario Cuomo?
2. Were the Crusades a social sign of "more religion" than exists in today's America?
3. Is it accurate to say that religion today has become "privatized?" Or is "personalized" a better word?
4. Is there any way that the Polish and African-American religious movements could be understood as unaffected by religion?

THE NEW AND THE OLD IN RELIGION
Thomas Luckmann

SOCIAL THEORY AND RELIGION

Religion, stubbornly refusing to disappear as a moving force in the conduct of human affairs, continued to pose a seemingly intractable problem for modern social theory. As the heir to eighteenth-century social philosophy, modern social theory was singularly ill-equipped to approach religion without rationalist prejudice. The immediate precursors of nineteenth-century social theory, the philosophers of the Enlightenment, were as one in assuming that the influence of religion would shrink in direct proportion to the ascendancy of reason. They were convinced that the ultimate victory of reason over superstition was inevitable as soon as the fetters imposed upon the minds of men by the unholy alliance of the church with the absolutist state were thrown off.[1]

As their successors in the first half of the nineteenth century learned to view religion as a complex, although deficient, social phenomenon rather than as a simple pathology of thought and emotion, some of them invested considerable effort in searching for a *rational and scientific* substitute. This Comtean motif continued to inspire Durkheim half a century later. After a pioneering analysis of the social roots of religion and of the function of religion in maintaining the bonds of solidarity under different structural conditions, he still seemed to hope that a universal morality might eventually replace the narrower values operative under the conditions of a mechanical division of labor, which were apparently weakening under the anomic conditions of modern life.

Compared to the attitudes toward religion set by the philosophers of the Enlightenment, the post-Hegelian critique of religion may be said to have had a better—and an astonishingly "modern"—grasp of the universal human basis of religion. Formulated successively by Anselm Feuerbach and Karl Marx, its premise is that *"man makes religion,* not religion man."[2] But Marx was far from abandoning the then-already traditional, not to say conventional, assumption of religion as an essentially deficient mode of human existence in the world or, more precisely, as a deficient mode of orientation in an as-yet deficient world. For Marx, this deficiency was rooted in an alienation caused fundamentally by the division of labor and historically by the capitalist mode of production.[3]

At the beginning of the present century, this range of positions regarding religion had not undergone substantial changes in the different camps of social theory. The Marxists, otherwise inclined to ignore the writings of the early "pre-

Source: Pierre Bourdieu and James S. Coleman, eds. *Social Theory for a Changing Society,* Boulder: Westview Press/Russell Sage Foundation, 1991.

scientific" Marx, kept repeating his characterization of religion as the opium of the people. They expected religion to disappear automatically after the revolutionary overthrow of the *objective* conditions of misery, which were assumed to produce the *subjective* illusions of religion. Their prognostic formula "no capitalism, no religion" was reversed in bourgeois social theory by a quasi-empirical formula: "modern capitalism, no religion." The blindness and deafness in social theory regarding religious matters remained remarkable. Although the Spencerian account of the evolution of functional differentiation in society became the dominant model for the interpretation of global social change, its implications for corresponding changes in institutional forms of religion were not pursued. It was ideologically more convenient to cling to both camps of the etiological myth of modernity as the age of the final decline of religion and the ultimate ascendancy of reason—now understood as science. In social theory, the myth was eventually transformed into a "theory" of secularization.[4]

Max Weber alone kept an open mind, although it was he who provided a detailed and convincing account of the process of *Entzauberung* of modern life and was convinced that functional differentiation was leading to a rational-bureaucratic social order—the "iron cage" of modern society. His account of the various factors encouraging rationalization—a process that, according to him, was ironically ushered in by religion as a systematizing and disciplining force—contributed to an understanding of the freeing of the economy and polity from overarching religious norms. But Weber saw no reason to assume that human nature was radically changed in this historical process, and thus he anticipated the advent of new and terrifyingly irrational gods in the minds of those who were to live in the rational cage of modern society.

Still another school of thought, which regarded religion in another perspective but did not exert much lasting influence on social theory, was instituted by the postrevolutionary traditionalists (Louis G. de Bonald, Joseph de Maistre) and found representatives in the first half of the twentieth century in thinkers such as Max Scheler (perhaps, one should say, one of the several "Schelers") as well as in various, more marginal proponents of an "organic" theory of the corporate state and society in which (traditional) religion was to play an essential role. A tenuous thread connects their intellectual positions with those held in contemporary neoconservatism.

These views on religion persisted in simplified versions, if anything. They were current well past the middle of the present century. They formed a rather loose paradigm that influences the social theory of religion to this day. The attitudes associated with these views were, of course, anything but identical. The decline of religion was regarded with smug satisfaction by enlightened progressives and with profound despair by traditional conservatives. The perception of facts as well as the imputation of specific causes also varied significantly. But whether structural differentiation, modern capitalism, industrial society, technology, or science were taken to have already dealt the deathblow to religion, or whether the communist *Aufhebung* of the social conditions responsible for alienation—and thus the religious illusion—was expected to do so shortly, the common denominator of these views is obvious. It is the assumption that the social structure and the culture of the modern world are intrinsically hostile to religion. A second common premise underlying these views was that religion and its traditional (Western) institutional forms could be considered identical for all practical purposes. Thus, the decline of doctrinal and ritual adherence to these forms that was registered at least in Europe during the nineteenth and twentieth centuries was naively generalized, extrapolated to the future, and taken as evidence for a global "theory" of secularization.

Yet, religion refused to behave as expected. Instead of fading away, it continues to show remarkable signs of life.[5] It must be admitted, however, that "religion" put on various disguises—disguises from the point of view, prevalent in the social sciences well into the 1960s, equating religion with its institutionally specialized Western Christian forms. This made it possible for general sociologists (with a few notable exceptions) no longer interested in such an outdated phenomenon as religion and for the somewhat marginalized sociologists of religion to cling to their preconceptions about the secular and rational character of modern society. Although Christianity (in Parsonian terms: the Judaeo-Christian tradition) was seen as the most important cultural factor in the motivation of social change and, eventually, modernization, few sociologists took note of Weber's prediction of the "new gods" to come, and most persisted in ignoring the continued presence of the old gods. In social theory, this state of affairs concerning religion began to change only in recent years, at least in part because of the visibly political consequences of Islamic antimodernist fundamentalism. Even in the sociology of religion, however, where there were signs of a less superficially motivated theoretical reorientation somewhat earlier, the rate of change is slow. The reason—I alluded to it with the "disguise" metaphor—is simple.

In most archaic and many traditional societies, only one social form of religion either existed or was dominant to the near exclusion of others.[6] In the West, this situation prevailed from the Middle Ages—with its Universal church, sects, and heresies—well into the early modern period. However, since the late nineteenth century, and at an accelerated pace after World War I (with the emergence of powerful political religions) and World War II (with the spread of privatization and subjective syncretism in religious matters), religious functions were incorporated into many different, apparently nonreligious institutions or were diffused into new semi-institutional and even noninstitutional (invisible) forms. With the exception of the formerly prevalent social form of religion for which the church-sect or the expanded church-denomination-sect-cult typology had proven adequate, religious phenomena fell through the conceptual meshes in use in the sociology of religion.

Political religions were therefore not considered to be "genuine" religions, even if their avowed goals were the Walhalla of the Third Reich or the Parousia of the classless society. And the most modern subinstitutional subjectivisms escaped attention until a supporting commercial and mass-media apparatus developed on such an order of magnitude that it simply could no longer be overlooked. Thus, only the "downs" and occasionally the "ups" of the traditional social form of religion to which the church-sect typology applied were registered.[7] Even from this limited point of view, the difference in the vitality of this social form of religion between traditional Europe and the modern United States, being the reverse of what one might expect, needed considerable explaining. But these forms, which appeared anachronistic to most social scientists steeped in the lore of rationalism, continued to do much better everywhere than could be expected on the basis of simple extrapolations from the statistics from the second half of the nineteenth and the first half of the twentieth centuries on church membership and various indicators of religious participation.

Religion in the modern world represents an extraordinary amalgam of old and new social forms of religion; the incorporation of religious functions by political movements; civil religions of modern states; fervent socialisms and nationalisms in modernizing states and similar self-declared secular entities; the involutions of modernism and fundamentalism in the established churches and denominations; and the spread of one version after another of romantic subjectivism, hedonism, and occultism and their subinstitutional coalescence around commercial and mass-medial support structures. It is not an overstatement to call this a challenge to social theory.

THE RELIGIOUS FUNCTION: COPING WITH TRANSCENDENCE

Social realities are the immediate and proximate results of human actions. Having become established as historical realities, they constitute the condition for further human actions. In other words, social realities are constructed, maintained, and changed in intersubjectively meaningful sequences of behavior. Therefore, they present a fundamental difficulty to the *social* sciences: How are interactionally *pre*constructed historical realities to be *recon*structed as data with such parsimony as to allow comparison (and more complex generalizing treatments) and yet with sufficient richness as to keep its intrinsically human historical quality?[8] Evidently another, equally fundamental methodological problem—that of adequate *explanations*—is shared by the social sciences with those sciences whose data are not preconstructed as human realities in ordinary human activities but are only constructed in scientific procedures of theoretically simple, if technologically complex, observation.

None of the social sciences can avoid the descriptive problem of adequate reconstruction of intersubjectively meaningful historical social realities. However, this problem must be faced in its most acute form by the social theory of religion. The reason is obvious: Religiously motivated actions, their anticipated and unanticipated results, the interpretations attached to them, and their historical institutionalizations are part of the ordinary, observable[9] social realities. To this extent, their sociological reconstruction as data is neither more nor less difficult than that of other kinds of social reality. But according to the *preconstructions* of the actors, the typical meanings of these actions refer to a reality that is not normally accessible through direct observation. The descriptive task of the sociology of religion, therefore, consists of a careful reconstruction of the structures of action that are part of observable reality and of the accounts given of their intrinsic meaning by the actors.

It is primarily through a systematic interpretation of the latter that a social theory of the *functions* of religion may be attempted. In my view, such a theory must be part of a general theory of religion. More specifically, it will help in identifying that which is common to the great variety of structures constituting the heterogeneous social forms of religion that so confusingly coexist in modern societies. A consideration of functions should play an important role in meeting the challenge religion today poses to contemporary social theory.[10]

Religion is commonly taken to refer to a particular part of human existence—the part that is concerned with the supernatural, with the ultimate meanings of life, with transcendence. Of course, in human life the supernatural is bound up with the natural; ultimate meanings only make sense in the context of the ordinary significance of everyday affairs; and the transcendent is only transcendent with respect to something that is immanent. Wherever these poles of human existence are kept apart with reasonable distinctness, one has little difficulty in applying the term *religion* to activities in which experiences pertaining to one of these poles are objectified and localized in symbols, sacred places, times, dates, persons, and the like. The familiar forms of tribal religions, ancestor cults, and the classical universal religions (especially when they are institutionalized in the form of church and sect) are obvious examples. Such historical institutionalizations of the symbolic (sacred) core of a world view are specific instances of a universal human social process. In this process, world views are constructed in long historical chains of communicative acts whereupon they serve as objective models of socialization.

The basic function of religion is to transform members of the natural species *homo sapiens* into actors in a historical social order—in a "cosmion illuminated from within."[11] Components of social reality that are essential to this function may legitimately be called religious, whether or not they explicitly refer to the supernatural. Religion is to be found wherever the behavior of the members of the species becomes morally accountable action—where a self finds itself in a world shared with other selves, interacting with them on the basis of the elementary principle of the reciprocity of perspectives.[12] The ethnographic and historical record of mankind shows a great variety of social phenomena that have served this basic religious function. However, all are products of two closely related elementary social processes in which the ordinary human reality of everyday life is linked to something that is taken to transcend that reality, to "another" reality.

The first of these processes—the intersubjective reconstruction of experiences of transcendence—consists of communicative acts in which subjective experiences of various kinds of this- and other-worldly transcendences are given an elementary social form as mythical narratives, as invocatory or commemorative rituals, as symbolic reminders and references. In the second of these processes—the social construction of "another" reality—the primary intersubjective reconstructions are interpreted, systematized, reformulated, and canonized—a process that may involve censoring deviant accounts. The reality to which these accounts refer is given firm and usually preeminent ontological status. The relation between ordinary and extraordinary reality is explained, and the norms that guide conduct in everyday life are systematically linked to the ultimate significance of the other reality.

The distinction between these two processes is rather artificial. Talking of universal human experiences of transcendence makes sense only in the context of phenomenological reduction. Concrete experiences of transcendence are necessarily historical, however, and are therefore determined to a large extent—in form and in content—by antecedent social constructions of reality, including those of the "other" reality. Nonetheless, there could be no social construction of transcendent realities without a logically antecedent intersubjective reconstruction of universal aspects of human experience. The historical selection, codification, and institutionalization involved in the second process presupposes the processes of the first. On the other hand, the concrete subjective experiences of transcendence are always molded to a greater or lesser extent by historical socially constructed models of such experiences.

What do I mean when I speak of experiences of *transcendence?* What are constructions of another, an *extraordinary* reality? Every normal human being knows the limits of his or her experience and the boundaries of his or her existence. There is a before, after, and behind one's ongoing, actual experience and a before and after one's own life. Nobody seriously doubts that the world into which he or she was born existed long before he or she became aware of its existence, and nobody expects the world to end when his or her consciousness of it ends. Furthermore, we take it for granted that many things happen that we do not want to happen and that many things occur that we do not want to occur. Sooner or later, every child discovers that the world is independent of its fears and hopes. In the naive realism of everyday life, we *know* the boundaries of our existence, even if we do not constantly *think* about them. Every normal human being knows about the transcendence of the world and knows that this knowledge is an essential part of the common sense—the practical theory of everyday life—of all societies.

In addition, all persons also know of things that transcend them *within* the world. We meet other beings and notice that some of them are remarkably like ourselves. We discover that we are not alone in the world—and this is another component of human awareness that is constitutive of normality. We see that other people are born and that other people die, and, given our knowledge that we are like other people in respect to birth, we are forced into the conclusion of an elementary syllogism. Even the experience of transcendence within the world, the experience of other selves, serves to remind us of the ultimate boundaries of our existence. Finally, we are constantly confronted with certain additional transcendences within the world of everyday life—but, as it were, on a smaller scale.

We must turn around to see what is behind us; sounds, pleasures, pains that are overwhelming in their actuality recede into the past, become memories. Not even the simplest perceptual experience is enclosed in itself. It contains some of the immediate past; it anticipates some of the immediate future. In other words, human experience is a continuous flow of transcendence.

A detailed and precise analysis of the experience of transcendence may not be necessary here, but a summary of its results may be helpful. First, whenever anything that transcends that which at the moment is concretely given in actual, direct experience can itself be experienced in the same manner as that which it now transcends, we may speak of the "little" (spatial and temporal) transcendences of everyday life. Second, when that which is actually experienced—such as the body of another self—is taken to refer to something that cannot be experienced directly—such as the consciousness, the inner life of the other self—we may speak of the intermediate transcendences of everyday life, *provided* that that which cannot itself be experienced directly is taken to belong to the same *everyday* reality as the self and its experiences. Third, when an experience presents itself as pointing to something that not only cannot be experienced directly but in addition is definitively not part of an ordinary reality (in which things can be seen, touched, handled), we may speak of the "great" transcendences.

There is more than one path in which everyday reality can be left behind: in dreams, ecstasy, meditation. These paths have one thing in common: They are departures from ordinary life, and they suspend its practical theory—common sense. In dreams, ecstasies, and meditation, everyday life loses its status as the preeminent reality for the human being, at least for the duration of these experiences. After one returns to everyday life, only recollections of such experiences remain.

Human societies differ significantly in the ways in which they organize subjective experiences of the little transcendences of time and space in ordinary life. Societies differ still more in the way in which they deal with the intermediate and the great transcendences. The importance for social structure of the ways in which the intermediate—the social—transcendences are interpreted and systematized is obvious. And the experiences of the great transcendences are by their very nature always close to disorder. Their organization and control represent a serious problem for all societies. Whether dreams are taken as other-worldly symbolic pointers, as this-worldly psychodynamic signs, or as symptoms of a heavy dinner the night before is not a trivial issue. Whether the realities we remember from ecstatic experiences are defined as illusions or as ultimate reality, and, if the latter, whether the ultimate is seen as radically different or as closely intertwined with everyday affairs constitutes an essential part of world views. *How* people interpret their experiences of transcendence on its different levels is neither a matter of a natural religiosity of the species nor of some archetypal religion. It is a matter of a variety of historical social processes and their products: of the ways in which subjective experiences of transcendence are being communicatively reconstructed, of the ways in which such reconstructions are being built into overarching social constructions of everyday and other realities, and of the ways in which such social constructions—in their turn—serve as models for subjective experiences of transcendence.

THE SOCIAL FORMS OF RELIGION

After these brief functional considerations, it is necessary to look at the structural foundations for the social constructions of "other" realities.[13] Until the late modern period in the industrial societies of the West, there were three basic kinds of arrangements. The first is characterized by the diffusion of religious functions throughout the entire social structure. In the second, there is a certain differentiation of religious functions; they tend to coalesce in institutions in close proximity to, or partial identity with, political institutions. In the third, religious functions are monopolized by a specialized institutional domain.

The first social form of religion was universal in the sense that all archaic societies (hunting and gathering, early nomadic, and horticultural) seem to have been characterized by one of the variants of this arrangement. The second developed after the agricultural revolution in the civilizations of the city-states and early empires. The third emerged from medieval beginnings in the early modern societies of the West and spread, to a certain extent, to the Americas and elsewhere in the footsteps of colonization. Although these forms succeeded one another in historical sequences, they are not stages in an evolutionary pattern. Furthermore, at least two of these forms may have coexisted in any given society for long periods.

In archaic societies, the maintenance and transmission of the sacred universe are based on the social structure in its entirety. To what extent transcendent realities are segregated from ordinary ones—to what extent sacredness is accented and isolated—varies from society to society, otherwise conforming to this basic arrangement. Nevertheless, in all such societies, religion is diffused among the various institutions of society, with minimal crystallizations at certain points in the kinship system (ancestors) and among the first transcendence specialists (shamans). Transcendence-oriented collective representations legitimize the norms of kinship (the dominant dimension of social organization), of the simple division of labor, and of the kinship-based exercise of authority. The meaning of all ordinary action, insofar as it is defined and sanctioned by institutions, is linked either directly—in symbols and rituals—or indirectly—in etiological narratives, proverbs, and the like—to transcendent realities. These motivate and legitimate social action in a great variety of situations and bestow ultimate significance on all relevant stages of an individual's course of life.[14]

The second social form of religion is much younger. Its development is best documented in Pharaohic Egypt and the hydraulic societies of the Near East nearly five thousand years ago.[15] Although the entire social structure still supported a sacred universe, just as transcendent realities legitimated the entire social structure, important religious functions were institutionalized separately and gained strong and highly visible ties with the differentiated institutions of power as, for example, in divine kingship. Increasing complexity in the division of labor, the production of a surplus over the subsistence minimum, central control over storage and distribution (as in the temple-based economy of Old Egypt), growth of supra-communal and supra-tribal political organizations, emergence of distinct occupational roles, and the formation of social classes are processes connected with functional differentiation of social institutions. Yet the logic of the sacred universe continued to dominate all other institutions. The supreme sense ascribed to transcendent realities joined together the meanings of the most diverse everyday actions. It endowed these actions with a certain coherence within the life of the individual, both in its routines and its crises, and linked them to the transcendent life of the family, the community. In any case, the rural majority of the population continued to live in archaic folk communities.

The third of these basic arrangements of religion in society is characterized by a radical change in the relationship between the sacred universe and social structure. Institution specialization of religion means that one particular set of institutions came exclusively to maintain and transmit the social constructions of transcendent reality, in ever-increasing separation from the transmission of the other parts of the social stock of knowledge. Religion acquired a visibly separate location in a special set of social institutions. This social form of religion emerged in societies that were already marked by a relatively high degree of structural complexity. The general differentiation of the social structure into functionally specialized institutional domains, far from being the result of unilinear evolution, was limited to one particular line of historical development. And within that general process of social differentiation of *some* societies, the institutional specialization of religion in the form of the Christian churches again represents a particular Western—although fateful—historical development.

The institutional specialization of religion in the historical form of the Christian churches in *conjunction* with a state of affairs that superficially approximated the social universality of religion in archaic and, partly, traditional societies—although structurally unlikely—was the result of a historically unique constellation of circumstances. Societies that have reached a certain level of complexity and achieved a high degree of functional differentiation cannot easily maintain the social universality of an essentially religious world view. In such societies, norms and orientations (including those that refer to transcendent realities) cannot be transmitted to everyone in basic socialization processes as generally and as successfully as mythical world views were transmitted to the entire community in archaic societies. Nor can functionally differentiated social institutions reinforce and support such a world view in the course of an individual's life in a manner analogous to social interaction in the face-to-face communities of archaic societies. As is well known, and as I indicated earlier, the long-range consequences of institutional specialization of religion have been customarily interpreted as a process of secularization.[16] However, in my view, the structural instability of the institutional specialization of religion leads to its partial replacement by an emerging fourth social form of religion. This form is linked to another profound change in the location of religion in society, a process best described as *privatization* of religion.

A NEW SOCIAL FORM OF RELIGION: PRIVATIZATION, INDIVIDUAL SYNCRETISM, AND MASS CULTURE

Privatization of religion is part of the general privatization of individual life in modern societies. The social condition most directly connected with privatization is, of course, the high degree of functional differentiation in the social structure.[17] The "big" institutions exert considerable control over individual conduct by their functionally rational norms and by the mixture of rewards and punishments characteristic of the political economy of modern capitalistic nation-states. But the institutional segmentation of the meaning of actions left large spheres of life without institutionally predefined meaning-structures and without obligatory models of biographical coherence.[18] The life-space that is not directly touched by institutional control may be called "the private sphere." As individual consciousness—not individual conduct—is liberated from social structural constraints, a process typically accompanied by legal provisions for freedom of opinion, people gain a sense of individual autonomy. Totalitarian reactions having been unsuccessful, the individual is given the freedom of choice from a variety of sacred universes. These sprang up as the cultural correlate of structural privatization.

Modern social constructions designed to cope with various levels of transcendence are extremely heterogeneous. For several generations, the traditional Christian sacred universe was no longer the only transcendent reality mediated in social processes of specialized churches and sects did not even retain their monopoly on specifically religious themes without challenge from secular ideologies. Collective representations originating in social constructions of the intermediate transcendences of nation, race, classlessness, and the like successfully shaped important aspects of modern consciousness. In recent decades, concern with minimal transcendences symbolized by notions such as self-fulfillment and the like has become widespread, if not dominant. The derivation of such notions from romanticism, certain branches of philosophic idealism, and the more recent depth-psychologies is obvious. But what were marginal bohemian, avant garde, and intellectualist phenomena at one time now seem to have become characteristic of the orientations of broad strata of *embourgeoisé* populations.

The shift of intersubjective reconstructions and social constructions away from the great other-worldly transcendences to the intermediate and, more and more, the minimal transcendences of modern solipsism cannot be said to have been directly determined by structural privatization of individual life in modern society. However, an elective affinity does seem to obtain between the latter and the sacralization of subjectivity that is celebrated in much of modern mass culture. Evidently, the traditional religious orientations (at whose center are social constructions of the great transcendences) have not disappeared. But their social distribution has become narrower, and the institutionally specialized basis of these orientations (the churches, sects, and denominations) no longer represents the socially dominant form of religion.

The ascendant privatized social form of religion is characterized by a wider range of different actors on the social scene being involved in the social construction of various kinds of transcendence.[19] The basic structure of the process is that of a demonopolized market supplied by (1) the mass media, (2) churches and sects that are trying to reinsert themselves into the processes of modern social constructions of transcendence, (3) the residual carriers of nineteenth-century secular ideologies, and (4) subinstitutional, new religious communities formed around minor charismatics, commercialized enterprises in astrology, the consciousness-expanding line, and the like. This social form of religion is thus characterized by immediate mass-cultural accessibility of the supply of representations referring to varied levels of transcendence.

However, this does not mean that no form of mediation exists between the market and potential consumers. Much of modern (Byronian or Baudelairean) consciousness is rooted in the cultivation of immediate sensations and emotions—which are notoriously unstable and offer considerable resistance to clear articulation in myths, symbols, and dogmas. Nonetheless, a variety of secondary institutions—typically arising in subinstitutional movements around charismatics, entrepreneurs, and small-group revival attempts of older occult, spiritualist, and similar movements—have taken the challenge and turned it into a profitable business. These institutions address the problem of the verbalization of topics arising in the private sphere, of packaging the results in easily digestible portions, and of distributing the results to potential consumers. Inner-worldly analogies to traditional devotional literature range from treatises on positive thinking to *Playboy* articles on the expansion of consciousness by various (for example, sexual) techniques, pocketbooks on popular psychology—especially psychoanalysis—Eastern mystical literature, astrological advice columns, offerings on bioenergetics and meditation, and the like. The products convey a more or less systematically arranged set of meanings (and, occasionally, techniques) referring to from minimal to intermediate and, rarely, great transcendences. The set can be bought and kept for a short or longer period. It can be individually combined with elements from other sets. The sets are, of course, not obligatory models characteristic of the older social forms of religion. They *can* be taken up by groups—typically on the periphery of modern society—and converted into a sectarian model, but the chances of success for such firm institutionalizations are not great.

This social form of religion can best be illustrated by recent syncretistic developments[20] such as the New Age movement and the new occultism and its predecessors, such as spiritism. The New Age movement lays stress on the spiritual development of each individual. Sometimes it revives elements of older religious traditions that had not been canonized and that it interprets in unorthodox (often far-fetched) ways. It collects abundant psychological therapeutic, magic, marginally scientific, and older esoteric materials,[21] repackages them, and offers them for individual consumption and further private syncretism. The New Age movement programmatically refuses organization in terms of big institutions; instead, it cultivates the notion of networks. This allows the formation of commercially exploitable cultic milieus, which are characterized by varied—generally weak—forms of institutionalization.[22] The New Age movement illustrates the social form of the invisible religion. It has no stable organization, canonized dogmas, recruitment system, or disciplining apparatus. This may be a structural precondition for the successful maintenance of its vague holistic approach, which meets—among other things—the rising demand for an overall hierarchy of meaning that overcomes the specialization of those cultural domains, such as science, religion, art, and the like that had found reasonably firm institutional bases. Instead of segmentation, it offers integration—no matter how superficial this may seem to the outside observer. Thus, the New Age and similar representatives of a holistic, magical world view supply individual searchers with the bricks and some straw for further individual bricolage.[23]

The structural conditions leading to various privatized forms of religion characterized by the search for a new wholeness—intended to overcome the segmentation of meaning into specialized institutional spheres and cultural regions—also give rise to another holistic option that is diametrically opposed to bricolage, that is to fundamentalism. One must distinguish between the sociostructural conditions (the specialization of institutional domains, the pluralism of mass culture, and the development of a market of world views—all of which are prevalent in modern industrial societies) and the strains similar conditions produce upon their emergence in modernizing societies. The relatively sudden loss of religious legitimations for everyday life seems to lead to anti-modernist reactions among substantial segments of the populations of modernizing countries.[24] But even in modern Western societies, Protestant and Catholic versions of fundamentalism have chosen traditional models of wholeness in reaction to modernity (institutional specialization, immorality of economic and political life, lack of obligatory controls for private life and pluralism and a lack of cognitive support for one's own world view, disorientation, and mass availability of immoral products and behavior).[25] It seems unlikely, however, that these reactions, which range from the Catholic *opus dei* to Protestant moral majorities, will prove successful in the long run. The fit between this kind of world view and the social structural determinants of modern life is rather poor. It can be improved, however, in closed communities of various kinds. On the whole privatized syncretism seems to have a better chance to become established as a (minimally) social form of religion.

Notes

1. It might be optimistically supposed that those philosophers of progress who lived to observe the pathetic symbolism of the revolutionary Cult of Reason were disabused of their illusions.

2. To quote the well-known passage written in 1843–1844 by Karl Marx in "Zur Kritik der Hegelschen Rechtphilosophie" (published in Siegfried Landsbut, ed., *Die Frühschriften* [Stuttgart: Kroener, 1955], p. 207).

3. "This means that religion is the consciousness of self and the sentiment of self on the part of human beings who have not yet attained to themselves or have already lost themselves again." (Ibid., p. 208, my translation.)

4. See Hermann Lübbe, *Säkularisierung. Geschichte Eines Ideenpolitischen Begriffs* (München: Alber, 1965), and my "Secularization—A Contemporary Myth," in Thomas Luckmann, *Life-World and Social Realities* (London: Heinemann, 1983), pp. 124–132 (first published in Italian in *Cultura e Politica* 14 [1969]:175–182). For an excellent review of various theories on the origins of modernity from Max Weber to Michel Foucault and Alan McFarlane, see Alois Hahn, "Theorien zur Entstehung der Europäischen Moderne." *Philosophische Rundschau* 31 (1984):178–202. A different view is presented by Franz-Xaver Kaufmann, "Religion und Modernität," in Johannes Berger, ed., *Die Moderne—Kontinuitäten und Zäsuren* (Sonderband 4 der "Sozialen Welt") (Göttingen: Schwartz, 1986), pp. 283–307. It is regrettable that those essays are not available in English.

5. I do not think that this indicates anything like an unexpected revival of religion, a New Age of spirituality, a return of repressed irrational forces, a breakdown of rationalism and science, or anything of the sort. I rather think, and thought a quarter of a century ago when I wrote *The Invisible Religion* (New York: Macmillan, 1967), that despite certain cyclical movements that had occurred at least in the most publicly visible forms of religion during the last two hundred years as well as in other epochs of human history, religion as a part of human life had never weakened substantially and that, in fact, it remained embedded in the lives of ordinary people, even in modern industrial societies.

6. By "social form" of religion, I refer to the basic model for the institutionalization of religious functions. For a detailed discussion of this concept and the sketch of a historical typology, refer to my *The Invisible Religion*.

7. The typology had served well in the sociological study of Western Christianity, which was for obvious reasons a central topic of interest in the sociology of religion since its professional inception roughly one hundred years ago. But even after interest extended to other cultural regions and historical epochs, the limited applicability of the typology was not readily recognized. The sense of epochal change was satisfied by the myth of secularization. Therefore, the notion that a *transformation* in the social forms of religion, rather than its final decline, might be occurring did not find easy acceptance.

8. I need not document here the successes and failures of the various attempts to solve the problem of the "subjective" adequacy (as Max Weber called it in the earliest clear articulation of this basic methodological issue) of scientific reconstructions of the social world.

9. I am not using this concept in a simple-minded behaviorist sense.

10. I shall not take up here the problem of functionalism in the abstract. It will be obvious that some of my elementary assumptions are Durkheimian but that I do not accept the notion that religion is a representation of society. Starting from Alfred Schutz's phenomenological analysis of the experience of various levels of transcendence (Alfred Schutz and Thomas Luckmann, *The Structures of the Life-World II* [Evanston, IL: Northwestern University Press. 1989]), I tried in several recent papers to add the outline of a specific theory of the functions of religion to the more generally functionalist assumptions made in *The Invisible Religion*. The last of these is "Religion and Modern Consciousness," in *Zen Buddhism Today* (Annual Report of the Kyoto Zen Symposium) 6 (1988):11–22.

11. To use a term coined by Eric Voegelin in *The New Science of Politics: An Introduction* (Chicago: University of Chicago Press, 1952).

12. Alfred Schutz, *Collected Papers I* (The Hague: Nijhoff, 1962), pp. 11 ff.

13. In order to stay closer to the terms and concepts commonly used in the social theory of religion, I shall refer to such constructions as "sacred universes."
14. A society with a single—and an essentially religious—world view presupposes a pattern of life based almost exclusively on face-to-face social relations and homogeneous socialization procedures.
15. See James H. Breasted, *The Dawn of Conscience* (New York and London: Russell, 1933): Jan Assmann, *Aegypten—Theologie und Frömmigketit Einer Frühen Hochkultur* (Stuttgart: Vohlhammer, 1984); Henri Frankfort, *Kingship and the Gods: A Study of Ancient Near Eastern Religion as the Integration of Society and Nature* (Chicago: University of Chicago Press, 1978); Karl A. Wittfogel, *Oriental Despotism: A Comparative Study of Total Power* (New Haven: Yale University Press, 1963).
16. As I also indicated, this notion is an etiological myth of modernity that usurped the status of social theory.
17. Previously multifunctional institutions, which regulated social interaction in archaic and also in traditional societies, slowly accented *one* function and lost most of the other functional components that originally constituted them. At the same time, institutions with similar functions coalesced into large specialized domains, such as the state and the economy. In contemporary industrial societies, institutions have become highly interdependent elements of social subsystems. These subsystems, however, are rather autonomous parts of the social structure. The norms of each subsystem are *comparatively* independent of the rules that govern action in other subsystems. Depending on the domain in which it is performed, institutionalized social interaction obeys rather heterogeneous norms. The connection of these norms—which have been described by Max Weber as functionally rational ones—to the "logic" of a transcendent reality is severed.
18. In this connection, Parsons spoke of "institutional interstices."
19. See Jacob Needleman and George Baker, eds., *Understanding the New Religions* (New York: Seabury Press, 1981) (especially Robert Wuthnow, "Religious Movements and the Transition in the World Order," pp. 63–79 and Joseph P. Chinnici. "New Religious Movements and the Structure of Religious Sensibility," pp. 26–33); James A. Beckford, ed., *New Religious Movements and Rapid Social Change* (London: Sage, 1986); and James A Beckford and Thomas Luckmann, eds., *The Changing Face of Religion* (London, Newbury Park, and New Delhi: Sage, 1989).
20. See Colin Campbell and Shirley McIver, "Cultural Sources of Support for Contemporary Occultism." *Social Compass* 34 (1987): 41–60.
21. For an early study, see Andrew Rigby and Bryan S. Turner, "Findhorn Community, Centre of Light: A Sociological Study of New Forms of Religion," in M Hill, ed., *A Sociological Yearbook of Religion in Britain*, Vol. 5 (London: SCM Press, 1972), pp. 72–86.
22. Not unlike what Troeltsch rather misleadingly called "mysticism." For "cultic milieus," see Danny L. Jorgensen, "The Esoteric Community: An Ethnographic Investigation of the Cultic Milieu." *Urban Life* 4 (1982):383–407; Rodney Stark and William S. Bainbridge, *The Future of Religion: Secularization, Revival and Cult Formation* (Berkeley: University of California Press, 1986).
23. Colin Campbell, "The Cult, the Cultic Milieu, and Secularization," in M. Hill. *A Sociological Yearbook of Religion in Britain*, Vol. 5 (London: SCM Press, 1972), pp. 119–136.
24. See, for example, Bassam Tibi, *Der Islam und das Problem der Kulturellen Bewältigung Sozialen Wandels* (Frankfurt: Suhrkamp, 1985).
25. See Frank J. Lechner, "Fundamentalism and Sociocultural Revitalization in America: A Sociological Interpretation." *Sociological Analysis* 46 (1985):243–259; Donald Heinz, "Clashing Symbols: The New Christian Right as Countermythology." *Archives de Sciences Sociales des Religions* 59 (1985):153–173.

COMMENTS
....
Andrew M. Greeley

First, this commentary allows me to express my gratitude to Professor Luckmann for the important contribution his work on the invisible religion made to my thinking at a critical time.

Second, my main dissent from his theory focuses on his use of the word "privatized" to describe religion in a complex multi-institutional society. The word can easily be interpreted to mean trivialized. I prefer the word "personalized." Instead of religion having a diffuse cultural impact on society it now has an indirect effect through the image systems of individual persons and groups. Is that impact greater or less than it was in the past? I am not sure the question can be answered. I am content with the different adjective.

Does Mario Cuomo's Catholicism have more or less impact on how he governs the state of New York than, say, did the Catholicism of Richard the Lion-Hearted on the latter's governance of England? (I have little doubt which is the better Catholic.) I do not think the impact of Cuomo's religious vision on his behavior is any less great because he does not permit the cardinal rear admiral of New York to dictate his policy stands any more than I think Rich Daley lacks a Catholic vision because the local cardinal cannot dictate his stand on gay rights.

It is usually difficult, even in a group of U.S. sociologists, to challenge the myth of secularization, no matter how much data one has. It is even more difficult to suggest that the myth is a classic example of the fallacy of misplaced concreteness when sociologists from other countries are present. Everyone knows that religion is less important than it used to be. Thus, attempts at verification and falsification are unnecessary and impossible; no one sees any need to operationalize either "important" or "used to be."

Gentlepersons, I know a dogma when I hear one.

In the present context, I would suggest that the proper way to state the question is: Under what sets of circumstances do which kinds of religions have what kind of effects in which sorts of societies? Usually one emerges from exercises that strive to answer such modest questions with very modest answers—significant correlations under, say, .15, if one is lucky. I must note for the theorists that such is the fate of almost every hypothesis in our discipline that is taken out of the sheltered protection of the cloistered monastery of theory and exposed to temptation in the mundane world of verification and falsification.

I understand that in the present context, Luckmann is asserting that in modern Western societies religious "fundamentalism cannot be organized into substantial politico-religious movements." He does concede that in modernizing societies, such movements can be transformed into powerful politico-religious movements, "at least temporarily."

I will leave aside the question of the modernizing countries and discuss Western society. I will also leave aside Ireland because social scientists are never made to take Ireland seriously. Patently the Irish do not count. Nonetheless, I will assert that when social theory leads one to conclude that religious movements have only occasional and marginal importance in developed nations, there is something profoundly wrong with the theory, and it ought to be either refined or jettisoned.

In my work on falsification, I will cite two cases—the United States and Poland. In the former, I will not discuss such issues as abortion or prohibition in which religious movements played and still play an important part. I will rather point at the black (or, if you wish, African-American) civil rights movement. Not to perceive that this movement is profoundly religious in its origins, organization, style, leadership, symbols, and goals is not to understand it at all. I have the impression that many white secularist social scientists do not take the religious aspects of the civil rights movement seriously. The religious symbols, they seem to imply, are a scam—albeit a legitimate one—used for political purpose and are not something that the leaders and followers, both in great part, take very seriously. Let me ask those who live in a major city how many nights in the last three months political rallies in black churches appeared on television. Surely that would suggest that the movement is both political and religious and that the two components cannot be separated, not even by the most convinced believer in secularization.

I would add that the black civil rights movement is fundamentalist, an assertion that will offend many secular sociologists. The blacks are a good cause, the fundamentalists are bad. How dare I link the two? Such a response only demonstrates ignorance of U.S. religion. The goals of the television evangelists and the Reverend Jesse Jackson may be quite different, but how can anyone who has watched both doubt the similarity of style? Both white fundamentalism and black civil rights are essentially Southern Baptist movements.

It is worth noting, incidentally, that true to their fundamentalist heritage, blacks are the group in the United States most likely to oppose abortion, even more than white Catholics: You will not read that fact in the *New York Times*.

I do not see how anyone can argue that the civil rights movement is either marginal or occasional. The New Age religion Luckmann cites is a trivial epiphenomenon in the contemporary United States. The religious nature of the civil rights movement is both durable and enormously important. How can it be missed?

My second case for the falsification of Luckmann's proposition is, if anything, even more powerful. While the black movement is Baptist and fundamentalist, Polish Catholicism is conservative, perhaps, but not fundamentalist. Again I do not comprehend how anyone with even a basic familiarity with the events in Poland can fail to see the profoundly religious nature of this unusual revolution.

There have probably been two authentic people's revolutions in the last forty years—the Iranian and the Polish. The first is surely a reaction to modernity, as Luckmann has suggested, and a bloody one at that. The second is an authentic liberal revolution—maybe the only one since 1776—with no loss of life, save for an occasional priest murdered by a zealous police force. It has been a very sophisticated, patient revolution whose final achievements are still in doubt. However, there is little question now as to which side has gained the advantage. It may also be the first case that disproves Max Weber's theory that all revolutions produce more centralized power than the regimes they replace.

I confess that I do not understand why the Polish revolution does not draw more sociological attention. Perhaps the reason is that the Poles, like the Irish, really do not count.

In Solidarity, as in the case of the civil rights movement in the United States, religion—both as a personalized faith of individuals and groups and as an ecclesiastical institution—is deeply and inextricably bound up with the political movement. Where does Lech Walesa have his meetings? At the same place Martin Luther King had his—in the local church. The simple-minded secularist observer may write off Solidarity as mere politics with a religious veneer, but this would be as unperceptive as to write off Martin Luther King as a politician with a ministerial veneer.

In both cases, there is a mutual and reciprocal causality in which religion and politics influence one another. Only the convinced dogmatist could fail to grasp this point. The dispassionate scholar should be interested not in dogmatically dismissing the religious factor but in understanding and analyzing the interaction of both religious and political factors.

I will surely be told that these two phenomena do not falsify the theory because they are exceptions. This is doubtless the case. Doubtless, too, is the fact that General-Secretary Gorbachev's almost unseemly haste in drawing the Orthodox church into his glasnost cause is only "marginal and occasional."

Thus, if I am asked what I feel will be the impact of religion on social structures in the next millennium, I would say that it may not be that different from what it has been in the past two or three millennia. In some societies, it will have only a slight impact on the functioning of other social structures. In other societies (such as the local one), it will have considerable impact. And yet, in other societies—east or west, north or south, modernizing or not—under certain circumstances it will have a powerful and even revolutionary impact. A social theory that does not consider the set of possibilities involved in such a prediction, I submit, is blinded by its own dogmatism.

Reading 20

CONTINUITY IN AMERICAN RELIGION— ANDREW M. GREELEY

This essay is an excerpt from the final chapter of my book, *Religious Change in America,* which was written for Harvard University Press as part of a project on social indicators, launched by the Social Science Research Council. Because social indicators exist to measure change and because change normally occurs, the title of the book was proper, if ironic. On almost all the survey measures dating from the 1940s, 1950s, and early 1960s there were no changes in the late 1980s—belief in God; belief in life after death, heaven, hell, and the divinity of Jesus; frequency of prayer; church membership, activity in church organizations, and etc., etc.

In fact, despite the turbulence of the last half century of American life, I could find only four changes in American religious behavior—a decline in acceptance of biblical literalism among Catholics, a shift away from main-line Protestant denominations (especially from Methodism), a decline in church attendance among Catholics, and a decline in Catholic financial contributions. The excerpt begins with a discussion of these four changes.

Questions for Reflection and Discussion

1. To what do you attribute the continuity in American religious attitudes and behavior?
2. What does this continuity do to the theory of secularization?
3. Can you suggest an alternative theory that better fits the data? How would you test it?
4. Do you think this evidence would trouble the writers of earlier readings in this section?

AMERICAN RELIGION
Andrew M. Greeley

... The first change, the result of the impact of the Second Vatican Council's revision of Catholic teaching about the Bible on younger and college-educated Catholics (and especially younger college-educated Catholics), is not a departure from Catholic orthodoxy. The third change has apparently stopped, with loyalty counteracting the impact of the birth control encyclical. We do not know whether the fourth change will also be terminated by loyalty.

The second change is real enough, especially rapid among more recent cohorts, and undeniably threatening to the mainline denominations, especially to the Methodists. It does not, however, represent a change in Protestant devotion or practice, but rather a shift in the distribution of membership to match the devotional aspirations of congregants. It is nonetheless the only continuing major change in American religion that we have been able to document.

With the exception of this shifting of denominational affiliations, Protestantism has not changed in the last half-century. Catholicism has changed, but not much, and the change is over.

As they stand, those two sentences of summary seem absurd. Protestantism has experienced the rise and fall of neoorthodoxy, the death and rebirth of the social gospel, migration from farm and small town to the city, the appearance of the electronic evangelist, the surge (or rediscovery) of fundamentalism and evangelicalism, the musical chairs of various denominational mergers, social and political conflict between activist clergy and conservative laity, the clerically launched and led civil rights movement, renewed controversy between literalist and nonliteralist interpretation of scripture, and the endless battle between science and religion.

Catholicism has experienced the twin transformation of the *embourgeoisement* of the children of immigrants and the *aggiornamento* of Vatican II. Its people have moved from the immigrant city to the professional suburbs, from unquestioning loyalty to frequently contentious independence, from Latin to English, from the Counter-Reformation to the ecumenical age, from pious and docile nuns to vocal supporters of the ordination of women, from the *Baltimore Catechism* to the Charismatic Renewal. Priests and nuns have left the active ministry by the thousands; others have become involved in radical political and social movements, some of them with Marxist tones; still others have doffed distinctive garb, insist on being called by first names, and instead of pretending that they have no personal problems, insist that their problems become the topic of constant conversation. Non-Catholic students flock to parochial grammar

Source: Andrew M. Greeley, *Religious Change in America,* Cambridge: Harvard University Press, 1989.

schools, Liberation Theology is taught in Catholic high schools, and professed atheists hold chairs of theology in Catholic universities.

How is it possible to argue that there has been no change in Protestantism and only minor change in Catholicism?

There are two possible responses to the question. One is to inquire whether there is as much change as meets the eye in the descriptions of the previous paragraphs insofar as it affects the daily religious life and faith of ordinary Catholic and Protestant laity. Is not the "changing church" a concern of the clergy, the lay elites, and the denominational journals of opinion rather than of typical congregants? Is not the "changing church" model an example of the future shock fallacy, which assumes that changes in technology and environment must change the fundamental dimensions of human life? Have not church members through the years shown remarkable skill in drawing from their faith what they want and need regardless of current organizational and theological fashions among their elites?

Priests on picket lines are news; but is there any reason to think that such activity has more than a peripheral effect on the religious life of Catholics? The protests of Catholic activists during the Vietnam war are frequently alleged to have turned the Catholic laity from hawks to doves, but survey data show that Catholics were always more dovish than typical white Americans, that their turn against the war antedated the Catholic peace movement, and that after each major public antiwar demonstration, there was an increase in support for the Nixon administration's conduct of the war. Are Catholics more likely than Protestants to oppose nuclear arms because of a pastoral letter by the American hierachy? Or is the letter itself a result of lay concern? The survey data in this book show that Catholics were more likely to think that too much money was being spent on weapons ten years ago, long before the pastoral letter.

In other words, the ecclesiastical changes so widely publicized in the mass media may in fact have little effect on the religious life of individuals, families, and local communities. Such an effect needs to be proved, not assumed.

A second response is to concede the fact and the importance of the changes in American Christianity, and then add that social indicator research cannot hope to describe all the aspects of a phenomenon but only those for which there exist time-series data. Social indicators are at best a skeleton of a body politic or a body religious, an incomplete trajectory, an outline, a sketch. They represent truth as far as they go, but not, surely, the whole truth.

The second response is of course merely a less contentious version of the first. A little less explicitly than the first it says, "Give us an operational measure of religious change and we'll try to find data to test it. Until then we must stand by the data we have; and these indicate that nothing much has changed."

Of the five models proposed in the first chapter, the secularization model fits only sexual ethics (and only some aspects of sexual ethics) and belief in literal interpretation of the Bible. Even the latter change is confined to younger and better-educated Catholics and represents a shift to a position which is, if anything, more orthodox for Catholics than strict literalism.

The kind of revivals predicted by the cyclic theory are certainly to be found in the AIPO question about the influence of religion in society, but the meaning of such an indicator is obscure; it may merely tell us that a lot of respondents see small fluctuations in religious influence, and it almost certainly represents a judgment about society and not about personal religious conviction. There may also be a revival of prayer and religious experience, although even at the presumed low points in such activities half of Americans prayed every day and one out of three had had at least a single intense religious experience. Interreligious attitudes, as measured by the SRC feeling thermometers, have fluctuated greatly during the years for which we have data, but there is no discernible pattern in such movement, and the relative positions of Protestants, Catholics, and Jews remain stable—with Catholics the losers in the tradeoff of warm feelings.

The episodic shock model seems to apply to Catholic church attendance rates, which fell sharply from 1969 to 1975 but have leveled off since. The decline was caused by the birth control encyclical, the stability by an underlying loyalty to the church.

Bible reading has increased over the last century, prayer may have increased in the last fifteen years, and certainly there is greater willingness to report ecstatic and paranormal experiences. So there is some confirmation for the increase of religion model which was noted at the beginning as a logical fifth possibility.

But most of the other social indicators discussed in the previous chapters best fit—sometimes with minor adjustments—the stability model. There has been no discernible change in belief in God, the divinity of Jesus, life after death, the existence of heaven, and divine influence on the Bible. The pattern of denominational affiliations has not changed (save for a possible decline in Methodism), nor have the propensities to become a church "member" and to belong to a church-affiliated voluntary organization (which still have the largest American organizational membership). The self-professed "strength" of religious affiliation has not changed, and this strength is proved by the fact that even among the most unreligious age group—those in their early twenties—half the Christians in the United States are inside a church at least once a month.

The position of the three major religious groups on the political spectrum has not changed: Protestants are still more likely to be Republican, Jews and Catholics more likely to be Democratic (with a decline in Democratic affiliation in the early 1970s which was marginally greater among Catholics than among Protestants). Jews are more likely to be liberal on political issues, Protestants to be conservative, and Catholics to be in the middle but to the left on the national averages and perhaps tilting somewhat more in the liberal direction during the last decade—despite their rapid movement up the social and economic ladder.

Basic doctrines, church attendance, prayer, organizational affiliation and activity, religious experience, location on the political spectrum—are not these indicators, superficial and naive as they might seem, at least a rough measure of the basic condition of religion in America? If they have not changed, is there not reason to assert that there is a certain long-term stability in American religious behavior whatever important changes might also be occurring? Is there not even more reason to assert that the secularization model, which is the conventional wisdom of many elite Americans, is unsupported by the available social indica-tors? Is it not true, then, that those who argue for or assume secularization now must labor under the burden of finding evidence to sustain their position?

Theodore Caplow and his colleagues, in their 1983 study of the religion of "Middletown" (Muncie, Indiana, first studied by Robert and Helen Lynd in 1924), note that in the late 1970s and early 1980s Middletown's religion had not changed on eleven major indicators for which there were measures at the beginning and the end of the sixty-year period:

> If secularization is a shrinkage of the religious sector in relation to other sectors of society . . . then it ought to produce some or all of the following indications: (1) a decline in the number of churches per capita of the population, (2) a de-cline in proportion of the population attending church services, (3) a decline in the proportion of rites of passage held under religious auspices (for example, declining ratios of religious to civil marriages and of religious to secular funer-als), (4) a decline in religious endogamy, (5) a decline in the proportion of the labor force engaged in religious activity, (6) a decline in the proportion of in-come devoted to the support of religion, (7) a decline in the ratio of religious to non-religious literature, (8) a decline in the attention given to religion in the mass media, (9) a drift toward less emotional forms of participation in religious services, (10) a dwindling of new sects and of new movements in existing churches, and (11) an increase in attention paid to secular topics in sermons and liturgy (Caplow et al., 1983, p. 34).

Though acknowledging that religion has changed greatly in Middletown since the 1920s, Caplow found no support for any of the eleven hypotheses (ibid., pp. 34–45). Muncie, Indiana, is the nation writ small in terms of the indi-cators analyzed in the previous chapters—a place of remarkable continuity in religious behavior.

Why, it is often asked by those who are prepared to accept the data gath-ered by researchers such as Caplow, is the United States so different from Europe, where "secularization" is so much further advanced? I suggest that if Europe is indeed secularized, then a consideration of religious practice in the rest of the world indicates that Europe, not the United States, is unique. Religion has lost none of its power in the Third World, despite the energies which we group under the label "modernization." Indeed the nonwestern religions all seem to be undergoing dramatic revivals. From a global perspective, the apparent failure of Christianity in some countries in Europe is the deviant case, not the norm, a fact which orthodox sociology—based as it is on the work of three great theorists of secularization (Karl Marx, Emile Durkheim, and Max Weber)—is most reluc-tant to admit. . . .

In the United States more than four-fifths of those who are born Catholic and more than nine-tenths of those who are born Protestant or Jewish eventu-ally opt for their own religious heritage. Why? I suggest that the reason for this is that in the calculus of benefits, the choice of one's own religion seems to most Americans, finally, to confer the most benefits. The choice of the religion of one's parents may suggest a certain propensity to choose the familiar because so much has been invested in the familiar, perhaps a phenomenon not unlike the decision to remain with one's original word-processing program even if other programs promise more benefits, because (quite rationally) it is calculated that the advantages of the new program do not offset the investment of startup time required to obtain skill in it. Stigler and Becker's (1977) theory of "addiction" or "consumption capital" may also be pertinent, although they were discussing "addiction" to classical music. Stated in terms of religious identification, the theory would assert that the marginal utility of time allocated to a given denomination is increased by an increase in the stock of religious capital. Thus the consumption of a given religious heritage could be said to rise with exposure to the heritage because the marginal utility of time spent on the heritage rose with exposure. Could people be said to be "addicted" to their religious heritage because they have acquired consumption capital in that heritage? It is difficult to learn the rituals, protocols, and doctrines of one religion; why bother learning another when the extra benefit does not seem all that great?

I propose the following paradigm. Most Americans are born into a religious heritage of some sort. There are five components of that heritage which may be conveniently considered: (1) a set of symbols which, *pace* Clifford Geertz, purport to explain uniquely the real, to provide answers to problems of injustice, suffering, and death; (2) a set of rituals which activate these symbols at crucial life-cycle turning points and inculcate the paradigms which the symbols can contain; (3) a community which is constituted by and transmits these symbols and rituals; (4) a heritage to pass on to one's children, should one wish; (5) a differentiation, thick or thin, from those who are not born inside the heritage.

Let us consider the schedule of benefits a person faces, say, in the middle twenties, when considering a religious decision. First of all, the community provides a pool of preferred partners, friends, marital partners, perhaps business or professional colleagues. Second, it offers familiar rituals for crucial turning points in one's life. Third, it offers symbols, usually absorbed very early in childhood, which express meaning when one is in a situation which requires meaning. Fourth, it offers various social and organizational activities which confer advantages of various sorts on its members. The more actively one engages in religious activities—up to a certain point, perhaps—the more available these resources may become. (There may also be a law of diminishing returns: attending Sunday mass may find someone a spouse, but attending daily mass may not notably increase the chances of doing so.)

In the case of each of these benefits there will be considerable cost in giving up their utility. Other partners may not respond to the most familiar interactive cues. Valuable relationship networks may be lost. It may be necessary to learn new symbols and integrate them into one's personality orientations—not an easy task in adulthood, perhaps for many not even a possible task—or to engage in unfamiliar ritual behaviors which might be distasteful. New organizational activities may involve relative strangers.

Or people may have to live without symbols, rituals, and community—or try to do so. . . .

Unintentionally, perhaps, American life seems to reinforce the loyalty factor which Hout and I (1988) found latent in both political affiliation and church attendance. The factor is both discrete and continuous. There is a threshold of loyalty that people apparently elect to cross or not to cross in their late teens or early twenties. Once they choose to be a religious and/or political alienate at that threshold, they are likely to remain so for the rest of their lives. On the other hand, if they cross the threshold, even to the extent of identifying with a political party by reporting that they are independents "leaning" toward one party or the other or by attending church at least once a year, then their level of political and/or religious affiliation is likely to increase over a lifetime. Perhaps age makes people more conservative and more in need of firm guidelines. Or perhaps with the passage of time people become more aware of the complexity of human existence and hence more tolerant of the imperfections of their church and party and more in need of clearly marked guideposts. Or perhaps they want to be able to pass on such useful guideposts to their children so that they can chart a safe and happy path through life's confusions. Or perhaps all three explanations come to the same thing: some guideposts and some community to set up the posts and maintain the signs on them are better than none.

These possible explanations can be converted into operational measures; but social scientists will begin to work on such measures only when they are convinced that religion is not losing its importance in American life and hence is still worth studying as a major component of social structure and of the glue which holds the society, however precariously at times, together.

The null hypothesis that religious attitudes and behaviors in America are not changing has not been appreciably weakened by the survey data available to us. Whatever may be said in theory about the success of science in its battle with religion, religion does not in general seem to have been notably weakened in the United States during the past half-century, insofar as we are able to measure its strength from survey items.

The secularization model, which has never been confirmed by the data and has often been disproved—as in this book—nonetheless remains as strong as ever in scholarly and journalistic circles, unshaken and apparently unshakable. Students of religion will be not surprised. They know a religion when they see one. They know that religious faith is difficult if not impossible to disprove. Secularization as a theory itself confirms the stability model.

Reading 21

THE GOOD OLD DAYS—ANDREW M. GREELEY

If the secularization theory provides little in the way of useful hypotheses for religious change in the last half century in America, what can it tell us about religious change over longer periods of time—say between medieval and contemporary Europe?

It seems to be assumed that the mass of Europeans were devout Catholics through the "Ages of Faith," although this assumption is hardly consistent with the fact that in the 11th Century the Church had to impose upon Catholics the obligation of Sunday Mass attendance and annual Easter reception of Communion.

It would appear that with some exceptions of time and place, religion was an urban phenomenon in the years between the fall of the Roman empire and the Reformation. Religious devotion was strong in the cities and towns and in the monastic communities, but the country folk, the *pagani* (the word pagan original meant "rural") were not particularly devout. The serfs and the *colons* (a social class lower even than the serfs) were Christian indeed, but often barely so. Their religion was strongly affected by magic and superstition and consisted in great part of devotions to the saints and to the Mother of Jesus. Their marriages were mostly common law (which is why the Catholic Church insisted that only the consent of the man and woman were required for a valid marriage). Their priests were almost as ignorant as the people—and as likely to have a wife or a concubine. They attended church services rarely (unless forced to by their lords or later by the civil government) and received the sacraments even more rarely.

It does not follow that they were not Christian, much less that, given the circumstances of that thousand years, they were inferior in the their basic Christianity to modern Christians. It only follows that the pious Breton (or Irish) peasant women so often cited as evidence of the "ages of faith" were in a distinct minority.

In this perspective, both the Reformation and the Counter Reformation were attempts to assert urban religion on the countryside, to improve the performance of the clergy and the orthodoxy and the devotion of the laity. Gabriel LaBras, the French sociologist, has shown that religious devotion today in France tends to correspond to those areas in which St. Vincent DePaul conducted missions in the 17th Century. Emmet Larkin (cited in the text of the excerpt) has told me that the Vincentians began the parish missions in Ireland in the 19th century, which contributed substantially to the devotional revolution in that country. Indeed one may think of pre-famine Ireland as the best example available, in times accessible to social science and social history, of a model of what rural Europe was like before the Reformation and the Counter Reformation. There was religious belief, indeed (though of a primitive sort mixed with superstition and magic), but almost no religious education and low levels of religious devotion. Patronal feasts (the "patterns") were occasions for drinking and fighting (actually brawls between large gangs of men with clubs), selling horses, arranging marriages, and bouts of lovemaking.

Jean Delumeau in his book (*Catholicism between Luther and Voltaire*) gives examples of the low level of religious devotion on the continent, and especially in France, which parallel those that I cite from England and the United States in the excerpt. In one sense, the Church dominated life. Its ceremonies, its festivals, its calendars, its rules shaped to a considerable extent, the course of the year and the course of human life. But it does not follow that in terms of devotion, purity of faith, and religious knowledge, the religion of the countryside represents a golden age from which our present times are a decline. Michael Carroll (whose work will be excerpted in subsequent section) has argued that the difference between the more devout northern Italy and the less devout southern Italy and Sicily is that the Counter Reformation (in the degrees of the Council of Trent) were enforced in the former relatively soon after the Council and not in the latter. Indeed contemporary religious practice in Sicily might be a useful approximation of what religious faith and devotion were like in rural medieval Europe.

Hardly the good old days.

The point here is not to demean the Christianity of rural Europeans throughout the thousand years we call the Middle Ages. The point is to suggest that those who celebrate that era as profoundly devout because the *Angelus* was recited in the fields have hardly taken a serious look at evidence about the period's actual religious practice. To view it as the *terminus a quo* of religious decline brought on by secularization is to display a dismaying lack of historical sophistication—as well as a failure to search for evidence to sustain one's model.

Questions for Reflection and Discussion

1. What does it mean when it is said that the challenge is not to explain the low levels of religious devotion in some countries but to explain the high levels in other countries?
2. Does it surprise you that the peasants of Europe before (and in many countries after) the Reformation and the Counter Reformation were not all that devout?
3. Have you seen the film "The Return of Martin Guere?" Does it seem to you that it gives us some idea of what the religion of late medieval and early modern Europe was like?
4. How would you explain the lack of devotion in medieval Europe? How do you explain its continued absence in both Catholic and Protestant countries even after the Reformation?

THE 'DECLINE OF RELIGION'
Andrew M. Greeley

. . . Much of the discussion of 'secularisation' presumes an earlier era (often not precisely designated) characterised by high levels of religious faith and devotion, a kind of golden age since when there has been an obvious and indisputable decline. However, the existence of this golden age is usually assumed rather than proven, and the most recent historical research casts doubt on the assumption. Instead, some scholars are beginning to question whether there was all that much devotion in western Europe even in the high middle ages. Finke and Stark (1992) note that most medieval rural churches were far too small to provide room for all the people in their parishes, and cite evidence that in 1738 thirty Oxfordshire parishes reported only a combined average total of 911 communicants on the four great festivals of Christmas, Easter, Whitsun, and Ascension. They calculate church membership in England as 11.5 per cent of the population in 1800, 16.7 per cent in 1850 and 18.6 per cent in 1900. As we shall see, the monthly attendance at religious services reported by British respondents in the present analysis is in fact higher even than this last figure.

The histories of the British churches in the 19th century are filled with quotes deploring the lack of devotion among the people. Earlier still, Wickham's (1957) study of Sheffield shows that there is little evidence of religious devotion at the beginning of the 18th century. Even allowing for the clerical propensity for alarmist views, it seems clear that the industrial urban working class was not devout. The portrait of the Church of England painted by the 19th century's most perceptive sociological novelist, Anthony Trollope, would hardly lead one to believe that congregants were elbowing each other to obtain admission to churches and chapels on Sunday morning.[1]

Was England 'burned out' religiously following the civil war? Or was there, even when the Puritans were fighting the King's men, just beneath the surface of events little propensity to religious devotion? Butler (1990), in perhaps the best account of religion in Britain and the USA in the 17th century, notes that Dissent (Congregationalism) declined rapidly after the end of the Cromwellian years, from a high of no more than five per cent in 1670 to less than two per cent of the population in 1700.[2] The real religion of Britain at the time (and of the USA too) was, it may be argued, magic. Indeed, there is some doubt as to whether the peasant populations of Europe were ever converted to orthodox and devout Christianity. They may have gone to church services when they were constrained to do so. But in the absence of this constraint, they participated irregularly (if at all) and mixed Christian practices with survivals of pagan superstition and magic

Source: Andrew M. Greeley, Religion in Britain, Ireland and the USA, in British Social Attitudes: the 9th Report, Roger Jowell, Lindsay Brook, Gillian Prior, and Bridget Taylor (eds). Social and Community Planning Research. Dartmouth Publishing Co., Ltd.: Hants, England and Brookfield, Vermont, 1992.

that have by no means disappeared even today (Carroll, 1992). It is not suggested that these peasants—the overwhelming majority of Europeans outside Britain *were* peasants until the present century—were not Christian. However, it now seems probable that they were Christian in their fashion and according to their own norms—a style of Christianity acceptable neither to the religious authorities of their time (though the authorities were able to do relatively little about it) nor to the sociologists of religious faith and religious devotion of the present time.

Clearly the starting point of the evolutionary 'secularisation' model needs to be re-examined. Moreover further work on the popular religious beliefs and practices of the so-called Ages of Faith has yet to be done (Greeley, 1992). In any event, the notion that the British were more religious at some time in the past than they are now is certainly not proven, may not be provable, and may in fact be untrue. Perhaps Britain was never all that religious; instead, an explanation is needed not for the low level of devotion in Britain but for the high level in Ireland and the United States.

Studies by scholars such as Larkin (1972, 1984)* trace current levels of devotion in Ireland to the time after the Great Famine of the 1840s when the Irish-speaking 'bog Irish' who had only loose ties to Catholicism were either wiped out by hunger and disease or left the country. One way for a country to become more devout is for it to lose people who are not devout, either to migration or death.

Moreover, religious affiliation in the United States at the time of the American Revolution was low and religious devotion hardly fervent. The Congregationalist zeal of Puritan New England was being replaced either by Unitarianism or a genteel Congregationalism which the Pilgrim Fathers would not have recognised. It was only after the so-called 'Second Great Awakening' in the early years of the last century that the United States began its path towards high levels of affiliation and devotion, a pilgrimage which Finke and Stark (1992) have called 'The Churching of America'.

Hatch (1989) attributes the remarkable flowering of religion after 1800 more to the 'democratisation' of the USA in the wake of the Revolution than to the techniques of religious revival. For three decades, he argues, the USA was swept by 'religious populism', led by lay leaders and preachers and supported by a popular press and popular hymnody. The ordinary people, he suggests, took religion away from the clergy and directed it themselves towards their own purposes and their own goals.

At about the same time as the Second Great Awakening in the USA, and shortly before the development of devotional Catholicism in Ireland under Cardinal Paul Cullen, Britain was experiencing an intense Methodist movement. The first two developments shaped the religious histories of their respective countries; the last petered out. Why was American Methodism able to generate enormous popular support, while British Methodism gradually lost whatever ability it might have had to attract the working class? According to Hatch (1989), it was because Thomas Coke, the British Methodist leader, insisted on

---

*See also Connolly (1982) and Greeley (1988).

social respectability; while the American Frances Asbury, with his camp meetings, appealed both to the immigrants pouring into the east and to the pioneers moving out to the west. So religion perhaps provided a community function that it did not in Britain (save perhaps for the Irish immigrants). Religion also became an essential part of the social location and self-definition of Americans; as Herberg (1955) argued several decades ago, most Americans identify themselves as either Protestant or Catholic or Jew, a kind of self-definition which is not nearly so powerful (to the extent that it exists at all) in Britain.

In Ireland, torn by religious and political conflict, religion was and is also a critically important component of identity. Although Catholicism was and is the religion of the majority in the island, Ireland also was and is a pluralistic society in which the majority religion was not an established church. Moreover the Catholic Church in the Republic is not an established church today, at least not in the way the Church of England is in Britain. The United States is *de jure* pluralistic, Ireland *de facto* pluralistic, and Britain in theory and in practice is not pluralistic.

Stark, Melton and Iannaccone (1992) have suggested that religion is more likely to flourish when various denominations are forced to compete in an open marketplace. According to this model, the USA has the most open market and Britain the least, with Ireland (north and south) somewhere in between. Little wonder then that the established Church in Britain fares relatively badly, while serious competition against it is discouraged.

CROSS-NATIONAL COMPARISONS

In the next section, we compare our findings in Britain with those in the United States, the Irish Republic and Northern Ireland. We look first at religious beliefs and religious observance, then at the place of God in people's lives, and lastly at the place of religion in public life.

Beliefs

Seven out of ten people in Britain believe in God, as opposed to more than nine out of ten in the other three societies; though as we shall see there are some ambiguities in the stance of British 'unbelievers'. Just over 60 per cent of British responders have 'always' believed in God as opposed to approximately 90 percent in the other three societies. Sixteen per cent of Britons once believed but no longer do and eight per cent once did not but do now—a net 'loss' to believers of eight percentage points. In Northern Ireland, in contrast, there is a net 'gain' to believers of three percentage points. In the USA and the Irish Republic, the figures balance out.

The God in whom Britons believe is notably less likely than the God of the Irish people and the Americans to be depicted as personally involved with the people. Only 37 per cent of British respondents picture God as concerned "with

Religious Beliefs (percentages)

	Britain	USA	Irish Republic	Northern Ireland
Believe in God	69	94	95	95
God concerned personally*	37	77	77	80
% believing in:**				
Life after death	55	78	80	78
Heaven	54	86	87	90
Religious miracles	45	73	73	77
Hell	28	71	53	74
The Devil	28	47	49	69
The Bible is the 'actual' or 'inspired word of God'	44	83	78	81

*The percentages combine 'strong agreement' with 'agreement' to the appropriate item. This pattern will be followed in all tables in this chapter unless otherwise noted
**The percentages combine 'definitely' and 'probably' believing in each item

every human being personally", as opposed to more than three quarters of respondents in the other societies. As the table above shows, Britain stands out in other ways too. For instance, just over half of Britons believe in life after death, while approximately four out of five respondents in the other countries do so. The same proportion of the British also believe in heaven, but approaching nine out of ten do in the USA and Ireland.

In summary, a little less than half of the British give reasonably 'orthodox' answers to most questions, compared with approximately three quarters of people in the other three societies. The detailed figures for belief in God and God's personal concern provide a useful thumbnail sketch of religion in Britain: about a quarter to a third are not religious at all, a little less than two-fifths are 'seriously religious' and the rest are somewhere in between—conventionally but not seriously religious.

Observance

Some two-thirds of Britons profess an affiliation to a religious denomination—again as opposed to more than nine out of ten in the other three societies. Although only six per cent of British respondents were raised with no affiliation, 35 per cent now say they have no affiliation. Almost 40 per cent of Britons are affiliated to the Church of England, 10 per cent are Roman Catholics, five per cent are Presbyterians (Church of Scotland), four per cent belong to the 'Free Churches' (Baptist and Methodist) and seven per cent have other denominations or faiths. 'Retention rates' (the proportion still belonging to the denomination in which they were brought up) are highest (68 per cent) among Roman Catholics followed by 62 per cent for the Church of England and the same for the Presbyterians. But higher still are retention rates (nine in ten) among the small number of people who were raised with no religious affiliation (and continue to have none). The steepest decline in affiliation is to the Church of England: 58 per cent of respondents were raised in the Established Church but only 39 per cent identify with it today.[3] Later we will search for an explanation of this apparent decline.

There are yet more differences between the British on the one hand and the Irish (whether Green or Orange) and the Americans on the other, as the next table shows. In religious attendance, frequency of prayer and participation in 'church activities' (other than attending services) the British stand out as conspicuously less devout.

Religious Observance and Experience (percentages)

	Britain	USA	Irish Republic	Northern Ireland
Affiliated with a denomination	64	93	98	92
Attend service two or three times a month	16	43	78	58
Pray weekly	27	58	75	65
'Church activity' monthly	11	31	17	28
Intense experience*	28	33	22	24
'Conversion' experience**	17	46	16	29
Feel close to God (*extremely/somewhat*)	46	85	79	76
Describe themselves as religious (*extremely/very/somewhat*)	43	73	77	68

*Ever felt "Close to a powerful spiritual force that seemed to lift you out of yourself"
**Ever been "A turning point in your life when you made a new and personal commitment to religion"

Although considerably less devout on all the measures, the British are about as likely as anyone else to report that they have had an 'ecstatic' religious experience—indeed, more likely than those in either sample of Irish respondents. If religion is ultimately founded on such experiences, then Britain seems to present an environment no more (or less) hostile to them than any other country. Some religious responses, it would seem, are more sensitive to social contexts than others (Greeley 1989): thus, respondents in Britain and in the Irish Republic who report an intense religious experience outnumber those who report a conversion experience. As far as self-description is concerned, however, the British self-image is once again more secular. A little less than half describe themselves as 'close to God' or as 'religious,' compared to between about 70 per cent and 85 per cent of people in the three other societies.

So the patterns for religious observance, practice and experience supplement those in respect of religious belief. More than two-fifths of the British are seriously religious and approximately a quarter could be considered devout. However none of the four societies seems to have a monopoly on intense religious experiences.

The Meaning of Life

There is somewhat more fatalism in the British Isles than there is in the United States. Only 13 per cent of Americans say "there is little people can do to change the course of their lives" but (as the next table shows) around a quarter or more of Britons and Irish (from north and south) take that grim view. The British alone are also more likely to think that life has no purpose. But the absence of religious devotion, it would seem, does not necessarily lead to *massive* fatalism and nihilism. Even in Britain, as many as one in five think that life is decided by God and that it is God who makes life meaningful, and only around one in seven believe that life is without purpose.

Attitudes Towards the Meaning of Life

% saying:	Britain	USA	Irish Republic	Northern Ireland
There is little that people can do to change the course of their lives (*strongly agree/agree*)	22	13	24	27
Life is meaningful only because God exists (*strongly agree/agree*)	21	49	50	54
Life does not serve any purpose (*strongly agree/agree/neither agree nor disagree*)	14	8	9	11
The course of our lives is decided by God (*strongly agree/agree*)	20	40	58	54
We each make our own fate (*strongly agree/agree*)	61	62	66	51
"Very happy these days"	33	37	41	37

The British are also a little less likely than other respondents to report that they are 'very happy', but compared with some of the differences we have found so far, these variations are small. In summary, the British seem to view life from a somewhat grimmer perspective than do the other three societies, and are less likely to see God as giving meaning to life. But who knows whether this pessimism is associated with a less vigorous religious faith, or whether it merely reflects a greater realism about the human condition?

Religion and Public Life

We also asked a series of questions to investigate the extent to which people believe that religion has a place in public life, and to try to gauge attitudes to churches and religious organisations. We found that the British have much less confidence in churches than do the Irish or the Americans, although (as the next table shows) the latter were far from unanimous in *their* vote of confidence. But criticism of churches for having too much power is most widespread in Ireland (north and south), though even there the critics are clearly in a minority.

Religion and Public Life—1 (percentages)

	Britain	USA	Irish Republic	Northern Ireland
Confidence in churches*	18	41	46	43
Churches have 'far too much' or 'too much power'	28	23	37	37
Religious leaders should not try to influence how people vote	74	65	76	72
Religious leaders should not try to influence government	59	63	70	62

*'Complete confidence' or 'a great deal of confidence'

However, solid majorities in all four societies think that church leaders ought not to try to influence voters or government decisions, the Irish (both north and south) being both united and especially emphatic about church leaders' relations with government.

When we move to questions of religious tolerance and the place of religion in society, the British and the Irish in the south are less likely than the Northern Irish and the Americans to think that atheists are unfit for public office. Again the British, but this time alongside the Americans, are less likely than the Irish (south and north) to be in favour of banning anti-religious books. The Americans are the most likely, and the British the least, to believe that their country would be better off "if more people with strong religious beliefs held public office". However, support for daily school prayers is widespread in all countries—even among the more secular British.

With the exception of school prayers then, the British are clearly the most secularist in their approach to the relationship between religion and public life. They are also less likely than their counterparts across the Irish Sea to view their churches as a political threat, almost certainly because in fact the British churches *are* less of a threat. But it is worth noting that large majorities in Northern Ireland and the Republic—both allegedly priest-dominated societies—also disapprove of church involvement in politics, an apparent indictment of a situation in which religious leaders both south and north of the border *do* seem to have considerable political influence.

Religion and Public Life—2 (percentages)

	Britain	USA	Irish Republic	Northern Ireland
Politicians who do not believe in God are unfit for public office (*strongly agree/agree/neither agree nor disagree*)	31	59	35	52
Books and films that attack religions should be prohibited by law (*definitely/probably*)	30	34	49	54
It would be better for [Britain] if more people with strong religious beliefs held public office (*strongly agree/agree*)	17	39	28	24
There should be daily prayers in all state schools (*definitely/probably*)	70	73	83	87

THE BRITISH PERSPECTIVE

We now turn from cross-national comparisons to an analysis of religion in Britain. We look at responses to a battery of eleven questions (eight about belief, observance and experience, and three about the relationship between religion and public life) which serve as a quick summary of Christian religious (or quasi-religious) attitudes and behaviour, and discuss interdenominational, demographic and other differences.

Denomination

As noted previously, 36 per cent of British respondents identify with the Church of England, 10 per cent with Roman Catholicism, four per cent each with Presbyterianism and with the Free Churches, three per cent with other Protestant denominations and three per cent with other religions. In addition, four per cent call themselves 'Christian' but give no denomination, and the remaining 35 per cent have no religion. Since most sub-sample sizes are small, only fairly large differences between groups are likely to be statistically significant. It is for this reason that we limit the analyses below to Christian denominations.

Catholics are consistently more devout and more believing than the other denominations and Anglicans generally the least devout (save, of course, for those with 'no religion').

As can be seen, those who profess no religion are by no means completely irreligious. Twenty-eight per cent of them believe in God, 35 per cent in life after

Religious Beliefs and Observance in Britain

	All	Church of England	Roman Catholic	Presby-terian	Free Churches	Other Protestant	No Religion
% believing in:							
God	69	84	92	88	91	89	28
Life after death	55	57	78	67	77	66	35
Religious miracles	45	49	80	46	78	61	22
Pray weekly	27	30	52	30	38	52	8
Attend service two or three times a month	16	14	36	25	31	49	1
Intense experience	28	27	32	29	51	42	19
Feel close to God	46	51	72	60	71	69	18

death; about one in six say they are close to God. However, as the table below shows, only a third have any confidence in churches, and they are much more likely than all the professed Christian groups to believe that the churches have too much power and much less likely to approve of prayer in schools. Even so, sizeable minorities of the non-religious are clearly ambivalent about religion. And from other analyses (not reported here for lack of space) it seems possible that part of the reason for some of these people's rejection of religion is that they have both more liberal moral and sexual attitudes and a greater suspicion of churches than their counterparts do.

Religion and Public Life in Britain (percentages)

	All	Church of England	Roman Catholic	Presby-terian	Free Churches	Other Protestant	No Religion
Confidence in churches*	58	66	77	76	78	81	34
Churches have too much power	28	24	20	18	12	6	45
In favour of school prayers	70	82	87	77	95	90	45

*'Complete', 'a great deal of' or 'some' confidence.

Almost five out of six Christian Britons are either Anglicans or Roman Catholics with the former four times as numerous as the latter. As noted, Catholics are more likely to be devout than Anglicans, and they are also more likely to have confidence in churches.[4]

Region

An examination of the eleven regions of Britain† reveals a common religious culture—as measured by our eleven-item battery—in eight of the regions, but differences from this common culture in three: Wales, Scotland, and the North-West.‡ Since these three regions were similar to each other in religious culture, we group them together for purposes of analysis and dub them (not altogether inaccurately as will be seen) 'the Celtic Fringe'.

As shown in the next table the 'Fringe' differs significantly from the rest of Britain on nine of the eleven items, proving to be consistently more devout and more religious on these items.

	All	'Celtic Fringe'	Rest of Britain
% believing in:			
God	69	75	66
Life after death	55	62	52
Religious miracles	45	51	43
Affiliated with a denomination	64	67	63
Pray weekly	27	32	25
Attend service two or three times a month	16	19	14
Intense experience	28	28	28*
Feel close to God	46	52	43
Confidence in churches	58	62	56
Churches have too much power	28	28	29*
In favour of school prayers	70	75	69

*Not significantly different from the 'Celtic Fringe'

But the explanation for this difference is not, as it turns out, surprising when one looks at the different religious composition of the 'Fringe'. In the rest of Britain, Anglicans make up 40 per cent of the population and Catholics and Presbyterians 10 per cent between them. However, in the 'Fringe' the combination of Catholics (15 per cent) and Presbyterians (14 per cent) exceeds the Anglican proportion (22 per cent). When this is taken into account, *all* the differences between the 'Fringe' and the rest of Britain decline not only to statistical insignificance but virtually to zero. So the 'Fringe' may be legitimately called Celtic because of the Scottish and Irish influences (for example, of the large Irish Catholic communities in Liverpool and Manchester). In sum, the only difference in regional religious culture we can detect is actually a difference in denominational composition.

---

†Registrar-General's Standard Regions of Scotland, Northern, North-West, Yorkshire and Humberside, West Midlands, East Midlands, East Anglia, South-West, South-East, Greater London and Wales.
‡Comprising Cheshire, Lancashire, Greater Manchester and Merseyside.

Gender

Women have traditionally been thought to be more devout and more religious than men. Not so long ago this difference was generally attributed (though sometimes only implicitly) to the chauvinistic view that women were neither as logical nor as realistic as men. A more plausible explanation, and one which fits at least some of the data, is that the difference has arisen out of women's role in the family, which involves more 'socio-emotional' (caring) responsibilities than men's more 'instrumental' (doing) responsibilities. Indeed, women's devoutness and religiosity are more like those of men (though by no means the same) *before* they acquire a spouse and children. Once you start 'taking care' of people, perhaps, you begin implicitly to assume greater responsibility for their 'ultimate' welfare.[5]

There has, however, been a suggestion that as women become more involved in the workforce and assume greater 'instrumental' responsibilities in life, gender differences on religious issues will diminish. We tested this assumption.

First of all, as the next table shows, women *are* clearly much more likely than men to be devout and religious. On only one item out of the eleven are women much the same as men; on all the rest, women are more orthodox.

| | | | | WOMEN | |
	All	Men	Women	Working Full-time	Not Working Full-time
% believing in:					
God	69	60	76	69	79**
Life after death	55	47	61	65	60**
Religious miracles	45	40	50	49	51**
Affiliated with					
a denomination	64	58	69	57	73
Pray weekly	27	21	33	25	36
Attend service two					
or three times a month	16	12	19	17	20**
Intense experience	28	30	26*	27	25**
Feel close to God	46	38	52	47	54
Confidence in churches	58	53	62	57	65**
Churches have					
too much power	28	33	24	26	24**
In favour of school prayers	70	66	74	64	78

*Difference from men not statistically significant
**Difference between women working full-time and women not working full-time is not statistically significant.

To what extent can these differences be explained by the supposedly less 'instrumental' role of women? Might the differences already be diminishing as women assume greater participation in the workforce? First of all, as the table above shows, non-working women are *not* significantly more religious than working women in respect of seven out of the eleven items in our battery. The other four differences are statistically significant—but not when one takes age into account. In other words it is the younger women who tend to be less religious regardless of whether they are in paid work or not.

Does this finding suggest that, as young working women grow older, they will continue to be different from older non-working women? Or will younger women grow more religious as they age, and hence sustain the similarities in respect of religious attitudes and behaviour between those women who work and those who do not? To answer this question we need to know how devout were young working women in the recent past. In the absence of such data, we must suspend judgment. The propensity of some sociologists to see an age correlation as a social trend ignores the possibility that an age correlation may be merely a life-cycle phenomenon. In the absence of data enabling us to follow a specific birth cohort through the life-cycle, we cannot reject the explanation that as men and women grow older they become more religious, and that there is thus no long-term trend in Britain towards a decline in devotion.[6]

Moreover, further analysis has shown that (when age is not taken into account) women in full-time jobs are still significantly more religious than are full-time working men. So whether or not workforce participation leads people to have less religious attitudes, it does not prevent women from being more religious than their male counterparts. However one looks at it, therefore, women in Britain are likely to continue to be more religious than men.[7]

Education

If religion, as it is often alleged, is a remnant of a 'pre-scientific' mentality, it might be expected to lose its importance as educational attainment increases. Are the better-educated more likely to be sceptics?

The data in the next table address that question. First of all, educational attainment (as measured by age at school leaving) does not correlate significantly with six out of our battery of eleven items. The negative, significant correlation between education and belief in God does not persist once age is taken into account. In fact, the only difference that remains statistically significant after controlling for age is support for daily prayer in schools, where the less educated are the more in favour.

Belief in religious miracles, perhaps a classic indicator of a 'pre-scientific' mentality, persists even among two in five of those who left school aged 19 or older (and hence were likely to have had some tertiary education). Education does not seem to be threatening religion in Britain.

Age and Gender

Research on religion and life-cycle carried out in the USA offers persuasive evidence that religious faith and observance begin to decline in the middle teens, reach bottom in the middle twenties and then slowly climb up, until they level off in the middle forties. Thus a simple correlation between religion and age cannot be seen to prove that there is any long-term decline in faith. However there

	All	AGE AT SCHOOL LEAVING		
		15 or less	16–18	19 or more
% believing in:				
God	69	75	66	43**
Life after death	55	55	58	48*
Religious miracles	45	51	43	41**
Affiliated with a denomination	64	72	57	36**
Pray weekly	27	31	24	26*
Attend service two or three times a month	16	14	13	26*
Intense experience	28	27	29	30*
Feel close to God	46	55	42	35**
Confidence in churches	58	60	56	60*
Churches have too much power	28	30	27	27*
In favour of school prayers	70	84	65	53

*Correlation with school leaving is not statistically significant
**Correlation with school leaving becomes statistically significant when age is taken into account.

is show an interesting pattern of difference in belief in God for men and women. The curve showing the relationship between age and faith for women fits exactly the pattern that our cohort research in the USA would lead us to expect; by the time they are in their thirties women are as likely as older women are to believe in God.

However, the pattern for men leads us to expect that cohort analysis might prove that men who are presently under fifty (born after 1942) will be less likely to believe in God all their lives than those who are over fifty. Future replications of the present survey will also enable that possibility to be explored.

We found a somewhat similar pattern for the proportion of men and women who have no religious affiliation. Only 10 per cent of women aged 70 and over and twenty per cent of men of the same age have no affiliation. For men this proportion increases almost linearly to 60 per cent of those under thirty with no religious affiliation, and for women the increase levels off to 45 per cent for those in their thirties.

Subsequent replications of this question will be necessary to confirm whether or not these correlations indicate a long-term trend.

Three points must be re-emphasised about the decline in belief in God. First, the phenomenon under analysis may well just be a life-cycle phenomenon, and it may be that men born since 1942 will turn out to grow more religious as they become older. Secondly, the decline is confined largely, if not entirely, to men. And thirdly, the level of unbelief does not rise among those born after 1952 (at present aged under 40). It looks very much like a one-shot phenomenon—a sharp decline which has since levelled off.

There is one more curious twist to the question of British belief in God which the next section will explain.

THE GOD OF THE UNBELIEVERS

We asked three different questions about the existence of God. In the first, respondents were asked to endorse one of six statements, ranging from "I don't believe in God" to "I know God really exists and I have no doubts about it". Ten per cent of Britons opted for the first statement; and a further 14 per cent gave the agnostic response that they did not know whether there is a God and knew of no way to find out. So it seems that around a quarter of Britons do not, or cannot, believe in God. Yet that figure is somewhat unstable, since in response to *the very next question*—"How close do you feel to God most of the time"—only 13 per cent of respondents chose the option "I do not believe in God"; seemingly the wording in this context implied too strong a rejection of God for many agnostics. To complicate the matter further, some 31 per cent of respondents chose one of the two options in a third question ("I don't believe in God now and I never have" or "I don't believe in God now, but I used to"). So we might think that somewhere under a third of the British are atheistic or agnostic.

But of those who say that they do not believe in God ("now" or "never have"), nearly three in 10 nonetheless profess to being *neither* atheist nor agnostic. Moreover, 15 per cent of non-believers report having had an intense religious experience, and three per cent say they pray at least once a week (to whom it may concern?). Two out of five of them support daily prayers in schools. And while unbelievers are twice as likely as believers to say that life has no purpose, still only one in five admit to such nihilism.

However, our data give little support to those theologians and clerics who think that the churches can reclaim 'relevance' by taking a strong stand on social issues: there is no difference between believers and unbelievers on the questions of equalisation of income or government provision of jobs.

In Britain, therefore, there seems to be considerable uncertainty about God, some inclined perhaps to believe despite themselves.

What about Ireland and the USA? Do the 'unbelievers' there have the same ambivalence?** The table below suggests that in the other societies 'unbelievers' are around half as likely as they are in Britain to choose the atheist response. The remaining 80 per cent of unbelievers in the USA and Ireland do not exclude the possibility of God (compared with 60 per cent in Britain). So not only are there considerably fewer 'unbelievers' in Ireland and the USA, those Irish and Americans who categorise themselves as 'unbelievers' are more inclined to give

---

** Our analyses are somewhat hampered by the very small number of non-believers in Ireland (south and north) and the United States. Ninety-four per cent of respondents in these three societies believe in God. So we have combined all their responses.

God the benefit of the doubt. Moreover, in Britain even the 'believers' are more likely to have doubts: only 44 per cent of them are 'theists' as opposed to 70 per cent in the other societies.

	BELIEVE IN GOD		DON'T BELIEVE IN GOD	
	Britain %	Other Societies %	Britain %	Other Societies %
Atheist	—	1	41	22
Agnostic	1	1	31	44
Uncertain	11	5	19	29
Doubter	37	21	4	3
Theist	44	70	—	2

While there are considerable ambiguities in both Britain and the other three societies, in the former they 'tilt' against God, but in the latter in favour.

Perhaps the social context affecting responses to questions about God is somewhat different in Britain than in other countries. It may be that to the British a confident acknowledgement of the existence of God is somehow perceived of as a limitation on their personal choice or intelligence. When asked about God, Britons certainly are inclined to hesitate and say "Yes, but . . . ," or to shift their responses from question to question. Perhaps the God in which one is asked to believe may also differ from society to society. Or are the British simply exhibiting the diffidence and lack of fervour that is supposedly (and stereotypically) a national trait? A comparison between Britain and other European societies more secular than Ireland (say Germany or the Netherlands or Norway) will become possible later and should yield very interesting results.

CONCLUSIONS

Britain is clearly a less religious society than the other three in this analysis, though by no means an irreligious society. How can one account for the differences? Why are the British less religious than the Americans or the Irish? The difference does not seem to be of recent origin. Church attendance in the USA and Ireland has long been higher. And even among Britons in the oldest age group, fewer believe in God and fewer are affiliated to a denomination.

We have already noted too that in the late medieval and early modern eras (as far as scholars can reconstruct them) Europeans were not particularly devout. High levels of religious observance in Europe are the result of rather recent historical developments. For instance, social and political structures seem to have aided and abetted the early to middle 19th century religious revival in Ireland (as they did in the USA), and to have impeded a parallel revival in England. Perhaps the worst thing for religion in England was the establishment of the Church of England. Or to put it differently, religion and religious devotion were unlucky in Britain and lucky in Ireland and the USA.

At least such an explanation may point in the right direction if we are trying to understand why religion seems so much more vigorous in Ireland and the USA, and to discover why they are the exceptions (along with Canada) within the North Atlantic world. The question can be reversed, however; we might just as well ask why religion is relatively weak in western and central Europe, and relatively strong in much of the rest of the world. According to this perspective, the exceptions are Britain and most countries of the European continent west of Poland, while Ireland and the United States are more typical of the human condition. In any event, religion certainly manifests itself differently in the three (or four) English-speaking cultures under consideration. None of the cultures is totally irreligious. None is without its ambiguities and inconsistencies. Perhaps all four societies can be accused of some measure of religious (or irreligious) hypocrisy. But the differences need to be taken seriously by anyone interested in the impact of political and social history, and existing social structures, on human culture and behaviour.

To end this chapter with—as is perhaps appropriate for its American-Irish author—an Irish 'bull': the British are more religious than they think they are. Indeed, as Rodney Stark has commented on an earlier draft of this paper, they are also possibly more religious than they used to be.

Notes

1. Brierley (1991a and 1991b) has provided a considerable amount of data from the English Church Census of 1989. The census however was essentially a census of churches and therefore of people who were affiliated with the churches. While it presents enormous amounts of data, it tells us very little about that vast majority of English men and women who are not affiliated with churches.

2. Butler (1990) adds that in Yorkshire in 1743 only 20 per cent of adults attended worship regularly and only 31 per cent attended at Easter.

3. But the picture is not quite as simple as that—it rarely is in religious matters in Britain as we shall see. When asked what their spouse's (or partner's) religious affiliation was, only 12 per cent—15 per cent of men and 10 per cent of women—said that he or she had no religious affiliation. Since the spouses (or partners) of a random sample of people are themselves a random sample, it is clear that almost a quarter of respondents are willing to attribute to their wife, husband or partner a religious affiliation the spouse does not claim (34 per cent of currently married or cohabiting Britons report no religious affiliation). Perhaps respondents have stricter criteria for their own religious affiliation than they apply to their partners. Perhaps married respondents remember how the issue of religion was negotiated at the time of marriage. Or perhaps in a country where there is a single established Church dominating the religious landscape, 'affiliation' is not a matter of great saliency to many Britons. If pushed, they might claim some vague affiliation with the 'C or E', but it is not a relationship of which they are sufficiently conscious spontaneously to claim it in response to a survey question.

4. In another paper the author will compare British Catholics and their counterparts in Ireland and the USA to determine whether living in a society which is less avowedly devout and religious has an effect on Roman Catholics.
5. Personal observation convinces the writer that the amount of prayer required of a woman (in her own mind) tends to increase with the number of children and grandchildren for whom she has assumed responsibility. If one adds to a woman's spouse the number of children and grandchildren under her 'jurisdiction', one might find a variable that goes a long way towards accounting for the greater religious devotion of women.
6. In cohort analysis the writer has done in the United States with Michael Hout of the University of California, the preponderance of the data supports the life-cycle explanation.
7. On the other hand, if intense religious experiences are the ultimate measure of receptiveness to religion, then women and men do not differ on this most fundamental religious dimension. A 'gender-linked' culture may create in women a greater disposition to religious participation and acceptance of cognitive religious propositions, but it does not make them any more likely to have experienced religious 'ecstasy'.

References

Brierley, P. (1991a), *Christian England: What the Church Census Reveals*, London: MARC Europe.

Brierley, P. (1992b), *Prospects for the Nineties: Trends and Tables from the 1989 English Church Census*, London: MARC Europe.

Butler, J. (1990), *Awash in a Sea of Faith*, Cambridge Massachusetts: Harvard University Press.

Carroll, M. (1992), *Madonnas that Maim*, Baltimore: John Hopkins University Press.

Connolly, S.J. (1982), *Priest and People in Prefamine Ireland*, Dublin: Gill and Macmillan.

Finke, R. and Stark, R. (1992), *The Churching of America*, (in press).

Greeley, A. (1988), 'The Success and Assimilation of Irish Protestants and Irish Catholics in the United States', *Sociology and Social Research*, 4: 229–236.

Greeley, A. (1989), 'Protestant and Catholic: Is the Analogical Imagination Extinct?', *American Sociological Review*, 54: 485–502.

Greeley, A. (1991), *The Pragmatics of Prayer*, Unpublished Paper, Chicago: NORC.

Greeley, A. (1992), *The Two Catholic Traditions*, Unpublished Paper, Chicago: NORC.

Hatch, N. (1989), *The Democratization of American Christianity*, New Haven: Yale University Press.

Herberg, W. (1955), *Protestant, Catholic, Jew*, London/New York: Doubleday.

Larkin, E. (1972), 'The Devotional Revolution in Ireland', *The American Historical Review*, 7: 623–652.

Larkin, E. (1984), *The Historical Dimensions of Irish Catholicism*, Washington D.C.: The Catholic University of America Press.

Martin, D. (1967), *A Sociology of English Religion*, London: SCM Press.

Martin, D. (1969), *The Religious and the Secular: Studies in Secularization*, London: Routledge & K. Paul.

Martin, D. (1978), *A General Theory of Secularization*, Oxford: Blackwell.

Stark, R., Melton, G. and Iannaccone, L. (1992), *The Secularization of Europe Reconsidered*, forthcoming.

Wickham, R. (1957), *Church and People in an Industrial City*, London: Lutterworth Press.

Wilson, B. (1969), *Religion in Secular Society*, Harmondsworth: Penguin.

Wilson, B. (1976), *Contemporary Transformations of Religion*, Oxford/New York: Oxford University Press.

Acknowledgement

Since 1989, the ESRC has (through its funding of the Joint Centre for the Study of Social Trends) helped ensure SCPR's continuing participation in the International Social Survey Programme. We thank the Council for its financial support.

Sociologists are fascinated by the development of religious institutions. Typically, these begin with a founder and a small group of followers. If the group survives, it gradually evolves into a more and more complex formal organization, in which means become ends and the original ends of the tradition are forgotten—a process that seems to mark all bureaucratic development. Ernest Troeltsch, working with an original insight of Max Weber's, established the paradigm for this process in his analysis of how Christianity changed from a sect to a church.

In recent years, sociologists have focused on sects and "cults," a pre-sect initial phase, which they have added to Troeltsch's model, and have paid rather less attention to the other end of the process, perhaps because churches seem to fit nicely into the models of formal organizational theory.

Cults come and go, though many of them become both so large and sufficiently well organized that they seem to be in fact mini-denominations. The appeal of cults seems to be similar to that of folk religion: both offer special knowledge and special practices for those who are confused or uncertain about their lives. In addition, the cults also frequently provide comprehensive communities that offer their members not only a faith in which to believe, but a strong (and often dominating) social group to which to belong. The appeal of the cults seems especially strong to young people and even more especially to those young people whose families have either no religious tradition or whose adherence to a tradition is perfunctory.

....

CHURCH AND SECT—ERNEST TROELTSCH

Ernest Troeltsch (1865–1923) was a friend and colleague of Max Weber's. Like Weber, he was interested in the relationship between religion and society and, like Weber, he believed that religion influences social structure and was not merely influenced by social and economic activity. Unlike Weber, who studied the great world religions, Troeltsch concentrated on Christianity and showed how it began as a religious movement (and not an economic protest) and developed into a formal institutionalized Church, which had powerful social influences, but was also shaped by the institutions with which it coexisted.

Troeltsch's distinction between sect and church (in his most important work—*The Social Teachings of the Christian Churches*—1912) and his account of how the former evolves into the latter has fascinated sociologists, who have applied the model to the study of religious institutions—not always with as much nuance or sophistication as one might have liked. Often it seems in such analyses that the sociologist's sympathy lies with the spontaneity, the enthusiasm, and fervor of the sect over against the formalized and bureaucratic church.

Some have made attempts to expand Troeltsch's typology, to insert "cult" before "sect" and denomination after it. Troeltsch, however, was less interested in developing a set of categories into which various religious groups could be inserted than he was in portraying a process that seems inevitable in any religious movement.

Formalization of a religious movement is inevitable if the movement is to survive. Organization is part of the process by which any group of human beings tries to preserve their community. (Someone has to bring the poker chips for a card game!) A religious cult or sect is on its way to becoming a denomination or a church when it buys its first copy machine or its first fax machine. The secret of keeping a religious institution alive and vital is whether it can make room for, if not guarantee, periodic revivals of sect-like fervor and enthusiasm. Most large denominations have sect-like groupings within their membership to the dismay or delight of the institutional leadership. Catholicism has tended to keep much movements within its boundaries (by defining the boundaries as broadly as possible) though it failed to do so in the 16th century. Protestantism has tended to accommodate to sect-like movements by founding new denominations. But the process of revitalization and institutionalization goes on constantly in any denomination that is still alive.

Questions for Reflection and Discussion

1. Did Christianity have to become a church?
2. Does Troeltsh disapprove of the journey from sect to church?
3. Would you rather belong to a sect or a church? What are the advantages of each?
4. Why does Catholicism tend to incorporate sect movements within its membership, while Protestantism tends to spin off new denominations?

SECT-TYPE AND CHURCH-TYPE CONTRASTED
Ernest Troeltsch

The importance of this element is the fact that at this point, alongside of the Church-type produced by Christianity in its sociological process of self-development, there appears the new type of the sect.

At the outset the actual differences are quite clear. The Church is that type of organization which is overwhelmingly conservative, which to a certain extent accepts the secular order, and dominates the masses; in principle, therefore, it is universal, i.e. it desires to cover the whole life of humanity. The sects, on the other hand, are comparatively small groups; they aspire after personal inward perfection, and they aim at a direct personal fellowship between the members of each group. From the very beginning, therefore, they are forced to organize themselves in small groups, and to renounce the idea of dominating the world. Their attitude towards the world, the State, and Society may be indifferent, tolerant, or hostile, since they have no desire to control and incorporate these forms of social life; on the contrary, they tend to avoid them; their aim is usually either to tolerate their presence alongside of their own body, or even to replace these social institutions by their own society.

Further, both types are in close connection with the actual situation and with the development of Society. The fully developed Church, however, utilizes the State and the ruling classes, and weaves these elements into her own life; she then becomes an integral part of the existing social order; from this standpoint, then, the Church both stabilizes and determines the social order; in so doing, however, she becomes dependent upon the upper classes, and upon their development. The sects, on the other hand, are connected with the lower classes, or at least with those elements in Society which are opposed to the State and to Society; they work upwards from below, and not downwards from above.

Source: Ernst Troeltsch, "Sect-Type and Church-Type Contrasted," from Ernst Troeltsch, *The Social Teaching of the Christian Churches* (trans. Olive Wyon), London: Allen and Unwin, 1931, vol. 1, pp. 331–343.

Finally, too, both types vary a good deal in their attitude towards the supernatural and transcendent element in Christianity, and also in their view of its system of asceticism. The Church relates the whole of the secular order as a means and a preparation to the supernatural aim of life, and it incorporates genuine asceticism into its structure as one element in this preparation, all under the very definite direction of the Church. The sects refer their members directly to the supernatural aim of life, and in them the individualistic, directly religious character of asceticism, as a means of union with God, is developed more strongly and fully; the attitude of opposition to the world and its powers, to which the secularized Church now also belongs, tends to develop a theoretical and general asceticism. It must, however, be admitted that asceticism in the Church, and in ecclesiastical monasticism, has a different meaning from that of the renunciation of or hostility to the world which characterizes the asceticism of the sects.

The asceticism of the Church is a method of acquiring virtue, and a special high watermark of religious achievement, connected chiefly with the repression of the senses, or expressing itself in special achievements of a peculiar character; otherwise, however, it presupposes the life of the world as the general background, and the contrast of an average morality which is on relatively good terms with the world. Along these lines, therefore, ecclesiastical asceticism is connected with the asceticism of the redemption cults of late antiquity, and with the detachment required for the contemplative life; in any case, it is connected with a moral dualism.

The asceticism of the sects, on the other hand, is merely the simple principle of detachment from the world, and is expressed in the refusal to use the law, to swear in a court of justice, to own property, to exercise dominion over others, or to take part in war. The sects take the Sermon on the Mount as their ideal; they lay stress on the simple but radical opposition of the Kingdom of God to all secular interests and institutions. They practise renunciation only as a means of charity, as the basis of a thorough-going communism of love, and, since their rules are equally binding upon all, do not encourage extravagant and heroic deeds, nor the vicarious heroism of some to make up for the worldliness and average morality of others. The ascetic ideal of the sects consists simply in opposition to the world and to its social institutions, but it is not opposition to the sense-life, nor to the average life of humanity. It is therefore only related with the asceticism of monasticism in so far as the latter also creates special conditions, within which it is possible to lead a life according to the Sermon on the Mount, and in harmony with the ideal of the communism of love. In the main, however, the ascetic ideal of the sects is fundamentally different from that of monasticism, in so far as the latter implies emphasis upon the mortification of the senses, and upon works of supererogation in poverty and obedience for their own sake. In all things the ideal of the sects is essentially not one which aims at the destruction of the sense life and of natural self-feeling, but a union in love which is not affected by the social inequalities and struggles of the world.

All these differences which actually existed between the late Mediaeval Church and the sects, must have had their foundation in some way or another within the interior structure of the two-fold sociological edifice. If, then, in reality both types claim, and rightly claim, a relationship with the Primitive Church, it is clear that the final cause for this dualistic development must lie within primitive Christianity itself. Once this point becomes clear, therefore, it will also shed light upon the whole problems of the sociological understanding of Christianity in general. Since it is only at this point that the difference between the two elements emerges very clearly as a permanent difference, only now have we reached the stage at which it can be discussed. It is also very important to understand this question thoroughly at this stage, since it explains the later developments of Church History, in which the sect stands out ever more clearly alongside of the Church. In the whole previous development of the Church this question was less vital, for during the early centuries the Church itself fluctuated a great deal between the sect and the Church-type; indeed, it only achieved the development of the Church-type with the development of sacerdotal and sacramental doctrine; precisely for that reason, in its process of development up to this time, the Church had only witnessed a sect development alongside of itself to a small extent, and the differences between them and the Church were still not clear. The problem first appears clearly in the opposition between the sacramental-hierarchical Church conception of Augustine and the Donatists. But with the disappearance of African Christianity this opposition also disappeared, and it only reappeared in a decisive form after the completion of the idea of the Church in the Gregorian church reform.

The word "sect," however, gives an erroneous impression. Originally the word was used in a polemical and apologetic sense, and it was used to describe groups which separated themselves from the official Church, while they retained certain fundamental elements of Christian thought; by the very fact, however, that they were outside the corporate life of the ecclesiastical tradition—a position, moreover, which was usually forced upon them—they were regarded as inferior side-issues, one-sided phenomena, exaggerations or abbreviations of ecclesiastical Christianity. That is, naturally, solely the viewpoint of the dominant churches, based on the belief that the ecclesiastical type alone has any right to exist. Ecclesiastical law within the modern State definitely denotes as "sects" those religious groups which exist alongside of the official privileged State Churches, by law established, groups which the State either does not recognize at all, or, if it does recognize them, grants them fewer rights and privileges than the official State Churches. Such a conception, however, confuses the actual issue. Very often in the so-called "sects" it is precisely the essential elements of the Gospel which are fully expressed; they themselves always appeal to the Gospel and to Primitive Christianity, and accuse the Church of having fallen away from its ideal; these impulses are always those which have been either suppressed or undeveloped in the official churches, of course for good and characteristic reasons, which again are not taken into account by the passionate party polemics of the sects. There can, however, be no doubt about the actual fact: the sects, with their greater independence of the world, and their continual emphasis upon the original ideals of Christianity, often represent in a very direct and characteristic way the essential fundamental ideas of Christianity; to a very great extent they are a most important factor in the study of the development of the sociological consequences of Christian thought. This statement is proved conclusively by all those who make a close study of the sect movements, which were especially numerous in the latter mediaeval period—movements which played their part in the general disintegration of the mediaeval social order. This comes out very clearly in the great works of Sebastian Franck, and especially of Gottfried Arnold, which were written later in defence of the sects.

The main stream of Christian development, however, flows along the channel prepared by the Church-type. The reason for this is clear: the Church-type represents the longing for a universal all-embracing ideal, the desire to control great masses of men, and therefore the urge to dominate the world and civilization in general. Paulinism, in spite of its strongly individualistic and "enthusiastic" features, had already led the way along this line: it desired to conquer the world for Christ; it came to terms with the order of the State by interpreting it as an institution ordained and permitted by God; it accepted the existing order with its professions and its habits and customs. The only union it desired was that which arose out of a common share in the energy of grace which the Body of Christ contained; out of this union the new life ought to spring up naturally from within through the power of the Holy Spirit, thus preparing the way for the speedy coming of the Kingdom of God, as the real universal end of all things. The more that Christendom renounced the life of this supernatural and eschatological fulfilment of its universal ideal, and tried to achieve this end by missionary effort and organization, the more was it forced to make its Divine and Christian character independent of the subjective character and service of believers; henceforth it sought to concentrate all its emphasis upon the objective possession of religious truth and religious power, which were contained in the tradition of Christ, and in the Divine guidance of the Church which fills and penetrates the whole Body. From this objective basis subjective energies could ever flow forth afresh, exerting a renewing influence, but the objective basis did not coincide with these results. Only thus was it possible to have a popular Church at all, and it was only thus that the relative acceptance of the world, the State, of Society, and of the existing culture, which this required, did no harm to the objective foundation. The Divine nature of the Church was retained in its objective basis, and from this centre there welled up continually fresh streams of vital spiritual force. It was the aim of the leaders of the Church to render this basis as objective as possible, by means of tradition, priesthood, and sacrament; to secure in it, objectively, the sociological point of contact; if that were once firmly established the subjective influence of the Church was considered secure; it was only in detail that it could not be controlled. In this way the fundamental religious sense of possessing something Divinely "given" and "redeeming" was ensured, while the universalizing tendency was also made effective, since it established the Church, the organ of Divine grace, in the supreme position of power. When to that was added the Sacrament of Penance, the power of spiritual direction, the law against heretics, and the general supervision of the faith, the Church was then able to gain an inward dominion over the hearts of men.

Under these circumstances, however, the Church found it impossible to avoid making a compromise with the State, with the social order, and with economic conditions, and the Thomist doctrine worked this out in a very able, comprehensive theory, which vigorously maintained the ultimate supernatural orientation of life. In all this it is claimed that the whole is derived, quite logically, from the Gospel; it is clear that this point of view became possible as soon as the Gospel was conceived as a universal way of life, offering redemption to all, whose influence radiates from the knowledge given by the Gospel, coupled with the assurance of salvation given by the Church. It was precisely the development of an objective sociological point of reference, its establishment on a stable basis, and its endeavour to go forward from that point to organize the conquest of the world, which led to this development. It is, however, equally obvious that in so doing the radical individualism of the Gospel, with its urge towards the utmost personal achievement, its radical fellowship of love, uniting all in the most personal centre of life, with its heroic indifference towards the world, the State and civilization, with its mistrust of the spiritual danger of distraction and error inherent in the possession of or the desire for great possessions, has been given a secondary place, or even given up altogether; these features now appear as mere factors within the system; they are no longer ruling principles.

It was precisely this aspect of the Gospel, however, which the sects developed still farther, or, rather, it was this aspect which they were continually reemphasizing and bringing into fresh prominence. In general, the following are their characteristic features: lay Christianity, personal achievement in ethics and in religion, the radical fellowship of love, religious equality and brotherly love, indifference towards the authority of the State and the ruling classes, dislike of technical law and of the oath, the separation of the religious life from the economic struggle by means of the ideal of poverty and frugality, or occasionally in a charity which becomes communism, the directness of the personal religious relationship, criticism of official spiritual guides and theologians, the appeal to the New Testament and to the Primitive Church. The sociological point of contact, which here forms the starting-point for the growth of the religious community, differs clearly from that upon which the Church has been formed. Whereas the Church assumes the objective concrete holiness of the sacerdotal office, of Apostolic Succession, of the *Depositum fidei* and of the sacraments, and appeals to the extension of the Incarnation which takes place permanently through the priesthood, the sect, on the other hand, appeals to the ever new common performance of the moral demands, which, at bottom, are founded only upon the Law and the Example of Christ. In this, it must be admitted that they are in direct contact with the Teaching of Jesus. Consciously or unconsciously, therefore, this implies a different attitude to the early history of Christianity, and a different conception of Christian doctrine. Scripture history and the history of the Primitive Church are permanent ideals, to be accepted in their literal sense, not the starting-point, historically limited and defined, for the development of the Church. Christ is not the God-Man, eternally at work within the Church, leading it into all Truth, but He is the direct Head of the Church, binding the Church to Himself through His Law in the Scriptures. On the one hand, there is development and compromise, on the other literal obedience and radicalism.

It is this point of view, however, which makes the sects incapable of forming large mass organizations, and limits their development to small groups, united on a basis of personal intimacy; it is also responsible for the necessity for a constant renewal of the ideal, their lack of continuity, their pronounced individualism, and their affinity with all the oppressed and idealistic groups within the lower classes. These also are the groups in which an ardent desire for the improvement of their lot goes hand in hand with a complete ignorance of the complicated conditions of life, in which therefore an idealistic orthodoxy finds no difficulty in expecting to see the world transformed by the purely moral principles of love. In this way the sects gained on the side of intensity in Christian life, but they lost in the spirit of universalism, since they felt obliged to consider the Church as degenerate, and they did not believe that the world could be conquered by human power and effort; that is why they were always forced to adopt eschatological views. On the side of personal Christian piety they score, and they are in closer touch with the radical individualism of the Gospel, but they lose spontaneity and the spirit of grateful surrender to the Divine revelation of grace; they look upon the New Testament as the Law of God, and, in their active realization of personal fellowship in love, they tend towards legalism and an emphasis upon "good works". They gain in specific Christian piety, but they lose spiritual breadth and the power to be receptive, and they thus revise the whole vast process of assimilation which the Church had completed, and which she was able to complete because she had placed personal Christian piety upon an objective basis. The Church emphasizes the idea of Grace and makes it objective; the sect emphasizes and realizes the idea of subjective holiness. In the Scriptures the Church adheres to the source of redemption, whereas the sect adheres to the Law of God and of Christ.

Although this description of the sect-type represents in the main its prevailing sociological characteristics, the distinctive significance of the sect-type contrasted with the Church-type still has a good concrete basis. (There is no need to consider here the particular groups which were founded purely upon dogma; they were indeed rare, and the pantheistic philosophical sects of the Middle Ages merge almost imperceptibly into sects of the practical religious kind.) In reality, the sects are essentially different from the Church and the churches. The word "sect", however, does not mean that these movements are undeveloped expressions of the Church-type; it stands for an independent sociological type of Christian thought.

The essence of the Church is its objective institutional character. The individual is born into it, and through infant baptism he comes under its miraculous influence. The priesthood and the hierarchy, which hold the keys to the tradition of the Church, to sacramental grace and ecclesiastical jurisdiction, represent the objective treasury of grace, even when the individual priest may happen to be unworthy; this Divine treasure only needs to be set always upon the lampstand and made effective through the sacraments, and it will inevitably do its work by virtue of the miraculous power which the Church contains. The Church means the eternal existence of the God-Man; it is the extension of the Incarnation, the objective organization of miraculous power, from which, by means of the Divine Providential government of the world, subjective results will appear quite naturally. From this point of view compromise with the world, and the connection with the preparatory stages and dispositions which it contained, was possible; for in spite of all individual inadequacy the institution remains holy and Divine, and it contains the promise of its capacity to overcome the world by means of the miraculous power which dwells within it. Universalism, however, also only becomes possible on the basis of this compromise; it means an actual domination of the institution as such, and a believing confidence in its invincible power of inward influence. Personal effort and service, however fully they may be emphasized, even when they go to the limits of extreme legalism, are still only secondary; the main thing is the objective possession of grace and its universally recognized dominion; to everything else these words apply: *et cetera adjicientur vobis.* The one vitally important thing is that every individual should come within the range of the influence of these saving energies of grace; hence the Church is forced to dominate Society, compelling all the members of Society to come under its sphere and influence; but, on the other hand, her stability is entirely unaffected by the fact of the extent to which her influence over all individuals is actually attained. The Church is the great educator of the nations, and like all educators she knows how to allow for various degrees of capacity and maturity, and how to attain her end only by a process of adaptation and compromise.

Compared with this institutional principle of an objective organism, however, the sect is a voluntary community whose members join it of their own free will. The very life of the sect, therefore, depends on actual personal service and co-operation; as an independent member each individual has his part within the fellowship; the bond of union has not been indirectly imparted through the common possession of Divine grace, but it is directly realized in the personal relationships of life. An individual is not born into a sect; he enters it on the basis of conscious conversion; infant baptism, which, indeed, was only introduced at a later date, is almost always a stumbling-block. In the sect spiritual progress does not depend upon the objective impartation of Grace through the Sacrament, but upon individual personal effort; sooner or later, therefore, the sect always criticizes the sacramental idea. This does not mean that the spirit of fellowship is weakened by individualism; indeed, it is strengthened, since each individual proves that he is entitled to membership by the very fact of his services to the fellowship. It is, however, naturally a somewhat limited form of fellowship, and the expenditure of so much effort in the maintenance and exercise of this particular kind of fellowship produces a certain indifference towards other forms of fellowship which are based upon secular interests; on the other hand, all secular interests are drawn into the narrow framework of the sect and tested by its standards, in so far as the sect is able to assimilate these interests at all. Whatever cannot be related to the group of interests controlled by the sect, and by the Scriptural ideal, is rejected and avoided. The sect, therefore, does not educate nations in the mass, but it gathers a select group of the elect, and places it in sharp opposition to the world. In so far as the sect-type maintains Christian universalism at all, like the Gospel, the only form it knows is that of eschatology; this is the reason why it always finally revives the eschatology of the Bible. That also naturally explains the greater tendency of the sect towards "ascetic" life and thought, even though the original ideal of the New Testament had not pointed in that direction. The final activity of the group and of the individual consists precisely in the practical austerity of a purely religious attitude towards life which is not affected by cultural influences. That is, however, a different kind of asceticism, and this is the reason for that difference between it and the asceticism of the Church-type which has already been stated. It is not the heroic special achievement of a special class, restricted by its very nature to particular instances, nor the mortification of the senses in order to further the higher religious life; it is simply detachment from the world, the reduction of worldly pleasure to a minimum, and the highest possible development of fellowship in love; all this is interpreted in the old Scriptural sense. Since the sect-type is rooted in the teaching of Jesus, its asceticism also is that of primitive Christianity and of the Sermon on the Mount, not that of the Church and of the contemplative life; it is narrower and more scrupulous than that of Jesus, but, literally understood, it is still the continuation of the attitude of Jesus towards the world. The concentration on personal effort, and the sociological connection with a practical ideal, makes an extremely exacting claim on individual effort, and avoidance of all other forms of human association. The asceticism of the sect is not an attempt to popularize and universalize an ideal which the Church had prescribed only for special classes and in special circumstances. The Church ideal of asceticism can never be conceived as a universal ethic; it is essentially unique and heroic. The ascetic ideal of the sect, on the contrary, is, as a matter of course, an ideal which is possible to all, and appointed for all, which, according to its conception, united the fellowship instead of dividing it, and according to its content is also capable of a general realization in so far as the circle of the elect is concerned.

Thus, in reality we are faced with two different sociological types. This is true in spite of the fact (which is quite immaterial) that incidentally in actual practice they may often impinge upon one another. If objections are raised to the terms "Church" and "Sect", and if all sociological groups which are based on and inspired by monotheistic, universalized, religious motives are described (in a terminology which is in itself quite appropriate) as "Churches", we would then have to make the distinction between institutional churches and voluntary churches. It does not really matter which expression is used. The all-important point is this: that both types are a logical result of the Gospel, and only conjointly do they exhaust the whole range of its sociological influence, and thus also indirectly of its social results, which are always connected with the religious organization.

In reality, the Church does not represent a mere deterioration of the Gospel, however much that may appear to be the case when we contrast its hierarchical organization and its sacramental system with the teaching of Jesus. For wherever the Gospel is conceived as primarily a free gift, as pure grace, and wherever it is offered to us in the picture which faith creates of Christ as a Divine institution, wherever the inner freedom of the Spirit, contrasted with all human effort and organization, is felt to be the spirit of Jesus, and wherever His splendid indifference towards secular matters is felt, in the sense of a spiritual and inner independence, while these secular things are used outwardly, there the institution of the Church may be regarded as a natural continuation and transformation of the Gospel. At the same time, with its unlimited universalism, it still contains the fundamental impulse of the evangelic message; the only difference is that whereas the Gospel had left all questions of possible realization to the miraculous coming of the Kingdom of God, a Church which had to work in a world which was not going to pass away had to organize and arrange matters for itself, and in so doing it was forced into a position of compromise.

On the other hand, the essence of the sect does not consist merely in a one-sided emphasis upon certain vital elements of the Church-type, but it is itself a direct continuation of the idea of the Gospel. Only within it is there a full recognition of the value of radical individualism and of the idea of love; it is the sect alone which instinctively builds up its ideal of fellowship from this point of view, and this is the very reason why it attains such a strong subjective and inward unity, instead of merely external membership in an institution. For the same reason the sect also maintains the original radicalism of the Christian ideal and its hostility towards the world, and it retains the fundamental demand for personal service, which indeed it is also able to regard as a work of grace: in the idea of grace, however, the sect emphasizes the subjective realization and the effects of grace, and not the objective assurance of its presence. The sect does not live on the miracles of the past, nor on the miraculous nature of the institution, but on the constantly renewed miracle of the Presence of Christ, and on the subjective reality of the individual mastery of life.

The starting-point of the Church is the Apostolic Message of the Exalted Christ, and faith in Christ the Redeemer, into which the Gospel has developed; this constitutes its objective treasure, which it makes still more objective in its sacramental-sacerdotal institution. To this extent the Church can trace its descent from Paulinism, which contained the germ of the sacramental idea, which, however, also contained some very unecclesiastical elements in its pneumatic enthusiasm, and in its urgent demand for the personal holiness of the "new creature."

The sect, on the contrary, starts from the teaching and the example of Jesus, from the subjective work of the apostles and the pattern of their life of poverty, and unites the religious individualism preached by the Gospel with the religious fellowship, in which the office of the ministry is not based upon ecclesiastical ordination and tradition, but upon religious service and power, and which therefore can also devolve entirely upon laymen.

The Church administers the sacraments without reference to the personal worthiness of the priests; the sect distrusts the ecclesiastical sacraments, and either permits them to be administered by laymen, or makes them dependent upon the personal character of the celebrant, or even discards them altogether.

The individualism of the sect urges it towards the direct intercourse of the individual with God; frequently, therefore, it replaces the ecclesiastical doctrine of the sacraments by the Primitive Christian doctrine of the Spirit and by "enthusiasm". The Church has its priests and its sacraments; it dominates the world and is therefore also dominated by the world. The sect is lay Christianity, independent of the world, and is therefore inclined towards asceticism and mysticism. Both these tendencies are based upon fundamental impulses of the Gospel. The Gospel contains the idea of an objective possession of salvation in the knowledge and revelation of God, and in developing this idea it becomes the Church. It contains, however, also the idea of an absolute personal religion and of an absolute personal fellowship, and in following out this idea it becomes a sect. The teaching of Jesus, which cherishes the expectation of the End of the Age and the Coming of the Kingdom of God, which gathers into one body all who are resolute in their determination to confess Christ before men and to leave the world to its fate, tends to develop the sect-type. The apostolic faith which looks back to a miracle of redemption and to the Person of Jesus, and which lives in the powers of its heavenly Lord: this faith which leans upon something achieved and objective, in which it unites the faithful and allows them to rest, tends to develop the Church-type. Thus the New Testament helps to develop both the Church and the sect; it has done so from the beginning, but the Church had the start, and its great world mission. Only when the objectification of the Church had been developed to its fullest extent did the sectarian tendency assert itself and react against this excessive objectification. Further, just as the objectification of the Church was achieved in connection with the feudal society of the Early Middle Ages, the reappearance of the tendency to form sects was connected with the social transformation, and the new developments of city-civilization in the central period of the Middle Ages and in its period of decline—with the growth of individualism and the gathering of masses of people in the towns themselves—and with the reflex effect of this city formation upon the rural population and the aristocracy.

Cult Formation—William Bainbridge and Rodney Stark

As Bainbridge and Stark note in the beginning of the selection, the formation of the Christian Churches happened long ago, but cult formation goes on at the present and can be observed. Despite the media attention to cults and sects, there is no reason to think they are a new phenomenon in American life. They have always been spinning into and out of existence. The two authors distinguish three kinds of cults, all of which offer religious compensations of one kind or another to their members in situations in which the recruits feel personal or social stress or deprivation. The first results from some kind of emotional disturbance in the founder; the second from the energies of a religious "hustler"; and the third evolves out of a distinctive subculture (as in the concern about flying saucers).

Cults fascinate sociologists both because, as the two authors note, they are available to watch and study here and now and because they are colorful and hence fun to investigate. They also prove that the human religious impulse has not died away—and neither has the tendency for this impulse to head in bizarre directions.

It is worth remembering, however, that despite the abundance of cults and their fascination, they are not the typical religious group. Most people do not join cults. Most of those who do choose not to remain in them indefinitely. The mortality rate on cults is high.

The three models in this selection help us to understand why people join cults and why they so rarely find in them that for which they are looking.

Questions for Reflection and Discussion

1. Have you ever belonged to a cult? Do you know someone who did? Into which of the three categories did it fit?
2. Why do people join cults? Why do they tend to leave them?
3. Can cults be dangerous? Why?
4. What do you think of the attempts of family members to de-program people who have belonged to cults?

THREE MODELS OF CULT FORMATION
William Bainbridge and Rodney Stark

The origins of the great world faiths are shrouded by time, but cult formation remains available for close inspection. If we would understand how religions begin, it is the obscure and exotic world of cults that demands our attention. This chapter synthesizes the mass of ethnographic materials available on cult formation as the necessary preliminary for a comprehensive theory. Although it represents an important step in our continuing work to formulate a general theory of religion, this chapter is primarily designed to consolidate and clarify what is already known about this subject.

The published literature on cults is at present as chaotic as was the material on which cultural anthropology was founded a century ago: an unsystematic collection of traveler's tales, mostly journalistic, often inaccurate, and nearly devoid of theory. For all the deficiencies of this mass of writing, three fundamental models of how novel religious ideas are generated and made social can be seen dimly. In this chapter we develop and compare these models. Although we find it convenient to discuss them separately, each is but a different combination of the same theoretical elements.

The three models of cult formation, or religious innovation, are (1) *the psychopathology model,* (2) *the entrepreneur model,* and (3) *the subculture-evolution model.* Other social scientists have presented the first in some detail, but the second and third have not previously been delineated as formal models.

Cult formation is a two-step process of innovation. First, new religious ideas must be *invented.* Second, they must be *socially accepted* by at least a small group of people. Therefore, we must first explain how and why individuals invent or discover new religious ideas. Many (perhaps most) persons who hit upon new religious ideas do not found new religions. So long as only one person holds a religious idea, no real religion exists. Therefore, we also need to understand the process by which religious inventors are able to make their views social—to convince other persons to share their convictions. We conceptualize successful cult innovation as a social process in which innovators both invent new religious ideas and transmit them to other persons in exchange for rewards.

RELIGIONS AS EXCHANGE SYSTEMS

To understand how cults are formed, a brief reprise of our general theory of religion is in order. We have noted that human action is governed by the pursuit of

Source: This commentary was originally published as William Sims Bainbridge and Rodney Stark, "Cult Formation: Three Compatible Models," *Sociological Analysis,* 1979, 40:4, pp. 283–295.

rewards and the avoidance of costs (Stark and Bainbridge, 1980). Rewards, those things humans will expend costs to obtain, often can be gained only from other humans; so people are forced into exchange relations. However, many rewards are very scarce and can be possessed by only some, not all. Other rewards appear to be so scarce that they cannot be shown to exist at all. Having learned to seek rewards through exchanges with other persons, in their desperation humans turn to each other for these highly desired scarce and nonexistent rewards. And from each other humans often receive compensators for the rewards they seek.

When rewards are very scarce, or not available at all, humans create and exchange compensators—sets of beliefs and prescriptions for action that substitute for the immediate achievement of the desired reward. Religions are social enterprises whose primary purpose is to create, maintain, and exchange supernaturally based general compensators. But how do new compensators and new systems of compensators get invented? Modest rates of compensator production may take place in any social organization, but, to see mass production and radical innovation, we must look to cults.

Cults are social enterprises primarily engaged in the production and exchange of novel or exotic compensators. Thus, not all cults are religions. Some offer only magic—for example, psychic healing of specific diseases—and do not offer such general compensators as eternal life. Magical cults frequently evolve toward progressively more general compensators and become full-fledged religions. Then they become true *cult movements*: social enterprises primarily engaged in the production and exchange of novel and exotic general compensators, based on supernatural assumptions.

Often, a cult is exotic and offers compensators that are unfamiliar to most people who encounter it because it migrated from another, alien society. In this chapter, we are not interested in these imported cults, but in those novel cult movements that are innovative alternatives to the traditional systems of religious compensators that are normal in the environment in which the cult originated.

Two points should be kept in mind about the three models of cult formation. First, they are *compatible*. Any pair, or even all three, could combine validly to explain the processes of innovation that produced a given cult. Second, the processes described can take place at a reduced rate in any religious organization—or even in secular organizations. Only if the compensators produced are very general and based on supernatural assumptions shall we speak of *religion*. Only when the degree of innovation is extreme shall we speak of a *cult*. But all the dimensions we describe are matters of degree, and the models could be applied in attenuated form to even very slight episodes of compensator innovation.

The first model appears to be the most extreme, although it also is the most familiar. It locates the creative spark of religion in human experiences of ultimate despair and confusion; yet there is no reason why diluted variants of the same processes could not also occur.

THE PSYCHOPATHOLOGY MODEL OF CULT INNOVATION

The *psychopathology model* has been used by many anthropologists and ethnopsychiatrists, and it is related closely to deprivation theories of revolutions and social movements (Smelser, 1962; Gurr, 1970). A similar approach has been used to explain involvement in radical politics (Lasswell, 1930; Smith et al., 1956; Langer, 1972). The model describes cult innovation as the result of individual psychopathology that finds successful social expression. Because of its popularity among social scientists, this model exists in many variants, but the main ideas are the following:

1. Cults are novel cultural responses to personal and societal crisis.
2. New cults are invented by individuals suffering from certain forms of mental illness.
3. These individuals typically achieve their novel visions during psychotic episodes.
4. During such an episode, the individual invents a new package of compensators to meet his own needs.
5. The individual's illness commits him to his new vision, either because his hallucinations appear to demonstrate its truth or because compelling needs demand immediate satisfaction.
6. After the episode, the individual will be most likely to succeed in forming a cult around his vision if the society contains many other persons suffering from problems similar to those originally faced by the cult founder, to whose solution, therefore, they are likely to respond.
7. Therefore, such cults most often succeed during times of societal crisis, when large numbers of persons suffer from similar unresolved problems.
8. If the cult does succeed in attracting many followers, the individual founder may achieve at least a partial cure of his illness because the self-generated compensators are legitimated by other persons and because the founder now receives true rewards from his followers.

The psychopathology model is supported by the traditional psychoanalytic view that all magic and religion are mere projections of neurotic wish fulfillment or psychotic delusions (Freud, 1927, 1930; Devereux, 1953; Roheim, 1955; La Barre, 1969, 1972). However, the model does not assume that cultic ideas are necessarily wrong or insane. Rather, it addresses the question of how individuals can invent deviant perspectives and then have conviction in them, despite the lack of objective, confirmatory evidence.

All societies provide traditional compensator systems that are familiar to all their members and that have considerable plausibility both because their assumptions are familiar and because of the numbers of people already committed to them. Then why should some persons reject the conventional religious tradition, concoct apparently arbitrary substitutes, and put their trust in these novel formulations? The psychopathology model notes that highly neurotic or psychotic persons typically do just this, whether in a religious framework or not. By definition, the mentally ill are mentally deviant. Furthermore, especially in the case of psychotics, they mistake the products of their own minds for external realities. Thus, their pathology provides them not only with abnormal ideas, but with subjective evidence for the correctness of their ideas, whether in the form of hallucinations or of pressing needs that cannot be denied.

A number of authors have identified occult behavior with specific psychiatric syndromes. Hysteria frequently has been blamed. Cult founders often do suffer from apparent physical illness, find a spiritual "cure" for their own ailment, then dramatize that cure as the basis of the cult performance (Messing, 1958; Lévi-Strauss, 1963; Lewis, 1971). A well-known American example is Mary Baker Eddy, whose invention of Christian Science apparently was a successful personal response to a classic case of hysteria (Zweig, 1932).

In other cases, a manic-depressive pattern is found. John Humphrey Noyes, founder of the Oneida community, had an obsessive need to be "perfect." In his more elevated periods, he was able to convince a few dozen people that he had achieved perfection and could help them attain this happy state as well. But the times of elation were followed by "eternal spins," depressive states in which Noyes was immobilized by self-hatred (Carden, 1969).

Classical paranoia and paranoid schizophrenia also have been blamed for producing cults. A person who founds a cult asserts the arrogant claim that he or she (above all others) has achieved a miraculous cultural breakthrough, a claim that outsiders may perceive as a delusion of grandeur. For example, L. Ron Hubbard (1950b: 9) announced his invention of Dianetics (later to become Scientology) by saying, "The creation of dianetics is a milestone for Man comparable to his discovery of fire and superior to his inventions of the wheel and arch."

Martin Gardner has shown that the position of the cultist or pseudoscientist in the social environment is nearly identical to that of the clinical paranoid. Neither is accorded the high social status he or she demands from conventional authorities, and each is contemptuously ignored or harshly persecuted by societal leaders. Gardner (1957: 12) notes that paranoia actually may be an advantage under these circumstances because, without it, the individual "would lack the stamina to fight a vigorous, single-handed battle against such overwhelming odds."

Many biographies of cult founders contain information that would support any of these diagnoses, and often the syndrome appears to be a life pattern that antedated founding the cult by a number of years. However, the symptoms of these disorders are so close to the features that define cult activity that simplistic psychopathology explanations approach tautology. Lemert (1967) has argued that social exclusion and conflict over social status can produce the symptoms of paranoia. It may be that some cult founders display symptoms of mental illness as a result of societal rejection of their cults. Another problem faced by the psychopathology model is the fact that the vast majority of mental patients has not founded cults.

The simplest version of the model states that the founder's psychopathology had a physiological cause. Religious visions may appear during psychotic episodes induced by injuries, drugs, and high fevers. If an episode takes place outside any medical setting, the individual may find a supernatural explanation of the experience most satisfactory (Sargant, 1959). Innumerable examples exist. Love Israel, founder of a cult called the Love Family, told us that his religious vision was triggered by hallucinogenic drugs that enabled him to experience a state of fusion with another man, who subsequently became a prominent follower. The stories of some persons who claim to have been contacted by flying saucers sound very much like brief episodes of brain disorder to which the individual has retrospectively given a more favorable interpretation (Greenberg, 1979).

More subtle variants of the psychopathology model present psychodynamic explanations and place the process of cult formation in a social context. Julian Silverman (1967) outlined a five-step model describing the early career of a shaman (sorcerer, witch doctor, magical healer) or cult founder. In the first stage, the individual is beset by a serious personal and social problem, typically severely damaged self-esteem, that defies practical solution. In the second stage, the individual becomes preoccupied with this problem and withdraws from active social life. Some cultures have even formalized rituals of withdrawal in which the individual may leave the settlement and dwell temporarily in the wilderness. The Bible abounds in examples of withdrawal to the wilderness to prepare for a career as a prophet.

Withdrawal immediately leads to the third stage, in which the individual experiences "self-initiated sensory depriviation," which can produce very extreme psychotic symptoms even in previously normal persons. Thus begins the fourth stage, in which the future cult founder receives a supernatural vision. "What follows then is the eruption into the field of attention of a flood of archaic imagery and attendant lower-order referential processes such as occur in dreams or reverie. . . . Ideas surge through with peculiar vividness as though from an outside source" (Silverman, 1967: 28).

In the fifth stage, which Silverman calls *cognitive reorganization,* the individual attempts to share this vision with other people. Failure drives the person into chronic mental illness. Success in finding social support for these supernatural claims transforms the person into a mentally stable shaman or cult leader. If the followers reward the leader sufficiently with honor, the originally damaged self-esteem that provoked the entire sequence will be repaired completely, and the cult founder may even become one of the best adapted members of the social group (cf. Boas, 1940).

The theory of *revitalization movements* proposed by Anthony F. C. Wallace (1956) is similar to Silverman's model but adds the important ingredient of social crisis. Wallace (1956: 269) suggests that a variety of threats to a society can produce greatly increased stress on members: "climatic, floral and faunal change; military defeat; political subordination; extreme pressure toward acculturation resulting in internal cultural conflict; economic distress; epidemics; and so on." Under stress, some individuals begin to go through the process Silverman outlined and, under favorable circumstances, achieve valuable cultural reformulations that they can use as the basis of social action to revitalize their society. Although Wallace (1956: 273) advocates a pure form of the psychopathology model, he concludes "that the religious vision experience per se is not psychopathological but rather the reverse, being a synthesizing and often therapeutic process performed under extreme stress by individuals already sick."

Wallace's suggestions that many historically influential social movements, and perhaps all major religions, originated according to its principles underscores the importance of the psychopathology model. This view is held by Weston La Barre (1972), who says that every religion originated as a *crisis cult*, using this term for cults that emerge according to the pattern Wallace described. He specifically describes Christianity as a typical crisis cult. Writing in an orthodox Freudian tradition, La Barre identifies the source of a cult founder's vision: "A god is only a shaman's dream about his father" (La Barre, 1972: 19; cf. Freud, 1946). He says the shaman is an immature man who desperately needs compensation for his inadequacies, including sexual incapacity. In finding personal magical compensations the shaman generates compensators for use by more normal persons as well (La Barre, 1972: 138).

Claude Lévi-Strauss, an exchange theorist as well as a structuralist, emphasizes that the shaman participates in an economy of meaning. Normal persons want many kinds of rewards they cannot obtain and can be convinced to accept compensators generated by fellow citizens less tied to reality than they. "In a universe which it strives to understand but whose dynamics it cannot fully control, normal thought continually seeks the meaning of things which refuse to reveal their significance. So-called pathological thought, on the other hand, overflows with emotional interpretations and overtones, in order to supplement an otherwise deficient reality" (Lévi-Strauss, 1963: 175). In shamanism, the neurotic producer of compensators and the suffering normal consumer come together in an exchange beneficial to both, participating in the exchange of compensators for tangible rewards that is the basis of all cults.

THE ENTREPRENEUR MODEL OF CULT INNOVATION

The *entrepreneur model* of cult innovation has not received as much attention from social scientists as has the psychopathology model. We have known for decades that the psychopathology model could not explain adequately all cultic phenomena (Ackerknecht, 1943), but attempts to construct alternate models have been desultory. It is difficult to prove that any given cult founder was psychologically normal, but, in many cases, even rather lengthy biographies fail to reveal significant evidence of pathology. Although the psychopathology model focuses on cult founders who invent new compensator systems initially for their own use, the entrepreneur model notes that cult founders often may consciously develop new compensator systems in order to exchange them for great rewards. Innovation pays off in many other areas of culture, such as technological invention and artistic creativity. If social circumstances provide opportunities for profit in the field of cults, then many perfectly normal individuals will be attracted to the challenge.

Models of entrepreneurship have been proposed to explain many other kinds of human activity, but we have not found adequate social scientific models specifically designed to explain cult innovation. Journalists have documented that such a model would apply well to many cases, as our own observations in several cults amply confirm. Therefore, we sketch the beginnings of an entrepreneur model, with the understanding that much future work will be required before this analytic approach is fully developed. The chief ideas of such a model might be the following:

1. Cults are businesses which provide a product for their customers and receive payment in return.
2. Cults are mainly in the business of selling novel compensators, or at least freshly packaged compensators that appear new.
3. Therefore, a supply of novel compensators must be manufactured.
4. Both manufacture and sales are accomplished by entrepreneurs.
5. These entrepreneurs, like those in other businesses, are motivated by the desire for profit, which they can gain by exchanging compensators for rewards.
6. Motivation to enter the cult business is stimulated by the perception that such business can be profitable, an impression likely to be acquired through prior involvement with a successful cult.
7. Successful entrepreneurs require skills and experience, which are most easily gained through a prior career as the employee of an earlier successful cult.
8. The manufacture of salable new compensators (or compensator packages) is most easily accomplished by assembling components of pre-existing compensator systems into new configurations or by further developing successful compensator-systems.
9. Therefore, cults tend to cluster in lineages. They are linked by individual entrepreneurs who begin their careers in one cult and then leave to found their own. They bear strong "family resemblances" because they share many cultural features.
10. Ideas for completely new compensators can come from any cultural source or personal experience whatsoever, but the skillful entrepreneur experiments carefully in the development of new products and incorporates them permanently in his cult only if the market response is favorable.

Cults can, in fact, be very successful businesses. The secrecy that surrounds many of these organizations prevents us from reporting current financial statistics, but a few figures have been revealed in various investigations. Arthur L. Bell's cult, Mankind United, received contributions totaling $4 million in the ten years preceeding 1944 (Dohrman, 1958:41). Between 1956 and 1959, the Washington, D.C., branch of Scientology took in $758,982 and gave its founder, L. Ron Hubbard, $100,000 plus the use of a home and car (Cooper, 1971:109). Today, Scientology has many flourishing branches, and Hubbard lives on his own 320-foot ship. In 1973, an English expatriate cult, The Process, was grossing $100,000 a month, $4,000 of this going directly to the husband and wife team who ran the operation from their comfortable Westchester County estate (Bainbridge, 1978c: 168). In addition to obvious material benefits, sucessful cult founders also receive intangible but valuable rewards, including praise, power, and amusement. Many cult leaders have enjoyed almost unlimited sexual access to their followers (Orrmont, 1961; Carden, 1969).

The simplest variant of the entrepreneur model, and the one preferred by journalists, holds that cult innovators are outright frauds who have no faith in their own product and sell it through trickery to fools and desperate persons. Certainly, we have many examples of cults that were pure confidence games, and we cite examples of fraud in three kinds of cult we defined in Chapter 2: audience cults, client cults, and cult movements.

In 1973, Uri Geller barnstormed the United States, presenting himself as a psychic who could read minds and bend spoons by sheer force of will. As James Randi (1975) has shown Geller's feats were achieved through trickery; yet untold thousands of people were fascinated by the possibility that Geller might have real psychic powers. The whole affair was a grand but short-lived audience cult.

Medical client cults based on intentional fraud are quite common. A number of con artists have discovered not only that they can use the religious label to appeal to certain kinds of gullible marks, but also that the label provides a measure of protection against legal prosecution (MacDougall, 1958; Glick and Newsom, 1974). In many of these cases, it may be impossible to prove whether the cult founder was sincere or not, and we can only assume that many undetected frauds lurk behind a variety of client cults.

In some cases, the trickery is so blatant that we can have little doubt. Among the most recent examples are the Philippine psychic surgeons, Terte and Agpaoa, and their Brazilian colleague, Arigo. These men perform fake surgery with their bare hands or brandishing crude jackknives. In some cases, they may actually pierce the patient's skin, but often they merely pretend to do so and then spread animal gore about to simulate the results of deep cutting. Through a skillful performance, they convince their patients not only that dangerous tumors have been removed from their bodies, but also that the surgeon's psychic powers have instantaneously healed the wound. But their failure actually to perform real operations in this manner must be clear to the psychic surgeons themselves (Flammonde, 1975).

Arthur L. Bell's cult movement was a fraud based on the traditional Rosicrucian idea that a vast benevolent conspiracy prepares to rule the world and invites a few ordinary people to join its elite ranks. Bell claimed only to be the superintendant of the Pacific Coast Division, in constant communication with his superiors in the (fictitious) organizational hierarchy. In this way, he was able to convince his followers that they were members of an immensely powerful secret society, despite the fact that the portion of it they could see was modest in size. Like several similar fraudulent movements, Bell's cult did not originally claim religious status, but became a "church" only after encountering legal difficulty (Dohrman, 1958).

In order to grow, a cult movement must serve real religious functions for its committed followers, regardless of the founder's private intentions. Many older cults probably were frauds in origin but have been transformed into genuine religious organizations by followers who deeply believed the founder's deceptions.

But fraud need not be involved in entrepreneurial cult innovation. Many ordinary businesspeople are convinced of the value of their products by the fact that customers want to buy them, and cult entrepreneurs may likewise accept their market as the ultimate standard of value. Many cult founders do appear to be convinced that their compensator packages are valuable by testimonials from satisfied customers. This was probably the case with Franz Anton Mesmer, who saw astonishing transformations in his clients, apparently the beneficial results of his techniques, and found in them ample evidence of the truth of his theories (Zweig, 1932; Darnton, 1970). Practitioners of all client cults frequently see similar evidence in favor of their own ideas, no matter how illogical, because all such cults provide compensators of at least some strength (Frank, 1961). We describe mechanisms that would encourage them in Chapter 7.

Another source of confidence for cult innovators is their experience with other cults. Early in their careers, innovators typically join one or more successful cults and honestly may value the cults' products themselves. However, they may be dissatisfied with various aspects of the older cults and come to the sincere opinion that they can create a more satisfactory product. Despite their often intense competition, cult leaders frequently express respect and admiration for other cults, including the ones with which they themselves were previously associated. L. Ron Hubbard of Scientology has praised Alfred Korzybski's General Semantics: Jack Horner of Dianology has praised Hubbard's Scientology: other examples abound.

Once we realize that cult formation often involves entrepreneurial action to establish a profitable new organization based on novel culture, we can see that concepts developed to understand technological innovation should apply here as well. For example, a study of entrepreneurship and technology by Edward B. Roberts (1969) examined the cultural impact of the Massachusetts Institute of Technology, the preeminent center of new technological culture. Over 200 new high technology companies had been founded by former M.I.T. employees who concluded they could achieve greater personal rewards by establishing their own businesses based on what they had learned at M.I.T. The current cult equivalent of M.I.T. is Scientology, which Bainbridge studied in 1970. Cultic entrepreneurs have left Scientology to found countless other cults based on modified Scientology ideas, including Jack Horner's Dianology, H. Charles Berner's Abilitism, Harold Thompson's Amprinistics, and the flying saucer cult described in the ethnography *When Prophecy Fails* (Festinger et al., 1956). Scientology, like M.I.T., is a vast storehouse of exotic culture derived from many sources. Social scientists studying patterns of cultural development should be aware that an occasional key organization can be an influential nexus of innovation and diffusion.

Future research can determine the most common processes through which entrepreneurial cult founders actually invent their novel ideas. We suspect that the main techniques involve the cultural equivalent of recombinant DNA genetic engineering. Essentially, the innovator takes the cultural configuration of an existing cult, removes some components, and replaces them with other components taken from other sources. The innovator may simply splice pieces of two earlier cults together. In some cases, the innovator preserves the supporting skeleton of practices and basic assumptions of a cult he or she admires and merely grafts on new symbolic flesh. Rosicrucianism affords a sequence of many connected examples (Hall, 1928; King, 1970; McIntosh, 1972). In creating the AMORC Rosicrucian order, H. Spencer Lewis took European Rosicrucian principles of the turn of the century, including the hierarchical social structure of an initiatory secret society, and grafted on a veneer of symbolism taken from Ancient Egypt, thus capitalizing on public enthusiasm for Egyptian civilization that was current at the time. His headquarters, in San Jose, California, is a city block of simulated Egyptian buildings. Later, Rose Dawn imitated Lewis in creating her rival Order of the Ancient Mayans. In great measure, she simply replaced AMORC's symbols with equivalent symbols. Instead of Lewis's green biweekly mail-order lessons emblazoned with Egyptian architecture and Egyptian hieroglyphics, she sold red biweekly mail-order lessons decorated with Mayan architecture and Mayan hieroglyphics.

The highly successful *est* cult is derived partly from Scientology and well illustrates the commercialism of many such organizations in contemporary America. Werner Erhard, founder of *est,* had some experience with Scientology in 1969. Later, he worked for a while in Mind Dynamics, itself an offshoot of Jose Silva's Mind Control. After Erhard started his own cult in 1971, he decided to emulate Scientology's tremendous success and hired two Scientologists to adapt its practices for his own use. Conventional businesses, such as auto companies and television networks, often imitate each other in pursuit of profit. Erhard's research and development efforts were rewarded, and, by the beginning of 1976, an estimated 70,000 persons had completed his $250 initial seminar (Kornbluth, 1976).

We suggest that cult entrepreneurs will imitate those features of other successful cults that seem to them most responsible for success. They will innovate either in nonessential areas or in areas where they believe they can increase the salability of the product. In establishing their own cult businesses, they must innovate at least superficially. They cannot seize a significant part of the market unless they achieve product differentiation. Otherwise, they will be at a great disadvantage in direct competition with the older, more prosperous cult on which theirs is patterned (cf. Hostetler, 1968; Cooper and Jones, 1969). The apparent novelty of a cult's compensator package often may be a sales advantage because the public has not yet discovered the limitations of the rewards that members actually will receive in the new cult, although older compensator packages may have been discredited to some extent. Much research and theory building remains to be done, but the insight that cults often are examples of skillful free enterprise immediately explains many of the features of the competitive world of cults.

THE SUBCULTURE-EVOLUTION MODEL OF CULT INNOVATION

Although the psychopathology and entrepreneur models stress the role of the individual innovator, the *subculture-evolution model* emphasizes group interaction processes. It suggests that cults can emerge without authoritative leaders, and it points out that even radical developments can be achieved through many small steps. Although much social psychological literature would be useful in developing this model, we are not aware of a comprehensive statement on cult innovation through subcultural evolution: so again we attempt to outline the model ourselves.

1. Cults are the expression of novel social systems, usually small in size but composed of at least a few intimately interacting individuals.
2. These cultic social systems are most likely to emerge in populations already deeply involved in the occult milieu, but cult evolution may also begin in entirely secular settings.
3. Cults are the result of sidetracked or failed collective attempts to obtain scarce or nonexistent rewards.
4. The evolution begins when a group of persons commits itself to the attainment of certain rewards.
5. In working together to obtain these rewards, members begin exchanging other rewards as well, such as affect.
6. As they progressively come to experience failure in achieving their original goals, they will gradually generate and exchange compensators as well.
7. If the intragroup exchange of rewards and compensators becomes sufficiently intense, the group will become relatively encapsulated, in the extreme case undergoing complete social implosion.
8. Once separated to some degree from external control, the evolving cult develops and consolidates a novel culture, energized by the need to facilitate the exchange of rewards and compensators, and inspired by essentially accidental factors.
9. The end point of successful cult evolution is a novel religious culture embodied in a distinct social group which must now cope with the problem of extracting resources (including new members) from the surrounding environment.

In writing about juvenile delinquency, Albert K. Cohen (1955) described the process of *mutual conversion*, through which interacting individuals could gradually create a deviant normative structure (cf. Thrasher, 1927). This process may result in criminal behavior, but it may also result in the stimulation of unrealizable hopes and of faith in the promise of impossible rewards. Thus, mutual conversion can describe the social process through which people progressively commit each other to a package of compensators that they simultaneously assemble. It begins when people with similar needs and desires meet and begin communicating about their mutual problems. It takes place in tiny, even imperceptible, exploratory steps, as one individual expresses a hope or a plan and receives positive feedback in the form of similar hopes and plans from fellow members.

> The final product ... is likely to be a compromise formation of all the participants to what we may call a cultural process, a formation perhaps unanticipated by any of them. Each actor may contribute something directly to the growing product, but he may also contribute indirectly by encouraging others to advance, inducing them to retreat, and suggesting new avenues to be explored. The product cannot be ascribed to any one of the participants; it is a real "emergent" on a group level. (Cohen, 1955:60)

Cohen (1955:50) says that all human action "is an ongoing series of efforts to solve problems." All human beings face the problem of coping with frustration because some highly desired rewards, such as everlasting life, do not exist in this world. Through mutual conversion, individuals band together to solve one or more shared problems, and the outcome presumably depends on a number of factors, including the nature of the problems and the group's initial conceptualization of them. We suspect that a cultic solution is most likely if the people begin by attempting to improve themselves (as in psychotherapy) or to improve their relationship to the natural world and then fail in their efforts. Criminal or political outcomes are more likely if people believe that other persons or social conditions are responsible for their problems.

The quest for unavailable rewards is not reserved for poor and downtrodden folk. Many elite social movements have been dedicated to the attainment of goals that ultimately proved unattainable. One well-documented example is the Committee for the Future, an institutionally detached little organization that formed within the network of technological social movements oriented toward spaceflight. Founded in 1970 by a wealthy couple, the CFF was dedicated to the immediate colonization of the moon and planets and to beginning a new age in which the field of human activity would be the entire universe. The biggest effort of the CFF, Project Harvest Moon, was intended to establish the first demonstration colony on the moon, planted using a surplus Saturn V launch vehicle. Ultimately, high cost and questionable feasibility prevented any practical accomplishments.

In struggling to arouse public support, the CFF held a series of open conventions at which participants collectively developed grand schemes for a better world. Blocked from any success in this direction, the CFF evolved toward cultism. The convention seminars became encounter groups. Mysticism and parapsychology replaced spaceflight as the topic of conversation. Rituals of psychic fusion were enacted to religious music, and the previously friendly aerospace companies and agencies broke with the committee. Denied success in its original purposes and unfettered by strong ties to conventional institutions, the

CFF turned ever more strongly toward compensators and toward the supernatural (Bainbridge, 1976).

Cults are particularly likely to emerge wherever numbers of people seek help for intractable personal problems. The broad fields of psychotherapy, rehabilitation, and personal development have been especially fertile for cults. A number of psychotherapy services have evolved into cult movements, including those created by some of Freud's immediate followers (Rieff, 1968; cf. Brown, 1967; Jung, 1969). Other independent human service organizations may also be susceptible to cultic evolution. The best known residential program designed to treat drug addiction, Synanon, has recently evolved into an authoritarian cult movement that recruits persons who never suffered from drug problems.

Two important factors render cultic evolution more likely. First, the process will progress most easily if there are no binding external constraints. For example, psychiatrists and psychologists who work in institutional settings (such as hospitals or universities) may be prevented by their conventional commitments from participating in the evolution of a cult, but independent practitioners are more free. Second, the process will be facilitated if the therapist receives compensators as well as gives them and thus will participate fully in the inflation and proliferation of compensators.

A good example is The Process, founded in London in 1963, which began as an independent psychotherapy service designed to help normal individuals achieve supernormal levels of functioning (Rowley, 1971; Cohen, 1975; Bainbridge, 1978c). The therapy was based on Alfred Adler's theory that each human being is impelled by subconscious goals, and it attempted to bring these goals to consciousness so the person could pursue them more effectively and escape inner conflict (Adler, 1927, 1929). The founders of The Process received the therapy as well as gave it, and frequent group sessions brought all participants together to serve each other's emotional needs. The Process recruited clients through the founders' preexisting friendship network, and the therapy sessions greatly intensified the strength and intimacy of their social bonds.

As bonds strengthened, the social network became more thoroughly interconnected as previously distant persons were brought together. The rudiments of a group culture evolved, and many individuals contributed ideas about how the therapy might be improved and expanded. Participants came to feel that only other participants understood them completely and found communication with outsiders progressively more difficult. A social implosion took place.

In a social implosion, part of an extended social network collapses as social ties within it strengthen and, reciprocally, those to persons outside it weaken. It is a step-by-step process that may be set off by more than one circumstance. In the case of The Process, the implosion was initiated by the introduction of a new element of culture, a "therapy" technique that increased the intimacy of relations around a point in the network. Correlated with the implosion was a mutual conversion as members encouraged each other to express their deepest fantasies and to believe they could be fulfilled. The Adlerian analysis of subconscious goals was ideally designed to arouse longings and hopes for all the unobtained and unobtainable rewards the participants had ever privately wished to receive. The powerful affect and social involvement produced by the implosion were tangible rewards that convinced participants that the other rewards soon would be achieved.

Concomitant estrangement from outside attachments led The Process to escape London to the isolation of a ruined seaside Yucatán plantation. Remote from the restraining influence of conventional society, The Process completed its evolution from psychotherapy to religion by inventing supernatural doctrines to explain how its impossible, absolute goals might ultimately be achieved. When the new cult returned to civilization in 1967, it became legally incorporated as a church (Bainbridge, 1978c).

Nonreligious groups can evolve into religious cults; so it is not surprising that cults also can arise from religious sects—extreme religious groups that accept the standard religious tradition of the society, unlike cults that are revolutionary breaks with the culture of past churches. An infamous example is the Peoples Temple of Jim Jones, which destroyed itself in the jungles of Guyana. This group began as an emotionally extreme but culturally traditional Christian sect, then evolved into a cult as Jones progressively became a prophet with an ever more radical vision. Either the psychopathology or entrepreneur models may apply in this case, but the committed members of the sect probably contributed to the transformation by encouraging Jones step by step and by demanding that he accomplish impossibe goals. Even when a single individual dominates a group, the subculture-evolution model will apply to the extent that the followers also participate in pushing the group toward cultism. In this case, the needs of the followers and their social relationships with the leader may have served as a psychopathology amplifier, reflecting back to Jones his own narcissism multiplied by the strength of their unreasonable hopes.

CONCLUSION

Each of the three models identifies a system of production and exchange of compensators. In the psychopathology model, a cult founder creates compensators initially for his or her own use, then gives them to followers in return for rewards. In the entrepreneur model, the cult founder sets out to gain rewards by manufacturing compensators intended for sale to followers. The subculture-evolution model describes the interplay of many individual actions in which various persons at different times play the roles of producer and consumer of novel compensators.

Although the models may appear to compete, in fact, they complement each other and can be combined to explain the emergence of particular cults. After cult founders have escaped a period of psychopathology, they may act as entrepreneurs in promoting or improving their cult. Entrepreneurs threatened with loss of their cult may be driven into an episode of psychopathology that provides new visions that contribute to a new success. The subculture-evolution model may include many little episodes of psychopathology and entrepreneurial enterprise participated in by various members, woven together by a complex network of social exchanges.

Taken together, the psychopathology, entrepreneur, and subculture-evolution models foreshadow a general theory of cult innovation that can be constructed using their elements connected logically within the framework of exchange theory. Although the technical derivation of a theory to accomplish this cannot be given here (cf. Stark and Bainbridge, 1980), several later chapters of this volume contribute detail to the three models and suggest how they might fit together. But even at the level of competing models, the three offer numerous explanatory hypotheses that could be tested using the store of historical information found in any large library or new data collected in future field research. The models provide a checklist of important questions to guide the ethnographer in studying a cult. Until now, the social science of cult innovation has lacked a clear body of theory and a research program. The three models developed in this chapter provide a solid basis for studying the emergence of new religions, and they have already begun to influence the teaching of the sociology of religion (Chalfant et al., 1981:260–263).

Section
7   WOMEN AND RELIGION

If the objects, events, and people can be occasions of experience of the sacred and become the narrative symbols that encode these experiences and provide meaning for human life and paradigms for human living, women certainly can occasion the sacred and encode it for both men and other women. As Eliade reports in the first selection, the image of woman as a hint of the divine exists in most nature religions.

However, with the vast social and cultural changes that are both the cause and the effect of the emancipation of women, the question has arisen as to whether the image of god-as-woman can make religion helpful to women in their struggle for freedom, dignity, and power. Did the goddess come before the god in antiquity? Can the goddess preside over a religion specifically for women? Is Mary, the mother of Jesus—the only "mother goddess" available in the Western World—an adequate religious narrative symbol for women?

In fact, the image of God as mother, hinted at even in the Jewish scriptures, seems available to many people today, regardless of age or gender, and may be even more important for men than for women. And if, despite Henry Adams, the Virgin of Chartres is a spoiled symbol for the "new women," this truth does not seem to have broken through to Catholic young people.

However, the implications of the insight that woman is a sacrament of God for both men and women requires and will doubtless obtain much further study, reflection, and development.

Reading 24

WOMEN AS SACRED—MIRCEA ELIADE

For ancient humans, fertility was the most powerful force in the universe and also the most important; the tribe depended on the fertility of the fields and the fertility of the forests, the fertility of the flocks, and the fertility of the crops to survive. Moreover, unless women were fertile, all the other fertilities would be in vain because the tribe would die off without children.

All nature religions were in one way or another fertility religions, and all festivals in one way or another were fertility festivals—prayers for the planting, the harvesting, the vintage, and survival to the next planting (February 2, May 1, August 15, and October 31, in the Celtic lands).

Therefore, women were sacred because they reflected the fertility of the gods, the life-giving power that was unleashed "in that time." Earth was a mother to be worshipped as the sun was the father. (Sometimes the roles were reversed.) While women might have been second-class humans, as they were in some cultures, or equals, as they were in others, the power that they represented was always treated with fear and respect. Eliade outlines a few of the ancient customs that pay tribute to the sacred fertility of women.

Questions for Reflection and Discussion

1. Why is the earth pictured as a mother more often than as a father?
2. Can we understand the ancients' enormous fear of and respect for the forces of fertility, which women represent in a special way? Are we not too far from the primitive fields and flocks to identify with such feelings?
3. Would this attitude tend to reduce women to a lower rank in the human species?
4. Would fertility worship tend to objectify women?

THE EARTH, WOMAN AND FERTILITY
The Earth Mother

". . . Earth [Gaia], herself, first of all gave birth to a being equal to herself, who could overspread her completely, the starry heaven [Ouranos], who was to present the blessed gods a secure throne forever."[1] This primeval pair gave birth to the innumerable family of gods, Cyclops and other mythical creatures (Cottos, Briareus, Gyges, "children filled with pride," each with a hundred arms and fifty heads). The marriage between heaven and earth was the first hierogamy; the gods soon married too, and men, in their turn, were to imitate them with the same sacred solemnity with which they imitated everything done at the dawn of time.

Gaia or Ge was fairly widely worshipped in Greece, but in time other earth divinities took her place. The etymology suggests that in her the earth element was present in its most immediate form (cf. Sanskrit *go,* "earth, place;" Zend *gava,* Gothic, *gawi, gauja,* "province"). Homer scarcely mentions her; a chthonian divinity—and one belonging pre-eminently to the pre-Hellenic substratum—would be unlikely to find a place in his Olympus. But one of the Homeric hymns is addressed to her: "It is the earth I sing, securely enthroned, the mother of all things, venerable ancestress feeding upon her soil all that exists . . . To thee it belongs to give life to mortals, and to take it from them . . . Happy the man favoured with thy good will! For him the soil of life is rich with harvest; in his fields, the flocks thrive, and his house is full of wealth."[2]

Aeschylus also glorifies her, for it is the earth that "gives birth to all beings, feeds them, and receives back from them the fertile seed."[3] We shall see in a moment how genuine and ancient is this formula of Aeschylus'. And there is another very old hymn which, Pausanias tells us, the Pleiades of Dodona sang: "Zeus was, is and shall be, O Great Zeus; it is through thy help that the Earth gives us her fruit. We call her our mother with good reason."[4]

A great many beliefs, myths and rituals have come down to us which deal with the earth, with its divinities, with the Great Mother. As the foundation, in a sense, of the universe, the earth is endowed with manifold religious significance. It was adored because of its permanence, because all things came from it and all things returned to it. If one studied the history of a single religion, one might manage to state fairly exactly the function and development of its beliefs about the chthonian epiphanies. But if one is simply dealing with a study of reli-

---

Source: Mircea Eliade, *Patterns in Comparative Religion.* Translated by Rosemary Sheed. New York: Sheed and Ward, 1958.

[1]Hesiod, *Theogony,* v, 126 ff.

[2]*To Earth,* 1 ff.

[3]*Choephori,* v, 127–8.

[4]x, 12, 10.

gious forms, the thing becomes impossible; here, as in all our other chapters, we are looking at acts, beliefs and theories belonging to cycles of civilization differing in age, differing in nature. Let us, however, attempt to see the main threads in the pattern whose elements are listed in the indexes of works on the subject under such headings as Earth, Mother Earth, Earth Divinities, Earth Spirits, etc.

THE PRIMEVAL PAIR: SKY AND EARTH

The divine couple, Heaven and Earth, presented by Hesiod, are one of the *leit-motiven* of universal mythology. In many mythologies in which the sky plays the part of supreme divinity, the earth is represented as his companion, and as we saw earlier (§12 ff.), the sky has a place almost everywhere in primitive religious life. Let us recall some examples of this. The Maoris call the sky Rangi and the Earth Papa; at the beginning, like Ouranos and Gaia, they were joined in a close embrace. The children born of this infinite union—Tumata-nenga, Tanemahuta and others—who longed for the light and groped around in the darkness, decided to separate from their parents. And so, one day, they cut the cords binding heaven to earth and pushed their father higher and higher until Rangi was thrust up into the air and light appeared in the world.[5]

The creation motif of a primeval pair, Heaven and Earth, occurs in all the civilizations of Oceania, from Indonesia to Micronesia.[6] You find it in Borneo, among the Minehassa, in the northern Celebes (where Luminuut, the goddess of earth, is the chief divinity);[7] among the Toradja of the central Celebes (I-lai and I-ndora), in innumerable other Indonesian islands, and so on. In some places one also meets the motif of the sky and earth separated by force; at Tahiti, for instance, it is believed that this was effected by a plant which raised the sky up by growing.[8] This motif is quite widespread in other areas of civilization too.[9] We find the primeval couple, heaven and earth, in Africa; for instance, the Nzambi and Nzambi-Mpungu of the Bawili tribe, in the Gabon,[10] Olorun and Oduna ("the black") among the Yoruba,[11] the divine couple of the Ewe, and of the Akwapim,[12] and so on. Among the Kumana, an agricultural tribe of southern Africa, the marriage between sky and earth takes on the same sense of cos-

---

[5]You remember that, in the myth Hesiod tells, too, Kronos castrates his father, but for a different reason: because Ouranos was giving birth unknowingly to monsters, which he then hid in Gaia's body. Lang thought the Greek myth could be explained in terms of the Maori. But while the latter is simply a creation myth, explaining the distance between sky and earth, the other can only be explained if one records the Indo-European religious notion of sovereignty, as G. Dumézil has shown in *Ouranos-Varuna* (Paris, 1934).

[6]Staudacher, *Die Trennung von Himmel u. Erde,* Tübingen, 1942,; Numazawa, *Die Weltanfänge in der japanischen Mythologie,* Lucerne, 1946, pp. 138 ff., 305 ff.

[7]Cf. Pettazzoni, p. 130.

[8]Krappe, *Genèse,* p. 79.

[9]Cf. Krappe, pp. 78–9; Numazawa, pp. 317 ff.

[10]Pettazzoni, pp. 210, 212.

[11]Pettazzoni, p. 246.

[12]Pettazzoni, p. 241.

mic fertility as it has in the hymns of the Pleiades of Dodona: "The Earth is our mother, the Sky is our father. The Sky fertilizes the Earth with rain, the Earth produces grains and grass."[13] And as we shall see, this formula covers a large part of the beliefs concerning agriculture. The divine couple also figure in the mythologies of the Americas. In southern California, the Sky is called Tukmit and the Earth Tamaiovit;[14] among the Navahos we find Yadilqil Hastqin (sky man) and his wife Nihosdzan Esdza (earth woman);[15] among the Pawnees, in north America,[16] with the Sioux, the Hurons (one of the main tribes of Iroquois),[17] the Hopi, the Zuñi, in the West Indies, and elsewhere we find the same cosmic duality. In the mythologies of the East, it plays an equally important part in the creation of the universe. The "queen of the lands" (the goddess Arinna) and her husband U or Im, the god of storm, are the Hittite version; the goddess of earth and the god of sky are the Chinese; Izanagi and Izanami the Japanese; and so on. Among the Germanic peoples, Frigga, the wife of Tyr, and later of Othin, is in essence a goddess of earth. And it is merely a chance of grammar that the Egyptians had a goddess, Nut, to represent the sky (the word for sky was feminine), and a god, Geb, for the earth. . . .

CHTHONIAN MATERNITY

One of the first theophanies of the earth as such, and particularly of the earth as soil, was its "motherhood," its inexhaustible power of fruitfulness. Before becoming a mother goddess, or divinity of fertility, the earth presented itself to men as a Mother, *Tellus Mater.* The later growth of agricultural cults, forming a gradually clearer and clearer notion of a Great Goddess of vegetation and harvesting, finally destroyed all trace of the Earth-Mother. In Greece, the place of Gaia was taken by Demeter. However, certain ancient ethnological documents reveal relics of the old worship of the Earth-Mother. Smohalla, an Indian prophet of the Umatilla tribe, forbade his followers to dig the earth, for, he said, it is a sin to wound or cut, tear or scratch our common mother by the labours of farming. And he defended his anti-agricultural attitude by saying: "You ask me to plough the ground? Shall I take a knife and tear my mother's bosom? Then when I die she will not take me to her bosom to rest. You ask me to dig for stone? Shall I dig under her skin for her bones? Then when I die I cannot enter her body to be born again. You ask me to cut grass and make hay and sell it, and be rich like white men! But how dare I cut off my mother's hair?"[18]

Such a mystical devotion to the Earth-Mother is not an isolated instance. The members of a primitive Dravidian tribe of central India, the Baiga, carried

---

[13]Krappe, p. 78.

[14]Pettazzoni, p. 279.

[15]Pettazzoni, p. 282.

[16]Pettazzoni, p. 284.

[17]Pettazzoni, pp. 291, 315.

[18]James Mooney, "The Ghost-Dance Religion and the Sioux Outbreak of 1890," *Annual Report of the Bureau of American Ethnology,* Washington, 1896, xiv, p. 721.

on a nomadic agriculture, sowing only in the ashes left when part of the jungle had burnt away. And they went to such trouble because they thought it a sin to tear their mother's bosom with a plough.[19] In the same way some Altaic and Finno-Ugrian peoples thought it a terrible sin to pluck the grass, because it hurt the earth as much as it would hurt a man to pluck out his hair or his beard. The Votyaks, whose custom was to place their offerings in a ditch, were careful never to do it in the autumn, as that was the time when the Earth was asleep. The Cheremisses often thought the earth was ill, and at such times would avoid sitting on it. And there are many other indications that beliefs about Mother Earth persisted, even though sporadically, among both agricultural and non-agricultural peoples.[20] Earth religion, even if it is not, as some scholars believe, the oldest of man's religions, is one that dies hard. Once established in an agricultural framework, thousands of years may go by without its altering. In some cases there is no break in the continuity from prehistoric times to the present. The "dead man's cake," for instance, (*coliva* in Rumanian) was known by the same name in ancient Greece, which had it as a heritage from prehistoric, pre-Hellenic times. Further examples of continuity within the enduring framework of agricultural earth religions will be mentioned later on.

In 1905 A. Dieterich published a book, *Mutter Erde, ein Versuch über Volksreligion*,[21] which soon became a classic work. Emil Goldmann[22] and others after him, and—more recently—Nilsson,[23] have put forward every sort of objection to Dieterich's theory, but it has never been totally disproved. Dieterich opens his study by recalling three customs practised in antiquity—the laying of newborn children upon the ground, the burial of children (by contrast with the cremating of adults), the placing of the sick and dying as near the earth as possible—from which he reconstructs the outline of the primitive earth-goddess, the "Earth-Mother-of-all-things" (*pammetor Ge*) mentioned by Aeschylus,[24] the Gaia of Hesiod's hymn. An impressive amount of material was gathered round these three primitive customs, and controversies took place which we need not go into here. But we may see what the things themselves teach us, and in what religious setting they are to be seen.

MAN'S DESCENT FROM THE EARTH

Saint Augustine,[25] following Varro, mentions the name of a Latin goddess, Levana, who raised children from out of the earth: *levat de terra*. Dieterich notes, in connection with this fact, the custom, still current in the Abbruzzi, of

[19]Frazer, *Adonis, Attis, Osiris,* vol. i, p. 89.

[20]Cf. Nyberg, pp. 63 ff.

[21]Leipzig-Berlin, 3rd ed., 1925, enlarged and completed by E. Fehrle.

[22]"Cartam levare," *MIOG*, 1914, vol. xxv, pp. 1 ff.

[23]*Geschichte*, pp. 427 ff.

[24]*Prometheus*, 88.

[25]*De Civ. Dei*, iv, 11.

placing babies upon the earth as soon as they are washed and swaddled.[26] The same ritual took place among the Scandinavians, the Germans, the Parsees, the Japanese, and other races. The child was picked up by its father (*de terra tollere*), who thus expressed his recognition of it.[27] Dieterich interprets this rite as a way of dedicating the child to the earth, *Tellus Mater,* which is its true mother. Goldmann objects that the placing of a baby (or an ill or dying person) on the ground does not necessarily imply any descent from the earth, nor even any consecration to the Earth-Mother, but is simply intended to make a contact with the magic powers in the soil. Others[28] are of the opinion that this rite is meant to procure the child a soul, which comes to it from *Tellus Mater.*

We are obviously faced with two different interpretations, but they contradict each other only on the surface; both follow from the same primordial conception: that of the earth as the source at once of force, of "souls," of fecundity—the fecundity of the Earth-Mother. Lying on the ground (*humi positio*) is a custom found frequently and among a great many peoples; among the Gurions of the Caucasus, and in some parts of China, women lie on the ground as soon as the pains of childbirth begin, so that they will be on the ground when their child is born;[29] the Maori women in New Zealand have their children beside a stream, in the bushes; in a lot of African tribes, it is usual for women to give birth in forests, sitting on the ground;[30] we find the same ritual in Australia, in Northern India, among the Indians of North America, Paraguay and Brazil.[31] Samter notes (p. 6) that this custom had been abandoned by the Greeks and Romans by historical times, but it certainly existed at one time; some statues of the goddesses of birth (Eilithyia, Damia, Auxeia) represent them kneeling in the exact position of a woman having a child straight on the ground.[32] In the Middle Ages in Germany, among the Japanese, in certain Jewish communities, in the Caucasus,[33] in Hungary, Rumania, Scandinavia, Iceland, and elsewhere, the same ritual can be found. The expression "to sit on the ground" in Egyptian, was used in demotic writings to mean "giving birth."[34]

The basic meaning of this extremely widespread ritual was undoubtedly the maternity of the earth. As we have seen, it was believed in a number of places that children came from wells, water, rocks, trees and so on; it goes without saying that in others, children were thought to have "come from the earth."[35] A

---

[26]*Mutter Erde,* p. 7.

[27]Nyberg, p. 31.

[28]For instance Rose, in *Primitive Culture in Italy,* London, 1926, p. 133.

[29]Samter, *Geburt, Hochzeit und Tod,* Berlin, 1911, pp. 5 ff.

[30]Nyberg, p. 131, gives sources.

[31]Ploss and Bartels, *Woman: An Historical, Gynæcological and Anthropological Compendium,* London, 1935, vol. ii, §§ 278–80.

[32]See also Marconi, *Riflessi mediterranei nella più antica religione laziale,* Milan, 1939, pp. 254 ff.

[33]Nyberg, p. 133.

[34]Nyberg, p. 134.

[35]Cf. Dieterich, pp. 14 ff.; the myth of the man made of earth among the Australians, etc.; Nyberg, p. 62.

bastard was known as *terrae filius*. When the Mordvinians want to adopt a child, they place it in a ditch in the garden where the protecting goddess, the Earth-Mother, is supposed to dwell.[36] This means that a child, to be adopted, must be born anew; and this is managed, not by the adopting mother imitating the act of giving birth on her knees (as e.g., with the Romans), but by placing the child on the bosom of its true mother, the earth.

It was natural that this notion of descent from the earth should, later, be replaced by a kindlier notion; a realization that the earth was the protectress of children, the source of all strength, and that it was to it (that is, to the maternal spirit dwelling in it) that newborn babies must be consecrated. That is why we so often find "earth cradles": tiny babies were put to sleep or rest in ditches, in direct contact with the earth, or with the bed of ashes, straw, and leaves their mothers made for them there. The earth cradle is common both in primitive societies (the Australians and various Turco-Altaic peoples) and in higher civilizations (the Inca empire, for instance).[37] Unwanted children were never killed, but left on the ground by the Greeks and others. The Earth-Mother must take care of them; she must decide whether they were to live or die.[38]

A child "exposed," abandoned to the will of the elements—water, wind, earth—is always a sort of defiance thrown in the face of fate. Entrusted to earth or water, the child will henceforward bear the social status of an orphan, and is in danger of dying, but he also has a chance to attain to some condition other than the human. Protected by nature, the abandoned child generally becomes a hero, king or saint. The legend giving his biography is simply repeating the myths about gods abandoned at birth. Remember that Zeus, Poseidon, Dionysos, Attis and innumerable other gods also shared the fate of Perseus, Ion, Atalanta, Amphion and Zethos, of Oedipus, Romulus and Remus and the rest. Moses too was abandoned to the water, like the Maori hero Massi who was thrown into the sea, like the hero of the *Kalevala,* Vainamoinen, who "floated above dark waves." The tragedy of the abandoned child is made up for by the mythological grandeur of the "orphan," the primeval child, with his utter and invulnerable loneliness in the universe, his uniqueness. The appearance of such a child coincides with a moment in the dawn of things: the creation of the cosmos, the creation of a new world, of a new epoch of history (*Jam redit et virgo* ...), a "new life"—at no matter what level of reality. A child abandoned to the Earth-Mother, saved and brought up by her, no longer has any part in the common destiny of mankind, for he re-enacts the cosmological instant of "beginning," and grows not in the midst of a family, but in the midst of the elements. That is why heroes and saints come from among abandoned children: merely by protecting the child, and preserving it from death, the Earth-Mother (or the Water-Mother) is dedicating it to a tremendous destiny which a common mortal could never attain. . . .

---

[36]Nyberg, p. 137.

[37]Cf. Nyberg, p. 160.

[38]Cf. Delcourt, *Stérilités mystérieuses et naissances maléfiques dans l'antiquité classique*, Paris, 1938, p. 64.

WOMAN AND AGRICULTURE

No one doubts that agriculture was discovered by women. Man was almost always in pursuit of game, or pasturing his flocks. Woman, on the other hand, with her keen, though circumscribed, powers of observation, was in a position to watch the natural phenomena of seeds falling and growing, and to try and reproduce those phenomena artificially. And then too, because she was linked up with the other centres of cosmic fertility—Earth and the Moon—woman also became endowed with the prerogative of being able to influence and distribute fertility. That is the reason for the dominant role played by women when agriculture was in its infancy—particularly when this skill was still the province of women—and which in some civilizations she still plays.[39] Thus, in Uganda, a barren woman is thought to be a danger to the garden, and her husband can seek a divorce simply on economic grounds.[40] We find the same belief in the danger to farming of female sterility in the Bhantu tribe, in the Indies.[41] In Nicobar it is thought that the harvest will be richer if the seed is sown by a pregnant woman.[42] In southern Italy, it is thought that everything undertaken by a pregnant woman will be a success, and that everything she sows will grow as the foetus grows.[43] In Borneo ". . . the women play the principal part in the rites and actual operations of the *padi* culture; the men only being called in to clear the ground and to assist in some of the later stages. The women select and keep the seed grain, and they are the repositories of most of the lore connected with it. It seems to be felt that they have a natural affinity to the fruitful grain, which they speak of as becoming pregnant. Women sometimes sleep out in the *padi* fields while the crop is growing, probably for the purpose of increasing their own fertility, or that of the *padi;* but they are very reticent on this matter."[44]

The Orinoco Indians left the task of sowing maize and planting roots to their women; for "as women knew how to conceive seed and bear children, so the seeds and roots planted by them bore fruit far more abundantly than if they had been planted by male hands."[45] At Nias, a palm tree planted by a woman has more sap than one planted by a man.[46] The same beliefs are to be found in Africa, among the Ewe. In South America, among the Jibaros, for instance, it is believed "that women exercise a special, mysterious influence on the growth of cultivated plants."[47] This solidarity of woman with fertile furrows was pre-

---

[39]See U. Pestalozza, "L'Aratro e la donna nel mondo religioso mediterraneo," *Rendiconti, Reale Instituto Lombardo di Scienze e Lettere, cl. di Lettere,* 1942–3, vol. lxxvi, no. 2, pp. 324 ff.

[40]Briffault, *The Mothers,* London, 1927, vol. iii, p. 55.

[41]Lévy-Bruhl, *L'Expérience mystique et les symboles chez les primitifs,* Paris, 1938, p. 254.

[42]Temple, in Hastings' *Encyclopædia of Religion and Ethics,* vol. ix, p. 362.

[43]Finamore, *Tradizioni populari abruzzesi,* p. 59.

[44]Hose and MacDougall, *Pagan Tribes of Borneo,* i, iii, quoted by Lévy-Bruhl, *L'Expérience mystique,* p. 254.

[45]Frazer, *Spirits of the Corn and of the Wild,* vol. i, p. 124; see the whole chapter, "The Role of Woman in Agriculture."

[46]Lévy-Bruhl, p. 254.

[47]Karsten, quoted by Lévy-Bruhl, p. 255.

served even after farming became a masculine skill, and the plough took the place of the primitive spade. This solidarity accounts for a great many rites and beliefs which we shall examine when we come to look at the various rituals of agriculture (§ 126).

WOMAN AND FURROW

The identification of woman with the ploughed earth can be found in a great many civilizations and was preserved in European folklore. "I am the earth," declares the beloved in an Egyptian love song. The *Videvdāt* compares fallow land to a woman with no children, and in fairy tales, the barren queen bewails herself: "I am like a field on which nothing grows."[48] On the other hand, a twelfth-century hymn glorifies the Virgin Mary as *terra non arabilis quae fructum parturiit*. Ba'al was called "the spouse of the fields."[49] And it was a common thing among all Semitic peoples to identify woman with the soil.[50] In Islamic writings, woman is called "field," "vine with grapes," etc. Thus the Koran:[51] "Your wives are to you as fields." The Hindus identified the furrow with the vulva (*yoni*), seeds with *semen virile*.[52] "This woman is come as a living soil: sow seed in her, ye men!"[53] The Laws of Manu also teach that "woman may be looked upon as a field, and the male as the seed".[54] Nārada makes this comment: "Woman is the field, and man the dispenser of the seed."[55] A Finnish proverb says that "maidens have their field in their own body."[56]

Obviously, to identify woman with a furrow implies an identification of phallus with spade, of tilling with the act of generation. Such anthropo-telluric comparisons could only come in civilizations which understood both agriculture and the true causes of conception. In certain Australasian languages, the word *lak* means both phallus and spade. Przyluski has suggested that a similar Australasian term is at the root of the Sanskrit words *laṅgūla* (tail, spade) and *liṅgam* (male generative organ).[57] The phallus-plough identification has even been represented pictorially.[58] The origins of this representation are much older:

---

[48]Van der Leeuw, *Religion in Essence and Manifestation*, London, 1938, p. 96.

[49]Robertson Smith, *Religion of the Semites*, London, 1923 ed., pp. 108, 536 ff.

[50]Robertson Smith, p. 537; cf. Dhorme, *La Religion des Hébreux nomades*, Brussels, 1937, p. 276.

[51]ii, 223.

[52]*Śatapatha-Brāhmaa*, vii, 2, 2, 5.

[53]*AV*, xiv, 2, 14.

[54]ix, 33.

[55]Cf. Pisani, "La Donna et la terra," *APS*, 1942–5, vol. xxxvii–xl, *passim*.

[56]Nyberg, p. 232, n. 83.

[57]Cf. Bagchi, *Pre-Aryan and pre-Dravidian in India*, Calcutta, 1929, p. 11; Eliade, *Yoga*, p. 291; *Le Yoga: Immortalité et Liberté*, p. 410.

[58]Cf. the reproductions in Dieterich, pp. 107–8.

a drawing of a plough of the Kassite period shows joined to it symbols of the generative act.[59] Primitive intuitions of this sort take a long time to disappear not only from the spoken tongue, but even from the vocabulary of serious writers. Rabelais used the expression "the member we call the husbandman of nature."[60]

And finally, for examples of the identification of agricultural labour with the act of generation, consider the myth of the birth of Sītā, the heroine of *Rāmāyana*. Her father Janaka (the name means "progenitor") found her in his field while he was ploughing, and called her Sītā, "furrow."[61] An Assyrian text brings to us the prayer addressed to a god "whose plough has fertilized the earth."[62]

Even to-day, a lot of primitive peoples still use magic amulets representing the generative organs to make the earth fruitful.[63] The Australian aboriginals practise a most curious fecundation ritual: armed with arrows which they carry in phallic fashion, they dance round a ditch shaped like the female generative organ; and conclude by planting sticks in the ground.[64] It must be remembered what a close connection there is between woman and sexuality on one hand and tilling and the fertility of the soil on the other. Thus, there is one custom whereby naked maidens must mark out the first furrows with the plough,[65] a custom which calls to mind the archetypal union of the goddess Demeter with Jason at the beginning of spring, in a freshly sown furrow.[66] All these ceremonies and legends will yield up their meaning when we come to study the structure of agricultural cults.

SYNTHESIS

In all the mythological and ritual patterns we have examined, the earth is primarily honoured for its endless capacity to bear fruit. That is why, with time, the Earth-Mother imperceptibly turned into the Corn Mother. But the theophany of the soil never totally disappeared from the picture of "Mothers," or earth divinities. To give but one example, we can perceive attributes that were originally those of the Earth-Mother in all the female figures of the Greek religion—

[59]Cf. Jeremias, *Handbuch der altorientalischen Geisteskultur,* Berlin, 1929, p. 387, fig. 214.

[60]*Gargantua,* bk. ii, ch. 1.

[61]*Rāmāyana,* ch. 66; cf. other references in Coomaraswamy, *The Rig Veda as landnama bok,* pp. 15, 33.

[62]Quoted by Langdon, *Semitic Mythology,* Boston, 1931, p. 99.

[63]Dieterich, p. 94.

[64]See references in Dieterich, pp. 94 ff.; on the erotic meaning of the stick, cf. Meyer, *Trilogie altindische Mächte und Feste der vegetation,* Zürich-Leipzig, 1937, vol. iii, pp. 194 ff.

[65]There is a wealth of material in Mannhardt, *Wald- und Feld-kulte,* Berlin, 1904–5, vol. i, pp. 553 ff.; Frazer, *The Magic Art,* vol. i, pp. 469ff.; 480 ff.

[66]*Odyssey,* v, 125.

Nemesis, the Furies, Themis. And Aeschylus[67] prays first to the Earth, then to Themis. It is true that Ge or Gaia was eventually replaced by Demeter, but the Hellenes never lost the consciousness of the bond between the goddess of cereals and the Earth-Mother. Euripides,[68] speaking of Demeter, says: "She is the Earth. . . . Call her what you will!"

Agricultural divinities took the place of the primitive divinities of the soil, but this substitution did not involve the abolition of all the primeval rites. Underlying the "form" of the agricultural Great Goddesses, we can still detect the presence of the "mistress of the place," the Earth-Mother, But the newer divinities are clearer in feature, more dynamic in their religious structure. Their history starts to involve emotion—they *live* the drama of birth, fertility and death. The turning of the Earth-Mother into the Great Goddess of agriculture is the turning of simple existence into living drama.

From the cosmic hierogamy of heaven and earth to the least of the practices that bear witness to the holiness of the soil, the same central intuition comes in as a constantly repeated *leitmotiv:* the earth produces living forms, it is a womb which never wearies of procreating. In every kind of phenomenon to which the epiphany of the soil has given rise—whether a "sacred presence," a still formless divinity, a clearly-defined divine figure, or merely a "custom" that results from some confused memory of subterranean powers—everywhere we can discern the activity of motherhood, of an inexhaustible power of creation. This creation may be of a monstrous kind, as in Hesiod's myth of Gaia. But the monsters of the *Theogony* merely illustrate the endless creative resources of the Earth. In some cases the sex of this earth divinity, this universal procreatrix—does not even have to be defined. A great many earth divinities, and some divinities of fertility, are bisexual.[69] In such cases the divinity contains all the forces of creation—and this formula of polarity, of the coexistence of opposites, was to be taken up again in the loftiest of later speculation. All divinities tend to become *everything* to their believers, to take the place of all other religious figures, to rule over every sphere of the cosmos. And few divinities have ever had as much right or power to become *everything* as had the earth. But the ascent of the Earth-Mother to the position of the supreme, if not unique, divinity, was arrested both by her hierogamy with the sky and by the appearance of the divinities of agriculture. And traces of this tremendous story are preserved in the bisexuality of certain of the earth divinities. But the Earth-Mother never entirely lost her primitive prerogatives of being "mistress of the place," source of all living forms, keeper of children, and womb where the dead were laid to rest, where they were reborn to return eventually to life, thanks to the holiness of Mother Earth.

---

[67]*Eumenides*, 1.

[68]*Bacchæ*, 274.

[69]Cf. Nyberg, pp. 231, n. 69 and 72.

Bibliography

The divine pair, Sky and Earth: Pettazzoni, R., *Dio,* vol. i, pp. 130, 210, 241, etc.; Krappe, A. H., *La Genèse des mythes,* pp. 68 ff.; Fischer, H. T., *Het Heilig Huwelik van Hemel en Aarde,* Utrecht, 1929; supplementary bibliographical suggestions in Thompson, Stith, *Motif-Index of Folk-Literature,* Helsinki, 1932, vol. i, p. 98; cf. also the bibliography following Chapter II. There is a great deal of ethnological research in Staudacher, W., *Die Trennung von Himmel und Erde,* Tübingen, 1942, and also in Numazawa, F. Kiichi, *Die Weltanfänge in der japanischen Mythologie,* Lucerne, 1946; cf. Eliade, M., "La Terre-Mère et les hiérogamies cosmiques," *EJ,* Zürich, 1954, vol. xxii.

On the Earth Mother: Lang, A., *Myth, Ritual and Religion,* London, 1887, pp. 299 ff.; Dieterich, A., *Mutter Erde,* 3rd ed., Berlin, 1925, *passim;* Lindenau, Max, "Ein vedischer Lobgesang auf die Mutter Erde als die grosse Allgottheit (*Ath. Ved.,* XII, 1)," *Festgabe Hermann Jacobi,* Bonn, 1926, pp. 248–58; Marconi, Momolina, *Riflessi mediterranei nella più antica religione laziale,* Milan, 1939, *passim;* Pestalozza, U., *Pagine di religione mediterranea,* Milan, 1942, vol. i, *passim;* Weinstock, S., "Tellus," *GLA,* 1933–4, vol. xxii, pp. 140–162; Noldecke, "Mutter-Erde bei den Semiten," *AFRW,* 1905, vol. viii, pp. 161 ff.; Dhorme, E. P., "La Terre-Mère chez les Assyriens," *AFRW,* 1905, vol. viii, pp. 550 ff.; Briem, E., "Mutter Erde bei den Semiten," *AFRW,* 1926, vol. xxiv, pp. 179–95; Nielsen, Dietlef, "Die altsemitische Mutter-göttin," *Zeitschr. der deutschen morgenländischen Gesel.,* 1938, pp. 504–31; Holmberg-Harva, Uno, *Finno-Ugric Mythology,* Boston, 1927, pp. 239–459; Werner, Alice, *African Mythology,* Boston, 1925, p. 125; Struck, B., "Nochmals 'Mutter Erde' in Afrika," *AFRW,* 1908, vol. xi, pp. 402 ff.; Alexander, H. B., *North American Mythology,* Boston, 1916, pp. 91 ff.; Fuchs, Stefan, "The Cult of the Earth-Mother among the Nimar-Balahis," *IAFE,* vol. xl, pp. 1–8; for the Bhils' prayers to the Earth-Mother, see Koppers, W., "Bhagwan, The Supreme Deity of the Bhils," *APS,* 1940–1, vol. xxxv–xxxvi, pp. 265–325, particularly 272 and 273.

On the divinities and cults of the soil: Thompson, Stith, *Motif-Index,* vol. i, p. 83; Nyberg, B., *Kind und Erde,* Helsinki, 1931, pp. 230–1, n. 69; Frazer, Sir J., *The Worship of Nature,* London, 1926, pp. 316–440; Walter, E., "Die Erdgöttin der Tschuwaschen und Litauer," *AFRW,* 1899, vol. iii, pp. 358 ff.; Wilke, George, *Die Religion der Indogermanen in archäologischer Betrachtung,* Leipzig, 1923, pp. 97–107; Von Wesendonck, "Aremati als arische Erd-Gottheit," *AFRW,* 1929, vol. xxxii, pp. 61–76; Nestle, E., "Die 'jungfräuliche' Erde," *AFRW,* 1908, vol. xi, pp. 415 ff.

On the myth of Adam born of the Virgin Earth: Vollmer, H., "Die Erde als jungfräuliche Mutter Adams," *ZNW,* 1911, vol. x, pp. 324 ff.; Starck, W., "Eva-Maria," *ZNW,* 1934, vol. xxxiii, pp. 97–109; on the creation of man from the earth, there is a rich bibliography in Briffault, R., *The Mothers,* London, 1927, vol. iii, p. 57.

On the placing of children on the ground: Dieterich, op. cit., pp. 7 ff.; Samter, E., *Geburt, Hochzeit und Tod,* Berlin, 1911, pp. 2 ff.; Goldmann, E., "Cartam levare," *MIOG,* 1914, vol. xxxv, pp. 1 ff.; Struck, B., "Niederlegen und Aufheben des Kindes von der Erde," *AFRW,* 1907, vol. x, p. 158; supplementary suggestions and bibliography, Nyberg, B., op. cit., pp. 158 ff.; Rose, H. J., *Primitive Culture in Italy,* London, 1926, p. 133; for a quantity of ethnographical research, see Ploss and Bartels, *Woman: An Historical, Gynæcological and Anthropological Compendium,* London, 1935, vol. ii, pp. 35 ff.; Delcourt, Marie, *Stérilités mystérieuses et naissances maléfiques dans l'antiquité classique,* Paris, 1938, pp. 31 ff.; Briffault, *The Mothers,* vol. iii, p. 58; Granet, Marcel, "Le Dépôt de l'enfant sur le sol. Rites anciens et ordalies mythiques," *RAR,* 1922; reprinted in the volume *Etudes Sociologiques sur la Chine,* Paris, 1953, pp. 159–202.

On the identification of woman and field: in addition to the suggestions already given in the text, see Dieterich, op. cit., pp. 46 ff.; Fehrle, E., *Die kultische Keuschheit im Albertum,* Geissen, 1910, pp. 170 ff.; Farnell, *The Cults of the Greek States,* Oxford, 1896–1909, vol. iii, pp. 106 ff.; Lévy-Bruhl, *Primitive Mentality,* London, 1923, pp. 315 ff.; Robertson Smith, *The Religion of the Semites,* 3rd ed., London, 1927, pp. 613 ff. (A propos Robertson Smith's remarks on Ba'al, "master of the earth," cf. Lagrange, *Etudes sur les religions sémitiques,* 2nd ed., p. 97; Dussaud, R., *Origines cananéennes du sacrifice israélite,* Paris, 1941, p. 206; id., *Les Découvertes de Ras Shamra,* 2nd ed., Paris, 1941, p. 102; Meyer, J. J., *Trilogie altindischer Mächte und Feste der Vegetation,* Zürich-Leipzig, 1937, vol. i, p. 202; Pestalozza, U., "L'Aratro e la donna nel mondo religioso mediterraneo, "*Rendiconti, Reale Instituto Lombardo di Scienze e Lettere, Cl. di Lettere,* 1942–3, vol. lxxvi, no. 2, pp. 321–30; Pisani, Vittore, "La Donna e la terra," *APS,* 1942–5, vol. xxxvii–xl, pp. 241–53; (a wealth of Indian and Græco-Latin material).

On ritual burials: Dieterich, op. cit., pp. 28 ff.; Nyberg, B., op. cit., p. 150; Frazer, Sir J., *Folklore in the Old Testament,* London, 1918, vol. ii, p. 33; Brelich, A., *Aspetti della morte nelle inscrizioni sepolcrali del'Impero Romano,* Budapest, 1937, pp. 9 ff.

On the rebirth of ancestors in newborn children: Eckhardt, K. A., *Indische Unsterblichkeit,* Weimar, 1937; Ashley-Montagu, M. F., "Ignorance of Physiological Paternity in Secular Knowledge and Orthodox Belief among the Australian Aborigines," *OA,* 1940–2, vol. xii, pp. 75–8.

On burial "in the shape of an embryo," cf. Van Der Leeuw, G., "Das sogenannte Hockerbegräbnis und der ägyptische Tjknw," *SMSR,* 1938, vol. xiv, pp. 150–67.

On the "literary mythologies" of the earth, see Bachelard, Gaston, *La Terre et les rêveries de la volonté;* id., *La Terre et les rêveries du repos,* Paris, 1948, 2 vols.

Reading 25

GOD AS MOTHER IN THE HEBREW SCRIPTURES—MAYER GRUBER

It is rightly said that the Hebrew Scriptures reflect a patriarchal society. However, hints of the motherhood of God survive in some places in the Scriptures, most notably in the book of Deuteronomy and the Second Part of the book of Isaiah (or the Third Part, depending on where you choose to make the break).

Mayer Gruber's essay does not prove that the world in which the various books of the Bible were written was not a patriarchy. But it does prove that by the time the books of the later prophets were written down, there were authors (perhaps women) who dissented from that position.

In contemporary America, a third of respondents think of God as either equally mother and father or more mother than father (12% for the latter). Moreover these proportions do not correlate either with gender or age, suggesting that the image of the motherhood of God has been part of the preconscious imagination for a long time and that feminism has forced religious elites to catch up with where their people have been, perhaps for generations.

Rosemary R. Reuther, a feminist theologian, writes that God is neither mother or father and both mother and father. This is a restatement of a long-held position (by Cardinal Nicholas of Cusa and Pope John Paul I for example) that God is androgynous and can be imagined as either Father or Mother.

Questions for Reflection and Discussion

1. In what ways might God be imagined as a mother? As a father?
2. Why do you think the author of the verses in Isaiah choose to write them in the way that they appear? Do you think they created shock?
3. Does equality between the genders depend on an androgynous image of God? Does it help?
4. Why are so many Americans willing to picture God as either equally mother or father or as more mother than father? Are you surprised that these figures correlate neither with age or gender?

THE MOTHERHOOD OF GOD
IN SECOND ISAIAH[1]

Mayer Gruber

Throughout the Hebrew Bible the LORD is compared to a father,[2] and only rarely in the Hebrew Scriptures is the LORD compared to a mother.[3] Thus, in Jer. 1:8 the LORD says, "For I have been to Israel as a father // while Ephraim is My firstborn son." According to the laws of Biblical poetry, the prophet could have written, "For I have been to Israel as a father // as a mother to Ephraim My firstborn son." It is noteworthy, however, that Jeremiah does not make use here of what Wilfred G. E. Watson has called "Gender-Matched Synonymous Parallelism."[4]

When Malachi, the last of the prophets, speaks about *lèse-majesté* toward the LORD, he also compares the LORD to a father when he says, speaking in the name of God (Mal. 1:6):

Source: Mayer Gruber, *The Motherhood of God and Other Stories.* Atlanta, Georgia: Scholars Press, 1992.

[1]This article is expanded from a paper presented at the Eighth World Congress of Jewish Studies in Jerusalem, August 1981.

[2]Examples, in addition to the four discussed in the text below, include Deut. 32:6; 2 Sam. 7:14; Isa. 63:16; 64:7; Jer. 3:4, 19; 1 Ch. 17:13; 22:10; 28:6. These texts range in date from the tenth century B.C.E. to the post-exilic times of Malachi and the Chronicler. See the extensive discussion of these texts in my "Feminine Similes Applied to the LORD in Second Isaiah," *Beer Sheva* 2 (1985) 75–84 (in Hebrew).

[3]Gen. 1:27, in which the creation of humankind in the image of God is juxtaposed with the creation of humankind "male and female" *can* be taken to *imply* that God is both male and female. If so, Deutero-Isaiah and Ps. 123:12 (see below, n. 4) and P's creation story, to which modern biblical scholarship has assigned Gen. 1:27, could all be cited to demonstrate a non-patriarchalizing tendency in post-exilic Judaism alongside of the anti-feminist tendency seen in post-exilic Judaism by Samuel Terrien, "The Omphalos Myth and Hebrew Religion," *VT* 30 (1970) 314–338. The latter study, which is often cited as "canonical" in the field of feminist scholarship manages to ignore Deutero-Isaiah's feminine similes for God, Ps. 123:2, and P's creation story while seeing in the exploits of Esther and even Judith examples of post-exilic Judaism's anti-feminism. I suggest that it would be more productive to consider each corpus of biblical texts independently of preconceived notions of post-exilic decadence or progress. Interestingly, Phyllis Trible, *God and the Rhetoric of Sexuality* (Philadelphia: Fortress Press, 1978) 15–21 argues that Gen. 1:27 shows that God is *neither* male nor female. See also Leonard Swidler, *Biblical Affirmations of Woman* (Philadelphia: Westminster Press, 1979) 35. For detailed analysis of other verses in the Hebrew Bible where according to Trible, followed by Swidler, it is *implied* that God is feminine see Gruber, "Feminine Similes," n. 9. The fact remains that the only instances in the Hebrew Bible where God is *explicitly* compared to a mother are those in Deutero-Isaiah discussed below.

[4]Wilfred G. E. Watson, "Gender-Matched Synonymous Parallelism in the Old Testament," *JBL* 99 (1980) 321–344; see also Adele Berlin, "Grammatical Aspects of Biblical Parallelism," *HUCA* 50 (1979) 27–30. For the word pair "father" / "mother" in synonymous parallelism in the Hebrew Bible see Ezek. 16:3, 45; Mic. 7:6; Prov. 1:8; 6:20; 10:1; 15:20; 19:26; 23:22; 30:11, 17; for the same pair in Phoenician see *KAI* 24:10; 26:3. In Ps. 123:2, which, it is generally agreed, postdates Deutero-Isaiah (see commentaries), we have two additional gender-matched pairs "slave" / "maidservant," "master" / "mistress" employed in similes applied to the Jews and God respectively. We render the verse as follows: "Behold, as the eyes of slaves are fixed upon the hand of their masters, as the eyes of a maidservant are fixed upon the hand of her mistress so are our eyes fixed upon the LORD our God until He shows us favor."

A son honors his father // and a servant his master.
Now if I be a father where is My honor?
And if I be a master where is the fear of Me?

Again it is worthy of note that Malachi does not make use of "Gender-Matched Synonymous Parallelism." Hence he does not have the LORD speak as follows:

A son honors his father // and a daughter her mother.
Now if I be a father where is My honor?
And if I be a mother where is the fear of Me?

According to Phyllis Trible, the expression *raḥēm 'ăraḥămennû* in Jer. 31:19 means "I will truly show motherly-compassion."[5] This rendering assumes that Heb. *riḥam* here corresponds to Akk. *rêmu* "have compassion," which is a cognate of Akk. *rēmu* = Heb. *reḥem* "womb,"[6] and not to Akk. *ra'āmu*

---

[5]*God and the Rhetoric of Sexuality,* p. 50. Trible's assertion (there) that in Jer. 31 "the uterine metaphor encompassed by the root *rḥm* signifies the image of God female" seems to rest upon the questionable assumption that Jeremiah and his contemporaries who were native speakers of Hebrew were fully conscious of the etymological relationship of the verb *riḥam* "be compassionate" and the noun *reḥem* "womb" whenever they heard or employed the verb *riḥam* or the adjective *raḥûm* "compassionate." Native speakers of a language tend to be far less conscious of the etymological history of words or the origin of idioms than are preachers, philologists, and students of Hebrew as a foreign language. Were Trible's assumptions correct, the following thirteen attestations of the masculine adjective *raḥûm* "compassionate," which is applied to the LORD exclusively would have to be construed as "the image of God female": Ex. 34:6; Deut. 4:31; Joel 2:13; Jonah 4:2; Ps. 78:38; 86:15; 103:8; 111:4; 112:4 (see LXX); 145:8; Neh. 9:17, 31; 2 Ch. 30:9. Moreover, the etymological relationship of the verb *riḥam* in Jer. 41:19 to the noun *reḥem* "womb" is open to question; see below, n. 7. I will grant, nevertheless, the *possibility* that *hāmû mē'ay* both in Jer. 31:19 and in Cant. 5:4 *can* mean "my womb trembles" (so Trible, there, p. 45) rather than "I get butterflies in my stomach" or "My heart aches." This *possibility may* suggest that Jer. 31:19 employs a maternal metaphor for God. For *mē'ayim* denoting "womb" see Gen. 25:23; Isa. 49:1; Ps. 71:6; Ruth 1:11. For *mē'ayim* denoting "heart," i.e., the seat of thought and emotional feeling, see Ps. 22:15; Job 30:27; Lam. 1:20; 2:11. For *mē'ayim* denoting "stomach" or "guts," see 2 Sam. 20:10; Jer. 4:19 (but see below); Ezek. 3:3; 7:19; Jonah 2:1, 2; 2 Ch. 21:18, 19. Note, however, that *mē'ayim* unequivocally denotes the male reproductive organs slightly more frequently than it unequivocally denotes "womb." For *mē'ayim* meaning "male reproductive organs" see Gen. 15:4; 2 Sam. 7:12; 16:11; Isa. 48:19; 2 Ch. 32:21. Moreover, the activity expressed by *hāmû mē'ayim* is compared to the function of a harp in Isa. 16:11. Perhaps, therefore, *mē'ayim* with the verb *hāmāh* "groan, murmur" (see dictionaries and see Marvin H. Pope, *The Song of Songs,* AB vol. 7C [Garden City, N.Y.: Doubleday, 1977] 519) like *lēb* with the verb *hāgāh* (see H. L. Ginsberg, "Lexicographical Notes," *VTS* 16 [1967] 80) may denote the organ of speech. Hence Isa. 16:11 should be rendered, "Therefore my voice, like a lyre, chants a lament for Moab // my throat for Kir-heres." For the realization that *hāmāh* here means "chant a lament" see Rashi *ad loc;* for the realization that *mē'ay* and *qirbî* are a pair of synonyms, see Radak, *ad loc.* Samuel David Luzzatto, *Il Profeta Isaia* (Padua: Bianchi, 1867) *ad loc* already observed that the palpitations of the heart cannot be compared to the sound of a harp! I shall deal with the possible implications of these observations for the meaning of Jer. 4:19–20 in a forthcoming study. For the present it should be sufficient to note that *hāmû mē'ay* in both Jer. 31:19 and Cant. 5:4 may very well mean "I groan(ed)." Hence it is incorrect to compare the remotely *possible* feminine metaphor of Jer. 31:19 with the unequivocal feminine similes of Isa. 40–66.

[6]Cf. Foster R. McCurley, Jr., "A Semantic Study of Anatomical Terms in Akkadian, Ugaritic, and Biblical Literature" (Unpublished Ph.D. dissertation, Dropsie College, 1968) 87, n. 287 and the literature cited there.

"love."[7] Just as Trible in our time has seen a connection between *riḥam* and *reḥem* so was it possible also in antiquity for poets and for those who read or heard peotry to see in *raḥămîm* "compassion" a characteristically motherly attribute. It is important to note, therefore, that this was not necessarily the case. Hence we find that the author of Ps. 103:13 treats *raḥămîm* as a specifically paternal attribute when he says, "As a father shows compassion for children, the LORD has shown compassion for His devotees."[8]

Against the background of the tendency in all strata of the Hebrew Bible to compare the LORD to a father it is possible to appreciate how unusual is the phenomenon of a whole series of maternal expressions applied to the LORD in Isa. 40–66. It appears that the presupposition that Isa. 56–66 is the work of Trito-Isaiah rather than the continuation of Second Isaiah may have prevented sensitive scholars from asking why it is that one anonymous prophet used an entire series of explicitly maternal expressions for the LORD, the like of which do not occur anywhere else in the Hebrew Bible.[9]

We have seen that when Malachi speaks about *lèse-majesté* toward God he uses a paternal expression, and he avoids the fixed pair father // mother. Instead he uses the pair father // master, which is found nowhere else in the Hebrew Scriptures. When, however, Second Isaiah speaks about *lèse-majesté* toward the LORD he says:

Alas for him who says to his father,
"What are you begetting?"
And to (his) mother,[10]
"To what are you giving birth?" (Isa. 45:10)

---

[7]While Akkadian distinguishes between *ra'āmu* "love" (from the root *r'm*) and *rêmu* "have compassion" (from the root *rḥm*), in Hebrew and Aramaic the two verbs coalesce as *rḥm* "love, have compassion." See Y. Muffs, *Studies in the Aramaic Legal Papyri from Elephantine* (Leiden: E. J. Brill, 1969) 132–135 and the literature cited there; see also id., "Joy and Love as Metaphorical Expressions of Willingness and Spontaneity in Cuneiform, Ancient Hebrew, and Related Literatures," in *Christianity, Judaism, and Other Greco-Roman Cults for Morton Smith at Sixty*, ed. J. Neusner (4 vols.; Leiden: E. J. Brill, 1975) 3:5, n. 13. Jonah Ibn Janah, *Sepher Haschoraschim*, ed. W. Bacher (Berlin: M'kize Nirdamim, 1896) 477 already argues, however, that *'erḥoměkā* "I love You" in Ps. 18:2 is a cognate of Targumic *rḥm*, which is employed to render Heb. *'hb* "love" and not a cognate of *rḥm* "have compassion," which is attested in Isa. 9:16; Ps. 103:13; etc.

[8]Contrast Trible, *God and the Rhetoric of Sexuality*, p. 34.

[9]Phyllis Trible, "Depatriarchalizing in Biblical Interpretation," *JAAR* 41 (1973) 33 writes concerning Isa. 42:15, "Deutero-Isaiah boldly employs gynomorphic imagery," and concerning Isa. 66:9 she states (there), "Third Isaiah continues the maternal picture." For a discussion of Trible's interpretation of Isa. 66:9 see my "Feminine Similes," n. 9. With reference to the features which unite Isa. 40–66 see M. Haran, "The Prophetic Message and Its Literary Form," in *Studies in the Book of Isaiah*, pt. 2, ed. Ben-Zion Lurie (Jerusalem: Kiryath Sepher, 1980) 1–17 (in Hebrew).

[10]Only in two places in the Hebrew Bible, here and in Isa. 49:15, is *'iššâ* "woman" employed in the secondary sense "mother." Here the rendering "mother" is suggested by the appearance of *'iššâ* in gender-matched synonymous parallelism with *'ab* "father."

The latter verse makes explicit what is implicit throughout the Hebrew Scriptures, namely, that the LORD is neither specifically male nor specifically female. God is above and beyond both sexes. Hence to the very same extent that the God of Israel can be compared to a father the God of Israel can and should be compared also to a mother.[11]

Hence in Isa. 42:13–14 the anonymous prophet compares the LORD both to a man of war and to a woman in labor when he says:

> The LORD will go forth like a hero,
> Like a warrior He will stir up (His) rage.
> He will shout; indeed He will roar.
> He will prevail over His enemies.
> "For a long time I kept quiet.
> I was silent. I restrained Myself."
> ["Now," says the LORD], "I will scream
> like a woman in labor. I will inhale,
> and I will exhale simultaneously."[12]

Many Bible commentators expressed amazement that the anonymous prophet should have juxtaposed the comparison of the LORD to a military hero with his comparison of the LORD to a woman in labor. Many scholars suggest that Isa. 42:13–14 juxtaposes two contradictory similes—the comparison to the warrior who acts upon others and the comparison to the woman in labor who is only acted upon.[13] What these scholars did not know or forgot is that in natural childbirth the woman's role is active rather than passive.[14]

The same prophet who in Isa. 42 compares the LORD to a woman in labor compares the LORD to a mother in Isa. 49. According to Isa. 49:14, "Zion said, 'the LORD has abandoned me, and my Lord has forgotten me.'" In Isa. 49:15 the LORD responds to this assertion with a double rhetorical question which should be restored as follows:

---

[11]Trible, "Depatriarchalizing," 31–32; Y. Kaufmann, *History of the Israelite Religion,* 8 vols. (Jerusalem: Bialik Institute, 1964; Tel Aviv: Dvir, 1964) 1:300, 302–303, 438–439 (in Hebrew).

[12]On the final clauses, "I will inhale, and I will exhale simultaneously," see Luzzatto, *Il Profeta Isaia,* p. 471. Interestingly, the prophet here describes precisely the breathing technique prescribed for the transition period of labor in Elisabeth Bing, *Six Practical Lessons for an Easier Childbirth,* rev. ed. (New York: Bantam Books, 1977) 88–91. Fernand Lamaze, *Painless Childbirth,* trans. L. R. Celestin (New York: Pocket Books 1972) 120 explains the rationale for this method of breathing (4 or 6 or 8 short inhalations followed by a quick exhalation through the lips) as follows: "Whether the dilation stage of labour or the delivery be considered, it still remains that the child must receive a constant and sufficient supply of oxygen. This means a good or a bad start in life for the child; and such a responsibility falls mostly on the mother."

[13]See A. B. Ehrich, *Mikrâ ki-Pheschutô* (3 vols.; Berlin: H. Itzkowski, 1901) 3:92 (in Hebrew); Antoon Schoors, *I am God Your Saviour* (VTS 24; Leiden: E. J. Brill, 1973) 91–92; John L. McKenzie, *Second Isaiah* (AB, no. 20; Garden City, N.Y.: Doubleday & Co., 1968) 4; contrast James Muilenberg in *IB* 5:472–473.

[14]See passim in Bing, *Six Practical Lessons.*

Will a mother[15] forget her infant?[16]
Or a woman the child of her womb? (Isa. 49:15a)[17]

Were there here not a double rhetorical question but a three-part question, the latter two clauses would be followed by the third part, "Why should I forget you?" The import of such a three-part question would be as follows: the LORD is the mother of Zion. Just as a mother does not abandon her children so does the LORD not abandon or forget Zion.

The anonymous prophet, however, is not satisfied to claim that the LORD is a mother like all mothers lest someone should point out that there are, in fact, mothers who abandon their children. Hence it might be inferred that the LORD also is liable to abandon Zion. The prophet therefore declares, speaking in the name of the LORD, "These,[18] indeed, may forget [their children], but I shall not forget you" (Isa. 49:15b). This is to say that even if it be asserted that sometimes a mother forgets her child, it should be known that the LORD, who is the Mother of Israel, is not like these wicked mothers but like the good mothers.

In light of the three references to the LORD as Mother noted above we should not be surprised that while in Ps. 103 the LORD's compassion is compared to that of a father, in Isa. 66:13 the LORD says to the people of Israel, "I shall comfort you like a

---

[15]See n. 9 above.

[16]It is generally recognized that Heb. *'ûl* "infant" derives from a root meaning "nurse;" see *BDB* 732a. Hence the LORD's question, "Can a woman forget her sucking child?" (KJV) may allude to the important role of nursing in establishing emotional "bonding" between mother and child. In this connection Derrick B. Jelliffe and E. F. Patrick Jelliffe, *Human Milk in the Modern World* (Oxford: Oxford University Press, 1978) 156 point out, "Apart from such operant conditioning to the pleasurable sensations resulting from the infant's sucking, hormonal differences, including increased levels of prolactin, may also affect the women's 'motherliness' and her attachment to the baby." It is conceivable, however, that the anonymous prophet may not have had in mind *BDB*'s etymology! Hence my rendering "infant."

[17]Robert Gordis, "Studies in the Book of Amos," in *American Academy for Jewish Research Jubilee Volume* (2 vols.; Jerusalem: American Academy for Jewish Research, 1980) 1:211 argues that the verse is to be rendered, "Shall a woman forget her sucking child, A mother the child of her womb? These may forget, but I shall not forget you." He states, "This interpretation is now incorporated in NEB, 'or a loving mother, the child of her womb?'" Note, that NEB, *unlike* Gordis, begins the second clause with "or," which appears to represent the Hebrew interrogative particle *'im*, which normally introduces the second part of a double rhetorical question in Biblical Hebrew. It appears, therefore, that NEB, *unlike* Gordis, has anticipated the suggestion defended in detail in my "Will a woman forget her infant . . . ?," *Tarbiz* 51 (1982) 491–492 (in Hebrew). Briefly, this suggestion is that the initial *mem* of MT's *mēraḥēm* derives from an ancient copyist's omission of the *'aleph* of an original *'im raḥam* . . . "Or a woman . . . " Gordis, on the other hand, simply revocalizes *mēraḥēm* as a *mem*-preformative noun. Note should be taken of the prophet's subtle play on words in the second clause of Isa. 49:15 where he points to the special bond which should link mother and child by referring to the mother as *raḥam* "woman," a cognate of *reḥem* "womb" and to the woman's progeny as *ben-bitnâ* "child of her womb." For the nuances of Heb. *raḥam* (Judg. 5:30) and its Ugaritic and Moabite cognates see my "Will a woman forget her infant," n. 2. In accord with what I have stated in n. 5 above (see also n. 16) it is conceivable that the play on words which is so obvious to moderns who study Biblical Hebrew as a dead language may have been less than obvious to the native speakers and writers of the language such as Jeremiah.

[18]Gordis, "Studies in the Book of Amos," 211; id., "Studies in the Relationship of Biblical and Rabbinic Hebrew," in *Louis Ginzberg Jubilee Volume* (New York: American Academy for Jewish Research, 1946) 186 demonstrates that in Biblical Hebrew a plural pronoun is used to refer to a single object or event which has previously been referred to by two separate terms in synonymous parallelism. Hence in Isa. 49:15 "these" refers to the hypothetical mother who earlier in the same verse is called both *'iššâ* and *raḥam*, the primary meaning of both of which is "woman."

man whose mother comforts him, and you shall be comforted through Jerusalem."

We have seen, therefore, that in four verses in Second Isaiah—Isa. 42:14, 45:10, 49:15, 66:13—at least one verse in each of the three principal divisions of Second Isaiah—two from Isa. 40–48, one from Isa. 49–57, and one from Isa. 58–66[19]—the anonymous prophet explicitly compares the LORD to a mother while throughout the rest of the Hebrew Scriptures the LORD is explicitly compared to a father but not to a mother.

The question arises, therefore, as to why in particular Second Isaiah should employ maternal similes for God, which are not employed elsewhere in the Hebrew Bible. In his book *Bible Studies,* S. D. Goitein writes, "Since the women were kept at a distance from the worship of the Temple the result was that they more than the males were attracted to the popular beliefs and cults which were widespread in the ancient Near East.[20]

Jeremiah and Ezekiel both stress the involvement of Israelite women in idolatrous cults.[21] These same prophets employ feminine similes and metaphors for the people of Israel and exclusively male expressions for the LORD.[22] Both of these prophets compare Israel to a harlot and the foreign deities to the men who patronize prostitutes.[23] Tragically, these prophets never compare the foreign

---

[19]For the threefold division of Deutero-Isaiah see Kaufmann, *History of the Israelite Religion* 8:76–77 (in Hebrew).

[20]2nd ed. (Tel Aviv: Yavneh, 1963) 271 (in Hebrew); cf. Phyllis Bird, "Images of Women in the Old Testament," in *Religion and Sexism: Images of Woman in the Jewish and Christian Traditions,* ed. Rosemary Radford Ruether (New York: Simon & Schuster, 1974) 85, n. 77: "It is significant that the syncretistic rites with which Israelite women are explicitly connected are associated solely with female deities or with deities whose cult is predominantly female." See also M. Cogan, *Imperialism and Religion,* SBL Monograph Series, no. 19 (Missoula, Montana: Society of Biblical Literature and Scholars Press, 1974) 84, n. 103.

[21]Jer. 7:18, 44; Ezek. 8:14.

[22]In Jer. 2:2 the LORD and Jerusalem are compared to husband and wife respectively while in Jer. 3:19 the LORD and Israel are compared to father and daughter respectively. In Ezek. 16:6–7 Jerusalem is pictured as a daughter who was abandoned by her mother and adopted by the LORD while in Ezek. 16:8 the LORD is pictured as the husband who married her. Deutero-Isaiah likewise compares the LORD to the husband of the people of Israel in Isa. 50:1. In Isa. 54:1–17 he pictures the LORD as the husband of the land of Israel while in Isa. 62:4–5 the LORD is pictured as the husband of both the land and the people of Israel. In Isa. 63:16 the people of Israel address God in prayer as "our Father."

[23]Typical of Jeremiah is Jer. 2:20, ". . . for on every high hill and under every leafy tree you lie down and whore;" see also Jer. 2:23, 24; 3:1, 2, 6–10; 4:30; 5:7; 13:20–27; 22:20–23. While Jeremiah compares idolatrous Israel to a whoring adulteress more frequently than any other prophet, Ezekiel makes up in intensity of detail in Ezek. 16 and 23 for his not employing the image so extensively as Jeremiah. Cf. also Isa. 57:7–8. As for the contention that Jer. 31:22b, "a woman will circumambulate a man," points to a women's liberation tendency in Jeremiah (see William L. Holladay, "Jer. xxxi 22b Reconsidered: The Woman Encompasses the Man," *VT* 16 [1966] 236–239; id., "Jeremiah and Women's Liberation," *Andover Newton Quarterly* 12 [1971–72] 213–223; Trible, *God and the Rhetoric of Sexuality,* pp. 47–50; id., "Woman in the Old Testament," *IDB Supplementary Volume* [Nashville: Abingdon, 1976] 865b; Swidler, pp. 31–32), I find the thesis completely unconvincing. For a much more plausible interpretation of Jer. 31:22 see my "Ten Dance-Derived Expressions in the Hebrew Bible," below, pp. 156–157. Crucial to Holladay's thesis is his contention that *geber* "man" "does not denote the male as a sexual being, but the male as a warrior" (*VT* 16, p. 237). This contention is clearly contradicted by Prov. 30:19 *derek geber běʾalmâ* "the way of a man with a maid" and Job 3:3 in which *geber* means "man child." Incidentally, the bride's circumambulation of the groom, to which Jer. 31:22 refers, was eliminated from the marriage ceremony in nineteenth and twentieth century Reform Judaism precisely because this symbolic act was perceived as degrading to women. I wish to record my personal thanks to Prof. William L. Holladay for his having provided me with a copy of his 1971–72 article.

deities to harlots nor the people of Israel to the men who patronize prostitutes.[24] It appears, therefore, that not only the fact that the women were kept at a distance from the official Israelite cult but also the fact that the great prophets continually compared the LORD to a husband and Israel to a wife and never used explicitly feminine expressions for the LORD may have contributed to Israelite women becoming attracted to cults in which femaleness existed as a positive value with which divinity could identify itself.

Deutero-Isaiah polemicized against idolatry more than any other prophet whose writings are preserved in the Bible.[25] This prophet believed that devotion to idolatrous cults was primarily the result of lack of understanding:

> They do not perceive, and they do not understand for their eyes are plastered over so that they do not see and their hearts so that they do not think. (Isa. 44:18)

Perhaps, therefore, the anonymous prophet understood that the women were especially attracted to idolatrous cults because of the insensitivity of his predecessors such as Jeremiah and Ezekiel who had intimated that in the religion of Israel maleness is a positive value with which divinity chooses to identify itself while femaleness is a negative value with which divinity refuses to identify itself. Perhaps, as a result of this realization our prophet deliberately made use of both masculine and feminine similes for God.

Perhaps also there is a lesson to be learned from the experience of Jeremiah and Ezekiel who failed to put an end to idolatry in Israel and from the experience of Deutero-Isaiah who succeeded in attracting even non-Jews to become "those who attach themselves to the LORD to minister to Him" (Isa. 56:6).[26] The lesson would seem to be that a religion which seeks to convey the Teaching of God who is above and beyond both sexes cannot succeed in conveying that Teaching if it seeks to do so in a manner which implies that a positive-divine value is attached only to one of the two sexes.[27]

---

[24]In Isa. 57:3, on the other hand, the people of Israel are called "brood of an adulterer."

[25]See Kaufmann, *History of the Israelite Religion* 1:272–273 (in Hebrew).

[26]The post-exilic prophets Haggai, Zechariah, and Malachi no longer polemicize against idolatry. The last prophetic references to Israelite idolatry are found in Isa. 57; 65; and 66. It appears that the prophetic author of the latter speeches succeeded in putting an end to idolatry in Israel. Cf. Kaufmann, *History of the Israelite Religion* 8:139, 143, 188–189 (in Hebrew).

[27]Having been asked repeatedly my opinion of Raphael Patai's treatment of the subject of this article in his famous work *The Hebrew Goddess* (New York: Ktav, 1967), I think it helpful to point out that he does not deal there with the key verses from Deutero-Isaiah, which are the basis for the thesis of this article.

THE WOMANLINESS OF GOD AND THE SURVIVAL OF MARY—ANDREW M. GREELEY

In 1980, my colleagues, William McCready, Joan Fee, and Teresa Sullivan, and I began a study at National Opinion Research Center (NORC), under a grant from the Knights of Columbus, of the attitudes and behaviors of young Catholic adults. From our findings it only follows that at this stage of the ongoing history of the Mary story, one cannot say unequivocally that the Mary story is obsolete. It seems to have some utility for some young women—and perhaps even more for some young men.

In the present condition of ecumenical conversation among Christians and the orientation of Catholic ecclesiastical authority towards women, it is too early to say whether the story does have the promise of becoming useful as an explanation for what should be the proper treatment of women in the human condition.

Questions for Reflection and Discussion

1. Why would a womanly God be even more appealing to men than to women?
2. Why did so many Catholic young people find the Mary image so appealing?
3. What would have to happen before the Mary story could become acceptable to others besides Catholics as a story for "new women?"

THE WOMANLINESS OF GOD
Andrew Greeley

I will contend in this chapter that men need the image of God as woman more than women do.

The most striking image of the womanliness of God in recent years was presented in Bob Fosse's film *All That Jazz* described in the opening chapter of this

Source: Andrew M. Greeley, *The Religious Imagination*, Chicago: William Sadlier, Inc., 1981.

book. It is, as we have said, the story of Fosse's brush with death during a massive heart attack. The death experience, however, turned out to be an interlude of grace. Death itself seemed to be very much like a woman—a tender, sensuous lover who sees through the phoniness of Joe Gideon (the fictional Fosse) and loves him anyway. Indeed, Angelique (Jessica Lange, King Kong's sometime girl friend) is a summation of all the women in Gideon's life. She gently wipes the sweat from his hands as he is dying as would his wife, threatens to absorb him with a passionate kiss at the very end as have his mistresses, and playfully mocks him as does his daughter (indeed in the final sequence the identification between Angelique and his daughter is heavily emphasized—the daughter's tears make Angelique sad).

Demanding, sexy, a bit sinister, inescapable, tender, and passionately loving—that's what the angel of death is like, Fosse tells us. The angel may also be God. Fosse is not sure, yet twice in the movie he brackets scenes with Ms. Lange in references to God; and at the end he gives us a choice: either life ends with a lifeless corpse being zipped up in a plastic bag or in the consummation of a love affair with a beautiful spouse.

According to *All That Jazz* then, death is a beautiful woman, and the beautiful woman may be God. Fosse doesn't insist. Like any good poet he merely suggests . . . yet what if he's right?

It seemed to me as I reflected on the film that in principle we men ought to have more invested in the image of God as someone like Jessica Lange than women might. God, we are told, is love. Our relationship to God is a love relationship. Normally, the most powerful love experiences we have are cross-sexual relationships. It is hard to fit these experiences into an imagery of God which is predominately male.

The usual reaction (even with college students, I find) to a comparison of human love with divine love is to insist that it is utterly different from sexual attraction ("not at all physical," my students tell me). Thus, to use scholastic terms, the word "love" is predicated equivocally of intimacy with humans and intimacy with God.

I do not believe, however, that such an equivocal predication will stand the test of either good spirituality or good exegesis. If love with God isn't really like human love at all, then it can hardly be very appealing, since human love is the most powerful emotion of which we are capable. Moreover, the sexual imagery of the Scriptures is washed away if the usage is equivocal.

Thus we must conclude that the use of "love" is analogous. God does passionately desire us in a way similar to how an attractive member of the opposite sex might desire us. And we desire God in a way similar to the way we might desire an appealing member of the opposite sex. (I trust I will be excused in this book from discussing images for Gays. While the subject is proper and important, it is beyond the goals of this preliminary essay.)

Of any analogy one must inquire how the two uses differ. There can be only one answer: divine love is more passionate than human love. God's desire for us is greater than that of any human spouse; and God's appeal is more powerful than that of any human bedmate. God is different from Jessica Lange mainly in that God is more attractive, more demanding, more tender, more passionate, more gentle.

If there is any validity in these reflections it would follow that men who have a womanly image of God will find it easier to think of God as a lover, will pray more often and more intensely, and will be more deeply committed to the social concerns which should come from intense religious devotion. Moreover, precisely because they are involved in a love relationship with a womanly God, they should have better relationships with human women. Finally, it seems not unlikely that their womanly image of God will be affected by their relationships with their mother and by strong, womanly images of Mary.

These predictions would substantiate my "theory" only if they did not also apply, or at least did not apply to such a great extent, to women's imagery of God-as-woman.

It is possible to test these hypotheses against data collected in the Knights of Columbus' study of young Catholics. All the hypotheses are sustained.

Some 10 percent of young American Catholics say that they are extremely likely to imagine God as a "mother." There are no differences between young men and young women in this proportion. However (Table 1), men with a womanly image of God are significantly more likely than men who do not have that image also to imagine God as a lover, to pray often, to offer prayers of gratitude, to consider a life of social concern and involvement to be important, to say that their sexual fulfillment in marriage is excellent, and to be in marriages in which both husband and wife report the sexual fulfillment excellent. They also are more likely to say they were very close to their mother and to score high on a scale which measures their image of Mary as "patient" and "comforting." In only two of the variables are there significant relationships in the same direction for women—the image of God as lover and closeness to mother.

Women who think of God as a mother are twice as likely to think of God also as a lover than those who do not imagine God as mother, but men with the picture of God as mother are three times more likely to imagine her also as a lover than are men without that picture.

They are also half again as likely to be in marriages in which both they and their wives say the sexual fulfillment is excellent. Picturing God as a mother is not only good for the prayer life of a man, it is also good for the sex life of his wife.

So the Fosse/Gideon experience of the womanliness of God is not as rare as one might have thought. While a tenth of the Catholic men under thirty is surely a minority, it is by no means a trivial number of young men who imagine God as a mother and who are likely to benefit in their spiritual and sexual lives from that image.

One is forced to wonder where the image comes from; surely it does not originate in any educational or spiritual direction experiences they have had. Perhaps it results from experiences with women in which they sense that God has disclosed herself to them.

TABLE 1

Correlates of God as Mother for Men and Women (Percent)

	MEN God as Mother		WOMEN God As Mother	
	"Extremely Likely"	Not "Extremely Likely"	"Extremely Likely"	Not "Extremely Likely"
God as Lover (extremely likely)	76*	22	57*	25
Prayer (several times a week at least)	63*	42	61	65
Prayers of Gratitude (often)	64*	46	60	60
Own Sexual Fulfillment "Excellent"	80*	38	38	47
Both husband and wife say sexual fulfillment "Excellent"	33*	22	15	27*
Social concerns "Extremely Important"	43*	21	21	25
Was very close to mother	42*	32	52*	31
High on Mary scale ("Patient" and "Comforting" both "Extremely likely" as image)	78*	58	77	75

*Differences statistically significant.

Confirmation of this explanation can be found in the data. Men who say their mothers had a strong impact on their religious development are almost three times as likely to report that they imagine God as mother as do those who do not report such maternal influence. Furthermore, men who say that their wives have a powerful impact on their religious development are more than three times as likely as are other men to imagine God as mother (Table 2). There is no parallel effect on the religious imagery of women respondents.

Women, then, seem to mediate the womanliness of God for men. Apparently they do so without seeking permission from the magisterium. Religious imagery with its profound effect on human life and human religion is shaped with little attention to and little support from or awareness of the institutional Church.

The implications of these findings for spiritual and pastoral theology as well as for prayer and spiritual direction are enormous. They are also shattering and revolutionary. A woman may well imagine herself as a bride of Christ (and a married woman or an unmarried lay woman has as much right to that image as

TABLE 2
Influence of Women on a Man's Image of God-As-Woman
Percent "Extremely Likely" to Imagine God as Mother

	MEN		WOMEN	
	Powerful Effect	Not Powerful	Powerful Effect	Not Powerful
Mother	18	7	9	10
Spouse	18	5	13	10

does a religious woman). But a man imagine himself as the husband of God? Or God as his paramour? Or God as a woman pursuing him with passionate desire? How shocking and scandalous. God may desire women but certainly not men.

Yet however scandalous and shocking the implications, the findings are hard to dispute. Some young men do benefit from cross-sexual images of God, and so do their spouses. . . .

MARY SURVIVES
Andrew M. Greeley

In John Power's play, "Patent Leather Shoes," there is a scene in which the second grade performs its annual May crowning. They begin to sing "Bring Flowers of the Rarest." The night two of us were there, the audience joined in the chorus, "O Mary, we crown thee with blossoms today. . . ." Mr. Powers was asked afterwards if it was an unusual event. "They do it every night," he replied. "If they stop singing it, I'll begin to worry." (The musical play, based on the author's novel, *Do Patent Leather Shoes Reflect Up?*, has been playing to packed houses for nine months in Chicago, and is now reported to be Boston, and perhaps even Broadway, bound.)

In the recent study of Catholic young adults, . . . graciously sponsored by the Knights of Columbus, the Mary image proved to be stronger than either the Jesus image or the God image. As Professor Teresa Sullivan remarked: "Bernard of Clairvaux was right: 'If you fear the father, go to the son. If you fear the son, go to the mother.'"

Source: Andrew M. Greeley, William McCready, Teresa Sullivan, and Joan Fee, "Mary Survives," *America*, Vol. 142, No. 7. February 23, 1980.

The technical details of the research project, question wording, significance tests and other such matters can be found in *The Young Catholic Family* (to be published shortly by the Thomas More Press), and the final report of the Knights of Columbus project, *The Young Catholic Adult.* For the purposes of the present article, we present only one question and state that the study was a probability sample of Catholics between 15 and 30 in the United States and Canada, screened by phone and administered mail questionnaires. . . . The data were collected in the winter and spring of 1979. The response rate was approximately 80 percent, and the total number of respondents was 2,504. All the findings reported in this article are statistically significant.

More than 75 percent of the young adults said they were "extremely" likely to think of Mary as "warm" or as "patient" or as "comforting" or as "gentle"; 65 percent of the respondents checked all four words as "extremely likely," while 50 percent rated Jesus as high on all four images.

Nor were the Mary images irrelevant. Our "madonna scale" (one point for each of the four words checked as "extremely likely") correlated positively with social commitment, frequency of prayer, concern for racial justice and sexual fulfillment in marriage. Mary is not only still fashionable, but, it seems, also still "relevant."

How can this be, one is asked. Have not the Catholic schools deemphasized Mary? Has not the church played down the doctrine in a quest for ecumenical understanding? Is not much of the old-fashioned Marian piety outdated and unappealing?

To begin with, there is no correlation between number of years of Catholic schooling and the madonna scale (or years of C.C.D., either). Secondly, we are dealing with religious images, not religious doctrines. Thirdly, however outdated, the "lovely lady dressed in blue" piety of the past may be, it was and is peripheral to the attractiveness of Mary. . . .

The most appealing "stories of God" (symbols) are those that present the Other as tender and caring. Hence, the near universality of mother symbols in religions. Everyone has had the experience of having a mother (or a mother surrogate). Similarly, everyone has the experience of either being potentially a mother or being able to join with a potential mother in an activity that enables her to become a mother. Conceding to the feminists all the ambivalences that one experiences in one's relationship to one's mother or in one's exercise of maternity, the appeal of a warm, gentle, patient, comforting mother is still powerful (if not biologically programmed) in the species. Consider the annual impact of the nativity scene or the attractiveness of a young mother holding a baby in her arms in an airport boarding lounge.

The motherhood experience, in short, is one of the most powerful "sacraments" in our lives. It can be an overwhelming experience of "grace," representing the persistence of life and, indeed, of life treated tenderly and caringly. A religious symbol that resonates with, and replicates, the "grace" experience in maternity will have perennial appeal. Hence, the presence of womanly deities (or Cosmic Personages, if you will) in most of the world's religions.

Each human being must decide whether there is a purpose and plan in the universe and in his or her life. Often the matter seems inconclusive. Yet, often, too, it appears that there is graciousness at work. The "stories of God" that resonate with the appearance of grace cannot be eradicated from the human condition. If Whoever is behind it all is kind and good—and sometimes it appears that He might not be—then there is reason to hope. If, additionally, the Whoever-is-behind-it-all loves us with the tenderness and warmth of a mother with a newborn babe, there is reason to celebrate Her love. Maternity may not be an accurate story of God, but the attractiveness of the possibility makes the "mother story" virtually irresistible and guarantees the survival of the story, no matter how much elites may think it outmoded and unfashionable.

Mary survives among young adults for the same reason that she has been an appealing "sacrament" for 1,500 years: She is too good a story of God to pass up. Whether the story she represents is too good to be true is another matter, though on this subject Catholic faith has traditionally been confident.

With that theoretical perspective, we formulated a number of hypotheses:

1. The madonna scale would correlate with positive experiences with motherhood as a child.
2. It would also correlate with positive experiences with a spouse, particularly in the most intimate aspect of the relationship—"sexual fulfillment," as our questionnaire called it.
3. Positive experiences of motherhood as a child would further correlate with sexual fulfillment in marriage and be channeled through (in whole or in part) the madonna image.
4. The madonna image would correlate at a much higher level with personal prayer than would doctrinal orthodoxy.
5. Arguing from history and from anecdotal evidence, we expected Hispanics and Poles to have the highest scores of any Catholic ethnic group on the madonna scale. Our "maternity" measure was composed of four items: a description of mother's approach to religion as "joyous," frequent Communion on the part of the mother, mother involved at least as an equal in family decision making and mother reported to have a strong religious effect on respondents. Sexual fulfillment was one of a list of dimensions of marital satisfaction ranked from "excellent" to "poor." The doctrinal orthodoxy scale was composed of such matters as papal infallibility, papal primacy, mortally sinful obligation to attend Mass every week, existence of the devil and of hell.

The first four hypotheses were all true at a statistically significant level for both men and women in the United States and Canada (women have higher scores on the madonna scale than men, but there are no important differences in the correlations or any of the other findings).

A positive experience with your mother while growing up leads to a positive experience with your spouse (the relationships are hardly strong enough to be determining). Your image of Mary is the conduit linking these two experiences. Mary connects the story of your childhood with the strory of your marriage. Small wonder that she's important.

There is no statistically significant relationship between doctrinal orthodoxy and prayer (in fact, the relationship is 0.07 in the opposite direction). But the madonna scale correlates with frequency of prayer as a 0.37 level, quite high in most social research. Images lead you to prayer, not doctrinal propositions.

On the ethnic group prediction, we were dead wrong, although the hypothesis did not flow from our theory. The Irish are most likely to score high on the scale, "significantly" higher than the rest of the population, perhaps because of their tradition of strong mother figures. . . .

Neither the Jesus scale nor the God scale correlates with experiences in either family of origin or family of procreation. Mary is the story of God that links the two aspects of "my" story.

She also plays a role in the process by which "my" story and "your" story fuse into "our" story. When husband and wife both are high on the madonna scale, it is half again as likely that they will both say that their sexual fulfillment is excellent (questionnaires were, of course, filled out independently, not that anyone would be likely to conspire on their image of Mary). Furthermore, among those families where both husband and wife are high on the madonna scale, the correlation between one spouse's description of the quality of the sexual relationship in marriage and the other's description of it becomes higher as the years together increase. If we both share a common story of God in the Mary image, we come to share more and more a common story of our own sexual relationship.

Some feminist critics of devotion to Mary, most notably Marina Warner in *Alone of All Her Sex,* have argued that the Mary symbolism traditionally was used to support a "conservative" approach to the role of women, emphasizing fulfillment in the home and family to the exclusion of all else and placing a high value on passivity and fertility. They have also contended that this tradition has "spoiled" the image for contemporary women. We are in no position to discuss the historical impact of Marian imagery on women (the data are, to put it mildly, scarce), and we will concede to writers like Marina Warner the possibility that the imagery has been spoiled for them. However, it does not seem to play any such conservative role for modern young men or women.

There is no difference between those who are high on the image and those who are low in attitudes toward birth control or divorce or abortion in the case of likely handicapped children. They marry at about the same age, have the same number of children, expect the same number of children and have the same estimates of ideal family size (low, but higher than non-Catholics). Nor does a strong Marian image impede college graduation or work after marriage or economic success or propensity to reject the idea that a working mother harms her children.

Those who are high on the madonna scale, however, are more likely to reject abortion on demand and to disapprove of living together before marriage. Only the most rigid ideologue will insist on the "conservative" nature of such responses, especially since the madonna scale also correlates with various measures of social commitment such as concern for the environment and for racial justice and emphasis on social activism as a source of life satisfaction.

Two questions are asked by colleagues with whom we have discussed our findings: Can the young people be fairly said to be "devoted" to Mary, and where did they get the story of God and Mother from if they did not learn it in the schools or C.C.D. class and are not likely to pick it up from Sunday sermons?

We do not know whether our respondents pray to the Virgin, nor do we know whether they are aware of the impact of the Mary story in their lives. We hope in further research to explore both these issues. However, it must be observed that it is the nature of preconscious imagery that it need not be conscious to have an impact, although the impact may be greater if it becomes conscious.

We presume that young people learn about Mary from their mothers. From whom else? We also speculate that they learn it very early in life as they are told the Christmas story. The woman by the crib, they are told, is God's "mommy," a proposition with which the child has no difficulty. Everyone has a mommy, doesn't he? From such an insight it is but a small jump to say that God loves like a mommy. The story is born again.

Our research, however startling, is still preliminary. Much more needs to be done to understand both the role of religious images in the lives of humans and the specific power of Mary. Obviously, Mary is an enormously useful resource for the church. Our teachers and thinkers and leaders, official and unofficial, should make much more of her than they do. They are wasting an opportunity. The waste is not going to cause Catholicism to lose the story of Mary. It's too good to be lost, ever.

We have no way of knowing how non-Catholics in general react to the Mary symbol. However, we can investigate the reactions of the non-Catholics who were married to our respondents. Rather surprisingly, Mary's image is almost as good with them as it is with Catholics: 62 percent say they are "extremely likely" to think of her as "warm," 67 percent as "gentle," 52 percent as "patient" and 56 percent as "comforting." Two-fifths of the non-Catholic spouses endorse as "extremely likely" *all four items* on the madonna scale, not quite as many as the two-thirds of the Catholic spouses, but still an astonishingly high number. There is also a correlation even among non-Catholic spouses between a high "madonna" score and frequent prayer; 52 percent of the spouses high on the madonna scale pray almost every day, as opposed to 40 percent of those who are low. (More than half of the

Methodists and Baptists endorse all four madonna items as do 37 percent of those spouses who report no religious affiliation.) Mary may actually be an asset to ecumenism instead of a liability.

APPROPRIATE IMAGES
from the oldest, if not the senior, researcher:

The broken Mary Myth cannot compete,
A loser in the symbolic marketplace,
like the mighty dollar now debased,
turned tinsel tattered in a slushy street
Rejected, Madonna, as obsolete,
Discarded in ecumenical distaste
A worn out image buried with all due haste
and quickly forgotten by a smug elite.

Yet sounds of happiness in the winter cold:
A young mother's joy shouted at the skies,
A young woman's laugh chasing dreary pain
Capricious, our universe will not stay closed,
Like the magic star Mary glows surprise,
And her hint that God is tender love remains.

—A.M.G.

Section 8 AMERICAN RELIGION

Religious practice and affiliation in the United States is the second highest in the Christian world (that is, in the countries where Christians are the majority of the population). Only Ireland has higher rates of devotion. This fact is an affront to the proponents of "secularization" theory, who dominate sociology of religion in Europe, and it embarrasses some American sociologists, who find it hard to see anything good in their own country. The three causes of "secularization" usually cited by its proponents—urbanization, industrialization, and scientific achievement and education—exist in their most advanced form in the United States, and yet Americans are insistently and stubbornly religious.

In an earlier selection, the editor of this volume suggested that the era of frantic religious populism in the last decades of the eighteenth century and the first decades of the nineteenth century may account for the continued fervor—and perhaps the continued variety—of American religion and the absence of such a phenomenon in Britain may account for lower levels of fervor in that country.

The response of many critics to this apparent fervor is to deny the "authenticity" of American religious belief and practice. American religion is a "culture religion" without content or without challenge to complacency; it is a "civil religion," a worship of America; it is a form of "Gnosticism," which has little in common with traditional Christianity; it is a "fundamentalist" religion, which supports conservative and reactionary political and social attitudes.

Perhaps all these assertions are true (though they are rarely accompanied by any evidence) and not true at the same time. In generalizations about American religion, the size and diversity of American society and of American religion is usually ignored. Yet from New England Unitarians to New York Jews to Chicago Irish Catholics to Texas Southern Baptists to California New Age cultists, America has more religious diversity than any country in the Western world. One can find almost anything one wants in American religion and then, often without traveling to far, find exactly the opposite. Almost every generalization about American religion that one cares to make is true at least of some Americans; and the opposite is true of other Americans.

Hence, the wise observer is skeptical of all generalizations that are innocent of nuance, qualification, and evidence (such as those of Robert Bellah in the selection in this section).

There are selections in this section about four major religious groups—Protestants, Catholics, Jews, and African Americans. Merely to list those four groups is to define a problem, because the last two of them are something more than merely religious groups—Jews because a case can be made that they are also an ethnic group, and African Americans because they are a racial group with many different religious components.

An editor has to choose labels under which the available material can be subsumed, but knows both that the typology implicit in the labels is inadequate and that within all four groups there is enormous diversity.

The statistical materials presented at the beginning of the section will be useful not only because they provide numbers, but perhaps even more because they reveal the astonishing diversity of American religion, a diversity that seems unlikely to go away.

Reading 27

AMERICAN DENOMINATIONALISM: THE STATISTICS—ANDREW M. GREELEY

Because the United States Census refuses to ask a religious question, we must rely on data from national surveys to present a statistical portrait of American Denominationalism. The two collections of tables and figures (based on a pooling of data from five years of NORC's General Social Survey) that begin this section are designed to present a statistical overview (as of 1992) of American denominations and their history during the last century. The first collection—"Data on American Denominations"—is a series of four sets of three tables: the first table in each set provides demographic statistics, the second gives family data, and the third provides information on the political and religious attitudes of each group. The first set is for all Americans, the second for Catholic ethnic groups, the third for African Americans, and the fourth for Hispanic Americans. Catholics are the largest denomination in America, counting a quarter of the population in their membership. A little less than two out of three Americans are Protestant. Between 2% and 3% are Jewish, 3% identify with "other" denominations, and 7% have no religious affiliation. More than half of African Americans are Baptists, only 8% are Catholic. Only 72% of American Hispanics are Catholic.

The second collection of figures is an outline of the history of Denominationalism, based on data from all the General Social Surveys (1972 to 1991) and compiled from responses to questions on the year of birth and religion in which one was raised. It presents a history of the decline of mainline Protestant Denominations ("Liberal" and "Moderate") and increase in "Fundamentalist" denominations. As Figure 8 demonstrates most of this change is the result of the decline of Methodists and the increase in Baptists.

Questions for Reflection and Discussion

1. Why has Methodist membership declined and Baptist increased?
2. Why are Hispanic Catholics only 72% of the Hispanic population?
3. Why are Catholics and Jews more likely to be Democrats than Protestants?
4. Where do Catholics and Jews tend to live?

Part 1

DATA ON AMERICAN DENOMINATIONS[1]
Andrew M. Greeley

TABLE 1
Demography of American Denominations

	Years of Education	%Professional or Manag	Annual Income*	Age	%South	%Rural**	%Metro***	%Black	%Same City since 16	N=
Catholic	12.5	29%	$30.3	44.5	19%	22%	44%	5%	43%	385
Baptist	11.4	19%	$21.9	45.4	63%	33%	34%	40%	48%	336
Method.	12.5	32%	$29.0	45.0	34%	34%	29%	16%	44%	156
Lutheran	12.7	31%	$29.7	44.8	12%	34%	32%	2%	43%	105
Presbyt.	13.6	42%	$36.6	45.0	28%	29%	34%	3%	38%	677
Episcop.	14.2	48%	$38.8	45.6	35%	20%	44%	8%	33%	373
Other Prot.	12.0	26%	$26.3	45.2	36%	32%	30%	16%	42%	232
Prot, No Denom.	12.9	31%	$29.8	45.8	24%	24%	38%	6%	32%	618
Jewish	14.7	60%	$47.9	45.9	20%	4%	80%	2%	32%	311
None	13.2	35%	$29.1	45.1	23%	20%	49%	11%	38%	113
Other	13.8	40%	$30.7	46.2	24%	15%	54%	16%	27%	310

*In 1986 Dollars (thousands)
**Less than 50,000
***Large Central City or Suburb

TABLE 2
Marriage and Children by Denominations

	%Married	%Ever Divorced	%Never Married	Siblings	Children
Catholic	55%	19%	22%	4.2	1.9
Baptist	50%	28%	18%	4.8	2.2
Method.	58%	24%	15%	3.7	2.0
Lutheran	59%	20%	15%	3.6	1.9
Presbyt.	59%	23%	15%	3.1	1.8
Episcop.	55%	27%	16%	2.8	2.6
Other Prot.	60%	25%	14%	4.5	2.3
Prot, No Denom	59%	31%	15%	3.5	1.9
Jewish	57%	18%	20%	2.3	1.6
None	43%	25%	35%	3.7	1.3
Other	50%	23%	30%	3.7	1.5

[1]The data are drawn from the General Social Survey, years 1982 to 1991, NORC, the University of Chicago.

TABLE 3
Religion and Politics by Denomination

	Attend Church 2 or 3 times a month	Pray Daily	Life After Death	%Bible Inspired	%Demo-cratic	%Conser-vative
Catholic	49%	56%	79%	26%	54%	31%
Baptist	42%	64%	77%	59%	62%	35%
Method.	38%	53%	79%	35%	48%	33%
Lutheran	45%	56%	82%	35%	41%	34%
Presbyt.	39%	53%	78%	25%	36%	34%
Episcop.	33%	50%	77%	25%	36%	39%
Other Prot.	52%	68%	77%	21%	35%	40%
Prot, No Denom	28%	51%	78%	55%	45%	42%
Jewish	16%	24%	80%	38%	38%	42%
None	3%	15%	79%	4%	71%	23%
Other	30%	57%	75%	18%	48%	23%
			81%	37%	51%	26%

TABLE 4
Demography of Catholic Ethnic Groups

	Years of Edu-cation	%Profes-sional or Manag	Annual Income*	Age	%South	%Rural**	%Metro***	%Same City since 16	N=*
Irish	13.3	35%	$33.8	46.4	16%	21%	45%	40%	548
German	12.9	32%	$30.1	44.4	13%	31%	36%	41%	507
Italian	12.2	26%	$32.4	44.4	12%	14%	52%	47%	508
Polish	12.4	26%	$31.3	44.7	14%	17%	54%	51%	292
French	12.4	31%	$32.7	44.2	14%	26%	29%	39%	217
Hispanic	11.1	17%	$20.9	44.6	39%	16%	48%	44%	473
British	13.4	37%	$34.6	45.4	22%	20%	41%	40%	256
East Europe	11.9	27%	$29.8	44.3	12%	30%	41%	49%	169
African	12.7	19%	$25.0	44.7	22%	2%	68%	46%	92
Other	12.7	31%	$30.2	45.3	22%	22%	44%	43%	797

*In 1986 Dollars (thousands)
**Less than 50,000
***Large Central City or Suburb

TABLE 5
Marriage and Children of Catholic Ethnic Groups

	%Married	%Ever Divorced	%Never Married	Siblings	Children
Irish	54%	18%	22%	3.9	2.0
German	54%	17%	23%	4.0	1.9
Italian	54%	17%	25%	3.7	1.6
Polish	60%	13%	20%	3.7	1.9
French	63%	19%	16%	3.9	2.0
Hispanic	60%	22%	20%	6.0	2.2
British	57%	23%	19%	3.4	2.2
East Europe	54%	14%	18%	3.8	2.2
African	38%	32%	29%	4.6	1.9
Other	53%	19%	22%	4.2	1.8

TABLE 6
Religion and Politics of Catholic Ethnic Groups

	Attend Church 2 or 3 times a month	Pray Daily	Life After Death	Bible Inspired	%Democratic	%Conservative
Irish	50%	59%	77%	14%	57%	26%
German	60%	57%	77%	20%	48%	36%
Italian	43%	52%	80%	26%	53%	28%
Polish	52%	53%	76%	24%	57%	41%
French	49%	61%	80%	23%	54%	25%
Hispanic	45%	62%	80%	49%	63%	25%
British	47%	52%	79%	14%	48%	36%
East Europe	58%	62%	78%	31%	56%	38%
African	39%	59%	77%	37%	78%	18%
Other	49%	53%	79%	26%	54%	32%

TABLE 7
Demography of African Americans by Denomination

	Years of Education	%Professional or Manag	Annual Income*	Age	%South	%Rural**	%Metro***	%Same City since 16	N=
Catholic	12.5	20%	$22.6	44.4	27%	5%	69%	47%	188
Baptist	11.1	14%	$17.6	44.0	54%	18%	52%	51%	1335
Method.	11.7	24%	$19.7	46.7	59%	16%	47%	48%	243
Other Prot.	11.8	17%	$20.1	45.2	46%	17%	56%	53%	468
None	12.1	21%	$19.9	41.9	32%	5%	66%	51%	125

*In 1986 Dollars (thousands)
**Less than 50,000
***Large Central City or Suburb

TABLE 8
Marriage and Children of African Americans by Denomination

	%Married	%Ever Divorced	%Never Married	Siblings	Children
Catholic	32%	26%	38%	4.9	1.8
Baptist	34%	25%	27%	5.7	2.4
Methodist	48%	23%	19%	5.5	2.2
Other Protestant	42%	28%	21%	5.6	2.4
None	23%	15%	55%	5.1	1.4

TABLE 9
Religion and Politics of African Americans by Denomination

	Attend Church	Pray Daily	Life After Death	Bible Inspired	%Democratic
Catholic	42%	57%	78%	42%	75%
Baptist	51%	72%	77%	60%	83%
Methodist	54%	77%	74%	59%	88%
Other Protestant	57%	81%	79%	62%	77%
None	6%	33%	82%	29%	68%

TABLE 10
Demography of Hispanic Americans by Denomination

	Years of Education	%Professional or Manag	Annual Income*	Age	%South	%Rural**	%Metro***	%Black	%Same City since 16	N=
Catholics	11.1	17.3	$20.9	44.1	39%	16%	48%	2%	44%	47
Baptist	12.1	17.8	$26.6	46.9	45%	29%	32%	16%	26%	31
Other Prot.	11.1	19.5	$23.8	45.4	27%	18%	41%	5%	40%	11
None	11.2	26.7	$17.9	47.7	29%	6%	69%	11%	38%	35

*In 1986 Dollars (thousands)
**Less than 50,000
***Large Central City or Suburb

TABLE 11
Marriage and Children of Hispanic Americans by Denomination

	%Married	%Ever Divorced	%Never Married	Siblings	Children
Catholic	57%	22%	20%	6.0	2.2
Baptist	61%	19%	22%	5.5	2.1
Other Protestants	64%	21%	14%	6.1	2.5
None	34%	26%	43%	5.5	1.9

TABLE 12

Religion and Politics of Hispanic Americans by Denomination

	Attend Church	Pray Daily	Life After Death	Bible Inspired	%Democratic
Catholic	45%	62%	82%	49%	63%
Baptist	53%	84%	69%	59%	48%
Other Protestants	59%	71%	81%	64%	45%
None	3%	20%	73%	14%	57%

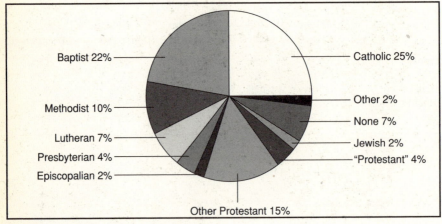

FIGURE 1. Denominational affiliation.

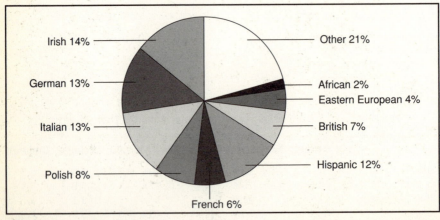

FIGURE 2. Catholic ethnics.

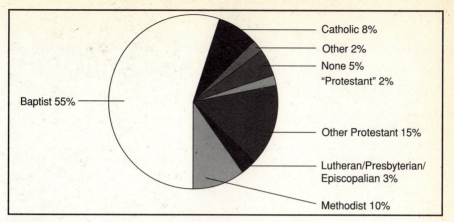

FIGURE 3. Denominational affiliation of African Americans.

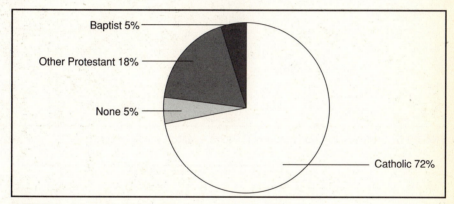

FIGURE 4. Denominational affiliation of Hispanic Americans.

Part 2

MEMBERSHIP OF DENOMINATIONS IN THE LAST HUNDRED YEARS

Andrew M. Greeley

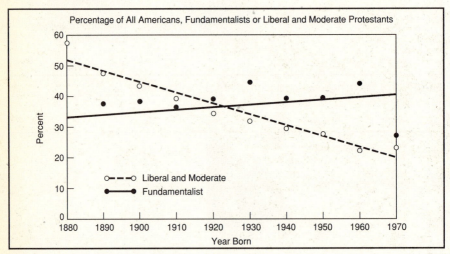

FIGURE 5. Protestant denominations (religion raised) by year of birth.

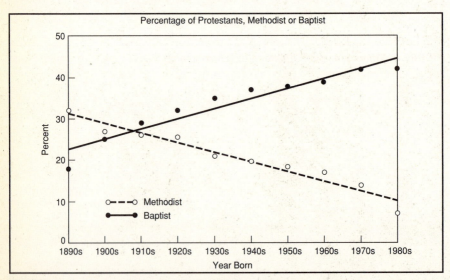

FIGURE 6. Protestant denominations (religion raised) by year of birth.

Source: The General Social Survey, years 1972 to 1991, NORC, the University of Chicago.

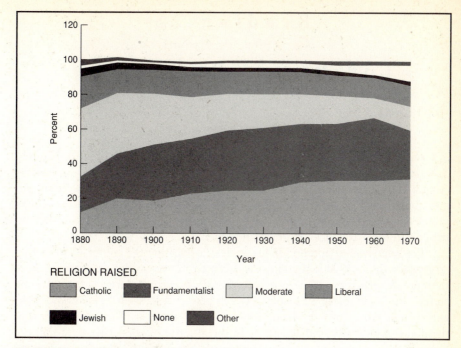

FIGURE 7. American religions by year of birth.

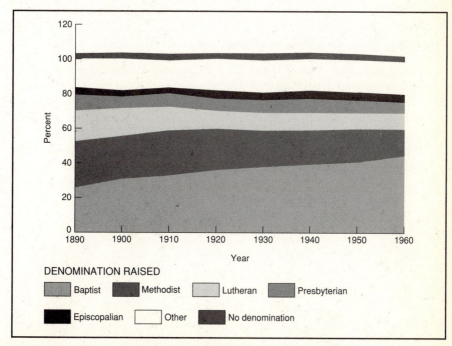

FIGURE 8. American Protestants by year of birth.

Reading 28

CIVIL RELIGION—ROBERT BELLAH

Robert Bellah—an American sociologist who pontificated about Italian religion without citing the work of Italian sociologists of religion—is severely critical about American religion in an oft-cited essay on American "civil religion," a religion of American self worship. He defines that religion as outlined in the inaugural addresses of American presidents and suggests that it contributes to the arrogance of American power.

The unanswered question in his analysis is whether the cult of America that emerges in the presidential address is accepted by Americans as anything more than political rhetoric. It did not, for example, prevent Americans from turning against the Vietnamese war, during which period Bellah wrote his essay. What exists in the words of a president does not necessarily play an important part in the minds and hearts of the citizens. In the absence of persuasive data that the "Civil Religion" does affect the attitudes and behavior of Americans, one must remain skeptical that it is an important aspect of American culture, much less a substitute for traditional religious faith.

Questions for Reflection and Discussion

1. Could one argue that it is the Civil Religion that is responsible for the increase in church affiliation in America during the last two centuries?
2. What evidence can you find that makes you believe that the Civil Religion is something more than political rhetoric? What evidence that it is only rhetoric?
3. What do you think of the methodology of arguing from a political address to the faith of a people?

CIVIL RELIGION IN AMERICA
Robert N. Bellah

While some have argued that Christianity is the national faith, and others that church and synagogue celebrate only the generalized religion of "the American Way of Life," few have realized that there actually exists alongside of and rather clearly differentiated from the churches an elaborate and well-institutionalized civil religion in America. This article argues not only that there is such a thing, but also that this religion—or perhaps better, this religious dimension—has its own seriousness and integrity and requires the same care in understanding that any other religion does.[1]

THE KENNEDY INAUGURAL

Kennedy's inaugural address of 20 January 1961 serves as an example and a clue with which to introduce this complex subject. That address began:

> We observe today not a victory of party but a celebration of freedom—symbolizing an end as well as a beginning—signifying renewal as well as change. For I have sworn before you and Almighty God the same solemn oath our forebears prescribed nearly a century and three quarters ago.
>
> The world is very different now. For man holds in his mortal hands the power to abolish all forms of human poverty and to abolish all forms of human life. And yet the same revolutionary beliefs for which our forebears fought are still at issue around the globe—the belief that the rights of man come not from the generosity of the state but from the hand of God.

And it concluded:

> Finally, whether you are citizens of America or of the world, ask of us the same high standards of strength and sacrifice that we shall ask of you. With a good conscience our only sure reward, with history the final judge of our deeds, let us go forth to lead the land we love, asking His blessing and His help, but knowing here on earth God's work must truly be our own.

These are the three places in this brief address in which Kennedy mentioned the name of God. If we could understand why he mentioned God, the way in which he did it, and what he meant to say in those three references, we would understand much about American civil religion. But this is not a simple or obvious task, and American students of religion would probably differ widely in their interpretation of these passages.

Let us consider first the placing of the three references. They occur in the two opening paragraphs and in the closing paragraph, thus providing a sort of

Source: *Daedalus,* Journal of the American Academy of Arts and Sciences, Winter, 1967, Cambridge, Massachusetts.

frame for the more concrete remarks that form the middle part of the speech. Looking beyond this particular speech, we would find that similar references to God are almost invariably to be found in the pronouncements of American presidents on solemn occasions, though usually not in the working messages that the president sends to Congress on various concrete issues. How, then, are we to interpret this placing of references to God?

It might be argued that the passages quoted reveal the essentially irrelevant role of religion in the very secular society that is America. The placing of the references in this speech as well as in public life generally indicates that religion has "only a ceremonial significance"; it gets only a sentimental nod which serves largely to placate the more unenlightened members of the community, before a discussion of the really serious business with which religion has nothing whatever to do. A cynical observer might even say that an American president has to mention God or risk losing votes. A semblance of piety is merely one of the unwritten qualifications for the office, a bit more traditional than but not essentially different from the present-day requirement of a pleasing television personality.

But we know enough about the function of ceremonial and ritual in various societies to make us suspicious of dismissing something as unimportant because it is "only a ritual." What people say on solemn occasions need not be taken at face value, but it is often indicative of deep-seated values and commitments that are not made explicit in the course of everyday life. Following this line of argument, it is worth considering whether the very special placing of the references to God in Kennedy's address may not reveal something rather important and serious about religion in American life.

It might be countered that the very way in which Kennedy made his references reveals the essentially vestigial place of religion today. He did not refer to any religion in particular. He did not refer to Jesus Christ, or to Moses, or to the Christian church; certainly he did not refer to the Catholic Church. In fact, his only reference was to the concept of God, a word which almost all Americans can accept but which means so many different things to so many different people that it is almost an empty sign. Is this not just another indication that in America religion is considered vaguely to be a good thing, but that people care so little about it that it has lost any content whatever? Isn't Eisenhower reported to have said, "Our government makes no sense unless it is founded in a deeply felt religious faith—and I don't care what it is,"[2] and isn't that a complete negation of any real religion?

These questions are worth pursuing because they raise the issue of how civil religion relates to the political society, on the one hand, and to private religious organization, on the other. President Kennedy was a Christian, more specifically a Catholic Christian. Thus, his general references to God do not mean that he lacked a specific religious commitment. But why, then, did he not include some remark to the effect that Christ is the Lord of the world or some indication of respect for the Catholic Church? He did not because these are matters of his own private religious belief and of his relation to his own particular church; they are not matters relevant in any direct way to the conduct of his public office. Others with different religious views and commitments to different churches or denominations are equally qualified participants in the political process. The principle of separation of church and state guarantees the freedom of religious belief and association, but at the same time clearly segregates the religious sphere, which is considered to be essentially private, from the political one.

Considering the separation of church and state, how is a president justified in using the word *God* at all? The answer is that the separation of church and state has not denied the political realm a religious dimension. Although matters of personal religious belief, worship, and association are considered to be strictly private affairs, there are, at the same time, certain common elements of religious orientation that the great majority of Americans share. These have played a crucial role in the development of American institutions and still provide a religious dimension for the whole fabric of American life, including the political sphere. This public religious dimension is expressed in a set of beliefs, symbols, and rituals that I am calling the American civil religion. The inauguration of a president is an important ceremonial event in this religion. It reaffirms, among other things, the religious legitimation of the highest political authority.

Let us look more closely at what Kennedy actually said. First he said, "I have sworn before you and Almighty God the same solemn oath our forebears prescribed nearly a century and three quarters ago." The oath is the oath of office, including the acceptance of the obligation to uphold the Constitution. He swears it before the people (you) and God. Beyond the Constitution, then, the president's obligation extends not only to the people but to God. In American political theory, sovereignty rests, of course, with the people, but implicitly, and often explicitly, the ultimate sovereignty has been attributed to God. This is the meaning of the motto, "In God we trust," as well as the inclusion of the phrase "under God" in the pledge to the flag. What difference does it make that sovereignty belongs to God? Though the will of the people as expressed in majority vote is carefully institutionalized as the operative source of political authority, it is deprived of an ultimate significance. The will of the people is not itself the criterion of right and wrong. There is a higher criterion in terms of which this will can be judged; it is possible that the people may be wrong. The president's obligation extends to the higher criterion.

When Kennedy says that "the rights of man come not from the generosity of the state but from the hand of God," he is stressing this point again. It does not matter whether the state is the expression of the will of an autocratic monarch or of the "people"; the rights of man are more basic than any political structure and provide a point of revolutionary leverage from which any state structure may be radically altered. That is the basis for his reassertion of the revolutionary significance of America.

But the religious dimension in political life as recognized by Kennedy not only provides a grounding for the rights of man which makes any form of political absolutism illegitimate, it also provides a transcendent goal for the political process. This is implied in his final words that "here on earth God's work must truly be our own." What he means here is, I think, more clearly spelled out in a previous paragraph, the wording of which, incidentally, has a distinctly Biblical ring:

> Now the trumpet summons us again—not as a call to bear arms, though arms we need—not as a call to battle, though embattled we are—but a call to bear the burden of a long twilight struggle, year in and year out, "rejoicing in hope, patient in tribulation"—a struggle against the common enemies of man: tyranny, poverty, disease and war itself.

The whole address can be understood as only the most recent statement of a theme that lies very deep in the American tradition, namely the obligation, both collective and individual, to carry out God's will on earth. This was the motivating spirit of those who founded America, and it has been present in every generation since. Just below the surface throughout Kennedy's inaugural address, it becomes explicit in the closing statement that God's work must be our own. That this very activist and non-contemplative conception of the fundamental religious obligation, which has been historically associated with the Protestant position, should be enunciated so clearly in the first major statement of the first Catholic president seems to underline how deeply established it is in the American outlook. Let us now consider the form and history of the civil religious tradition in which Kennedy was speaking.

THE IDEA OF CIVIL RELIGION

The phrase *civil religion* is, of course, Rousseau's. In Chapter 8, Book 4, of *The Social Contract,* he outlines the simple dogmas of the civil religion: the existence of God, the life to come, the reward of virtue and the punishment of vice, and the exclusion of religious intolerance. All other religious opinions are outside the cognizance of the state and may be freely held by citizens. While the phrase *civil religion* was not used, to the best of my knowledge, by the founding fathers, and I am certainly not arguing for the particular influence of Rousseau, it is clear that similar ideas, as part of the cultural climate of the late eighteenth century, were to be found among the Americans. For example, Franklin writes in his autobiography:

> I never was without some religious principles. I never doubted, for instance, the existence of the Deity; that he made the world and govern'd it by his Providence; that the most acceptable service of God was the doing of good to men; that our souls are immortal; and that all crime will be punished, and virtue rewarded either here or hereafter. These I esteemed the essentials of every religion; and, being to be found in all the religions we had in our country, I respected them all, tho' with different degrees of respect, as I found them more or less mix'd with other articles, which, without any tendency to inspire, promote or confirm morality, serv'd principally to divide us, and make us unfriendly to one another.

It is easy to dispose of this sort of position as essentially utilitarian in relation to religion. In Washington's Farewell Address (though the words may be Hamilton's) the utilitarian aspect is quite explicit:

> Of all the dispositions and habits which lead to political prosperity, Religion and Morality are indispensable supports. In vain would that man claim the tribute of Patriotism, who should labour to subvert these great Pillars of human happiness, these firmest props of the duties of men and citizens. The mere politician, equally with the pious man ought to respect and cherish them. A volume could not trace all their connections with private and public felicity. Let it simply be asked where is the security for property, for reputation, for life, if the sense of religious obligation *desert* the oaths, which are the instruments of investigation in Courts of Justice? And let us with caution indulge the supposition, that morality can be maintained without religion. Whatever may be conceded to the influence of refined education on minds of peculiar structure, reason and experience both forbid us to expect that National morality can prevail in exclusion of religious principle.

But there is every reason to believe that religion, particularly the idea of God, played a constitutive role in the thought of the early American statesmen.

Kennedy's inaugural pointed to the religious aspect of the Declaration of Independence, and it might be well to look at that document a bit more closely. There are four references to God. The first speaks of the "Laws of Nature and Nature's God" which entitle any people to be independent. The second is the famous statement that all men "are endowed by their Creator with certain inalienable Rights." Here Jefferson is locating the fundamental legitimacy of the new nation in a conception of "higher law" that is itself based on both classical natural law and Biblical religion. The third is an appeal to "the Supreme Judge of the world for the rectitude of our intentions," and the last indicates "a firm reliance on the protection of divine Providence." In these last two references, a Biblical God of history who stands in judgment over the world is indicated.

The intimate relation of these religious notions with the self-conception of the new republic is indicated by the frequency of their appearance in early official documents. For example, we find in Washington's first inaugural address of 30 April 1789:

> It would be peculiarly improper to omit in this first official act my fervent supplications to that Almighty Being who rules over the universe, who presides in the councils of nations, and whose providential aids can supply every defect, that His benediction may consecrate to the liberties and happiness of the people of the United States a Government instituted by themselves for these essential purposes, and may enable every instrument employed in its administration to execute with success the functions allotted to his charge.
>
> No people can be bound to acknowledge and adore the Invisible Hand which conducts the affairs of man more than those of the United States. Every step by which we have advanced to the character of an independent nation seems to have been distinguished by some token of providential agency. . . .
>
> The propitious smiles of Heaven can never be expected on a nation that disregards the eternal rules of order and right which Heaven itself has ordained. . . . The preservation of the sacred fire of liberty and the destiny of the republican model of government are justly considered, perhaps, as *deeply*, as *finally*, staked on the experiment intrusted to the hands of the American people.

Nor did these religious sentiments remain merely the personal expression of the president. At the request of both Houses of Congress, Washington proclaimed on October 3 of that same first year as president that November 26 should be "a day of public thanksgiving and prayer," the first Thanksgiving Day under the Constitution.

The words and acts of the founding fathers, especially the first few presidents, shaped the form and tone of the civil religion as it has been maintained ever since. Though much is selectively derived from Christianity, this religion is clearly not itself Christianity. For one thing, neither Washington nor Adams nor Jefferson mentions Christ in his inaugural address; nor do any of the subsequent presidents, although not one of them fails to mention God.[3] The God of the civil religion is not only rather "unitarian," he is also on the austere side, much more related to order, law, and right than to salvation and love. Even though he is somewhat deist in cast, he is by no means simply a watchmaker God. He is actively interested and involved in history, with a special concern for America. Here the analogy has much less to do with natural law than with ancient Israel; the equation of America with Israel in the idea of the "American Israel" is not infrequent.[4] What was implicit in the words of Washington already quoted becomes explicit in Jefferson's second inaugural when he said: "I shall need, too, the favor of that Being in whose hands we are, who led our fathers, as Israel of old, from their native land and planted them in a country flowing with all the necessaries and comforts of life." Europe is Egypt; America, the promised land. God has led his people to establish a new sort of social order that shall be a light unto all the nations.[5]

This theme, too, has been a continuous one in the civil religion. We have already alluded to it in the case of the Kennedy inaugural. We find it again in President Johnson's inaugural address:

> They came here—the exile and the stranger, brave but frightened—to find a place where a man could be his own man. They made a covenant with this land. Conceived in justice, written in liberty, bound in union, it was meant one day to inspire the hopes of all mankind; and it binds us still. If we keep its terms, we shall flourish.

What we have, then, from the earliest years of the republic is a collection of beliefs, symbols, and rituals with respect to sacred things and institutionalized in a collectivity. This religion—there seems no other word for it—while not antithetical to and indeed sharing much in common with Christianity, was neither sectarian nor in any specific sense Christian. At a time when the society was overwhelmingly Christian, it seems unlikely that this lack of Christian reference was meant to spare the feelings of the tiny non-Christian minority. Rather, the civil religion expressed what those who set the precedents felt was appropriate under the circumstances. It reflected their private as well as public views. Nor was the civil religion simply "religion in general." While generality was undoubtedly seen as a virtue by some, as in the quotation from Franklin above, the civil religion was specific enough when it came to the topic of America. Precisely because of this specificity, the civil religion was saved from empty formalism and served as a genuine vehicle of national religious self-understanding.

But the civil religion was not, in the minds of Franklin, Washington, Jefferson, or other leaders, with the exception of a few radicals like Tom Paine, ever felt to be a substitute for Christianity. There was an implicit but quite clear division of function between the civil religion and Christianity. Under the doctrine of religious liberty, an exceptionally wide sphere of personal piety and voluntary social action was left to the churches. But the churches were neither to control the state nor to be controlled by it. The national magistrate, whatever his private religious views, operates under the rubrics of the civil religion as long as he is in his official capacity, as we have already seen in the case of Kennedy. This accommodation was undoubtedly the product of a particular historical moment and of a cultural background dominated by Protestantism of several varieties and by the Enlightenment, but it has survived despite subsequent changes in the cultural and religious climate.

CIVIL WAR AND CIVIL RELIGION

Until the Civil War, the American civil religion focused above all on the event of the Revolution, which was seen as the final act of the Exodus from the old lands across the waters. The Declaration of Independence and the Constitution were the sacred scriptures and Washington the divinely appointed Moses who led his people out of the hands of tyranny. The Civil War, which Sidney Mead calls "the center of American history,"[6] was the second great event that involved the national self-understanding so deeply as to require expression in the civil religion. In 1835, Tocqueville wrote that the American republic had never really been tried, that victory in the Revolutionary War was more the result of British preoccupation elsewhere and the presence of a powerful ally than of any great military success of the Americans. But in 1861 the time of testing had indeed come. Not only did the Civil War have the tragic intensity of fratricidal strife, but it was one of the bloodiest wars of the nineteenth century; the loss of life was far greater than any previously suffered by Americans.

The Civil War raised the deepest questions of national meaning. The man who not only formulated but in his own person embodied its meaning for Americans was Abraham Lincoln. For him the issue was not in the first instance slavery but "whether that nation, or any nation so conceived, and so dedicated, can long endure." He had said in Independence Hall in Philadelphia on 22 February 1861:

> All the political sentiments I entertain have been drawn, so far as I have been able to draw them, from the sentiments which originated in and were given to the world from this Hall. I have never had a feeling, politically, that did not spring from the sentiments embodied in the Declaration of Independence.[7]

The phrases of Jefferson constantly echo in Lincoln's speeches. His task was, first of all, to save the Union—not for America alone but for the meaning of America to the whole world so unforgettably etched in the last phrase of the Gettysburg Address.

But inevitably the issue of slavery as the deeper cause of the conflict had to be faced. In the second inaugural, Lincoln related slavery and the war in an ultimate perspective:

> If we shall suppose that American slavery is one of those offenses which, in the providence of God, must needs come, but which, having continued through His appointed time, He now wills to remove, and that He gives to both North and South this terrible war as the woe due to those by whom the offense came, shall we discern therein any departure from those divine attributes which the believers in a living God always ascribe to Him? Fondly do we hope, fervently do we pray, that this mighty scourge of war may speedily pass away. Yet, if God wills that it continue until all the wealth piled by the bondsman's two hundred and fifty years of unrequited toil shall be sunk, and until every drop of blood drawn with the lash shall be paid by another drawn with the sword, as was said three thousand years ago, so still it must be said "the judgements of the Lord are true and righteous altogether."

But he closes on a note if not of redemption then of reconciliation—"With malice toward none, with charity for all. . . ."

With the Civil War, a new theme of death, sacrifice, and rebirth enters the civil religion. It is symbolized in the life and death of Lincoln. Nowhere is it stated more vividly than in the Gettysburg Address, itself part of the Lincolnian "New Testament" among the civil scriptures. Robert Lowell has recently pointed out the "insistent use of birth images" in this speech explicitly devoted to "these honored dead": "brought forth," "conceived," "created," "a new birth of freedom." He goes on to say:

> The Gettysburg Address is a symbolic and sacramental act. Its verbal quality is resonance combined with a logical, matter of fact, prosaic brevity. . . . In his words, Lincoln symbolically died, just as the Union soldiers really died—and as he himself was soon really to die. By his words, he gave the field of battle a symbolic significance that it had lacked. For us and our country, he left Jefferson's ideals of freedom and equality joined to the Christian sacrificial act of death and rebirth. I believe this is a meaning that goes beyond sect or religion and beyond peace and war, and is now part of our lives as a challenge, obstacle and hope.[8]

Lowell is certainly right in pointing out the Christian quality of the symbolism here, but he is also right in quickly disavowing any sectarian implication. The earlier symbolism of the civil religion had been Hebraic without being in any specific sense Jewish. The Gettysburg symbolism (". . . those who here gave their lives, that that nation might live") is Christian without having anything to do with the Christian church.

The symbolic equation of Lincoln with Jesus was made relatively early. Herndon, who had been Lincoln's law partner, wrote:

> For fifty years God rolled Abraham Lincoln through his fiery furnace. He did it to try Abraham and to purify him for his purposes. This made Mr. Lincoln humble, tender, forebearing, sympathetic to suffering, kind, sensitive, tolerant; broadening, deepening and widening his whole nature; making him the noblest

and loveliest character since Jesus Christ. . . . I believe that Lincoln was God's chosen one.[9]

With the Christian archetype in the background, Lincoln, "our martyred president," was linked to the war dead, those who "gave the last full measure of devotion." The theme of sacrifice was indelibly written into the civil religion.

The new symbolism soon found both physical and ritualistic expression. The great number of the war dead required the establishment of a number of national cemeteries. Of these, the Gettysburg National Cemetery, which Lincoln's famous address served to dedicate, has been overshadowed only by the Arlington National Cemetery. Begun somewhat vindictively on the Lee estate across the river from Washington, partly with the end that the Lee family could never reclaim it,[10] it has subsequently become the most hallowed monument of the civil religion. Not only was a section set aside for the Confederate dead, but it has received the dead of each succeeding American war. It is the site of the one important new symbol to come out of World War I, the Tomb of the Unknown Soldier; more recently it has become the site of the tomb of another martyred president and its symbolic eternal flame.

Memorial Day, which grew out of the Civil War, gave ritual expression to the themes we have been discussing. As Lloyd Warner has so brilliantly analyzed it, the Memorial Day observance, especially in the towns and smaller cities of America, is a major event for the whole community involving a rededication to the martyred dead, to the spirit of sacrifice, and to the American vision.[11] Just as Thanksgiving Day, which incidentally was securely institutionalized as an annual national holiday only under the presidency of Lincoln, serves to integrate the family into the civil religion, so Memorial Day has acted to integrate the local community into the national cult. Together with the less overtly religious Fourth of July and the more minor celebrations of Veterans Day and the birthdays of Washington and Lincoln, these two holidays provide an annual ritual calendar for the civil religion. The public-school system serves as a particularly important context for the cultic celebration of the civil rituals.

In reifying and giving a name to something that, though pervasive enough when you look at it, has gone on only semiconsciously, there is risk of severely distorting the data. But the reification and the naming have already begun. The religious critics of "religion in general," or of the "religion of the 'American Way of Life,'" or of "American Shinto" have really been talking about the civil religion. As usual in religious polemic, they take as criteria the best in their own religious tradition and as typical the worst in the tradition of the civil religion. Against these critics, I would argue that the civil religion at its best is a genuine apprehension of universal and transcendent religious reality as seen in or, one could almost say, as revealed through the experience of the American people. Like all religions, it has suffered various deformations and demonic distortions. At its best, it has neither been so general that it has lacked incisive relevance to the American scene nor so particular that it has placed American society above universal human values. I am not at all convinced that the leaders of the churches have consistently represented a higher level of religious insight than the spokesmen of the civil religion. Reinhold Niebuhr has this to say of Lincoln, who never joined a church and who certainly represents civil religion at its best:

> An analysis of the religion of Abraham Lincoln in the context of the traditional religion of his time and place and of its polemical use on the slavery issue, which corrupted religious life in the days before and during the Civil War, must lead to the conclusion that Lincoln's religious convictions were superior in depth and purity to those, not only of the political leaders of his day, but of the religious leaders of the era.[12]

Perhaps the real animus of the religious critics has been not so much against the civil religion in itself but against its pervasive and dominating influence within the sphere of church religion. As S. M. Lipset has recently shown, American religion at least since the early nineteenth century has been predominantly activist, moralistic, and social rather than contemplative, theological, of innerly spiritual.[13] Tocqueville spoke of American church religion as "a political institution which powerfully contributes to the maintenance of a democratic republic among the Americans"[14] by supplying a strong moral consensus amidst continuous political change. Henry Bargy in 1902 spoke of American church religion as "la poésie du civisme."[15]

It is certainly true that the relation between religion and politics in America has been singularly smooth. This is in large part due to the dominant tradition. As Tocqueville wrote:

> The greatest part of British America was peopled by men who, after having shaken off the authority of the Pope, acknowledged no other religious supremacy: they brought with them into the New World a form of Christianity which I cannot better describe than by styling it a democratic and republican religion.[16]

The churches opposed neither the Revolution nor the establishment of democratic institutions. Even when some of them opposed the full institutionalization of religious liberty, they accepted the final outcome with good grace and without nostalgia for an *ancien régime*. The American civil religion was never anticlerical or militantly secular. On the contrary, it borrowed selectively from the religious tradition in such a way that the average American saw no conflict between the two. In this way, the civil religion was able to build up without any bitter struggle with the church powerful symbols of national solidarity and to mobilize deep levels of personal motivation for the attainment of national goals.

Such an achievement is by no means to be taken for granted. It would seem that the problem of a civil religion is quite general in modern societies and that the way it is solved or not solved will have repercussions in many spheres. One needs only to think of France to see how differently things can go. The French Revolution was anticlerical to the core and attempted to set up an anti-Christian civil religion. Throughout modern French history, the chasm between traditional Catholic symbols and the symbolism of 1789 has been immense.

American civil religion is still very much alive. [In 1963] we participated in a vivid reenactment of the sacrifice theme in connection with the funeral of our assassinated president. The American Israel theme is clearly behind both

Kennedy's New Frontier and Johnson's Great Society. Let me give just one recent illustration of how the civil religion serves to mobilize support for the attainment of national goals. On 15 March 1965 President Johnson went before Congress to ask for a strong voting-rights bill. Early in the speech he said:

> Rarely are we met with the challenge, not to our growth or abundance, or our welfare or our security—but rather to the values and the purposes and the meaning of our beloved nation.
>
> The issue of equal rights for American Negroes is such an issue. And should we defeat every enemy, and should we double our wealth and conquer the stars and still be unequal to this issue, then we will have failed as a people and as a nation.
>
> For with a country as with a person, "What is a man profited, if he shall gain the whole world, and lose his own soul?"

And in conclusion he said:

> Above the pyramid on the great seal of the United States it says in Latin, "God has favored our undertaking."
>
> God will not favor everything that we do. It is rather our duty to divine his will. I cannot help but believe that He truly understands and that He really favors the undertaking that we begin here tonight.[17]

The civil religion has not always been invoked in favor of worthy causes. On the domestic scene, an American-Legion type of ideology that fuses God, country, and flag has been used to attack nonconformist and liberal ideas and groups of all kinds. Still, it has been difficult to use the words of Jefferson and Lincoln to support special interests and undermine personal freedom. The defenders of slavery before the Civil War came to reject the thinking of the Declaration of Independence. Some of the most consistent of them turned against not only Jeffersonian democracy but Reformation religion; they dreamed of a South dominated by medieval chivalry and divine-right monarchy.[18] For all the overt religiosity of the radical right today, their relation to the civil religious consensus is tenuous, as when the John Birch Society attacks the central American symbol of Democracy itself.

With respect to America's role in the world, the dangers of distortion are greater and the built-in safeguards of the tradition weaker. The theme of the American Israel was used, almost from the beginning, as a justification for the shameful treatment of the Indians so characteristic of our history. It can be overtly or implicitly linked to the idea of manifest destiny which has been used to legitimate several adventures in imperialism since the early nineteenth century. Never has the danger been greater than today. The issue is not so much one of imperial expansion, of which we are accused, as of the tendency to assimilate all governments or parties in the world which support our immediate policies or call upon our help by invoking the notion of free institutions and democratic values. Those nations that are for the moment "on our side" become "the free world." A repressive and unstable military dictatorship in South Viet-Nam becomes "the free people of South Viet-Nam and their government." It is then part of the role of America as the New Jerusalem and "the last best hope on earth" to defend such governments with treasure and eventually with blood. When our soldiers are actually dying, it becomes possible to consecrate the struggle further by invoking the great theme of sacrifice. For the majority of the American people who are unable to judge whether the people in South Viet-Nam (or wherever) are "free like us," such arguments are convincing. Fortunately President Johnson has been less ready to assert that "God has favored our undertaking" in the case of Viet-Nam than with respect to civil rights. But others are not so hesitant. The civil religion has exercised long-term pressure for the humane solution of our greatest domestic problem, the treatment of the Negro American. It remains to be seen how relevant it can become for our role in the world at large, and whether we can effectually stand for "the revolutionary beliefs for which our forebears fought," in John F. Kennedy's words.

The civil religion is obviously involved in the most pressing moral and political issues of the day. But it is also caught in another kind of crisis, theoretical and theological, of which it is at the moment largely unaware. "God" has clearly been a central symbol in the civil religion from the beginning and remains so today. This symbol is just as central to the civil religion as it is to Judaism or Christianity. In the late eighteenth century this posed no problem; even Tom Paine, contrary to his detractors, was not an atheist. From left to right and regardless of church or sect, all could accept the idea of God. But today, as even *Time* has recognized, the meaning of the word *God* is by no means so clear or so obvious. There is no formal creed in the civil religion. We have had a Catholic president; it is conceivable that we could have a Jewish one. But could we have an agnostic president? Could a man with conscientious scruples about using the word *God* the way Kennedy and Johnson have used it be elected chief magistrate of our country? If the whole God symbolism requires reformulation, there will be obvious consequences for the civil religion, consequences perhaps of liberal alienation and of fundamentalist ossification that have not so far been prominent in this realm. The civil religion has been a point of articulation between the profoundest commitments of the Western religious and philosophical tradition and the common beliefs of ordinary Americans. It is not too soon to consider how the deepening theological crisis may affect the future of this articulation.

THE THIRD TIME OF TRIAL

In conclusion it may be worthwhile to relate the civil religion to the most serious situation that we as Americans now face, what I call the third time of trial. The first time of trial had to do with the question of independence, whether we should or could run our own affairs in our own way. The second time of trial was over the issue of slavery, which in turn was only the most salient aspect of the more general problem of the full institutionalization of democracy within our country. This second problem we are still far from solving though we have some notable successes to our credit. But we have been overtaken by a third great problem which has led to a third great crisis, in the midst of which we stand. This is the problem of responsible action in a revolutionary world, a world seeking to attain many of the things, material and spiritual, that we have already attained. Americans have, from the beginning, been aware of the responsibility and the significance our republican experiment has for the whole world. The first internal political polarization in the new nation had to do with our attitude toward the French Revolution. But we were small and weak then, and "foreign entanglements" seemed to threaten our very survival. During the last century, our relevance for the world was not forgotten, but our role was seen as purely exemplary. Our democratic republic rebuked tyranny by merely existing. Just after World War I we were on the brink of taking a different role in the world, but once again we turned our back.

Since World War II the old pattern has become impossible. Every president since Roosevelt has been groping toward a new pattern of action in the world, one that would be consonant with our power and our responsibilities. For Truman and for the period dominated by John Foster Dulles that pattern was seen to be the great Manichaean confrontation of East and West, the confrontation of democracy and "the false philosophy of Communism" that provided the structure of Truman's inaugural address. But with the last years of Eisenhower and with the successive two presidents, the pattern began to shift. The great problems came to be seen as caused not solely by the evil intent of any one group of men, but as stemming from much more complex and multiple sources. For Kennedy, it was not so much a struggle against particular men as against "the common enemies of man: tyranny, poverty, disease and war itself."

But in the midst of this trend toward a less primitive conception of ourselves and our world, we have somehow, without anyone really intending it, stumbled into a military confrontation where we have come to feel that our honor is at stake. We have in a moment of uncertainty been tempted to rely on our overwhelming physical power rather than on our intelligence, and we have, in part, succumbed to this temptation. Bewildered and unnerved when our terrible power fails to bring immediate success, we are at the edge of a chasm the depth of which no man knows.

I cannot help but think of Robinson Jeffers, whose poetry seems more apt now than when it was written, when he said:

> Unhappy country, what wings you have! . . .
> Weep (it is frequent in human affairs), weep for the terrible magnificence
>   of the means,
> The ridiculous incompetence of the reasons, the bloody and shabby
> Pathos of the result.

But as so often before in similar times, we have a man of prophetic stature, without the bitterness or misanthropy of Jeffers, who, as Lincoln before him, calls this nation to its judgment:

When a nation is very powerful but lacking in self-confidence, it is likely to behave in a manner that is dangerous both to itself and to others.

Gradually but unmistakably, America is succumbing to that arrogance of power which has afflicted, weakened and in some cases destroyed great nations in the past.

If the war goes on and expands, if that fatal process continues to accelerate until America becomes what it is not now and never has been, a seeker after unlimited power and empire, then Vietnam will have had a mighty and tragic fallout indeed.

I do not believe that will happen. I am very apprehensive but I still remain hopeful, and even confident, that America, with its humane and democratic traditions, will find the wisdom to match its power.[19]

Without an awareness that our nation stands under higher judgment, the tradition of the civil religion would be dangerous indeed. Fortunately, the prophetic voices have never been lacking. Our present situation brings to mind the Mexican-American war that Lincoln, among so many others, opposed. The spirit of civil disobedience that is alive today in the civil rights movement and the opposition to the Viet-Nam war was already clearly outlined by Henry David Thoreau when he wrote, "If the law is of such a nature that it requires you to be an agent of injustice to another, then I say, break the law." Thoreau's words, "I would remind my countrymen that they are men first, and Americans at a late and convenient hour,"[20] provide an essential standard for any adequate thought and action in our third time of trial. As Americans, we have been well favored in the world, but it is as men that we will be judged.

Out of the first and second times of trial have come, as we have seen, the major symbols of the American civil religion. There seems little doubt that a successful negotiation of this third time of trial—the attainment of some kind of viable and coherent world order—would precipitate a major new set of symbolic forms. So far the flickering flame of the United Nations burns too low to be the focus of a cult, but the emergence of a genuine transnational sovereignty would certainly change this. It would necessitate the incorporation of vital international symbolism into our civil religion, or, perhaps a better way of putting it, it would result in American civil religion becoming simply one part of a new civil religion of the world. It is useless to speculate on the form such a civil religion might take, though it obviously would draw on religious traditions beyond the sphere of Biblical religion alone. Fortunately, since the American civil religion is not the worship of the American nation but an understanding of the American experience in the light of ultimate and universal reality, the reorganization entailed by such a new situation need not disrupt the American civil religion's continuity. A world civil religion could be accepted as a fulfillment and not a denial of American civil religion. Indeed, such an outcome has been the eschatological hope of American civil religion from the beginning. To deny such an outcome would be to deny the meaning of America itself.

Behind the civil religion at every point lie Biblical archetypes: Exodus, Chosen People, Promised Land, New Jerusalem, Sacrificial Death and Rebirth. But it is also genuinely American and genuinely new. It has its own prophets and its own martyrs, its own sacred events and sacred places, its own solemn rituals and symbols. It is concerned that America be a society as perfectly in accord with the will of God as men can make it, and a light to all the nations.

It has often been used and is being used today as a cloak for petty interests and ugly passions. It is in need—as is any living faith—of continual reformation, of being measured by universal standards. But it is not evident that it is incapable of growth and new insight.

It does not make any decision for us. It does not remove us from moral ambiguity, from being, in Lincoln's fine phrase, an "almost chosen people." But it is a heritage of moral and religious experience from which we still have much to learn as we formulate the decisions that lie ahead.

Notes

1. Why something so obvious should have escaped serious analytical attention is in itself an interesting problem. Part of the reason is probably the controversial nature of the subject. From the earliest years of the nineteenth century, conservative religious and political groups have argued that Christianity is, in fact, the national religion. Some of them have from time to time and as recently as the 1950's proposed constitutional amendments that would explicitly recognize the sovereignty of Christ. In defending the doctrine of separation of church and state, opponents of such groups have denied that the national polity has, intrinsically, anything to do with religion at all. The moderates on this issue have insisted that the American state has taken a permissive and indeed supportive attitude toward religious groups (tax exemption, et cetera), thus favoring religion but still missing the positive institutionalization with which I am concerned. But part of the reason this issue has been left in obscurity is certainly due to the peculiarly Western concept of "religion" as denoting a single type of collectivity of which an individual can be a member of one and only one at a time. The Durkheimian notion that every group has a religious dimension, which would be seen as obvious in southern or eastern Asia, is foreign to us. This obscures the recognition of such dimensions in our society.
2. Quoted in Will Herberg, *Protestant-Catholic-Jew* (New York, 1955), p. 97.
3. God is mentioned or referred to in all inaugural addresses but Washington's second, which is a very brief (two paragraphs) and perfunctory acknowledgment. It is not without interest that the actual word *God* does not appear until Monroe's second inaugural, 5 March 1821. In his first inaugural, Washington refers to God as "that Almighty Being who rules the universe," "Great Author of every public and private good," "Invisible Hand," and "benign Parent of the Human Race." John Adams refers to God as "Providence," "Being who is supreme over all," "Patron of Order," "Foundation of Justice," and "Protector in all ages of the world of virtuous liberty." Jefferson speaks of "that Infinite Power which rules the destinies of the universe," and "that Being in whose hands we are." Madison speaks of "that Almighty Being whose power regulates the destiny of nations," and "Heaven." Monroe uses "Providence" and "the Almighty" in his first inaugural and finally "Almighty God" in his second. See *Inaugural Addresses of the Presidents of the United States from George Washington 1789 to Harry S Truman 1949.* 82nd Congress, 2d Session, House Document No. 540, 1952.
4. For example, Abiel Abbot, pastor of the First Church in Haverhill, Massachusetts, delivered a Thanksgiving sermon in 1799, *Traits of Resemblance in the People of the United States of America to Ancient Israel,* in which he said, "It has been often remarked that the people of the United States come nearer to a parallel with

Ancient Israel, than any other nation upon the globe. Hence 'Our American Israel' is a term frequently used; and common consent allows it apt and proper." Cited in Hans Kohn, *The Idea of Nationalism* (New York, 1961), p. 665.

5. That the Mosaic analogy was present in the minds of leaders at the very moment of the birth of the republic is indicated in the designs proposed by Franklin and Jefferson for a seal of the United States of America. Together with Adams, they formed a committee of three delegated by the Continental Congress on July 4, 1776, to draw up the new device. "Franklin proposed as the device Moses lifting up his wand and dividing the Red Sea while Pharoah was overwhelmed by its waters, with the motto 'Rebellion to tyrants is obedience to God.' Jefferson proposed the children of Israel in the wilderness 'led by a cloud by day and a pillar of fire by night.'" Anson Phelps Stokes, *Church and State in the United States*, Vol. 1 (New York, 1950), pp. 467–468.

6. Sidney Mead, *The Lively Experiment* (New York, 1963), p. 12.

7. Quoted by Arthur Lehman Goodhart in Allan Nevins (ed.), *Lincoln and the Gettysburg Address* (Urbana, Ill., 1961), p. 39.

8. Ibid., "On the Gettysburg Address," pp. 88–89.

9. Quoted in Sherwood Eddy, *The Kingdom of God and the American Dream* (New York, 1941), p. 162.

10. Karl Decker and Angus McSween, *Historic Arlington* (Washington, D.C., 1892), pp. 60–67.

11. How extensive the activity associated with Memorial Day can be is indicated by Warner: "The sacred symbolic behavior of Memorial Day, in which scores of the town's organizations are involved, is ordinarily divided into four periods. During the year separate rituals are held by many of the associations for their dead, and many of these activities are connected with later Memorial Day events. In the second phase, preparations are made during the last three or four weeks for the ceremony itself, and some of the associations perform public rituals. The third phase consists of scores of rituals held in all the cemeteries, churches, and halls of the associations. These rituals consist of speeches and highly ritualized behavior. They last for two days and are climaxed by the fourth and last phase, in which all the separate celebrants gather in the center of the business district on the afternoon of Memorial Day. The separate organizations, with their members in uniform or with fitting insignia, march through the town, visit the shrines and monuments of the hero dead, and, finally enter the cemetery. Here dozens of ceremonies are held, most of them highly symbolic and formalized." During these various ceremonies Lincoln is continually referred to and the Gettysburg Address recited many times. W. Lloyd Warner, *American Life* (Chicago, 1962), pp. 8–9.

12. Reinhold Niebuhr, "The Religion of Abraham Lincoln," in Nevins (ed.), *op. cit.*, p. 72. William J. Wolfe of the Episcopal Theological School in Cambridge, Massachusetts, has written: "Lincoln is one of the greatest theologians of America—not in the technical meaning of producing a system of doctrine, certainly not as the defender of some one denomination, but in the sense of seeing the hand of God intimately in the affairs of nations. Just so the prophets of Israel criticized the events of their day from the perspective of the God who is concerned for history and who reveals His will within it. Lincoln now stands among God's latter-day prophets." *The Religion of Abraham Lincoln* (New York, 1963), p. 24.

13. Seymour Martin Lipset, "Religion and American Values," Chapter 4, *The First New Nation* (New York, 1964).

14. Alexis de Tocqueville, *Democracy in America*, Vol. 1 (New York, 1954), p. 310.

15. Henry Bargy, *La Religion dans la Société aux Etats-Unis* (Paris, 1902), p. 31.

16. Tocqueville, *op. cit.*, p. 311. Later he says, "In the United States even the religion of most of the citizens is republican, since it submits the truths of the other world to private judgment, as in politics the care of their temporal interests is abandoned

to the good sense of the people. Thus every man is allowed freely to take the road which he thinks will lead him to heaven, just as the law permits every citizen to have the right of choosing his own government" (p. 436).

17. U.S., *Congressional Record*, House, 15 March 1965, pp. 4924, 4926.
18. See Louis Hartz, "The Feudal Dream of the South," Part 4, *The Liberal Tradition in America* (New York, 1955).
19. Speech of Senator J. William Fulbright of 28 April 1968, as reported in *The New York Times,* 29 April 1968.
20. Quoted in Yehoshua Arieli, *Individualism and Nationalism in American Ideology* (Cambridge, Mass., 1964), p. 274.

Reading 29

A RELIGION OF REVIVALS—
EDWARD A. TIRYAKIAN

In an original and proactive article intended for French readers, Edward Tiryakian argues that religious revivals to a considerable extent shape American religious culture. Certainly revivals have been important—the First Great Awakening in the middle of the eighteenth century, the Second Great Awakening at the beginning of the nineteenth, and the Third Great Awakening at the turn of the twentieth. Tiryakian thinks there was another revival in the 1970s, but in retrospect that does not seem to have been true.

Or perhaps, to be more precise, the 1970s were a time of continuing revival.

More recent histories argue that the Awakenings were not so much turning points as continuations of an ongoing process in American life. Instead of three or four awakenings, American religion is in a condition of permanent revivalism. The most decisive period in American religious history was the first three decades of the last century. While the Second Great Awakening was part of the era, even more important seems to have been a surge of religious populism in which the egalitarian ideology of the American Revolution swept into American religion—producing, among other phenomena, new denominations such as the Mormons and the Adventists. Populism and revivalism account for the great vitality and creativity of American religion—and also for its unpredictability and instability.

Tiryakian is certainly correct that historians in the next century will see revivals as important. Presumably revivals will be occurring then, too.

Questions for Reflection and Discussion

1. Compare the portraits of American religion made by Bellah, and Tiryakian. What do they have in common? How are they different?
2. Can you find anything in these two theories or combinations thereof that can account for the decline of the Methodists and the increase of the Baptists?
3. Can you find anything that would help you to understand why there are always new religions emerging in American?
4. And anything that accounts for Catholicism's ability to adjust to American culture?

THE UNITED STATES AS A RELIGIOUS PHENOMENON
Edward A. Tiryakian

> *"Je n'ai point vu de pays ou le christianisme s'enveloppât moins de formes, de pratiques et de figures qu'aux Etats-Unis, et présentât des idées plus nettes, plus simples, plus générales à l'esprit humain. Bien que les chrétiens d'Amerique soient divisés en une multitude de sectes, ils aperçoivent tous leur religion sous ce meme jour.... les prêtres americains n'essayent point d'attirer et de fixer tous les regards de l'homme vers la vie future; ils abandonnent volontiers une partie de son coeur aux soins du present ... L'Amerique est la contrée la plus democratique de la terre, et c'est en même temps le pays ou, suivant des rapports dignes de foi, la religion catholique fait le plus de progrès."*
>
> —Alexis de Tocqueville, *De la Democratie en Amerique*, II, 2 (*"Democratie et Religion"*).

I

At the dawn of a new age for Africa, Georges Balandier seized the essence of that continent's situation in the famous title of the book he first published twenty years ago: *Afrique Ambiguë*. Nearly 150 years ago Alexis de Tocqueville saw at first hand the new age of modernity being unfurled in America, and his analysis of its institutions and their underlying values might well have had as an alternative title, *L'Amerique Ambiguë*. There are many dimensions to the ambiguity of the United States, but certainly no dimension is more salient than the ambiguity of the religious situation, in de Tocqueville's time as well as in our own. What I shall seek to do is to offer the reader of this volume a perspective on religion and society in the United States which will stress the factor of ambiguity; America's religious ambiguity is multi-faceted but perhaps at the core of this is that the United States is the first real Protestant country.

There are two sides of Protestantism, I would suggest, which are opposite in tendencies, yet strangely complementary: on the one hand, there is a strong, rationalistic this-worldly orientation, so well analyzed by Max Weber in his great studies in the sociology of religion,[1] and on the other, there is an equally strong evangelical, Christocentric current. Both of these produce in the United States a very powerful activist element which—unlike the situation of Europe—manifests itself in institutions that for the European mind would be regarded as "secular." Activism and voluntarism are another way of saying that in the United States a fundamental value is that individuals should take, on their own

Source: Published (in French) in Jean Delumeau, ed., *Histoire Vécue de Peuple Chrétien*, v. 2. Toulouse, France: Editions Privat, 1979.

initiative, a major part in freely choosing their own social situation; this entails above all their own economic and religious situation. As a result, I would suggest that *both* the economic and the religious life in the United States are positively emphasized by greater proportional numbers of lay persons than in any other large, complex society. The two have permeated each other so that a good deal of American capitalism is not simply an economic system, but one which has many religious features. Here I would point out the service-orientation of American capitalism, the unwritten rule that individuals and corporations have a duty to contribute to the societal community; a cynic may say that it is "good business" or good public relations to be civic-minded, but I would argue that the very extensive corporate giving to educational and scientific institutions—a sort of modern "tithing"—is not found in other capitalist countries on the same proportional scale, and that this is very much a Protestant "this-worldly" moral obligation towards the societal community.

However, although I think that there is a remarkable integration of the "sacred" and the "secular" in American society, I do not wish to suggest that the ambiguity is without tension. There is as much a fundamental tension between the secular rationalism and the evangelical orientations of American Protestantism, as there is between the political left and right in political regimes. On the one hand, we can see at different moments in the history of the United States a tendency for the country to become a religious exemplar for the world—a modern Christian nation whose members form a total "community of saints"; on the other hand, there is a tendency for the United States to be totally nothing other than "the bourgeois republic," as Marx labelled it.

This tension if not ambiguity was noted by de Tocqueville in the course of his famous visit. He noted the flourishing of religious life in a country whose constitution forbade the establishment of a state religion, but he also drew attention to the emphasis on the acquisition of wealth. Calling this "The Cult of Money," de Tocqueville observed that a distinguishing feature of the American people is the extent to which business and industry permeate social life.[2] Had de Tocqueville lived a few more years beyond his allotted time, he could have pointed out a dramatic symbol of America's dualistic "sacred" and "profane" orientations, for in the closing days of the Civil War, the 2¢ coin issued in 1864 bore the motto "In God we trust," which the American Congress had adopted as the federal motto, at the suggestion of Salmon Chase, Secretary of the Treasury under President Lincoln. And on July 11, 1955 the American Congress decreed that *all* United States currency should bear this motto. What other country in the modern world invokes the name of God in its money? And if this is not bewildering enough, bear in mind that the symbols of the Great Seal of the United States, which appear on the $1 bill are those of American Freemasonry. Further, although the United States' religious message is found on all its coins, yet in 1963 the Supreme Court decided that Bible reading and repeating the Lord's Prayer in public schools was unconstitutional.

We can add other features to the ambiguity of the religious situation in the United States. For example, between 1957 and 1970 the percentage of U.S. adults feeling that religion was losing its influence on American life increased from 14% in 1957 to 45% in 1965 and to 75% in 1970.[3] However, for every person who belonged to a church in 1900, there were two in 1973—nearly three out of 4 Americans are church members, about 40% of the total population goes to church weekly.[4] And this is not concentrated in the older age categories—as is typically the situation in Europe—for a study of graduate students showed that 47% of Protestants and 87% of Catholics attended church at least monthly.[5]

II

Thus, one feature of the American religious situation is a high level of religious identification and participation. There is another feature which is as much, if not more conspicuous. It is that *the United States is par excellence the land of religious revivals*. I want to dwell on this for several reasons, not the least of which is that the United States today, in the midst of a profound identity crisis, is also in the midst of a religious revival. In fact, since the end of World War II, there have been not one but *three* succeeding religious revivals, which I will discuss shortly. Moreover, what gives the religious historical process of the United States, from colonial times to the present, a distinct flavor is a fairly regular periodicity to religious revivals (or should we call them renewals?), for they seem to succeed each other in about 50-year intervals, beginning with the first "Great Awakening" in New England in the 1730s.[6] Just a few years after the United States had become an independent country, in the wake of secularism and religious lethargy, the "Second Awakening" began in the frontier territory of Kentucky in 1800. The open camp meetings which brought together Baptists, Methodists, and Presbyterians were scenes of a religious effervescence that recall in some aspects the convulsionaries of Saint-Medard. Instead of the "grands secours" of the Jansenists, one reads about the incredible array of 'exercises'— falling, barking, catalepsy, rolling, running. There were shrieks, laughter, outcries, incantations.[7] Although the form was similar, the consequences were different, for the American religious revival spread throughout the country, not being specific to any one denomination nor to any one social stratum. Revivalism became, in effect, an integral part of the "American way of life," for as the great American intellectual historian, Perry Miller, comments, "for the mass of the American democracy, the decades after 1800 were a continuing, even though intermittent, revival."[8]

After this would come, on the eve of the Civil War, the Third Awakening of 1857–58, which had its major concentration in large urban centers such as Philadelphia, New York and the rapidly growing Chicago. In the year 1858, the total of those converted at revivals who joined the churches was about 10% of total church membership in the United States, and by the outbreak of the Civil War two years later, 1,000,000 converts had been made in a total population of 30,000,000.[9]

The next great flurry of religious outpouring has two sides. On the one hand, extensive urbanization, industrialization and immigration from Europe rapidly changed the American physical and socioeconomic landscape in the 1880s, bringing about another crisis in collective identity. Capitalism changed from being entrepreneurial, individual or family-centered, to being a vast enterprise with absentee ownership; with urbanization increasing rapidly at the expense of the rural countryside—so that by 1900 the majority of Americans now lived in cities or urban areas—the small-town, relatively culturally homogeneous character of American society became submerged into a more cosmopolitan, heterogeneous, impersonal atmosphere of big city life. The Protestant churches, particularly the more "progressive" elements launched an active drive to make the churches responsive to urban social needs. For this wing of Protestantism there was an urgency to the religious renewal, to adapting or "modernizing" the Christian message so as to be in keeping with the new urban social order. The dramatic influx of new immigrants, who were overwhelmingly non-Protestant, was challenging the traditional moral order and cultural unity of American life. Besides, the absence of the social controls of rural America in the new sprawling metropolitan centers, and the importation of political radicalism in some of the immigrant groups who viewed America through the prism of their Old World experiences (especially those coming from the political turmoils of Eastern Europe) added fuel to the feeling of malaise at the end of the century. The liberal aspect of Protestantism rose to the occasion with what became known as "The Social Gospel" movement. The Movement was contemporary with Leo XIII's *Rerum Novarum,* the great Catholic social encyclical: its two most influential works are Josiah Strong's *Our Country: Its Possible Future and Its Present Crisis* (1885) and Walter Rauschenbusch's *Christianity and the Social Crisis* (1907). Just as in previous religious awakenings, the Social Gospel movement, particularly in the vision of Rauschenbusch, was eschatological, with millenarian and socialist-communitarian aspects in hailing the imminence of the Second Kingdom of God on earth.[10] The Social Gospel movement has both older roots and a longer extension than its manifestation at the turn of the century. Looking backwards, the Social Gospel movement, though not yet labelled so, was a major driving force behind the anti-slavery abolitionist movement in the decades preceding the Civil War:

> The churches were slow in joining the antislavery cause, but they did most of the pioneering, and as the movement gained momentum the countriless auxiliary organizations of mainstream Protestantism became radiating centers of concern and agitation. The national antislavery societies ... were superseded by ecclesiastical organization in which an antislavery 'social gospel' was forging ahead. . . .[11]

I would also propose that the Social Gospel movement surfaced anew in the 1960s when the liberal Protestant clergy—particularly those associated with universities—took an active role, first in agitation for civil rights for Blacks in the South, and after this second abolitionist movement was won, the liberal clergy took an active role in the denunciation of the American involvement in Vietnam.

There was a different revival of religion at the turn of the century which complements the social gospel movement, and that is the Pentecostal movement. It began at Bethel Bible College in Topeka, Kansas in 1900 and spread west to California. This movement, giving centrality to the experience of "speaking in tongues," itself followed in the wake of an earlier revival movement known as the Holiness movement that began at the end of the Civil War.[12] As in the case of the Social Gospel movement—to which it was diametrically opposed—the Pentecostal movement has deep roots in the American religious soil, for in its democratic, multidenominational, camp setting (the outdoors is a profound American symbol of freedom and individual self-assertion), the movement was the heir to the Second Awakening on the Kentucky frontier a century earlier. And, I would like to propose that the Pentacostal movement, although it became associated with lower class enthusiasm and credulity, would surface again in the latest religious revival which is so much part of the American present situation.

I have suggested that religious revivals are basic features of the historical unfolding of the United States. If I may be permitted a metaphor from the field of genetics, it seems as if the "double helix" of the religious life is liberal Protestant orientation that seeks maximal involvement in perfecting the social order so as to conform to the divine plan. That side will give the religious life a strong political and cultural activism in activities which European observers would think are "secular" matters. On the other hand, there is a strong evangelical tradition that seeks maximal personal involvement in the spiritual and emotional attainment of a Christian life here and now. I see these orientations, not so much as "progressive" and "conservative" respectively, but rather as both having a strong this-worldly activism. In a sense, if the United States has been seen as an "achievement-oriented" society, it would be well to understand that there is a strong current of "religious achievement" at the personal level; periodically, particularly in crisis situations where the social and the moral fabric of the society has become strained, a revival appears in one part of the country and spreads rapidly to all corners.

I have begun with a brief glimpse at the background of revivals and religious awakenings in America. They are a recurrent feature and have been instrumental in producing much social change in the United States, while they themselves would undoubtedly not have happened unless extensive social change were taking place to disturb the social and moral equilibrium of American society. I have suggested that although revivals are, like mushroom spores, always latent in the American soil awaiting proper moisture to appear almost overnight, one can point to their more extensive manifestations in terms of 50 year intervals. That is, a new wave of revival begins and reaches a crest about 50 years or so after the previous one; it may then go on, with diminishing intensity for several additional years.

Before we consider the post-World War II situation, it might be worth noting in passing that a phenomenon unique to the United States took place in the 1920s in the wake of, and as a result of, the religious revival at the turn of the century. This was the "noble experiment" of Prohibition, when an entire nation adopted a constitutional amendment prohibiting the sale of alcoholic beverages in the land. In Prohibition we have a joint enterprise of the liberal, social gospel wing of Protestantism, seeing in liquor a vice undermining the productivity of labor, and the evangelical wing seeing in alcohol the moral ruin of the person. The "temperance movement" had old roots, going straight back to the Puritans of the colonial period, and appearing in the first half of the nineteenth century. Cleaning up America of saloons and alcoholic spirits was a sort of moral ecological movement, in which all Protestant churches could unite. It was perhaps the last direct social influence that could be exerted at the national level by the Protestant churches as standard bearers of "native" American culture. Even after the federal repeal of the Prohibition Amendment, many states and municipalities have retained the forbidding of the sale of alcoholic beverages; this is particularly so in areas of high Baptist and Methodist concentrations.

III

In the years which have followed World War II, the United States has been the scene of three new waves of religious life. The first, which began 50 years or so after the combined Social Gospel–Pentecostal religious renewals at the turn of the century, took place in the 1950s. This movement has not received any particular name but it may be termed an "institutional religious revival" because its major characteristic was a notable increase in the membership of existing religious denominations. It was not marked by qualitative changes in the religious life, such as new sects or new forms of worship. This took place in a decade which, in retrospect, seems like one of tranquility and traditional American "normalcy." President Eisenhower was a collective representation of the American way of life, and the symbiotic relationship between religion and society noted by de Tocqueville in the citation we have quoted at the beginning of this essay was expressed in his own way by Eisenhower in 1954: "Our government makes no sense unless it is founded on a deeply felt religious faith—and I don't care what it is."[13] Although the revival of religious interest was predominantly the return to Protestantism, Catholicism, and Judaism by adult members who had at an earlier phase of their life cycle left or neglected the religious identity of their fathers or grandfathers, there were also some other manifestations. On the one hand, at the intellectual level, a more positive perspective on religion as a matter worthy of scholarly study appeared in many leading universities in "secular" departments rather than traditional divinity schools. Here I think in particular of the disciplines of psychology and sociology, with the sociology of religion emerging as an important field of both empirical and theoretical investigations. Also in connection with this were the beginnings of new interdisciplinary professional organizations that would bring together scholars in religious studies and social scientists interested in comparative aspects of religious life. On the other hand, it is also in this period that began the evangelistic work of Billy Graham whose ministry also crosses denominational boundaries and who brought back to urban America something of the camp-meeting revival tradition.

Although the societal context of the 1950s seems in today's light a rather quiet, even blissful time in American life, the actual situation was a good deal more complex with various tensions and conflicts at both the domestic and the international level providing, if not a readily manifest "crisis," at least an underlying malaise. Revivals of religion do not occur where there is no dissension or severe pressures in the larger social body. In the case of the United States in the 1950s, part of the strains related to a renewal of religious membership and religious interest must be understood in terms of severe uncertainties concerning the nation at the international level. The United States found itself at the helm of the "free world," in a leadership position made precarious by the omnipresent threat of a thermonuclear war; the emerging strong countries of the "free world" were its vanquished foes of World War II, while its chief antagonist in the "Cold War" was its wartime ally. International relations had become ambiguous, and the threat of a devastating Armageddon further clouded the political meaning of the world. Thus, the Korean War was the first war that the United States fought in which the nation had to accept a stalemate, with this being very much against the basic American temper of winning. One should also note that the successful launching of "sputnik" by Russia added to the sense of crisis because this constituted a challenge to the superiority of American technology. I would here suggest that somehow for many Americans a demonstration that God is on the side of the United States is that technological superiority is a sign of divine grace. Hence, the possibility of no longer being supreme in technological advances was a crisis that added to the loss of confidence in science and technology, and which favored reconsidering alternative approaches to finding ultimate meaning of the world. In addition, at the domestic level, a growing cleavage of "left" and "right" began in the 1950s, first over McCarthyism and later over the growing civil rights movement. This intense fissure in the American polity went beyond the traditional "Democratic" and "Republican" two-party system; there was a note of political discord which might possibly grow into an outright civil war. I think therefore that internal political strains—which would dramatically erupt in the next decade—also played a part in seeking a certain reassurance of the meaning of the world in the traditional religious bodies.

Undoubtedly, however, it is the subsequent revival which drew a great deal more of attention than the one of the 1950s. The second revival, that of the later 1960s, took on the name of the "Occult Revival." It is characterized by belonging to the "counter-culture" movement of the period, one which saw the unexpected emergence of new religious movements, some being old wine in new casks, some being new wine in old casks. A few remarks about the societal context of the United States in the 1960s are needed.

The university setting in the United States went through a major transformation in that decade. Unlike the European scene where the university has been closely involved in the country's political situation, in the United States, until the

1960s, the university campus (and the great majority of students live on the campus where they study) had been a rather halcyonic place, free from the political cares of the outside world. The emphasis was on leisurely developing the mind or else, in more vocational colleges, on imparting practical knowledge. But in the 1960s the university became the primary place for political mobilization and "consciousness raising." The Kennedy administration recruited heavily from academic ranks, and this was one sense in which the universities felt more involved in national politics. Second, Kennedy drew a very responsive chord from college students with his launching of the Peace Corps. This may be seen as a secular missionary movement that echoed the college-based foreign missions movement in the closing decades of the 19th century. The latter, itself, was part of a broader missionary movement which also had a major "home missions" aspect that sent evangelical young people to both large urban centers run over by new migrants, as well as to the western lands which had poorly developed religious institutions to provide moral integration of recent newcomers. One can readily see in both the overseas-oriented Peace Corps and the domestic-oriented VISTA a modern version, albeit in a "secular" framework, of the strong this-worldly service impulse of American Protestantism which on previous occasions had mobilized American youth (many of whom were not Protestants, either in practice or in background). What is involved here is a raising of the "social consciousness" of American youth people, and Kennedy himself and his youthful entourage played a great part in this.

But there were other dimensions. The university setting also became a forum for political consciousness, initially conducted by "progressive" faculty members who sought to get their students involved in the civil rights struggle at home and in opposition to the Vietnam War overseas. The students learned their lessons well, and in a few years' time, the American university setting completely lost the atmosphere of the cloister that had so long stamped it. However, for the purpose of this essay, what remains to be noted is that from about 1965 or so onward, the "drug culture" became a feature of the university setting. It may have originated with a communal experiment at Harvard organized by a sometime-member of the faculty whose psychological studies led him to experiment with the drug LSD. In any case, it spread rapidly to metropolitan-environment universities, and seemed particularly widespread in California and New York. The "drug culture" had some affinity with political radicalism; it flourished almost overnight, not only *on* the university campus but also in the cultural setting surrounding contiguous to the university. That is, one could (and still can) find former students living close to the university who form communal living arrangements where one bond in common is the use of some drug or stimulant which will send consciousness on a distant "trip"; there may be stores that will in effect provide the necessary commodities; and there are means of communication, newspapers and periodicals which publish articles catering to those living in this culture.

Within a very short time after the "drug culture" appeared on the scene— one that recruited its membership heavily from the college population, therefore from the young and fairly affluent members of society—there came what has been termed the "Occult Revival." Given the image of the United States as a highly rationalistic society and of its people as practical and "this-worldly," the interest in the broad category of phenomena designated as "occult" is most puzzling. If one looked at magazines and movies depicting life in the United States in 1969, give or take a year, it would seem as if half of the college-aged population was preparing for a political revolution, and the other half was raising its consciousness by taking to astrology, the tarot, Zen Buddhism, yoga, Curdjieff, Hara Krishna, and even witchcraft and satanism! In reality, much smaller numbers were really committed to either the political or the cultural revolution; nonetheless, the "counter culture," with which the Occult Revival is identified, did represent an important turning point in the religious life of young Americans. It certainly seemed to many to be symbolic of the waning of the "Protestant Ethic" beyond the point of no return, for the counter culture seemed to be a total refusal of American technological civilization and its underlying values of rationality and this-worldly salvation in one's occupation.[14] The counter culture, in its ideological aspects as a critique of American culture was not only a critique of an industrial, technological economic order, but also a critique of the lack of spirituality and the lack of interpersonal intimacy in American life. The strong emphasis on "subjectivism" led in the direction of a new search for transcendence not filled by Western Christianity.[15] It also led to an affirmation of hedonism (the phrase "doing your own thing" became a catchword), which underlies the truly extensive "sexual revolution" that is, in my opinion, the most important revolutionary and destructuring force operative on human society since capitalism. One linkage between the Occult Revival and the sexual revolution is that in recent years one finds, as part of the sexual revolution the theme of "androgyny," which strives to eliminate at the cultural level (in clothes, hairdos, as well as in textbooks and professional writings) differences in gender. In this sense, the sexual revolution is not only the breaking of traditional monogamous relationships in an ideology of sexuality which seeks the "liberation" of the person from traditional socio-religious conventions. It is also the neutralization and levelling of sexual differences. But the concept of the "androgyne," which is appearing in print,[16] is very much part of an older esoteric tradition, owing much to gnostic and kabalistic inspiration, that appears in earlier periods of history, sometimes in marginal religious sects such as the Adamites who find in original man a divine whole sexual being. The Occult Revival, then, was the revival of archaic, pre-modern, modes of relating to transcendental reality; moreover, these modes had been in generations past denounced by both Protestant and Catholic churches for being "false," "irrational," "superstitious," and even "demonic."

It is no wonder that by the beginning of the present decade, the combined thrust of religious radicalism and political radicalism seemed on the edge of turning the social order on its head. Many professors, who a few years before had complained of student "apathy" and had sought to have students become "engage," began to wonder if they had not created a Frankenstein which would bring the reign of *unreason* to the university.

The great sociologist Max Weber had indicated that a central underlying historical development of the West was the complex process of *rationalization,* and that as part of this, the authority structure of the modern Western setting came to approximate more and more one type of authority, namely, legal-rational authority. But Weber in his famous essay on *The Protestant Ethic and the Spirit of Capitalism* concluded with a tone of uncertainty as to the future direction of a civilization that in its rationalization of its religious-ethical impulse, had become estranged from its foundation. At the end of the 1960s, legal-rational authority seemed to have lost its meaning, and all the traditional values of American life—political and religious values—which had given so much stability to American society were on the point of exhaustion. The society undergoing such rapid change was not only one where authority of all sort was in a twilight zone,[17] but also, a society proceeding to the extremes of secularization.

There was to be a third revival, however, which has been as unexpected as was the Occult Revival, and this revival is what marks the religious situation of the United States at the time of this writing. It is what may be called the "Jesus Revival" as a mass, popular movement that has several features worth noting.

I am tempted to invoke Hegelian terminology in calling this movement a "synthesis" of the first two—that is, the religious revival of the 1950s was a thesis affirming the importance of institutional religious membership as part of the "American way of life." The "Occult Revival" was the antithesis of the objective, traditional, American institutions—the counterculture which frames the "Occult Revival" placed a stress on new forms of subjectivity, on new forms of social relationships, on the spontaneous or what for a short time was called "the happening." This implied a rejection of the value of postponing present gratification for the future; certainly, traditional American society was very much a future-oriented society, and the counter culture rejected this temporal horizon in favor of the present, the immediate. How is the "Jesus Revival" a synthesis of its two predecessors? The emphasis in one major direction of the movement is to experience the reality of the subject's relation to Jesus, so that one's life is transformed by the encounter. Further, a good deal of the movement (though not all of it) is marked by Charismatic Renewal, that is, by experiencing the gifts of the Holy Spirit. This personal encounter—although it may be in a group setting—with the divine being is an affirmation of the subjective realm of being, which was an important value of the counter culture. That the Jesus revival or Jesus movement partook of the anti-establishment aspect of the counter culture is indicated in that many of the church leaders (higher clergy and intellectuals) representing the official religious establishment of Protestantism, Catholicism, and Judaism, showed great doubts, skepticism, disapproval, and misgivings about the Jesus movement.[18]

One has to understand that the Jesus revival grew up in an unexpected context, namely, it arose in the same setting as did the drug culture and the Occult Revival. If one had to pinpoint a geographical local for its debut, it would be the metropolitan centers of California—Los Angeles and San Francisco—which were cultural centers of the drug culture. Somewhere in 1969 and 1970 the new religious culture developed among segments of college-age population, including converts from the drug culture who brought into their radical discovery of Jesus elements of the drug culture: ecstasy, folk music and the musical instrument of cultural protest, the guitar; they also brought styles of life from the drug culture, namely communal living, which went against traditional American individualism and which was seen as an aspect of the return to the primitive Christian community. The emphasis upon the charismatic experience and the speaking in tongues was also quite unorthodox in terms of established religious practices. A few years before, the adolescents and young adults who identified and participated in the counterculture—in fact, who gave up living in the larger society to become members of the everyday counterculture—became called "Hippies"; they had their own style of life and even their own language. Those who around 1969 or 1970 converted to a new Christian way of life also made this a total commitment, a whole way of life; because of the totality of their religious involvement they were called "Jesus Freaks." They took up living in houses with such names as the "House of Acts," "Tree of Life," "Fish House," and formally their corporate name is the Christian World Liberation Front, evocative of the political radicalism of the counterculture. Even the religious language of the Jesus movement shows the imprint of the Hippie drug culture; note for example the following testimony:

> "I've been through 'grass,' the heavyweight stuff, LSD and speed, and all the meditation-breathing bit, and it just freaked me out and down. But Jesus is very true, very hip, very with it. He's our thing."[19]

The expressions used are not only hard to translate in another language; they are also beyond the vocabulary of Americans born before World War II. Still, the new religious culture, drawing upon the rock 'n roll music of the drug culture, could be understood across generations and across nations in such musical forms as "Jesus Christ Superstar" and "Godspell." Just as the revival of 1858 was an urban revival, so was the revival of 1969–70. It was very much part of the American youth culture, for its initiative was very much with persons under 30. The Christian communities in the metropolitan areas of California exist side by side with the most advanced forms of the hedonistic culture; in a sense, they are mutual aid religious groupings that are today's modern "home missions."

Of course, that was not the only center of religious renewal, though it was its most dramatic one. The American evangelical tradition has its outstanding figure in Billy Graham, whose crusades are readily seen by millions on television and who is consistently ranked in opinion surveys as one of the most respected men in the United States. One notable aspect of Graham's revivalistic activities is that they utilize modern technology while delivering fundamentalist religious messages, including belief in the eschatological ending of the world; another aspect is that Graham's crusades are interracial and intergenerational, that is, they are important bridges between social strata. Another component in the religious revival has been the charismatic movement which has come from traditional and more ritualistic churches that have not in the past been associated with religious enthusiasm. On the one hand, starting as an isolated phenomenon in some California churches, glossolalia (tongue speaking) appeared in the Episcopalian Church; on the other hand, the charismatic movement is also notable in the Catholic Church. In the latter it began in 1967 at Duquesne University (a Catholic university heavily influenced after World War II by phenomenology imported from the Netherlands), then spread to the University of Notre Dame and other campuses.[20] The higher clergy has shown ambivalence to this, but since it is in the spirit of the Vatican II emphasis on greater laity participation, it has become increasingly accepted. It may be noted in passing that the ecumenical movement has really two tiers or levels. In one tier, ecclesiastical authorities and theologians are crossing former boundaries to develop a greater cognitive understanding of one another's teachings and doctrines. I would say that this is really a meeting of elites and academics. The second ecumenical movement is the meeting of charismatics, where denominational boundaries may also be rejected in the common acceptance of the Holy Spirit. The latter movement is popular, and I know of such prayer groups where laity and clergy come together at the initiative of the laity.

*   *   *

What is the present situation of the United States? I have stressed in the course of this cursory overview the factor of religious revivals. I do believe that the social historian of the 21st Century—assuming that history will still be written and reinterpreted fifty or a hundred years from now—will look back and see that the religious revival of the 1970s was of paramount importance in the United States, whether or not the movement realized its aspiration of preparing America for the Second Coming. Perhaps I need to correct this, for the religious movement is not like a political movement that has a given political objective to achieve. The religious revival lacks a central leadership, except that it takes the Godhead as its leader. It seeks the spiritual and therefore inner transformation of the individual, and in that sense it is a reaffirmation of traditional American values of individualism. Very broadly speaking the "Jesus movement," or the "Born Again" movement is a this-worldly salvation movement which cross-cuts sacred and profane, cross-cuts denominations, cross-cuts age groups. It is a movement that takes satisfaction in having the present president of the United States a "born again" Christian. Yet, there is no indication that President Carter would do anything official as a Christian president—in fact, during the first year of his administration what had come to be a traditional religious Christmas stamp with religious figures (for example, portraits of the Nativity scene, of the Madonna, etc.) was now secularized with a portrait of George Washington. This is part of the ambiguity of the United States with which I began this essay.

The present religious awakening is very broadly based and has many directions. It extends into two "profane" or secular spheres, the world of business and the world of leisure. I have in mind two voluntary associations which are entirely organized by laymen: The Fellowship of Christian Athletes and the Full Gospel Businessmen Group. The former began in the state of Oklahoma in the 1950s and has spread to high schools (lycées), universities, and to professional sports. FCA holds week-long conferences which combine athletics and devotional religious activities; over 10,000 athletes and coaches of all ages have been participating in these modern "retreats" which implicitly take to heart the old Latin phrase *mens sana in corpore sano*. The Businessmen's Group is more recent, again starting on the West Coast and now spreading to the East rapidly. Its endeavor is to establish the priority of Christian commitment even in the modern commercial world, and members commit themselves to observing a code of Christian ethics and fair pricing; those familiar with "the Yellow Pages" of telephone books will appreciate that these "Born Again" businessmen have started a Christian "Yellow Pages" Directory.

These two illustrations are suggestive that there is an extension of religion in America in spheres which one might think outside of the religious pale. Although this renewal is part of the "Jesus Revival," one may also see it as a modern extension of the American Puritan religious tradition, at least in that sector of Puritanism which sought to rationalize all spheres of life so as to contribute to the greater glory of God. What this leads me to observe is that, paradoxically, while one trend of rationalization is toward increasing secularization, a divergent trend in American life is toward sacralization—that is, toward making activities (such as sports and business) which are thought of as "profane" into activities which get an added religious element.

I don't want to leave the impression that all of America is partaking in the new religious revival, nor that the presence of this revival should be taken as indicating that the United States is in a state of religious unity and harmony. That is obviously not the case. For one thing, in all instances where an extensive revival has occurred in American history, there has been a serious state of social crisis as a background factor. Today's crisis is more than the economic crisis (including here the worsening of the quality of life for millions of essentially middle and working class Americans, the apprehension of increasing scarcity of resources, etc.). It is also more than the recent political crisis of 1973–74 which shook the basic trust of Americans in their government, and before that the bitter political cleavage over American involvement overseas.

The religious revival may also be seen as conveying a response to a crisis in urban life. Social relationships in the city have become more precarious, more impersonal as neighborhood communities have become increasingly dissolved, not only due to the spread of street violence (which received an important increase from the drug culture) but also as an indirect consequence of racial integration in the public school system. If nature abhors a vacuum, one can also say that human beings abhor a vacuum in social life. The new religious communities that have developed in urban settings provide a renewed sense of fellowship and common denominators to persons who find an absence of such ties in weakened social structures.

It is also certainly a crisis of moral meaning as to the sense of the United States, as to where stands the United States in the historical process and where stands the virtues of the nation.[21] Americans had grown up obviously certain that their technology and scientific know-how, that the American form of government, and in general the American economic system formed the greatest nation on earth. This youthful and naive self-confidence has for just about the past twenty years been going through a series of traumatic shocks. The institutional structure, while still existing, has been severely strained, and the traditional American ethnic group which had in effect been the cultural majority is no longer an effective elite. The present situation would quite likely have been described by Emile Durkheim as one of "anomie."

It is a condition where not only are there new—or renewed—forms of Christianism but also where several of the "new religious movements" of the counterculture flourish, awaiting the test of time.[22] And of course, if Charismatics or Hare Krishnas, respectively, attract much attention, it must be kept in mind that both of these are not the majority of religious Americans, for the latter are to be found in traditional religious institutional ties. Moreover, it is simplistic to portray the United States as if its entire population is "religious." The United States does have an active, well-organized, anti-religious, secularizing segment of the population which, if small in numbers, exerts great influence through the legal system. As in practically every other Western industrial society, there is a Gnostic presence as the antithesis to the religious thesis.

A generation ago we all knew what it meant to be an American and well knew what the United States stood for. In the past ten years it has become painfully the case that national identity is more and more problematic and uncertain. The quest for re-establishing identity has received much attention in the search for "roots." I consider much of the recent religious revival—both that of the counterculture and that of the "Jesus Movement"—to be a personal search for both old and new roots. And for many of yesterday's ethnic and racial minorities who had suppressed or placed in brackets their ethnic or racial identity, the rediscovery of their ethnicity has been something of a religious "born again" experience. But some of these persons and a larger number of others have found the deepest waters of their personality to be religious waters. What remains ambiguous is whether the nation itself as an entity can rediscover its authentic religious identity.

Ambiguous America is likely to remain so in terms of its religious situation. Whether "sacralization" of American social life can provide new cultural and social alternatives to "secularization," that is, whether as in previous periods of crises the religious renewal can revitalize creatively social institutions, is a most uncertain matter. Yet, if the past is an indicator, one can foresee that religious activism will continue to characterize the American population. Moreover, it will be young adults who will take the initiative in this activism. For a final observation, I would suggest that religion and society in the United States are as close to being in a state of "permanent revolution" as any modern nation is likely to witness.

Notes

1. For an explication of Weber's *Religionssoziologie,* see J. A. Prades, *La Sociologie de la Religion chez Max Weber.* Paris: Beatrice-Nauwelaerts, 1966.
2. *De la Démocratie en Amérique.* Paris: Union Generales d'Editions, Collection October 18, 1963, p. 332. De Tocqueville felt uneasy that the American penchant for wealth and well-being might be a fatal flaw in the American democracy, leading its citizens in the long run to forsake freedom for the servitude of the Welfare State.
3. *U. S. News and World Report,* March 23, 1970, p. 45.
4. "Religion in the U. S.—Where It's Headed," *U. S. News and World Report,* June 4, 1973, p. 54.
5. Andrew M. Greeley, *The Denominational Society,* Glenview, Ill.: Scott, Foresman, 1975, p. 146. In contrast, Greeley reports only 11% of Jewish graduate students indicate at least a monthly religious attendance.
6. For a brief overview, see Timothy L. Smith, "Historical Waves of Religious Interest in America," *The Annals of the American Academy of Political and Social Science,* v. 332 (November 1960): 9–19. For materials on the first revival, see Edwin S. Gaustad, *The Great Awakening in New England* (Chicago: Quadrangle, 1968); Alan Heimert and Perry Miller, eds., *The Great Awakening* (Indianapolis and New York: Bobbs Merrill, 1967).
7. Perry Miller, *The Life of the Mind in America.* New York: Harcourt, Brace and World, 1965, p. 7.
8. *Ibid.,* p. 7.
9. J. Edwin Orr, *The Second Evangelical Awakening in Britain* (London: Marshall, Morgan and Scott, Ltd., 1949), pp. 35–37.
10. Millenial and eschatological expectations are of course closely related to the theme of religious revivals, and they have been very much part of the American experience, in a dialectical relationship with the more linear view of the future as "progress." See my essay, "The Time Perspectives of Modernity," in *Society and Leisure/Loisir et Societé,* I, no. 1 (avril, 1978). For an illustrative study of one American millenary community, see Henri Desroches, *Les Shakers americains: D'un néo-Christianisme à un pré-socialisme?* Paris: Editions Minuit, 1955. English translation, *The American Shakers: From Neo-Christianity to Presocialism.* Amherst, Mass.: University of Massachusetts Press, 1971.
11. Sydney E. Ahlstrom, *A Religious History of the American People,* vol. 2. Garden City, N. Y.: Doubleday Image, 1975, p. 102.
12. Morton T. Kelsey, *Tongue Speaking.* Garden City, N. Y.: Doubleday, 1964.
13. Quoted in Sydney E. Ahlstrom, *A Religious History of the American People,* vol. 2. Garden City, N. Y.: Doubleday Image Books, 1975, p. 450.
14. Theodore Roszak, *The Making of a Counter Culture.* Garden City, N. Y.: Doubleday Anchor, 1969.
15. In this respect there is an important linkage between the counter culture of the 1960s and the Romantic Movement of the 19th Century.
16. For example, Carolyn G. Heilbrun, *Toward A Recognition of Androgyny,* New York: Harper Colophon, 1973; June Singer, *Androgyny, Toward a New Theory of Sexuality,* Garden City, N. Y.: Anchor Press/Doubleday, 1976.
17. See the sensitive analysis of Robert Nisbet, *Twilight of Authority.* New York: Oxford University Press, 1975.
18. For example, the Campus Crusade for Christ in 1974 became the object of a determined campaign to halt it by those fearful of a wave of religious enthusiasm.

Likewise, Reverend Moon's Christian Unity Church has become the target of great hostility by established denominations and by parents of teenagers converted to the new religious community.

19. French readers may get an approximation of this from "Les Chretiens de Los Angeles," in *Paris Match*, No. 1195, ler avril 1972. The feature of this issue is "Jesus Idole de Notre Temps." They might also wish to read the dialogue between Cardinal Danielou and Jean Duvignaud in *Le Figaro Literaire* No. 1350, ler avril, 1972.

20. See Ralph Lane, Jr., "Catholic Charismatic Renewal," in Charles Y. Glock and Robert N. Bellah, eds., *The New Religious Consciousness*. Berkeley, Cal.: University of California Press, 1976, pp. 162–179.

21. For a sensitive interpretation of the moral crisis, see the study of the American sociologist Robert N. Bellah, *The Broken Covenant*. New York: Seabury Press, 1975.

22. For studies of the new religious movements, see Irving I. Zaretsky and Mark P. Leone, eds., *Religious Movements in Contemporary America*. Princeton: Princeton University Press, 1975; and Glock and Bellah, eds., *The New Religious Consciousness*, 1976.

Reading 30

....

RELIGIOUS CHANGERS—WADE CLARK ROOF AND WILLIAM MCKINNEY

In the 1960s, Dean M. Kelley wrote a book that startled many Protestant leaders, *Why the Conservative Churches Are Growing*. He argued that the "conservative" churches—those that we would call "fundamentalist"—were growing rapidly, while the mainline churches were having a difficult time holding their own. Kelley's data, however, were based on denominational statistics that are of such value that along with a dollar and a half, they will get you a ride on the Chicago subway.

It would appear that the "fundamentalist" denominations may tend to exaggerate their membership and the mainline churches may tend to underestimate their membership for reasons of different institutional pressures. However, when Kelley wrote, he used what were the only statistics available. With the beginning of the General Social Survey in 1972, reliable national sample data on denominational membership became available for the first time (such as the tables and graphs presented in the first two selections of this section). Two qualifications of Kelley's thesis became necessary. First of all, the change was not new, but had been proceeding for all of the present century—as my graphs in the second selection demonstrate. Secondly, as I discussed in my book *Religious Change in America*, the shifting shape of American Protestantism (what Finke and Stark call, in *The Church of America*, "winners and losers") takes place *without any change in either religious practice or doctrinal belief*. American Protestants change their denominational affiliation without changing their beliefs or practice. Methodists become Baptists without abandoning old doctrines or acquiring new ones. Perhaps rather than the faithful leaving denominations, the denominations leave the faithful—possibly because divinity-school trained clergy preach a religion that is too advanced for their own congregants, who then go down the street to a church where the minister has not attended divinity school.

In this selection Roof and McKinney trace the nature of religious change by looking closely at those who change and those who do not. They detect three movements:

1. The change of older and better educated people to more liberal denominations. This may be similar to the movements of some blacks into Catholicism, which will be discussed in a subsequent selection.

2. The change of younger, less well educated, and more conservative people—often with more traditional doctrinal and social attitudes (in reference to ERA, abortion, gay rights, etc.) to more conservative denominations.
3. The movement away from all religion of a younger, and especially younger male, population.

The second movement is much stronger than the first.

The third movement is problematic, however, because Roof and McKinney did not attempt cohort analysis such as Michael Hout and I have done: they did not follow a population group from their early twenties to their middle twenties and then their early thirties. Hence, they did not take into account the "change back" to religion of young people as they mature. To be fair to Roof and McKinney, their study was written before ours and indeed before a method of cohort analysis had been developed by sociologists.

Hout and I established that the defection rate for Catholics (those who were born Catholic but no longer described themselves as Catholic) was 15% in 1960; thirty years later after all the turbulence in the Catholic Church it was still 15%.

Questions for Reflection and Discussion

1. Do the analyses of American religion in the last three selections shed any light on the changes that Roof and McKinney describe?
2. If you were in charge of a liberal denomination, what would you try to do to hold your members?
3. How can it be that men and women can change their denominations without changing their doctrines?
4. Where does Catholicism seem to fit in this pattern of religious switching?

THE DEMOGRAPHY OF RELIGIOUS CHANGE
Wade Clark Roof and William McKinney

Are the churches dying?

—*Dean M. Kelley*

For so blunt a question to be asked in the early seventies about the future of the churches was a sure sign that times were changing. The fact that the question was posed by an executive of the National Council of Churches, long the coordinating headquarters of the Protestant mainline, underscored the point even

Source: Wade Clark Roof, and William McKinney, *American Mainline Religion: Its Changing Shape and Future*, New Brunswick: Rutgers University Press, 1987.

more. Kelley's book *Why the Conservative Churches Are Growing* became a conversation piece, capturing the mood of the times much as had Will Herberg's *Protestant—Catholic—Jew* in an earlier period. Many cults, sects, and religious movements appear on the scene and then disappear; indeed, we have come to expect that many of them will be short-lived. But what about the more established, mainline churches and synagogues? Were they too following a course of institutional decline? Was their future really that uncertain?

Kelley's data gave little basis for optimism. With a massive array of membership figures and related statistics, he documented sharp growth for conservative and sectarian bodies but precipitous decline for many of the older, historic religious traditions. The mood of the country had changed since the more expansive and optimistic growth period of the 1950s, when virtually all religious institutions as well as "religion in general" seemed to flourish. Growth was now more selective, and the demographics offered proof of the changing religious fortunes. The mainline churches were not about to die, but they were in trouble.

From the vantage point of the mid-1980s we can ponder why Kelley's book attracted so much attention. Much of it had to do with the "shock" of facing up to a changing religious milieu and hearing about it from the establishment itself, yet in some respects the facts presented were not all that new. It was not the first time we learned that the conservative churches were experiencing a great surge in growth. The sectarian wing of Protestantism has been expanding throughout most of this century. Ever since the modernist-fundamentalist struggles of the 1920s and 1930s, this wing has grown. Even in the more conformist 1950s there had been signs of mounting conservative momentum. Henry P. Van Dusen, in what is surely one of the few *Life* magazine articles ever regularly cited in scholarly footnotes, called attention to a rapidly emerging "Third Force" in Christendom (alongside traditional Protestantism and Catholicism), composed of Adventists, Pentecostals, Nazarenes, Jehovah's Witnesses, and many small holiness sects.[1] Nor had religious conservatives suddenly overtaken liberals in rates of membership growth. The annual yearbooks had shown for decades that many of the newer, conservative bodies were growing far more rapidly than the older, more established groups. The division within Protestantism into liberal and conservative camps had been widening for some time and was apparent to anyone who took the time to tally the membership figures of the churches.[2]

What was eye-catching, however, and quite alarming for some were the *minus* signs in the growth rates. Minus signs pointed to absolute declines in the membership statistics, and year after year for an extended period of time—which was a new phenomenon in American religious history. To be sure, there had been drop-offs in membership at one time or another in the past. One such period was the "religious depression" of the late 1920s and early 1930s, but it neither lasted as long nor had so significant an impact on the membership base of the churches as did the declines beginning in the 1960s. By the time Kelley wrote his book in 1972, the memberships of some liberal Protestant churches had dropped by hundreds of thousands; by the end of the decade they were lower still. The fact that other religious traditions showed parallel losses helped underscore the significance of the changes. Catholic growth slowed, and many

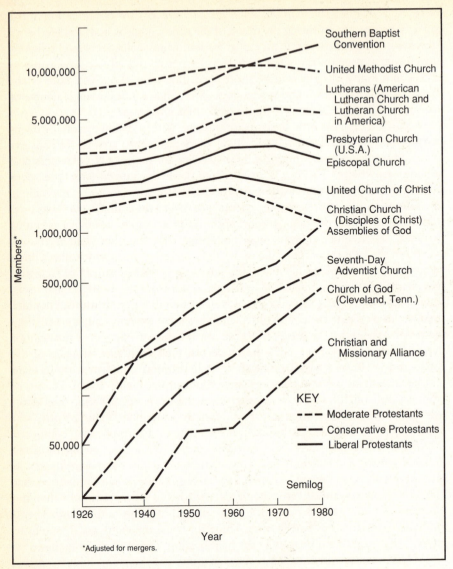

FIGURE 1. Growth patterns for selected denominations.

Reform synagogues experienced declines. The minus signs stood out all the more when compared with the conservative churches, which continued to grow in both decades, often at exceedingly high rates of 50 percent or more. Even the huge Southern Baptist Convention, the largest of the conservative bodies, continued to grow at rates well over 15 percent per decade. A glance at the membership statistics made clear that the denominations were on differing trajectories, some growing and others not (see Figure 1).

Now it appears the mainline decline may have bottomed out. Some of the churches that suffered losses are reporting modest gains, and others, while not growing, at least appear more stable.[3] Yet there is no evidence that a genuine turnaround has begun. The liberal Protestant community is mired in a depression, one that is far more serious and deeper than it has suffered at any time in this century. Large numbers of Catholics and Jews have also defected. All of this points to a changing religious establishment and changing relations of religion and culture in the modern period. Twenty years of membership decline and loss of the young have left a fundamentally altered religious mainline. Even if the declines have leveled off, these institutions will bear the imprint of these demographic shifts for many years. Imbalances of this magnitude work themselves out slowly, and not without lasting scars.

One thing the differential patterns of growth and decline has done is to raise concern about the changing social and demographic profile of religious America. Kelley's charts and graphs jolted us into recognizing that religious communities have quite differing demographics and that the ways in which they grow, or fail to grow, bear directly on their institutional destinies. Recent developments have made us newly aware that congregations are very much "earthen vessels"—no less so than other social institutions, they are shaped by a myriad of influences in their environments. Sometimes they grow, and sometimes they suffer losses, depending on both their internal and external conditions; not to understand them in this way is to overlook their fundamental human character. Increasingly, religionists and social analysts alike are turning to religious demographics for church planning and helping religious groups understand their growth potential. Indeed, compiling and interpreting these facts is one of the new growth industries in religious research today. George Gallup, Jr.'s Princeton Religion Research Center, for example, is one of many thriving research enterprises now collecting and analyzing data on religion. A growing storehouse of reliable and representative data on varied aspects of religion makes it possible to describe, better than ever before, the trends now reshaping the religious mainline in the United States.

TWO BASIC DEMOGRAPHICS: AGE AND FAMILY PATTERNS

Of all the information now available, two basic demographics are the age structures and family patterns for the religious groups. By examining these we are able to determine, in the first instance, the "location" of a particular group in the larger American population and, in the second, the fundamental relations between religion and family. Far from being constants, or common features of the mainline groups, these two can vary in ways that are important for understanding how religion fits into the social structure. In both instances the demographics point to significant shifts since midcentury and changing institutional patterns for religion in America.

Aging Constituencies

Normally religious involvement varies by age, which means that churches and synagogues have a disproportionate number of older people within them. This observation has long been made by commentators, indeed for as long as we have had reliable data on congregations. In the 1930s the Lynds, for example, commented on "the same preponderance of gray-haired persons" that they observed in Middletown's churches.[4] Returning to Middletown in the late seventies, Theodore Caplow and his research associates found much the same patterns; they concluded that "regular attendance and intermittent attendance increase for each increment of age."[5]

Age differentials in religion have become even more pronounced since midcentury. The reason for this is simple: the American population is growing older. Low birth and death rates have pushed the average age upward. This finding might not be of much significance if all groups were affected uniformly, but such is hardly the case. Some religious groups, depending on their location relative to the mainstream culture, are far more influenced by general population trends than are others.

Mainline Protestants especially have aged. For some Protestant denominations there have been noticeable increases in the average age levels.[6] The proportion of members fifty years of age or older within these churches has grown considerably in just the last twenty-five years:

	1957	1983
Episcopalians	36%	46%
Methodists	40%	49%
Lutherans	36%	45%
Presbyterians	42%	49%
Baptists	33%	40%

While this trend is most evident in the Protestant mainline churches (both old-line and moderate), the Catholic and Jewish communities have aged as well. Similar proportions of members fifty or older increased for Catholics during this period from 31 percent to 34 percent and for Jews from 33 percent to 39 percent. Religious constituencies generally have aged while just the opposite is true for those with no religious preference: nonaffiliates are considerably younger today than they were a quarter century ago. As the social composition of this secular constituency has undergone a metamorphosis, so too has its demographics. With large numbers of youth dropping out of the churches in the 1960s, and religious nonaffiliation becoming more acceptable, the average age within this sector declined significantly.

Among the religious communities there are disparities in age structures, some being more lopsided than others. This is apparent in table 1, which looks at the percentage distribution of mainline religious group members by age. Affiliates of all faiths are older than nonaffiliates; Jews are older than both Protestants and Catholics; Protestants are older than Catholics. Within Protestantism there are some striking differences: white Protestants are older than black Protestants, and liberal Protestants are older than conservative Protestants.

TABLE 1

Percentage Distribution of Religious Families by Age

Family	18–34	35–54	55+
Liberal Protestants	27	34	39
Moderate Protestants	31	32	38
Black Protestants	37	31	32
Conservative Protestants	35	34	31
Catholics	40	34	27
Jews	31	31	38
No religious preference	59	26	15

More is involved here than simply the aging of the American population: in the seventies and eighties the greater voluntarism of young Americans took many out of the churches and synagogues and in turn "pushed" the average age levels upward. Protestants, Catholics, and Jews all felt the impact of growing numbers of disaffected and "unchurched" members, the upshot of which was to shift the location of religious mainstream in the direction of a somewhat older age base. Age would thus join the list of social correlates, along with class, ethnicity, and region, as an aspect of fundamental change for these historic traditions. Perhaps no other feature is so apparent in observing many congregations today.

The age shift would have its most profound consequences for Protestantism. Within this community a growing age gap now exacerbates existing tensions and cleavages between liberals–moderates and conservatives. By the 1980s liberal Protestants were on the average almost four years older than conservative Protestants. United Church of Christ members have, along with Christian Scientists, the oldest constituencies, with mean ages greater than fifty years of age. Forty-three percent of the United Church of Christ, 41 percent of Methodists, and 42 percent of Disciples of Christ are age fifty-five or older. This stands in marked contrast to the lower mean ages of the conservative Protestant denominations, the lowest being 41.2 for Pentecostal/holiness members. Not one of the conservative Protestant groups has as many as 40 percent of its members over fifty-five years of age; fewer than one-third of Jehovah's Witnesses, Pentecostals, and Assemblies of God members are this age or older.

Young adults under the age of thirty-five, on the other hand, account for only 26 percent of the members of the Reformed church, 21 percent of the United Church of Christ, and 28 percent of the Methodists. Proportionately these numbers are small, a fact that becomes clear when one considers that almost 40 percent of the nation's adult population belongs to the eighteen-to-thirty-four age category. Young adults are far better represented in the conservative churches: more than 50 percent of Jehovah's Witnesses belong to this younger category. Compared with moderate and liberal Protestants, the conservative churches are more successful in holding on to their young members.

The fact is that liberal, mainline Protestant denominations are aging more rapidly than the more evangelical, fundamentalist faiths. A lopsided age distribution obtains broadly within the liberal Protestant sector, resulting in death rates that are high and likely to become higher still unless the denominations are able to replenish their ranks with younger members in their child-rearing years. As it stands at present, the situation amounts to what Benton Johnson describes as a fundamental "demographic weakness" for liberal Protestantism, and one that does not augur well for its future.[7] For the other religious traditions the age shifts are not as critical, although they are discernible and creating institutional repercussions.

The youthful rebellion against the churches served also to broaden the age gap between the religious and secular cultures. Fifty-nine percent of nonaffiliates are under thirty-five years of age, which is much higher than for any of the religious clusters; only 15 percent of nonaffiliates are age fifty-five or older. The age profile for this more secular constituency has shifted dramatically in the post-1960s period. Nonaffiliates have on the average become younger as they have become more educated and more affluent, all of this happening when the mainline churches were aging. The combination of trends now creates a widening cultural rift between the religious and nonreligious sectors.

Family Patterns

Another set of demographic changes are underway in the relations between family life and religion. Both of these fundamental institutions have had to adjust to the dominant values of individualism, freedom, and equality in the modern world. Both also have had to accommodate the massive social and cultural upheavals of the post-1960s period. New life-styles, changing roles for women, increased divorce rates, and new family forms all pose serious challenges to the traditional family—especially the Norman Rockwell portrait of the normative American family consisting of the husband who is the breadwinner, the wife who is the homemaker, and young children in the home.

Today almost one-fifth of all families are maintained by single parents, about two-fifths have dual wage earners, and one-tenth of the population lives in nonfamily arrangements.[8] Varying patterns of family and household types have become more and more common, and the highly sentimentalized view of the traditional family is now very much a minority family type. Consequently, a huge "gap" exists between the idealized image of the American family and the great diversity of family patterns that now exist. And increasingly, as the range of new family and household types has expanded, so too have ways in which religious institutions accommodate these changes.

Family patterns vary across religious traditions, more so than is often realized. Norman Rockwell's normative family is most commonly found among conservative Protestants and next among moderate Protestants. Seventy-one percent of the conservatives and 68 percent of the moderates are married. For many Protestants of the center and right, the more evangelical and fundamen-

TABLE 2
Percentage Distribution of Religious Families by Marital Status

Family	Married	Widowed	Separated/ Divorced	Never Married
Liberal Protestants	66	12	10	12
Moderate Protestants	68	12	9	11
Black Protestants	46	14	21	19
Conservative Protestants	71	10	10	9
Catholics	65	9	9	18
Jews	65	12	7	16
No religious preference	48	4	14	34

talist ones especially, the nuclear family is considered not only normative in American culture but God given. This pattern is viewed as in keeping with the "biblical concept of the family," which defines marriage as heterosexual and life-long and the primary function of the family as that of home building and parenting. Roles in the family are traditional: the conservatives strongly prefer that women remain in the home or that, if they must work outside, it not interfere with child-rearing responsibilities. Theological conservatives encourage churches and synagogues to exercise social control and socialization functions that support the traditional family, though not without some difficulty in the face of secular pressures.

For Jews, Catholics, and liberal Protestants, there is a wider diversity of marital and family styles. All three have large numbers of singles, reflecting the growing number of Americans choosing not to marry or, more commonly, to postpone marriage until a later age, and sizable numbers of widowed. That the numbers of the widowed would be high for Jews and liberal Protestants is understandable given their above-average age structures. The proportion who are separated or divorced is not unusually high (except for Episcopalians); the proportion of Jews who are separated or divorced is actually the lowest, at 7 percent of all the major groupings. While the nuclear family is held up as a model, norms of pluralism and freedom of choice are deeply ingrained within these traditions. There is less emphasis upon maintaining a particular family style and more openness to diversity. Even within the Catholic community, where traditional family norms are deeply ingrained, there is awareness of diversity among the laity and among many parish priests and a growing effort to deal with changing family forms. Most mainline churches and synagogues recognize a variety of family patterns and life-styles, and in official stands and statements religious authorities have moved toward a greater nurturance and support. Such emphasis does not mean abandoning values crucial for the survival of the family but rather, as William V. D'Antonio points out, helping people to "draw out the love and caring features of religious teachings."[9]

Two of the religious constituencies differ significantly from the mainstream family norms. Black Protestants have the lowest proportion of married persons, the highest separated or divorced and widowed, and large numbers of singles, which is not surprising in view of the long history of strains on the black family. The growing number of single-parent families and serial marriages within this community suggests that it may become even more distinctive in its religious and family patterns. Also not surprising, the nonaffiliates have the highest number of singles and, next to blacks, the highest number of separated and divorced—34 percent and 14 percent respectively. Considering that many of the nonaffiliates are young, many will likely marry in time, but it is also evident that this subculture will remain distinctive for its large number of "alternative" households. Neither of the two groups is likely to become an exemplar of, much less a strong advocate for, the traditional family.

FACTORS AFFECTING RELIGIOUS GROWTH

Both the aging of the mainline religious constituencies and their changing relations with the family bear upon the theme that has become of such paramount concern in recent years—whether the churches are growing or declining. This is a complex issue involving internal institutional as well as contextual factors, and one that has attracted much attention in both scholarly and popular circles. Here our concern is not so much to identify the various reasons why some churches grow and others do not as it is to describe specifically the demography of religious change.

The size of a group's membership over time is dependent upon two fundamental sets of factors: its natural growth and its net gains or losses from conversion. Most faiths are able to hold the loyalty of a majority of the children born to members, and thus the higher the fertility among members the greater the likelihood of numerical growth. Such growth is so obvious that it is usually taken for granted. In contrast, conversion involves the addition or subtraction of members by means of willful choice. Persons join or leave on their own accord—"religious switching" as sociologists describe such movement. A group with a sufficiently high birth rate can, within limits, lose substantial numbers to other faiths and still grow faster than its rivals. Provided it does not lose too many of its members, the group will grow simply because of the large numbers of children born to its members. By the same token, a group with a low birth rate and a high death rate can be a net gainer as a result of conversions and still show membership declines over time. Its losses due to deaths exceed its gains from membership transfer.

These two sets of factors are critically important in the demographic balance and thus determine whether a congregation, or church, grows or shrinks in its membership base (see Figure 2). So important are they for understanding the changing American religious mainline that we give extended treatment to them in the pages that follow.

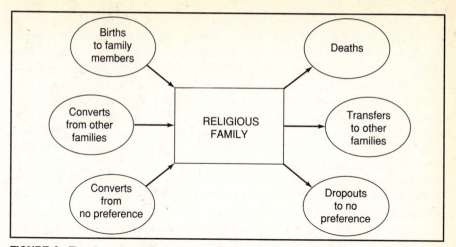

FIGURE 2. The demography of religious family growth and decline.

Birth Rates

Within the natural growth equation the most significant variable is the birth rate, which varies across traditions and over time as well. Factors of theological heritage as well as group experience combine to create differential fertilities, which once in place tend to be perpetuated. Norms of family size and birth control all vary from one religious subculture to another. Conformity to religious norms is itself a factor. Among Catholics, for example, John Scanzoni found that religious devoutness and traditional attitudes toward sex were mutually supportive: "Wives who have been more traditional have been more devout, which in turn reinforces and perhaps increases traditionalism, and so forth. Acting together, both elements have evidently resulted in larger families."[10]

Catholics' birth rates are higher than Protestants' or Jews', Protestants' are higher than Jews', and blacks' higher than whites'. Among white Protestants there are differences that, for the most part, reflect the wide span of class and educational levels found within this large religious family. Thus Methodists typically have had more children than Episcopalians, but fewer than Nazarenes, Jehovah's Witnesses, or many other conservative Protestants. In some instances where fertility levels are high, class may not be so important; for example, the Mormons, Hutterites, and Mennonites lay great emphasis upon the regeneration of the community of believers and have created close ties between kinship and religious roles. But these are minority faiths outside the mainstream, where, generally speaking, fertility varies in direct relation to a group's socioeconomic standing. As with political party affiliation, personal and family styles, and social attitudes, fertility is a fairly sensitive index of status and class.

Those groups that have collectively moved upward in the social structure have typically experienced declining fertility. Churches originating as working-class movements a hundred years or more ago and evolving into middle-class constituencies in the early decades of this century have experienced this pattern.

The number of children born to Methodists, for example, dropped as members moved from the farms and small towns to the cities and adopted more middle-class values and life-styles. With the exception of Catholics, whose church prohibits artificial birth control, only small minorities in other religious communities have recognized any religious direction on matters of contraception—maybe as few as 20 percent of the most religious Protestants and 30 percent of the most devout Jews. Consequently, nonreligious factors have had a greater influence in shaping fertility patterns. Urbanization, the changing relations of work and family, women in the work force, and better methods of birth control have all contributed to a reduced fertility.

More generally, norms of family size vary from one period to another. The postwar baby boom of the 1950s is a good example. At midcentury, birth rates were at an all-time high for the modern period, and familial and child-centered themes (for example, The Family That Prays Together, Stays Together) figured prominently in the religious milieu of the period. Middle-class families with three or more children were not uncommon in those years, and more often than not, new parents followed their children to the Sunday schools and churches. "A Little Child Shall Lead Them" was the title of Dennison Nash's popular essay on the role of children in bringing about the so-called religious revival at the time.[11] The symbolism of religion, family, and country was pervasive; for the religious establishment, the market was bullish indeed.

In the late 1950s, however, birth rates began trending downward. The postwar baby boom peaked and was followed by an extended period of declining or stabilized low fertility. The declines affected virtually all sectors of the society. Among young Catholics, for example, the declines throughout this period were especially evident. In a Gallup poll conducted in 1971, 58 percent of Catholics interviewed agreed that one could ignore *Humanae Vitae,* the pope's encyclical proscribing birth control, and still be a good Catholic.[12] Only 40 percent of the priests surveyed in 1969 agreed with the encyclical, and opposition was almost unanimous among the younger priests.[13] For a variety of reasons the gap in birth rates for Protestants and Catholics was narrowing. Even by the late fifties, overall birth rates for Protestants and Catholics under forty-five years of age were already coming together.[14] Throughout the sixties and seventies, the gap continued to diminish. Broad changes in the society and within Catholicism led in the direction of greater convergence—in fertility as in many other cultural aspects.

Today Catholic and mainline Protestant birth rates are roughly similar, but differences remain among the Protestant communities. Table 3 shows the number of children born per woman, both the total figures and those broken down by age. With the exception of blacks, conservative Protestants have the highest birth rates of any of the religious families (for older women the rates are even higher than that of blacks). Despite declining birth rates and converging patterns generally in the United States, historic differentials within Protestantism are still readily apparent. At present, differences *within* Protestantism far transcend those between Protestants and Catholics.

The patterns are indeed striking. Among women under forty-five years of age, the child-to-woman ratio is 2.01 within the conservative Protestant family

TABLE 3
Average Number of Births per Woman by Religious Family

Family	Total	Age 45+	Under Age 45
Liberal Protestants	1.97	2.27	1.60
Moderate Protestants	2.27	2.67	1.80
Black Protestants	2.62	3.08	2.24
Conservative Protestants	2.54	3.12	2.01
Catholics	2.20	2.75	1.82
Jews	1.69	1.96	1.37
No religious preference	1.39	2.30	1.18
National	2.25	2.75	1.73

as compared to 1.60 for liberal Protestants. This translates into four-tenths of a child less for every liberal Protestant adult female under forty-five. If indeed liberal Protestant women had as many babies as do conservative Protestant women, the size of the liberal sector would increase by more than 2.2 million! Not only, however, do liberal Protestant women have fewer children, but there are fewer women in these churches in the child-bearing ages. Thus numbers and fertility work against a strong and sustained liberal mainline: the natural growth potential for the liberal denominations is fairly weak, while the opposite is true for conservative bodies.

Against conservative Protestantism's strong demographic base, the other white religious communities have far less potential for growth. None of the others are positioned as well in age structure and family patterns—the essential prerequisites for a strong fertility. Except for Northern Baptists and Reformed members, birth rates for the under-forty-five females in the moderate Protestant family are relatively low, almost as low as for liberal Protestants. Catholics' birth rates are similar to those of moderate Protestants: both hover around the national average. Young Jewish women have the lowest fertility of any comparably aged, religiously affiliated Americans. The nonaffiliates have the lowest of all of the major groupings, especially for the under-forty-five category. The nonaffiliates, Unitarian-Universalists, and Christian Scientists have, in that order, the lowest birth rates among younger women. In contrast, black Protestants have exceedingly high birth rates, the very highest in fact among young women.

Religious Switching

Religious switching is another significant factor in the demographic equation of mainline religion. Inflow and outflow amount to a migratory stream of religious movement—in and out of the established faith communities. Some churches benefit from what is described as the "circulation of the saints," that is, they pick up members from other churches; other churches pick up fewer members this way and must aggressively proselytize from among those who have no religious background. As with inflow, so with outflow. Churches and synagogues lose members either to another faith community or to the more secular, nonreligious sector. Losing members to the former does not mean that these members have lost faith, but rather that they are simply opting for a different religious style; losses to the ranks of the nonaffiliated are more serious and may suggest a general secular drift as a competitor to faith.

Movement from one church to another is common in the United States, especially among Protestants. The most common pattern is an "upward movement" of switching from low-status to high-status denominational affiliations. Long observed in Protestant church life, this type of switching has contributed to the making of a diverse and socially conscious denominational order. Much impressionistic evidence, throughout the nineteenth century and much of the twentieth, points to religious movement associated with upward social mobility. Closely linked symbolically with the prevailing mobility ethos, religious switching has often been celebrated as part of the American Way of Life. Abraham Lincoln's own celebrated life course was not all that atypical religiously: from a hard-shell Baptist background, through a "good" marriage and a successful law practice, to regular Presbyterian attendance.[15] Americans can generally relate to the character type that Peter Berger describes as "the young Baptist salesman who becomes an Episcopalian sales executive."[16] Education, hard work, success, good marriage, recognition—all are values given expression in the upward religious movement, which Jay Demerath amusingly describes as "playing musical church to a status-striving tune."[17]

The best "hard" evidence on religious switching is found in Rodney Stark and Charles Y. Glock's *American Piety*. Using 1963 survey data from California and a 1965 national survey, they observed "upward" movement among Protestants from conservative to more liberal denominations.[18] Liberal churches benefited for two reasons: first, upward social mobility tended to propel people into more liberal, higher-status churches; and, second, people found the demythologized beliefs of the liberal churches more congruent with modern life. While the pattern of liberal movement was especially pronounced in California, there was ample evidence of similar switching nationally as well. The groups with the greatest gains were the Episcopalians, Presbyterians, and to a lesser extent the Congregationalists. Conservative Protestant bodies lost in the switching process, as did Methodists and Lutherans. By far the greatest losses were experienced by non-Christian groups and those with no religious preference. Religious nonaffiliates declined by 31 percent in the national study. Overall, in the sixties the pattern demonstrated conservative Protestant switching losses, modest gains for moderate Protestants, and the greatest gains for liberal Protestants.

Stark and Glock's findings offer a portrait of upward shifts in a bullish religious market. Whether their description accurately fits the past or is an inflated pattern peculiar to the period we do not know. Unfortunately, historical data on which to judge either the amount of movement or its significance are lacking. But we believe it is reasonable to conclude that in this century such movement was a source of growth and vitality for many mainline religious institutions. Especially in times of economic growth and middle-class expansion such as the post–World War II era, high-status Protestant churches likely benefited from above-average levels of religious switching. Old-line establishment churches such as the Episcopal and Presbyterian often received membership transfers from lower-status churches; so did Congregationalism, particularly in New England and the Midwest. A dynamic, achievement-oriented society generated a secular, accommodating religious stance favoring these churches. Higher-status churches have benefited up the line; upwardly mobile Nazarenes and Baptists often became Methodists, affluent Methodists joined the Presbyterians, and many out of diverse backgrounds, if successful, found a home with the Episcopalians. Thus one religious tradition after another in the mainline has enjoyed gains from this pattern of membership flow.

The portrait given us by Stark and Glock underscores another observation: sectarian and conservative Protestant bodies recruit more successfully among the nonaffiliated than do liberal Protestants. This finding is in keeping with the more evangelical character of these traditions and hardly comes as any surprise. But it is an important observation about the basic historic structure of religious movement in the United States. An inflow of members at the "bottom" of the religious establishment has served to replenish low-status memberships and has assured a continuing large pool of upward religious switchers. Large numbers of Americans, whatever their current religious affiliation, were first introduced to, or indoctrinated into, Christianity within the more conservative and moderate branches of American Protestantism.

This portrait of religious America was no longer fitting after the tumultuous sixties. To claim a religious affiliation was "in" during the fifties and early sixties; religious belonging was consistent with the conformist pressures of the period. In an era of expansion and mobility generally, upward religious movement created a favorable milieu for the mainline churches. Conformist cultural and religious themes helped create something of an artificial prosperity and gave the impression that mainline Protestantism (and to a lesser extent an Americanized Catholicism and Judaism) was healthier than it really was. The religious institutions were on the brink of a "gathering storm"—confronting civil rights and other divisive issues of the 1960s. The counterculture, Vietnam, and the crisis of authority for the established structures would shatter the older bourgeois styles of status-driven religiosity. Both the culture and the role of religion within it were to change and so would patterns of religious switching.

Current Patterns of Switching

What about religious switching today? Is the proportion of switchers relative to nonswitchers still fairly high? How have the patterns of switching changed? The following news release issued in June of 1980 is worthy of note:

> LESS THAN HALF REMAIN IN SAME DENOMINATION
>   Princeton, N.J. Fewer than half of U.S. adults (43 percent) say they have always been a member of their present religion, or denomination, as determined by a recent Gallup survey.[19]

Many surveys and studies show that at least 40 percent of American Protestants have at one time or another switched denominational affiliations.[20] Switching within this tradition remains much higher due to its size and diversity of churches. For Catholics and Jews there is less switching "in" or "out," but all indications are that it has increased in recent years. Not only has switching increased since the 1960s, but patterns of movement generally have changed. The new voluntarism, involving greater individual choice and preference, has produced more diverse types of switching and far more value-laden and symbolic movement into and out of the religious communities.

To grasp the full import of switching, we must look at both its quantitative and qualitative aspects. Even the quantitative switching, which in one sense is obvious, must be sorted out carefully. We begin with levels of stability for the religious groups. By *stability* we mean the extent to which those who grow up in a religious group stay with it throughout their lives. The more stable a group, the stronger most likely will be its institutional attachments and religious bonds and the more likely it will add the children of its members. Obviously a crucial dimension, stability points to a group's capacity to sustain and "hold on" to its members in what is a fluid and competitive religious market.

Groups vary far more than might be expected in how well they hold on to their members. Jews and Catholics do much better than Protestants: 87 percent and 85 percent, respectively, remain in their faiths. Eighty percent of Mormons and 78 percent of Jehovah's Witnesses continue to maintain their original religious ties. Among more mainline Protestants, the range is wide—from 75 percent (Lutherans) to 37 percent (evangelicals and fundamentalists). A ranking of Protestant denominations shows the following groups to be the most stable: Lutherans, 75 percent; black Northern Baptists, 73 percent; white Southern Baptists, 73 percent; Pentecostals and holiness, 70 percent; Adventists, 69 percent; and black Methodists, 69 percent. At the bottom of the rank order, or the least stable, are three disparate groups: Christian Scientists, 39 percent; Unitarian-Universalists, 39 percent; and evangelicals and fundamentalists, 37 percent.

Most of the large, Protestant mainline denominations fall in the middle. Episcopalians (65 percent), Methodists (63 percent), United Church of Christ (61 percent), Disciples (58 percent), and Presbyterians (60 percent) all have majorities that have remained stable, yet there are large numbers of switchers. This is not too surprising: to be in the mainline is to be in the middle, tending toward neither extreme. By virtue of their size and social location, they are the religious institutions most likely to experience tensions arising out of the larger society. The cross-pressures of switching versus nonswitching are felt most acutely within these structures.

One thing is clear—membership stability is not a matter simply of liberal or conservative theology. Groups in the most stable category do not all share a strong conservative theology, nor are those least stable necessarily similar in this respect. Christian Scientists and Unitarian-Universalists are among the most liberal; many evangelicals and fundamentalists are known to switch to other churches. Stability appears to be more a reflection of communal belonging. Mormons, Lutherans, Jehovah's Witnesses, black Baptists and Methodists, and white Southern Baptists all have strong ethnic or quasi-ethnic loyalties, at least compared with more mainline groups. The role of communal attachments in creating stability becomes even more apparent in view of the fact that nonaffiliates are also among the least stable of all groupings. Only 45 percent of those reared as nonaffiliates have retained a nonreligious preference. Known to be highly individualistic and to have weak communal attachments, they are also unstable as a constituency of nonbelievers or, more correctly, nonbelongers.

Looking at the religious families, we see even better the significance of ethnic and group ties. Stability in this context refers to the percentage of persons raised in a family group who remain within that family; for example, a person raised an Episcopalian who is now a Presbyterian is classified as remaining in the liberal Protestant family. Of course this means the amount of switching is less than when grouped in more specific denominational categories, but such grouping helps show levels of stability for the larger religiocultural traditions in America today. Arranged on the basis of the percentage remaining within the family, the ordering is as follows: Jews, 87 percent; black Protestants, 87 percent; Catholics, 85 percent; conservative Protestants, 78 percent; moderate Protestants, 74 percent; liberal Protestants, 67 percent; and no religious preference, 45 percent. The relation between group identity and membership stability within the family is evident: the stronger the quasi-ethnic bonds, the more likely members will stay within their traditions. Jews, Catholics, and black Protestants are more likely to remain within their families than are conservative and moderate Protestants, who in turn are more likely to do so than liberal Protestants. That levels of stability parallel so closely *gemeinschaft*-like group attachments is itself revealing about the contextual boundaries that set limits on religious switching even in the highly individualized culture of modern America.

There is another aspect to switching: a group's capacity to *attract* new members. Net gains or losses for a particular group are a function of both its stability (or the number it retains) and its attractiveness (or the number who switch in). Thus very stable religious groups need not attract many persons in order to show a net gain, but denominations that lose many of their members must attract large numbers of new members if they are to avoid net losses through switching.

With this in mind, we can begin to see how the flow of members varies for the various religious traditions. Table 4 shows switching patterns for the seven mainline groupings. For each the table gives the number of sample members who were raised in the family, the number who were raised in another family or without a religious preference, and the number brought up in the tradition who have switched out either to another family or to no religious preference. To illustrate: there were 1,255 members raised in liberal Protestant denominations. To this number were added 431 persons from other families and 27 with no religious preference. Subtracted were 311 persons raised as liberal Protestants who are now affiliated with another religious family and 101 who now list no religious preference. Overall, the liberal Protestant family has a net gain of 46 members, or 3.7 percent. By looking closely at the membership flows, we can draw several conclusions about religious change today.

TABLE 4

Family Gains and Losses Due to Switching

Denominational Family	TOTAL		UNDER AGE 45		AGE 45+	
	Number in Sample	Percent	Number in Sample	Percent	Number in Sample	Percent
Liberal Protestants						
Base (age 16)	1,255	100.0	635	100.0	620	100.0
From other families	431	34.3	154	24.3	277	44.7
From nonaffiliation	27	2.2	18	2.8	9	1.5
To other families	(311)	−24.8	(159)	−25.0	(152)	−24.5
To nonaffiliation	(101)	−8.0	(73)	−11.5	(28)	−4.5
Net gain/loss	46	3.7	(60)	−9.4	106	17.1
Moderate Protestants						
Base (age 16)	3,896	100.0	1,862	100.0	2,034	100.0
From other families	708	18.2	353	19.0	355	17.5
From nonaffiliation	84	2.2	41	2.2	43	2.1
To other families	(796)	−20.4	(340)	−18.3	(456)	−22.4
To nonaffiliation	(225)	−5.8	(167)	−9.0	(58)	−2.9
Net gain/loss	(229)	−5.9	(113)	−6.1	(116)	−5.7
Black Protestants						
Base (age 16)	1,499	100.0	814	100.0	685	100.0
From other families	33	2.2	20	2.5	13	1.9
From nonaffiliation	3	0.2	3	0.4	0	0
To other families	(133)	−8.9	(62)	−7.6	(71)	−10.4
To nonaffiliation	(63)	−4.2	(55)	−6.8	(8)	−1.2
Net gain/loss	(160)	−10.7	(94)	−11.5	(66)	−9.6
Conservative Protestants						
Base (age 16)	2,307	100.0	1,278	100.0	1,029	100.0
From other families	550	23.8	272	21.3	278	27.0
From nonaffiliation	53	2.3	32	2.5	21	2.0
To other families	(448)	−19.4	(208)	−16.3	(240)	−23.3
To nonaffiliation	(90)	−3.9	(72)	−5.6	(18)	−1.7
Net gain/loss	65	2.8	24	1.9	41	4.0
Catholics						
Base (age 16)	4,012	100.0	2,438	100.0	1,574	100.0
From other families	331	8.3	178	7.3	153	9.7
From nonaffiliation	37	0.9	18	0.7	19	1.2
To other families	(287)	−7.2	(175)	−7.2	(112)	−7.1
To nonaffiliation	(294)	−7.3	(245)	−10.0	(49)	−3.1
Net gain/loss	(213)	−5.3	(224)	−9.2	11	0.7
Jews						
Base (age 16)	357	100.0	171	100.0	168	100.0
From other families	19	5.3	12	7.0	7	4.2
From nonaffiliation	3	0.8	3	1.8	0	0
To other families	(12)	−3.4	(7)	−4.1	(5)	−3.0
To nonaffiliation	(36)	−10.1	(23)	−13.5	(13)	−7.7
Net gain/loss	(26)	−7.3	(15)	−8.8	(11)	−6.5
No religious preference						
Base (age 16)	387	100.0	247	100.0	140	100.0
From other families	809	209.0	635	257.1	174	124.3
To other families	(207)	−53.5	(115)	−46.6	(92)	−65.7
Net gain/loss	602	155.6	520	210.5	82	58.6

Liberal Gains Offset By Losses

Many mainline Protestant churches enjoy membership gains from other church-es but lose equal numbers, if not more, to the ranks of the nonaffiliates. Liberal Protestants show a gain of 34.3 percent through transfers *from* other families, which is offset by a loss of 24.8 percent *to* other families, or a resulting net inter-family gain of 9.5 percent. This suggests that liberal Protestantism is attractive as a religious alternative and actually does better in interfamily switching than any other religious family. Liberal churches continue to pick up members out of the conservative churches. But with other types of membership flow they do not come out as well. Liberal churches show a gain of 2.2 percent from the nonaf-filiates, which is offset by a loss of 8.0 percent to them, or a net loss of 5.8 per-cent. This leads to the observation, one which goes against popular wisdom, that the challenge to liberal Protestantism comes not so much from the conservative faiths as from the growing secular drift of many of their not-so-highly-commit-ted members.

Secular Drift Across the Religious Spectrum

The big "winner" in the switching game is the growing secular constituency. Of all seven groupings, nonaffiliates are the greatest beneficiary of switching; all the groups lose more persons to this category than they receive from it. In the exchange, Jews, liberal Protestants, and Catholics have the greatest losses, while conservative Protestants come closest to holding their own. The liberal religious traditions especially have a serious institutional problem of holding on to their own.

Stark and Glock hypothesized some twenty years ago that the leftward trend of switching might not end with movement into the liberal churches, but that in time many liberals might simply drop out of the churches altogether. They surmised that should this happen, what had seemed like a favorable situ-ation for liberal Protestantism could turn into a serious problem of membership collapse.[21] To some extent, their predictions appear to have been borne out. Liberal Protestantism's greatest losses come from those dropping out of religion altogether. But Catholics and Jews, and to a lesser extent some conservative Protestants, also lose considerable numbers to the nonaffiliate ranks. What was once a liberal Protestant "problem" is now more generally one for the mainline faiths.

The only group showing net gains among younger members is the nonaffil-iates. All the religious families lose considerably higher proportions of their younger members to this group than they receive from it. In this exchange, Jews, liberal Protestants, and Catholics experience exceptionally high losses among those under forty-five years of age. All three families lose great numbers of youth and young adults to the nonaffiliates. Conservative Protestants do somewhat better; they hold on to more of their younger members, yet still lose in the exchange. In every case the rate of loss to nonaffiliation for the younger group exceeds that of persons forty-five and older. This trend differs from the 1950s and 1960s, when proportionately more were leaving the ranks of the "unchurched" to affiliate with one or another of the major national faiths. Disaffiliation, and indifference generally to organized religion, is much more of a reality today for the churches and synagogues. Maybe it was the case, as Dennison Nash said, that the religious revival of the fifties came about as a result of "A Little Child Leading Them," but we might add with just a little whimsy that in the seventies and eighties a religious depression resulted when "A Teen-Ager or Young Adult Dropped Out."

Older Switchers Within the Religious Communities

Many of the mainline Protestant and Catholic churches pick up more recruits from other religious communities than they lose, yet it is important to note who these persons are. The net switching gains for liberal Protestants are wholly accounted for by *older* switchers. Among older persons this community experiences a net gain of 17.1 percent, among younger persons a loss of 9.4 percent. Conservative Protestants and Catholics pick up older members and break even or lose the young. Both increasing numbers of switchers to nonaffiliation and a decline in the number of persons switching from other religious communities have contributed to this more pronounced age-related phenomenon. Generally, religion's "market share" of potential recruits has grown older.

Losses in the Middle

The big "losers" are the moderate Protestants. The large middle America denominations—Methodists, Lutherans, Disciples, Northern Baptists, Reformed—have disproportionately lost to other groups since the 1960s. Because of their size and close identity with the mainstream culture, they have been unable to hold their own and have become the major suppliers of recruits to other faiths. As the nation's cultural and religious center has weakened, movement is greatest at the extremes—in the conservative religious and the secular, nonaffiliated directions. Such switching reflects the more fragmented and polarized culture that so rocked the religious establishment in the sixties and seventies. The strains run deep in the large moderate Protestant bodies, those truly mainline in faith and cultural experience.

THE SWITCHERS

Who are the switchers? What are their social and life-style characteristics? How do they differ from nonswitchers? Considering how many switchers there are and their importance for American religion, we must inquire further about them. As we have seen, patterns of switching currently are much too complex for simple generalizations about the switchers. In recent years switching patterns have become more diverse, reflecting the greater variety of styles of belief and behavior. By looking at the switching profiles, we can learn a great deal about the religious disestablishment of the sixties and seventies and about the many currents of change now reshaping the religious landscape (see table 5).

Again, we draw several conclusions:

1. *The overriding factor of age.* The profile data confirm what we already know—age is a major predictor of switching patterns. Young persons are vastly overrepresented among those who switch to nonaffiliation. As many as 80 percent of those who have disaffiliated from some of the religious families are under forty-five years of age. Age differences stand out in Protestant interfamily switching. Those switching into the liberal Protestant family from other traditions are older. Sixty-four percent of those who switch into liberal Protestantism from another religious family are over forty-five years of age. Fifty percent of those switching from other families to both moderate and conservative Protestant families are of this age. While we do not know the age of individuals when they made a change of affiliation, the data suggest two possible conclusions: switching to liberal Protestantism occurs mainly among older persons or switching to this family may have been more common in earlier periods than in the recent past. Very likely both are correct and, if so, bear implications for the future course of change within American Protestantism.

Switching currently contributes to the lopsided age composition of the liberal churches. Because these churches lose so many of their young and receive as members a disproportionate share of older persons, their constituencies continue to age. No other religious family is so adversely affected. Disaffiliation by the young has raised the average age levels in all the families, but in most instances this is somewhat offset by a favorable membership transfer. Among conservative Protestants, for example, there is almost no discrepancy between the ages of those switching in and those switching out (among religious families); the overall age level of these denominations is essentially unaffected by interfamily switching. The members moderate Protestants pick up are younger than those they lose to other denominations. Catholics pick up members who are older than the ones they lose in the exchange, but whatever demographic imbalances may result are "made up" by a favorable fertility.

2. *Upward switching.* All evidence points to less upward switching, or conservative-to-liberal transfer of religious membership, now than in the past. Net gains resulting from switching for liberal Protestants are not as marked today as they were in previous decades; there seems to have been a falloff in what had once been an important source of their growth during the 1950s and 1960s. Conservative Protestants show net gains from switching today, in contrast to their earlier losses; they are losing proportionately fewer to other faiths today because of their greater attraction and appeal in the religious marketplace. Because greater numbers of affluent, well-educated persons are becoming nonaffiliates, liberal churches are drained of many who in times past were more likely to join these churches. There appears to be little question that the old historic pattern of intragenerational switching—from conservative to liberal Protestant denominations—has declined and no longer

TABLE 5
Selected Characteristics of Switchers
....

Family	Percent under 45	Mean Age	Mean Education	Mean Occupational Prestige	%Regular Worship % Attenders	%Strong Members
Liberal Protestants						
No change	48	47.2	13.2	43.8	34	32
From other families	36	51.2	13.3	45.6	48	37
From nonaffiliation	67	41.7	13.6	42.8	33	28
To other families	51	46.8	13.1	42.5	57	43
To nonaffiliation	72	36.8	14.1	45.4	2	—
Moderate Protestants						
No change	47	47.6	12.0	39.5	39	36
From other families	50	46.7	12.0	40.4	50	38
From nonaffiliation	49	45.4	11.5	37.3	42	33
To other families	43	49.3	12.3	41.3	57	45
To nonaffiliation	74	37.3	13.1	40.0	3	—
Black Protestants						
No change	54	44.5	10.4	31.0	55	13
From other families	*	*	*	*	*	*
From nonaffiliation	*	*	*	*	*	*
To other families	47	44.8	11.1	32.2	74	56
To nonaffiliation	87	34.0	11.5	32.2	3	—
Conservative Protestants						
No change	56	43.9	10.8	36.4	54	52
From other families	50	47.5	10.9	36.3	69	59
From nonaffiliation	60	39.9	9.9	35.6	70	54
To other families	46	47.4	11.7	40.6	49	39
To nonaffiliation	80	35.8	11.0	37.0	4	—
Catholics						
No change	59	42.5	11.9	38.8	53	43
From other families	54	44.9	12.3	38.8	52	32
From nonaffiliation	49	45.9	11.9	37.9	62	34
To other families	61	42.1	11.8	38.6	50	39
To nonaffiliation	83	34.4	13.5	41.8	4	—
Jews						
No change	46	49.2	14.0	47.3	13	43
From other families	*	*	*	*	*	*
From nonaffiliation	*	*	*	*	*	*
To other families	58	41.3	12.5	34.8	*	*
To nonaffiliation	64	39.7	15.4	53.8	0	—
No religious preference						
No change	73	35.3	12.0	38.5	2	—
From other families	79	35.9	13.1	41.1	3	—
To other families	56	43.3	11.5	37.7	51	38

*Too few cases for meaningful analysis.

plays as important a role in sustaining a vital membership for the liberal churches.

Some upward switching still occurs primarily among those with higher levels of education and occupational prestige. As in the past, contemporary switching helps enhance status differences among Protestants. The social characteristics and status trajectories for the several streams of switchers differ. Those leaving the liberal churches for other churches have lower educational and occupational standing than "stayers," or those remaining, or than those who switch in from other churches. In other words, interfamily switching contributes to the higher social status of liberal Protestants. But the opposite is true for conservative Protestantism. While switchers into this family have education and occupational prestige that are close to those of stayers, the status levels are lower for the joiners than for persons raised in the family who switch to other groups. Much the same holds for moderate Protestants. Unquestionably there remains an upward switching pattern within Protestantism of older, well-educated, and higher-status members.

Upward switching is not simply a Protestant phenomenon. Catholics too appear to enjoy status gains as a result of the circulation of the saints. Those switching into this faith have a higher socioeconomic standing than those who leave for another religious affiliation. New recruits to Catholicism have equal if not greater status than those who are born and reared within the faith. More distinct switching patterns here indicate broad changes in Catholicism, especially in its relation to American culture. As Catholicism has moved into the religious mainstream, its patterns of recruiting have changed to reflect the greater mobility and status of its members.

3. *Mobility and secular drift.* There is an emerging second type of religious movement associated with upward mobility: switching into the ranks of the nonaffiliated. Those who switch to no religious preference have significantly more education and higher occupational prestige than those who remain religiously affiliated. This is true across all the religious families, for Protestants, Catholics, and Jews. Many born and reared in the established faiths and who are upwardly mobile are dropping out and becoming a part of the growing nonaffiliated sector. At the same time, recruits into the churches from the nonaffiliated have less education and lower occupational prestige than those who switch the opposite way—from a faith to nonaffiliated. Switching thus contributes to the emergence of a more sharply crystallized image of nonaffiliates as an increasingly mobile, high-achieving group.

By and large, interfamily switching serves to maintain rather than lessen status differences among the religious communities in America. Even the more diverse switching patterns of recent times and the emergence of a more distinct secular, nonaffiliated constituency appear not to have eroded historic class differences among Protestants. If anything, switching has enhanced these contrasts and contributed to the greater religious and ideological pluralism of contemporary America.

THE "QUALITY" OF CONVERTS

In the circulation of the saints that occurs within Protestantism, mainline Protestant churches take in many affluent, well-educated, upwardly mobile members. But what about the level of *religious* commitment of those picked up? As church members are they more or less committed than converts to conservative Protestant churches? There is reason to expect that the liberal denominations fail to attract the highly committed. Rodney Stark and Charles Y. Glock two decades ago concluded that "liberal denominations fare badly in generating member commitment."[22] More recently Kirk Hadaway, in a study of the "quality" of switchers to various denominations, concluded that while more liberal groups have larger net gains as a result of switching, "conservative denominations pick up the 'better' converts."[23]

The data at hand shed some light on these interesting questions. The evidence in table 5 suggests that "joiners" make good attenders and strong members, often better ones than those who have remained all their lives in a particular tradition. Among "stayers," regular worship is highest for Catholics and conservative Protestants, but lower for black Protestants, moderate Protestants, and liberal Protestants. It is very low for Jews and those with no preference. In contrast, religious "joiners" have significantly higher rates of religious participation (more true in the case of religious attendance than "strong" membership). This is particularly true of persons switching to conservative Protestantism and Catholicism; persons raised with no preference who switch to these groups have the highest participation rates shown in the table (70 percent and 62 percent, respectively). Even for liberal Protestants, those switching in tend to participate about as much as those who have been with the tradition all their lives. Across the religious spectrum, then, it appears that recruits are a source of on-going institutional vitality.

Thus there is little basis for believing that religious switching itself undermines institutional commitment or leads persons to lessened religious involvement; if anything, switching from one faith to another is probably the occasion for greater clarity of choice and deliberateness. As conformity has given way to greater choice in lifestyle and religious affiliation, opportunity for a more genuine type of commitment becomes possible. In an age of religious voluntarism, switching may well be a means of enhancing personal faith as well as institutional commitment and should not be viewed as simply an expression of how secular forces erode faith.

But the "quality" of switchers does indeed vary. Liberal and moderate mainline Protestants attract persons who are less active than those they lose to other groups, whereas those who switch to the conservative Protestant family are more active than those who leave. A difference is evident among those both switching in and switching out. For example, 48 percent of the "new" liberal Protestants raised in other families are regular attenders as compared to 69 percent of those switching to conservative Protestantism and

52 percent of those switching to Catholicism. Those picked up by the liberal churches are, as Hadaway suggests, less committed. And it is also true that these churches lose their most faithful participants. Among those switching out of the liberal Protestant tradition to other faiths, 57 percent are regular attenders—a much greater percentage than that of its stayers. Forty-three percent of those leaving are "strong" members—a higher percentage than that for the stayers or for any new recruits. Typically those leaving a liberal church for another church find one in which they can become more involved. A principle of consistency seems to operate: persons whose levels of religious commitment differ from the prevailing norms within their respective traditions, whether liberal or conservative, tend to switch to a group more in keeping with their particular styles.

The quality of converts thus adds to the list of woes for liberal churches. To compensate for their low natural growth and high death rates, they must rely upon transfers from other faiths in order to maintain a steady membership. But falloff in membership transfers of this kind places the churches in a weak demographic position, and the fact that they fail to pick up the better converts further erodes their institutional strength. Both numbers and levels of member commitment work against them.

This lack of commitment helps explain a puzzling feature about switching and church growth. While liberal Protestant churches enjoy net gains from switching, these churches have suffered severe membership losses for two decades now. Why would the churches benefiting from the switching not also be growing? Of course the survey data on switching have to do with "religious preference," not church membership, which may account partly for the discrepancy. And we do not know when individuals in the surveys may have switched. The average age of switchers into these churches may have risen, which might also be a factor. The most likely explanation is that some may say they have switched but in fact are mental affiliates—that is, they do not actually join or become active participants with these churches. Mental affiliates show up in the polls but not on the churches' rolls.

For Catholics, patterns are similar to those for conservative Protestants. Both tend to pick up "better" converts than they lose. Both of these large communities show considerable power in attracting highly committed members, and they do so across a broad spectrum of social and religious backgrounds. Both recruit persons from the nonaffiliated category as well as from other religious families. Sixty-two percent of those switching from nonaffiliation to Catholicism, and 70 percent of those switching to conservative Protestantism, are regular worshipers. Levels of commitment for the recruits are in each instance considerably higher than those of long-standing members. The more liberal and moderate Protestants fare less well in reaching the unchurched and reactivating their faiths. Those switching from a nonreligious background appear to adopt a style of institutional commitment in keeping with standards of practice within the churches they join. They truly "join" and often become good members.

408 • AMERICAN RELIGION

THREE STREAMS OF RELIGIOUS MOVEMENT

Today there are three distinct streams of religious movement reshaping the religious mainline: two amount to circulation of the saints within the religious establishment, and the third involves a drift out of the religious communities. The first stream is the liberal movement, characterized generally by rising status levels for many Americans. Those shifting into liberal churches are typically older, more educated, and hold more prestigeous occupations; they tend to be relatively liberal on many moral and social issues. They are less active religiously than those they leave behind in other churches and synagogues. While such switching has declined somewhat in recent decades, it is still a discernible pattern accompanying upward mobility and entry into the mainstream. Liberal Protestants and Catholics, and to a lesser extent Reform Jews, all benefit from such switching. Older switchers account for a disproportionate amount of such movement. In the United States in the 1980s, the moral and ideological views of the switchers have become more pronounced, suggesting that those who choose to identify with these traditions may do so with greater awareness of, and possible conviction for, what they represent in the larger framework of American religious pluralism at present.

A second stream is the conservative movement, perhaps best understood primarily as a reaction to the secular trends of modern society and accommodation of the mainline faiths to the culture. Those switching to the conservative churches tend to be somewhat younger, less educated, and of lower social standing; they are often opposed to such issues as the ERA, abortion, gay rights, and the extension of civil liberties. They are more committed to traditional religious values and moral principles. Such switching is very much ideological in character and seems to have increased in recent years as a response to the moral and religious ambiguities of the times. Largely it is a white Protestant phenomenon, and the losses it creates are felt most within the large, moderate bodies.

The third movement, or growth of the secular constituency, is qualitatively different. It cuts across religious families and breaks with the cognitive and moral worlds associated with the religious traditions. Amid all the flux of the recent period, this group has become the main beneficiary. For every person raised without religion who adopts a church, three persons forsake the churches for no institutional religious affiliation. Those who become nonaffiliates are young, predominately male, well educated, more committed to alternative lifestyles, and oriented generally to an ethic of personal growth and self-fulfillment. Though we have no hard data on which to judge, these persons appear to be more "new class" in outlook and ideology. They may be religious in a deeply personal sense, but affiliation with a congregation is not deemed essential to their spiritual quests.

This greater diversity in switching patterns signifies, as noted earlier, the migratory character of faith in a modern, pluralistic society: people move "in" and "out" of faith communities with considerable ease. Americans have always been known for how easily they cross boundaries of faith, and they seem to be doing so even more now than in the past. A new religious order appears to be in the making in which life-style choice and moral values play a bigger part in the selection of a religious (or nonreligious) affiliation. The religious individualism of modern America encourages sifting and sorting on the basis of shifting perceptions of institutions and definitions of personal need. Individual preferences in matters of faith operate more freely; believers are less bound by the strictures of group belonging, by custom and tradition. As conformity in religious life has declined, choice has become a more important factor.

CONCLUSION

The demography of American religion offers many clues to how and why the religious establishment is changing. Age structures and family patterns are becoming more diversified in the religious mainline. These fundamental shifts in the social and demographic structure have implications for the social location and institutional characteristics of religion, now and for the future.

Generally demographers who study population dynamics concern themselves with three basic variables—births, deaths, and migration. All three of these bear upon the changing religious scene. As we have seen, differential birth rates are important, death rates are crucial especially for those traditions with low birth rates, and religious switching, or the migration equivalent, has become more significant in the modern period. A particular church or tradition may enjoy added numbers as a result of a favorable birth rate or net gains from switching, or both; similarly it may suffer serious institutional losses depending upon how the numbers fall. Both natural growth and additions by switching are crucial elements that figure in the formula of institutional and group survival. It is difficult to imagine that either will become any less important as considerations in the future, and one or the other may well become even more critical. Switching as a factor especially is likely to take on greater significance.

Demography has proven to be destiny for American Protestantism. Since midcentury, demographic and switching trends have literally reshaped the Protestant establishment. Declining birth rates have diminished the chances that liberal Protestants will reproduce themselves. Liberal churches continue to attract upwardly mobile switchers but at a reduced rate, and those they attract tend not to be very active. The liberal churches at present suffer from a severe demographic weakness: they have aging constituencies and have become, or are dangerously close to becoming, in Hadaway's phrase, "unstable destination denominations."[24] Large numbers of members who are only nominally committed and many who now are leaving the churches altogether make the liberal churches vulnerable as continuing vital religious institutions. With their lopsided age distributions, death rates are high and likely to become higher still unless the churches are able to replenish their ranks with younger people. Of all the major traditions, liberal Protestantism is suffering the most from the secular drift of the post-1960s. Lack of strong group cohesion means that many individuals either disaffiliate or simply become nominal members having little to do with congregational life. The greater religious voluntarism of modern life produces "alumni associations," or collectivities with vague ties to the churches. Even though many are attracted to a liberal stance of openness and pluralism, such traits tend not to generate strong institutional commitment.

Protestant conservatives, in contrast, fare better. Fewer of them are now switching to liberal denominations, and they hold on to more of their younger members. Their death rates are lower, and their birth rates higher—a winning combination in the game of religious growth. Compared with other Protestants, they gain the most committed converts, retain the most committed members, and lose those who are least likely to be regular participants and supporters. Loyalty to traditional doctrines runs deeper, and mechanisms of member commitment are stronger. Perhaps most important, conservative churches have stronger socioreligious group attachments, which play an important role in undergirding them as communities of belief. More emphasis upon the gathered community of believers and a sense of responsibility and accountability to one another serve as a "buffer" protecting the conservative churches more from the privatizing forces of modern society. Secular forces are strong, of course, and are propelling these churches in the direction of greater religious voluntarism, but relatively speaking they still enjoy greater social cohesiveness.

In some respects, Catholics and moderate Protestants have similar demographies. Neither are suffering from great decline in birth rates; death rates are about average; and both are losing increasing numbers of their members to the secular drift. Catholics choose, as Greeley says, "to go their own way," meaning that many now believe and practice in a manner in keeping with their personal preference and set their own conditions for religious belonging.[25] Traditional and rigid Catholic styles are giving way to a more voluntaristic style of "selective Catholicism"; many Catholics are functionally "unchurched," "nonpracticing," or "communal." Moderate Protestants, long a supplier of recruits to the liberal establishment, now lose members to liberal and conservative churches as well as many to the unchurched ranks. Both traditions enjoy a mainline status, which in recent years has become not just a mark of privilege but a burden as well—including the possibility of rejection and defection. Mainline Catholics and Protestants alike are feeling the effects of greater religious migration, or increasing numbers of persons moving in and out of the religious establishment on their own terms.

The American Jewish community, more self-contained and in some ways more removed from the trends toward greater voluntarism, suffers from a low birth rate and losses brought about by increased intermarriage and large numbers of "alternative families." Increased numbers of singles, intermarrieds, and divorcés contribute to a decline in Jewish ritual practices and communal loyalties. But this community also testifies to the fact that religious mobility can have positive effects. Many born-Gentile spouses of Jews convert to Judaism, and on average they are more religiously observant than the average born Jew. "Jews by choice," as the converts prefer to be called, often contribute a spirituality and piety that are rare among born Jews and thereby raise the religious consciousness of the community. Marginal Jews drop out and are replaced, so to speak, by those of another background who choose to be Jews. The result is what Milton Himmelfarb describes as a positive balance of trade: "Our imports," he says, "are better than our exports."[26]

The new voluntarism of which we speak is a significant aspect of the contemporary religious scene—whether Protestant, Catholic, or Jewish. Greater individualism as expressed in more diverse switching patterns suggests the growing importance of the migration analogy, or the possibility of easy movement from one tradition to another. Tocqueville recognized this potential in American religion more than a century ago, but it took the post-1960s period of religious and cultural disestablishment to bring these populist tendencies into clear focus. Tocqueville wrote: "If we examine it very closely, it will be perceived that religion itself holds sway there much less as a doctrine of revelation than as a commonly received opinion."[27]

Perhaps it should be said that the greater individualism as we have described it embodies both the best and the worst of religious trends today. By *worst* we mean simply that in the exercise of greater choice, individuals often become so cut loose from their groups that they lose the support needed for reinforcing institutional commitment. The plight of the liberal Protestant churches is an example: a lack of cohesion, too much openness and diffuseness, and absence of any clear sense of institutional identity. Those switching into these churches come already highly individualized and privatized in matters of faith, and many switch out into the ranks of the disaffiliated without much of a sense of having left any particular group. In this sense liberal Protestants are on the forefront of the confrontation with modernity, though hardly alone and distinct; increasingly Catholics and many conservative Protestants follow a similar path of enfranchising individuals with greater responsibility and choice in religious matters. Growing numbers of secular nonaffiliates drawn from all the major religious families is evidence enough of where the paths of greater individualism and privatism often lead.

Best refers to the enhancement of personal religious choice and emancipation of faith from ascriptive loyalties. The diverse types of switching we have described is a positive factor in shaping a more responsible, conscientious mode of religious commitment. Moral and ideological commitments play more of a role in determining religious loyalties today: people increasingly choose on the basis of their values and preferences whether to affiliate, and if so, with which church or tradition. This had led to the rise of a more self-conscious secular constituency but also to a better sense of religious alternatives. The boundaries of moral and religious communities have become more sharply distinguished and the range of life-style and belief systems expanded in a more genuinely pluralistic manner. America's many religious traditions and faith communities have taken on greater clarity in a market increasingly governed by individual choice and personal preference.

What all of this means—the changing demographies and greater voluntarism—for the future of American religion is a matter of no small significance. At stake is not just the shape of the changing religious establishment but the place of religion generally in public life. The new demographics and diversity of switching patterns have helped sharpen moral and cultural cleavages now so prominent within the religious mainline. The faiths have become more divided in the face of difficult and controversial issues, and it is to these new morally based divisions that we now turn.

Notes

1. Henry P. Van Dusen, "The Third Force's Lessons for Others," *Life* 44 (June 9, 1958), 122–123. Also see William G. McLoughlin, "Is There a Third Force in Christendom?" *Daedalus* 96 (Winter 1967), 43–68.
2. Throughout the period from the 1920s to the 1960s, conservative churches were growing at a rapid rate, sometimes as much as 100 percent per decade. By comparison, the more liberal churches grew on an average of 19.2 percent per decade. See William R. Hutchinson, "Does Liberal Protestantism Have an American Future?" in Michaelsen and Roof, *Liberal Protestantism: Realities and Prospects,* 65–82.
3. The 1985 *Yearbook of American and Canadian Churches* is the best source of these institutional statistics. Also see Hutchinson, "Does Liberal Protestantism Have an American Future?"
4. Robert Lynn and Helen Lynn *Middletown in Transition: A Study in Cultural Conflicts* (New York: Harcourt and Brace, 1937), 298.
5. Theodore Caplow, Howard M. Bahr, and Bruce A. Chadwick, *All Faithful People: Change and Continuity in Middletown's Religion* (Minneapolis: University of Minnesota Press, 1983), 77.
6. The 1957–1958 data are taken from Lazerwitz, "Major United States Religious Groups," table 2. More recent data on age composition can be found in the Gallup report *Religion in America, 1984* Report No. 22.
7. See Benton Johnson, "Liberal Protestantism: End of the Road?" in *Annals of the American Academy of Political and Social Science* 480 (July 1985), 39–52.
8. These data are taken from William V. D'Antonio and Joan Aldous, eds., *Families and Religions: Conflict and Change in Modern Society* (Beverly Hills: Sage Publications, 1983), p. 81ff.
9. Taken from William V. D'Antonio, "Family Life, Religion, and Societal Values and Structures," in D'Antonio and Aldous, *Families and Religions,* 106.
10. John Scanzoni, *Sex Roles, Life Styles and Childbearing: Changing Patterns in Marriage and the Family* (New York: Free Press), 87.
11. Dennison Nash, "A Little Child Shall Lead Them: A Statistical Test of the Hypothesis That Children Were the Source of the American 'Religious Revival,' " *Journal for the Scientific Study of Religion* 7:238–240.
12. Reported in Leo Rosten, *Religions of America: Ferment and Faith in an Age of Crisis* (New York: Simon and Schuster 1975), 393.
13. Reported in Wilson, *Religion in American Society,* 252.
14. These patterns were evident in the special Census Bureau study, conducted in March 1957. See U.S. Bureau of the Census, *Statistical Abstract of the United States, 1958,* 79th ed., no. 40, Washington, D.C. 1958. Differences in birth rates among Protestant denominations were greater than those between Protestants and Catholics.
15. Sydney E. Ahlstrom draws this observation. See *Religious History of the American People,* 847.

16. Peter L. Berger, *The Precarious Vision* (Garden City, N. Y.: Doubleday, 1961), 74.

17. N. J. Demerath III, *Social Class in American Protestantism* (Chicago: Rand McNally, 1965), 71n.

18. Stark and Glock, *American Piety,* 10.

19. Reported in *Emerging Trends,* June 1980.

20. Much research confirms this estimate for Protestants. Stark and Glock's earlier study reported 46 percent switching in their California sample and slightly more than 40 percent nationally. Comparable estimates are found in more recent research. See Frank Newport, "The Religious Switcher in the United States," *American Sociological Review* 44 (August 1979), 528–552; and Wade Clark Roof and C. Kirk Hadaway, "Denominational Switching in the Seventies: Going Beyond Stark and Glock," *Journal for the Scientific Study of Religion* 18 (December 1979), 363–377. Switching for Catholics and Jews is much lower.

21. This is also the argument of Steven Bruce in "A Sociological Account of Liberal Protestantism," *Religious Studies* 20, no. 3 (September 1984), 414.

22. Stark and Glock, *American Piety,* 203.

23. Kirk Hadaway, "Changing Brands: Denominational Switching and Membership Change," in *Yearbook of American and Canadian Churches, 1983* (Nashville: Abingdon Press, 1983), 262–268.

24. Ibid.

25. Greeley, "American Catholics," 28ff.

26. Reported in Silberman, *A Certain People,* 299. Also see Silberman's chapter "Jews by Choice."

27. Alexis de Toqueville, *Democracy in America,* vol. 2 (New York: Vintage Books, 1945), 12.

PROTESTANTS—NANCY T. AMMERMAN AND JEFFREY K. HADDEN

Two primary, and converging themes have preoccupied sociologists who study American Protestantism—the decline of the mainline churches and the growth of the fundamentalist churches. In three papers in this selection, these themes—already described in part in previous selections—are developed. Nancy Ammerman traces the history of the fundamentalist churches in America for the last hundred years and shows how the fundamentalist thrust is an attempt to retrieve a (partially imaginary) past. Jeffery K. Hadden proposes a mostly anecdotal account of the "rise of the Religious Right" during the 1980s.

The "surge" of membership and of political power in the fundamentalist churches during the 1980s has produced various reactions—astonishment, anger, and fear being some of them—among the leaders and scholars of the mainline and liberal denominations. Their theologians were telling them that a new "secular man" (more recently, they would have said "secular human") was emerging and that the churches should strive to become "relevant" to the men and women who felt they had no need of God. Yet in the real world, just the opposite was happening: their own membership was decamping to more conservative, not to say reactionary denominations.

Secular humankind, it turned out, may have existed on the divinity school faculties and in the social science and humanities departments and in the pages of the denominational journals, but he or she had not quite taken over the local congregations as yet.

Hence, the more radical fundamentalists became the villains of the 1980s, both because they were attracting more members to a religion that was devoid of serious intellectual content and was inconsistent with the thinking of the best minds in the country and because they were striving for political power so they could impose their own rigid morality on the rest of the country.

During this "swing to the right" in the Reagan years, Rev. Jerry Falwell and his "Moral Majority" became the favorite bogeyman of the alarmed and threatened liberals. The national media became obsessed with the threat from the right, often in tones which seemed to picture cavemen with clubs pouring out of the caves to attack civilization.

In fact, during the years of the "fundamentalist revival" there was no change in the proportion of Americans believing in the literal interpretation of the scripture. In fact, as I pointed out in a previous section, the proportion actually declined because of a liberalization of attitudes towards the scripture among

Catholics. Moreover, there was no change in the three-measure Gallup index of fundamentalism (literal interpretation, born again, and attempts to convert others). Twenty percent of the population measured in as fundamentalists in the 1960s; the rate was exactly the same a quarter century later. Finally, there was no evidence in NORC's General Social Survey of any shift to the right on moral or social issues like premarital sex and abortion.

As for the "rise of the Moral Majority," a case could be made that all three of its claimed qualities were untrue. It didn't rise, it wasn't a majority, and it was not all that moral.

As Ammerman's essay makes clear, fundamentalism has been an important part of American life for a long time. Fundamentalists have always been politically active. There is no evidence that the movement has grown either larger or more politically active in the years since 1980. What seems to have happened is that with the Republican electoral sweeps in the early 1980s and claims by the "religious right" to be responsible for these victories, the New York and Washington media discovered for the first time what most Americans had known all along—fundamentalism is and has been a vigorous and important part of American life.

More sober statistical studies cast doubt that the rightwing components of these denominations increased their political power during the 1980s or notably influenced voting patterns. Their members always voted for conservative candidates and continued to do so, with perhaps more noise and more media attention than in the past.

It is also important to note that even though one may belong to a fundamentalist denomination, it does not follow that one is necessarily conservative or reactionary politically. The election of the Clinton-Gore ticket in 1992 was hardly a triumph for the religious right although both men were devout and practicing Southern Baptists.

In fact in his book, *What Does the Lord Require*, Stephen Hart analyzed 39 questions on economic issues in the General Social Survey (years 1984 to 1989) with all pertinent control variables held constant. He found no relationship between traditionalism as measured by belief in the literal interpretation of the Bible and economic conservatism and that indeed (p. 161) biblical literalists are more likely to support the notion that "The government should provide a decent standard of living for the unemployed." So, too, are those who are pro-life more likely to support such a policy than those who are pro-choice.

The near hysteria of the Hadden articles, therefore, indeed tells a story; it is the result of a narrative symbol. As a symbol, it may be useful for men and women to understand the world in which they live and a template according to which they might respond to the world they perceived. However, it is not a good model for generating hypotheses that can be verified by empirical data.

Questions for Reflection and Discussion

1. Did the "religious right" and their critics cooperate (unintentionally) to create the myth of increased political power? Why did this happen?

2. Is there anything wrong with conservative Christians advocating their own political agenda? Are all the authoritarians on the right politically?

3. If there is, as Patrick Buchanan said at the 1992 Republican convention, a culture war going on for the future of America, who is fighting in this war? Do the leading generals on either side really represent broad constituencies? Or are they simply elite groups who wish to create the impression of massive public support?

Part 1

NORTH AMERICAN PROTESTANT FUNDAMENTALISM
Nancy T. Ammerman

As fundamentalism re-emerged in the United States in the late twentieth century after a period of apparent hibernation, no two words better captured its public image and agenda than "Moral Majority." In 1979 independent Baptist pastor Jerry Falwell declared that people who were concerned about the moral decline of America were a majority waiting to be mobilized. He set out to accomplish that task, and for the next decade conservative voters were registered, rallies were held, and legislators elected. Ronald Reagan came to see religious conservatives as an important constituency, speaking at their rallies and inviting their leaders to the White House. And in 1988, politically active conservative pastors again had the ear of Republican George Bush.[1] By 1989 Falwell could declare his mission was accomplished, that conservative consciences had been raised; he could return to pastoring his church and leading his growing Liberty University.

Pastoring churches and establishing schools had long been the more likely strategies of people who called themselves fundamentalists. Not all saw politics and social change as their mission, and many had discounted such activities as useless, even counterproductive. At the same time that some fundamentalists were lobbying in the White House, others were waiting anxiously for the Rapture, the time when they would be transported to heaven. A new book had appeared that set 1988 as the date for this eschatological event, and many were convinced by its claims that the Jewish New Year, Rosh Hashana, would be the appointed time.[2] Like many dates before it, this appointment with the End Times went unkept, but believers were reminded again of how important it was to be "Rapture ready" and to seek the salvation of others.

Source: Martin E. Marty and R. Scott and Appleby (eds.). *Fundamentalism Observed*, Chicago: Univ. of Chicago Press, 1991.

Fundamentalists in North America could be found in both camps—waiting for the Rapture and lobbying in the White House. In both cases believers were drawing on a distinctive view of the world that had emerged about a century earlier. They were willing to argue that certain beliefs were "fundamental," and they were willing to organize in a variety of ways to preserve and defend those beliefs.

A BRIEF INTRODUCTION AND DEFINITION

In the last quarter of the nineteenth century, many leaders in American Protestantism were actively seeking ways to adapt traditional beliefs to the realities of "modern" scholarship and sensibilities. They were met head-on, however, by people who saw the adaptations as heresy and declared that they would defend traditional beliefs from such adaptation. In the first two decades of the twentieth century, they produced a number of publications that furthered this defensive cause. Among the most important was a series of short scholarly essays issued over a five-year peiod (1910–15) and entitled "The Fundamentals"—a name that was being widely used as the designation for the threatened beliefs. In 1920 Curtis Lee Laws, editor of the Northern Baptist newspaper *The Watchman Examiner,* wrote that a "fundamentalist" is a person willing to "do battle royal" for the fundamentals of the faith.[3] It was both a description and a call to action, and the name stuck.

During the 1920s fundamentalists actively fought against modernism in their churches and against evolution in their schools. They lost those battles but retreated and reorganized into a network of institutions that has housed much of the conservative wing of American Protestantism ever since.

However, the name fundamentalist is not synonymous with "conservative." It is, rather, a subset of that larger whole. Fundamentalists share with other conservative Christians their support for "traditional" interpretations of such doctrines as the Virgin Birth of Jesus, the reality of the miracles reported in Scripture (including the Resurrection of Jesus from the dead), and the eventual return of Christ to reign over this earth. In spreading these teachings, conservatives tend to support the more supernatural interpretation of events, while liberals tend to seek naturalistic explanations.

In American society such conservatism in religion is widespread. Seventy-two percent of Americans say the Bible is the Word of God, with over half of that number (39 percent of the total) saying that it should be taken literally. Almost two-thirds say they are certain that Jesus Christ rose from the dead. Nearly three-fourths say they believe in life after death.[4] And almost half (44 percent) could be called "creationists," since they believe that God created the world in "pretty much its present form" sometime in the last ten thousand years.[5]

Not all these people, however, are fundamentalists. Even within conservatism there are a number of significant divisions. Among other things, not everyone agrees on that most central of doctrines—how people are saved, that is, how they make themselves acceptable to God. One branch of conservative

Protestantism places primary emphasis on the historic creeds of the faith and membership in a church that confesses those beliefs. People are baptized (initiated) as infants into a community of faith.[6] These "confessional" churches are often conservative, but they are not often the home of fundamentalists.[7]

Fundamentalists are more often found in the other, much larger, branch of conservative Protestantism that identifies itself as "evangelical." These are people for whom only an individual decision to follow Jesus will suffice for salvation. They are concerned not only about their own eternal fate but also about the destiny of those around them. They seek to "win souls for Christ" by their words and deeds, testifying to the necessity of a life-changing decision to become a Christian. They often speak of that experience as being "born again." It is an experience that gives them a sense of personal and intimate communion with Jesus and often shapes their lives and conversations in noticeably pious ways.

But even within the evangelical branch there are significant subdivisions. Almost all black Protestants belong here, for instance, but they have developed independent traditions over two centuries of segregation that have made them quite distinctive from many white evangelicals. Blacks hold to many of the conservative doctrines of other evangelicals, and three-fourths of black churchgoers are in one of the black Baptist or Methodist denominations. They are likely to hold Scripture in high regard and to emphasize the necessity of being saved.

These churches were born out of the Great Awakening and the later southern revivals, and they have retained much of that evangelical heritage. But the distinctive style of African American worship and the distinctive relationship of African Americans to society make the label *fundamentalist* less than apt. Theirs is a style of worship that is distinctive not for its doctrinal content but for the way in which it celebrates a separate ethnic tradition. C. Eric Lincoln has described the function of separateness as protecting the black believer from distortions that whites might introduce and as reinforcing and enhancing the very characteristics of African American worship belittled in white society. He claims that "black ethnicity denies the relevance of white styles of worship for black people and sanctions the ritual patterns developed in the churches of the black experience."[8] Theirs is not, then, a religiously based separation from a secular world but a racially based separation in which church and community are bound tightly together. In Lincoln's words, "in the black community the Black Church is in a real sense a universal church, claiming and representing all Blacks out of a tradition that looks back to the time when there was *only* the Black Church to bear witness to 'who' or 'what' a black [person] was."[9] When a black preacher speaks, he or she speaks for more than a mere congregation. In that sense, black evangelicals have yet to experience the modern secularization that has separated religious institutions from the political and economic mainstream. Theirs is not a rebellion against modernist compromises. Although they share many beliefs with other evangelicals, those beliefs function quite differently in their very different social world.[10]

Pentecostal and charismatic Christians in North America also belong in the evangelical family but are a distinct group within it. Beginning with the Pentecostal revivals near the turn of the twentieth century, new denominations such as the Church of God, the Church of God in Christ, and the Assemblies of God were formed, in which "gifts of the spirit" (such as speaking in tongues and healing) were emphasized as evidence of the believer's spiritual power. By the 1960s an emphasis on the Holy Spirit's power had also found its way into many mainline denominations, with prayer and healing groups meeting around the country in the parish halls of Catholic, Episcopal, Presbyterian, Methodist, and many other local churches. The *Christianity Today*–Gallup poll estimated that only about one-third of the nation's twenty-nine million charismatics are in traditional Pentecostal denominations.[11] Whatever their denominational location is, charismatics tend toward becoming "evangelical" in their insistence on a personal experience of salvation. But their religious experiences go considerably beyond the "rebirth" noncharismatic evangelicals claim.[12]

Another group sometimes called "evangelical" or "fundamentalist" is the Church of Jesus Christ of Latter Day Saints, the Mormons. This group's reverence for its scripture, their disciplined way of life, and their aggressive evangelism sometimes cause them to be referred to as "fundamentalist." The term, "Protestant Christian fundamentalism," however, is not appropriate in the case of the large majority of Mormons. While they share some religious and social characteristics with fundamentalists, they are certainly not Protestant. They accept few of the traditional doctrines Protestant fundamentalists hold sacred, and their adoption of a unique sacred text, *The Book of Mormon,* sets them firmly at odds with Protestant fundamentalists.[13] In fact in recent years Mormons have experienced a fundamentalist movement within their own ranks, in groups seeking to purify their tradition and return to orthodox interpretations of their scripture.

These groups occupy the same general religious territory as fundamentalists. They are all conservative and evangelical, but they are still distinct from each other and from fundamentalists. Mormons have their own scripture, African Americans are defined more by race than by doctrine, and Pentecostals trust the revelatory power of experience more than do the more rationally oriented fundamentalists who seek to confine revelation to Scripture alone.

While we may be able to identify these other distinct subgroups, it is less clear that we can identify fundamentalists as distinct from evangelicals in general and on what basis that might be done. During most of the first half of the twentieth century "fundamentalist" and "evangelical" meant roughly the same things. People might use either name to describe those who preserved and practiced the revivalist heritage of soul winning and maintained a traditional insistence on orthodoxy.

But as orthodox people began to organize for survival in a world dominated by the non-orthodox, two significantly different strategies emerged. Seeking a broad cultural base for their gospel, one group saw benefits in learning to get along with outsiders. They did not wish to adopt the outsiders' ways, but they wanted to be respected. They began, especially after World War II, to take the name "evangelical" for themselves. Billy Graham can be seen as their primary representative.[14] The other group insisted that getting along was no virtue and that active opposition to liberalism, secularism, and communism was to be pursued.[15] This group retained the name "fundamentalist." To this group we now turn our attention.

CENTRAL FEATURES OF FUNDAMENTALISM IN NORTH AMERICA

Evangelism

When fundamentalists describe how they are different from other people, they begin with the fact that they are saved. They clearly affirm their kinship with other evangelicals on this point. Much of their organized effort is aimed at seeking out converts. They invite the "lost" to church, broadcast evangelistic messages over radio and television, print millions of pages and record millions of words on cassette tapes—all aimed at convincing the unconvinced that eternity in heaven is better than the eternal damnation in hell that surely awaits the unsaved. Preachers proclaim the hopeless conditions of lives not entrusted to Jesus. And individual believers invest much in prayer and testimony directed at the eternal fate of their families and friends. Evangelism and the salvation of individual souls remains at the heart of the message fundamentalists proclaim to American society in the late twentieth century.

Inerrancy

Fundamentalists also claim that the only sure path to salvation is through a faith in Jesus Christ that is grounded in unwavering faith in an inerrant Bible. As fundamentalists see the situation, if but one error of fact or principle is admitted in Scripture, nothing—not even the redemptive work of Christ—is certain. When asked what else makes them distinctive, fundamentalists will almost invariably claim that they are the people who "really believe the Bible." They insist that true Christians must believe the whole Bible, the parts they like along with the parts they dislike, the hard parts and the easy ones. The Bible can be trusted to provide an accurate description of science and history, as well as morality and religion. And only such an unfailing source can be trusted to provide a sure path to salvation in the hereafter and clear guidance in the here and now. As Kathleen Boone has pointed out, fundamentalists imagine "themselves either steadfast in absolute truth or whirling in the vortex of nihilism."[16]

Such contemporary use of ancient texts requires, of course, careful interpretation. Studies of fundamentalists invariably point to the central role of pastors and Bible teachers in creating authoritative meanings out of the biblical text.[17] Fundamentalists live in communities that are defined by the language they use and the stories they tell. Community leaders, teachers in Christian schools, and Christian media personalities give shape to the way ordinary believers understand their world by offering interpretations that give the infallible text its concrete human reality. The more people are immersed in this fundamentalist community of discourse, the more easily they accept the Bible as completely accurate. They are more likely to question the validity of science than to doubt the unfailing Word of God.[18]

Some aspects of modern science, of course, are *not* questioned (the earth's roundness and orbit around the sun, for instance). The interpretive task fundamentalists undertake, then, requires a careful balancing of facts about the world presumed by moderns to be true with the assumption that the Bible contains no factual errors. Phrases that seem to indicate a modern view of the solar system (such as "circle of the earth") are highlighted, while statements clearly reflecting an ancient view (such as references to "waters" above and below the earth) are said to be poetic and not intended to be "scientifically precise."[19] Likewise, moral teaching in Scripture that seems to condone slavery or polygamy must be neutralized. Such teaching is neither endorsed as eternally relevant (with the notable exception of patriarchy) nor rejected as a mistake of ancient writers. Rather, such practices are deemed irrelevant to salvation, to be accepted if in keeping with the cultural custom and abandoned if not. Within any social arrangement individuals can live fully Christian lives by virtue of their personal relationship with Jesus.

Because this idea of inerrancy is so central to the identity of fundamentalists, it is an idea that receives considerable attention and development. Theologians and church leaders worry about all the nuances of interpretation and arrive at various theories that seem best to support the Bible's truthfulness. They often argue vociferously among themselves, but their worrying rarely affects the people in the pews. The primary affirmation of ordinary believers is simply that the Bible is a reliable guide for life. It contains systematic rules for living that have been proven successful over six thousand years of human history. Fundamentalists are confident that everything in Scripture is true, and if they have questions about a seemingly difficult passage, they know that prayer, study, and a visit with the pastor are guaranteed to provide an answer.[20]

Premillennialism

Fundamentalists do not simply read the Bible to learn history or moral principles. They also expect to find in Scripture clues to the future destiny of this world, what will happen in the End Times. From the beginning of the fundamentalist movement, traditionalists who were concerned about Scripture and doctrine were closely linked with people who were concerned about interpreting the Bible's prophecies. The legacy of that connection is that today most fundamentalists are "pretribulation dispensational premillennialists." The ideas that go with that label are almost as complicated as the label, but one of the most important is the idea of the Rapture. For fundamentalist readers of Scripture, one of the most central stories is Jesus' description of how it will be when the "Son of Man comes" (Matt. 24:37–41). "There will be two men in a field; one will be taken, the other left; two women grinding at the mill; one will be taken, the other left." Combined with words in 1 Thessalonians (4:15–18) about being "caught up in the air to meet the Lord," a picture of heavenly escape is created. True believers will one day soon simply hear the heavenly trumpet and disappear into the sky, leaving those around them bewildered. That is the Rapture for which they seek to be ready. If the Rapture does not come before death, believers have, of course, the "hope of heaven" after death. But the Rapture might come first, meaning that even those with no reason to expect death do not know how long they have on this earth. The belief in an "any moment" Rapture, then, lends both urgency to the evangelistic task and comfort to persecuted believers.

While the Rapture is perhaps the most central feature of fundamentalist eschatology (that is, their beliefs about the climax of history), it is nearly overshadowed by the emphasis on prophecy that accompanies it. Believers are not content to know that Jesus is coming for them; they want to know when and what will happen next. For these clues they turn to the apocalyptic books of Daniel (in Hebrew Scripture) and the Revelation (at the end of the New Testament). Here there are great images of destruction and horror preceding the ultimate triumph of God. Believers interested in prophecy dissect these images to create a systematic scheme (often pictured in elaborate charts) that chronicles the "Tribulation" of the earth following the departure of believers, the rise of a world ruler (the Antichrist), and the final battle (Armageddon) in which the forces of good and evil will meet. Only then will Christ establish a kingdom of peace and righteousness on this earth. That fundamentalists believe Christ will have to return before the millennium (one-thousand-year reign on earth) makes them "premillennialists" (in contrast to the more optimistic "postmillennialists" who thought human effort might usher in the reign of God). That they think the Rapture will happen before the upheavals of the Tribulation makes their position "pretribulation." (There are also "mid" and "post" tribulation positions, but they are less popular.) That they divide history into such clear-cut periods, separated by climactic acts of God, is at the heart of being "dispensationalist."

Dispensationalists take their name from a reading of history that divides time into distinct periods (usually seven) in which salvation is "dispensed" in unique ways. The period from the time of Jesus' death until the Rapture is known as the "Church Age," in which salvation is by grace, obtained through belief in Jesus. Both before and after this age, salvation is granted differently. Therefore scriptures addressed to people in different ages may not apply to our own. Likewise, Scripture addressed to God's earthly people, the Jews, is distinct from Scripture addressed to God's heavenly people, the church. Sorting all of this out requires a good deal of effort, and many fundamentalists turn for help to the Scofield Reference Bible (1909) or the more recent Ryrie version (1978). Both contain extensive footnotes explaining the true intent of each passage of Scripture.

It is in these interpretations of prophecy, then, that fundamentalists depart most dramatically from a literal reading of Scripture. Prophetic words do not mean what they seem to mean to the uninitiated. Weeks are really sets of seven years, armies coming from the north refer to Soviet forces, "Tubal" is Turkey, and so forth. In these prophecies, believers discern a kind of secret road map to the unfolding of human history. They can cross-reference Scripture and the nightly news. They only occasionally set dates for the Rapture—they are, after all, repeatedly warned against that in the Bible—but they are constantly watching for the signs that it might be soon. And they distrust claims to orthodoxy made by people who do not take prophecy seriously.

Strict inerrancy, then, is taken by fundamentalists as demanding a premillennial interpretation of Scripture and attention to its "inerrant" prophecy alongside its inerrant history, science, and moral teaching. In this view, the truth of Scripture can be "proved" by its accurate predictions of future events, as well as by its practical advice about salvation and Christian living. The systematic derivation of facts and principles that is at the heart of fundamentalist interpretation lends itself to the systematic outlining of history and future found in dispensationalism.

Separatism

The conservative orthodoxy and evangelism of fundamentalists clearly do not make them unique. As we have already seen, there are many nonfundamentalist conservatives. Even inerrancy and premillennialism are not fully sufficient defining characteristics. Among nonfundamentalist evangelicals there are inerrantists and premillennialists, but those views are both less dominant and held less dogmatically in nonfundamentalist circles of evangelicals. And more importantly, few nonfundamentalist evangelicals would insist that eschatology is a critical test of faith. The ultimate characteristic that has distinguished fundamentalists from other evangelicals has been their insistence that there *can be* tests of faith. Fundamentalists insist on uniformity of belief within the ranks and separation from others whose beliefs and lives are suspect. The fundamentalist, then, is very likely to belong to a church with strict rules for its own membership and for its cooperative relations with others. It is likely to be an "independent" church, since so many of the denominations are seen as infected with apostasy and compromise. The true believer will also adhere to strict rules for her own life, shunning any person or practice that might reduce the effectiveness of her life's witness to the message of salvation. When confronted with unbelief, doubt, error, or sinful ways, fundamentalists weigh the possibility that direct confrontation might avert a brother or sister from eternal damnation. If pickets at the doors of a movie such as "The Last Temptation of Christ"[21] will keep even a single soul from the fires of hell, then the effort is worth it. But if confrontation is likely only to drag the believer down to the level of the sinner, better to avoid the situation. Even if the believer might be able to witness to his buddies while they are drinking after work, the possibility for misinterpretation of his presence (or even slipping into sin himself) is too great to risk. He would rather lose his friends than his soul. Simply getting along, not making waves, accepting the ways of the world, is not characteristic of those evangelicals who deserve (and claim) the label "fundamentalist.". . .

NOTES

1. One strategy meeting of conservative ministers with Bush included Presbyterian James Kennedy and Southern Baptist Convention president Jerry Vines, both pastors in Florida. See S. Hastey and M. Knox, "Bush Meets with Evangelicals, including Southern Baptists," *Baptist Press*, 4 August 1988.

2. The source of the prediction was a book called *88 Reasons Why the Rapture Will Be in 1988*, written by engineer Edgar C. Whisenant and published by the World Bible Society in Nashville. While admitting that he could not know the "day or hour" of the Lord's return (due to multiple time zones), he nevertheless was sure that he could calculate "the year, the month, and the week of the Lord's return" from the Bible's many "end time" prophecies (p. 3).

3. George M. Marsden, *Fundamentalism and American Culture* (Oxford: Oxford University Press, 1980), p. 158.

4. George Gallup, Jr., *Religion in America: 50 Years, 1935–1985* (Princeton: The Gallup Report, 1985).

5. George Gallup, Jr., *Public Opinion 1982* (Wilmington, Del.: Scholarly Resources, 1983).

6. J. D. Hunter makes this distinction between confessional and "born again" evangelicals in "Operationalizing Evangelicalism," *Sociological Analysis* 42 (1982): 363–72.

7. The notable exception, of course, is the Missouri Synod Lutheran Church, taken over by fundamentalists in the early 1970s, to be discussed below.

8. C. E. Lincoln, *Race, Religion, and the Continuing American Dilemma* (New York: Hill and Wang, 1984), pp. 92–93.

9. Ibid., p. 96.

10. On the black church, see E. F. Frazier, *The Negro Church in America*, and C. Eric Lincoln, *The Black Church since Frazier* (bound together; New York: Schocken Books, 1973); and J. R. Washington, Jr., "The Peculiar Peril and Promise of Black Folk Religion," in David E. Harrell, Jr., ed., *Varieties of Southern Evangelicalism* (Macon, Ga.: Mercer University Press, 1981), pp. 59–69.

11. See K. S. Kantzer, "The Charismatics Among Us," *Christianity Today*, 22 February 1980, pp. 245–49.

12. Meredith B. McGuire, *Pentecostal Catholics: Power, Charisma, and Order in a Religious Movement* (Philadelphia: Temple University Press, 1982); Mary J. Neitz, *Charisma and Community: A Study of Religious Commitment Within the Charismatic Renewal* (New Brunswick, N.J.: Transaction Books, 1987); and Joseph H. Fichter, *The Catholic Cult of the Paraclete* (New York: Sheed & Ward, 1975), offer helpful accounts of the charismatic movement.

13. For overviews of Mormon history and practice, see Jan Shipps, *Mormonism* (Urbana: University of Illinois Press, 1985); and Thomas O'Dea, *The Mormons* (Chicago: University of Chicago Press, 1964).

14. On Billy Graham, see William Martin, "Bill Graham," in *Varieties of Southern Evangelicalism*, pp. 71–88. On the development of evangelicalism since the 1940s, see George M. Marsden, *Reforming Fundamentalism: Fuller Seminary and the New Evangelicalism* (Grand Rapids, Mich.: Wm. B. Eerdmans, 1987); and J. D. Hunter, *Evangelicalism: The Coming Generation* (Chicago: University of Chicago Press, 1987).

15. Jerry Falwell, The *Fundamentalist Phenomenon* (Garden City, N.Y.: Doubleday-Galilee, 1981), contains a discussion of the contrasts from his point of view.

16. Kathleen C. Boone, *The Bible Tells Them So* (Albany: State University of New York Press, 1989), p. 24.

17. Cf. Alan Peshkin, *God's Choice: The Total World of a Fundamentalist Christian School* (Chicago: University of Chicago Press, 1986); and Nancy T. Ammerman, *Bible Believers: Fundamentalists in the Modern World* (New Brunswick, N.J.: Rutgers University Press, 1987).

18. On fundamentalist ideas about the relationship between science and religion, see also S. D. Rose, *Keeping Them Out of the Hands of Satan* (New York: Routledge, 1988).

19. *The Proceedings of the Conference on Biblical Inerrancy* (Nashville: Broadman Press, 1987) contains a number of interesting examples of fundamentalist modes of interpretation. See especially Robert Preus, "The Inerrancy of Scripture," pp. 47–60. For a discussion of more "everyday" processes of interpretation in a fundamentalist congregation, see Ammerman, *Bible Believers*, chap. 4; and Boone, *The Bible Tells Them So.*

20. On the role of the fundamentalist pastor, see Ammerman, *Bible Believers*, chap. 7; and Boone, *The Bible Tells Them So*, chap. 6.

21. The 1988 film by Martin Scorsese depicts Jesus as doubtful about his mission and subject to human lusts.

Part 2

CONSERVATIVE CHRISTIANS, TELEVANGELISM, AND POLITICS: TAKING STOCK A DECADE AFTER THE FOUNDING OF THE MORAL MAJORITY
Jeffrey K. Hadden

Throughout this century right-wing Christian activism has periodically reappeared. And with each new wave of activism, the press and intellectuals have reacted with expressions of disbelief that religious fanatics could again be entering into the political arena. This tendency to see conservative Christian activism as an aberration in American politics has the quality of cultural schizophrenia. On the one hand there is a cynical snickering at these poor misguided religious extremists. H. L. Mencken and Sinclair Lewis, writing in the third decade of this century, set the tone and style of a genre of lambasting literature that subsequent generations have admired and sought to emulate. But nearly simultaneous to unconcealed mocking are shrill warnings that these fanatical fundamentalist fools pose a grave threat to the health and well-being of the political system. These mixed signals are reminiscent of the old military folk adage: "The situation is desperate, but not serious."

How can we account for the simultaneous presence of these diametrically opposed viewpoints? A good beginning point is the recognition that intellectuals and political pundits largely view religion in the modern world from a perspective that is grounded in secularization theory. While often unarticulated explicitly, this perspective is nevertheless held with considerable confidence. Secularization theory postulates either the eventual erosion of religious senti-

Source: Thomas Robbins, and Dick Anthony, (eds.). *In Gods We Trust: New Patterns of Religious Pluralism in America*, New Brunswick: Transaction Publishers, 1990.

ment from the modern world or the retreat of religion to the private realm. These unwelcome and unsuited intrusions into the political arena, thus, will eventually pass as aging cohorts of old-time Bible believers die off. In the interim, the periodic reappearance of conservative Christians as a political force amounts to so much noxious noise that disrupts the eighteenth-century accommodation of church and state.

Secularization theory can incorporate the notion that intermittent waves of political activism are to be expected as this archaic belief system moves toward extinction. But this does not explain why the reappearance of Christian political activism produces the hysteria and shrill cries that warn that the fundamentalists are taking over America. Even more ironic is the fact that this reaction tends to come from the same people who steadfastly believe in the inevitability of secularization. Perhaps they experience temporary amnesia. Or perhaps the surges of religious political activism lead to a brief loss of confidence in the inexorableness of the secularization process. The mere contemplation of a dark age in which irrational religious sentiment, rather than reason, guides the ship of state is so horrible that it brings forth a fighting instinct.

However these vacillations are to be explained, America experienced another episode of alarm and amusement during the 1980s. The religious fanatics were called the New Christian Right (NCR), and for most of the decade the undisputed leader was a television preacher named Jerry Falwell who, in 1979, created an organization called the Moral Majority to do battle with the evils of secular humanism.

Seldom in modern history has the emergence of an interest group attracted so much attention. When the 1980 elections were over Ronald Reagan had scored a stunning victory that resulted in the defeat of several ranking liberal Democrats in the House and Senate. Falwell wasted no time in stepping forward to claim responsibility in the name of Moral Majority. Several defeated senators and congressmen agreed with Falwell's assessment, and so did pollster Louis Harris.

Countermovement organizations (for example, Americans for Common Sense and People for the American Way) sprang up all across the nation and joined with traditional liberal organizations (for example, the American Civil Liberties Union and Common Cause) to mobilize resources to do battle with the NCR. After the 1982 congressional elections, the absence of evidence to indicate that the NCR had made further political gains led many to conclude that the movement had been only a brief flash in the pan. Other analysts went even further, contending that the movement never had been anything more than media hype. Downplaying the significance of the NCR took on credibility as both movement and countermovement organizations either closed up shop, or bore evidence of merely being direct-mail organizations.

But Jerry Falwell's ability to gain the attention of the mass media, President Reagan's ongoing courtship of evangelical Christians, and the nagging presence of antiabortion and antipornography protesters made it difficult for the media and scholars to write an obituary and close the books of the NCR.

Then, in early 1986, Jerry Falwell made a surprise announcement that he was abandoning the Moral Majority name in favor of a new organization he would call the Liberty Federation. While he promised that the new organization would tackle a broader range of issues, there was a lot of evidence to indicate that Falwell wanted to move out of the public limelight to concentrate his time and energies on building Liberty University.

Falwell's disestablishment of the Moral Majority corresponded closely with the first national news that fellow Virginia televangelist Pat Robertson was serious about making a bid for the Republican presidential nomination. Robertson, however, had a difficult time persuading the press that his candidacy should be taken seriously. The televangelism scandals that erupted in March of 1987 made his task even more difficult. PTL's Jim Bakker, the focal personality in the sex and financial scandals at Heritage U.S.A., had begun his broadcasting career with Robertson at the Christian Broadcasting Network. Before the PTL scandal began unfolding, the mass media were having a grand time with Oral Roberts' scheme to raise eight million dollars by 1 April 1987 in order to keep God from "calling him home." A few months earlier Roberts had endorsed Robertson's candidacy in a gala occasion in Washington's Constitutional Hall, which was simulcast via satellite in over two hundred auditoriums across the nation.

But as the nation moved closer to the kickoff of the presidential primary sweepstakes, the media became increasingly impressed with Robertson's grass-roots organizational skills. He outorganized Vice President George Bush in Michigan only to lose his grip on the majority of delegates in an unusual and controversial legal maneuver by Bush operatives. Robertson further embarrassed Bush by finishing second in the Iowa caucuses behind Senator Robert Dole. And in Hawaii, where the delegate-selection process was locked-in before the New Hampshire primary, Robertson secured 80 percent of the delegates. For a brief moment, at least, it appeared that Pat Robertson really did have an "invisible army," and that he was staged to make a serious bid for the Republican nomination.

But George Bush's control of the resources of the Republican National Committee led to a swift elimination of all of his rivals. With Bush's nomination early assured, media attention shifted to the Democratic primaries where Jesse Jackson's surprising performance provided good news copy. Little effort was devoted to looking back and assessing the Robertson campaign.

In the brief time span between Robertson's gaining of national visibility and Bush's effective smashing of his opposition on Super Tuesday, several things happened that contributed to undermining Robertson's candidacy. First, candidate Robertson made several gaffs that drew widespread media attention. Then, without warning, another televangelism scandal broke—this one involving Jimmy Swaggert. Robertson, who was already having difficulty shaking the negative image of televangelist, first claimed that the Bush campaign was responsible for the timing of the revelations of Swaggert's involvement with a New Orleans prostitute, and then he traveled to Louisiana to express solidarity with Swaggert. Finally, on the eve of Super Tuesday, Robertson withdrew a libel suit against former Congressman Paul McClosky, who had accused him of using his father's influence to avoid active duty in the Korean War.

These developments led to a hasty conclusion that Pat Robertson had not been a serious candidate. And with his conclusion came yet another swift vacillation in the perceived threat of the NCR. The new conventional wisdom held that the NCR "poli-preachers," as syndicated columnist William Safire (1986) labeled them, never were serious players in the conservative movement of the 1980s. They were merely perceived to be so because of the support the religious broadcasters had received from Ronald Reagan. In the twilight of his administration, and the failed candidacy of Pat Robertson, the NCR seemed destined for oblivion.

This interpretation of the fate of the NCR appeared to have considerable credibility. After eight years of high media visibility, the religious factor seemed to vanish during the general election. If the Robertson and Falwell and Southern Baptist political contingents were working for George Bush, they appeared to be as quiet as church mice. They were neither heard from nor visible in the media. And in the headlines of postelection analyses, there was virtually no mention of the "evangelical vote." At last, it appeared that the skeptics were right.

But once again, the rush to count the NCR down and out was premature. With virtually no fanfare, evangelical Christians played a major role in George Bush's impressive 54 percent to 46 percent victory over Michael Dukakis. While they received virtually no publicity, three major news service exit polls showed that Bush received 80 percent or greater of the evangelical vote (Menendez 1988). The *New York Times/CBS News* exit poll (1988) reported that 81 percent of white fundamentalist or evangelical Christians voted for Bush compared with 78 percent who voted for Reagan in 1984.

Evangelical support for Bush was probably even stronger than indicated by these exit polls. During the 1988 primary and general elections, the Times Mirror Corporation, publishers of the *Los Angeles Times,* using factor analytic techniques, developed a sophisticated method for measuring ten independent sectors of the electorate. The sector they identified as "moralists" is a purer measure of the conservative religious community than the measures "fundamentalists" or "evangelicals" used by most pollsters. In the last Times Mirror poll conducted before the general election, the moralists favored Bush over Dukakis by a margin of 93 percent to 3 percent (Times Mirror 1988). Furthermore, George Gallup, who conducted the polling for Times Mirror, reported that while the moralists constituted 12 percent of the electorate, they were expected to represent 14 percent of all voters (Gallup 1988).

Bush's solid sweep of the South and Southwest, where evangelical Christian concentration is the greatest, was impressive and the margin of victory can substantially be attributed to the evangelical vote. Albert Menendez (1988), an authority on religion and voting who has been reluctant to acknowledge that the NCR has ever had any political clout, concluded that the evangelical vote was also probably the margin of victory for Bush in the tightly contested states of Pennsylvania, Illinois, and Missouri. Menendez reported, for example, that seventeen strongly evangelical counties in Pennsylvania delivered a 134,000 plurality for Bush to offset a Dukakis margin of 34,000 for the rest of the state. And in a sample of campus precincts of ten evangelical colleges, Menendez reported that Bush did almost as well as did Reagan in 1984 (84 percent to 86 percent).

The evangelical vote is not to be equated with the NCR, but neither can we dismiss the role of this political and social movement in the growing alliance between the Republican party and evangelical Christians. In 1980, 63 percent of white evangelicals voted for Reagan, up from 55 percent voting Republican in 1976. Even though critics are right in pointing out that none of the major stated goals of the NCR movement have been achieved—curbing abortion and pornography, reinstating prayer in school, etc.—evangelical Christians seem to be moving toward a consensus that their best chance for achieving these goals is through the Republican party. Their allegiance to the Republican party is now approaching the strength of blacks' allegiance to the Democratic party. This is a remarkable shift of allegiance away from the Democratic party, and it has mostly taken place in a fairly brief time span.

The role of the NCR in this shift of allegiance to the Republican party can't be easily quantified, but the case for the impact of the televangelist-led movement seems more plausible than the argument against this claim. First of all, the moral content of religious broadcasters on television and radio is highly similar; one can virtually say that it is monolithic. Second, very large proportions of evangelicals view some religious broadcasting. Third, the high visibility in the secular media of some politically aroused televangelists has served to heighten evangelical consciousness about politics in general as well as about specific issues.

A serious assessment of the NCR as a social movement, and the role the televangelists have played in forging this movement, must take seriously the presidential candidacy of Pat Robertson. Contrary to the impression created by the media, Robertson achieved some rather remarkable successes in his first bid for political office. Foremost was the fact that he cultivated genuine grass-roots political organization. Until the Robertson candidacy, the NCR had relied primarily on direct-mail and mass media to communicate with adherents and potential adherents. People were enlisted to vote, or occasionally to participate in a demonstration. Aside from contributing to organizations like the Moral Majority or Christian Voice, little was asked of people. There was little development of local organizational chapters. Even piggybacking on existing organizations, primarily churches, was ad hoc.

Robertson effectively utilized churches, but he built organizations independent of local churches. People were enlisted to participate in the political process in a variety of ways at local, congressional district, and state level. To do so, a cadre of local activists had to develop an understanding of both the minutia and complexity of the political process. The degree of success varied, but by the end of the primary season, the Robertson forces were within striking distance of controlling the Republican party in at least ten states. Robertson chose not to flaunt his strength but, rather, to demonstrate that he was a team player.

Robertson is unlikely to win the GOP nomination for the presidency at some future date, but he has established himself as an important player. Furthermore, there are thousands that Robertson drew into active leadership roles who, having learned how the political process works, will remain active in GOP politics.

The alliance between evangelical Christians and the Republican party is an uncomfortable one; one might even say a marriage of convenience. Many traditional Republicans are uncomfortable with the emotionally charged moral agenda of the Christian right. Furthermore, the infusion of newly politicized Christians is viewed as a threat to status-quo party politics at every level. But in spite of the success of the GOP in presidential elections over the past two decades, Republicans remain the minority party. They need the evangelical Christians if they are to build a majority party. The Democratic party, on the other hand, is too staunchly aligned with left-wing special interests to provide an accommodating environment for the Christian right, at least within the foreseeable future. Thus, from a pragmatic perspective, the moralist Christians and the traditional probusiness Republicans are a likely alliance.

The future of the NCR and the Republican party in the immediate future will hinge on whether Republicans seek to accommodate evangelicals mobilized by Robertson or attempt to roust them out of the party. Accommodation will keep NCR movement concerns focused within normal party politics. Hostility toward evangelical Christians could trigger a sustained effort to take over the GOP. But the bitter battles fought by Robertson and Bush forces in states like Michigan and Georgia could leave many alienated from party politics, which could have the effect of renewing more aggressive activity outside of established party politics.

Precisely how the interests of the Christian right will be worked out in the political process during the last decade of the twentieth century is uncertain. What is not in doubt is their presence as a significant interest group. They can no more be ignored than blacks, Catholics, feminists, hispanics, or Jews. While scarcely being recognized as such by the media and the general public, they have already become one of the more politically effective interest groups in American politics.

Unlike previous waves of Christian right-wing politics during this century, the NCR has demonstrated the ability to be politically pragmatic, even in dealing with issues on which they hold absolutist positions. Ronald Reagan is to be credited with having dealt with the NCR in a highly effective manner. From the moment he first addressed the Christian activists during his 1980 presidential campaign, they never doubted his commitment to support their agenda and they, in turn, supported the president's agenda. At the same time, Reagan can probably be credited with having taught them the value of patience and being willing to take what you can get in the political process, recognizing that there will be another day.

Jerry Falwell claims to be the first public figure in America to endorse George Bush's presidential candidacy. This represented both political astuteness and pragmatism. Similarly, once it was evident that the vice president had a lock on the nomination, Pat Robertson moved to heal campaign wounds and to build bridges to Bush and the Republican National Committee.

The most important lesson to be learned about the leadership of the NCR, and what separates it from earlier waves of conservative Christian activists during this century, is the pragmatism that we have seen demonstrated by Falwell, Robertson, and others. They are resolute and determined to be serious players in American politics.

The second most important lesson is to recognize that they have considerable resources to sustain a significant political movement. The single most important resource is the unique access they have to the airwaves (Hadden and Shupe 1988, 291–92). Evangelicals have battled with mainline Protestants for access to the airwaves from the very beginning of radio broadcasting. They developed a clear advantage in 1960 when the Federal Communications Commissions (FCC) ruled that local broadcasters could sell air time and also receive public service "credit." Unlike the mainline churches who have always been dependent upon broadcasters for free air time, Evangelicals have never been hesitant to solicit funds over the air to pay for their broadcast time.

Clearly the televangelism scandals of 1987 and 1988 served to undermine the credibility of all religious broadcasters. Viewing and contributions were down sharply for almost *all* religious broadcasters. Only time will reveal whether the scandals will have a long-term impact on the religious broadcasting industry. But so long as the FCC, the Congress, and the courts do not significantly alter the rules for access to the airwaves, religious broadcasters will communicate both overt and latent political messages. Thus, both directly and indirectly the televangelists will contribute to the mobilization of conservative Christians who are committed to turning back the tide of secular humanism.

This essay began with the assertion that the presence of conservative Christians in the political arena has, for most of this century, been viewed as an aberration. In light of the growing sophistication of conservative Christians during the 1980s, and the large number of U.S. citizens who consider themselves to be fundamentalists or evangelicals, the continued denial of their presence in politics seems itself to be the aberration. But still the idea persists, along with the assumption that conservative Christians constitute a unique threat. How is this to be explained?

It has already been suggested that a subtle commitment to secularization theory has contributed to an assumption that religion can be expected to play a diminishing role in public life. For those who are committed to a liberal social agenda—which includes a fairly large proportion of scholars and political analysts in America—the involvement of liberal Christians in politics should similarly be viewed as an aberration (Williamsburg Charter Foundation 1988). But since they share a common social agenda with liberal Christians, the presence of the latter in politics is not viewed as threatening. Hence, the involvement that is equally anomalous to secularization theory is missed.

Social scientists have frequently addressed the question of how personal values intrude in efforts at objective analysis. Stanley Lieberson, a distinguished scholar of ethnic and race relations, recently explored the issue in his presidential address to the Pacific Sociological Association. Writes Lieberson:

> I am convinced that our discipline follows certain implicit rules of thinking that are totally inappropriate, illogical, and ultimately undermine our ability to advance knowledge about society (1988, 379).

The discipline of sociology, argues Lieberson, carries unspoken social norms regarding what kinds of findings are acceptable and unacceptable with respect to political and social policy issues. When findings are unacceptable, "illogical procedures and inappropriate ways of thinking" are employed to discount or discredit research. Ad hominem arguments and the application of double standards are among several techniques used to discredit "unacceptable" information.

While Lieberson is addressing his sociology colleagues, his argument is equally pungent for the broader community of scholars, intellectuals, and opinion makers in America. Evangelical Christians, and particularly those who would make known their sentiments through the political process, are an anathema to educated secular persons. They are not a phenomenon to be understood, but objects of ridicule and scorn. As long as they are silent and remain on the periphery of society, they can be tolerated. When they threaten to enter the mainstream of political life, they become dangerous. The thought that evangelical Christians might have real political power produces such intense cognitive dissonance (Festinger et al. 1964, 26) that the information suggesting the presence, or even potential for power, is discounted. The bringers of the "bad" news are subjected to ad hominem arguments, double standards are applied to discredit research evidence, etc. "We have a set of illogical but punishing conclusions about those whose results do not meet certain predetermined notions," argues Lieberson (1988, 394).

Evangelical Christians and the political movement they have propagated over the past decade are not well understood because of the immense intellectual barrier to objective analysis. Rather than cool analysis, the introduction of any datum about the Christian right almost automatically produces an ideological response. Some are prone to respond by viewing almost any datum with alarm; others can see the folly in any argument that asserts real or potential political power grounded in evangelical Christian principles. So long as ideology serves as the foundation for understanding the Christian right, our insights will not be very profound and we shall continue to be surprised by their tenacious persistence in the political arena.

References

Festinger, Leon, H. W. Riecken, and S. Schacter. 1964. *When Prophecy Falls*. New York: Harper and Row.
Gallup, George Jr. 1988. "The Impact of Religion in the 1988 National Elections." Address at the annual meetings of the Society for the Scientific Study of Religion, Chicago (Oct. 29).
Hadden, Jeffrey K., and Anson Shupe. 1988. *Televangelism: Power and Politics on God's Frontier*. New York: Henry Holt.
Lieberson, Stanley. 1988. "Asking Too Much, Expecting Too Little." *Sociological Perspectives* 31 (4) (Oct.): 379–97.
Menendez, Albert J. 1988. "Evangelicals Helped Win It for Bush." *National and International Religion Report* 2 (23) (21 Nov.).
New York Times/CBS News Poll. 1988. "Portrait of the Electorate." *New York Times* (10 Nov.), B6.
Safire, William. 1986. "The Poli-Preachers." *New York Times* (9 June).
Times Mirror. 1988. "The Static Dynamic Electorate." *New York Times* (6 Nov.).
Williamsburg Charter Foundation. 1988. *The Williamsburg Charter Survey on Religion and Public Life*. Washington, D.C.

Reading 32

CATHOLICS—ANDREW M. GREELEY

1) Who are American Catholics?
2) How are they different from other Americans?
3) Why do they stay in the Catholic Church?

The answer to the first question is that they are, in great part, the third and fourth generation offspring of the European immigrants who arrived in the United States at the turn of the century. The new immigration, that which is taking place now, is also heavily Catholic, although the Church is losing many of its Hispanic members.

The answer to the second question—which I address in the article in this section—is that they differ from other Americans in the way in which they imagine reality.

The answer to the third question is that they remain Catholic because they like being Catholic, they find the Catholic narrative symbol system appealing, even if they are not enamored with the institutional leadership of the Church.

Questions for Reflection and Discussion

1. Why do Catholics imagine the world differently? What effect does it have?
2. How can they be good Catholics and ignore what the Pope says?
3. If they don't like what the Church teaches, wouldn't they be better off if they simply got out of the Church?

THEOLOGY AND SOCIOLOGY: ON VALIDATING DAVID TRACY

Andrew M. Greeley

In this paper I propose to outline my efforts to find empirical validation for David Tracy's theory of the Analogical Imagination and then to engage in some

Source: Andrew M. Greeley, "Theology and Sociology: On Validating David Tracy," *Journal of the American Academy of Religion,* Vol. 59, No. 4, Winter 1991.

speculation on the nature of the religious enterprise and its relationship to theological "classics." To summarize my findings, I was indeed able to find that hypotheses derived from the Tracy theory were sustained by social science data in two multi-nation studies involving ten countries (UK, BRD, Australia, Ireland, Italy, Austria, Canada, Hungary, the Netherlands, and the United States). On the basis of these findings I will suggest that religious sensibilities generate theological "classics" and not vice versa and that theology, even the theology of the "classics," is merely part of the superstructure of a religious heritage.[1]

I must outline as a prelude my sociological theory of religion as imagination, which parallels Tracy's theological theory. Religion, I am convinced, is imaginative before it is propositional. It begins in (1) experiences which renew hope, is encoded in (2) images or symbols which become templates for action, is shared with others through (3) stories which are told in (4) communities and celebrated in (5) rituals. This model is a circle, not a straight line, and hence permits stories, communities and rituals in their turn to influence hope renewal experiences.

Because we are reflective creatures we must reflect on our imaginative religion. Because we are creatures who belong to communities that have heritages we must critique our imaginative religion. Creeds, catechisms, theological systems, even teaching authorities are an inevitable and essential result of reflection on and critique of experiential religion. Religion must be intellectual, but it is experiential before it is intellectual. Religion takes its origins and its raw power from experiences, images, stories, communities, and rituals. Most religious socialization (transmission of a culture) takes place through narrative before it takes place in non-fiction. Jesus was a story teller, the parables are the essential Jesus; they share with us Jesus's experience of the generous, hope-renewing love of the Father in heaven (who, be it noted, in the stories of Jesus loves with a mother's forgiving tenderness as much as She loves with a father's vigorous protection).

The Jewish tradition is passed on especially in the stories of the Holidays and the Passover. The Catholic tradition is passed on especially in the stories of Christmas and the Christian passover. Indeed I often think that maybe half our heritage is transmitted to children around the crib at Christmastime—and especially in the wonderfully mysterious explanation of the Incarnation to little kids that Mary is God's mommy.

The analogical or Catholic imagination, to summarize and simplify Tracy, emphasizes the presence of God in the world and its creatures and relationships and social structures. The analogical imagination stresses the metaphorical dimension of creation as a sacrament of God. I often illustrate the theory

---

[1] I must presume that readers are familiar with David Tracy's *The Analogical Imagination* (New York: Crossroad Books, 1981) and are willing to grant that I make the same qualifications in my use of its model as he does. Moreover, again because of limitations of space, I must also ask that those who are interested in the technical sociological details of my work to consult my book-length development of the article The Behaviour and Beliefs of American Catholics in *The Catholic Myth* (New York: Charles Scribner's Sons, 1990).

by noting that Catholics have angels and saints and souls in purgatory, statues and stained glass windows, votive candles and holy water, and an institutional church which itself is thought to be a sacrament. Protestant denominations, on the other hand, either do not have this imagery or do not put so much emphasis on it. The Catholic imagination is defined by the practice of devotion to Mary the Mother of Jesus. Catholics practice this devotion and Protestants on the whole do not practice it or at least do not grant it so much importance.

One side leans in the direction of immanence, the other leans in the direction of transcendence. Which is better? Neither. Which is necessary? Both.

The Analogical and the Dialectical imaginations are not mutually exclusive. No individual is completely possessed by one or the other, nor does any denomination or group have a monopoly on one or the other. The two "imaginations" represent propensities, tendencies, emphases, or, in the lexicon of my own discipline, modest but statistically significant correlations.

It occurred to me that the theory of the two religious imaginations seemed to converge with the "classic" sociological theories (we have "classics" too, only they're not so old) of Emile Durkheim and Max Weber. Might not a religious sensibility which stresses the sacramentality, the metaphorical power, of human relationships underpin a social and ethical orientation which could be called "communal," and a religious sensibility which emphasizes the "sinfulness" of human social order (in the sense that God is absent from it) underpin a social and ethical orientation which could be called "individualist"?[2]

To support this speculation I had to prove, it seemed to me, first, that differences between the two sensibilities could be found among Catholics and Protestants in different countries (and hence was not an American phenomenon). Or, to put the challenge in terms of my discipline, I had to prove that the theory would permit me to generate hypotheses which would not be falsified by empirical data. Then I had to establish that these differences were not part of an archaic past that was disappearing under the impact of "modernization." Finally I had to show that the differences could be accounted for by different images of God and world.

The data bases were exceptionally rich—items about political and social attitudes and behaviors, ethical orientations, attitudes toward equality, religious orientations, and family structure attitudes and behaviors. I was able to formulate more than seventy hypotheses to be tested against these data. More than three quarters of them were confirmed (or in technical language not falsified). Moreover, in general these differences persisted not only in the entire sample but within each country (except Hungary[3]). A theory of the religious imagination therefore did indeed predict different attitudes and behaviors in the whole sample *and* within each country.

---

[2] I emphasize again that neither denominational heritage has a monopoly on either orientation.

[3] My colleague Tamas Kalashi explains to me that Hungarian Lutherans have a highly distinctive and strongly communal subculture, to a considerable extent because of their proximity to Romania.

The differences were especially striking on measures of attitudes towards inequality and on measures of attitudes and behavior with regard to family structures. Catholics were much more likely than Protestants to live with their families or near parents and siblings and children and to be in constant and frequent touch with parents and siblings and children. Moreover, they were more likely to turn to family for help, major or minor, than were Protestants. The differences were often in the range of twenty percentage points.

The correlations in the international samples did not diminish when either age or education were taken into account. They were the same among both the young and the well educated. Moreover, for those variables in which I had measures of the religious imagination, either pictures of God[4] or attitudes on the relationship between God and world,[5] these measures reduced the correlation between denomination and attitudes and behavior to statistical insignificance.

To summarize: the differences between Catholics and Protestants that one might expect from Weber[6] and Durkheim are not diminishing. Moreover, these differences can be accounted for by different patterns of religious imagery, different sensibilities about the relationship between God and world. The Tracy theory of the religious imaginations can be confirmed, therefore, not only by the "classics" but also by data on attitudes and behaviors of ordinary people living the *fin de siècle* of the Twentieth Century.

Or, again to use the lexicon of my discipline, Tracy was not falsified by the data. Perhaps I should have called this paper "On the Nonfalsification of David Tracy."[7]

In subsequent analysis, reported in *The Catholic Myth,* I was able to establish that it was the appeal of the Catholic religious sensibility which keeps

---

[4]Mother versus father, lover versus judge, spouse versus master, king versus friend—on seven point scales.

[5]A measure which I call the Tracy Scale!

[6]For those who remember Weber's work on the Protestant ethic, there is no longer a correlation between denomination and educational achievement in Germany—or anywhere else. Nor is there a correlation between religion and income. The "communal ethic" no longer impedes educational and economic success or, if you wish, the spirit of capitalism.

[7]In my kind of sociology no theory is ever "verified." We always admit the possibility that someone else may find data which will force us to abandon or, more likely, to refine our theory. It is a methodological modesty that I would commend to others. Mind you such falsification—significant differences in the opposite direction—must be established by empirical evidence and not by speculations in faculty lounges or in question periods at scholarly meetings.

This footnote is as good a place as any to respond to criticisms of "survey" or "positivist" sociology (often advanced by devotees of "critical" sociology who are unaware that empiricists have long since routed the Frankfurt school even at Frankfurt).

All generalizations about human behavior, even those offered by Professor Bellah and his colleagues, are based on surveys—on conversations with people or observations and impressions of their behavior. The only difference between their reports and ours is that we are explicit about our sample designs, our questionnaire items, and our statistical methods. Thus Bellah's assertion that Americans have less civic responsibility than they used to have is a generalization based on interviews and observations of a sample of people in the present (and by implication in the past)—either that or it is nothing more than a highly personal opinion or the result of some special divine revelation. Incidentally the data gathered by my colleagues Norman Nie and Sidney Verba demonstrate conclusively that the proposition that Americans are more civic minded than they were a quarter century ago cannot be falsified—thus strongly challenging the Bellah thesis.

American Catholics in their Church (and loyally and stubbornly in that Church) despite their sharp disagreements with ecclesiastical authority. I noted that in any conflict between sacramental imagery and propositional teaching, the former would win going away. Thus in the conflict between the image of marriage as a sacrament of God's love (not articulated that way but experienced that way) and the formal teaching on birth control, the former won easily. It always will.[8]

Tracy's theory of the religious imaginations also can be an enormously useful tool in cultural analysis. An excellent conscious and explicit example of this utility can be found in Lee Lourdeaux's brilliant *Italian and Irish Film Makers in America,* a study of Ford, Capra, Coppola, and Scorsese.[9]

There are two broad questions with which we are left when we have discovered that Tracy's Analogical Imagination does exist in ordinary men and women of our time as well as in the Catholic classics of the past.

The first is, where did it come from? My guess is that it arose from the decision of the early Church (implicit and extended over centuries) to make its peace

---

[8]In response to some questions and objections;

1) I do not discuss differences among Protestant denominations:

The distribution of Protestants even in a large international sample is such that the various denominations tend to be found in specific countries rather than in all countries. There are precious few German Methodists, Italian Lutherans, Austrian Anglicans. So such analysis becomes much more problematic. However, I was not able to find significant differences among the Protestant denominations, save that Anglicans (some of whom would obviously resent the categorization) are more like Catholics than they are like (other) Protestants on matters of family structure, a finding which perhaps is not all that surprising.

2) I say nothing about the religious imagination of the orthodox or of non-Christians, even that of Jews:

To which I reply that my silence is because of lack of data. I suspect that the Orthodox will be like Catholics, that the Jews will occupy a middle ground, and that most non-Christians (Moslems excepted) will also tend in the Catholic direction.

The International Social Survey Program, whence my best data comes, will shortly launch a survey in which a religious module will be used. If I can persuade my colleagues in the Philippines, Israel, Slovenia, and the Soviet Union to ask religious image questions we might be able to say more on the subjects of these other religions in the future. The serious problem of course is that the analogical dialectical distinction may well be specific to the religious cultures of the four great religious traditions of the Holy One of Israel—Judaism, Protestantism, Catholicism, and Islam.

3) I do not discuss the religious imagery of the Third World, even of Catholics and Protestants in the Third World (or of Protestant Hispanics in the United States—a population which would be very interesting to study from the perspectives of a theory of the religious imagination):

Again I would be happy to do so if the data were available. However, data collection from probability samples is prohibitively expensive; and funding agencies are generally not interested in religion (foolishly so, given its importance in affecting human behavior). The best one can hope for is that one can piggyback religious questions on other surveys. Under those circumstances one does the best one can with the data one has.

The participation of the Philippines in the International Social Survey Program (with money furnished by the Catholic hierarchy!) will provide at least the possibility of a beginning of possible Third World analysis.

[9]I believe that Martin Scorese, for all his flaws (including most especially his blood obsession), is one of the great Catholic artists of our time. The Church's condemnation of "The Last Temptation" was a foolish and stupid action, the result of bishops listening to dialogue and paying no attention to imagery. The best way to watch the film on videotape is simply to turn off the soundtrack and give oneself over to the imagery.

with the pagan nature religions and absorb whatever is good from these religions, a decision which to some extent went against the formal injunctions of prophetic Judaism in the TNK.[10]

Thus in Ireland the intercourse symbol of male and female combined became the Celtic cross. God was pictured as rather like Dagda and Jesus like Lug. The ancient goddess Brigid (Bride), goddess of poetry and spring and new life, was converted to the Christian saint of the same name who enjoyed similar responsibilities (in addition to the more recent one of having charge of Radio Telefis Eirean). Her cross, a sun symbol, became the Brigid Cross of Catholic piety which, hanging over the doorway in west of Ireland cottages even today, asks Brigid's intercession till the warmth of spring returns.[11]

The Irish used the Analogical Imagination with a vengeance—and with the constant risk of corruption into folk religion and superstition which is always a danger for the Catholic imagination.[12]

The revulsion against the admixture of pagan superstitions in folk Catholicism, which revulsion was always part of the Catholic tradition, was perhaps such an important element in the Reformation that the Reformation Churches were fated to emphasize the transcendental pole of the heritage. In a sense the Reformation could be said to represent a splitting of the Analogical and the Dialectical Imaginations. In fact, it may have been that more than anything else and certainly more than a battle between Aristotle (and Aquinas) and Augustine.

I leave this issue to others and turn at somewhat greater length to the relationship between the "classic" expression of religious sensibility and that which for the lack of a better name I call the popular.

Which comes first?

I respond by asking how many people read theology books? How many have read the *City of God* or the *Summa Contra Gentiles* or the *Institutes?* How many have read *The Analogical Imagination,* for which God forgive them, says I!

How many people read Aquinas or Augustine even in their own day?

Is not theology, in other words, a manifestation in the superstructure of the religious enterprise, the infrastructure of which is the religious sensibility?

---

[10]Excavations of Jewish synagogues from the first century of the common era suggest that the Judaism of that era was open to pagan artistic influence.

[11]Not at that warm it is to be feared in Ireland.

[12]The Church has bitterly fought three Irish religious customs, patent hold-overs from paganism, for the last two centuries—the "pattern" (festival at a shrine of a patron saint on the saint's feast day), the holy wells, and the wake. In recent years the Church had seemed to have won all three—though not thereby gained any respect from the Occupying Power and its people for abandoning "superstition." More recently, however, the "pattern" (purged for the moment of its heavy drinking and rowdy fighting) is in the process of being restored, holy wells have been re-evaluated; and the wake is at least being reconsidered. The analogical imagination finds it hard to give up on the symbols of the past. Nor is it persuaded that the rearticulation of superstitious customs so that they have authentic Christian meaning is all that impossible. It is much less fearful of such an effort than would be the dialectical imagination.

Did Aquinas acquire his Catholic sensibility because of his theory of analogy or did the theory flow out of his Catholic sensibility? Was it not, in the good sense of the word, a rationalization of his imaginative instincts instead of constituting those instincts?

Did Father Tracy become an Irish Catholic from New York (about which background he is honest) because he wrote *The Analogical Imagination?* Or is *The Analogical Imagination* the kind of book that would be most unlikely to have an author who was not an Irish Catholic?

Has not, to put the issue in modern terms, ecumenical dialogue made far easier progress on *Sola Fides* than it has on the veneration of the saints and of the Mother of Jesus and terribly scandalizing presence of statues in Catholic churches?[13]

Is theology then an epiphenomenon? While it might be risky to say so in present company, I would respond at least as a model for further investigation that it is indeed an epiphenomenon, though a necessary epiphenomenon. I am always impressed in the ongoing debates within Catholicism between the Magisterium (so-called[14]) and theologians by how important both sides of the discussion think they are and how little attention they pay to a third party—the laity who listen but little to either of them.

Theology is necessary because pre-intellectual experience, image, and story need to be critiqued by intellect. Each tradition needs a group of people who engage in such formal critique. Moreover, theology makes available the tools for rational reflection to those in a heritage who for one reason or another need or desire to engage in sustained formal reflection on their religious sensibility. Finally, formal theology clarifies and confirms the religious sensibility and thus reenforces its continuity and stability (and I think Father Tracy's work does that brilliantly).

Thus the distinction between person and nature, however obscure it may seem to us today, has been necessary and essential as a model by which elites within the Catholic heritage have critiqued certain manifestations of the heritage and around which they have organized their formal instruction so that the Catholic instinct about the dual nature of Jesus may be transmitted adequately on the formal and verbal level.

Am I daring to suggest that the sociologist is more important than the theologian? Rather, I am saying that both become equally unimportant (though still

---

[13]Some priests and Church architects think they can finesse this issue by eliminating statues and vigil lights from new Catholic churches. Such an attempt at compromise betrays their own heritage. The veneration of Mary and the Saints is a matter for dialogue between the two imaginations and not of premature compromise in which one side abandons its position, especially because there is no sign that the Catholic people are willing to give up saints, to say nothing of the Mother of Jesus. It must be said in all candor to our brothers and sisters of other denominational backgrounds that Catholics are not ashamed of our veneration of Mary and the saints and we will not give it up. If we respect your fears about what it might mean, you should also listen to what we say it means, not what your visceral reactions are convinced that it does mean. I wonder if there is a more difficult issue in Protestant-Catholic dialogue than this one.

[14]An eighteenth-century Lutheran term I am told!

equally necessary) when compared with the poet, the artist, the story teller, the mystic, the saint.

In the religious culture of both the group and the individual, intellect is never absent. Both the community and the individual must reflect on experiential religion. The Catholic religious sensibility as it manifests itself in both community and individual always has a rational and reflective component. There is no such thing in the mature human adult as purely experiential religion. Formal theology will always have some influence on this reflective component, but for most people and for most of Catholic history this influence would seem to have been both remote and indirect.

I draw three conclusions from this speculation:

1) We know very little about the components of the ordinary Catholic religious sensibility (or any other), both experiential and reflective, or how the sensibility[15] is transmitted. From parents to children, from parish clergy to people, in works of art and story, in ritual and song, with festivals and celebrations, one might suspect. How much of the Catholic heritage, for example, is transmitted to children at Christmas time and especially around the crib? How much of the Jewish at seder? We need to know far more than we do about these matters.

2) Secondly, while the "faith of the Christian people" has always been considered an important "locus theologicus," perhaps theologians could treat the orientations and behaviors of the ordinary faithful with more respect than they do. They ought not look for the raw material for theological reflection only in the experiences of people who are not their own. I note that such sensitive sympathy to their own faithful is not incompatible with criticism of their narrowness and rigidities. Quite the contrary; the critic who understands sympathetically those whom he is criticizing is likely to be far more effective than the one who simply denounces. If you write off your own people as materialist, individualist, consumerist chauvinists and polluters, it may be great fun, but you shouldn't be surprised that they don't listen to you.

John Shea has suggested to me that it is difficult to reflect on the religious sensibility of your tradition if you have, one way or another, alienated yourself from the community which embodies (incarnates if you wish) that tradition. You cannot, for example, fashion a theology of Catholic marriage unless you are open to the religious sensibility of Catholic marriage.

3) Finally and perhaps merely a restatement of the previous conclusion, it is a serious mistake for those who attempt to educate, one way or another, under the influence of the categories of current formal theology (liturgists and "reli-

---

[15] I am suspicious of the use of the term "piety" to describe this religious sensibility or subculture. "Piety" seems to imply a person making the stations of the cross or fingering the rosary beads (both unobjectionable behaviors) with little religious sophistication. I also object to the use of the adjective "popular," which seems to imply inferior. Therefore I strongly object to the use of the dismissive term "popular piety" to describe a religious sensibility or subculture. In fact, a religious sensibility in both individual and community can be a sophisticated narrative system with a subtle blend of the experiential and the reflective. One does not begin to learn how to respect such a system by using a demeaning terminology to describe it. All that can be said about the religious sensibility of ordinary people is that it is not the same as that of academic theologians.

gious educators" in my Church) to think that because the faithful are illiterate in the terminology of contemporary theology (I almost said theological fashion) they are also religiously illiterate, graceless and spiritless people.[16] Quite the contrary; educators must realize that they will succeed only if they are interacting with people in the grip (to a greater or lesser extent) of an ancient, rich, variegated, and powerful religious sensibility. The educators' success in providing their students with a new vocabulary with which to reflect on that heritage will depend to a considerable extent on the educators' sensitive and sympathetic understanding of it. You may modify the religious sensibility but you won't eliminate it. If you try it will eliminate you as an effective educator.

You won't make much progress in your religious education or your liturgy, for example, if you write off the Holy Souls or abolish May Crownings. You'd be much better advised to help your students to rearticulate the experience and the stories which those two images encode.

In conclusion, I know of no other occasion in which a sociologist has drawn his theoretical orientation and his hypotheses for falsification from the work of a theologian. It is a tribute to Father Tracy's work that such an exercise can be performed and that indeed the hypotheses are strongly sustained (not falsified). Thus I am inclined to believe that the publication of *The Analogical Imagination* may well be an axial event in the history not only of theology but of all religious thought, a new Catholic classic in-the-making.

References

Greeley, Andrew. 1989. "Protestant and Catholic: Is the Analogical Imagination Extinct?" *American Sociological Review* 54:485–502.

Greeley, Andrew. 1990. *The Catholic Myth*. New York: Scribner.

Lourdeaux, Lee. 1990. *Italian and Irish Film Makers in America*. Philadelphia: Temple University Press.

Tracy, David. 1981. *The Analogical Imagination*. New York: Crossroad Books.

---

[16] I think of those who seem to be influenced by the work of Monika Helwig and Aidan Kavanagh and of many of the enthusiasts of the Rite of Christian Initiation of Adults.

Reading 33

JEWS—JACOB NEUSNER AND BERNARD LAZERWITZ

Jews are somewhere between two and three percent of the American population —at the most six million people. They are the largest of the non-Christian religious groups, though perhaps the Mormons will catch up to them after the turn of the century. They have a (not illegitimately) disproportionate influence on American culture because of their mix of talent and hard work, their superb organizational abilities, and their concentration in a few critically important population centers (New York, Los Angeles, and Chicago).

Jewish scholars see the Jewish community caught in a number of dialectical tensions: Is Judaism a religion or an ethnic group? Does there have to be a religious component in Jewish activity for it to be Jewish? How can Jews be socially and politically liberal and still fight for their own political agenda? Can Jews be tolerant of others and still oppose religious intermarriages, which seem to be eroding their population base? Is there a conflict between loyalty to America and concern about the nation of Israel? How should Jews react when minority groups (most notably African Americans), once their allies, appear to turn against them? Should Jews relax in their apparently secure place in American society or be constantly on the watch for a resurgence of anti-Semitism?

Sociology can provide no easy answers to these questions, but it can perhaps shed some light on the circumstances in which the questions must be answered. The question of Jewish "identity" is a value question that cannot be resolved by sociology. In this section, Rabbi Neusner sketches the two "Judaisms which he sees shaping American Jewish life, one private life and the other public life. Bernard Laserwitz sees a drift of many Jews away from denominational affiliation and a more vigorous denomination among those who remain.

Questions for Reflection and Discussion

1. How are the two "Judaisms" which Rabbi Neusner describes related to one another?
2. Are American Jews drifting away from their Jewish identity?
3. Is Judaism a religion, an ethnic group, or something else altogether?

Part 1

JUDAISM IN CONTEMPORARY AMERICA
Jacob Neusner

THE TWO JUDAISMS OF AMERICA: THE DUAL TORAH AT HOME, THE JUDAISM OF HOLOCAUST AND REDEMPTION IN THE COMMUNITY

The largest group of practitioners of Judaism in the world today are in America, where, among approximately 5.5 million Americans who call themselves Jewish, more than four million surveyed in 1990 declared that they were "Jewish" because they practice the religion, Judaism. The answer to the question provoked by the human situation is, "This is Judaism and this is what I do because it is Judaism." Two Judaisms form the question, one practiced at home and in the family, the other characteristic of the Jewish community at large. We have already examined those components of the Judaism of the dual Torah that thrive in home and family. The other Judaism, which appeals to different stories and involves different rites from the familiar one, is called "the Judaism of Holocaust and redemption," and it thrives within Jewry at large, defining the civil religion of American Jews.

DEFINING THE JUDAISM OF HOLOCAUST AND REDEMPTION

The Judaism of Holocaust and redemption focuses on the murder of nearly six million Jews in Europe in World War II and the creation of the State of Israel afterward and in consequence of those murders. Appealing across the sectarian lines of Reform, Orthodox, Reconstructionist, Conservative, or other Judaisms, the Judaism of the Holocaust and redemption brings together all who differ on everything else. In politics, history, in society, Jews in North America—the United States and Canada—as well as in other western democracies, respond to the Judaism of the Holocaust and redemption as they respond to the Passover seder, the Seven Blessings at the marriage canopy and nuptial meal, or the other

Source: Jacob Neusner, *A Short History of Judaism: Three Meals, Three Epochs,* Minneapolis, MN: Fortress Press, 1992.

rites of the Judaism of the dual Torah. That is to say, the Judaism of Holocaust and redemption makes them imagine that they are someone else, living somewhere else, at another time and circumstance. That vision transforms families into an Israel, a community.

The somewhere else is Poland in 1944 and the earthly Jerusalem, and the vision turns them from reasonably secure citizens of North America into insecure refugees finding hope and life in the land and State of Israel. Public events are commemorated in such a way that "we" were there in "Auschwitz" (which represents all of the centers for the murder of Jews) and "we" share, too, in the everyday life of that faraway place in which we do not live but should, the State of Israel. That transformation of time and of place, no less than the recasting accomplished by the Passover seder, or the rite of circumcision, or the marriage rite turns people into something other than what they are in the here and now.

The Judaism of Holocaust and redemption supplies the words that make another world of this one. Those words, moreover, change the assembly of like-minded individuals into occasions for the celebration of the group and the commemoration of its shared memories. Not only so, but events defined, meetings called, moments identified as distinctive and holy, by that Judaism of Holocaust and redemption mark the public calendar and draw people from home and family to collectivity and community—those events, and, except for specified reasons, not the occasions of the sacred calendar of the synagogue, that is, the life of Israel as defined by the Torah. Just as in the United States religions address the realm of individuals and families but a civil religion defines public discourse on matters of value and ultimate concern, so the Judaism of the dual Torah forms the counterpart to Christianity, and the Judaism of Holocaust and redemption constitutes Jewry's civil religion. The way-of-life Judaism of Holocaust and redemption requires active work in raising money and political support for the State of Israel.

Different from Zionism, which held that Jews should live in a Jewish State, this system serves, in particular, to give Jews living in America a reason and an explanation for being Jewish. This Judaism therefore particularly emphasizes the complementarity of the political experiences of mid-twentieth-century Jewry: the mass murder in death factories of six million of the Jews of Europe, and the creation of the State of Israel three years after the end of the massacre. These events, together seen as providential, bear the names *Holocaust,* for the murders, and *redemption,* for the formation of the State of Israel in the aftermath. The system as a whole presents an encompassing myth, linking one event to the other as an instructive pattern and moves Jews to follow a particular set of actions, rather than other sorts, as it tells them why they should be Jewish. In all, the civil religion of Jewry addresses issues of definition of the group and the policies it should follow to sustain its ongoing life and protect its integrity.

The Judaism of Holocaust and redemption affirms and explains in this-worldly terms the Jews' distinctiveness. It forms, within Jewry, a chapter in a larger movement of ethnic assertion in America. Attaining popularity in the late 1960s, the Judaism of Holocaust and redemption came to the surface at the same time that black assertion, Italo-American and Polish-American affirmation, feminism, and movements for self-esteem without regard to sexual preference attained prominence. That movement of rediscovery of difference responded to the completion of the work of assimilation to American civilization and its norms. Once people spoke English without a foreign accent, they could think about learning Polish or Yiddish or Norwegian once more. Then it became safe and charming. Just as when black students demanded what they deemed ethnically characteristic food, so Jewish students discovered they wanted kosher food too. In that context the Judaism of Holocaust and redemption came into sharp focus, with its answers to unavoidable questions deemed to relate to public policy: Who are we? Why should we be Jewish? What does it mean to be Jewish? How do we relate to Jews in other times and places? What is the State of Israel to us? and, What are we to it? Who are we in American society? These and other questions form the agenda for the Judaism of Holocaust and redemption.

EXPLAINING THE SUCCESS OF THE JUDAISM OF HOLOCAUST AND REDEMPTION

The power of the Judaism of the Holocaust and redemption to frame Jews' public policy—to the exclusion of the Judaism of the dual Torah—may be shown very simply. The Holocaust formed the question, redemption in the form of the creation of the State of Israel, the answer, for all universally appealing Jewish public activity and discourse. Synagogues except for specified occasions appeal to a few, but activities that express the competing Judaism appeal to nearly everybody. That is to say, nearly all American Jews identify with the State of Israel and regard its welfare as more than a secular good, but a metaphysical necessity—the other chapter of the Holocaust. They also regard their own "being Jewish" as inextricably bound up with the meaning they impute to the Jewish state. In many ways these Jews relive the terror-filled years in which European Jews were wiped out every day of their lives—and every day they do something about it. It is as if people spent their lives trying to live out a cosmic myth, and, through rites of expiation and regeneration, accomplished the goal of purification and renewal. Access to the life of feeling and experience, to the way of life that made one distinctive without leaving the person terribly different from everybody else emerged in the Judaic system of Holocaust and redemption. The Judaism of Holocaust and redemption presents an immediately accessible message, cast in extreme emotions of terror and triumph, its round of endless activity demanding only spare time. That Judaism realizes in a poignant way the conflicting demands of Jewish

Americans to be intensely Jewish, but only once in a while, providing a means of expressing difference in public and in politics while not exacting much of a cost in meaningful everyday difference from others.

The Judaism of the dual Torah, and the Judaism of Holocaust and redemption flourish side by side, the one viewed as self-evidently valid at home, the other in the public discourse. The words that evoke worlds that transform for the community at large in its assembly, that reach public and socially shared emotions and turn occasions into events, speak in the Jews' life as a group. The topic now is public policy, politics, how we should relate to the world beyond. In the nature of public life in North America, that topic is taken to be not otherworldly and supernatural, but this-worldly and political, involving the affairs of nations and states. The Judaism of the dual Torah—with its Adam and Eve, Abraham, Isaac, and Jacob, slaves in Egypt, Moses on Sinai, sanctification in the here and now and salvation at the end of time—exercises power at home. That Judaism does not pertain to the issues of public policy and politics that Jewry, as a collectivity, chooses to address. That other Judaism, which speaks of history and politics, things that have really happened and their implications in the here and now, takes over when the Jew leaves home.

Rabbinic Judaism in its American formulation thrives in the private life of home and family, where, in general, religion in North America is understood to work its wonders. The Judaism of Holocaust and redemption makes its way in the public arena, where, in general, politics and public policy function, viewed as distinct from religion. When we ask why the bifurcation between the personal and the familial, subjected to the Judaism of the dual Torah, perceived as religion, and the public and civic, governed by the Judaism of Holocaust and redemption, perceived as politics, we turn to the situation of religion in the United States. The explanation of the difference between Judaism for home and family and the civil religion for the Jewish community lies in the definition of permissible difference in North America and the place of religion in that difference. In North American society, defined as it is by Protestant conceptions, it is permissible to be different in religion, and religion is a matter of what is personal and private. Hence Judaism as a religion encompasses what is personal and familial. The Jews as a political entity then put forth a separate system, one that concerns not religion, which is not supposed to intervene in political action, but public policy. Judaism in public policy produced political action in favor of the State of Israel, or Soviet Jewry, or other important matters of the corporate community. Judaism in private affects the individual and the family and is not supposed to play a role in politics at all. That pattern conforms to the Protestant model of religion, and the Jews have accomplished conformity to it by the formation of two Judaisms. A consideration of the Protestant pattern, which separates not the institutions of church from the activities of the state, but the entire public polity from the inner life, will show us how to make sense of the presence of the two Judaisms of North America.

JUDAISM IN THE PROTESTANT MODEL

In Protestant (but also Roman Catholic and Judaic) North America, people commonly see religion as something personal and private. For example, prayer speaks for the individual. No wonder, then, that those enchanted words and gestures that, for their part, Jews adopt transform the inner life, recognize life's transitions and turns them into rites of passage. It is part of a larger prejudice that religion and rite speak to the heart of the particular person. What can be changed by rite then is first of all personal and private, not social, not an issue of culture, not effective in politics, not part of the public interest. What people do when they respond to religion, therefore, affects an interior world—a world with little bearing on the realities of public discourse: What, in general terms, should we do about nuclear weapons? or, in terms of Judaism, How should we organize and imagine society? The transformations of religion do not involve the world, or even the self as representative of other selves, but mainly the individual at the most particular and unrepresentative. If God speaks to me in particular, then the message, by definition, is mine, not someone else's. Religion, the totality of these private messages (within the present theory) therefore does not make itself available for communication in public discourse, and that by definition too. Religion plays no public role. It is a matter not of public activity but of what people happen to believe or do in private, a matter mainly of the heart.

DEFINING JUDAISM AT THE END

Christianity divides up into Christianities, Buddhism into Buddhisms, and Islam into Islams. Relationships among Christianities and Islams, past and present, produced major war and social upheaval. So too, as we have seen, Judaism comprises various Judaisms, of which we have surveyed the important ones past and present. In a second way, Judaism is like Christianity, Buddhism, and Islam. Like the other three religions, Judaism bears a universal message, addressing all of humanity with God's will for everybody. Like them, it is geographically a world religion, because, for most of its history Judaism has flourished in many places, not only in the land of Israel but also all over Europe, in Africa, and in Asia, in Christendom, and in Islam. People who originated in diverse groups became "Israel" whenever and wherever they adopted the Torah, that is, the religion, Judaisms. By practicing Judaism, they became members of "Israel," meaning, the holy family and people to whom the Torah was revealed. Therefore Judaism is not a religion that has limited itself to a single ethnic group or geographical area but has been and still is an international and multiracial religion. Nevertheless, like Buddhism, Christianity, and Islam, Judaism began in one place within a single group, utilizing a received tradition in a fresh way.

Up to now we have defined Judaism. But, as a matter of fact, a variety of religious systems—comprising a worldview or ethos, a way of life or ethics, and a theory of the social group that lives by that worldview and way of life—appealed to that same Torah, revealed by God to Moses. All of them called their followers "Israel," and all of them set forth rules of life on how to live, as Israel, by the Torah. While each of these systems, on its own, in its context, saw itself as Judaism, the differences among them require us to call them, as a group, Judaisms, and to recognize that each stands on its own, in its context, not connected, fore or aft, to some other Judaism. We have therefore to define not "Judaism," meaning, the one, harmonious religion, tracing itself in a single, linear relationship back to Sinai, but rather, "Judaisms," meaning, a family of religions sharing important traits in common.

On the basis of our survey, now completed, how shall we describe *a Judaism?* A Judaism is a religion that (1) takes as its Scripture the Torah revealed by God to Moses at Mount Sinai, meaning, the Five Books of Moses (Genesis, Exodus, Leviticus, Numbers, and Deuteronomy—the Pentateuch) and certain other records of revelation in addition; (2) believes that its adherents through all times and places form part of that one and the same extended family, or "Israel," the singular or holy people of whom the Pentateuch speaks; and (3) requires "Israel" to live in accord with the teachings of the Torah.

A religion has three components: worldview, definition of the social entity, way of life. The worldview of Judaism is defined by how the Torah is read. The social group of Judaism—its "church" in Christian terms—comprises Israel, the holy people. The way of life is set forth in the Torah. Therefore the definition of Judaism is in three aspects: the components of the canon as displayed in its sacred writings as they emerge at a particular time and place; the context of the social group that constituted Judaism; and the system of questions and answers that served that group of Jews. The Judaism that emerged as the normative religious system in a given period answered its particular problems. The problems persisted and because they were adequately answered by Judaism, the Judaism that solved that problem endured and enjoyed success among the Jewish people. We can define Judaism, in any of its several systems over time, when we can define the critical questions addressed by a given system and specify valid answers to those questions. The question that recurs in Judaism is, Who and what is "Israel," God's holy people? or, in current language, Who is a Jew? The reason is that while Judaism is a world religion, it does not have many adherents, so the definition of who is in and who is not, for a tiny group, forms a critical issue.

JUDAISM AND ITS ENEMIES: ANTI-JUDAISM, ANTI-SEMITISM, ANTI-ZIONISM

No account of Judaism is complete without attention to the enemies of Judaism, because so much of the history of Judaism forms a response to what those enemies have found it possible to say about Judaism and to do to Jewish people. In Christian America, and throughout the West, there are two assumptions about

Judaism that are misleading and dangerous notions. The first is that Judaism is the religion of the Old Testament. That is true but not true. Judaism is the religion of the Torah, which begins with the Five Books of Moses and encompasses the Old Testament. But Torah stands for more than the Pentateuch or even the whole Old Testament. The second is that Judaism is virtually the same as the Jews' history and culture. That is an error based on the fact that what happens to Israel, the Jewish people, defines the critical questions to be addressed by Judaism. Nevertheless, the answers that comprise Judaism are not represented as the result of public opinion but of God's will and word. A religion that appeals to revelation contained in authoritative and holy writings and presented by qualified teachers by its own word cannot be reduced to whatever a group of people say and do at a given time or place. The theology of Judaism—authoritative truth, set forth in a systematic way—cannot be confused with the sociology or the politics of the Jews.

When people identify Judaism as "the religion of the Old Testament" in contradistinction to Christianity, which has both the Old and the New Testaments, they do not realize that the Old Testament, in particular the Pentateuch, forms only part of the Torah of Judaism, and that other holy books take their place within the canon, just as Christianity appeals to both the Old Testament as well as other holy books. They furthermore take for granted that the religion that is portrayed within the Old Testament is the same religion to which we refer when we speak of Judaism. Like Christianity, Judaism draws upon the writings of the Old Testament, reading these writings within the framework of the worldview and way of life that came to expression only later, with the formation of the Pentateuch and in the centuries beyond. When people take for granted that Judaism is the same as the history and culture of the Jews as an ongoing group in history, Judaism as a religion is identified with the Jews' ethnicity and their history. Yet a religion that appeals to holy books cannot be defined merely by appeal to history and culture, and the Torah cannot be confused with whatever a given group of Jews happens to think at any given time or place.[1] It is important to recognize how, in general, what people assume that they know as fact about Judaism is wrong.

These errors in fact about Judaism are significant because they form the basis for anti-Judaism, the dismissal of Judaism as a dead religion, and the judgment that it is inferior to Christianity. For example, as eminent a scholar as Harvard Divinity School professor John Strugnell, former chief editor of the Dead Sea Scrolls, created a furor in 1990 when he told a reporter for an Israeli newspaper that "Judaism is a horrible religion," a Christian heresy, and "The correct answer of Jews to Christianity is to become Christian." In his defense, Strugnell's Harvard friends said he was insane. But people do not have to be insane to allege that Judaism is a dead religion, merely the religion of the Old Testament, now superseded by Christianity, or that Jews should become Christians because they have no religion. On the contrary, Christianity has set

---

[1]William Scott Green, "Old Habits Die Hard: Judaism in *The Encyclopedia of Religion*," *Critical Review of Books in Religion* 1989, 24.

forth anti-Judaism as standard doctrine for centuries. No account of Judaism should pretend that the Jews and Judaism did not resist enormous pressure, over many centuries, to give up the faith and accept Christianity or Islam.

Anti-Judaism denies the legitimacy of Judaism as a religion and declares it a fossil that ought to disappear. Anti-Semitism denies the Jews the human rights accorded others, ultimately the right to life. Anti-Zionism denies the State of Israel the right to legitimate national existence. Anti-Judaism, anti-Zionism, and anti-Semitism concur that Jews and Judaism ought to die, and, among religious and political programs, the one at Auschwitz came close to succeeding in its goals. While anti-Semitism often appeals principally to racism, anti-Judaism and anti-Zionism in the West commonly draw upon teachings of one stream of Christianity. It is not the only one. In his exposition of the standard anti-Semitic evaluation of Judaism, Harvard's John Strugnell reminds us of another stream of Christianity, the one of reconciliation—Vatican II and its Protestant counterparts in Europe and the United States. Some thought Christian anti-Semitism on theological grounds was over, but among many (not all!) Christian theological scholars of Judaism, Harvard's Strugnell shows that it thrives in Christian theological education.

Anti-Semitism on Christian grounds teaches that Judaism, the religion, is racist, that Jews are racist by continuing their distinct life as a people, and of course, by definition, that the State of Israel is as well. Carrying forward a nearly two-thousand-year-old theological position of Christianity, Judaism is further maligned as a religion that ought to have perished at the advent of Christianity. Judaism is moreover to be evaluated by the "higher" standard of Christianity, with the "religion of love" invidiously contrasted to the "religion of law." Christian anti-Judaism on religious grounds helped pave the road to Auschwitz. How are we to identify the intellectual foundations of this religiously based anti-Semitism broadly believed among devout and learned Christians? As we have noted, broadly held myths about Judaism circulate, and these have long nurtured anti-Judaism and now feed anti-Semitism and anti-Zionism among Christians in particular.

First, nearly all Christians view Judaism as not a religion in its own terms but merely Christianity without Christ, virtually the same religion, but deeply flawed by the rejection of Jesus. Judaism is the religion of "the Old Testament," so they suppose, and since, within Christianity, the Scriptures of ancient Israel that Judaism knows as the written Torah are to be read in light of "the New Testament," Judaism perverts revelation, and has no Torah of its own. Few grasp that Judaism is not merely "not-Christianity" or that Judaism reads the written Torah in light of the other, orally formulated and orally transmitted, Torah of Sinai. Some professors of Christianity only hear the Jewish twenty centuries of no to Christianity, not their eternal yes to God and the Torah.

Second, many Christians view Judaism as the culture or history of the Jews and, disliking Jews because, not being Christians, they are "different," or they remember some Jew they did not like. In most extreme form, this identification of the ethnic with the religious leads Christians who find Jews "clannish"—

meaning, Jews happily form a distinct and distinctive community, as everybody else does—to accuse Judaism of racism. That accusation then exculpates the Jew hater, just as it was meant to delegitimate the State of Israel in the 1975 United Nations resolution.

Third, many Christians deny that Judaism is a valid religion, which, time and again, has formulated compelling and persuasive answers to the urgent questions facing Israel, the Jewish people, in one crisis after another. Jews find the meaning of their life in the joy of Judaism. An ancient, enduring people that has so resolutely and happily found the center of its being in its religion (the Torah), under such unremitting Christian and Muslim pressure, for so many centuries, clearly identifies with a religion of considerable enduring appeal, and success.

NEVER AGAIN: TO A JEW, IT IS A SIN TO DESPAIR

Why people facing many alternatives have chosen and now choose to be Jewish and to practice Judaism (in the United States, two Judaisms, the personal and the political, as we have seen), is not a question readily answered. Within the Judaic system, the answer is, because that is how God wants things. Outside of it, answers may derive from whatever larger system of explaining the world people find plausible, for example, psychology, economics, sociology, or politics. But one answer is suggested even by this examination of how a Judaic system comes into being and why it thrives when it does, or meets plausible competition when it does.

First, Judaism thrives in home and family because the foundations of how we perceive the world are laid there. Judaism therefore endures in the eternal exchange from mother and father to son and daughter. Second, Judaism succeeds when it identifies a question that is both chronic and urgent: chronic, so people will need an answer from one generation to the next; and urgent, so that people will pay attention to the answer all their waking moments. A question of that order must derive not from home and family but from politics and the social order. The triumph of Judaism is attested, third, because its message finds a hearing among the survivors, the losers of war after war, the suffering who look back on the murder of millions but find plausible the insistence that catastrophe has meaning and may be called "the Holocaust."

The astonishing moment of success for Judaism has come in the century that now draws to a close. After World War II, when survivors of the German war against the Jews, emerged from hiding or were liberated by the American and Soviet armies, considerable numbers determined, "never again," and so adopted the ruling religion of their nation, whether Orthodox Christianity in Rumania, Roman Catholic Christianity in Poland and Hungary, or a form of Protestant Christianity elsewhere. They wanted to make sure that their children would never undergo the horrors they had now survived. To most Jews in post-war Europe, and nearly all Jews in the United States and elsewhere, the meaning of "never again" was to create the State of Israel and to reaffirm the legitimate difference of Israel, the Jewish people, from others, in the diaspora. Far from giving up, Jews renewed the covenant. They found language appropriate to their circumstance. The language, in contemporary terms, expressed the age-old affirmation of themselves as Israel, God's first love. They found in Judaism the meaning and message that their life mattered, that what happened to them bore meaning, and that to be Israel meant to find one's bearings in time, en route to eternity. That is evidence of the success of Judaism in explaining the issue that the Torah addressed from the outset: how to treat the given as a gift. Through Judaism, Israel the holy people—whether in the State of Israel or anywhere in the world—continued to ask itself, What does it mean to be a kingdom of priests and a holy people? and, How do I live my life in a manner appropriate to what the Torah says that I am, which is humanity "in God's image, after God's likeness"?

Part 2

THE AMERICAN JEWISH COMMUNITY AT THE END OF THE TWENTIETH CENTURY
Bernard Lazerwitz

As this book readily shows, the United States is a religious and denominational society and has been so for a considerable time. Greeley (1972, 231) has pointed out that "denominations are . . . groups providing means of identification and location within the American social structure. Loyalty to the . . . denomination . . . involves loyalty to the denominational tradition." Carroll and Roof (1993, 349) also state that "insofar as denominations do not absolutize their traditions and practices, they provide alternative places and occasions in which individuals experience belonging and meaning in a multicultural and diverse society." Other students of American religion, such as Swatos (1981) and Roof (1993) emphasize the importance of America's denominational system.

Into this denominational system entered wave upon wave of European Orthodox Jews. As Jick (1992) shows, the foundation of the American Jewish population began in the 1820's with the commencement of a relatively sizable immigration of Jews from Germany. In the course of the next 50 years, Jick's historical work shows how the various waves of these Jews from Germany gradu-

Source: Originally published as "American Jewish Denominations: A Social and Religious Profile," by Bernard Lazerwitz and Michael Harrison, The American Sociological Review 44 (1979). Revised and submitted specifically for this publication.

ally evolved the Jewish Reform denomination with its strong emphasis upon the integration of Jews into American society together with whatever religious changes were necessary to accomplish this integration.

Starting in 1881 a massive stream of Eastern European Jews began arriving in the United States. These immigrants came from very traditional Jewish communities locked into the Russian and Austro-Hungarian empires or newly created Balkan states such as Rumania. With their arrival, the revival of the American Jewish Orthodox denomination commenced. The religious traditions of this denomination looked with disdain upon secular society and strongly clung to the historic Jewish religious and ethnic approaches. Out of the clash between American modernity and secularism with Orthodox Judaism arose a third American denomination which sought a religious and ethnic approach between the radical changes introduced by the Reform denomination and the considerable resistance to modern American life of the Orthodox denomination. This third denomination is the Conservative movement. The Conservative denomination began with the founding in 1886 in New York City by Rabbi Sabato Morais of what has become the Jewish Theological Seminary of America. Rapid growth began in 1902 with the assumption of the head of this seminary by Rabbi Solomon Schechter. Adherents of this denomination have sought to retain the flavor of "that old-time religion" yet have moved near to the surrounding American social environment. (For more information on these denominations, readers can refer to Bulka, 1983; Davidman, 1991; Danzger, 1989; Greenberg, 1981; Heilman and Cohen, 1989; Waxman, 1983; Sklare, 1955; and Furman, 1987.)

By 1990, American Orthodoxy has, itself, modernized and established an extensive Jewish day school movement (akin to the Catholic parochial system). The Reform denomination has restored a variety of traditional Jewish practices and now supports Israel as strongly as the other sectors of the American Jewish community. It has also become more tolerant of the traditional Jewish dietary laws. The Conservative denomination for a considerable period of time has been the largest American Jewish denomination. It also has created a growing network of day schools. As will be seen for American Jews, as for other Americans, denominationalism is based on variations of belief and religious life style.

DATA SOURCE

In 1990 the Council of Jewish Federations, the national roof organization of the various local community Jewish federations, financed a large scale survey of the American Jewish population. This survey was the second such study done by the Council with the first having been conducted in 1971. This 1990 national survey of the American Jewish population (NJPS) is based on a sample obtained by random digit dialing selections from among all United States residential telephones. This approach obtained a probability sample of households whose residents were screened for those who state that they were Jewish or who had a

Jewish parent. After this screening, at a later date, eligible households were recontacted and one sample respondent per household was obtained from all who screened in as Jewish by the "next birthday method of respondent selection." (For a detailed explanation of this technique see Salmon and Nichols, 1983.)

The screening response rate was 63%; the recontact interviewing response rate was 68%. Obtained were 2,441 interviews. This search for respondents who declared themselves to be Jewish or who had a Jewish parent resulted in 471 respondent households consisting of people all of whom were reported as Christians and as not having been born Jewish; 25 adults who had been born Jewish but who had converted into a Christian faith; and 40 interviews with Jewish respondents under 20 years of age. All these have been dropped from analysis work. The number of analysis cases are, then, 1905 Jewish respondents 20 years old or older.[2]

The Denominational Characteristics of American Jewish Adults

With America being a denominational society, the most effective way of viewing the social and religious characteristics of American Jewish adults is through their denominational affiliations. Furthermore, prior research on American Jews by Lazerwitz and Harrison (1979) shows the importance of viewing Jews both by their denominational preference and by whether or not they are synagogue members. This shall be done throughout this presentation. Table 1 presents this distribution.

American Jews are overwhelmingly in two denominations which are just about equal in size. The once dominant Orthodox denomination is down to a mere 6% of American Jewish adults, and 15% of Jewish adults have no denominational preferences. When the denominational distribution of synagogue members is observed, there is a clear shift to the more traditional denominations. The Orthodox denomination almost doubles and the Conservative denomination is, by far, the leader. The no preference group is tiny among synagogue members. The sector of those who are not synagogue members has a shift to the opposite end with the Reform becoming the leader and the no preference category increasing to just about a quarter of those not synagogue members. (There are small denominational groups, such as the Reconstructionists, that are active in the American Jewish community. However, they furnished too few interviews for statistical treatment.)

---

[2]The sampling errors for random digit dialing samples are close to simple random sampling levels. For the 1905 interviews analyzed here, sampling error (two standard errors) for percentages is 2.4%. However, this survey's overall response rate was 43%. The possible bias resulting from this less than desirable response rate is estimated to be approximately 10% for religious and ethnic questions. The total survey error for percentages, a combination of sampling error and nonresponse bias, will be determined by the larger bias and will be at least 10%. The conclusions reached in this paper do not rest only on significance testing. Rather the patterning of results among denominational groups, and the support for such patterns from the 1971 National Jewish Population Survey, must also be considered. When all these factors are combined, it is judged highly unlikely that the findings presented here are random patterns.

TABLE 1

Jewish Adult Denominational Preferences by Synagogue Membership

Denominational Preference	All Jewish Adults	Synagogue Members	Not Synagogue Members
Orthodox	6%	10%	4%
Conservative	40%	51%	31%
Reform	39%	35%	41%
No Preference	15%	4%	24%
Base	100%	100%	100%

Overall, 47% of Jewish adults are synagogue members. Among those preferring the Orthodox denomination, synagogue members are 72%; among the Conservatives, members are 59%; among the Reform, they are 43%. Finally, a mere 13% are synagogue members among those without any denominational preferences. With so few Orthodox adherents not being synagogue members and so few no preference people being members, there are too few interviews with these two subgroups to permit additional analysis consideration.

Demographic and Socio-Economic Characteristics of Denominational Adherents

Table 2 indicates various demographic and socio-economic characteristics for the six denominational-membership groups. Men predominate among the Orthodox; women predominate among the two Conservative categories and the Reform members. The Reform-not members are equally split, while the no preference group is the most predominately male.

The adherents of the traditional denominations, the Orthodox and Conservative, are more concentrated in the 60 years and over category than are the other three. However, the Orthodox also have a sizable concentration in the young 20–39 age category. The Reform categories are the youngest ones among the six groups followed closely by the no preference adherents.

The Orthodox denomination has both more foreign born and U.S. born of foreign born parents than do any of the others. The Conservatives are concentrated in the parents-foreign born and parents-U.S. born categories. The Reform and no preference categories are still more generations in the United States with concentrations in the parents or grandparents U.S. born categories.

The households of the Conservative-not synagogue members have the least number of children under 17, followed by Reform-not members and then Conservative members. The no preference households have a bit more with children under 5 and relatively fewer children from 6–17. It is the Orthodox and Reform-members whose households have the most children with the Orthodox leading on children under 5 and the Reform members on children 6–17.

TABLE 2
Demographic and Socio-Economic Characteristics by Denominational Preferences and Synagogue Membership

Characteristics	Orthodox Member	CONSERVATIVE Memb.	Not Memb.	Memb.	REFORM Not Memb.	No Preference Not Member
DEMOGRAPHIC						
a) Gender						
Men	52%	47%	47%	47%	50%	59%
Women	48%	53%	53%	53%	50%	41%
b) Age						
20–39	46%	32%	37%	42%	48%	44%
40–59	24%	36%	32%	42%	32%	30%
60+	30%	32%	31%	16%	20%	26%
c) U.S. Generation						
Foreign born	28%	11%	7%	5%	4%	10%
US born, parents foreign born	50%	45%	46%	26%	29%	34%
Parents US born	13%	35%	34%	48%	49%	42%
Grandparents US born	9%	9%	13%	21%	18%	14%
d) Children in home						
5 yrs. or younger	26%	13%	13%	17%	15%	19%
6–17	18%	16%	9%	23%	12%	13%
SOCIO–ECONOMIC						
a) Education						
Undergrad. degree	38%	38%	28%	49%	42%	35%
Graduate work	25%	32%	25%	30%	22%	31%
b) Income						
$80,000 or more	7%	26%	11%	35%	20%	17%
$40,000–$79,999	62%	51%	49%	43%	45%	47%
Under $10,000	31%	23%	40%	22%	35%	36%

The Conservative-not members have the least amount of education followed by the Orthodox and then the no preference groups. The Reform members and Conservative members have the most education.

Finally, on income the Orthodox have the least percentage earning $80,000 or more and the most earning in the middle range of income. The two synagogue membership groups of the Reform and Conservative have the most income. The Reform-not members and the no preference groups have similar income distributions and follow after the Reform and Conservative members. The Conservative-not members have the lowest income distribution.

Now, what does this sum up to for the six denominational-membership groups? First of all, the Orthodox, despite their older foreign born adherents, have a considerable proportion of young adults and children. They also have almost two-thirds with an undergraduate degree or better, but lack high income earners. They represent a denominational group one would expect to have increased income as their young adults advance in their careers.

The adherents of the Conservative denomination are an aging social group with relatively few children in their homes. They are the children of either foreign born or U.S. born parents (but not grandparents.) However, the Conservative synagogue members are much better educated and have substantially more income than their not-member fellow denominational adherents. In fact, Conservative members rank just behind the leading Reform members on socio-economic status.

Reform members are relatively young with a substantial number of children at home and predominantly a multi-U.S. generation group. Reform-not members are similar in age and U.S. generation to Reform members. Yet they have fewer children, less education, and lower incomes than the members.

No preference people are considerably more often male, older, and fewer generations in the United States than the Reform adherents. They have more children 5 or younger but fewer older children than the Reform adherents. However, their socio-economic status is akin to that of the Reform-not members.

Religious and Ethnic Characteristics of Denominational Adherents

Table 3 presents a variety of religious and ethnic involvement measures for the six denomination-membership groups. Here, the findings are much more clear cut than those of Table 2. The Orthodox adherents customarily rank first on the measurements followed by Conservative synagogue members. Conservative-not members and Reform members are similar and rank next. Ranking last come the similar percentages of Reform-not members and the no preference groups.

There are interesting exceptions to this general rank ordering. The Jewish education percentage for the Orthodox is less than that for Conservative members. Membership in synagogues raises the involvement levels of Reform Jews to beyond that of Conservative-not members on Jewish education, synagogue attendance, and activity in Jewish organizations. Reform members are especially active in Jewish organizations. Reform-not members are more involved than no preference people in home religious practices, Jewish primary groups, and especially in activity in Jewish organizations.

The differential patterns of these six groups carries over to activities and attitudes outside of the Jewish community. Table 4 shows that Conservative and Reform synagogue members together with no preference people are most active in general community organizations. The two non-member groups are less, and about equally, active in these general organizations with Orthodox Jews being much less active than the rest. When questioned as to how politically liberal they regarded themselves, no preference people declared themselves to be liberal much more than the rest. They are followed by Reform-not members, Conservative and Reform members with Conservative-not members ranking behind the two member groupings. Orthodox Jews are least likely to consider themselves politically liberal.

TABLE 3
Jewish Involvement by Denominational Preferences and Synagogue Membership

Jewish Involvement	Orthodox Members	CONSERVATIVE			REFORM	
		Memb.	Not Memb.	Memb.	Not Memb.	No Preference Not Member
8 years or more of Jewish education	54%	59%	33%	39%	20%	19%
Attends synagogue 25 times or more in a year	76%	30%	7%	18%	2%	2%
Home Religious Practices*	91%	57%	23%	21%	10%	5%
J. Primary Groups**	92%	57%	35%	31%	16%	10%
J. Org. Activ.***	74%	64%	26%	52%	21%	6%
Has visited Israel	75%	51%	30%	28%	20%	19%

*Shabbat candles; Kiddush, chanukah candles; Kosher home
**Most friends Jewish; neighborhood Jewish; opposes intermarriage
***Member several J. org.; works 20 hrs. + per mo. for J. orgs.; gave money to J. orgs.

TABLE 4
General Community Involvement and Liberalism by Denomination and Synagogue Membership

Indices	Orthodox Members	CONSERVATIVE			REFORM	
		Memb.	Not Memb.	Memb.	Not Memb.	No Preference Not Member
General Community Organization Activity*	17%	42%	27%	44%	31%	41%
Considers Self Politically Liberal	23%	40%	34%	39%	44%	56%

*Member sev. gen. org.; gave nonJ. charity.

Geographic Distribution of Denominations

Goldstein (1993) estimates the number of Americans who declare themselves to be Jewish by religious and/or ethnicity to be approximately 5,500,000. This relatively small number, in comparison to the total American population, is highly concentrated in major population centers. Accordingly, it would be best to show the geographic distribution of Jewish denominations by estimated size of Jewish communities. This has been done in Table 5. (Synagogue members and not members have the same distributions. Hence Table 5 shows denominational preferences.)

TABLE 5

Jewish Denominations by Jewish Community Size

Jewish Community Size	Orth.	Conserv.	Reform	No. Pref.	Base
1 million plus (NYC metro area)	12%	39%	33%	16%	100%
Around 500,000 (Los Angeles and Miami metro areas)	3%	45%	41%	11%	100%
200,000–300,000 (Chicago, Philadelphia, Boston, Washington, DC metro areas)	3%	48%	35%	14%	100%
40,000–150,000 (11 Jewish communities)	8%	34%	46%	12%	100%
15,000–39,999 (18 Jewish communities)	2%	44%	42%	12%	100%
3,000–14,999	6%	32%	44%	18%	100%
Under 3,000	1%	39%	39%	21%	100%
Nationally	6%	40%	39%	15%	100%

The Jewish community size scale is composed of seven ranks. The first is New York City and its metropolitan area; the second rank (500,000 Jews) consists of the Los Angeles and Miami metropolitan areas; the third rank (200,000–300,000 Jews) is composed of the metro areas of Chicago, Philadelphia, Boston, and Washington, DC. The fourth rank consists of eleven Jewish communities estimated to have from 40,000 to 150,000 Jews. The fifth rank consists of eighteen Jewish communities estimated to have from 15,000 to 39,999 Jews. The sixth rank consists of those Jewish communities estimated to have from 3,000 to 14,999 Jews. The seventh rank consists of those Jewish communities estimated to have less than 3,000 Jews. Clearly New York City and its metropolitan area have, by far, the most respondents preferring the Orthodox denomination. It is barely below the national percentage for the Conservative denomination, somewhat below this percentage for Reform Jews, and barely above it for no preference respondents.

Those who prefer the Conservative denomination are more common in Jewish communities of 200,000 to 300,000, than in the 500,000 category (the combined category of Los Angeles and Miami metro areas) and in Jewish communities of an estimated 15,000 to 39,999 Jews. In the remaining size categories the Conservatives fall below their national average.

Where the Conservatives are "weak," the Reform respondents rise above their national average. This occurs in communities with estimated Jewish populations of 40,000 to 150,000 and 3,000 to 14,999. Both the Conservative and Reform are above their national averages in Jewish communities with estimated populations of 15,000 to 39,999. On the whole, Reform respondents live disproportionately in the smaller Jewish communities.

Respondents without any denominational preference are above their national percentage in the New York City metro area and in the two smallest size categories. On the whole, the no preference group falls below its national average in the Jewish communities with estimated populations of 15,000 on up apart from the New York metro area.

Denominational Shifting

The 1990 NJPS asked respondents for both their childhood denomination and their current denomination. These two questions enable an examination of the extent of denominational shifting since childhood by family generations in the United States as seen in Table 6. (Since nothing was ascertained about parental synagogue membership when respondents were children, there is no splitting by membership.)

The denominational shifts are dramatic and reflect the age differences among denominations that are presented in Table 2. The Orthodox denomination has undergone an extreme decline through the generations. The childhood denomination for the foreign born was 41% Orthodox. Currently, only 3% of respondents with United States born parents are Orthodox. Meanwhile, the no preference group has declined a bit among respondents with native born parents.

The dramatic gains are by the Conservative and Reform denominations. The Conservative adherents peak at 50% for the current preferences of respondents who are native born with foreign born parents. Then, the Conservatives decline for the next generation.

The adherents of the Reform denomination display a steady increase across the generations until they are, by far, the largest denomination among those with parents born in the United States.

Intermarriage

Not only have there been major shifts in denominational preferences among American Jews but there also has been a major shift in the extent to which American Jews are marrying out of the Jewish community. This change is shown in Table 7.

Before 1960, Jews rarely married outside of the Jewish community. In the decade of the 1960's, the percentage marrying outside of the Jewish community more than doubled. Since 1970, almost half of adult Jewish men and women have married outside of the Jewish community.

Before 1970 Jewish men were more likely to marry out than were Jewish women. Since 1970 both genders are equally likely to marry out.

The number of converts to Judaism, in one of its denominational forms, has also increased by about four times since before 1960. Also, converts are typically women who were born into a branch of Christianity.

The American Jewish Community at the Start of the Twenty-First Century

The statistics introduced so far picture an American Jewish Community which contains a small Orthodox denomination, an aging Conservative denomination, with a growing Reform denomination. What is the impact of intermarriage upon this situation? This is pictured in Table 8 which breaks up Jewish marriages entered into since 1970 into those between two Jewish born persons, those involving converts to a branch of Judaism, and those marriages which

TABLE 6

Childhood Denomination and Current Denomination by U.S. Generation

Denomination	FOREIGN BORN		U.S. BORN PARENTS FOREIGN BORN		PARENTS U.S. BORN	
	Child.	Curr.	Child.	Curr.	Child.	Curr.
Orthodox	41%	21%	40%	9%	10%	3%
Conservative	27%	43%	35%	50%	40%	34%
Reform	12%	19%	14%	28%	36%	48%
No Preference	20%	17%	11%	13%	14%	15%
Base	100%	100%	100%	100%	100%	100%

TABLE 7

All First Marriages by Sex and Time of Occurrence

	TIME OF OCCURRENCE					
	BEFORE 1960 JEWISH BORN		1960–1969 JEWISH BORN		1970–1990 JEWISH BORN	
First Marriage Type	Men	Women	Men	Women	Men	Women
Both Spouses Born Jewish	89%	95%	79%	87%	54%	54%
Convert-in	3%	1%	7%	1%	12%	5%
Jewish-Christian	5%	3%	11%	9%	25%	31%
Jewish-None or Other	3%	1%	5%	3%	9%	10%
Base	100%	100%	100%	100%	100%	100%
N	221	314	123	129	356	315

have remained religiously heterogeneous. Then these younger couples are contrasted with all Jewish respondents.

Marriages in which both spouses were born Jewish are consistently more likely to be synagogue members and to rank higher than all Jewish respondents on indices measuring activity in Jewish voluntary associations, ethnicity, Jewish education, home religious practices, and interest in Israel. They are as likely (perhaps a little less likely) to be active in general community voluntary associations than are all Jewish respondents. Both spouses born Jewish couples are more likely to attend synagogue than are all Jewish respondents with almost a quarter attending nineteen or more times yearly.

Conversion to Judaism seems successful with almost 80% of convert couples claiming synagogue memberships, and reporting somewhat greater synagogue attendance than that of the both spouses born Jewish couples. Convert couples do fall somewhat below both spouses born Jewish couple on activity in Jewish organizations and home religious practices. Convert couples, as would be expected, are less ethnically involved than couples in which both spouses were born Jewish. Their interest in Israel is also a lot less. (The number of Jewish

TABLE 8
Religio-Ethnic Characteristics of Jewish Marriages
Entered Into From 1970 to 1990

Religio-Ethnic Characteristics	MARRIAGE TYPES			
	Both Spouses Born Jewish	Convert-In	Hetero-geneous	All Jewish Respondents
Synagogue Member				
Yes	58%	78%	14%	47%
No	42%	22%	86%	53%
Jewish Org. Act. Index				
High	50%	43%	12%	38%
Moderate	32%	34%	28%	33%
Low	18%	23%	60%	29%
Ethnicity Index				
High	56%	27%	3%	35%
Moderate	26%	36%	13%	28%
Low	18%	37%	84%	37%
Denomination				
Orthodox	12%	3%	1%	6%
Conservative	43%	27%	21%	40%
Reform	36%	63%	44%	39%
None	9%	7%	34%	15%
Jewish Education Index				
High	50%	—	24%	36%
Moderate	27%	—	32%	33%
Low	23%	—	44%	31%
Home Religious Practices Index				
High	43%	39%	5%	29%
Moderate	36%	41%	34%	35%
Low	21%	20%	61%	36%
Interest in Israel Index				
High	41%	25%	14%	33%
Moderate	28%	26%	19%	23%
Low	31%	49%	67%	44%
Gen. Community Org. Activ. Index				
High	33%	53%	41%	35%
Moderate	48%	34%	39%	44%
Low	19%	13%	20%	21%
Synagogue Attendance				
19+ times per year	22%	27%	4%	16%
12–18 times	14%	23%	4%	11%
3–11 times	28%	27%	15%	22%
1–2 times	28%	15%	52%	34%
0 times	8%	8%	25%	17%

TABLE 9
Denomination by Jewish Marriages Entered into from 1970 to 1990

Denomination	Both Spouses Born Jewish	Marriage Types Convert In	Heterogeneous	Base
Orthodox	83%	6%	11%	100%
Conservative	53%	9%	38%	100%
Reform	31%	14%	55%	100%
No Preference	15%	3%	82%	100%

born respondents in convert marriages were too few to estimate properly their Jewish education.)

The religious and ethnic involvement of the heterogeneous couples is much less than the other two groups of couples. They are seldom synagogue members; they rank disproportionately low on the indices of Jewish organizational activities, home religious practices, and interest in Israel. They rarely, if at all, attend synagogue services. Convert couples are the most involved in general community voluntary associations followed by heterogeneous couples with both spouses born Jewish couples coming in last.

These various between-couple differences are best pictured by their denominational preferences. Over half of the both spouses born Jewish couples prefer either the Orthodox or Conservative denominations. Just about two-thirds of the convert couples prefer the Reform denomination. A bit less than half of the religiously heterogeneous couples prefer the Reform denomination and about one-third have no preference.

Up to now our statistics have been based on Jewish adults. Now let us shift to Jewish families as the base. This will indicate the backgrounds of the parents of the next generation of Jewish children. This tilts the presentation away from Jewish born adults since it takes two Jews to form one Jewish family but just one Jew to form a religiously heterogeneous family. When this is done, Table 9 indicates that 83% of the Orthodox Jewish families formed between 1970 and 1990 consists of couples in which both spouses were born Jewish. The Orthodox denomination, then, will overwhelmingly be able to retain its religious and ethnic characteristics in so far as they depend on husbands and wives having the same religious backgrounds.

However, Conservative denomination families will consist of just 53% both born Jewish couples. This denomination faces a need to absorb 47% of its young families in which just one spouse has been born Jewish. The Reform denomination will be one in which only 31% of the young couples have both spouses born Jewish. Practically all no preference families will have heterogeneous religious backgrounds.

Tables 8 and 9 clearly indicate that both major American Jewish denominations, the Reform and Conservative movements, are shifting from a historic Jewish combination of religion and ethnicity to being more religiously and less ethnically oriented. In particular, the Reform denomination will have its Jewish born adults be a bare majority (57%) of its adult adherents.

SUMMARY

The Jews of the United States have undergone constant change. They have moved out of their immigrant neighborhoods, such as the lower East Side of New York, to the pleasant greenery of suburbia. They have greatly improved their socio-economic status. Along with this has come a great decline of the Orthodox denomination, the rise of the Conservative denomination to being the largest denomination; then it's gradually being edged out of first place by the Reform denomination. Since 1970, there has been a considerable growth in the proportion of Jewish marriages that are between Jews and spouses from non-Jewish backgrounds.

Since the end of World War II, the declining Orthodox denomination has created an extensive network of all day Jewish schools and has maintained its traditional pattern of intensive and religious and ethnic involvement of its adherents. Orthodox Jews also are quite family oriented. They marry at a more rapid rate than other Jews and have more children. Mott and Abma (1992) found in their work with fertility data from the 1990 survey that Orthodox Jews are more likely to be married, have a greater number of children and expect to have more children than Jews of the other denominations. The age and children in the home data of Table 2 indicate that this denomination has a large percentage of young adults and children. It is thought likely that the Orthodox denomination has ended its long history of decline and could well begin to be a small, but increasing, proportion of the future American Jewish community.

The Conservative denomination is an aging one. The current small size of the Orthodox denomination makes it difficult for the Conservatives to continue to recruit sizable numbers for the Orthodox. Meanwhile, the Conservatives are losing sizable numbers of those raised in its ranks to the Reform denomination.

The Reform denomination adherents are young, and of high social status. However, a majority of those who prefer the Reform denomination fail to affiliate with a synagogue. As a religious body, its adherents display a low level of religious and ethnic involvement. However, those Reform adherents who do join a synagogue are active in both Jewish and general community organizations.

The impact of marriages outside of the Jewish community is felt somewhat among the Conservatives and to a considerable extent by the Reform denomination. It also widens the Orthodox-Conservative and Reform gaps. Those Jews who live disproportionately in the larger metropolitan areas and who are involved both religiously and ethnically with their Jewish communities customarily affiliate with the Orthodox and Conservative denominations. Those Jews who prefer the Reform denomination and are religiously active in it have far less ethnic attachments to their Jewish communities.

Among the results of the NJPS 1990 is the finding that women who attend synagogue on a regular basis (once a month or more) expect to have at least 0.4 more children than those who attend synagogue less frequently. Also, marriages between two Jewish born spouses have a lower divorce rate than religiously heterogeneous marriages. With marriages between two Jewish born spouses more religiously and ethnically involved and more religious women expecting larger families, the overall Jewish community is likely to have a slow trend back toward more traditional positions.

Converts to Judaism are a product of religious intermarriage. About two-thirds of such converts, primarily women, affiliate with Reform synagogues. As a group, converts are successfully absorbed religiously. Yet they are but 16% of the intermarriages.

Most marriages between people of Jewish backgrounds and Christian backgrounds form families which have little or no association with either the Jewish or Christian communities. Data from this survey show that while 70% of Jewish-Christian families have Christmas trees, only 17% attend church services three or more times a year.

It is possible that the families formed by people who wish to disassociate from their religious backgrounds, and do not wish to associate with any other historic religio-ethnic community, are forming a fourth American melting pot. This possible secular sector is yet to be thoroughly studied to see if it is a stable one which retains its children or merely a way station for a generation or so for those moving among the three basic American religio-ethnic communities.

Such a secular community also serves as a "safety valve" for the three historic religio-ethnic communities. People growing up in any of these three communities who strongly wish to leave them now have a socially acceptable place to enter in their personal search for a new overall orientation. When such people leave their childhood communities, those remaining behind will be the ones who are more involved with their own historic communities. When the least involved leave, this raises the religious and community involvement averages for the overall community. This is clearly happening in the American Jewish Community.

Acknowledgments

The Council of Jewish Federations is thanked for permission to work with the data from the 1990 national survey of the American Jewish population which it sponsored and financed. Also, thanks are due to my colleagues, Professor Arnold Dashefsky, Jerry Winter, and Ephraim Tabory, for their ongoing advice on the interpretation of this 1990 survey of American Jewry.

References

Bulka, Reuven P. (ed.) 1983. Dimensions of Orthodox Judaism. New York: KTAV.
Carroll, Jackson, and Wade Roof. 1993. Beyond Establishment: Protestant Identity in a Post-Protestant Age. Louisville, KY: Westminster/John Knox Press.

Danzger, Herbert. 1989. Returning to Tradition: The Contemporary Revival of Orthodox Judaism. New Haven, CT: Yale University Press.

Davidman, Lynn. 1991. Tradition in a Rootless World: Women Turn to Orthodox Judaism. Berkeley, CA: University of California Press.

Furman, Frida. 1987. Beyond Yiddishkeit: The Struggle for Jewish Identity in a Reform Synagogue. Albany, NY: University of New York Press.

Goldstein, Sidney. 1993. Profile of American Jewry: Insights from the 1990 National Jewish Population Survey. Occasional Papers No. 6, North American Jewish Data Bank. New York: Council of Jewish Federations.

Greeley, Andrew M. 1972. The Denominational Society. Glenview, IL: Scott, Foresman.

Greenberg, Blu. 1981. On Women and Judaism: The View from Tradition. Philadelphia: Jewish Publication Society of America.

Heilman, Samuel, and Steven Cohen. 1989. Cosmopolitans and Parochials: Modern Orthodox Jews in America. Chicago: University of Chicago Press.

Jick, Leon. 1992. The Americanization of the Synagogue, 1820–1870. Hanover, NH: Brandeis University Press/University Press of New England.

Lazerwitz, Bernard, and Michael Harrison. 1979. "American Jewish Denominations: A Social and Religious Profile." American Sociological Review, 44 (August), 656–666.

Mott, Frank, and Joyce Abma. 1992. "Contemporary Jewish Fertility: Does Religion Make a Difference?" Paper presented at the 1992 Meeting of the Population Association of America.

Roof, Wade. 1993. A Generation of Seekers: The Spiritual Journey of the Baby Boom Generation. New York: HarperCollins.

Salmon, Charles, and John Nichols. 1983. "The Next-Birthday Method of Respondent Selection." Public Opinion Quarterly. 47: 270–276.

Sklare, Marshall. 1955. Conservative Judaism. New York: Free Press.

Swatos, William. 1981. "Beyond Denominationalism? Community and Culture in American Religion." Journal for the Scientific Study of Religion, 20: 217–227.

Waxman, Chaim. 1983. America's Jews in Transition. Philadelphia: Temple University Press.

Reading 34

....

AFRICAN AMERICANS—LARRY L. HUNT AND JANET G. HUNT

Church and religion are and always have been extremely important to American blacks. The church was the one institution beyond the family that the slaves were permitted to keep (and often the only one when family ties were violated by slave owners). African-American religion is Protestant, mostly Baptist, indeed in liturgical style if not in doctrine or political attitudes very like Southern Baptists. Furthermore, from Rev. Martin Luther King to Rev. Jesse Jackson, African-American civil-rights leadership has been drawn from the ranks of the African-American clergy. Nonetheless, some African-American critics of religion have charged that the churches have more often cooperated with the white ruling class to keep African-American people "in their place."

Larry and Janet Hunt address themselves to this question. The Hunts find that when pertinent variables are considered, only sect-like groups (not unlike Benton Johnson's Holiness groups) seem to impede African-American militancy while the other denominations reinforce it.

The Hunts also find that African-American Catholics are more likely to be upwardly mobile than African-American Protestants—though the upward mobility may be the cause of their becoming Catholics (as in Wade Clark Roof's model)—and also more militant than African-American Protestants.

Clearly there is both ambiguity in the data and ambivalence in the analyses. But there can be no doubt that African-American churches are a major force in the African-American community, both religious and political.

Questions for Reflection and Study

1. On balance, have the churches been a help or a hindrance in the African-American struggle?
2. How do you account for the somewhat unusual role Catholicism seems to play in the African-American community? Might it be that upward mobile people who are also politically militant are attracted to Catholicism, so that their Catholic affiliation is more an effect than a cause?
3. Can you think of any African-American group that might replace the church and the clergy in the community's struggle?

BLACK RELIGION AS BOTH OPIATE AND INSPIRATION OF CIVIL RIGHTS MILITANCE: PUTTING MARX'S DATA TO THE TEST

Larry L. Hunt, and Janet G. Hunt

Alternative views of the influence of black religion on orientations toward protest have received empirical support in the last decade. In one of the major studies of black attitudes in the sixties, Gary Marx (a, b) concludes that the religious involvement of blacks serves largely as an accommodative opiate, producing a highly otherworldly focus and little concern with social change. More recently, Hart Nelsen and associates (a, b) have suggested that the black church is not simply a conservative, otherworldly institution inculcating quietism and rationalizing social inequality, but may also be an agency of creative change in the social order. The present study explores these contrasting interpretations of black religion through a secondary analysis of the 1964 Marx data base in terms of the suggestions and analytical distinctions proposed by Nelsen.

Marx is clearly sensitive to the possibility that black religion may historically have been significant for the mobilization of protest and acknowledges the temporal concern with social justice of such groups as the followers of Dr. Martin Luther King, Jr. His analysis of survey data on representative samples of urban blacks, however, was organized in such a way as to emphasize the traditional view of black religion (Frazier) as a conservative, accommodative institution of a disfranchised, subordinate population. Generally acknowledged as the definitive empirical study into black religion and civil rights activism, Marx's work identified particular features of black religious involvement that have appeared to be barriers to the mobilization of protest. Analyzing denominational differences, Marx reports that blacks in "largely white" denominations (Episcopalians, Presbyterians, Congregationalists, and Roman Catholics) are more militant than those in predominantly and/or all-black denominations— even those black denominations most visibly identified with the civil rights struggle. Further, Marx observed that those more religiously inclined—as indexed, in part, by church attendance and orthodoxy of belief—are least likely to hold a militant stance on civil rights issues.

Recognizing that these conclusions rest on empirical patterns that might be heavily shaped by secular factors (for example, social class was positively correlated with militance and negatively correlated with religiosity), Marx controlled sequentially (not simultaneously) for a variety of these factors and reports his findings to be stable even after these controls. Thus, the image of black religion generated by Marx's study is that membership in black denominations and black

Source: SOCIAL FORCES, v. 56, no. 1 Sept., 1977.

piety in general are religious factors which dampen the impact of secular factors, such as increasing education and urbanization, that may be conducive to racial equity.

Nelsen et al. (b) take exception to this essentially opiate view of black religion and argue that a dual role of the black church—producing both quietism and activism—is particularly apparent in light of trends that strengthen black religion's "Promethean motif." In their research, they use two data sets: the 1964 Marx data and a 1971 community study based on interviews in an urban center in the upper South. Using the Marx data, the authors show that the impression of a general tension between religiosity and militance is considerably reduced when multiple statistical controls for secular factors are employed. On the new data set, refining the religiosity dimension by distinguishing churchlike and sectlike belief systems proves crucial in isolating different attitudes toward militancy issues: only sectarian beliefs were inversely correlated with civil rights militance, while churchlike orthodoxy was positively associated with militance. These findings suggest that it is sectarianism that detracts from militance, while those forms of religiosity that have stressed the social gospel themes in Christian theology and the church's potential influence on other social institutions may well contribute to black activism. Furthermore, the authors speculate that secular trends, such as rising educational levels of blacks, may work to reduce sectarianism and enhance those churchlike religious orientations in the black community that provide a stimulus for protest.

Reconciliation of the divergent perspectives in Marx and Nelsen is difficult, owing to strategic differences in the two data bases. Marx's analysis rests on samples from several major urban centers, both North and South, while the new data in Nelsen et al. (b) come from a single community study. Additionally, Marx's data were collected before the rise of the black power and black theology movements (Cone), while the findings of Nelsen may reflect such later developments. Thus, Nelsen's findings which qualify Marx's general conclusions may be due to timebound, local conditions and may or may not reflect more broadly based and longstanding patterns in the black experience. To resolve some of these issues, we have reanalyzed Marx's data from the standpoint of Nelsen's criticisms and suggestions.

The first phase of our analysis employs Marx's original indexes and is motivated by Nelsen's concern about Marx's reliance on singular, sequential controls for secular factors. Consequently, we explore whether multiple controls for relevant secular variables (social class, region of current residence, region of birth, size of community during early childhood, sex, and age) alter Marx's conclusions. Specifically, we ask whether controlling on secular factors in this manner in any way changes the impression that: (1) blacks in largely white denominations are more militant than those in black denominations, and (2) blacks with higher attendance and more orthodox beliefs are lower in civil rights militance. The second aspect of the analysis involves a reevaluation of the presumed tension between religiosity and militance by separating churchlike and sectlike patterns of religious involvement and belief. Here we ask whether a Promethean motif associated with churchlike religiosity can be identified in Marx's as well as Nelsen's data, indicating a broader national pattern discernible at earlier stages of the civil rights movement than can be inferred from Nelsen's new findings.

THE SAMPLE

The data reported here were collected for the Survey Research Center of the University of California at Berkeley in October 1964. Marx (b) provides a detailed discussion of the sampling and interviewing procedures and a complete description of the questionnaire. His study focused on urban black adults, included representation of northern and southern cities, and was initiated to survey the climate of opinion among black Americans immediately following a summer of urban riots and the passage of landmark civil rights legislation. From the total of 1,119 interviews, we developed a working sample of 1,057 cases for whom identification of conventional forms of Christian religious affiliation could be determined. We excluded those reporting no religious affiliation, or extremely minor affiliations such as Jewish or Muslim, most of whom Marx erroneously included in his Roman Catholic category.

THE VARIABLES

Denomination

Denominational affiliation was determined by the self-definition of respondents. In the case of initial responses of "Protestant" or "Baptist" more detailed queries were made to provide for more precise specification. Our effort to identify denominational effects on militance independent of secular factors includes three ways of categorizing this variable. First, we used Marx's classification of respondents into five major denominational groupings: (1) Episcopalians, Presbyterians, and Congregationalists—hereafter termed "EPCs," (2) Roman Catholics, (3) Methodists, (4) Baptists, and (5) a composite category of various sects and cults—hereafter termed "sects." Then, following Nelsen's practice, we refined the large Baptist category into three subgroups: American Baptists, Southern Baptists, and a residual category of other Baptists. Finally, based on the results of analyses of previous categories, we developed our own threefold classification of denominations (explained later).

Religiosity

In the first part of the research, we use two of Marx's indexes of religiosity: church *attendance* and *orthodoxy* of belief. Attendance was measured by the respondent's report of the frequency of attendance at religious services.

Orthodoxy was measured by agreement with questions about belief in the existence of God, the Devil, and life after death.

In the second part of the analysis, we use refined measures which introduce the churchlike/sectlike distinction into both the attendance (or *involvement*) and orthodoxy (or *belief*) dimensions of religiosity. The involvement indexes are based on frequency of church attendance, supplemented by information on participation in religious and secular associations. Following Demerath, the key factor separating churchlike and sectlike involvement is the articulation of one's religious and secular participation: churchlike involvement entails participation in both religious and secular spheres; sectlike involvement rests on participation in the religious sphere exclusively. Our index of churchlike involvement yields three categories: "high" includes those with membership in secular voluntary associations combined with both high church attendance and membership in a church group (e.g., a prayer group, religious circle or club, etc.), "medium" includes those with secular memberships combined with high church attendance or membership in a church group; and "low" is a residual category capturing all of those with neither high church attendance nor church-group membership and all of those without secular memberships. The index of sectlike involvement also produces three categories: "high" includes those without secular memberships but with both high church attendance and membership in a church group, "medium" includes those without secular memberships and either high attendance or membership in a church group, and "low" includes all of those with neither high attendance nor church-group membership and all of those with secular memberships. In our sample, sectlike involvement is clearly the most prevalent, with 54 percent evidencing high or medium sectlike patterns, 25 percent evidencing high or medium churchlike patterns, and the remaining 21 percent low on both indexes.

Indexes for churchlike and sectlike beliefs, as differentiated by Nelsen, were derived from factoring a set of eight interview items reflecting *both* some conventional features of the Christian tradition and some parochial attitudes which are probably religiously linked but not intrinsic expressions of the Christian faith. As indicators of a churchlike orientation, we used: (1) the knowledge that the Ten Commandments are part of both Christianity and Judaism; (2) the affirmation of belief in life after death; (3) the awareness that the Old Testament identifies the Jews as God's chosen people; and (4) the belief that God exists. As indicators of a sectlike orientation, we used: (1) the belief that the Devil exists, (2) the conviction that without believing in Jesus, one cannot be saved, (3) the view that a person not believing in God should be prohibited from teaching in a public high school, and (4) the belief that a wrathful God punishes Jews for not accepting Jesus. A principal components factoring procedure with a criterion of eigenvalues greater than one identified two major attitudinal dimensions. Following varimax rotation, factor scores computed for the two dimensions proved to be statistically independent ($r = .03$, $p < .40$). Factor score coefficients for churchlike and sectlike beliefs (in that order) for the eight items are: (1) "Ten commandments" (.19, −.01); (2) "Life after death" (.31, .18); (3) "Chosen people" (.31, −.06); (4) "God exists" (.22, .12); (5) "Devil exists" (.13, .23); (6)

TABLE 1

Intercorrelations Among Selected Variables (Pearsonian *r*)*

	X2	X3	X4	X5	X6	X7	X8	X9	X10	X11	X12	X13
X1—Militance	−.08	−.18	.06	−.14	.08	−.26	.32	.18	.23	.17	.16	.20
X2—Attendance		.36	.26	.52	.16	.32	−.10	−.14	−.17	−.10	−.14	−.22
X3—Orthodoxy			.17	.27	.51	.76	−.25	−.24	−.18	−.22	−.17	−.24
X4—C-like invol.				−.10	.15	.08	.15	−.07	.04	−.08	.04	−.10
X5—S-like invol.					.03	.22	−.15	−.17	−.14	−.11	−.23	−.20
X6—C-like belief						.03	.08	−.07	.00	−.06	−.03	−.11
X7—S-like belief							−.39	−.27	−.24	−.24	−.15	−.26
X8—Social class								.18	.29	.18	.12	.32
X9—Region									.12	.66	.02	.16
X10—Community										.19	.05	.31
X11—Reg. of birth											.04	.16
X12—Sex												−.05
X13—Age												

*Correlations greater than ±. 10 are significant at .001 level

"Jesus saves" (−.14, .33); (7) "Not allow teaching" (−.16, .25); and (8) "God punishes" (−.08, .10).

Inasmuch as factor-score scales should not only have a clear statistical interpretation but should be linked with external criteria to establish validity (Schuessler), we correlated the belief indexes with the involvement indexes. As reported in Table 1, this check on the meaning of our measures reveals that churchlike belief is related to churchlike involvement ($r = .15$, $p < .001$) but unrelated to sectlike involvement ($r = .03$). Similarly, sectlike belief correlated with sectlike involvement ($r = .22$, $p < .001$) but not with churchlike involvement ($r = .08$).

Civil Rights Militance

The eight-item index central to Marx's analyses reported in *Protest and Prejudice* is our measure of civil rights militance. (We chose this index rather than the shorter version reported in the 1967 "Opiate" article because the two are very highly correlated ($r = .97$), and the book provides more complete discussion and documentary information.) Militance reflects a set of interrelated attitudes involving, among others, the feeling that there are definite barriers to personal achievement for blacks, that integration of American life is proceeding too slowly, that blacks deserve equal public accommodations, and that more demonstrations against racial inequality are desirable. (See Marx, b, 44–48, for complete listing of items and discussion of this index.) The index was thus designed to tap opposition to racial discrimination and advocacy of change in American society to make racial justice a reality.

Secular Factors

Marx's analysis used two major controls for status variables affecting militance, "social class" and "exposure to values legitimizing protest." The social class index, which is based on the education, occupation, and income of respondents is used in our analysis in two ways: (1) as a linear variable in most analyses (dummy coded when adjusted means were computed); and (2) as a contextual variable when classifying respondents into middle-, working-, and lower-class strata. We elected to decompose the "exposure" index into its four components because, unlike social class, there was no clear rationale for employing it as a linear variable. These components are identified and coded as follows: (1) "community," reflecting the size of the respondent's community during early childhood, coded 1 if nonfarm, (2) "birth," reflecting the region of birth, coded 1 if outside the deep South, (3) "sex," coded 1 if male, and (4) "age," coded 4 if under 30, 3 if 30–44, 2 if 45–59, and 1 if 60 or over. Finally, consistent with Nelsen et al. (b), we also control for region—current residence in a northern versus southern city—in most analyses, coded 1 if respondent lives in a northern city.

Intercorrelations

Table 1 summarizes the interrelationships among all variables except denominational affiliation. These correlations show that there are strong direct associations between the secular variables, used in our main analyses as control and conditional variables, and the major dependent variable, militance. They indicate further that Marx's measures of religiosity are negatively associated with militance, while the refined measures of churchlike and sectlike religiosity are associated differently with militance, positively and negatively respectively. Finally, it is noteworthy that churchlike forms of religiosity are less correlated with the secular variables than are the sectlike forms, the latter appearing to be tied to lower status, southern origins and residence, rural socialization, and the like, a pattern which closely parallels that observed in the Nelsen et al. (b) study.

THE FINDINGS

Table 2 presents three sets of analyses designed to evaluate Marx's conclusion that large white denominations are conducive to greater militance than all-black denominations. These analyses use multiple regression procedures in which militance is regressed on denomination before and after controls for secular factors. Denomination was measured by dummy variables where a score of 1 is assigned to membership in a given affiliation, and no dummy is entered for the least militant denomination in order to avoid indeterminate solution. The least militant denomination thus serves as a reference category for assessing effects attributable to the other denominational memberships. Two ways of summarizing denominational militance are presented: (1) actual means and predicted means, after secular factors are controlled, gauge the level of militance associated with

TABLE 2
Militance by Three Classifications of Denomination

Denomination	N	Actual	MEANS FOR DENOMINATIONS — PREDICTED MEAN CONTROLLING FOR — Class	All	BETAS FOR DENOMINATION CONTRASTS — O-order	CONTROLLING FOR[†] — Class	All
EPC	60	4.75	4.45	4.35	.130***	.085*	.061
Catholics	75	4.60	4.37	4.20	.126***	.084*	.049
Methodist	141	4.35	4.22	4.25	.120**	.086*	.074
Baptist	657	4.11	4.17	4.20	.106*	.107*	.095*
sects	106	3.70	3.79	3.84			
EPC	60	4.75	4.46	4.43	.130***	.085*	.062
Catholic	75	4.60	4.38	4.21	.126***	.084*	.050
Methodist	141	4.35	4.23	4.25	.120***	.087*	.075
Am. Baptist	257	4.35	4.35	4.24	.150***	.137**	.091*
So. Baptist	154	4.26	4.29	4.35	.106*	.106*	.096*
O. Baptist	246	3.76	3.91	4.08	.015	.036	.032
sects	106	3.70	3.79	3.84			
Predominantly white	135	4.67	4.42	4.25	.165***	.098*	.049
Activist-black	552	4.33	4.30	4.27	.155***	.121***	.073*
Retreatist-black	352	3.74	3.87	3.97			

*Indicates statistical significance: *$p < .05$; **$p < .01$; ***$p < .001$
[†]The effects for the secular factors employed as controls were quite stable in each denominational analysis. B-weights for these factors in the first analysis are: Class = .222*; Region = .101**; Community = .125**; Birth = .015; Sex = .122***; and Age = .072**

denominational categories, and (2) standardized betas indicate the extent of greater militance of a given denomination compared with the least militant reference category and provide a basis for assessing the effects of the secular factors compared to the effects of denominational membership.

In the first analysis, which uses Marx's five denominational categories, we find that the actual means point to the same general ordering of denominational militance Marx observed: the EPCs are the most militant, followed by Roman Catholics, Methodists, Baptists, and "sects" in that order. And, the zero-order betas indicate that membership in all denominations is associated with greater militance than that of the sects, with effects greatest for the EPCs and Catholics. Thus, the largely white denominations do appear to be the most militant, the otherworldly sects the least, with Methodists and Baptists somewhere in between. This picture changes, however, when secular factors are controlled. After controls for social class and then all secular factors, the predicted means show considerable leveling of denominational differences, and the betas, while not as large and significant as those for the secular factors, show that membership in the Methodist and Baptist denominations is most predictive of militance and that only the Baptists have markedly greater militance than the sects.

The second section of Table 2 uses the more refined breakdown of the large Baptist category and shows that, with secular controls, the American and Southern Baptists are more militant than the sects, while the other Baptists are not different from the sects. (In analyses not presented here, the same pattern of differentiation for the Baptist category was observed on all of Marx's measures of religiosity, with the other Baptists being even more otherworldly than the sects in some instances.) These considerations lead us into the third portion of Table 2 to differentiate predominantly white," "activist black," and "retreatist black" denominations by merging the EPCs and Catholics into the first category, the Methodists, American Baptists, and Southern Baptists in the second category, and the other Baptists and sects in the third. This classification shows that the predominantly white denominations have higher militance only when secular controls are absent. With controls, the "activist black" denominations exhibit the highest level of militance and are the only category with significantly greater militance than the retreatist blacks.

These lines of analysis suggest that Marx's conclusion of greater militance among blacks in white denominations is equivocal at best. Secular factors have a considerable leveling influence on denominational differences and the betas suggest that such factors, more so than denominational membership, are most critical in shaping orientations toward protest. Thus, the irony Marx thought present when concluding that white denominations conduce to greater militance than even the black denominations most involved in the civil rights struggle is explained by secular factors, not religious factors. That black religion may provide an opiate is a possibility, but our analysis of denominational differences cautions against any sweeping generalization.

Turning to an examination of the proposition of a general tension between religiosity and militance, Table 3 presents the correlations between two of Marx's measures of religiosity—attendance and orthodoxy—and militance before and after controlling for secular factors. The zero-order correlations show, as reported by Marx, that attendance and orthodoxy appear to be incompatible with militance. The partial correlations, however, show that this is not the case when secular factors related to both militance and religiosity are controlled. Thus, the apparently lower militance of those with high levels of religiosity is largely a consequence of variables such as social class and region.

Thus, once again, multiple controls for secular factors show that the inference of a general opiate quality to black religion is questionable. However, to explore the possibility that this particular method of introducing controls conceals such an effect, we elected to examine the religiosity-militance relationship conditionally by social class level and type of denomination. Table 4 presents these conditional relationships, which make even more apparent the limitations of Marx's view of the opiate features of black religion.

Marx assumed that the dimensions of the religious tradition of American blacks that most attenuate militance are its accommodative or escapist features of otherworldliness and sectarianism. Assuming further that these features were

TABLE 3

Total and Partial Correlations of Militance with Marx's Measures of Religiosity Attendance and Orthodoxy

Religiosity Index	Zero-order r	PARTIAL R CONTROLLING FOR	
		Social Class	All Secular Factors
Attendance	−.08**	−.02	−.01
Orthodoxy	−.18***	−.09*	−.03

*p < .05
**p < .01
***p < .001

TABLE 4

Correlation of Militance with Marx's Measures of Religiosity: Attendance and Orthodoxy by (a) Type of Denomination and (b) Social Class Level

Religiosity Index	White	Activist Black	Retreatist Black
Type of Denomination			
Attendance	−.12	−.09	−.02
Orthodoxy	−.25**	−.13*	−.11
	Middle	Working	Lower
Social Class Level			
Attendance	−.22**	−.05	−.01
Orthodoxy	−.27**	−.10*	−.07

*p < .05
**p < .01

most clearly embodied in the least militant of black religious groups, the sects, his major research question was whether a tension (negative correlation) between religiosity and militance might also obtain among the more affluent blacks with nonsect affiliations. Table 4 shows that a general tension between orthodoxy and militance exists in all denominational groups, but that it is most acute among blacks in the largely white rather than black denominations. The incompatibility is also most evident in the middle class rather than at lower socioeconomic levels. These patterns indicate that whatever opiate qualities religion may have for blacks, it cannot be simply identified with the black church or black religion as a low-status accommodative pattern.

Having shown that Marx's characterization of black religion as an impediment to civil rights militance is overdrawn, we turn to an examination of Nelsen's distinction between churchlike and sectlike types of religiosity. At issue is whether this distinction identifies kinds of religious involvement and/or belief that influence different militant stances.

TABLE 5
Relationships (Standardized Betas) Between Militance and
Churchlike/Sectlike Religiosity Without and with Secular Controls

RELIGIOSITY			
Dimension	Orientation	O-order BETA	BETA after Controls[†]
Involvement	Churchlike	.041	.027
	Sectlike	−.132***	−.024
Belief	Churchlike	.095***	.093***
	Sectlike	−.264***	−.099***

***$p < .001$
[†]Controls employed are: Class, Region, Community, Birth, Sex and Age.

Table 5 presents the relationships between militance and the four refined measures of religiosity. The zero-order relationships suggest that both sectlike involvement and sectlike belief are linked with nonmilitance, while churchlike involvement and particularly churchlike belief are conducive to greater militance. When controls for secular factors are applied, the tensions between militance and both sectlike measures are diminished, but the effects of sectlike belief remain significant. The controls have little impact on the churchlike measures although, again, it is the belief dimension that remains predictive of militance.

The data in Table 5 provide a measure of support for the views of both Marx and Nelsen. The fact that sectlike belief has a depressing effect on militance net of secular controls indicates that Marx's imputation of a religious factor inhibiting protest is partially accurate. But the extent to which controls reduce the relationships between the sectlike measures and militance suggests that the opiate quality of black religion is very much intertwined with secular conditions. Moreover, it is apparent that some forms of the black religious tradition are conducive to high levels of militance, and the greater stability of these relationships after secular controls suggests even more clearly the operation of a religious factor. Identification of this "Promethean motif" in black religion qualifies the generality of Marx's conclusions and documents the dual role of black religion in shaping secular attitudes.

To specify more accurately the dual orientation of black religion revealed by these analyses, we turn, finally, to an analysis of the relationship of churchlike and sectlike religiosity to militance by social class level and type of denomination. Table 6 reports the standardized betas after controlling on secular factors. These data show a negative relationship between sectlike belief and militance in all denominations, although it is not marked in the case of the activist blacks, and is strongest as class increases. Conversely, the positive relationship between churchlike religiosity and militance is most apparent in the activist black denominations and is strongest as social class decreases. These patterns indicate that

TABLE 6

Relationships (Standardized Betas) Between Churchlike/Sectlike Religiosity and Militancy by (a) Type of Denomination and (b) Social Class Level. Controlling for Relevant Secular Factors

RELIGIOSITY		TYPE OF DENOMINATION[†]			SOCIAL CLASS LEVEL[†]		
Dimension	Orientation	White	Activist Black	Retreatist Black	Middle	Working	Lower
Involvement	Churchlike	−.036	.022	.117*	−.020	.049	.058
	Sectlike	.097	.014	−.008	−.091	−.047	.005
Belief	Churchlike	.128	.131**	.053	.057	.111*	.120*
	Sectlike	−.139*	−.057	−.118*	−.209**	−.103*	−.023

*p < .05.
**p < .01.
[†]Secular factors controlled are: Class, Region, Community, Birth, Age and Sex.
[†]Secular factors controlled are: Region, Community, Birth, Age and Sex.

any opiate qualities of black religion are clearly not associated with low secular status and all types of black denominations. They suggest, rather, that sectarianism may have some of its most corrosive effects among those blacks most exposed to and assimilated into white society, while forms of religiosity which are churchlike may offer the clearest inspiration for secular protest within the activist black churches and among the least affluent.

CONCLUSIONS

The investigation has shown that Marx's inference of a general opiate quality in black religion is incomplete and potentially misleading. Using his own indices with more extensive controls, we find that the effects attributed to black denominational membership and black religiosity across denominations are more properly attributed to secular factors, such as social class, region, and nonurban origins. Moreover, what denominational effects remain after controls show that it is black activist rather than predominantly white affiliation that conduces to militance, and the religiosity effects indicate a positive as well as negative impact on activism when churchlike and sectlike modes are differentiated. Where attitudes and social participation are highly sectarian and membership is in one of the retreatest black denominations, we find religiosity linked with low levels of militance. On the other hand, where religious orientation is more churchlike, especially where membership is in a black activist denomination, religiosity is associated with high levels of militance.

These findings mean that Marx's original conclusions that have informed much later sociology of the black experience need qualification and specification. They show—indeed they demonstrate beyond what can be shown with Marx's own indices—that religiosity can militate against protest. And they indicate that this type of religious factor can operate in a wide range of contexts, including white denominations and middle-class social worlds. But they also show that the opiate interpretation of black religion is a limited and one-sided image of black religion, which in many of its forms has probably made a significant contribution to the mobilization of the black community for protest. Thus, the fact that we uncover patterns in the Marx data collected on a national sample during the early stages of the civil rights movement that are basically similar to those Nelsen found among a more geographically delimited and recent sample, indicates the presence for some time of those developments in black religion and within black denominations that Marx argues must accompany a more positive role of black religion in securing secular-status gains.

Perhaps both Marx's original inquiry and its widespread acceptance were heavily conditioned by the longstanding view in sociology of black institutions as obstacles to assimilation (Metzger). The present research, together with the work of Nelsen, suggests that a reevaluation of black religion may yield a more complex and differentiated image of its place in black experience. If this is the case, it may well be found that, just as the disorganized black family has been unduly blamed for perpetuating the status difficulties of blacks, black religion may also have been inappropriately seized upon as a critical factor holding blacks down.

References

Cone, James. 1969. *Black Theology and Black Power.* New York: Seabury Press.

Demerath, N.J., III. 1965. *Social Class in American Protestantism.* Chicago: Rand McNally.

Frazier, E. Franklin. 1964. *The Negro Church in America.* New York: Schocken.

Marx, Gary T. a:1967. "Religion: Opiate or Inspiration of Civil Rights Militancy among Negroes?" *American Sociological Review* 32(February):64–72.

———. b:1969. *Protest and Prejudice.* Rev. ed. New York: Harper & Row.

Metzger, L. P. 1971. "American Sociology and Black Assimilation: Conflicting Perspectives." *American Journal of Sociology* 76(January):627–47.

Nelsen, Hart, and Anne Kusener Nelsen. a:1975. *Black Church in the Sixties.* Lexington: University Press of Kentucky.

Nelsen, H., T. W. Madron, and R. L. Yokley. b:1975. "Black Religion's Promethean Motif: Orthodoxy and Militancy." *American Journal of Sociology* 81(July):139–46.

Schuessler, Karl. 1971. *Analyzing Social Data: A Statistical Orientation.* Boston: Houghton Mifflin.

Acknowledgments

....

READING 1: PARTS I AND II: Karl Marx and Friedrich Engels, *On Religion*. Scholar's Press, 1982, pp. 41–43, 69–72. Reprinted by permission.

READING 2: From *Moses and Monotheism* by Sigmund Freud. Copyright 1939 by Alfred A. Knopf Inc. and renewed 1967 by Ernst L. Freud and Anna Freud. Reprinted by permission of the publisher.

READING 5: Reprinted with the permission of Macmillian College Publishing Company from *The Protestant Ethic and the Spirit of Capitalism* by Max Weber, translated by Talcott Parsons. Copyright © 1958 Charles Scribner's Sons.

READING 6: Reprinted with the permission of The Free Press, an imprint of Simon & Schuster from *Essays in Sociological Theory* by Talcott Parsons. ©1954 by The Free Press; copyright renewed 1982 by Helen W. Parsons.

READING 7: Reprinted from "Religion as a Cultural System" in *Anthropological Approaches to the Study of Religion* edited by M. Banton (1966) by permission of Tavistock Publications Ltd.

READING 8: Reprinted from *The Idea of the Holy* by Rudolf Otto, translated by John W. Harvey (2nd ed. 1950), by permission of Oxford University Press.

READINGS 9 AND 10: Excerpt from "Sacred Space and Making the World Sacred" and "Sacred Time and Myths" from *The Sacred and the Profane: The Nature of Religion* by Mircea Eliade, copyright © 1957 by Taschenbuch Verlag Gmbh, English translation by William R. Trask, copyright 1959 and renewed 1987 by Harcourt Brace & Company, reprinted by Harcourt Brace & Company.

READING 11, PART I: Philip H. Ennis "Ecstasy and Everyday Life." Reprinted with permission from the *Journal for the Scientific Study of Religion*. Vol. VI, 1, 1967.

READING 11, PART II: *Mysticism: A Study and an Anthology* by F. C. Happold, Baltimore, Maryland: Penguin Books pp. 51–55. Copyright © Penguin Books 1963, revised edition 1970. Copyright © F. C. Happold, 1963, 1964, 1970. Reprinted by permission of Penguin Books Ltd.

READING 15: Michael Carrol. *Madonnas That Maim: Popular Catholicism in Italy Since the Fifteenth Century*. The Johns Hopkins University Press, 1992, pp. 129-137. Reprinted with permission.

READING 16: Robert Orsi, *The Madonna of 115th St.* Copyright © 1985 Yale University Press, pp. 1–13, 219–231. Reprinted with permission.

READINGS 17, PART II, AND 18: Thomas Luckman, *The Invisible Religion: The Transformation of Symbolism in Industrial Society.* Macmillan, 1967 pp. 28–37. Reprinted by permission of the author.

READING 19: Thomas Luckman and Andrew Greeley, "The New and the Old in Religion" from *Social Theory for a Changing Society.* Pierre Bourdieu and James Coleman, eds. Copyright 1991 by Westview Press. Reprinted by permission.

READING 21: "Religion in Britain, Ireland and the USA" in *British Social Attitudes: The 9th Report.* Edited by Roger Jowell, Lindsay Brook, Gillian Prior and Bridget Taylor. Copyright 1992 by Dartmouth Publishing Company. Reprinted with permission.

READING 23: William Bainbridge and Rodney Stark, "Cult Formation: Three Compatible Models," *Sociological Analysis,* 1979, 40:4 p. 283. Reprinted with permission.

READING 25: Mayer Gruber, *The Motherhood of God and Other Stories,* pp. 3–15. Copyright 1992 by Scholars Press. Reprinted with permission.

READING 26: Andrew M. Greeley, *The Religious Imagination,* pp. 209–213. Copyright 1981 by William H. Sadlier Inc. Reprinted with permission.

READING 28: Robert N. Bellah, "Civil Religion in America." Reprinted with permission of *Daedelus: Journal of the American Academy of Arts and Sciences,* from the issue entitled, "Religion in America," Winter 1967, Volume 96, Number 1.

READING 30: Wade Clark Roof and William McKinney, *American Mainline Religion: Its Changing Shape and Future.* Rutgers University Press, pp. 145–185, 1987. Reprinted by permission.

READING 31, PART I: Nancy T. Ammerman, "North American Protestant Fundamentalism" in *Fundamentalism Observed,* Martin E. Marty and R. Scott Appleby, eds. University of Chicago Press, 1991. pp 1–8. Reprinted with permission.

READING 31, PART II: Jeffrey K. Hadden, "Conservative Christians, Televangelism and Politcs: Taking Stock a Decade after the Founding of the Moral Majority" in *In God We Trust: New Patterns of Religious Pluralism in America.* Thomas Robbins and Anthony Dick, eds. Copyright 1990 Transaction Publishers. Reprinted with permission.

READING 32: Andrew M. Greeley, "Theology and Sociology On Validating David Tracy," *Journal of the American Academy of Religion,* LIX: 4. Used by permission.

READING 33, PART I: Reprinted by permission from *A Short History of Judaism* by Jacob Neusner. Copyright © 1992 Augsburg Fortress.

READING 34: Reprinted from *Social Forces* (Volume 56, no. 1, September 1977). "Black Religion as Both Opiate and Inspiration of Civil Rights Militance: Putting Marx's Data to the Test" by Larry L. Hunt and Janet G. Hunt. Copyright © The University of North Carolina Press.